APULEIUS MADAURENSIS

GRONINGEN COMMENTARIES ON APULEIUS

APULEIUS MADAURENSIS
METAMORPHOSES

Book VIII
Text, Introduction and Commentary

B. L. HIJMANS Jr. – R. Th. VAN DER PAARDT
V. SCHMIDT – C. B. J. SETTELS
B. WESSELING – R. E. H. WESTENDORP BOERMA

EGBERT FORSTEN, GRONINGEN 1985

CIP-Gegevens Koninklijke Bibliotheek, Den Haag

Apuleius

Metamorphoses / Apuleius Madaurensis ; text, introd. and comment.
B.L. Hijmans...[et al.]. - Groningen :
Forsten . - (Groningen commentaries on Apuleius) Book VIII
Met index, lit. opg.

ISBN 90-6980-005-5
SISO klas-1 851.6 UDC 871
Trefw.: Latijnse letterkunde ; teksten / Apuleius Madaurensis 'Metamorphoses'.

© Egbert Forsten Publishing, Groningen 1985.

Alle rechten voorbehouden. Niets uit deze uitgave mag worden verveelvoudigd,
opgeslagen in een geautomatiseerd gegevensbestand, of openbaar gemaakt,
in enige vorm of op enige wijze, hetzij elektronisch, mechanisch,
door fotokopieën, opnamen, of op enige andere manier, zonder voorafgaande
schriftelijke toestemming van de uitgever.

All rights reserved. No part of this publication may be reproduced, stored in a retrieval system, or transmitted, in any form or by any means, electronic, mechanical, photocopying, recording, or otherwise, without the prior written permission of the publisher.

This book was printed with financial support from the Netherlands Organisation for the Advancement of Pure Research (Z.W.O.)

CONTENTS

Preface	VII
Abbreviations	IX
Bibliography	XIII
Introduction	1
Note to the text	11
Text-Liber VIII	13
Commentary	27
Appendix I Funeral practices in the *Met.*	278
Appendix II Apuleius *Met.* 8, 12 (186, 19–21)	280
Appendix III The Dea Syria	286
Appendix IV Lucius' representation of the Dea Syria and her priests as the antithesis of Isis and her worshippers	287
Appendix V Public confession	299
General Index	301

PREFACE

The present volume of the Groningen Commentaries on Apuleius, third in the series, appears after roughly the same period of time that was needed for the preparation of the second volume. We were fortunate in having Prof. Dr. R. E. H. Westendorp Boerma with us during the earlier stages of the work and it was with regret that we accepted his decision to give up participation, a decision he announced after his contribution to the commentary on book VIII had been completed. Too soon afterwards we were saddened by the news of his final illness. We remember him as the one who, from its inception, guided the project with energy, wit and an admirable sense of detachment.

The name of Dr. A. G. Westerbrink is missing from the title page. This is not to say that he no longer took an interest: chapter by chapter he sent in his thoughtful remarks even though he had formally resigned from the group; particularly helpful, too, was his willingness to read the proofs. He deserves our gratitude.

Two new members joined the project: Drs. C. Settels and Drs. B. Wesseling. Both worked on a part time research grant at first provided by the Faculty of Letters of Groningen University, later by the Netherlands Organisation for the Advancement of Pure Research. Their task was divided into providing supportive work on narrative motifs in the Greek and Roman novel on the one hand, and preparing direct contributions to the commentary on the other. Their names will appear on the title page of the commentary on book IX as well.

Prof. Dr. H. Hofmann took the chair of Latin at Groningen University: his interest in, and support for, the project is manifest through his lively participation in the monthly sessions.

The English version of the commentary is owed to the painstaking and intelligent work of Dr. C. Ooms, whose work was scrutinized by Prof. Philippa Goold. Our debt of gratitude to the latter has now been tripled. As usual she did not confine her remarks to the English: she has read the entire commentary with critical acumen and as a result a whole series of notes have been improved immeasurably – or dropped entirely.

Once again we mention the Thesaurus Institute at Munich with gratitude: our yearly visits there are as productive as they are pleasant.

As in the case of the two previous volumes thanks are due to the Netherlands organisation for the Advancement of Pure Research for financial help with the publication. The University Library at Groningen and the Buma Bibliotheek at Leeuwarden were willing to continue the long term loan arrangements without which the work would have been almost impossible.

B. L. Hijmans Jr.
V. Schmidt

ABBREVIATIONS

We refer to all publications by author, year and page. For that reason we here list the publications mentioned for the first time in the present volume. For items not mentioned here we refer to R. Th. van der Paardt 1971 IX–XIII, *GCA* 1977, IX–XVI, *GCA* 1981, IX–XV and to the Bibliography in the present volume, below p. XIII. Generally known commentaries (e.g. Tarrant on Seneca's Agamemnon) have not been included in this list of abbreviations.

J. N. Adams, *The Latin Sexual Vocabulary*, London 1982.

M. v. Albrecht, *Meister römischer Poesie*, Heidelberg 1977.

B. Andreae, *Die Sarkophage mit Darstellungen aus dem Menschenleben, 2. Die römischen Jagdsarkophage*, Berlin 1980.

G. Appel, *De Romanorum precationibus*, New-York [r]1975.

J. Aymard, *Essai sur les chasses romaines des origines à la fin du siècle des Antonins. Bibl. Ecol. Franç. d'Athèn. et Rome* 170, Paris 1951.

M. Bieber, *Entwicklungsgeschichte der griechischen Tracht*, Berlin 1934.

H. Blümner, *Die römischen Privataltertümer*, München 1911.

F. Boll – C. Bezold – W. Gundel, *Sternglaube und Sterndeutung*, Darmstadt [5]1966.

F. Bömer, *Untersuchungen über die Religion der Sklaven in Griechenland und Rom (3. Teil: die wichtigsten Kulte der griechischen Welt)*, Wiesbaden 1961.

J. C. Bramble, *Persius and the Programmatic Satire*, Cambridge 1974.

H. Brandenburg, *Studien zur mitra*, Münster 1966.

W. Büchner, *Ueber den Begriff der Eironeia*, Hermes 76 (1941), 339 f.

F. Cairns, *Tibullus. A Hellenistic Poet at Rome*, Cambridge 1979.

F. Capponi, *Ornithologia Latina*, Genova 1979.

L. Castiglioni, *Apuleiana III*, RIL 71 (1938), 545 f.

J. D. Cloud, *The lex Cornelia de sicariis*, ZRG 86 (1969), 258 f.

F. Cumont, *Les religions orientales dans le paganisme romain*, Paris [4]1929.

J. De Bie (ed.), *Griekse mythologie en Europese cultuur*, Antwerpen 1979.

J. Esteve-Forriol, *Die Trauer- und Trostgedichte der römischen Literatur*, München 1962.

W. Fauth, *Dea Syria*, in: *Kleine Pauly*, Stuttgart 1964.

R. Fellman, *Der Sabazios-Kult*, in: *Die orientalischen Religionen im Römerreich*, ed. J. M. Vermaseren, EPRO 93, Leiden 1981.

E. Fraenkel, *Selbstmordwege*, Phil. 87 (1932), 470 f. (= *Kleine Beiträge zur klassischen Philologie* I, Roma 1964, 465 f.).

S. Frei-Korsumsky, *Griechische Wörter aus lateinischer Überlieferung*, Zürich 1969.

E. Frenzel, *Motive der Weltliteratur*, Stuttgart 1976.

M. Fuhrmann, *Persona, ein römischer Rollenbegriff*, in: *Poetik und Hermeneutik* VIII, München 1979, 83 f.

V. Gardthausen, *Augustus und seine Zeit*, Leipzig 1891.

G. Genette, *Figures III*, Paris 1972.

H. Goelzer, *Comptes rendus des séances de l'Académie des Inscriptions et Belles-Lettres*, Paris 1925, 37–39.

W. Gundel, *Sterne und Sternbilder im Glauben des Altertums und der Neuzeit*, Hildesheim r1981.

R. Hakamies, *Étude sur l'origine et l'évolution du diminutif latin et sa survie dans les langues romanes*, Helsinki 1951.

W. E. Heitland, *Agricola. A study of Agriculture and Rustic Life in the Greco-Roman World from the Point of View of Labour*, Cambridge 1921.

M. Helbers-Molt, *De vocabuli 'denique' apud Apuleium usu*, Mnem. III 11 (1943), 129 f.

L. Heller, *Lucius, the Ass as a Speaker of Greek and Latin*, ClJ 37 (1941/42), 533.

L. Heller, *Another Word from Lucius, the Ass*, ClJ 38 (1942/43), 96 f.

J. Henderson, *The Maculate Muse. Obscene Language in Attic Comedy*, New Haven – London 1975.

W. Heraeus, *Die Appendix Probi*, ALL 11 (1900), 324 f.

S. Hiller, *Bellerophon*, München 1970.

K. Hopkins, *Conquerors and Slaves. Sociological Studies in Roman History*, Cambridge 1978.

W. Hottentot e.a., *Juvenalis' tweede satire. Die mietjes zijn verdomde solidair*, Groniek 77 (1982), 65–76.

H. Th. Johann, *Trauer und Tod: eine quellen- und strukturanalytische Untersuchung der philosophischen Trostschriften über den Tod*, München 1968.

M. Kaser, *Das römische Privatrecht*, Zweiter Abschnitt, München ²1975.

R. Kassel, *Untersuchungen zur griechischen und römischen Konsolationsliteratur*, München 1958.

K. Kerenyi, *Die griechisch-orientalische Romanliteratur*, Tübingen 1927.

G. Kittel, *Theologisches Wörterbuch zum Neuen Testament*, Stuttgart r1966.

W. Klei, *L. Annaeus Seneca, Dialogorum II*, Utrecht 1950.

B. Kötting, *Wohlgeruch und Heiligkeit*, in: Jenseitsvorstellungen, in: Antike und Christentum, Gedenkschrift für A. Stuiber (Jahrbuch für Ant. und Christent. Ergänzungsband 9), Münster 1982, 168 f.

P. Lambrechts – P. Noyen, *Le culte d'Atargatis dans le monde grec*, NClio 6 (1954), 258 f.

R. Lattimore, *Themes in Greek and Latin Epitaphs*, Urbana 1962.

S. Lilja, *Dogs in Ancient Greek Poetry*, Helsinki 1976.

E. Lohmeyer, *Vom göttlichen Wohlgeruch*, Sitzungsberichte Heidelberg 1919, Abh. 9.

J. Marouzeau, *Traité de stylistique latine*, Paris ²1946.

R. H. A. Merlen, *De canibus. Dog and Hound in Antiquity*, London 1971.

P. von Moos, *Consolatio. Studien zur mittellateinischen Trostliteratur über den Tod usw.* München 1971/72.

L. A. Moritz, *Grain-mills and Flour in Classical Antiquity*, Oxford 1958.

C. F. W. Müller, *Syntax des Nominativs und Akkusativs im Lateinischen*, Leipzig 1908.

R. Müller, *Motivkatalog der römischen Elegie*, Zürich 1951.

D. van Nes, *Die maritime Bildersprache des Aischylos*, Groningen 1963.

R. Petri, *Ueber den Roman des Chariton*, Beiträge zur klassischen Philologie 11, Meisenheim 1963.

R. Pettazzoni, *Essays on the History of Religions*, Leiden 1954.

E. Pianezzola, *Gli aggettivi verbali in -bundus*, Firenze 1965.

K. Quinn, *Latin Explorations. Critical Studies in Roman Literature*, London 1963.

O. W. Reinmuth, *Vergil's Use of interea, a Study of the Treatment of Contemporaneous Events in Roman Epic*, AJPh 1933, 323 f.

M. Rostovtzeff, *Two Homeric Bowls in the Louvre*, AJA 41 (1937), 87 f.

C. Salles, *Assem para et accipe auream fabulam*, Latomus 40 (1981), 31 f.

G. Sanders, *Bijdrage tot de studie der latijnse metrische grafschriften van het heidense Rome*, Brussel 1960.

G. N. Sandy, *Heliodorus*, Boston 1982.

T. Sinko, *De Romanorum viro bono*, Cracovia 1903.

F. K. Stanzel, *Theorie des Erzählens*, Göttingen 1979 (^{2}1982).

H. R. Steiner, *Der Traum in der Aeneis*, Bern 1952.

C. Stöcker, *Humor bei Petron*, Erlangen 1969.

W. Stroh, *Ovids Liebeskunst und die Ehegesetze des Augustus*, Gymn. 86 (1979), 333 f.

R. A. Stucky, *Prêtres Syriens* II, *Hiérapolis*. Syria 53 (1976), 127 f.

E. H. Sturtevant, *The Pronunciation of Greek and Latin*, Philadelphia ^{2}1940.

J. Toynbee – J. Ward Perkins, *The Shrine of St. Peter. The Vatican Cemetary*, London 1956.

S. Trenkner, *The Greek novella in the Classical Period*, Cambridge 1958.

P. G. Walsh, in: *The Cambridge History of Classical Literature* II, *Latin Literature* (E. J. Kenney – W. V. Clausen edd.), Cambridge 1982, 774 f.

P. G. van Wees, rec. Callebat, *Sermo Cotidianus dans les Métamorphoses d'Apulée*, Gnomon 44 (1972), 780 f.

O. Weinreich, *Zu Apul. Metam. V 4*, Hermes 55 (1920), 111 f.

M. Wigodsky, *Vergil and Early Latin Poetry*. Hermes Einzelschriften 24. Wiesbaden 1972.

U. von Wilamowitz Moellendorff, *Der Glaube der Hellenen*, Berlin 1931/32.

A. E. Wilhelm-Hooyberg, *Peccatum. Sin and Guilt in Ancient Rome*, Groningen 1954.

G. Wille, *Musica Romana*, Amsterdam 1967.

G. Williams, *Some Aspects of Roman Marriage Ceremonies and Ideals*, JRS 48 (1958), 16 f.

E. Wölfflin, *Der Reim im Lateinischen*, ALL 1 (1884), 350 f.

Addenda to the abbreviations in *GCA* 1981 (p. IX f.)

R. J. Charleston, *Roman Pottery*, London 1955.

F. Cumont, *Recherches sur le symbolisme funéraire des Romains*, Paris 1942.

I. Hadot, *Seneca und die griechisch-römische Tradition der Seelenleitung*, Berlin 1969.

E. Kieckers, *Historische lateinische Grammatik mit Berücksichtigung des Vulgärlateins und der romanischen Sprachen*, München ^{r}1960.

A. D. Leeman, *Orationis ratio*, Amsterdam 1963.

P. H. Schrijvers, *La pensée de Lucrèce sur l'origine du langage*, Mnem. 27 (1974), 337 f.

W. C. Summers, *Seneca. Select Letters,* London ʳ1965.

H. S. Versnel, *Triumphus. An Inquiry into the Origin, Development and Meaning of the Roman Triumph,* Leiden 1970.

M. Vogel, *Onos Lyras. Der Esel mit der Leier (Orpheus Schriftenreihe zu Grundfragen der Musik* XIII), Düsseldorf 1973.

H. Wagenvoort, *Seneca. Brieven aan Lucilius.* Hilversum ⁴1967 and 1968.

J. F. Westermann, *Archaische en archaistische woordkunst,* Amsterdam 1939.

BIBLIOGRAPHY

We continue here the bibliography given in *GCA* 1981, XIII f. Reviews: G. Augello, Orpheus 1 (1980), 184–186; R. Heine, *Gnomon* 54 (1982), 496–499; J. A. Willis, *Mnem.* 35 (1982), 184–186.

Texts with translation

Apuleius, *Fabula de Amore et Psyche: das Märchen von Amor und Psyche*. Mit der Übersetzung von A. Rode, hrsg, und erl. von C. Loehning, München 1980.
Apuleius, *Der goldene Esel*. Herausgegeben und übersetzt von Edward Brandt und Wilhelm Ehlers, München ³1980 (with 'Nachwort zur dritten Auflage').

Studies

K. Alpers, Innere Beziehungen und Kontraste als hermeneutische Zeichen in den Metamorphosen des Apuleius von Madaura, *WJA* N.F. 6a (1980), 197–207.
G. Augello, *Nota Apuleiana. Un erroneo fortunato emendato del Koehler a Met. IV, 31 e la semantica di sudus*, ALGP 14–16 (1977–1979), 175–180.
J. Bergman, *Zum Zwei-Wege-Motiv, religionsgeschichtliche und exegetische Bemerkungen*, Svensk exegetisk årsbok (Lund) 41–42 (1976–1977), 27–56.
I. Cazzaniga, *Il supplizio del miele e delle formiche: un motivo novellistico nelle Metamorfosi di Apuleio VII 22*. SPh 66 (1949), 1–5.
G. Cooper, *Sexual and Ethical Reversal in Apuleius: the Metamorphoses as Anti-Epic*, in C. Deroux ed., *Studies in Latin Literature and Roman History*, II, Bruxelles 1980, 436–466.
F. Desbordes, *De la littérature comme digression. Notes sur les Métamorphoses d'Apulée*, in: *Questions de sens*, Paris 1982, 31–51.
M. Donnini, *Apul. Met. X, 2–12. Analogie e Varianti di un racconto*, MCSN 3 (1981), 145–160.
K. Dowden, *Eleven Notes on the Text of Apuleius' Metamorphoses*, CQ 30 (1980), 218–226.
K. Dowden, *Psyche and the Gnostics*, in: *SAG* 1981, 157–164.
K. Dowden, *Psyche on the Rock*, Latomus 41 (1982), 336–352.
K. Dowden, *Apuleius and the Art of Narration*, CQ 32 (1982), 419–435.
N. Fick, *Les Métamorphoses d'Apulée et le monde du travail*, in: *Recherches sur les Artes à Rome*, prol. de J. M. André, Paris 1978, 86–99.
M.-L. von Franz, *A psychological interpretation of the golden ass of Apuleius*, Dallas-Irving, ²1980.
G. Galimberti Biffoni, *Le Metamorfosi di Apuleio, Commedia umana?* in: *Studi su Varrone, sulla retorica, storiografica e poesia latina. Scritti in onore di Benedetto Riposati*, Rieti etc. 1979, 185–194.
R. W. Garson, *The faces of Love in Apuleius' Metamorphoses*, Mus. Afr. 6 (1977/78), 37–42.
G. F. Gianditi, *Memoria letteraria e giuridica nell' episodio di Chryseros e Lamachos (Apul. Met. 4, 9–11)*, QFC 3 (1981), 61–83.
J. Gil, *La novela entre los latinos*, Elias 22 (1978), 375–398.
P. Grimal, *Le conte d'amour de Psyché*, VL 1978, 71, 2–9.
J. Gijsel, *Lectuur van enkele teksten*, Kleio 12 (1982), 156–170.
C. Harrauer, *Lector intende, laetaberis (Zur Textstruktur der Metamorphosen)* in: *SAG* 1981, 144–155.

M. J. Hidalgo, *Organización social y económica en la obra de Apuleyo*, MHA 1 (1977) 109–114.
M. J. Hidalgo, *La magia y la religión en las obras de Apuleyo*, Zephyrus 30–31 (1980), 223–230.
N. M. Horsfall, *Allecto and natura: a pattern of allusion in Apuleius*, LCM 7 (1982), 41.
B. L. Hijmans Jr., *Boccaccio's Amor and Psyche*, in SAG 1981, 30–45.
B. L. Hijmans Jr.-V. Schmidt Edd., *Symposium Apuleianum Groninganum* (23–24 Oct. 1980), Groningen 1981.
J. E. Ifie – L. A. Thompson, *Rank, social status and esteem in Apuleius*, Mus. Afr. 6 (1977/78), 21–36.
C. P. Jones, *Apuleius' Metamorphoses and Lollianus' Phoinikika*, Phoenix 34 (1980), 243–254.
A. A. M. van Kempen, *A note on Apul. Met. I 6 (5, 15)*, Mnem. 33 (1980), 362–364.
D. M. Levin, *To whom did the ancient novellists address themselves?*, RSC 25 (1977), 18–29.
C. Marchesi, *Giovanni Boccaccio e i codici di Apuleio*, in: *Scritti minori di filologia e letteratura*, Firenze 1978, 1009–1011.
F. Millar, *The world of the Golden Ass*, JRS 71 (1981), 63–75.
D. Novaković, *Lucius ou l'âne et les Métamorphoses d'Apulée*, L & G 15 (1980), 25–46.
R. Th. van der Paardt, *The unmasked 'I': Apuleius Met. XI 27*, Mnem. 34 (1981), 96–106.
R. Th. van der Paardt, *The Story of Mr. 'Overbold' as specimen historiae (on Apul. Met. VIII 1–14)*, in: SAG 1981, 19–28.
R. Th. van der Paardt, *Sporen van de Gouden Ezel in de Nederlandse letterkunde*, Maatstaf 29, 5 (1981), 9–19.
R. Th. van der Paardt, *Louis Couperus en de romanciers van Rome*, in: *Antieke motieven in de moderne Nederlandse letterkunde*, Amsterdam 1982, 11–28.
M. Pizzica, *Su alcuni luoghi controversi delle Metamorfosi di Apuleio*, QC 1 (1979). 373–383.
M. Pizzica, *Apul. Met. II 30, 19–20; XI, 29, 3*, QILL 1 (1979), 95–99.
M. Pizzica, *La critica testuale e le metamorfosi di Apuleio. A proposito di un recentissimo volume di G. Augello*, RCCM 31–32 (1979/80), 179–194.
D. Quartuccio, *Sull' origine dell' affectio maritalis*, Labeo 24 (1978), 51–56.
S. Rocca, *Mellitus tra lingua familiare e lingua letteraria*, Maia 31 (1979), 37–43.
L. Rychslewska, *De Apulei Metamorphosibus cum Graecorum fabula romanensi comparatis*, Meander, 35 (1980), 145–155.
SAG 1981, see B. L. Hijmans-V. Schmidt Edd.
G. N. Sandy, *Interpolated Narratives in Apuleius: Listeners and Readers*, in SAG 1981, 4–17.
A. Savio, *La moneta romana in Apuleio*, NAC 5 (1976), 205–209.
C. C. Schlam, *Man and animal in the Metamorphoses of Apuleius*, in: SAG 1981, 115–142.
V. Schmidt, *Die Dea Syria und Isis in Apuleius' Metamorphosen*, in: SAG 1981, 70–76.
V. Schmidt, *Apuleiana Groningana VII: Apuleius Met. III 15 f.*, Mnem. 34 (1982), 269–282.
A. Scobie, *A Quechua Eselmensch*, Fabula 23 (1982), 287–291.
J. H. Tatum, *Apuleius*, in: T. J. Luce Ed., *Ancient Writers: G & R*, New York 1982, 1099–1116.
J. J. M. Tobin, *Apuleius and Ophelia*, Cl.B 56 (1980), 69–71.
P. G. Walsh, *Apuleius*, in: E. F. Kenney – W. V. Clausen Edd., *The Cambridge History of Classical Literature*, II, Cambridge 1982, 774–786.
J. Winkler, *Auctor & Actor: Apuleius and his Metamorphoses*, Pac. Coast Phil. 14 (1979), 84–92.
L. Zurli, *Il Modello Attanziale di una Novella Apuleiana*, MCSN 3 (1981), 397–410.

INTRODUCTION

1. Book VIII of Apuleius' Metamorphoses may roughly be subdivided as follows:
 – chapters 1–14: the tale of the deaths of Tlepolemus, Charite and Thrasyllus,
 – chapters 15–25 the ass's travels and adventures with the band of fugitive slaves,
 – chapters 26–31 the ass's sojourn with the priests of the Dea Syria.

The final section continues up to 9, 10 (210, 8 f.). Within this rough division chapters 1 and 15 contain transitional passages (176, 15–20 and 188, 7–14), chapter 22 a tale which on the surface has nothing to do with the preceding travel adventures (and which is explicitly 'marked' insertion: 193, 21–22), whereas the sale of the ass, related in chapters 23–25, may also be characterized as a transitional passage, but one which in the elaborateness of its narration is clearly marked as bridging a completer narrative shift than those of chapters 1 and 15. Nevertheless the casual reader will experience the narrative shift between chapters 14 and 15 as a sharp one. This is mainly due to the fact that at that point the sub-narrator's tale ends and with it the story of Charite. Lucius now continues with his own experiences as an ass (see also below 4.1). On some problems concerning the sub-narrator's tale see below 4.2.

2. In fact the break at 8, 25 may well be regarded as even sharper than the one at 7, 13–14 where the ass passes from the hands of the robbers to those of Charite, Tlepolemus and their *familia rustica*. The latter transition had been much more elaborately prepared for by the presence of Charite (from 4, 23 onwards) and her rescue by Haemus/Tlepolemus (7, 4–12), in which the ass had played a definite rôle. The transition of 8, 23–25, then, may be regarded as the first major one since Lucius' metamorphosis and capture by the robbers at 3, 25–28.

The beginning of book 8 coincides with a break within the story of Charite (see also below 4.2.3): the ass, still with the *familia rustica*, is among the audience to whom a messenger reports the deaths of their masters. On the function of this sub-narrator see below 4.2.1.1. The end of the book cuts through the middle of a sojourn of the priests of the Dea Syria with a religious man, at the point where the story of the cook's desperate measures ends and the rabies episode begins. It is noteworthy that the book ends with an element of suspense, not unlike, but rather more marked than, the suspense at the end of book 6. Book 7, too, ends with a threat to the ass's life, but in the last sentence the immediate threat is removed. On Apuleius' careful marking of the ends of books[1] see Junghanns 1932, 126 n. 13; in addition to his remarks it should be

---

[1] The explicits of all books except 1 and 11 contain an annotation by Sallustius preserved in F. The most elaborate of these, at the end of book 9 mentions a second reading in the year 397 A.D. The division into books therefore predates the end of the 4th cent. and most probably is due to Apuleius himself.

noted not only that Apuleius varies his methods in ending a book, but that the ends coincide with narrative shifts of varying completeness.

3. Both time and geographical situation in this section of the novel are kept vague.

3.1 The messenger's tale in chapters 1–14 takes place *noctis gallicinio* (176, 15). We may infer that the events described take place within the same period of time as that described in 7, 14–28, but the actual indications of time in that section (165, 26 *per diem,* 166, 7 *serius, aliquando, tandem,* 168, 24 *quadam die,* 169, 20 *nec multis interiectis diebus;* 171,20 *spatio modico interiecto,* 172, 9 *matutino,* 174, 19 *crastino,* 174, 23 *in alterum diem*) are all more important as time experienced than as objective time. If we compare the indications in 8, 1–14, only one fixed point of time is mentioned: 177,20 f. the day of Charite's rescue from the robbers. For the rest the reader's attention in this section, too, is entirely directed towards time as it is experienced by the characters involved, with the one, rather vague, exception that the events come to a head before Charite's mourning period is over (184, 19 f.). As far as time experienced is concerned, the major difference between 7, 14–27 and 8, 1–14 is that in the former section it always refers to time experienced by the experiencing I (= Lucius-ass), in the latter by one or the other of the main actors.

Immediately after this tale a number of successive days appears to be enumerated objectively (188, 22 f. one night; 193, 20 one night and one day; 195, 2 three days; 198, 11 the next day), but at 200, 10–11 this progression is dropped in favour of a vague indication which may imply a lengthier period. In fact, if we re-examine the passages in which 'objective' time is mentioned, we note that even there an element of experience is not lacking, at least in some cases: thus at 188,22 *iam uespera semitam tenebrante* connotes (after the previous colon in which a mountain was climbed and a long distance travelled) an element of fatigue, 189, 15 the dangers in store. The three days of 195, 2 – during which the *iumenta* are fattened – function rather as a prelude to the sale of the ass than as an indication of objective time.

3.2 Much the same may be noted with regard to the locality or localities in which the action takes place. As to 8, 1–14: the tale is told in the rural area where Charite's *familia rustica* resides. She herself lived in a *ciuitas proxima* (176, 15), but comparison with 7, 15 (165, 16) *procul a ciuitate* casts some doubt on the proximity of that *ciuitas*. When at 8, 15 the group of fugitives starts travelling, much attention is paid to the (usually dire) quality of the landscape, none to the direction they take; the *castella,* villages and houses mentioned remain nameless.

4. The book presents the reader with some interesting problems of interpretation with respect to

– the rôle of the ass, who is much less the central actor, much more the observer

– the structure of the tale of Charite, Tlepolemus and Thrasyllus
– the use of narrative motifs in that tale
– its significance
– the type of tales inserted in the remainder of the book, and the way in which they are linked with the framing tale

– the significance of the episode in which the ass sojourns with the priests of the Dea Syria.

4.1 The narrator, who reported in books 4, 6, 25–end and 7 a great many of his own experiences and, in particular, his sufferings as an ass, in this book is rather less ass-centered. Chapters 1–14 consist entirely of a tale he hears, and to which he does not react; at least his reaction to the tale is not recorded. The flight of the *familia rustica* admittedly gives him occasion to remark that he was glad to escape castration (188, 17 f., cf. 7, 26: 174, 16 f.) and there is a reference to his fear (189, 16 f.), but when everyone is bitten by savage dogs, it is only by implication that we may suppose the ass to have been bitten as well (cf. 191, 16 f.). The frame of the dragon tale (ch. 19–21) contains no reference to the ass at all, nor does that of the honey punishment (ch. 22). The only event that is apparently of great importance to the ass is his sale (ch. 23–25). After his sale, the ass's participation in events increases somewhat as his stay with the priests of the Dea Syria is reported – an event which marks almost the nadir, in moral terms, of his existence as an ass.

4.2 The tale of Charite, Tlepolemus and Thrasyllus warrants a fuller discussion.

4.2.1 It falls into the following sections:

a. 176, 15–20 link with the framing tale

b. 176, 21–177, 4 sub-narrator's introduction

c. 177, 5–178, 20 Thrasyllus: character and intentions

d. 178, 21–180, 25 hunting expedition and death of Tlepolemus

e. 181, 1–13 message for Charite, burial of Tlepolemus

f. 181, 14–182, 14 Thrasyllus' mourning and attempts at consolation, Charite's mourning

g. 182, 14–183, 21 Thrasyllus proposes to Charite, who sees through his scheme. Tlepolemus' ghost appears to Charite in a dream

h. 184, 1–185, 22 Charite sets a trap for Thrasyllus

i. 185, 23–187, 2 Thrasyllus walks into the trap, Charite addresses her drugged victim

j. 187, 3–26 Charite blinds Thrasyllus, runs to Tlepolemus' grave, where she explains events to the bystanders, commits suicide and is buried

k. 188, 1–6 Thrasyllus commits suicide in the same tomb.

4.2.1.1 The insertion of the tale within the framing tale presents a problem: Thrasyllus is presented as a wholly new character (177, 5 f.), in terms that seem to imply that the audience of *equisones opilionesque* etc. has never heard of him: there is no such phrase as 'as you probably know'. This seems strange when one remembers that it is Charite's *familia rustica* who form the audience and who might be supposed to have been aware of the *fama* referred to at 177, 10. On the one hand one may argue that the introduction, though addressed to the audience, also functions as an introduction to the readers. On the other hand it should be noted that the tale starts with the words *Erat in proxima ciuitate*, a phrase which evokes the opening of the tale of 'Amor and Psyche' (cf. 4, 28. 96, 16 *Erant in quadam ciuitate rex et regina*), another tale told by a sub-narrator to an audience.[2] The latter tale is largely one of *curiositas, amor* and *uoluptas*. Our

---

[2] See also vdPaardt in *SAG* 1981, 23.

present tale is one of an evil *libido* and its dire consequences and it is termed a *historiae specimen*[3]. The insistence on the truth of the description of Thrasyllus' character, and therefore the truth of the tale, may well be thought to support this aspect.[4] Nevertheless the tale is not smoothly inserted in the framing story (cf. below 4.3 on the tale of the punished slave). One palpable discrepancy has been noted in the commentary on 177, 11 *inter praecipuos proces:* at 4, 26 (94, 20 f.) Charite herself had said that she had been promised to Tlepolemus (whose name we learn at 7, 12:163, 7) from early youth. Here we have an instance of a discrepancy between information provided by two different characters. For that reason one of these may have to be branded as unreliable (cf. 4.5 below on the unreliability of the chief narrator). Presently (4.2.1.3) it will become clear that the reader has difficulty in deciding which of the two characters has to be so branded.

4.2.1.2 Though the tale is not structured as a formal prosecutor's oration, it is obvious throughout that many of the rhetorical devices of the prosecutor are used. It is the sub-narrator's obvious aim to convince the audience of Thrasyllus' guilt. The ancient orator however was trained to produce equally convincing speeches for both the defence and the prosecution in the same case. In the following paragraph it will be argued that the author whose rhetorical proficiency is beyond doubt, admittedly has his sub-narrator present his tale from a 'prosecutor's' point of view, but at the same time allows his readers glimpses of the tale as it might have been presented by the defence.

4.2.1.3 For the reader inclined to ask the question 'How do you know?' the author has constructed a careful, though not always obvious, chain of information that the reader can follow back from the tale he is reading to the events related. The usual link between the (implied) author and the narrator (Lucius) presents no problems: the author makes the ass part of the audience of the messenger (the sub-narrator), and so accounts for his knowledge of the tale. At this point in the chain, matters become less clear, although, at least at first sight, there seem to be no problems about section *d* (see 4.2.1 above), where the sub-narrator as one of the drovers (179, 14 *nos quidem*), looks like an eye-witness to the murder, nor about sections *g-i*, where Charite herself is the informant (cf. 187, 19–21) and has the sub-narrator among her audience (cf. 187, 9 f. *at nos et omnis populus*). But the report of Charite's dream ends with the words *et addidit cetera omnemque scaenam sceleris inluminat* (183, 20–21). This looks remarkably like another link in the chain of information, in particular since Charite's own tale at 187, 19–21 contains a reference to this sentence in the words *quae sibi per somnium nuntiauerat maritus*. Another look at the eye-witness status of the sub-narrator with respect to the death-scene of

---

[3] 177, 3 f. The expression should be compared on the one hand with Diophanes' prophecy at 2, 12 (35, 9 f.) *nunc enim gloriam satis floridam, nunc historiam magnam et incredundam fabulam et libros me futurum* (the prophecy concerns Lucius and therefore the framing tale), and on the other hand with Charite's utterance at 6, 29 (151, 4 f.) *uisetur et in fabulis audietur doctorumque stilis rudis perpetuabitur historia 'asino uectore uirgo regia fugiens captiuitatem'* (referring to the Charite tale up to 7, 15).

[4] At another level such insistence on the truth of his tale by the narrator may well arouse suspicions in the reader. For a similar, but more extensive, insistence on the truth of his tale see Aristomenes at 1, 5 (4, 18 f.).

Tlepolemus shows that it is less than certain that the drovers, hidden as they were (179, 16 f. *tegumentis frondis uel arboribus latenter abscondimus*), were in a position to observe the actual murder. Two arguments, both of them weak, may be adduced to support the notion that the drovers did not see the actual murder: *Thrasyllus culpam bestiae dabat* (180, 25) and the drovers (apparently) do not report the murder. The first argument may be reasoned away by translating 'tried blaming the boar' rather than 'kept blaming the boar', the second by assuming fear on the part of these slaves.

A second possibility is that the sub-narrator has indeed seen how Thrasyllus' lance entered Tlepolemus' thigh, but that the interpretation as murder rather than accident is faulty. See also comm. below on 180, 14 *dimisit*, and below 4.2.4 on the significance of the tale. Another slight difficulty in the tale is presented by the sub-narrator's sketch of Thrasyllus[5], his continual harping on the man's evil character and his knowledge of Thrasyllus' inner thoughts, in particular in section *c* and generally throughout the tale. In the case of a first-person narrator with limited point of view this may be understood in terms of interpretation after the event. If however the information about the events ultimately depends on what the ghost has told Charite in her dream, even the interpretation of Thrasyllus' character may have its source there rather than in the sub-narrator.

Charite, after her dream, reacts by trapping Thrasyllus and committing suicide. After a previous dream, the *anus* had reacted: 4, 27 (96, 5–14) '*Bono animo esto, mi erilis, nec uanis somniorum figmentis terreare. Nam praeter quod diurnae quietis imagines falsae perhibentur, tunc etiam nocturnae uisiones contrarios euentus nonnumquam pronuntiant. Denique flere et uapulare et nonnumquam iugulari lucrosum prosperumque prouentum nuntiant, contra ridere et mellitis dulciolis uentrem saginare uel in uoluptatem ueneriam conuenire tristitie animi, languore corporis damnisque ceteris uexatum iri praedicabant.*' As to the meaning of the dream to which the *anus* reacts see *GCA* 1977, 203 f., as to her theories ibid. 205. In her view, then – and the author nowhere indicates that she is wrong – dreams are less than trustworthy. Charite had dreamt that, when she was kidnapped by robbers, her husband[6] had pursued the kidnappers, but was killed by one of those robbers. That dream does not come true, but there seems to be a link between the robber-element there and the characterisation of Thrasyllus in the present tale as *factionibus latronum male sociatus* (177, 8).

If the author allows the reader to trace the information as to both the events and Thrasyllus' characterisation to Charite's second dream and links the two dreams in this manner, it would seem that he leaves the possibility open for the reader to treat the murder as a figment of Charite's (subconscious) imagination – a figment to which she overreacts in her punishment of Thrasyllus and her own suicide.

---

[5] The fact that the sub-narrator derives part of his characterization from the name Thrasyllus (182, 14 f.) may be seen as strongly persuasive with respect to his immediate audience. At the level author – reader one must reckon with an awareness of the playful aspect of the use of significant names in ancient literature.

[6] On the question whether Charite and Tlepolemus are married at that point see 4, 26 (95, 2) and *GCA* 1981, 168 on 7, 13 (164, 14).

Two elements in the tale seem to support the possibility of this view. (1) The phrase *iam scaenam pessimi Thrasylli perspiciens* (183, 6 f.) may imply that Charite has decided that Thrasyllus is the culprit. The subsequent dream, then, does not have its usual pivotal function. Indeed, far from being a message from the hereafter, it may be a reaction to, or a confirmation of, Charite's suspicions. Suspicions, not knowledge, since nothing in the preceding tale indicates that she had been informed by anybody concerning the details of the death of Tlepolemus – whether it was an intentional deed on the part of Thrasyllus, or an accident with his lance, or even merely due to the boar. The phrase, then, may have been inserted here by the author as a deliberate clue to enable the reader to come to the conclusion that Charite regards Thrasyllus as guilty on insufficient grounds. (2) The entire narrative strategy excludes any presentation by Thrasyllus of his own case, with the exception of the words *culpam bestiae dabat* (180, 25), and even these are the words of the sub-narrator, not a direct quotation. This fact throws an interesting light on the ambiguous abl. abs. *cognitis omnibus* at the beginning of section *k* (188, 1). The phrase allows at least two interpretations: (a) 'after Thrasyllus had become aware of the situation' – with the implication that earlier he was not, ergo had no guilty conscience, and (b) 'after he had heard of Charite's tale and suicide' with the implication suggested by the sub-narrator that Thrasyllus now knows that his criminal intents and actions have become common knowledge.

4.2.2 As to the tale pattern Rohde [5]1974, 590 noted a resemblance to the tale of Camma, Sinatus and Sinorix as told by Plutarch (*Mul. virt.* 20, 257 E f. and *Amat.* 22, 768 B f.) and Polyaenus (8, 39). The points of resemblance include the triangle, the murder of the husband and the revenge by the wife. For the hunting expedition with the sudden appearance of the boar the Adonis parallel as well as the Atys tale in Herodotus (1, 34 f.) can be added. See e.g. Apuleiana Groningana VIII under 4.1.3.3.1 (to appear shortly in *Mnemosyne*). The latter tale is also used by Lucian (*Jup. Conf.* 12, cf. Anderson 1976, 63). A similar tale occurs in Ach. Tat. 2, 34 where a young man attacked by a boar is accidentally killed by his lover. The combination of these two tale patterns is supported and enriched by the use of numerous more or less well known narrative motifs and topoi. As a result the tale is much more colourful and nuanced than those mentioned above and has become one allowing interpretation at more than one level. The motifs and topoi are discussed in the comm. ad loc. Here we list exempli gratia among motifs:

a. the treacherous friend

b. the faithful wife (with several subordinate motifs, e.g. her vengeance and suicide)[7]

c. the *custodia pudicitiae uxoris* (178, 9 f.)[8]

---

[7] The motif of the faithful wife (or husband) wishing to die with her (or his) husband (or wife) occurs frequently in the Greek novel, e.g. Chariton 1,5,2; 3,3,1; 3,10,4; Xen. Eph. 3,6,3; 3,10,2; 5,4,11; Ach. Tat. 3,16,2; 5,7,5; 7,6,1; Heliod. 1,31,6; 2,1,1; 2,4,4; 5,24,3; 10,20,2. Cf. also Longus 2, 22 and Petr. 111. It is noteworthy that the intended suicide never comes to pass, since the situation in almost all cases refers to the chief characters who cannot die without spoiling the happy end. In the Apuleian elaboration of the motif there is no such limitation.

[8] The motif of the *custodia pudicitiae uxoris* is elaborated more fully in the tale of Philesitherus (9, 17–21).

d. the *imagines defuncti* (182, 12)
e. the ruse/the drugged wine (184, 11 f./186, 1 f.)
f. blinding the culprit (187, 3 f.)
g. Thrasyllus' suicide in the tomb of the dead couple (188, 1 f.)

4.2.3 The tale as it appears in Apuleius, then, is a combination of tale patterns, motifs and topoi. The fact that *Onos* 34, 1 presents an entirely different ending to the tale of the kidnapped and rescued girl and her husband presumably indicates that Apuleius did not find the model for his tale in his 'Vorlage'. It is indeed highly likely that it is to be regarded as his own composition. The sources for his material were probably wide-spread. Apart from the items mentioned under 4.2.2 much may have been absorbed during his rhetorical training (cf. 4.2.1.2). It is noteworthy e.g. that the motif mentioned under 4.2.2 *c* also occurs in Quint. *Decl.* 363. As to *f*, there are declamations under the heading *adulter excaecatur*, cf. e.g. Quint. *Decl.* 357. For the vengeance (4.2.2 *b*) cf. also Val. Max. 9, 10 ext. 1. The faithful wife wishing to die with her husband occurs several times in Seneca's *Controuersiae* (e.g. 2,2,1).

In this context the many literary reminiscences merit mention as well. They have been noted in the commentary. Two instances of the use that Apuleius makes of them may be mentioned here. On several occasions Charite seems to be compared to Dido (see in particular comm. on 181, 1 f. 184, 1 f. and 187, 7 f.). The parallel shows an obvious element of inversion in so far as it is Charite's characterisation as the *uxor pudica* or *uniuira* that leads to her tragic end. In view of the absence of any element of the ridiculous it does not do to speak of parody here, though that element is by no means lacking in the *Met.* Another instance is Thrasyllus' tearless mourning of Tlepolemus (180, 23/181, 15), which is very much akin to Caesar's reaction to the death of Pompey in Lucan (9, 1035 f. and 1061 f., see comm. on 181, 15). This instance differs from the previous one in that Charite's kinship with Dido is suggested by means of verbal reminiscences, whereas the parallel Thrasyllus-Caesar is situational.[9]

4.2.4 If the provenance of Apuleius' material poses a problem, so do the function and significance of the tale within the novel as a whole. Here we can but touch upon a few aspects.

Apuleius himself has his sub-narrator refer to the tale as a *historiae specimen* (177, 3 f.). The phrase *ut cuncta noritis* in the same sentence touches upon the relation sub-narrator – audience and throughout the tale it is obvious that the sub-narrator is concerned to persuade (in the rhetorical sense of the word) his audience of the evil of Thrasyllus' character. A sentence like 178, 6–8 *quidni, cum flamma saeui amoris parua quidem primo uapore delectet, sed fomentis consuetudinis exaestuans inmodicis ardoribus totos amburat homines* is characteristic of his rhetorico-moralist attitude. He shares this attitude with the chief narrator e.g. in his depiction of the priests of the Dea Syria. But where the chief narrator on occasion pokes fun at himself (e.g. 7, 10: 162, 1 f. with *GCA* 1981,

---

[9] On the connection of the tale with Petronius' tale of the Widow of Ephesus (*Sat.* 111), which was noted by Dornseiff 1938, 226, see now Walsh in *AAGA* 1978, 20 f. and vdPaardt in *SAG* 1981, 20 f. The connection is mainly one of contrast. See also below comm. on 181, 19 f.

147 f. ad loc.), no such relief is offered by the sub-narrator.[10] At his level the tale constitutes an unmitigated condemnation of moral wrong, in particular Thrasyllus' *uoluptas,* see 178, 19 f. *Spectate denique, sed, oro, sollicitis animis intendite, quorsum furiosae libidinis proruperint impetus.* While the theme *libido* doubtless is to be linked with the general theme of *uoluptas* in the *Met.,* the sub-narrator's appeal to his audience may also be compared with the phrase – presumably to be placed at the level of the (implied) author – *lector, intende: laetaberis* (1,1: 2, 3 f.). The contrast is obvious: horror aroused at one level may be enjoyed at another; and if the ambiguities noted above under 4.2.1.3 are acceptable as such, the reader may enjoy discovering behind the tale as told a hidden one of a tragic mistake. At the chief narrator's level, however, the tale is characterised by the words *mira ac nefanda* (176, 19). The phrase clearly indicates that Lucius is here represented on the one hand as accepting the tale as told, on the other as placing it among the many other *mirabilia* he is relating.

Different approaches, leading to different types of significance are of course possible and have often been attempted. Thus e.g. Merkelbach 1962, 72 f. relates the tale to the myth of Osiris, Isis and Seth. Among the many reactions to his views we cite Gwyn Griffith's in *AAGA* 1978, 151 f.; see also Apuleiana Groningana VIII sub 4.1.2. A Jungian approach was attempted by Von Franz [2]1980, 113 f., who accepts Merkelbach's Isis- Osiris and Attis parallels. In her scheme of interpretation these parallels are pointers to the motif of the 'puer aeternus' in this part of the tale represented by Tlepolemus.

4.3 The remainder of the book shows a number of heterogeneous episodes. The unheeded warning against wolves, who actually do not materialise (ch. 15–16), leads to the sublimation of the ass's fear by means of the Pegasus parallel (189, 20 f.), as wel as to the arming of the band of fugitives (189, 26 f.). This in turn constitutes a natural transition to the battle of chapters 17 and 18, from which the band recuperates in a *locus* apparently *amoenus,* but actually the scene of the adventure with the shape shifting dragon (chapters 19 -21). On the latter scene see comm. ad loc. Whereas the first two scenes are linked to the ass's fears and the theme of self-preservation (cf. e.g. Heine in *AAGA* 1978, 27), the scene with the dragon is marked as belonging to the list of *mirabilia* in the *Met.* (cf. 193, 11 *mira*).[11] It is followed by the tale of the punished slave (ch. 22), a tale like the one of 1–14 heard by the ass. Not only the manner of insertion but also the theme of adultery link the two tales. The way they are inserted at least superficially removes them from the description of the ass's experiences. For interpretations and parallels of the tale of the punished slave see comm. ad loc.

The episode of the ass's first sale – the most elaborate of the episodes in which he changes hands (cf. 9, 10: 210, 12–17; 9, 31: 226, 22–26; 9, 42: 235, 23 f.; 10, 13:

---

[10] Of course the chief narrator presents his tale from a considerably greater distance than the present sub-narrator. In Lucius' case the distance is both a psychological one – the Isis-initiate relates the adventures of his previous existence as an ass – and one of time – the initiations of book 11 alone take months. The present sub-narrator's tale is told shortly after the events discribed.

[11] 8, 1–14 belongs to the same category, cf. 176, 19 *mira ac nefanda.* See also 195, 25 with our comm.

246, 5–7; 10, 17: 249, 22–26), even the final escape at 10, 35 is less elaborate – is mainly an elaboration of the theme of the humiliation and ridicule of Lucius/ass (cf. e.g. Heine in *AAGA* 1978, 30).

4.4 That humiliation culminates in the ass's being sold to the priests of the Dea Syria. For the interpretation of the episode in which the ass serves these priests see Appendix IV.

Here it may be noted that the humiliating ridicule to which the ass is subjected during his sale is balanced by the ridicule to which the priests are exposed when caught in depraved sexual activities (201, 1 f.).

The progressive humiliation, however, runs parallel with a gradual lessening of the physical violence to which the ass is subjected. In book 7 he had repeatedly complained of the heavy labour he was made to do (e.g. 7, 18) and of the many beatings that went with that labour (7, 18: 168, 9 f.; 7, 25: 173, 2; cf. also 7, 28: 176, 5 f.). In book 8, too, the violent treatment by the *coloni* and their dogs is mentioned emphatically. When the ass is transferred to the priests however, all violence ceases and his physical situation actually improves (198, 6 *adpositis largiter cibariis*). Even at 199, 20, where the ass evinces fear of the foreign goddess's bloodthirstiness, physical violence forms no part of the picture: his fear is unfounded. No danger threatens before 200, 22 f., when the ass in his moral indignation attempts to cry *'porro Quirites'* and thus arouses the anger of the priests, disturbed as they are in their abject activities. But the dangerous moment passes as swiftly as it had appeared: here, too, physical violence is absent. Real danger, indeed death, threatens, at the end of the book, from an unexpected source: a cook in dire straits prepares to kill the ass (202, 18 f.). The theme of violence, thus resumed, is continued in book 9.

4.5 As to the highly unfavourable picture of the band of priests it is perhaps not superfluous to note that it must be seen as part and parcel of the characterisation of the chief narrator rather than as representing the author's abhorrence of the sect. The author's attitude towards various religious practices as described in *S.* 14 (22, 4–22) makes it less than likely that he shares his chief narrator's tastes in this respect.[12] For the unreliability of the latter see e.g. vdPaardt in *AAGA* 1978, 80 n. 39.

5 With respect to style several questions have engaged the group throughout the sessions. Here we mention a few items only:

5.1 – the question whether stylistic features such as assonance, alliteration, rhyme, preponderance of certain vowels etc. may be regarded as functional, and, if so, in what sense of the word. For the present volume of the commentary the group has preferred to note the phenomena rather than to attempt specification of function, since the subjective element in any such attempt remains until dependable statistics have been compiled and agreed criteria for

---

[12] How far the implied author (as distinct from the historical Apuleius, but to be defined as those aspects or that image of himself that he allows to figure within the novel) agrees with the judgement is much more difficult to determine. If there is an autobiographical element in 11, 27 (289, 7) *Madaurensem* (cf. Walsh 1982, 783; see however also the more detailed study of the problem by vdPaardt 1981, 96–106 and Mason 1983, 142), there is something to be said for such agreement.

the interpretation of such statistics have been formulated. See also *AAGA* 1978, 189 f.[13]

– the question whether stylistic features are employed to characterise speakers within the book and the novel. On the whole it would seem that this is not the case. At ch. 20 we have noted in the commentary that the high-flown style of the speaker only apparently contrasts with his emotional state.

The same may be said of the sub-narrator of chapters 1–14, whose rhetoric must be seen as the very *stilus* of the *doctiores* whom he pretends to provide with raw material (177, 3).

Our general impression is that throughout the *Met.*, and also in the present book, an increased incidence of stylistic flourishes occurs at moments of heightened emotionality. One notable instance is Charite's speech to the drugged Thrasyllus (186, 8–187, 2).

5.2 An especially noteworthy aspect of Apuleian narrative style are the changes of pace. Thus e.g. we find after the elaborate descriptive passages of the hunting scene a brief passage (181, 1–13) packed with the events of Fama reaching Charite, Charite's mad rush towards the corpse of her husband and the burial of Tlepolemus. See also our note on 181, 11–13. Similarly Charite's death and burial (187, 21–26) are described very briefly in comparison with the elaboration of the preceding entrapment of Thrasyllus. This feature may be described in terms of Chausserie-Laprée (récit dramatique vs. récit soutenu) and belongs to the realm of narrative economy. Narrative economy, too, offers an explanation for the quick, often unremarked, disappearance of secondary characters from the pages of the novel. At the level of the first person narrator it is true that nothing can enter his narrative that he has not witnessed, but at the level of the author it is easy enough to provide information by means of an 'as I heard afterwards'. For an explanation in terms of generic laws see Heine in *AAGA* 1978, 28, who notes that the tale of the deaths of Tlepolemus and Charite forms an exception. See also Scobie ibidem 48.

5.3 As to the text adopted we follow the practice of the two previous volumes of discussing our reasons for a particular choice in the commentary ad loc. The reading of F is always basic, and is adhered to wherever and whenever possible. Spelling variations in F may possibly represent less than rigid standards on the part of the author. Our practice has been to follow F also in this respect, if there is evidence that for a given word the ancient spelling was inconsistent. Thus we spell e.g. *karissimum* at 184, 14, just as we preferred *nanque* at 7,7 (159, 12; see *GCA* 1981, 128 ad loc.). The list of words whose spelling differs within the Apuleian tradition is rather long. See e.g. Oldfather's Index on *Carthago/Karthago; Diofanes/Diophanes; dirrumpo/dirumpo; faetor/fetor; penna/pinna; reccino/recino*. It should be emphasized, however, that in retaining the variation we do not pretend to reconstruct Apuleius' spelling habits, but merely indicate that the available evidence does not allow us to assume consistency on his part.

---

[13] See also N. A. Greenberg, Aspects of Alliteration, a statistical study, Latomus 35, 1980, 585–611.

NOTE TO THE TEXT

We have followed Helm's text, as printed in his latest Teubner-edition (1931, reprinted with Addenda and Corrigenda 1955). However, we have used capitals at the beginning of new sentences, added paragraph numbers throughout, and omitted commas marking off participle constructions, as e.g. dormiens 184,2 and ablatives absolute. In the following places we have chosen a different reading:

	Our text	Helm's text
176,15	proxima	⟨e⟩proxima
177,6	quo clarus et pecuniae fuit	qui*dem*, clarus *et* pecuniae *fructu*
178,5	cupidinis	Cupidinis
179,1	generosae	generosae,
179,4	musitatione	mus⟨s⟩itatione
179,20	Qui stupore	Qui⟨d⟩ stupore
179,24	Et: 'cape	en cape
180,10	lania*uit* . Nec	lania*uit* nec
181,1	Fama	fama
182,8	oboediens	ob[oed]iens
182,9	munia	munia,
	penit*is*	penitus
182,19	imprudentiae	imp[r]udentiae
183,3	procella[s]que	procellaque
183,9	sane	san⟨i⟩e
183,11	coniux – quod licebit – :	coniux, quod licebit:
183,12	perman⟨e⟩at	perma*rce*t
183,13	intercidit, Quouis	intercidit, – quouis
183,20	alienum'. ⌐Et	alienum' *et*
183,21	inlumi⌐nat	inlumi*nauit*
184,3	quieti	quiete
184,4	he⟨i⟩ula⌐t	h[eu]eiu*lat*
184,9	†imperor uide†	nuper ⟨f⟩eruide (but see Addenda)
184,14	karissimi	carissimi
185,3	exitum	exit⟨i⟩um
185,6	linguae satia⟨n⟩ti⟨s⟩	lingu⟨a⟩ aestua⟨n⟩ti
186,14	ego gladio	ego ⟨te⟩ gladio
186,24	sepulchrum	sepulchro
187,8	se procul	se ⟨et⟩ procul
187,9	gestiens. Recta contendit, at	gestiens recta contendit. at
187,23	perflauit	⟨e⟩fflauit
187,25	*in*unita	[m]unita
188,2	exitium praesenti clade	exit[i]um praesenti cladi
188,7	spiritus	⟨su⟩spiritus
188,15	passares	passeres
188,18	quanquam enormis	,quanquam enormis,
188,25	numerosos,...sarcinosos,	numerosos...sarcinosos

11

189,7	uiae reddi	*in*gre[d]di
190,22	inscindere	ins*c*endere
191,6	munitis	[m]uu*l*tis
192,15	decepto	dec⟨*r*⟩ep⟨*i*⟩to
192,18	passarem	passerem
192,29	miseruit, sed	miseruit. sed
193,8	hora	*m*ora
193,11	trepidus: mira	trepidus ⟨*et*⟩ mira
193,16	⟨*aequ*⟩aeuum	⟨*s*⟩aeuum
193,17	⟨*tes*⟩corum	*l*ocorum
193,21	Ibi	*in*ibi
194,14	luxurie sua	uxori suae
194,17	†nidifici aburrĭbant†	nidificia borriebant
194,29	longe quaesituris	longe ⟨*a*⟩ quaesituris
195,18	*adeo*	*ideo*
197,18	fracta e⟨*t*⟩	fractae
198,23	prouolant	peruolant
201,8	nancti	nacti
201,20	exumie	ex*i*mie

TEXT

LIBER VIII

1 ¹Noctis gallicinio uenit quidam iuuenis proxima ciuitate, ut   H. 176
quidem mihi uidebatur, unus ex famulis Charites, puellae illius,
quae mecum aput latrones pares aerumnas exanclauerat. ²Is de
eius exitio et domus totius infortunio mira ac nefanda, ignem
propter adsidens, inter conseruorum frequentiam sic annuntia-   20
bat: ³'Equisones opilionesque, etiam busequae, fuit Charite
nobisque misella et quidem casu grauissimo nec uero incomita-   H. 177
ta Manis adiuit. ⁴Sed ut cuncta noritis, referam uobis a capite,
quae gesta sunt quaeque possint merito doctiores, quibus stilos
fortuna subministrat, in historiae specimen chartis inuoluere.

⁵Erat in proxima ciuitate iuuenis natalibus praenobilis, quo   5
clarus e*t* pecuniae fuit satis locuples, sed luxuriae popinalis
scortisque et diurnis potationibus exercitatus atque ob id
factionibus latronum male sociatus nec non etiam manus
infectus humano cruore, Thrasyllus nomine. Idque sic erat et   10
fama dicebat.
2 ¹Hic, cum primum Charite nubendo maturuisset,
inter praecipuos procos summo studio petitionis eius munus
obierat et quanquam ceteris omnibus id genus uiris antistaret
eximiisque muneribus parentum inuitaret iudicium, morum
tamen inprobatus repulsae contumelia fuerat aspersus. ²Ac   15
dum erilis puella in bon⟨*i*⟩ Tlepolemi manum uenerat, firmiter
deorsum delapsum nutriens amorem et denegati thalami permiscens indignationem, cruento facinori quaerebat accessum.
³Nanctus denique praesentiae suae tempesti*u*am occasionem,   20
sceleri, quod diu cogitarat, accingitur. ⁴Ac die, quo praedonum
infestis mucronibus puella fuerat astu uirtutibusque sponsi sui
liberata, turbae gratulantium exultans insigniter permiscuit sese
⁵salutique praesenti a⟨*c*⟩ futurae suboli nouorum maritorum
gaudibundus ad ho⟨*no*⟩rem splendidae prosapiae inter praeci-   25
puos hospites domum nostram receptus, occultato consilio   H. 178
sceleris, amici fidelissimi personam mentiebatur. ⁶Iamque
sermonibus assiduis et conuersatione frequenti, nonnunquam
etiam cena poculoque communi carior cariorque factus in
profundam r*ui*nam cupidinis sese paulatim nescius praecipi-   5
tauerat. ⁷Quidni, cum flamma saeui amoris parua quidem
primo uapore delectet, sed fomenti⟨*s*⟩ consuetudinis exaestuans inmodicis ardoribus totos amburat homines.
3 ¹Diu denique deliberauerat secum Thrasyllus, quo⟨*d*⟩ nec   10
clandestinis colloquiis opportunum repperiret locum et adulte-

rinae Veneris magis magisque praeclusos aditus copia custodientium cerneret nouaeque atque gliscentis affectionis firmissimum uinculum non posse dissociari perspiceret et puellae, si uellet, quanquam uelle non posset, furatrinae coniugalis incommodaret rudimentum; ²et tamen ad hoc ipsum, quod non potest, contentiosa pernicie, quasi posset, impellitur. ³Quod nunc arduum factu putatur, amore per dies roborato facile uidetur effectu. Spectate denique, sed, oro, sollicitis animis intendite, quorsum furiosae libidinis proruperint impetus.

4   ¹Die quadam uenatum Tlepolemus assumpto Thrasyllo petebat indagaturus feras, quod tamen in capreis feritatis est; nec enim Charite maritum suum quaerere patiebatur bestias armatas dente uel cornu. ²Iamque apud frondosum tumulum ramorumque densis tegminibus umbrosu⟨m⟩ prospectu uestigatorum obseptis capreis ³canes uenationis indagini[s] generosae mandato cubili residentes inuaderent bestias, immittuntur statimque sollertis disciplinae memores partitae totos praecingunt aditus tacitaque prius seruata musitatione signo sibi repentino reddito latra[n]tibus feru*i*dis dissonisque miscent omnia. ⁴Nec ulla caprea nec pauens dammula nec prae ceteris feris mitior cerua, sed aper immanis atque inuisitatus exsurgit toris callosae cutis obesus, pilis inhorrentibus corio squalidus, setis insurgentibus spinae hispidus, dentibus attritu sonaci spumeus, oculis aspectu minaci flammeus, impetu saeuo frementis oris totus fulmineus. ⁵Et primum quidem canum procaciores, quae comminus contulerant uestigium, genis hac illac iactatis consectas interficit, dein calcata retiola, qua primos impetus reduxerat, transabiit.

5   ¹Et nos quidem cuncti pauore deterriti et alio[n]quin innoxiis uenationibus consueti, tunc etiam inermes atque inmuniti tegumentis frondis uel arboribus latenter abscondimus, ²Thrasyllus uero nactus fraudium opportunum decipulum sic Tlepolemum captiose compellat: ³'Qui stupore confusi uel etiam cassa formidine similes humilitati seruorum istorum uel in modum pauoris feminei deiecti tam opimam praedam mediis manibus amittimus? ⁴Quin equos inscendimus? Quin ocius indipiscimur?' Et: 'Cape uenabulum et ego sumo lanceam!' ⁵Nec tantillum morati protinus insiliunt equos ex summo studio bestiam insequentes. ⁶Nec tamen illa genuini uigoris oblita retorquet impetum et incendio feritatis ardescens dente compulso, quem primum insiliat, cunctabunda rimatur. ⁷Sed prior Tlepolemus iaculum, quod gerebat, insuper dorsum bestiae contorsit. At Thrasyllus ferae quidem peperci*t*, set equi, quo uehebatur Tlepolemus, postremos poplites lancea feriens amputat. ⁸Quadrupes reccidens, qua sanguis effluxerat, toto ⟨t⟩ergo supinatus inuitus dominum suum deuoluit ad terram. ⁹Nec diu, sed eum furens aper inuadit iacentem ac primo

lacinias eius, mox ipsum resurgentem multo dente lania*uit*. Nec
coepti nefarii bonum piguit amicum uel suae saeuitiae litatum
saltem tanto periculo cernens potuit expleri, ¹⁰ sed percito atque
plagosa crura [uulnera] contegenti suumque auxilium miseriter
roganti per femus dexterum dimisit lanceam tanto ille quidem
fidentius quanto crederet ferri uulnera similia futura prosectu
dentium. ¹Nec non tamen ipsam quoque bestiam facili manu
transadigit.

6   Ad hunc modum definito iuuene exciti latibulo suo quisque
familia maesta concurrimus. ²At ille quanquam perfecto uoto,
prostrato inimico laetus ageret, uultu tamen gaudium tegit et
frontem adseuerat et dolorem simulat et cadauer, quod ipse
fecerat, auide circumplexus omnia quidem lugentium officia
sollerter adfinxit, sed solae lacrimae procedere noluerunt. ³Sic
ad nostri similitudinem, qui uere lamentabamur, con*f*ormatus
manus suae culpam bestiae dabat.

⁴Necdum satis scelere transacto Fama dilabitur et cursus
primos ad domum Tlepolemi detorquet et aures infelicis nuptae
percutit. ⁵Quae quidem simul percepit tale nuntium, quale non
audiet aliud, amens et uecordia percita cursuque bacchata
furibundo per plateas populosas et arua rurest⟨r⟩ia fertur
insana uoce casum mariti quiritans. ⁶Confluunt ciuium maestae
cateruae, secuntur obuii dolore sociato, ciuitas cuncta uacuatur
studio uisionis. Et ecce mariti cadauer accur*r*it labantique
spiritu totam se super corpus effudit ac paenissime ibidem,
quam deuouerat, ei red⟨*d*⟩idit animam. ⁷Sed aegre manibus
erepta suorum inuita remansit in uita, funus uero toto feralem
pompam prosequente populo deducitur ad sepulturam.

7   ¹Sed Thrasyllus nimium nimius clamare, plangere et, quas in
primo maerore lacrimas non habebat, iam scilicet crescente
gaudio reddere et multis caritatis nominibus Veritatem ipsam
fallere. ²Illum amicum, coaetaneum, contubernalem, fratrem
denique addito nomine lugubri ciere, nec non interdum manus
Charites a pulsandis uberibus amouere, luctum sedare, heiulatum cohercere, ³uerbis palpantibus stimulum doloris obtundere, uariis exemplis multiuagi casus solacia nectere, cunctis
tamen mentitae pietatis officiis studium contrectandae mulieris
adhibere odiosumque amorem suum perperam delectando
nutrire.

⁴Sed officiis inferialibus statim exactis puella protinus festinat ad maritum suum demeare cunctasque prorsus pertemptat
uias, certe illam lenem otiosamque nec telis ullis indigentem, sed
placidae quieti consimilem: ⁵inedia denique misera et incuria
squalida, tenebris imis abscondita, iam cum luce transegerat.
⁶Sed Thrasyllus instantia peruicaci partim per semet ipsum,
partim per ceteros familiares ac necessarios, ipsos denique
puellae parentes extorquet tandem, iam lurore et inluuie paene

conlapsa membra lauacro, cibo denique confoueret. ⁷At illa, parentum suorum alioquin reuerens, inuita quidem, uerum religiosae necessitati subcumbens, uultu non quidem hilaro, uerum ⌐pau⌐lo sereniore oboediens, ut iubebatur, uiuentium ⌐mu⌐nia pro[ru]rsus in [s]pectore, immo uero penitus i⌐n medul-⌐ lis luctu ac maerore carpebat animum; ⌐diesque to⌐tos totasque noctes insumebat l⌐uctuoso desi⌐derio et imagines defuncti, qu⌐as ad habitum dei⌐ Liberi for⟨m⟩auerat, adfixo s⌐eruitio
8 diuinis percolens⌐ honoribus ipso se solac⌐io cruciabat. ¹Sed Th⌐rasyllus, praeceps alioq⌐uin et de ipso nomine⌐ temerarius, priusquam dolorem lacrimae satiarent et percitae mentis resideret furor et in sese ni*m*ietatis senio lassesceret luctus, ²adhuc flentem maritum, adhuc uestes lacerantem, adhuc capillos distrahentem non dubitauit de nuptiis conuenire ³et imprudentiae labe tacita pectoris sui secreta fraudesque ineffabiles detegere. ⁴Sed Charite uocem nefanda⟨m⟩ et horruit et detestata est et uelut graui ton⟨i⟩tru procella[s]que sideris uel etiam ipso diali fulmine percussa corruit corpus et obnubilauit animam. ⁵Sed interuallo reualescente paulatim spiritu, ferinos mugitus iterans et iam scaenam pessimi Thrasylli perspiciens, ad limam consilii desiderium petitoris distulit. ⁶Tunc inter moras umbra illa misere trucidati Tlepolemi sane cruentam et pallore deformem attollens faciem quietem pudicam interpellat uxoris:

⁷'Mi coniux – quod tibi prorsus ab alio dici non licebit –: etsi pectori tuo iam perman⟨e⟩at nostri memoria, uel acer*b*ae mortis meae casus foedus caritatis intercidit. ⁸Quouis alio felicius maritare, modo ne in Thrasylli manum sacrilegam conuenias neue sermonem conferas ne⟨c⟩ mensam accumbas nec toro adquiescas. ⁹Fuge mei percussoris cruentam dexteram. Noli parricidio nuptias auspicari. Vulnera illa, quorum sanguinem ⌐tu⌐ae lacrimae proluerunt, non sunt tota dentium uul⌐nera⌐: lancea mali Thras*y*lli me tibi fecit alienum'. ⌐Et addi⌐dit cetera omnemque scaenam sceleris inlumi⌐nat.
9 ¹A⌐t illa, ut primum maesta quieuerat, toro ⌐faciem impressa, et⌐ iamnunc dormiens lacrimis ema⌐nantibus genas cohu⌐midat ²et uelut quo[d]dam tormen⌐to inquieta quieti excussa⌐ luctu redintegrato prolixum he⟨*i*⟩ula⌐t discissaque interu⌐la decora b⟨*ra*⟩chia saeuientibus palmulis conuerberat. ³Nec tamen cum quoquam participatis nocturnis imaginibus, sed indicio facinoris prorsus dissimulato et nequissimum percussorem punire et aerumnabili uitae sese subtrahere tacita decernit. ⁴Ecce rursus †imperor uidet† uoluptatis detestabilis petitor aures obseratas de nuptiis obtundens aderat. ⁵Sed illa clementer aspernata sermonem Thrasylli astuque miro personata instanter garrienti summisseque deprecanti:

⁶'Adhuc', inquit, 'tui fratris meique karissimi mariti facies

pulchra illa in meis deuersatur oculis, adhuc odor cinnameus ambrosei corporis per nares meas percurrit, adhuc formonsus Tlepolemus in meo uiuit pectore. ⁷Boni ergo et optimi consules, si luctui legitimo miserrimae feminae necessarium concesseris tempus, quoad residuis mensibus spatium reliquum compleatur anni, ⁸qu*ae* res cum meum pudorem, tum etiam tuum salutare commodum respicit, ne forte inmaturitate nuptiarum indignatione iusta manes acer*b*os mariti ad exitum salutis tuae suscitemus'. ¹Nec isto sermone Thrasyllus sobriefactus uel saltem tempestiua pollicitatione recreatus identidem pergit linguae satia⟨n⟩ti⟨s⟩ susurros improbos inurguere, ²quoad simulanter reuicta Charite suscipit: 'Istud equidem certe magnopere deprecanti concedas nece*ss*e est mihi, Thrasylle, ut interdum taciti clandestinos coitus obeamus ³nec quisquam persentiscat familiarium, quo⟨a⟩d dies reliquos metiatur annu*s*'.

⁴Promissioni fallaciosae mulieris oppressus subcubuit Thrasyllus et prolixe consentit de furtiuo concubitu noctemque et opertas exoptat ultro tenebras uno potiundi studio postponens omnia. ⁵'Sed heus tu', inquit Charit[at]e, 'quam probe ueste contectus omnique comite uiduatus prima uigilia tacitus fores meas accedas unoque sibilo contentus nutricem istam meam opperiare, quae claustris adhaerens excubabit aduentui tuo. ⁶Nec setius patefactis aedibus acceptum te nullo lumine conscio ad meum perducet cubiculum'.

¹Placuit Thrasyllo scaena feralium nuptiarum. Nec sequius aliquid suspicatus, sed expectatione turbidus de diei tantum spatio et uesperae mora querebatur. ²Sed ubi sol tandem nocti decessit, ex imperio Charites ad[h]ornatus et nutricis captiosa uigilia deceptus inrepit cubiculum pronus spei. ³Tunc anus de iussu dominae blandiens ei furtim depromptis calicibus et oenoforo, quod inmixtum uino soporiferum gerebat uenenum, crebris potionibus auide ac secure haurientem mentita dominae tarditatem, quasi parentem adsideret aegrotum, facile sepeliuit ad somnum. ⁴Iamque eo ad omnes iniurias exposito ac supinato introuocata Charite masculis animis impetuque diro fremens inuadit ac supersistit sicarium.

¹'En', inquit, 'fidus coniugis mei comes, en uenator egregius, en carus maritus. Haec est illa dextera, quae meum sanguinem fudit, hoc pectus, quod fraudulentas ambages in meum concinnauit exitium, oculi isti, quibus male placui, qui quodam modo tamen iam futuras tenebras auspicantes uenientes poenas antecedunt. ²Quiesce securus, beate somniare. Non ego gladio, non ferro petam; absit, ut simili mortis genere cum marito meo coaequeris: uiuo tibi morientur oculi nec quicquam uidebis nisi dormiens. Faxo, feliciorem necem inimici tui quam uitam tuam sentias. ³Lumen certe non uidebis, manu comitis indigebis,

Chariten non tenebis, nuptias non frueris, nec mortis quiete 20
recrea*b*eris nec uitae uoluptate laeta*b*eris, sed incertum simulacrum errabis inter Orcum et solem et diu quaeres dexteram, quae tuas expugnauit pupulas, quodque est in aerumna miserrimum, nescies de quo queraris. ⁴At ego sepulchrum mei Tlepolemi tuo luminum cruore libabo et sanctis manibus eius 25 istis oculis parentabo. ⁵Sed quid mora temporis dignum cruciatum lucraris et meos forsitan tibi pestiferos imaginaris amplexus? Relictis somnolentis tenebris ad aliam poenalem euigila caliginem. ⁶Atto*ll*e uacuam faciem, uindict*a*m recognosce, infortunium intellege, aerumnas computa. Sic pudicae 30 mulieri tui placuerunt oculi, sic faces nuptiales tuos illuminarunt thalamos. Vltrices habebis pr*o*nubas et orbitatem comitem H. 187 et perpetuae conscientiae stimulum'.

13   ¹Ad hunc modum uaticinata mulier acu crinali capite deprompta Thrasylli conuulnerat tota lumina eumque prorsus 5 exoculatum relinquens, dum dolore[m] nescio crapulam cum somno discutit, ²arrepto nudo gladio, quo se Tlepolemus solebat incingere, per mediam ciuitatem cursu furioso proripit se procul dubi⟨o⟩ nescio quod scelus gestiens. ³Recta monimentum mariti contendit, at nos et omnis populus nudatis totis 10 aedibus studiose consequimur hortati mutuo ferrum uaesanis extorquere manibus. ⁴Sed Charite capu*lum* Tlepolemi propter assistens gladioque fulgenti singulos abigens, ubi fletus uberes et lamentationes uarias cunctorum intuetur, 'abicite', inquit, 'importunas lacrimas, abicite luctum meis uirtutibus alienum. 15 ⁵Vindicaui in me*i* mariti cruentum peremptorem, punita sum funestum mearum [mearum] nuptiarum praedonem. Iam tempus est, ut isto gladio deorsus ad meum Tlepolemum uiam quaeram'.

14   ¹Et enarratis ordine singulis, quae sibi per somnium nun- 20 tiauerat maritus quoque astu Thrasyllum inductum petisset, ferro sub papillam dexteram transadacto [c̄]corruit ²et in suo sibi peruolutata sanguine postremo balbu*t*tiens incerto sermone perflauit animam uirilem. ³Tunc propere familiares miserae Charites accuratissime corpus ablutum *in*unita sepultura ibi- 25 dem marito perpetuam coniugem reddidere. ⁴Thrasyllus uero H. 188 cognitis omnibus, nequiens idoneum exitium praesenti clade reddere certusque tanto facinori nec gladium sufficere, sponte delatus ibidem ad sepulchrum ⁵'ultronea uobis, infesti Manes, en ades⟨t⟩ uictima' saepe clamitans, ualu*i*s super sese diligenter 5 obseratis inedia statuit elidere sua sententia damnatum spiritum.'

15   ¹Haec ille longo⟨s⟩ trahens spiritus et nonnunquam inlacrimans grauiter adfectis rusticis adnuntiabat. Tunc illi mutati dominii nouitatem metuentes et infortunium domus erilis altius 10 miserantes fugere conparant. ²Sed equorum magister, qui me

curandum magna ille quidem commendatione susceperat, quidquid in casula pretiosum conditumque seruabat, meo atque aliorum iumentorum dorso repositum a[d]sportans sedes pristinas deserit. ³Gerebamus infantulos et mulieres, gerebamus pullos, passares, aedos, catellos et quidquid infirmo gradu fugam morabatur, nostris quoque pedibus ambulabat. ⁴Nec me pondus sarcinae quanquam enormis urguebat, quippe gaudiali fuga detestabilem illum exectorem uirilitatis meae relinquentem.

⁵Siluosi montis asperum permensi iugum rursusque repo[s]sita camporum spatia peruecti iam uespera semitam tenebrante peruenimus ad quoddam castellum frequens et opulens, unde nos incolae nocturna, immo uero matutina etiam prohibebant egressione: ⁶lupos enim numerosos, grandes et uastis corporibus sarcinosos, ac nimia ferocitate saeuientes passim rapinis adsuetos infestare cunctam illam regionem iamque ipsas uias obsidere et in modum latronum praetereuntes adgredi, immo etiam uaesana fame rabidos finitimas expugnare uillas, exitiumque inertissimorum pecudum ipsis iam humanis capitibus imminere. ⁷Denique ob iter illud, qua nobis erat commeandum, iacere semesa hominum corpora suisque uisceribus nudatis ossibus cuncta candere ac per hoc nos quoque summa cautione uiae reddi debere ⁸idque uel in primis obseruitare, ut luce clara et die iam prouecto et sole florido uitantes undique latentes insidias, cum et ipso lumine dirarum bestiarum repigratur impetus, non laciniatim disperso[s], sed cuneatim stipato commeatu difficultates illas transabiremus. ¹Sed nequissimi fugitiui ductores illi nostri caecae festinationis temeritate ac metu incertae insecutionis spreta salubri monitione nec expectata luce proxuma circa tertiam ferme uigiliam noctis onustos nos ad uiam propellunt. ²Tunc ego metu praedicti periculi, quantum pote, turbae medius et inter conferta iumenta latenter absconditus clunibus meis ⟨ab⟩ adg⟨r⟩essionibus ferinis consulebam; iamque me cursu celeri ceteros equos antecellentem mirabantur omnes. ³Sed illa pernicitas non erat alacritatis meae, sed formidinis indicium; denique mecum ipse reputabam Pegasum inclutum illum metu magis uolaticum fuisse ac per hoc merito pinnatum proditum, dum in altum et adusque caelum sussilit ac resultat, formidans scilicet igniferae morsum Chimaerae. ⁴Nam et illi pastores, qui nos agebant, in speciem proeli manus obarmauerant; hic lanceam, ille uenabulum, alius gerebat spicula, fustem alius, sed et saxa, quae salebrosa semita largiter subministrabat; ⁵erant qui sudes praeacutas attol⟨l⟩erent; plerique tamen ardentibus facibus proterrebant feras. ⁶Ne⟨c⟩ quicquam praeter unicam tubam deerat, quin acies esset proeliaris. Sed nequicquam frustra timorem illum satis inanem perfuncti longe peiores in⟨h⟩aesimus laqueos. ⁷Nam

lupi, forsitan confertae iuuentutis strepitu uel certe nimia luce flammarum deterriti uel etiam aliorsum grassantes, nulli contra nos aditum tulerunt ac ne procul saltem ulli comparuerunt.

17 ¹Villae uero, quam tunc forte praeteribamus, coloni multitudinem nostram latrones rati, satis agentes rerum suarum eximieque trepidi, canes rabidos et immanes et quibusuis lupis et ursis saeuiores, ²quos ad tutelae praesidia curiose fuerant alumnati, iubilationibus solitis et cuiusce modi uocibus nobis inhortantur, qui praeter genuinam ferocitatem tumultu suorum exasper[n]ati contra nos ruunt et undique laterum circumfusi passim insiliunt ac sine ullo dilectu iumenta simul et homines lacerant diuque grassati plerosque prosternunt. ³Cerneres non tam hercules memorandum quam miserandum etiam spectaculum: canes copiosos ardentibus animis alios fugientes arripere, alios stantibus inhaerere, quosdam iacentes inscindere, et per omnem nostrum commeatum morsibus ambulare. ⁴Ecce tanto periculo malum maius insequitur. De summis enim tectis ac de proxumo colle rusticani illi saxa super nos raptim deuoluunt, ut discernere prorsus nequiremus, qua potissimum caueremus clade, comminus canum an eminus lapidum. ⁵Quorum quidem unus caput mulieris, quae meum dorsum residebat, repente percussit. Quo dolore commota statim fletu cum clamore

18 sublato maritum suum pa⟨*sto*⟩rem illum suppetiatum ciet. ¹At ille deum fidem clamitans et cruorem uxoris ab⟨*s*⟩tergens altius quiritabat: 'Quid miseros homines et laboriosos uiatores tam crudelibus animis inuaditis atque obteritis? ²Quas praedas munitis? Quae damna uindicatis? At non speluncas ferarum uel cautes incolitis barbarorum, ut humano sanguine profuso gaudeatis'. ³Vix haec dicta et statim lapidum congestus cessauit imber et infestorum canum reuocata conquieuit procella. ⁴Vnus illinc denique de summo cupressus cacumine: 'A*t* nos', inquit, 'non uestrorum spoliorum cupidine latrocinamur, sed hanc ipsam cladem de uestris protelamus manibus. Iam denique pace tranquilla securi potestis incedere'. ⁵Sic ille, sed nos plurifariam uulnerati reliquam uiam capessimus alius lapidis, alius morsus uulnera referentes, uniuersi tamen saucii. ⁶Aliquanto denique uiae permenso spatio peruenimus ad nemus quoddam proceris arboribus consitum et pratentibus uirectis amoenum, ubi placuit illis ductoribus nostris refectui paululum conquiescere corporaque sua diuerse laniata sedulo recurare. ⁷Ergo passim prostrati solo primum fatigatos animos recuperare ac dehinc uulneribus medelas uarias adhibere festinant, hic cruorem praeterfluentis aquae rore deluere, ille spongeis inacidatis tumores comprimere, alius fasciolis hiantes uincire plagas. Ad istum modum saluti suae quisque consulebat.

19 ¹Interea quidam senex de summo colle prospectat, quem circum capellae pascentes opilionem esse profecto clamabant.

Eum rogauit unus e nostris, haberetne uenui lactem uel adhuc liquidum uel in caseum recentem inchoatum. ²At ille diu capite quassanti: 'uos autem', inquit, 'de cibo uel poculo uel omnino ulla refectione nunc cogitatis? An nulli scitis, quo loco consederitis?', et cum dicto conductis ouiculis conuersus longe recessit. Quae uox eius et fuga pastoribus nostris non mediocrem pauorem incussit. ³Ac dum perterriti de loci qualitate sciscitari gestiunt nec est qui doceat, senex alius, magnus ille quidem, grauatus annis, totus in baculum pronus et lassum trahens uestigium ubertim lacrimans per uiam proximat uisisque nobis cum fletu maximo singulorum iuuenum genua contingens sic adorabat:

20 ¹'Per Fortunas uestrosque Genios, sic ad meae senectutis spatia ualidi laetique ueniatis, decepto seni subsistite meumque paruulum ab inferis ereptum canis meis reddite. ²Nepos namque meus et itineris huius suauis comes, dum forte passarem incantantem sepiculae consectatur arripere, delapsus in proximam foueam, quae fructicibus imis subpatet, in extremo iam uitae consistit periculo, ³quippe cum de fletu ac uoce ipsius auum sibi saepicule clamitantis uiuere illum quidem sentiam, sed per corporis, ut uidetis, mei defectam ualetudinem opitulari nequeam. ⁴At uobis aetatis et roboris beneficio facile est subpetiari miserrimo seni puerumque illum nouissimum successionis meae atque unicam stirpem sospitem mihi facere'.

21 ¹Sic deprecantis suamque canitiem distrahentis totos quidem miseruit, sed unus prae ceteris et animo fortior et aetate iuuenior et corpore ualidior quique solus praeter alios incolumis proelium superius euaserat, exurgit alacer et percontatus, quonam loci puer ille decidisset, monstrantem digito non longe frutices horridos senem illum inpigre comitatur. ²Ac dum pabulo nostro suaque cura refecti sarcinulis quisque sumptis suis uiam capessunt, clamore primum nominatim cientes illum iuuenem frequenter inclamant, mox hora diutina commoti mittunt e suis arcessitorem unum, qui requisitum comitem tempestiuae uiae commonefactum reduceret. ³At ille modicum commoratus refert sese buxanti pallore trepidus: mira super conseruo suo renuntiat: conspicatum se quippe supinato illi et iam ex maxima parte consumpto immanem draconem mandentem insistere nec ullum usquam miserinum senem comparere illum. ⁴Qua re cognita et cum pastoris sermone conlata, qui ⟨aequ⟩aeuum prorsus hunc illum nec alium tescorum inquilinum praeminabatur, pestilenti deserta regione uelociori se fuga proripiunt nosque pellunt crebris tundentes fustibus.

22 ¹Cele⟨r⟩rime denique longo itinere confecto pagum quendam accedimus ibique totam perquiescimus noctem. Ibi coeptum facinus oppido memorabile narrare cupio. ²Seruus quidam, cui

cuncta⟨m⟩ familiae tutelam dominus permiserat suus quique possessionem maximam illam, in quam deuerteramus, uillicabat, habens ex eodem famulitio conseruam coniugam, liberae cuiusdam extrariaeque mulieris flag⟨r⟩abat cupidine. ³Quo dolore paelicatus uxor eius instricta cunctas mariti rationes et quicquid horreo reconditum continebatur admoto combussit igne. ⁴Nec tali damno tori sui contumeliam uindicasse contenta, iam contra sua saeuiens uiscera laqueum sibi nectit infantulumque, quem de eodem marito iam dudum susceperat, eodem funiculo nectit seque per altissimum puteum adpendicem paruulum trahens praecipitat. ⁵Quam mortem dominus eorum aegerrime sustinens adreptum seruulum, qui causam tanti sceleris luxurie sua praestiterat, nudum ac totum melle perlitum firmiter aligauit arbori ficulneae, ⁶cuius in ipso carioso stipite in⟨h⟩abitantium formicarum †nidifici aburribant† et ultro citro commeabant multiiuga scaturrigine. ⁷Quae simul dulcem ac mellitum corporis nidorem persentiscunt, paruis quidem, sed numerosis et continuis morsiunculis penitus inhaerentes, per longi temporis cruciatu⟨m⟩ ita, carnibus atque ipsis uisceribus adesis, homine consumpto membra nudarunt, ut ossa tantum uiduata pulpis nitore nimio candentia funestae cohaererent arbori.

23 ¹Hac quoque detestabili deserta mansione, paganos in summo luctu relinquentes, rursum pergimus dieque tota campestres emensi uias ciuitatem quandam populosam et nobilem iam fessi peruenimus. ²Inibi larem sedesque perpetuas pastores illi statuere decernunt, quod et longe quaesituris firmae latebrae uiderentur et annonae copiosae beata celebritas inuitabat. ³Triduo denique iumentorum refectis corporibus, quo uendibiliores uideremur, ad mercatum producimur magnaque uoce praeconis pretia singulis nuntiantis equi atque alii asini opulentis emptoribus praestinantur; a*t* me relictum solum ac subsiciuum cum fastidio plerique praeteribant. ⁴Iamque taedio contrectationis eorum, qui de dentibus meis aetate*m* computabant, manum cuiusdam faetore sordentem, qui gingi*u*as identidem meas putidis scalpebat digitis, mordicus adreptam plenissime con*t*erui. ⁵Quae res circumstantium ab emptione mea utpote ferocissimi deterruit animos. Tunc praeco dirruptis faucibus et rauca uoce saucius in meas fortunas ridiculos construebat iocos: ⁶'Quem ad finem cantherium istum uenui frustra subiciemus et uetulum ⟨et⟩ extritis ungulis debilem et dolore deformem et in hebeti pigritia ferocem nec quicquam amplius quam ruderarium crib⟨r⟩um? Atque *adeo* uel donemus eum cuipiam, si qui tamen faenum suum perdere non grauatur'.

24 ¹Ad istum modum praeco ille cachinnos circumstantibus commouebat. Sed illa Fortuna mea saeuissima, quam per tot regiones iam fug⟨i⟩ens effugere uel praecedentibus malis

placere non potui, rursum in me caecos detorsit oculos et
emptorem aptissimum duris meis casibus mire repertum obiecit.
²Scitote qualem: cinaedum et senem cinaedum, caluum quidem,
sed cincinnis semicanis et pendulis capillatum, unum de triuiali
popularium faece, qui per plateas et oppida cymbalis et crotalis
personantes deamque Syria⟨m⟩ circumferentes mendicare
compellunt. ³Is nimio praestinandi studio praeconem rogat,
cuiatis essem; at ille Cappadocum me et satis forticulum
denuntiat. Rursum requirit annos aetatis meae; sed praeco
lasciuiens: 'mathematicus quidem, qui stellas eius disposuit,
quintum ei numerauit annum, sed ipse scilicet melius istud de
suis nouit professionibus. ⁴Quanquam enim prudens crimen
Corneliae legis incurram, si ciuem Romanum pro seruo tibi
uendidero, quin emis bonum et frugi mancipium, quod te et
foris et domi poterit iuuare?' Sed exinde odiosus emptor aliud
de alio non desinit quaerere, denique de mansuetudine etiam
mea percontatur anxie. ¹At praeco: 'ueruecem', inquit, 'non
asinum uides, ad usus omnes quietum, non mordacem nec
calcitronem quidem, sed prorsus ut in asini corio modestum
hominem inhabitare credas. ²Quae res cognitu non ardua. Nam
si faciem tuam mediis eius feminibus i⟨m⟩miseris, facile
periclitaberis, quam grandem tibi demonstret patientiam'.

³Sic praeco lurchonem tractabat dicacule, sed ille cognito
cauillatu similis indignanti: 'at te', inquit, 'cadauer surdum et
mutum delirumque praeconem, omnipotens et omniparens
dea[s] Syria et sanctus Sabadius et Bellona et mater ⟨I⟩daea
⟨et⟩ cum suo Adone Venus domina caecum reddant, qui
scurrilibus iam dudum contra me uelitaris iocis. ⁴An me putas,
inepte, iumento fero posse deam committere, ut turbatum
repente diuinum deiciat simulacrum egoque misera cogar
crinibus solutis discurrere et deae meae humi iacenti aliquem
medicum quaerere?' ⁵Accepto tali sermone cogitabam subito
uelut lymphaticus exilire, ut me ferocitate cernens exasperatum
emptionem desineret. ⁶Sed praeuenit cogitatum meum emptor
anxius pretio depenso statim, quod quidem gaudens dominus
scilicet taedio mei facile suscepit, septemdecim denarium, et
ilico me stomida spartea deligatum tradidit Philebo; hoc enim
nomine censebatur iam meus dominus. ¹At ille susceptum
nouicium famulum trahebat ad domum statimque illinc de
primo limine proclamat: 'puellae, seruum uobis pulchellum en
ecce mercata perduxi'. ²Sed illae puellae chorus erat cinaedorum, quae statim exultantes in gaudium fracta e⟨t⟩ rauca et
effeminata uoce clamores absonos intollunt, rati scilicet uere
quempiam hominem seruulum ministerio suo paratum. ³Sed
postquam non ceruam pro uirgine, sed asinum pro homine
succidaneum uidere, nare detorta magistrum suum uarie cauillantur: non enim seruum, sed maritum illum scilicet sibi

perduxisse. ⁴Et 'heus', aiunt, 'caue ne solus exedas tam *bellum* scilicet pullulum, sed nobis quoque tuis palumbulis nonnunquam inpertias'.

⁵Haec et huius modi mutuo blaterantes praesepio me proximum deligant. Erat quidam iuuenis satis corpulentus, choraula doctissimus, conlaticia stipe de mensa paratus, qui foris quidem circumgestantibus deam cornu canens adambulabat, domi uero promiscuis operis partiarius agebat concubinus. ⁶Hic me simul domi conspexit, libenter adpositis largiter cibariis gaudens adloquitur: 'uenisti tandem miserrimi laboris uicarius. Sed diu uiuas et dominis placeas et meis defectis iam lateribus consulas'. Haec audiens iam mea⟨s⟩ futuras nouas cogitabam aerumnas.

27 ¹Die sequenti uariis coloribus indusiati et deformiter quisque formati facie caenoso pigmento delita et oculis obunctis grafice prodeunt, mitellis et cro[cro]co*t*is et carbasinis et bo*m*bycinis iniecti, ²quidam tunicas albas, in modum lanciolarum quoquouersum fluente purpura depictas, cingulo subligati, pedes luteis induti calceis; ³deamque serico contectam amiculo mihi gerendam imponunt bracchiisque suis umero tenus renudatis, adtollentes immanes gladios ac secures, euantes exsiliunt incitante tibiae cantu lymphaticum tripudium. ⁴Nec paucis pererratis casulis ad quandam uillam possessoris beati perueniunt et ab ingressu primo statim absonis ululatibus constrepentes fanatice prouolant ⁵diuque capite demisso ceruices lubricis intorquentes motibus crinesque pendulos in circulum rotantes et nonnunquam morsibus suos incursantes musculos ad postremum ancipiti ferro, quod gerebant, sua quisque brachia dissicant. ⁶Inter haec unus ex illis ba⟨c⟩chatur effusius ac de imis praecordiis anhelitus crebros referens uelut numini⟨s⟩ diuino spiritu repletus simulabat sauciam uecordiam, prorsus quasi deum praesentia soleant homines non sui f⟨i⟩eri meliores,

28 sed debiles effici uel aegroti. ¹Specta denique, quale caelesti prouidentia meritum reportauerit. Infit uaticinatione clamosa conf[l]icto mendacio semet ipsum incessere atque criminari, quasi contra fas sanctae religionis dissignasset aliquid, et insuper iustas poenas noxii facinoris ipse de se suis manibus exposcere. ²Arrepto denique flagro, quod semiuiris illis proprium gestamen est, contortis taenis lanosi uelleris prolixe fimbriatum et multiiugis talis ouium tesseratum, indidem sese multinodis commulcat ictibus mire contra plagarum dolores praesumptione munitus. ³Cerneres prosectu gladiorum ictuque flagrorum solum spurcitia sanguin*i*s effeminati madescere. ⁴Quae res incutiebat mihi non paruam sollicitudinem uidenti tot uulneribus largiter profusum cruorem, ne quo casu deae peregrinae stomachus, ut quorundam hominum lactem, sic illa sanguinem conc*u*pi⟨s⟩ceret asininum. ⁵Sed ubi tandem fatigati

uel certe suo laniatu satiati pausam carnificinae dedere, stipes aereas, immo uero et argenteas multis certatim offerentibus sinu recepere patulo nec non et uini cadum et lactem et caseos et farris et siliginis aliquid et nonnullis hordeum deae gerulo donantibus, ⁶auidis animis conradentes omnia et in sacculos huic quaestui de industria praeparatos farcientes dorso meo congerunt, ut duplici scilicet sarcinae pondere grauatus et horreum simul et templum incederem.

29 ¹Ad istum modum palantes omnem illam depraedabantur regionem. Sed in quodam castello copia laetati largioris quaesticuli gaudiales instruunt dapes. ²A quodam colono fictae uaticinationis mendacio pinguissimum deposcunt arietem, qui deam Syriam esurientem suo satiaret sacrificio, probeque disposita cenula balneas obeunt ³ac dehinc lauti quendam fortissimum rusticanum industria laterum atque imis uentris bene praeparatum comitem cenae secum adducunt paucisque admodum praegustatis olusculis ⁴ante ipsam mensam spurcissima illa propudia ad inlicitae libidinis extrema flagitia infandis uriginibus efferantur passimque circumfusi nudatum supinatumque iuuenem execrandis oribus flagitabant. ⁵Nec diu tale facinus meis oculis tolerantibus 'porro Quirites' proclamare gestiui, sed uiduatum ceteris syllabis ac litteris processit 'O' tantum sane clarum ac ualidum et asino proprium, sed inoportuno plane tempore. ⁶Namque de pago proximo complures iuuenes abactum sibi noctu perquirentes asellum nimioque studio cuncta deuorsoria scrutantes intus aedium audito ruditu meo praedam absconditam latibulis aedium rati, coram rem inuasuri suam inprouisi conferto gradu se penetrant palamque illos execrandas foeditates obeuntes deprehendunt; iamiamque uicinos undique percientes turpissimam scaenam patefaciunt, insuper ridicule sacerdotum purissimam laudantes castimoniam.

30 ¹⟨H⟩ac infamia consternati, quae per ora populi facile dilapsa merito inuisos ac detestabiles eos cunctis effecera[n]t, noctem ferme circa mediam collectis omnibus furtim castello facessunt ²bonaque itineris parte ante iubaris exortum transacta[m] iam die claro solitudines auias nancti, multa secum prius conlocuti, accingunt se meo funeri deaque uehiculo meo sublata et humi reposita cunctis stramentis me renudatum ac de quadam quercu destinatum flagro illo pecuinis ossibus catenato uerberantes paene ad extremam confecerant mortem; ³fuit unus, qui poplites meos eneruare secure sua comminaretur, quod de pudore illo candido scilicet suo tam deformiter triumphassem: sed ceteri non meae salutis, sed simulacri iacentis contemplatione in uita me retinendum censuere. ⁴Rursum itaque me refertum sarcinis planis gladiis minantes perueniunt ad quandam nobilem ciuitatem. ⁵Inibi uir principalis, et

alias religiosus et exumie deum reuerens, tinnitu cymbalorum et 20
sonu tympanorum cantusque Frygi*i* mulcentibus modulis excitus procurrit obuiam deamque uotiuo suscipiens hospitio nos omnis intra conseptum domus amplissimae constituit numenque summa ueneratione atque hostiis opimis placare conten- 25
dit.

31 ¹Hic ego me potissimum capitis periclitatum memini. Nam quidam colonus partem uenationis inmanis cerui pinguissimum femus domino illi suo muneri miserat, quod incuriose pone H. 202
culinae fores non altiuscule suspensum canis adaeque uenaticus latenter inuaserat, laetusque praeda propere custodientes oculos euaserat. ²Quo damno cognito suaque reprehensa neglegentia cocus diu lamentatus lacrimis inefficacibus iamiamque 5
domino cenam flagitante maerens et utcumque metuens altius filio suo paruulo consalutato adreptoque funiculo mortem sibi nexu laquei comparabat. ³Nec tamen latuit fidam uxorem eius casus extremus mariti, sed funestum nodum uiolenter inuadens 10
manibus ambabus: 'adeone' inquit, 'praesenti malo perterritus mente excidisti tua nec fortuitum istud remedium, quod deum prouidentia subministrat, intueris? ⁴Nam si quid in ultimo fortunae turbine resipiscis, expergite mi ausculta et aduenam istum asinum remoto quodam loco deductum iugula femusque 15
eius ad similitudinem perditi detractum et accuratius in protrimentis sapidissime percoctum adpone domino ceruini uicem'. ⁵Nequissimo uerberoni sua placuit salus de mea morte et multum conseruae laudata sagacitate destinatae[t] iam lanienae 20
cultros acuebat.

CHAPTER I

One of Charite's slaves arrives in the early morning while it is still dark and tells 176, 15-18
the shepherds of the young woman's sad end.

Noctis gallicinio uenit quidam iuuenis proxima ciuitate, ut quidem mihi uidebatur, unus ex famulis Charites, puellae illius, quae mecum aput latrones pares aerumnas exanclauerat: "During the night at cockcrow a young man came from the nearest town; to me it seemed that he was one of the servants of Charite, the girl who had, along with me, endured the same hardships at the robbers' hideout."

noctis gallicinio: There is no need to assume an interval of time between the events narrated at the end of book 7 and the arrival of the *iuuenis*; see Introduction 3.1. *Noctis* can be regarded as a partitive genitive: Servius on Verg. *A*. 3, 587 reports that the night can be divided into seven parts, the fourth of which is *gallicinium quo galli cantant*. In Latin literature this indication of time is found first in Petronius in the story of the werewolf (*Sat.* 62, 3) *Apoculamus nos circa gallicinia, luna lucebat tamquam meridie* (Walsh *AAGA* 1978, 22 also compares the two passages and concludes that Petronius was presumably not Apuleius' direct model because of the plural). Callebat 1968, 28 calls *gallicinium* a 'mot de formation populaire'; cf. also Amm. 22, 14, 4 and Macr. 1, 3, 12.

So it is still dark and, together with the fire and the group of people sitting around it, the expression creates a striking atmosphere for the story that is to follow; cf. Anderson 1909, 537-549.

proxima ciuitate: in F and φ there is no preposition, but in ς *e* is supplied before *proxima*, which is accepted by most modern editors (Robertson, Helm, Frassinetti); vdVliet wishes to insert *de* on account of 9, 10 (210, 14) *quidam pistor de proximo castello* (at 9,33: 227, 19 *quidam e proximo pago* is usually printed, although the mss. have *de*; he is now supported by Augello 1977, 176, who points out that Apuleius uses the preposition *de* frequently. It is, however, possible to defend the text without a preposition, as do Baehrens 1912, 357, Giarratano, and Médan 1925, 58. Médan gives three other examples from Apuleius of a construction without a preposition: 9, 20 (218, 7) *procurrit cubiculo*; 9, 39 (233, 6) *dorso meo proturbat* and 10, 9 (244, 2) *iussi de meis aliquem...taberna...adferre*, but he fails to point out that those passages all contain a compound, the prefix of which justifies the construction; he would have done better to cite 3, 10 (59, 14) *theatro facessunt*. Although the construction of such an ablative with simple verbs is indeed rare, yet LHSz 2, 103 and KSt 1, 361 mention several examples; at first in poetry (cf. Titin. *Com.* 53 *aedibus facessere*; Verg. *G*. 4, 80 *aëre grando/...pluit*; *A*. 6, 191 *columbae...caelo uenere uolantes*), and from Livy (e.g. 4, 58, 7) onward also in prose, cf. Tac. *Ann.* 15, 54 *promptum uagina pugionem.* Oudendorp's *proxima e ciuitate* seems paleographically attractive but for the fact that anastrophe of a preposition in Apuleius occurs rarely or not at all; see Bernhard 1927, 28. We believe, although with some hesitation, that the transmitted reading is correct.

ciuitate = urbe; see vdPaardt 1971, 41 on 3, 3 (54, 3) and *GCA* 1977, 101 on 4, 13 (84, 15). For the town see 7, 13 (163, 20-22).

unus ex famulis Charites: for the role of this slave, who is emphatically linked with Charite and not with Tlepolemus or Charite's parents, and for his dependency on Charite's version of the events, see Introduction 4. 2. 1. 3.

aerumnas: for this somewhat solemn word, of which Apuleius is fond (see Tatum 1969[a], 45), cf. *GCA* 1981, 90 on 7, 2 (155, 18).

exanclauerat: this word (ἐξαντλεῖν, with a nautical metaphor, see Neuenschwander 1913, 90 and van Nes 1963, 143-145) also has an archaic coloration; cf. Enn. *scen.* 102 *Quantis cum aerumnis...exanclaui diem*; Lucil. 1083 *quantas...aerumnas quantosque labores exanclaris*; Cic. *Ac.* 2, 108 *Herculi quendam laborem exanclatum a Carneade.* Quint. *Inst.* 1, 6, 40 emphatically advises against the use of this word as being outdated: *ab ultimis et iam oblitteratis repetita temporibus.* Apuleius likes to use it, e.g. 6, 4 (131, 14); 6, 11 (136, 15); 7, 6 (159, 5); 11, 2 (267, 20); 11, 12 (275, 20); 11, 15 (277, 5), usually in elevated passages and in combination with *aerumnae*, as at 1, 16 (14, 20) *qui mecum tot aerumnas exanclasti*, where the pathetic exaggeration has a comical effect. See on this verb also Bernard 1927, 131 and 202.

It is curious that, by means of this relative clause *quae...exanclauerat*, the girl is introduced to the reader once more.

176, 18-20 Is de eius exitio et domus totius infortunio mira ac nefanda, ignem propter adsidens, inter conseruorum frequentiam sic annuntiabat: "About her death and the ruination of the entire house he bore stange, even outrageous tidings; sitting down at the fire, in the middle of the large group of fellow-slaves, he announced the following:"

infortunio: in the sense of 'misery' also 4, 27 (95, 18; see *GCA* 1977, 201 ad loc.) and 5, 12 (113, 10). There is a certain climax in *de eius exitio* and *domus totius*, which is accentuated by the rhyme.

mira ac nefanda: here, too, a distinct climax. Cf. 1, 11 (10, 8) *mira...nec minus saeua...memoras*.

ignem propter adsidens: Bernhard 1927, 28 argues (against Koziol 1872, 338) that anastrophe of prepositions does not occur in Apuleius: in the cases where *propter* occurs, *propter* ought to be regarded as an adverb and the accusative of the noun should be taken with the verb. He cites five such passages: 2, 23 (44, 8) *quam propter adsistens*; 4, 4 (77, 13) *riuulum quendam...propter insistens*; 5, 28 (125, 11) *natantemque propter assistens*; 187, 12 *capulum Tlepolemi propter assistens*; 9, 30 (225, 27) *cubiculum propter adstantes*, forgetting our passage. Anastrophe of *propter* is not entirely unknown in early Latin (LHSz 2, 247) but is found mainly with pronouns. On the other hand it is remarkable that in all the above- mentioned examples an accusative is found close to the compound.

See also *GCA* 1977, 47 on 4, 4 (77, 13)

ignem: it is conceivable that the fire is the same as the *focus* mentioned 7, 28 (176, 8).

adsidens: is it ī or ĭ? Vallette opts for the former ('s'asseyant'), Helm for the latter ('sitzend'). Both occur in Apuleius: *assīdo* is found 1, 23 (21, 3) *ut...adsidam iubet* and 2, 13 (36, 3) *ut adsidat effecit; assĭdeo* is found 1, 22 (20, 18) *assidebat pedes uxor*; e.g. 186, 4 (see our comm. ad loc.); 9, 17 (216, 3). In our context 'sit down' is somewhat more appropriate.

inter conseruorum frequentiam = *inter conseruos frequentes*: Apuleius has a preference for abstract nouns which take the place of an adjective; from book 8 alone we can cite 179, 21 *humilitati seruorum*; 180, 1 *incendio feritatis*; 185, 2 *inmaturitate nuptiarum*; 188, 9 *dominii nouitatem*; 195, 1 *annonae...celebritas*; see Médan 1925, 317 and Bernhard 1927, 97.

annuntiabat: F read first *annuntiauit* but the same hand changed the perfect into an imperfect, which indeed fits better (cf. its echo 188, 8). The verb is attested from Sen. onward; according to *ThLL* s.v. 788, 8 it is only here constructed with *de*, followed by direct discourse.

For the following narrative see Introduction 4.2.

'Equisones opilionesque, etiam busequae, fuit Charite nobisque misella et quidem casu grauissimo nec uero incomitata Manis adiuit: "'Grooms and shepherds and you too, cowhands! Charite is no more; the poor girl has gone from us to the shades – and by a most tragic disaster, indeed, but not unaccompanied." 176, 21-177, 1

Equisones...busequae: the narrator starts out with a pathetic opening and immediately after discloses the essence of the message: *fuit Charite*. Then, carefully and minutely, he builds up his narration, which in its style and structure recalls a messenger-speech in classical tragedy; cf. 1. 20 *annuntiabat*.

On *equisones* see *GCA* 1981, 176 on 7, 15 (165, 8). *Opilio*, with a variant form *upilio* (5, 25 : 122, 28 and *Fl.* 3 : 3, 16; for other passages see *ThLL* s.v. 707, 30) is also found 191, 30; 10, 33 (264, 6); *Apol.* 10 (12, 8) and 87 (96, 24 *upilio*). The first element of *opilio* is etymologically connected with *ouis*. The second element is less clear: Ernout thinks of a relation with οἰοπόλος, αἰπόλος; Walde-Hofmann, on the other hand, connect *-pilio* with I.E. **pel* 'drive', Lat. *pello*; they believe that the variant with *u-* is the urban (Roman) form. The word is already found in Pl. *As.* 540.

busequa: this word, which is just found in Apuleius, is used *Fl.* 3 (3, 16) *Vergilianus upilio seu busequa; Socr.* 5 (12, 10); *Apol.* 10 (12, 8) *Aemilianus, uir ultra Virgilianos opiliones et busequas rusticanus*. It is understandable that the scribe of F did not know the word and distorted it into *buses que*; this was already corrected by ς. Later it occurs only Sidon. *Epist.* 1, 6, 3 *inter busequas rusticanos subbulcosque rhonchantes* und In *Gloss.* (5, 657, 10) *busequa boum prouisor*.

fuit Charite nobisque misella; this dramatic beginning, which reminds one of Vergil's *Fuimus Troes, fuit Ilium*)*A.* 2 325), is accentuated by the clausula heroica and the preceding dactyls; see Schober 1904, 13 f. Cf. Westerbrink *AAGA* 1978, 70.

nobisque: it is far from certain what the correct reading should be here; F and φ have *nobis q* (which presumably means *qui*), ς offers *nobis quae* or *quam misella* (in the sense of *miserrima*). It is possible to accept *quae* with Frassinetti, which does not make for a smooth dependent clause, however. Another possibility is to emend, e.g. with Gruter *nobis quoniam*, with vdVliet *nobisque misella ⟨periuit⟩*, with Lütjohann *nobis! quippe misella*, or with Rohde, who, using the preceding emendations and believing that the ethic dative is too colloquial for this pathetic passage and that *casu grauissimo* does not make a good combination with *adiuit*, proposes *fuit Charite! obiit quippe. . .grauissimo: nec uero. . .* We do not share these objections and believe that the scribe has made a small error: with *nobisque* the clause runs satisfactorily (thus also Eyssenhardt, Giarratano and Helm). *Nobis* is then an ethic dative, comparable to e.g. 2, 13 (36, 6); 4, 21 (90, 24) *sic. . .nobis periuit*; 9, 5 (206, 14) *sicine uacuus. . .ambulabis mihi*; see Médan 1925, 46. *Nobis* confirms the ass's impression in l. 16.

misella: on Apuleius' preference for diminutives see Bernhard 1927, 137 and *GCA* 1977 and 1981 passim (see index). *Misellus* is especially frequent, e.g. 1, 13 (12, 11); 1, 19 (18, 10); 4, 27 (96, 2); 7, 27 (175, 17), particularly when it refers to recently deceased persons. Cf. also Catul. 3, 6 *o miselle passer* and Tert. *Test. An.* 4, p. 138, 25 *cum alicuius defuncti recordaris, misellum uocas eum*; this is confirmed by the frequent use in grave inscriptions, e.g. *CIL* 1, 2525 HEIC SITVS MISELLVS BEIMVS. See also the remark made by Stefenelli 1962, 127 in reference to Petr. 65, 10 *scissa lautum nouendialem seruo suo misello faciebat, quem mortuum manu miserat*; *GCA* 1981, 266 on 7, 27 (175, 17); Abate 1978, 41 and 49 on the hypocoristic diminutive (and in particular *misellus*) in Apuleius.

nec uero incomitata: as far as narrative technique is concerned, it is not unimportant that a preliminary indication is given here that there has been more than one victim. For the expression cf. 2, 18 (40, 8) *nec tamen incomitatus ibo* (Lucius goes accompanied by his sword).

Manis: a robber uses this term also 6, 30 (151, 27) and so will Thrasyllus at a dramatic moment (188, 4 below); cf. 186, 25.

adiuit: for the form with *-u-* see 4, 21 (91, 1) and Médan 1925, 6.

177, 1-4 Sed ut cuncta noritis, referam uobis a capite, quae gesta sunt quaeque possint merito doctiores, quibus stilos fortuna subministrat, in historiae specimen chartis inuoluere: "But in order that you may know everything, I will tell you from the beginning what has happened – things so bad that people more learned, upon whom fortune bestows the gift of penmanship, could rightly put them in a book as an exemplary tale."

ut cuncta noritis: on the topos 'der Besitz von Wissen verpflichtet zur Mitteilung' ('Exordialtopik') see Curtius 1969[7], 95 f.

noritis: thus originally F, which a different hand wrongly changed into *ueritis*; φ gives the correct reading *noritis*.

a capite; a common expression; cf. Cic. *Leg.* 1, 18 *a capite...repetis; Top.* 39 *usque a capite arcessere* (*argumentum*). For more examples see *ThLL* s.v. 415, 57 f.

sunt...possint: by the moods the author makes a clear distinction between what the narrating young man presents as facts (*sunt*) and their emotional evaluation as a potential subject for a literary rendering (*quae...possint*, a consecutive subjunctive). F's reading *possint* is to be preferred to *possent* (φ) and *possunt* (A).

Concerning the possibility that the narrator's presentation even of the facts may have been coloured by an emotional evaluation, see Introduction 4. 2. 1. 2. The discrepancy between the *iuuenis*' implicit claim to simplicity (*quae gesta sunt*) and the highly rhetorical handling of emotions in the subsequent tale is a striking instance of a common Apuleian procedure. One may also find an expression of modesty (in itself a rhetorical topos): writing *historiae* is not for him; it is a task rather for gentlemen whose fortune has endowed them with an adequate education. The thought is quite different from the ass's playful remark at 6, 25 (147, 4-6) *ego...dolebam..., quod pugillares et stilum non habebam, qui tam bellam fabellam praenotarem* (see also *GCA* 1981, 25 ad loc.). But the passages are akin in their irony at the level of the author. Apuleius himself is so proficient in handling the *stilus* that the end result remarkably resembles *historiae* and, what is more, *historiae* which neatly leave the reader in doubt whether he should allow himself, with the *conserui*, to be persuaded as to their veracity, or whether he should rather insert his own question marks, as in the case of the robber tales of book 4.

doctiores: vdPaardt in *SAG* 1981, 25 notes that 'with Ciceronian pride the writer behind the narrator refers to himself'.

historiae; this probably means 'story', as 7, 16 (166, 21) *sic apud historiam de rege Thracio legeram* (see *GCA* 1981, 190 ad loc.) and Gel. 1, 8, 1 *librum multae uariaeque historiae refertum*. It seems to us that Apuleius does not make a clear distinction everywhere between *historia, fabella*, and *fabula*; cf. 2, 12 (35, 10) *historiam magnam et incredundam fabulam et libros me futurum*. He does make a distinction 6, 29 (151, 4; see *GCA* 1981, 56 ad loc.) between *fabulis* 'stories told by people' and *historia* 'literature'. Here *historia* is (within fiction) reality, a piece of history, a true story (cf. e.g. Gel. 5, 18, 6 *historias esse aiunt rerum gestarum...expositionem* and Isid. *Orig.* 1, 41 *historia est narratio rei gestae, per quam ea, quae in praeterito gesta sunt, dinoscuntur*), while *fabula* refers to a work of fiction, which does not have to be true.

specimen historiae: an important expression for the interpretation of the entire novel: it is an exemplary tale, which holds many lessons. It also points out to the reader, who belongs to the *doctiores*, that the entire novel, too, should be read in that sense: one can learn something from it. See also vdPaardt in *SAG* 1981, 19 f.

In the material of the *ThLL* no other example could be found of the expression *in specimen* with a genitive or of *specimen historiae*. In the sense of 'example' *specimen* is quite common. For the etymology see LHSz 1, 370.

inuoluere: in this meaning 'include' (in a book) cf. Sen. *Ep.* 25,4 (*Epicurus,*) *cuius aliquam uocem huic epistulae inuoluam*. In *AAGA* 1978, 116 Hijmans

177, 5-10 Erat in proxima ciuitate iuuenis natalibus praenobilis, quo clarus et pecuniae fuit satis locuples, sed luxuriae popinalis scortisque et diurnis potationibus exercitatus atque ob id factionibus latronum male sociatus nec non etiam manus infectus humano cruore, Thrasyllus nomine. Idque sic erat et fama dicebat: "There was in a nearby town a young man, very noble by birth (on account of which he was famous and considerably wealthy) but always in action with dissipations in taverns, with harlots, and with drinking in broad daylight; therefore he had fallen into the bad company of robbers and, moreover, his hands were stained with human blood; his name was Thrasyllus. This was so and his reputation declared it."

Erat: as Apuleius has his 'Amor and Psyche' begin with the familiar fairy-tale opening (4, 28 : 96, 16) *Erant in quadam ciuitate rex et regina*, so he often has other tales, too, begin in a similar fashion: the verb comes first, e.g. 198, 1 *Erat quidam iuuenis satis corpulentus*; 7, 6 (158, 19) *Fuit quidam multis officiis...clarus*; 10, 9 (251, 20) *Fuit in illo conuenticulo matrona quaedam*. See Bernhard 1927, 12 on this usage in Apuleius; on a similar opening in general see Fehling 1977, 79 f. Anhang 1, 'Es war einmal', with numerous examples in many languages.

One might wonder why Thrasyllus is introduced here in so much detail to an audience that might be supposed to know him. This can be explained on the basis of narrative technique: if our (sub-)narrator took only his own audience into account, the tale would become incomprehensible for Lucius – and consequently for the reader of the novel – because of too many 'gaps'. Therefore additional information is needed. This happens often in a narrative text; usually the author solves the difficulty by a sentence like 'as you know' (then the reader knows, too). For a possible implication of the absence of a reminder of this nature, see Introduction 4. 2. 1. 1.

natalibus: this plural noun in the sense of 'parentage', 'origin' is also found 5, 15 (115, 9) *sciscitari, qualis ei maritus et unde natalium*; see also *GCA* 1981, 143 on 7, 9 (161, 15).

praenobilis: this adjective, also used by Apuleius *Met.* 11, 25 (257, 1) and *Fl.* 16 (27, 20), is not attested before him. On similar reinforcing prefixes, see Bernhard 1927, 109. They can replace the somewhat heavy superlatives.

quo clarus et pecuniae fuit satis locuples: F has *quo clarus eo*, ς reads *qui* (or *loco*) *clarus et*. Of the many attempts at emendation the following deserve to be mentioned: *qui eo* vdVliet, *quidem...et...fructu* Helm (later rejected in Helm-Krenkel). We believe that the most persuasive emendation is that of Goelzer 1925, 37-39: he proposes to retain *quo* and to combine it with *et* (ς), thus keeping very close to the transmission; this results in a relative clause beginning with *quo*, which describes the consequence of his noble origin (it could be printed as a parenthesis as is done by Helm-Krenkel); the subsequent *sed* forms the antithesis of *praenobilis*. The alternation of tenses *Erat...fuit* is not objectionable in an author who has e.g. 'Amor and Psyche' (4, 28 : 96, 16) start with *Erant in quadam ciuitate rex et regina* and continues with *hi tres...filias...habuere*. All modern editors except Helm have accepted this emendation.

pecuniae...locuples: this is the only passage in Latin litterature where *locuples* is constructed with a genitive, but for similar expressions (*refertus, largus, prodigus*, etc.) see LHSz 2, 77. Presumably there is some Greek influence; see vGeisau 1916, 249, who compares Cic. *Agr.* 1. 15 *locupletatis...inuidiae*.

luxuriae popinalis scortisque et...potationibus exercitatus: first a genitive, then twice an ablative; cf. 3, 2 (52, 22) *magistratibus...et turbae...cuncta completa* with vdPaardt 1971, 29 f. ad loc., who cites two examples from Sallust. See also Bernhard 1927, 150 f. and *GCA* 1977, 165 on 4, 21 (91, 6-8). Hildebrand's emendation *luxurie popinali* is unnecessary.

luxuriae: Apuleius uses the forms in *-ia* and *-ies* indiscriminately.

scortisque: referring to a *meretrix* Apuleius uses the word *scortum* also 1, 8 (8, 2) and *Apol.* 98 (108, 23, but in the same chapter 108, 3 *meretrix*); only once (9, 26 : 222, 17) he uses *prostituta*, which in the second century A.D. becomes the usual word in colloquial language. See Callebat 1968, 29.

diurnis: drinking parties by day always had a bad reputation in antiquity; cf. Plin. *Nat.* 14, 143 *Tiberio Claudio principe ante hos annos XL institutum est ut ieiuni biberent potiusque uinum antecederet cibos, externis et hoc artibus ac medicorum placitis nouitate semper aliqua sese commendantium* (if we can believe Suet. *Tib.* 42, 2, Tiberius was a notorious drinker, who acquired the nickname Biberius Caldius Mero). See also Petr. 31; Juv. 6, 424 f.; Sen. *Ep.* 122, 6; and the remark of Balsdon 1969, 41.

potationibus: Gargantini 1963, 39 points out Apuleius' frequent use of (usually) abstract deverbative nouns in *-tio*. *Potatio* is quite rare; it occurs e.g. Pl. *Bac.* 79; *St.* 211; it is not found in classical prose except in a quotation from Cic. in Quint. *Inst.* 8, 3, 66.

exercitatus: a military metaphor such as we find often in Apuleius, not only in the robbers' episode (see *GCA* 1977, 208 App. 1) but passim. Cf. e.g. 1, 1 (1, 9) *linguam Attidem primis pueritiae stipendiis merui*; 1, 16 (14, 18) *telum...Fortuna...subministrat*; 4, 22 (92, 2) *fauces...exerceo*; 5, 21 (119, 18) *Veneris proeliis*. The military connotation of *exercitatus* seems somewhat worn in this passage; it is still apparent 4, 17 (87, 25) *tota familia per diutinam consuetudinem nutriendis ursis exercitata est* and Hirt. *Gal.* 8, 25, 2 *ciuitas...cotidianis exercitata bellis*.

male: the narrator expresses his disapproval here; with a somewhat different nuance 186, 11 *oculi...quibus male placui*. vdVliet's conjecture *clam* should be rejected, if only because *clam* is always a preposition in Apuleius.

nec non etiam: for this and similar combinations, in which the litotes is emphasized (e.g. *nec non et, etiam, quoque*), see Callebat 1968, 418, who concludes that they are always found in rather dramatic and emotional passages; this is also true for Varro and Vergil (see Austin 1977 on *A.* 6, 595). *Nec non etiam* is also found 9, 9 (209, 14) and 11, 10 (274, 10); see Bernhard 1927, 172.

manus: Apuleius frequently uses this so-called accusativus Graecus in the *Met.* and *Fl.*; see vGeisau 1916, 81; Médan 1925, 34; LHSz 2, 36 f.

Thrasyllus nomine: the name has been chosen after θρασύς (if the text is correct, it is explained 182, 15 *de ipso nomine temerarius*); see Hijmans *AAGA* 1978, 116. The man's characterization is twofold: after a short preamble about his origin we hear that he degenerates and gets into bad company: *factionibus latronum male sociatus* – a reference to his past. Though grammatically referring to unmentioned bloody deeds in the past, *manus infectus humano cruore* – more than any other aspect of the present characterisation – persuades the audience to cast Thrasyllus in the role of the villain of the subsequent tale.

By this characterization of Thrasyllus the sub-narrator at once imposes his view on the audience at the beginning of his story; he continues to do so throughout his account until his very last words 188,6 *damnatum spiritum Thrasylli*). The name Thrasyllus, finally, is in keeping with his reckless way of life; the mentioning of this name is postponed until the end of the sentence, with a certain climax.

idque. . .dicebat: it is not entirely clear what is meant here; perhaps 'his name was "Overbold" (Merkelbach 1962, 75 n. 7 identifies him with Seth) and that was the way people spoke about him'; in this case the author gives a kind of explanation of the name Thrasyllus. Another interpretation is: 'these were the facts, and that was the way people spoke about him'; in this case the verity is emphatically underscored, which might have a negative effect on the *lector doctus*; see Introduction 4. 2. 1. 1 with note 4.

On short sentences like this instead of a period see Bernhard 1927, 39 f.; Callebat 1968, 443; *GCA* 1981, 152 on 7, 11 (162, 15).

CHAPTER II

Thrasyllus contends for Charite's hand but is declined; in spite of that he manages to become a family friend and keeps making overtures.

Hic, cum primum Charite nubendo maturuisset, inter praecipuos procos summo studio petitionis eius munus obierat et quanquam ceteris omnibus id genus uiris antistaret eximiisque muneribus parentum inuitaret iudicium, morum tamen inprobatus repulsae contumelia fuerat aspersus: "As soon as Charite had become ripe for marriage, he had among the principal suitors devoted himself with the greatest zeal to the task of wooing her and, although he ranked above all the other men of that kind and sought to win a favourable opinion of her parents by choice gifts, he had nevertheless been rejected on account of his way of life and had had to suffer the insult of a rebuff." 177, 10-15

cum primum...maturuisset: for the subjunctive cf. 7, 7 (159, 7) *cum primum litus Actiacum...appulisset* with *GCA* 1981, 126 ad loc. A similar use of *maturescere*, a metaphor from agriculture, is found Ov. *Met.* 14, 335 *Haec ubi nubilibus primum maturuit annis* and Sen. *Ep.* 102, 23 *sic per hoc spatium, quod ab infantia patet in senectutem, in alium maturescimus partum*. These are the only passages where the verb is used of people growing up; the adjective *maturus*, referring to people, is found often, cf. e.g. Verg. *A.* 5, 73 *aeui maturus Acestes*; Ov. *Met.* 14, 617 *Remulus maturior annis*. The minimal age for a girl to be married legally (Ulp. *Reg.* 5, 2; *Cod. Iust.* 5, 60, 3) was 12 years, and 14 years was quite usual; see Balsdon 1969, 21 with references 375, n. 18 and 380, n. 125; Summers 1967, 264.

inter praecipuos procos: Charite says that she has been engaged to Tlepolemus from childhood and other *proci* are not mentioned anywhere. Cf. 4, 26 (94, 23) with *GCA* 1977, 192 f. ad loc.; see also Introduction 4.2. 1. 1.

petitionis...munus obierat: many similarly prolix expressions are found in Apuleius, e.g. 1, 16 (15, 5) *ut...restis ad ingluuiem adstricta spiritus officia discluderet*, cf. Bernhard 1927, 174.

ceteris omnibus...antistaret: on *antistare* with a dative see *GCA* 1977, 72 on 4, 8 (80, 16-17). The use of the subjunctive after *quanquam* is customary in the *Met.*; see vdPaardt 1971, 31.

id genus: originally an apposition, this common adverbial accusative is also found e.g. 2, 1 (25, 5) *id genus pecua*; 2, 5 (29, 3) *id genus friuolis*; 5, 1 (103, 18) *id genus pecudibus*. See LHSz 2, 47 on the origin and frequency of this adverbial accusative. In this passage it probably refers to Thrasyllus' social position.

morum...inprobatus: it is not clear how this genitive is to be interpreted (according to *ThLL* 688, 48 this is the only instance where *improbare* is combined with a genitive). We see three possibilities: a) a genitive of the charge, cf. *furti damnare, accusare*; b) a causal genitive as 2, 15 (37, 7) *fatigationis... saucio* (see de Jonge ad loc.; vGeisau 1916, 250; Médan 1925, 41); c) a genitive of relation as 5, 4 (106, 3-4) *nouam nuptam interfectae uirginitatis curant*, explained by Weinreich 1920, 111 as 'they attend to the newlywed with regard to her lost virginity'; cf. 5, 2 (105, 2 *corporis curatae*; See also LHSz 2, 75.

For a similar embarrassment of riches cf. 4, 11 (82, 22) *trepidi re[li]gionis* (a genitive of relation?). See also *GCA* 1977, 51 on 4, 5 (78, 3) *postumae spei fatigati* and vdPaardt 1971, 126 on 3, 16 (64, 7) *maleficae disciplinae perinfames sumus* (a genitive of relation). Apuleius construes a similar verb with an ablative elsewhere, *Apol.* 61 (69, 17) *moribus comprobatus*.

repulsae: the messenger again uses ornate language: *repulsae* is a word from the sphere of constitutional law; it is used in poetry and post-Augustan prose in the sense of 'refusal', 'rebuff'. With reference to 'love' first in Prop. 3,14,26.

contumelia fuerat aspersus: the position of the verbal forms is somewhat mannered. The metaphor of 'sprinkling', 'spattering' is found several times, e.g. Cic. *Cael.* 23 *qui... non modo suspicione sed ne infamia quidem est aspersus*; Nep. *Alc.* 3, 6 *Aspergebatur etiam infamia*. Val. Max. 9, 14, 3 (Cornelius Scipio) *hac contumelia aspergeretur*; Suet. *Nero* 3, 2 *nonulla et ipse infamia aspersus*. Thus far the information presented by the sub-narrator is historical and the reader is by no means inclined to question the basis of his knowledge. See, however, Introduction 4. 2. 1. 3.

177, 15-19 **Ac dum erilis puella in bon⟨i⟩ Tlepolemi manum uenerat, firmiter deorsus delapsum nutriens amorem et denegati thalami permiscens indignationem, cruento facinori quaerebat accessum:** "And while the daughter of our master had entered into the custody of the good Tlepolemus, he persistently kept nursing his downfallen love, with which he mingled indignation about the rejected marriage, and he looked for an opportunity for a bloody crime."

erilis puella = *filia eri*; see our remark in *GCA* 1981, 175 on 7, 14 (165, 6) *greges equinos*. Callebat 1968, 482 calls *erilis* a 'terme archaïque', which is a dubious qualification: the adjective also occurs in Verg., Hor., Ovid., Stat., V.Fl., etc., so that it is not limited to Pl. and Ter. as he suggests. For *puella* = *filia* see *OLD* s.v. 1 b.

boni: in F the *i* has been added by a later hand and is written over the *n*. The epithet itself shows the messenger's estimation: there is a clear contrast between the villainous Thrasyllus and the good Tlepolemus (see our comm. on 177, 7 *male*).

in... manum uenerat: manus is the legal term for 'the power of the husband or paterfamilias'; see Norden 1912, 113. Cf. 6, 24 (146, 25) *Sic rite Psyche conuenit in manum Cupidinis*; below 183, 14 *modo ne in Thrasylli manum sacrilegam conuenias*. Cicero uses the same terminology *Top.* 3 *si ea (materfamilias) in manum non conuenerat, nihil debetur*. For the pluperfect after *dum* see LHSz 2, 613; Callebat 1968, 346.

firmiter: on Apuleius' preference for adverbs in *-ter* see Callebat 1968, 175; vdPaardt 1971, 46 and 119.

deorsus delapsum: observe alliteration and assonance; cf. 1, 19 (17, 13) *deorsum demeare* and 9,40 (234,17) *deorsus...derepit*. For the redundancy see Callebat 1968, 543. The *ThLL* s.v. *delabor* 415, 53 f. gives no other example of a combination with *amor*, but we may compare e.g. Sen. *Ep*. 16, 6 *ne patiaris impetum animi tui delabi et refrigescere*; Calp. *Decl*. 26 *nostra (uirtus) delabitur*.

nutriens amorem: a poetical expression; cf. Prop. 1, 12, 5 *nec mihi consuetos amplexu nutrit amores*; Ov. *Met*. 1, 496 *sterilem sperando nutrit amorem*. The mixed metaphor (*delapsum nutriens*) is remarkable.

accessum: this word is quite rare in the figurative sense of 'means or mode of approach'; cf. Sen. *Cons. P*. 8, 1 *nullum illa (tristitia) ad te inueniet accessum*. Of course Apuleius is seeking variation because of the immediately following *occasionem*, but perhaps he chose this word in reference to the *thalamus* which Thrasyllus was forbidden to enter.[1]

Nanctus denique praesentiae suae tempestiuam occasionem, sceleri, quod diu cogitarat, accingitur: "When at last he had found a suitable occasion for his presence, he prepared himself for the evil deed he had long contemplated."

denique: the meaning 'consequently' is possible, but we prefer 'finally' as at 7, 13 (165, 1); see *GCA* 1981, 173 ad loc.

tempestiuam: F has *tempestillam*; the correction occurs in ς. According to the *ThLL tempestillus* is not attested elsewhere. Nevertheless one may well hesitate before accepting the correction because Apuleius has a very high incidence of new or unique diminutives of nouns, adjectives, and adverbs. Of the adjective diminutives occurring only in the *Met*. we note *astutulus* 6, 27 (149, 5), *perastutulus* 9, 5 (206, 10), *lautiusculus* 7, 9 (160, 17), *semiadopertulus* 3, 14 (62, 22), *tantillulus* 2, 25 (45, 19). See for complete listings Abate 1978, 29 f. On the other hand Abate's chapter on diminutives in Apuleius (ibid. 65 f.) suggests a consciously applied artistic usage, as significant in its presence as in its absence (ibid. 89). In fact, the present passage (177,5-178,8) has no diminutives at all if *puella* and *poculum* are discounted. Since, moreover, a misreading of *-iu-* as *-ill-* is palaeographically quite plausible, adoption of the correction seems warranted.

diu = *iam dudum*, cf. 1, 24 (22, 24) *sat pol diu est, quod*. See Médan 1925, 224.

accingitur: middle voice, here combined with a final dative; cf. 201, 9 *accingunt se meo funeri*; Verg. *A*. 1, 210 *illi se praedae accingunt*; [Tib.] 3, 7, 179 *magnis se accingere rebus*. Elsewhere the verb is followed by *ad*, cf. 9, 18 (216, 11) *ad expugnandam...disciplinam...accingitur*.

---

[1] Angèle van Kempen suggests that the instrumental ablative *facinore* be read here and points to 178, 11 *praeclusos aditus*.

177, 20-178,2 Ac die, quo praedonum infestis mucronibus puella fuerat astu uirtutibusque sponsi sui liberata, turbae gratulantium exultans insigniter permiscuit sese salutique praesenti a⟨c⟩ futurae suboli nouorum maritorum gaudibundus ad ho⟨no⟩rem splendidae prosapiae inter praecipuos hospites domum nostram receptus, occultato consilio sceleris, amici fidelissimi personam mentiebatur: "And on the day when the girl had been saved from the deadly blades of the robbers by the cunning and courage of her fiancé, he mingled, conspicuously exultant, with the crowd of well-wishers; he expressed his joy at the rescue of the moment and the future offspring of the young couple, and in honour of his splendid parentage he was received into our house among the most distinguished guests, hiding his criminal plan and deceitfully playing the part of a most faithful friend."

die, quo...liberata: cf. 7, 13 (163, 21 f.). The events described at 7, 13-28 and 8, 1-4 apparently occupy the same amount of (unspecified) time. See also Introduction 3. 1.

infestis mucronibus: see *GCA* 1977, 198 on 4, 26 (95, 10), where the same combination is found.

fuerat...liberata: the two elements of the verb are separated by the instrumental modifier; the hyperbaton gives more emphasis to *astu uirtutibusque*.

insigniter: this adjective is found from Cicero onward, e.g. *Part.* 80 *parentibus...praecipue atque insigniter diligendis*. It should be linked with *exultans*: by displaying an excessive joy Thrasyllus seeks to attract attention and thus gain permanent access to the house.

saluti praesenti a⟨c⟩ futurae suboli: chiasmus with evenly distributed syllables and alliteration of *s*. The emendation is by Lipsius: F and φ read *p̄sentia*. The mention of future offspring on the wedding-day was quite common in antiquity; e.g. Catul. 61, 204 *ludite ut lubet, et breui / liberos date* (see Kroll ad loc.); cf. also Pl. *Aul.* 148 *liberis procreandis...uolo te uxorem domum ducere* (said already during the engagement).

saluti praesenti: this can refer to her well-being at this moment, but also to Tlepolemus' successful rescue operation.

suboli: this word, which rarely occurs in prose, has a distinctly poetic sound. Apuleius likes using it (as often as ten times), mostly in elevated passages; e.g. 5, 12 (112, 17) *diuinae subolis*; 11, 2 (267, 9) *aeterna subole*.

nouorum maritorum: Callebat 1968, 152 observes that this is the first time in Latin that *mariti* means 'spouses', 'man and wife'. In this meaning it is found more than once in the 2nd century (Tert. *Exh. Cast.* 9; Papin. 24, 1, 52). See also our comm. on 186, 9.

gaudibundus: this word is not found before Apuleius; after him it occurs only Cypr. *Ep.* 76, 4 *quis non appetat gaudibundus et laetus...in quo retribuat* and in a list of nouns in *-bundus* in Virg. Gramm. *Ep.* 5, p. 166, 19. Remarkably enough, it is combined here with a dative. Apuleius uses adjectives of this type several times; see Bernhard 1927, 139; Pianezzola 1965, 100 and 225 f.; vdPaardt 1971, 26.

prosapiae: on this archaic noun see vdPaardt 1971, 87.

domum nostram receptus: domum without *in* also in this combination, as e.g. Cic. *Arch.* 5 *eum domum suam receperat.*

personam mentiebatur: mentiri is construed here with a direct object in the sense of 'deceitfully play the role of', as at 5, 14 (114, 14) *sorores nomine mentientes.* Cf. also Ov. *Ep.* 20, 183 *mentiris amorem; Paneg.* 2, 25, 2 *cogebamur mentiri beatos.* See Callebat 1968, 180. On lying and deceit as one of the 'Leitmotive' in Apuleius, see Heine 1962, 206; see also *GCA* 1981, 220 and 227 on 7,21 (170,7) and 7,22 (171,4) respectively. The author uses a theatrical metaphor with *personam*; cf. 185,23 *scaena.*

From 177, 15 onward the sub-narrator has seemed aware of the thought and emotions of Thrasyllus (cf. also ch. 3); yet he does not retain this omniscience throughout the story. See below on 181, 15 *scilicet.*

Iamque sermonibus assiduis et conuersatione frequenti, nonnunquam etiam cena poculoque communi carior cariorque factus in profundam ruinam cupidinis sese paulatim nescius praecipitauerat: "And by continual conversations and frequent discussions, sometimes also by eating and drinking together, he had already become an ever dearer friend and had gradually and unknowingly plunged into the deep abyss of passion." 178, 2-6

poculoque: Vallette 33, n. 1 argues that, in addition to its concrete meaning 'cup' and its extended meaning 'drink' (as at 192, 4), *poculum* can acquire the abstract meaning of a verbal noun, as here 'drinking' (cf. 1, 19 : 18, 3 *auidus adfectans poculum*). Drinking usually takes place after the meal; here it is done together. See Balsdon 1969, 49-51.

carior cariorque: a repeated comparative adjective does not often occur in Latin; in Apuleius this is even the only example. On the other hand he likes to use a repeated comparative adverb, as *magis magisque* 3, 9 (58, 18) with vdPaardt 1971, 78-79 ad loc.

ruinam cupidinis: apparently passion is seen here as a ravine, in which one can perish by a deep fall (cf. 177, 17 *delapsum...amorem*). *Ruinam* is an emendation in ς (F has *roinã*); see Wiman 1927, 60, who in addition offers some parallels in defence of *ruinam* = 'ravine': Cic. *Sest.* 93 *ut eorum...diuitias in profundissimum libidinum suarum gurgitem profundat*; Cassian. *Coen.* 9, 6 *in barathrum concupiscentiae*; Hier. *Ep.* 100, 16 *barathrum uoluptatum.* Apuleius, too, uses *barathrum* metaphorically a few times: 2, 6 (29, 18), where Lucius craves to be initiated into magic in order to *prorsus in ipsum barathrum* (= 'undoing') *saltu concito praecipitare*; of a deep sleep 2, 25 (46, 2) *cum me somnus profundus in imum barathrum repente demergit*; cf. also *Apol.* 83 (92, 16) *ueritas...uelut alto barathro calumnia se mergit.* See Otto 1965, 53 s.v. *barathrum.* Partly on the ground of these parallels we see no reason to write *cupidinis* with a capital letter, as Helm and Frassinetti do. We regard *cupidinis* as an explicative genitive.

nescius praecipitauerat: Schober 1904, 72 points out that this conclusion almost agrees metrically with the beginning of the sentence *iamque sermonibus assidu(is).*

178, 6-8 Quidni, cum flamma saeui amoris parua quidem primo uapore delectet, sed fomenti⟨s⟩ consuetudinis exaestuans inmodicis ardoribus totos amburat homines: "No wonder: for the flame of a fierce love delights us, while it is still small, with its first heat, but when it is fed regularly it flares and consumes people completely by its excessive heat."

Quidni: after the metaphor of the abyss, into which passion plunged Thrasyllus, the narrator proceeds to philosophize in more general terms about the dangers of the fire of love. On *quidni* as an enlivening element in narrative style, see Callebat 1968, 424 f. and *GCA* 1977, 179 f. on 4, 24 (93, 5).

Apuleius, following in Plato's footsteps, gives *Pl*. 2, 14 (117, 3) a tripartition of the kinds of *amores: tres amores...unus diuinus cum incorrupta mente et uirtutis ratione conueniens, non paenitendus; alter degeneris animi et corruptissimae uoluptatis; tertius ex utroque permixtus* (see the remark of Beaujeu ad loc.). Thrasyllus' *amor* clearly fits into the second category.

saeui: the choice of words throughout the sentence illustrates the violence of Thrasyllus' emotions.

primo uapore: presumably to be linked with *delectet*: as long as the flame is still small, it warms with its first glow.

fomenti⟨s⟩: the omission of *s* can be explained by the fact that a series of words in this sentence ends in *s*. The emendation is by Eyssenhardt; F has *fomenti*, ς *fomento*, which is arguable as well. The word is used often, either in the plural or as a collective singular, for 'wood for kindling'; at 7, 19 (169, 3) *iamque fomento tenui calescens et enutritus ignis surgebat in flammas* it refers to hemp as a readily combustible fuel.

exaestuans: figuratively used (as it is here) the verb refers to the flaring passions, e.g. anger: Verg. *A*. 9, 798 *mens exaestuat ira*; violent grief: Ov. *Tr*. 5, 1, 63 *strangulat inclusus dolor atque exaestuat intus*; and also love: Apul. *Met*. 10, 2 (237, 17) *ubi completis igne uaesano totis praecordiis inmodice bacchatus Amor exaestuabat* in a description similar to this one. Cf. Firm. *Math*. 8, 21, 3 *ut in amorem eorum regis desideria semper exaestuent*.

amburat: according to *ThLL* s.v. 1878, 8, this is the only passage in which the verb is used figuratively of the *flamma amoris*. The metaphor is quite common; see *ThLL* s.v. *flamma* 867, 46 f., where one may note that the instances cited up to c. 200 A.D. belong to poetry; for *flamma* specified by *amoris* there are also prose instances in addition to our passage, e.g. Cic. *Ver*. 6,92 (see *ThLL* 867, 67 f.).

CHAPTER III

Thrasyllus starts on a malicious plan.

Diu denique deliberauerat secum Thrasyllus, quo⟨d⟩ nec clan- 178, 9-15
destinis colloquiis opportunum repperiret locum et adulterinae
Veneris magis magisque praeclusos aditus copia custodientium
cerneret nouaeque atque gliscentis affectionis firmissimum uinculum non posse dissociari perspiceret et puellae, si uellet,
quanquam uelle non posset, furatrinae coniugalis incommodaret
rudimentum: "Consequently, Thrasyllus had deliberated with himself for a
long time: for he did not find a suitable place for clandestine conversations with
her and he realized more and more that access to adulterous love was barred by
the great number of guards; he also perceived that the firm bond of a new and
growing affection could not be dissolved; and even if the girl was willing –
though, in fact, she could not possibly be willing – still her inexperience in
deceiving her husband was a handicap."

Tatum 1969, 82 points out that *uoluptas* is one of the dominant motifs in the *Met*. Even the lovable couple, Tlepolemus and Charite, paragons of loyal marital behaviour, fall victim to the lecherous Thrasyllus. The narrator emphatically points out again 1. 19-20 the results of *furiosa libido*.

Diu denique deliberauerat: with alliteration; for the combination *diu denique* see also 3, 26 (71, 8). For the meaning of *denique* see our comm. on 177, 19. There is no need for the conjecture of Blümner 1894, 309 *diu diuque* (cf. 11, 20: 281, 18).

quo⟨d⟩: this correction by Salmasius must be correct; F has *quo*, ç has *quo uel* (defended by Wower and Oudendorp) or *cum nec*; vdVliet proposes *quo⟨modo⟩ uel*. These conjectures are less radical (especially in view of the usual compendia) than Novák's *quo pacto* or *qui*. It is understandable for a scribe to make this mistake (cf. 10, 24 : 256, 11) because *quo* and *quod* tend to be confused in late Latin; cf. LHSz 2, 680. The use of the subjunctive is in keeping with classical usage: the causal clause contains Thrasyllus' train of thought. The use of the moods with *quod* is somewhat freer in later Latin; see LHSz 2, 577f.

clandestinis colloquiis: the adjective is found already in the *Lex XII tabularum* and in Plautus. Apuleius uses it five times, sometimes in an amorous context like 5, 18 (117, 7) *clandestinae ueneris* and 185, 10 *clandestinos coitus*. The word is naturally used quite often by historians in connection with e.g. *insidiae*, *coniuratio*, etc. The combination *clandestinis colloquiis* is found Amm. 14, 11, 1 (see de Jonge ad loc.) and 29, 5, 52; in the singular Amm. 20, 7, 9.

adulterinae Veneris: this is the only place in Latin literature where *adulterinus* is linked with *Venus*. Ambr. *Psalm*. 118, 12, 31 has *(uxor) quae adulterinos a*

41

seruolo concubitus flagitaret; cf. Aug. *C. Iul. op. imp.* 5, 24. Elsewhere Apuleius uses the adjective in a figurative sense 'false', e.g. 4, 16 (86, 25) *cum litteris...adulterinis*; and 6, 13 (138, 5) (referring to Amor) *huius...facti auctor adulterinus*; in both cases we have a common metaphor, used specifically of counterfeit coins etc. See Médan 1925, 353 and *GCA* 1977, 126 on 4, 16 (86, 25).

Summers 1967, 69f. and 266 rightly remarks that the relationship to which Thrasyllus is aspiring is, indeed, a penal offence in the 2nd century A.D. and that his caution is well-warranted: according to the *Lex Iulia de adulteriis coercendis*, the adulterer who has an affair with a married woman, whatever her rank, is liable to specific punishment; see Gardthausen 1891, 1, 905 and 2, 526; Austin on Verg. *A.* 6, 612 *ob adulterium caesi*.

Remarkably enough, the situation here is the reverse of most episodes of adultery in the *Met.*: usually the deceiver is the married woman, who fools her husband with cunning schemes. See Tatum 1969, 166.

magis magisque: although at first sight the words may be taken with *praeclusos*, it is hardly likely that this is an objective statement that Charite is supervised with increasing strictness. Because the entire sentence describes Thrasyllus' perception subjectively, it seems better to take the phrase with *cerneret*. For repetition in general in Apuleius see our comm. on 178, 4 *carior cariorque* above.

copia custodientium: Robertson transposes these words to stand before l. 15 *furatrinae*; vdVliet goes even further and shifts *nouae...perspiceret* to stand after l. 15 *rudimentum*. Both proposals arise from the consideration that, if the transmitted text is retained, *rudimentum* cannot have here the usual meaning of 'initiation' and must rather mean 'inexperience'; this was already the interpretation of Floridus, which seems plausible to us. Cf. 5, 12 (112, 19) *sarcinae nesciae rudimento miratur...incrementulum...uteri* (Helm-Krenkel 'unerfahren mit der ihr unbekannten Bürde'). Cf. also *Apol.* 92 (102, 11 f.), in reference to a girl: (*uirgo*) *affert...ad maritum nouum animi indolem, pulchritudinis gratiam, floris rudimentum*. In later Latin, too, *rudimentum* closely approaches the meaning of 'inexperience'; cf. e.g. Rufin. *Orig. in Rom.* 7, 6 *et uelut magister suscipiens rudem discipulum, et ignorantem penitus litteras, ut eum docere possit et instituere, necesse habet inclinare se ad discipuli rudimenta et ipse prius dicere nomen litterae*; perhaps also Rufin. *Orig. in Num.* 1, 3 *prius tamen paedagogo utentes Moyse et apud eum rudimenta infantiae deponentes, sic...*; *Paneg.* 8, 1, 1 *Si mihi, Caesar inuicte, post diuturnum silentium sola esset uincenda trepidatio qua rudimenta quaedam uocis meae rursus experior*. Finally *Gloss.* 2, 234, 14 *rudimentum*: ἀπειρία. The adjective *rudis*, too, sometimes means 'inexperienced'; cf. e.g. Ov. *Ep.* 17, 143 *sum rudis ad Veneris furtum*.

We have to admit that elsewhere in Apuleius *rudimentum (-ta)* is always a variant of *initium*; this meaning can, if necessary, be defended for our passage as well ('a first attempt', 'a trial' *OLD*; cf. Suet. *Ner.* 22, 2 *rudimentum ponere* 'pass the first test'); in that case *incommodare* would mean 'to cause difficulties'.

Finally one could follow Helm's suggestion (in his app. crit.) and write *incommodare*. In that case *rudimentum* retains its normal meaning 'first attempt' and is the direct object of *incommodare*; like *posse dissociari*, *incommodare* is part of the indirect discourse dependent on *perspiceret*. The difficulty is that *puellae* is then unconnected and, more important, that the harmonious structure *repperiret...cerneret...perspiceret...incommodaret* ('wachsende Glieder'!) is disturbed. For further remarks on *rudimenta* see *GCA* 1981, 172 on 164, 22.

copia custodientium cerneret: with triple alliteration and ending in a double cretic; in the latter respect it corresponds with *repperiret locum*; see Schober 1904, 47. For the *custodientes* see Introduction 4. 2. 2. c.

nouaeque: for the inconsistency with 4, 26 (94, 21 f.) see above on 177, 11 *inter praecipuos procos*.

quanquam...posset: the subjunctive is usual in the *Met.*; see LHSz 2, 602; Callebat 1968, 350. See also Waszink on Tert. *An.* 38, 1.

furatrinae coniugalis = adulterii. The rare noun has the figurative meaning of 'adultery' or 'stealthy deceit' only here; it has the literal meaning 'theft' in its other two occurrences in the *Met.*: 6, 13 (138, 1) *furatrina facili flauentis auri mollitie congestum gremium Veneri reportat* and 10, 14 (246, 25) *et diu...mihi furatrinae procedebat artificium*. The *ThLL* mentions in addition only Iul. Val. 2, 26 *pocula hoc furatrinae genere auertisti?* Apuleius has a liking for adjectives and nouns in *-inus* and *-ina*, e.g. *rupina* 6, 26 (148, 14) and 7, 13 (164, 10); *uncinus* 3, 15 (63, 2).

coniugalis: cf. also 5, 6 (107, 13) *amplexus coniugales*; 5, 8 (109, 11) *coniugale illud praeceptum*; 5, 28 (125, 18) *nuptiae coniugales*; all these examples occur in 'Amor and Psyche'. The adjective is found from Varro onward, according to Non. 848, 14 L *dis coniugalibus*, but is avoided by classical authors. Tac. *Ann.* 11, 27 writes *noctem...actam licentia coniugali*. The adjective is quite common in inscriptions and in late Latin; see Callebat 1968, 164.

et tamen ad hoc ipsum, quod non potest, contentiosa pernicie, quasi posset, impellitur: "and yet the very thing he cannot attain he is driven to by a pernicious passion, as if he could attain it." 178, 16-17

contentiosa pernicie: hypallage for *perniciosa contentione*; cf. e.g. 9, 2 (204, 12) *pestilentiae letalis peruicaci rabie possessus = pestilentia letali peruicacis rabiei possessus*. *Contentiosus* in the sense of 'persistent, 'obstinate' (*OLD*) is a rather rare adjective, first attested Plin. *Ep.* 2, 19, 5 *oratio...pugnax et quasi contentiosa*; by using *quasi* Pliny apologizes for this apparently mannered word. It occurs quite frequently in Christian authors. See Ernout 1949, 58 s.v.

potest...posset: presumably Thrasyllus is the subject in both cases, because otherwise *fieri* would almost certainly have been added.

Quod nunc arduum factu putatur, amore per dies roboratu facile uidetur effectu: "Wat is now considered difficult to do seems easy to accomplish when love has become daily more intense." 178, 17-19

arduum factu putatur...facile uidetur effectu: this sentence has both a fine parallel structure and a variation in the position of its parts and in the number of syllables. A statement of proverbial nature is offered here, rather than a remark specifically about Thrasyllus; therefore we do not favour the proposal made by Castiglioni 1938, 546 to insert ⟨et⟩ before *quod* in order to achieve a syndetic connection.

178, 19-20 **Spectate denique, sed, oro, sollicitis animis intendite, quorsum furiosae libidinis proruperint impetus**: "So observe, indeed examine attentively, I beg you, to what eruption the impetuosity of a furious passion has led."

Spectate...sed...intendite: the narrator (and of course also the author behind the narrator) now demands the audience's full attention, pointedly emphasising *spectate* by *sed, oro,* and *sollicitis animis intendite*; see Bétolaud 1884, 1, 468. In our opinion we have here a climax rather than a 'Wechsel synonymer Wörter' (Bernhard 1927, 147 f.). It is fascinating to compare the characterisation of Thrasyllus with the reflections at Apul. *Pl.* 2, 4 (107, 14 f.) and especially 2, 16 (118, 14 f.) on the *homo pessimus*, with whom Thrasyllus has many traits in common. The passages are analysed by Beaujeu 286 f. and 297 f.

denique: here equivalent to *ergo* (see our comm. on 177, 19). The narrator draws a conclusion from the previous sentence; what is about to follow is the illustration of that statement.

sed: this use of *sed*, which serves to give a special emphasis ('indeed', 'yes, and what's more' *OLD* s.v.3), originates in colloquial language; cf. e.g. Pl. *Cas.* 491 *abi atque obsona, propera, sed lepide uolo*. This usage becomes increasingly frequent in later Latin, e.g. in Firm., Arn., and the *Per. Aeth.* (see Löfstedt 1911, 179 f.); cf. also *Met.* 2, 5 (28, 16) *caue tibi, sed caue fortiter*; 7, 12 (163, 16) *cuncti denique, sed prorsus omnes*; 10, 22 (254, 3) *totum me prorsus, sed totum recepit*; etc.

oro...quorsum: a complete dactylic hexameter cf. Tatum 1979, 147.

oro: LHSz 2, 472 says about a parenthesis of this kind 'Parenthetische Satzwörter sind vor allem in der Umgangssprache häufig und neigen zu halbinterjektionaler Erstarrung'. This is the case with e.g. *amabo, oro* (especially *oro te*), *quaeso, rogo, obsecro*, etc. Apuleius uses *oro* especially often (14 times in the *Met.*) as an animated request for attention. See Hofmann *LU* 3 1951, 129; Bernhard 1927, 51; Callebat 1968, 106.

quorsum: also 6, 30 (151, 25) *quorsum...festinanti*; 9, 39 (233, 2) *quorsum...duceret asinus*. The variant *quorsus* is transmitted 11, 29 (290, 9) and *Fl.* 2 (3, 1).

furiosae libidinis: Heine 1962, 244 has collected all the passages in the *Met.* referring to fury, madness, etc.; they amount to a considerable number. Though the often exaggerated language of these passages loses some of its strength because of its frequency, still the image of a somewhat warped, eccentric world remains.

proruperint: as so often, the verb is in the penultimate position in the sentence, yielding a clausula consisting of a double cretic.

impetus: Apuleius seems to prefer the plural of this noun even when it is uncertain that it refers to a plural notion; cf. 6,5 (132,10) *saeuientes impetus*; 6,23 (145,27) *iuuentutis caloratos impetus*; 7,21 (170,12) *furiosos...impetus*; 179,14; 11,2 (267,14).

CHAPTER IV

The fatal hunting-party.

178, 21-24 Die quadam uenatum Tlepolemus assumpto Thrasyllo petebat indagaturus feras, quod tamen in capreis feritatis est; nec enim Charite maritum suum quaerere patiebatur bestias armatas dente uel cornu: "One day Tlepolemus wanted to go hunting in the company of Thrasyllus; he intended to track wild animals, in so far as there is any wildness in roe deer; for Charite culd not bear her husband to hunt animals armed with tusk or horn."

Die quadam: *dies* is masculine and feminine in Apuleius; see *GCA* 1977, 22 on 4, 1 (74, 9).

uenatum...petebat: it seems most plausible to connect these words and to regard *uenatum* as the accusative of the noun *uenatus* rather than as a supine, so that our interpretation is 'he sought the hunt', 'he wanted to go hunting'. Médan 1925, 242 includes the expression *uenatum petere* among the 'expressions nouvelles'.

indagaturus: the future participle expressing purpose is not very frequent in classical Latin but, partly under the influence of Greek idiom (vGeisau 1916, 278), it develops in Livy and in poetry; cf. LSHz 2, 390 f. An example is Verg. *A.* 2, 511 *fertur moriturus in hostis*. Apuleius often uses participles of this type; the same participle e.g. 7, 10 (162, 5).

quod: F has qδ (= *quod*), φ seems to offer q̅ (= *quid*); Robertson 1934, 94 categorically states 'Both abbreviations mean *quod* and nothing else...Probably *quod* is the true reading'. Robertson does not mention in this article (but does in his app. crit.) that qδ in F has been tampered with; consequently, one should not exclude the possibility that F, too, originally had *quid* (a few *recentiores* have, indeed, that reading). The meaning is clearly supposed to be 'in so far, at least, as..'. We think, therefore, that it is quite possible that Apuleius, fond as he is of archaic turns of phrase, has used *quod* here in the sense of *quoad* with a partitive genitive. LHSz 2, 57 declares in this connection that *quod* (= *quoad*) *eius* is found in early Latin and in the 'Umgangssprache' (Cato, *Rhet. Her.*, Cic. in early works and letters). In the discussion of *quoad* at LHSz 2, 654 f., the contraction *quōd* is mentioned in connection with the formula *quoad eius fieri poterit* (*Rhet. Her.* 1, 2, 2), in which the spelling *quod* is also possible. The contraction *quod* occurs also in inscriptions and sometimes in mss. (cf. e.g. Lucr. 2, 850, where Bailey ⌈1967, accepts Lambinus' conjecture *quoad* (monosyllabic) where the main mss. read *quod*; in his commentary he prefers to read *quod* = *quoad* and refers to 2, 248 *quod cernere possis*).

An alternative possibility is to follow Colvius and insert ⟨*si*⟩ before the pronoun (Colvius opts for *quid*), as does Oudendorp. Admittedly the combination *si quid tamen* and *si qui tamen* occurs elsewhere in Apuleius, e.g. 1, 8 (7, 22) *tu dignus. . . es extrema sustinere, si quid est tamen nouissimo extremius*; 195, 18 *si qui tamen faenum suum perdere non grauatur*; in general the combination of *si* with the restrictive *tamen* (see Löfstedt 1911, 27 and LHSz 2, 496) is frequently found in Apuleius; e.g. 6, 9 (135. 4); 7, 8 (160, 13); 9, 15 (214, 7); 11, 3 (268, 4). Since this is, nevertheless, a rather drastic intervention, one might consider *Quid tamen in capreis feritatis est?*, to be read as an interjection by the narrating shepherd. This solution is advocated by Hildebrand, Eyssenhardt, vdVliet and Schober 1904, 11, who calls attention to the dactylic rhythm; *ThLL* s.v. *caprea* 356, 37 also takes this view. Such a parenthetic question addressed to the audience, so soon after 178, 19-20 (*Spectate. . . impetus*) seems unlikely, however, and therefore we prefer the reading *quod* with the explanation = *quoad*.

nec. . . Charite. . . patiebatur: for the motif compare e.g. Herodotus 1, 34 f., where Croesus does not allow his son Atys to go hunting; Westerbrink *AAGA* 1978, 70 compares the details of that story to our passage and does not exclude the possibility that Apuleius is parodying Herodotus here. A famous example in mythology is that of Venus and Adonis; cf. Ov. *Met.* 10, 545 (Venus is speaking) *Parce meo, iuuenis, temerarius esse periclo / neue feras, quibus arma dedit natura, lacesse*. Another example is in the Nibelungen saga: Kriemhilde, worried by a dream, tries to prevent Siegfried from going on a hunt, but in vain; on this motif see Frenzel 1976, 771 with references 792. Heine 1962, 239 note 2 points out that it is remarkable that, after having massacred a whole band of robbers in book 7, Tlepolemus is now no longer allowed to hunt big game; similarly Thibau 1965, 126 refers to the 'degeneration' of Tlepolemus in book 8 as compared to his character in book 7.

armatas dente uel cornu: wild boars and e.g. red deer respectively; cf. Cic. *N.D.* 2, 121 *alias (animantes) esse cornibus armatas*. The verb *armare* is used regularly of animals' natural means of defense; see *ThLL* s.v. *armo* 618, 52 f. The use of the singular seems poetical; see LHSz 2, 14.

Iamque apud frondosum tumulum ramorumque densis tegminibus umbrosu⟨m⟩ prospectu uestigatorum obseptis capreis canes uenationis indagini[s] generosae mandato cubili residentes inuaderent bestias, immittuntur statimque sollertis disciplinae memores partitae totos praecingunt aditus tacitaque prius seruata musitatione signo sibi repentino reddito latra[n]tibus feruidis dissonisque miscent omnia: "And now on a wooded hillock, shady with dense foliage, the roe deer were hemmed in through the beaters' foresight and the dogs were turned loose; the bitches, bred to corner game, got the command to seize the animals as they lay in their lairs. At once, mindful of their expert training, they scattered and blocked all approaches. First they growled silently for a while, then, when suddenly a signal was given to them, they filled everything with their fiery and jarring barks." 178, 24-179, 5

Iamque: this indicates a leap in time: all at once we are on the hunting-ground. Quinn 1963, 220 f. gives under the title 'Elliptical Narrative' some examples of this technique in Vergil but rightly adds: 'All skilful writers do this to some extent.'

apud...tumulum: for the use of *apud* instead of the classical *in* with an ablative, see Callebat 1968, 216 and *GCA* 1981, 190 on 7, 16 (166, 21) *apud historiam*.

frondosum: Callebat 1968, 384 calls this a 'synonyme expressif de *frondens*'; found already in Ennius (*Ann.* 190 *omne sonabat / arbustum fremitu siluai frondosai*), it remained in use in Latin of all periods; cf. e.g. Verg. *A.* 8, 351 *frondoso uertice*. Note the rhyming *umbrosum* in the next phrase.

tegminibus: this noun has a poetic ring (cf. the beginning of Vergil's first Eclogue: *sub tegmine fagi...lentus in umbra*) but also occurs in postclassical prose writers (in Cic. only *Tusc.* 5, 90, spelled *tegimen*, in a translation from Greek). Apuleius has a liking for the plural in abstract nouns of this type; see Médan 1925, 54.

umbrosu⟨m⟩: F has *umbrosu*, and it is out of the question, according to Robertson, that it ever read anything else; φ and a* have *umbroso*, which makes what already is a complicated construction even harder to understand. The correction *umbrosum* is made in ς.

prospectu: Butler 1910 translates: 'And now they had come to a leafy hill roofed with a dark covert of shady boughs, which concealed the roedeer from the eyes of the hunters'. It is true that elsewhere in Apuleius the word always has the meaning 'the action of looking out' or 'prospect', 'view', but just in the second century A.D. it begins to develop the meaning of *prouidentia, cura*, which is frequent in Christian Latin. This development starts at Gel. 5, 11, 10 *cuius rationem prospectumque Bias non habuit*, where *prospectus* has detached itself from the merely sensory meaning: 'that possibility Bias did not observe or regard'. (We prefer to exclude Plin. *Ep.* 10, 18, 2 *prouinciales, credo prospectum sibi a me intellegent* because *prospectum* (sc. *esse*) could be an infinitive.) In Tertullian the meaning *cura*, 'precaution', becomes the rule, e.g. *Spect.* 1, 5 *ut hoc, consilio potius et humano prospectu, non diuino praescripto definitum existimetur* (see Büchner 1935 ad loc., who, in addition to many passages from Tertullian, also refers to our passage; Castorina 1961 ad loc. follows him in this). Further, the verb *prospicere* sometimes has the meaning 'take care of' in the *Met.*, e.g. 9, 6 (206, 23) *cenulae nostrae prospexi*. We are therefore inclined to follow Helm-Krenkel ('durch Fürsorge der Treiber') and Brandt-Ehlers ('schon haben...die Pirschjäger umsichtig die Rehe eingekreist').

uestigatorum: 'stalkers'; cf. e.g. Var. *L.* 5, 94 (where, however, the reading is uncertain); Col. 9, 8, 10 (of someone hunting a swarm of bees); at 179, 16 below it appears that these assistant-hunters (Brandt-Ehlers' translation 'Pirschjäger' is inexact) are unarmed. They are to be differentiated from the actual hunters: Ulp. *Dig.* 33, 7, 12, 12 *si in agro uenationes sint, puto uenatores quoque et uestigatores et canes...* makes a clear distinction.

obseptis capreis: the phrase is best taken as an abl. abs. To take it as a dative with *immittuntur* is less attractive in view of the distance between *capreis* and *immittuntur*.

uenationis: for the concrete sense 'animals hunted' see *OLD* s.v. 1b.

indagini[s]: F has *indaginis*, but the *s* has been erased; AUS show -*i*, φ -*is*. The genitive *indaginis* creates difficulties: it would have to be explained as a genitivus relationis (KSt 2,2, 443 f.) dependent on *generosae*, and *uenationis indago* would have to be taken as expressing a single notion 'game hunting'. We prefer to drop the *s* as a scribal error and join the modern editors who print *indagini*, a dative of purpose depending on the verbal idea residing in *generosae* (see below on that word). It is not necessary to follow Robertson, who places *uenationis indagini* after *bestias* making the dative depend on *immittuntur*.

generosae: 'of good stock', a frequent epithet of carefully bred animals, see *ThLL* s.v. 1801,41 f.; in the *Met.* also at 10,18 (251,4), where it qualifies *iumenta*. *ThLL* ibid. notes that the word refers to the excellent qualities and usefulness of animals. We propose to take it with the subsequent final dative *indagini* in the sense 'bred for': the nobility of the stock consists in their usefulness for man as good hunting dogs.

It is not unusual for bitches to be used for hunting: their sense of smell seems to be better and they are easier to train. Apuleius follows a Greek exemplar here, e.g. Xen. *Cyn.* 3, 1, where their qualities are described in detail. In Latin literature e.g. Pl. *St.* 139 *stultitiast, pater, uenatum ducere inuitas canes*; Ov. *Met.* 3, 140 (addressing Actaeon's dogs) *uosque canes satiatae sanguine herili* with Bömer ad loc.; Grat. *Cyneg.* 185 *canis illa...taciturna* with Enk ad loc. See Neue-Wagener I[3] 920 f. on this aspect. Apuleius always uses the masculine for hounds in other passages; cf. 4, 19 (89, 10) *canes...uenaticos auritos illos*; 8, 31 (202, 2); 9, 2 (203, 22). On dogs in general see Orth *RE* 8, 2561, 49 f. s.v. Hund; id. 9, 1, 558 f. s.v. Jagd; Merlen 1971; Lilja 1976.

mandato...inuaderent: it seems that this construction without *ut*, or, more generally, the preference for parataxis over hypotaxis, originates in colloquial language; see Bernhard 1927, 51; Callebat 1968, 358.

mandato: = *cum mandatum esset*. Apuleius often uses the abl. abs. participle with a noun-clause in place of a noun; e.g. 1, 5 (5, 5) *comperto...caseum recens...distrahi*; 7, 4 (157, 2) *cognitoque quosdam...oppetisse* (see *GCA* 1981, 104 ad loc.); 10, 16 (248, 23) *cognito:* 10, 24 (255, 29) *addito*; 10, 26 (258, 5) *mandato* again. Summers 1967, 266 seems to exaggerate when he says: 'It is possible to see in this phrase a metaphor based on the institution of Roman law known as *mandatum*'; for this he refers to 6, 7 (133, 10), where Venus instructs Mercurius (*fac ergo mandatum matures meum*) to find Psyche. In our opinion there is no connection between these two passages.

cubili residentes: *cubili* is presumably a dative; cf. 3, 27 (72, 4) *simulacrum residens aediculae* with vdPaardt 1971, 192 ad loc.; 3, 16 (64, 2) *iuuenem...tonstrinae residentem*. On the strength of these passages we may assume a dative both in our passage and at 11, 11 (274, 24) *residens umeris suis*, rather than a locative ablative without *in*, as Médan 1925, 57 maintains.

inuaderent: this is the reading of φ; F has *inuadere*, followed by erased -*nt*. The subjunctive is undoubtedly correct (see Lütjohann 1873, 467); cf. 4, 3 (76, 18) *conclamant canes atque...ferrent impetum,...cohortantur*; 7, 9 (160, 17) *uostemque...proferunt, numeret* (see *GCA* 1981, 138), 9, 23 (220, 28) (*uxor*) *non cessat optundere...fabulam proderet*. The strongest argument is found 10, 26 (258, 5) *mandato saltem...deposceret*. Observe that *KSt.* 1, 681 still – wrongly – read *inuadere...immittuntur* ('Infinitive nach den Verben der Bewegung').

49

immituntur: in the meaning 'let go' the verb is used absolutely e.g. 9,36 (230,19) *canes pastoricios...laxari...atque immitti praecepit*; 9,41 (235,16) *inmissis...lictoribus*.

sollertis disciplinae memores partitae: these words most probably belong together; the dogs divide into small groups (*partitae* is used here with the force of a Greek middle) as they have been trained to do.

totos...aditus: for *toti* in the sense *omnes* see *GCA* 1977, 51 and 165; Callebat 1968, 287. From the hunters' point of view these are, indeed, *aditus*. Often *aditus* has a much broader meaning than only 'access' or 'approach'; it is quite possible to leave by an *aditus*, cf. e.g. Sen. *Breu.* 14, 4 *per obscuros aedium aditus profugient*; Curt. 6, 8, 10 *occulto aditu...elabi*. See *ThLL* s.v. 696, 69 f. On the dactylic rhythm in *totos...seruata* see Schober 1904, 12 with many examples.

tacitaque...seruata musitatione: there are two slightly different possibilities. First, if *seruata* is taken in the quite common meaning *obseruata* (cf. Liv. 33, 4, 2 *qui neglegenter custodias seruassent*; 34, 9, 6 *seruabant uigilias*) the phrase must mean 'observe a silent growling'. The apparent contradiction is not without parallel: Luc. 5, 104 *haud illic tacito mala uota susurro / concipiunt*. Another possibility is to take *tacita* proleptically and *seruare* in the sense 'keep (down)' and translate 'keeping their growling down to the point of silence'; cf. Claud. *carm. min.* 2, 5 *aequor / clauditur et placidam discit seruare quietem* (Platnauer: 'and learns to lie in undisturbed tranquillity'). In both interpretations there is a distinct contrast with the subsequent *latratibus feruidis*, and *tacita* is used from the point of view of the hunted animals who are not to hear the dogs.

musitatione: this noun is not attested before Apuleius, who uses it only here (but *mussitare* in *Apol.* 71 : 80, 6). It is nowhere else used of dogs; later it is used more frequently, especially in Christian authors, but mostly in the sense of 'muttering', 'grumbling'. *ThLL* s.v. gives some ten passages, e.g. Tert. *Pudic.* 7, p. 231, 9 *nihil ad Pharisaeorum mussitationem respondisse...dominum*. The spelling with one *s*, used by F and φ, is quite common.

signo sibi repentino reddito: alliteration and assonance.

latra[n]tibus feruidis: F and φ have *latrantibus ferundis*; the first word is corrected in the margin of F by a second hand; the second word is corrected in ς (a similar mistake occurs in Veg. *Mulom.* 2, 42, 2, where the editio princeps and ms. A read *ferunta*, while the correct reading *feruore* is found in P). *Feruidus*, of course, always retains some of its fundamental meaning 'intensely hot' even when it is used in a figurative sense; cf. Verg. *A.* 12, 894 *non me tua feruida terrent / dicta, ferox*; [Tib.] 3, 18, 1 *Ne tibi sim...aeque iam feruida cura*.

miscent omnia: this expressive use of *miscere* = 'fill with confused noise' is known from poetry; cf. Verg. *A.* 2, 298 *diuerso...miscentur moenia luctu* (see Austin ad loc. 'noise and confusion'); 4, 160 *magno misceri murmure caelum / incipit* (Austin 'the sky is all a mass of noise'). Cf. in Apuleius e.g. 7, 7 (159, 13) *cuncta miscuit* with *GCA* 1981, 128 ad loc.

latratibus feruidis dissonisque miscent omnia: Möbitz 1924, 123 argues that the position of *miscent* can be explained here by the wish to avoid a *clausula heroica*. These words form indeed a rhythmically beautiful conclusion to a carefully composed period. The tension is mounting also from the point of view of content: the woods are closed off, the dogs are given their instructions and kept quiet; then, at a given sign, they start baying and everything is suddenly in motion and full of noise. Thus there is careful preparation for the climax in the next sentence.

Nec ulla caprea nec pauens dammula nec prae ceteris feris mitior cerua, sed aper immanis atque inuisitatus exsurgit toris callosae cutis obesus, pilis inhorrentibus corio squalidus, setis insurgentibus spinae hispidus, dentibus attritu sonaci spumeus, oculis aspectu minaci flammeus, impetu saeuo frementis oris totus fulmineus: "But no roedeer, nor timid antelope, nor doe, gentler than all the other wild creatures, rose up, but a wild boar, huge and of a size never seen before, thick muscles under his horny skin, his hide rough with coarse hair, his mane bristling along his spine, noisily whetting his foam-covered tusks, his eyes flaming with a menacing glare, the whole animal blazing with the fierce assault of his snarling mouth." 179, 5-11

This sentence is impressive in many respects, as to both content and style:

a) as to content, because we see here again how the author uses wild animals in order te describe a turn in the life of human beings. This is especially frequent in books 7-10: e.g. the she-bear at 7, 24 (see *GCA* 1981, 244 on 172, 20 *immanem ursam*) who mangles the sadistic *puer*; the wolves who threaten the runaway servants 8, 15; the *immanis draco* (with the same attribute as the boar here) of 8, 21 who devours a young man. The preferred epithets are *immanis* and *uastus*, which accentuate the overwhelming impression the animal makes. See Penwill 1975, 82 n. 71.

Amat 1972, 122 calls our attention to the fact that the image of a wild boar in full action was very fashionable in the arts during the time of Hadrian; there are, for instance, many scenes of this type on mosaics in Africa, although the deer-hunt is even more popular there. In literature one is reminded of the Erymanthian or the Calydonian boar; Ov. *Met.* 8, 338 f. describes Meleager's hunt; such descriptions have some features in common with representations in the arts and it is quite probable that there has been some interaction. But this scene in Apuleius with its baroque, almost barbaric savagery surpasses everything in this domain to such a degree that it is quite likely that he is deliberately ridiculing this trend.

b) stylistically: with a smile, the reader will recall the quasi-modest opening words of our narrator at 177, 2-4. Numerous rhetorical devices are pressed into service here: after we have been told what does not appear by means of *nec...nec...nec*, the climax comes with full force: *sed aper immanis atque inuisitatus* with alliteration and assonance; then the monster is characterized by means of six elements, asyndetically following each other, harmoniously composed and ending with rhyme:

toris callosae cutis obesus	(10 syllables)
pilis inhorrentibus corio squalidus	(12 syllables)
setis insurgentibus spinae hispidus	(11 syllables)

dentibus attritu sonaci spumeus (12 syllables)
oculis aspectu minaci flammeus (12 syllables)
impetu saeuo frementis oris totus fulmineus (16 syllables)

Bernhard especially points out the four cola with twelve syllables each (we follow him in regarding *corio* as disyllabic but elide *-ae* of *spinae*)[1] and sighs (1927, 91): 'Auf die Spitze getrieben ist die Sucht nach Entsprechung der Silbenzahl.' Apart from that the four middle cola run remarkably parallel, not only in their number of syllables, but also in their homoeoteleuton (*-īs* alternating with *-is*; twice *-entibus*; twice *-idus*; three times *-eus*), alliteration (*callosae cutis, sonaci spumeus, flammeus...frementis...fulmineus*), assonance (*sonaci, minaci*) and especially in the analogous position of the words (Strilciw 1925, 113 speaks of *harmonia*). The rhyming method used here is already discussed by Wölfflin 1884, 360.

This whole episode is absent in the *Onos*. Vallette 34 n.1 thinks that Apuleius is drawing from another source, which likes to use laboured effects (he also refers to 10, 2 and 3, where similar traits 'd'affectation ou de pédanterie' appear) – an unreasonable contention in our view, when one recalls the many rhetorical flowers of speech in the *Apol.* and the even greater number in the *Flor.* (See Bernhard 1927, 286 f., who speaks of 'asianische Beredsamkeit'.)

Nec ulla caprea nec pauens dammula nec prae ceteris feris mitior cerua; a tricolon with 'wachsende Glieder'; Cornelissen 1888, 68 proposes *nec fugax caprea* (cf. Verg. *A.* 10, 724 *fugacem...capream*); this is unnecessary. It is not entirely clear which three species are meant here. *Capreae* refers to all kinds of goat-like animals, but also to the doe; *dammula* is not attested before Apuleius and occurs only a few times afterwards, e.g. *VL Deut.* 12, 22 *si uidetur dammula* (= δορκάς) *aut cerua*, and in Christian authors (see *ThLL* s.v. 8, 59 f.). There is a gloss which explains *dammula* as *capra agrestis*; it is a diminutive of *damma* (the spelling *dama* is also common), which can refer to many species: goat, chamois, antelope, gazelle, etc.

prae ceteris feris mitior: the comparative notion is expressed twice; cf. 192, 29 *unus prae ceteris et animo fortior et aetate iuuenior*. See Médan 1925, 74 and KSt 2,2, 468.

inuisitatus: 'unseen', but also 'not previously seen', as here. Helm refers to Gel. 5, 14, 7 (concerning a hunting party in the *Circus Maximus*) *multae ibi saeuientes ferae, magnitudines bestiarum excellentes omniumque inuisitata aut forma erat aut ferocia*; cf. also Plin. *Nat.* 10, 132 *inuisitata genera alitum* (variant reading *inusitata*). Morelli 1913, 181 cites Iul. Val. 30, 39 *inuisitatae magnitudinis aquila* as a proof of Apuleius' influence on later writers. Much closer to Apuleius is e.g. Gel. 7, 3, 1 (of a snake) *inuisitatae insanitatis*.

toris callosae cutis obesus: literally 'fat with the muscles of the calloused skin': the swelling muscles are visible under the horny skin, so that the entire animal looks enormously heavy. It seems incorrect to punctuate with Rode-Rüdiger 318 n. 3 after *toris*: 'erhebt sich vom Lager, fett die Schwarte'; it would mean the

---

[1] Cf. Hijmans *AAGA* 1978, 202. But whether there are 11 or 12 syllables makes no essential difference to the generally symmetrical composition.

loss of symmetry in the composition. The same is true for Brandt-Ehlers 'erhebt sich von seinem Lager'.

cutis: according to Callebat 1968, 51 this is a 'mot specialisé du sermo cotidianus'; the *ThLL* s.v. also speaks of a 'vox sermonis vulgaris, sed praeter Cels.... et Plin. Nat. omnibus temporibus rara'. Apuleius always uses it, except here and 11, 13 (276, 5), of human skin; for animals he prefers *corium* and once *pellis* (4, 14 : 86, 4 referring to a bear skin). It is possible that Apuleius chooses this word for the sake of variatio in respect to the following colon and for the alliteration of *c* (the same is true for 276, 5 *cutis crassa*).

obesus: this adjective occurs three other times in Apuleius: 7, 16 (166, 18); 10, 15 (248, 8); 11, 13 (276, 6). Callebat 1968, 147 remarks that this too is a word from the *sermo vulgaris*; cf. Gel. 19, 7, 3 *uulgus enim* ἀκύρως *uel* κατ' ἀντίφρασιν *'obesum' pro 'uberi' atque 'pingui' dicit*. This apparently meaningless statement makes sense when one realises that Gellius is quoting a passage from the archaic poet Laevius, in which *obesus* has the unique meaning 'emaciated' (the passive participle of *obedo*), the exact opposite of the regular meaning 'fat', 'plump'. This meaning is found everywhere else and is certainly not confined to vulgar language. (see e.g. *OLD* s.v.). Ernout 1951, 806 remarks that the word does not occur in this meaning before the Empire, but this is incorrect: see Catul. 39, 11 *obesus Etruscus*.

corio: used in particular of an animal, e.g. an elephant (Pl. *Mil.* 235), an ass (Apul. *Met.* 7, 11 : 163, 3 and 11, 6 : 270, 17), a hippopotamus (Plin. *Nat.* 11, 227), snakes (Gel. 7, 3, 1), etc.; when it is used of the skin of a person, it usually is contemptuous. It is not certain whether *corio* here is a locative ablative or an ablative dependent on *inhorrentibus* (the dative does not occur with this verb); cf. Liv. 8, 8, 10 *hastas...in terra fixas, haud secus quam uallo saepta inhorreret acies, tenentes*. The verb is used more than once of hair standing on end; cf. [Quint.] *Decl. exc. Monac.* 12, p. 376, 25 *inhorrebant pili et artus*.

This and the next colon say practically the same thing: the boar's bristles are shaggy and are standing on end on his back. Obviously Apuleius is interested here in the rhetorical effect: most ingeniously the two cola are exactly parallel in construction.

spinae: probably a dative, which is not unusual with *insurgere*; cf. e.g. Verg. *A.* 3, 207 *uela cadunt, remis insurgimus*. Apuleius construes the verb with an accusative at 1, 2 (3, 6) *iugi quod insurgimus aspritudinem*. It is unlikely that *spinae* is a locative, as Médan 1925, 55 argues; he refers to 3, 2 (53, 22) *orchestrae mediae sistunt*; 3, 16 (64, 2) *tonstrinae residentem* (incorrect, see above on 179, 1 *cubili*); 3, 27 (72, 3) *pilae mediae* (also incorrect, see vdPaardt 1971, 191 ad loc.); 72, 4 *residens aediculae* (probably a dative); 9, 33 (228, 1) *spinae meae residens* (also probably a dative).

dentibus: while in the previous cola we read an instrumental ablative at the beginning, this is better taken as an ablative of respect; see LHSz 2, 134. Rohde 1885, 104 wants to read *dentis* and *oculi*, which he justifies thus: 'Der Singular wie p. 136, 31 *dente* (= 180, 1 H); 137, 7 *multo dente* (= 180, 10 II). Erst so entsteht volle Concinnität im Ausdruck; denn Ap. fährt fort: *impetu fulmineus*'. Robertson agrees: 'fortasse recte'. Our analysis above shows that this would disturb the parallelism of the cases.

attritu: 'the process of grinding'. Cf. Sen. *Ira* 3, 4, 2 *non alium sonum quam est apris tela sua adtrita acuentibus*; Sid. *Carm.* 23, 293 (Mars in the shape of an *aper*) *uel ille fingit / hirtam dorsa feram repanda tela / attritu adsiduo cacuminantem*.

sonaci: this word, also used by Apuleius 4, 31 (99, 20) *concha sonaci*, does not occur earlier according to the *ThLL* material. Apuleius has undoubtedly chosen the unusual attribute because of the rhyme with *minaci*; cf. the citation from Seneca s.v. *attritu*.

spumeus: the tusks are covered with foam as the animal whets them noisily. The element *spumare* is traditional in the description of a boar-hunt of this kind; cf. Verg. *A.* 1, 324 *aut spumantis apri cursum clamore prementem*; 4, 158 (Ascanius at the hunt) *spumantemque dari...optat aprum*; Mart. 14, 221, 2 *spumeus in longa cuspide fumet aper*.

flammeus: 'flaming', 'fiery' refers to eyes in several passages; cf. Acc. *trag.* 443 *rubore ex oculis fulgens flammeo*; Verg. *A.* 7, 488 *flammea torquens / lumina*; Ov. *Ep.* 12, 107 (Medea to Jason) *flammea subduxi medicato lumina somno*. Here, too, the idea will be that his eyes are showering sparks, as it were; this is emphasized by the next colon, which ends with the climax *totus fulmineus*.

oris: Damsté 1928, 24 praises vdVliet's idea that there is a lacuna after *oris*, which he proposes to fill with ⟨*toruus*⟩. In that case *totus fulmineus* would make a fine, summarizing conclusion, preceded by yet another 12-syllabe colon *impetu...toruus*. But this is unnecessary and smells of wishful thinking.

fulmineus: this is the third colon ending in an adjective in *-eus*. The animal appears like a flash of lightning to make a fierce counter-attack on the assaulting dogs. Ovid also uses it of a wild boar at *Ars* 2, 373 *sed neque fuluus aper media tam saeuus in ira est / fulmineo rabidos cum rotat ore canes*. In general the adjective suggest flashing speed; one is reminded of e.g. Verg. *A.* 4, 579, where Aeneas hurriedly draws his sword to cut the cables *uaginaque eripit ensem / fulmineum* (Austin: 'it suggests brightness, speed, sharpness'). Bernhard 1927, 211 includes *fulmineus* and *flammeus* in a list of adjectives which contribute to Apuleius' poetic coloration; for *fulmineus* he refers to Verg. *A.* 9, 442, for *flammeus* to Enn. *Sat.* 7 and Catul. 64, 341.

179, 11-14 Et primum quidem canum procaciores, quae comminus contulerant uestigium, genis hac illac iactatis consectas interficit, dein calcata retiola, qua primos impetus reduxerat, transabiit: "And first of all he rent and killed the boldest of the dogs, who had engaged him at close quarters, his tusks darting out left and right; then he trampled the flimsy nets where he had slowed his first attack and went off right through them."

comminus contulerant uestigium: although we cannot find an exact parallel for *comminus conferre* (again alliteration), we presume that the expression is analogous to *pedem conferre, gradum conferre*.

genis: Purser 1906, 48 proposes to read *genuinis* 'tusks' and refers to the end of ch. 5 *prosectu dentium* (cf. also 6, 15 : 140, 4 where Heinsius proposes *inter genuinos saeuientum* [*dentium*]); Purser does not take into account *Gloss.*

4,522,21, where *maxillae* is given as a synonym of *genae*. The glossator is right: *gena* in the sense of *maxilla* is sometimes used of wild animals; cf. e.g. Stat. *Th.* 2, 130 (*tigris*) *bella cupit laxatque genas et temperat ungues* and 10, 290 *tigris...lassauitque genas.* Amm. 22, 15, 19 refers to the *genae* of a crocodile and Apuleius himself (140, 5 cited above) writes *inter genas saeuientium dentium.* Therefore we do not find it objectionable to use *genae* of a wild boar's tusks.

consectas: older editions (e.g. Floridus, Scriverius, Puteanus, etc.) have *confectas*. This is rightly criticized by Oudendorp, who remarks that *secare* is typical of boars, who fight with their tusks; cf. below 180, 16 *prosectu dentium*. The verb *consecare* 'cut to pieces', which Apuleius uses 2, 7 (30, 16) in a culinary context (stuffing is being prepared) *pulpam frustatim consectam*, is therefore quite appropriate here.

retiola...transabiit: later the word *retiolum* is attested in Serv. on Verg. *A.* 4, 138 *ueluti retiolum dicit, quod colligit comas* (cf. also Isid. *Orig.* 19, 31, 7); Aug. *Ep.* 211, 10 (referring to hair-nets); Arn. *ad Greg.* 13 *retiola pauperis eius causa nominis contempserunt* (the nets of the disciples). In all these passages the diminutive has retained its force, as it does here, where the nets are light and intended for catching small deer. That nets of this kind were set is implied in the preparation as described at 178, 24 -79, 5. It is possible that the diminutive is also chosen to contrast with the *immanitas* of the boar.

qua: as so often in Apuleius not 'along what way' but 'where'.

impetus reduxerat: there are two possibilities: a) *impetus* refers to the *aper*: 'after he had slowed down his attack'; cf. Ov. *Met.* 6, 107 *timidasque reducere plantas* and Sen. *Ira* 2, 35, 2 *uelocitas...quae...cursu ad gradum reduci potest*; b) *impetus* refers to the attacks of the dogs 'where he had checked their first attacks'. We have not found a good parallel for this; Sen. *Ben.* 1, 14, 2 *nemo haec ita interpretetur, tamquam reducam liberalitatem et frenis artioribus reprimam* is not entirely comparable. Therefore we opt for the first possibility.

transabiit: for this poetic compound see *GCA* 1981, 134 on 7, 8 (160, 3). It is used in a figurative sense 189, 12. For a boar escaping by trampling the nets cf. also Hor. *C.* 1,1,28 with Nisbet-Hubbard ad loc.

CHAPTER V

A violent death.

179, 14-19 Et nos quidem cuncti pauore deterriti et alio[n]quin innoxiis uenationibus consueti, tunc etiam inermes atque inmuniti tegumentis frondis uel arboribus latenter abscondimus, Thrasyllus uero nactus fraudium opportunum decipulum sic Tlepolemum captiose compellat: "And all of us, overcome by fear and accustomed for that matter to hunting without risks and also at that time unarmed and unprotected, hide ourselves under the cover of leaves and in trees. But Thrasyllus, having got a ready chance to ambush Tlepolemus by fraud, traps him with these words:"

Tlepolemus' death is inevitable. The section of the tale describing it is introduced by a period in which first the fact that he cannot count on any assistance and second Thrasyllus' hostile intentions are underlined. The phrase *cuncti pauore deterriti* stands in obvious contrast to the name Thrasyllus. For the similarity of the tale to other tales of antiquity and for the question whether the narrator may be regarded as a true eye-witness of the event see Introduction 4.2.2 and 4.2.1.3 respectively.

Et nos quidem...abscondimus: the presence of a retinue of slaves (cf. 178,26 *uestigatorum*, line 21 below: *seruorum istorum* and 180,17-19), and in particular that of the narrator, apart from being the usual practice, may be seen as part and parcel of the series of indications answering the question how the narrator can be aware of the details of his story; see Introd. 4.2.1.3.

cuncti pauore deterriti: slaves' fear in physical danger is not a common motif in the *Met.*: the only other instance is Lucius' slave who flees when robbers invade Milo's house (3, 27 : 72,18 f.). The audience of the present tale consists of slaves who at 188,9 appear afraid of a change of masters. For the rest the slaves in the novel seem to differ from one another as much as their masters – this is what one would expect in a novel of which large parts are set in the lower strata of society (cf. Sandy 1968,82).

innoxiis uenationibus consueti: this agrees whith Charite's objection to dangerous quarries, cf. 178,23. We must take *innoxiis* in the sense of 'producing no danger to the hunter', in itself quite an ordinary meaning (cf. e.g. 9,37 : 231,25 *lapis...innoxius*), but parallels for *innoxius* qualifying an abstract notion are hard to find and do not seem to occur in hunting context, cf. perhaps 6,25 (122,18) *fluuius...eam* (sc. *Psychen*) *innoxio uolumine super ripam...exposuit*, and Tac. *Hist.* 4,20,1 *innoxium iter*.

inermes atque inmuniti: the text is uncertain. F's *imminiti* has been rewritten; φ has *attoniti* but the word was written in a gap by a second hand. Other mss. have *immuniti*. *Inmuniti* is the most likely reading. *Attoniti* ('panic-stricken') in φ is probably a conjecture. If *inmuniti* is right, this rare adj. was doubtless chosen for its parallel prefix. It occurs nowhere else in Apuleius, but cf. e.g. Fron. *Str.* 4,1,19.

tegumentis frondis uel arboribus: refers back to the landscape of 178,25 *frondosum tumulum ramorumque densis tegminibus umbrosum*. Whether the slaves climb the trees, like Nestor at Ov. *Met.* 8,366 f., is not entirely clear.

latenter abscondimus: this type of pleonastic expression is not infrequent in Apuleius, see 189,18 and comm. ad loc. There is no need for *abscondimur* (thus ς and Scaliger), cf. 6,12 (137,16). See Flobert 1975, 217.

nactus fraudium opportunum decipulum: cf. 177,18-20 and comm. ad loc. Note the homoeoteleuton.

opportunum decipulum: another rare expression. Apul. employs *decipulum* at *Met.* 10,24 (256,7) in a similar context, *Fl.* 18 (36,10) in a context of rhetorical or legal tricks. The word (also feminine from Hier. on, e.g. *Ep.* 98,5 *sophismatum decipulas proponentes*) is glossed *laqueus* (*CGL* 4,50,13) and *tenticula(m) qua aues capiuntur* (*CGL* 5,416,37). The Glossaries tend to distinguish between *decipulum* and *decipula*, a distinction not mentioned by *ThLL* s.v., which gives for both forms 'proprie rete ad aues capiendas', a meaning which metaphorically fits the present context.

sic Tlepolemum captiose compellat: note the alliteration. The challenge to Tlepolemus tends to ensnare him. The combination in one period with *decipulum* is more or less reproduced at 185,27 *nutricis captiosa uigilia deceptus*, see comm. ad loc. For *captiosus* see also 9,8 (209,1) *astu captioso*. So far the narrator reports from his own observation. Since the slaves are now hidden, however, the reader has difficulty in deciding whether the narrator has heard, or is inventing the subsequent speech on the grounds of Charite's dream. See introd. 4.2.1.3.

'Qui stupore confusi uel etiam cassa formidine similes humilitati 179, 20-24 seruorum istorum uel in modum pauoris feminei deiecti tam opimam praedam mediis manibus amittimus? Quin equos inscendimus? Quin ocius indipiscimur?' Et: 'Cape uenabulum et ego sumo lanceam!' '"Why are we in such numb confusion or rather act like those low slaves in groundless fear or are so paralysed in the manner of terrified women that we allow such a rich prey to slip through our very fingers? Why don't we mount the horses? Why don't we catch up with it quickly?' And: 'You take a hunting spear and I'll take a lance!'"

Qui: thus F and φ. The reading aroused suspicion at an early stage: in ς *quid* was substituted. Most editors adopt the correction. Hildebrand defends *qui* ('in what manner', 'why') referring to several instances in comic authors, e.g. Pl. *Epid.* 96 *qui lubidost male loqui*? (see also Duckworth 1940, 162 ad loc.). A long list of instances, including several in Cicero, is to be found in Neue-Wagener 2,458 f., most of them however requiring the translation 'in what manner' rather than 'why'. Apuleius uses *qui* in direct questions *Met.* 6,5 (132,11) *qui scias, an*; *Apol.* 35 (41,8) *qui minus possit*; *Soc.* 12 (20,16) and *Pl.* 2,11 (114,4) *qui potest*, as well as in the exclamatory *qui istum di perduint* (*Apol.* 75 : 83,20). The

57

fact that the two subsequent questions are introduced by *quin* (= negative *qui*) may well support *qui* rather than *quid*. Thrasyllus' speech, then, consists of one long question (incorporating three alternative descriptions with cumulative effect) and two short questions with an anaphoric element, followed by a brief instruction: all in all the impact is one of increasing urgency.

stupore...deiecti: the three qualifications (note the stylistic variation) move from close by to far distant: *stupore confusi* points the finger at Tlepolemus and Thrasyllus themselves, the comparison with the slaves still keeps within the scene described, the reference to women's fear passes beyond that boundary. For *stupore confusi* cf. e.g. 2,13 (36,4) *attonitus repentinae uisionis stupore*; 3,22 (68,18) and vdPaardt 1971, 164 ad loc.

similes humilitati seruorum istorum: for abstractum pro concreto see *GCA* 1977, 80 on 4,10 (82,1); and above on 176,19 *inter conseruorum frequentiam*; Janus Vlitius (van der Vliet), in his 1645 ed. of Grattius, *Cyneg.*, proposed *ceruorum*, a conjecture rightly rejected by Pricaeus and Oudendorp. There would be no reason to mention the conjecture if it were not for the facts that Helm mentions it in his app. crit. (where it is wrongly ascribed to de Rhoer) and that the proposer apparently felt that a slave could not speak of slaves in this manner. Of course the slave quotes (or pretends to quote) Thrasyllus and it is quite obvious that our slave-narrator is sketched as capable of all kinds of rhetorical devices including imitation of character.

in modum pauoris feminei deiecti: on the surface a simple challenge to Tlepolemus' masculine courage and an invitation to neglect Charite's wishes (178,23). When subsequently Charite assumes masculine courage (186,6) and Thrasyllus commits suicide in a feminine manner (comm. on 188,6) the contrast with the mood of the present phrase is complete.

Tam opimam praedam mediis manibus amittimus: the frequency of *m* in this phrase is noteworthy, cf. 7,14 (165,7) *multas mulas alumnas* and *GCA* 1981, 175 ad loc. and below comm. on 188,9 f.

Quin equos inscendimus? Cf. Liv. 1,57,7 *quin...conscendimus equos* (at the start of the tale of the rape of Lucretia). So far the narrator has not mentioned any horses, let alone the fact that the hunters had dismounted. The fact that Apuleius introduces horses in his description of the fatal hunting party may be thought a little puzzling. The most likely models (Meleager, *Il.* 9, 529 f.; Atys, Herod. 1,34 f. and Adonis, Ov. *Met.* 10,710 f.) omit them.

On the other hand the Dioskouroi are hunting on horseback during the Caledonian hunt as described in Ov. *Met.* 8, 372 f., where Bömer notes (in a rich an informative annotation) that they cut an odd figure among the other heroes. Aymard 1951, 322 discusses the fact that boarhunting on horseback becomes more frequent only in late Antiquity and that it has imperial or princely associations. Here, of course, we have no boar hunt at all, but the accidental appearance of a boar, to which Thrasyllus immediately reacts by calling for the horses. No deep reasons should be looked for: the boar is making its escape (above 179,14 *transabiit* and here *amittimus*) and horses are the only means to catch up with it.

ocius: a rare adverb in Apuleius (also at 10,5 : 240,15); the positive *ociter* occurs 1,23 (21,21). For instances in exhortative questions see *ThLL* s.v. 415,35 f. (e.g. Pl. *Cur.* 312; Petr. 96,6).

indipiscimur: it is perhaps easiest to supply *praedam* (or with *ThLL* s.v. 1197,37 *aprum*) and to take the word in its quite usual meaning 'catch up with' However, Gel. 1,11,8 suggests the meaning 'start', 'begin': *sed enim Achaeos Homerus pugnam indipisci ait non fidicularum tibiarumque, sed mentium animorumque concentu conspiratuque tacito nitibundos* (follows a quotation of Il. 3,8 f.). This meaning is accepted by *OLD* s.v. which cites Plin. *Nat.* 2,139 *Vocant et familiaria* (sc. *fulmina*) *in totam uitam fatidica, quae prima fiunt familiam suam cuique indepto. ThLL* s.v. 1197,40 queries this meaning. In fact the second instance cited by *OLD* seems to admit the meaning 'obtain'. Support for the possibility suggested by the Gellius instance may be found in the corrupt entry in *CGL* 5,76,23 *Inde piscis est aliquid incipere et perficere ac potari* where (teste Thesauro s.v. 1197,18) the correct reading may be *Indipisci[s] est...potiri*. Therefore and in view of the insertion of *Quin equos inscendimus* the possibility of taking *indipiscimur* in an absolute sense cannot be rejected outright.

Et: '*Cape:* & *cape* F.Most editors now read (with Haupt) *En cape uenabulum et ego sumo lanceam*, after Heinsius' conjecture: *I cape uenabulum, en ego sumo lanceam*. Both conjectures make excellent sense, Haupt's is the simpler one. But Apuleius quite often leaves out *dixit* or *ait*, cf. e.g. 1,17 (15,19) *Emergo laetus atque alacer...et: 'ecce'*; see for lists of comparable instances Bernhard 1927, 156 f.; Callebat 1968, 448.

The other possibility, that Thrasyllus says '*Et cape uenabulum et ego sumo lanceam*', while not absolutely impossible (and defended by Hildebrand), is less attractive, since there is no obvious reason for a heavily underscored link and, if there were, one would expect '*Et tu cape...*'. On the other hand the one instance of *en* + imperative in Apuleius (*Met.* 1,19 : 18,1) has '*en*', *inquam, 'explere...*'. Apart from that passage *ThLL* s.v. 547,26 f. provides instances of *en* + imperative from poetry only. All in all there seems to be no compelling reason to change F's reading, rather than its punctuation.

cape...et ego sumo lanceam: instead of the expected future *sumam*: according to LHSz 2,481e this substitution of present for future belongs to the sermo cotidianus. See also *ThLL* s.v. *et* 894,55 f.

uenabulum...lanceam: the text gives no indication of the difference between the two weapons. Both weapons appear to have been used for throwing (for the *uenabulum* see below 180,3; for the *lancea* see Grosse in *RE* 12,618 f.). The *uenabulum* may have been broad-bladed, cf. Verg. *A.* 4,131 *lato uenabula ferro* and Ov. *Her.* 4,83. The *lancea* is longer; in Antiquity the word was regarded as a foreign loan word, cf. Var. fr. 108 Ag.: *Lanceam quoque dixit non Latinum, sed Hispanicum uerbum esse*. Festus 105,17 L prefers to connect it with Gr. λόγχη. Walde-Hofmann en Ernout-Meillet s.v. suggest a Celtic origin. It was usually provided with a leather throwing strap; though commonly used in warfare, it is also used for hunting, cf. *Met.* 1,4 (4,5) *uenatoriam lanceam*; Amm. 24,5,2 and *ThLL* s.v. 917,63 f. The difference in weapons cannot be construed to be another item in the list of Thrasyllus' tricks, even though presently (180,10-16) Thrasyllus is said to count on the similarity of the wounds produced by his *lancea* and those effected by the boar's teeth. Adonis in Ov. *Met.* 10,713 is armed with *uenabula*; Meleager finally slays the Caledonian boar with that

179, 24-26   Nec tantillum morati protinus insiliunt equos ex summo studio bestiam insequentes: "And without the slightest delay they jump on their horses in all eagerness to go after the animal."

tantillum: see *GCA* 1977, 198 on 4,26 (95,12-15).

insiliunt equos: cf. *GCA* 1981, 200 on 7,18 (167,22) *lumbos meos insiliens*; add Bömer on Ov. *Met.* 8,142 for the interchange of dat. and acc.

ex summo studio: see *GCA* 1981, 244 on 7,24 (172,20). For parallels see Callebat 1968, 207, whose term 'instrumental' may well be right against *ThLL* s.v. *ex* 1121,60 f. 'de modo'.

insequentes: see above 23 *indipiscimur*; the animal had trampled the nets and was making off, cf. 179,14.

179, 26-180,2   Nec tamen illa genuini uigoris oblita retorquet impetum et incendio feritatis ardescens dente compulso, quem primum insiliat, cunctabunda rimatur: "But the animal, by no means forgetful of its native vigour, changes direction in its swift course, and, burning with the fire of ferocity and gnashing its teeth, checks itself to spy out whom to attack first."

retorquet impetum: the animal was moving away (179,14 *transabiit*). It seems most likely that *impetus* here (unlike 179,14 *qua primos impetus reduxerat*) implies 'speed' rather than 'attack'. The combination also occurs Fron. *Str.* 4,1,8.

incendio feritatis: see above on 176,19 *inter conseruorum frequentiam*.

dente compulso: thus Fφ; in F however there remains a bare trace of a marginal annotation: ...ċp; several other mss. have *dentium compulsu*, which may derive from F's marginal annotation. Helm thought he read *dentē c̄pulsū* in F's margin; Kronenberg emended to *dente compulsum* (taking *compulsum* as a supine), with reason. Neither *compellere dentes* nor the noun *compulsus* are attested elsewhere. That is not to say however that either manuscript reading is impossible. It is hard to choose between them: Augello 1977, 170 defends *dentium compulsu*, but since F's marginal reading must be reconstructed from later mss. it is perhaps safer to read *dente compulso*. Hildebrand thinks the words imply the activity described 179,9 with the words *attritu sonaci*, and he is followed by Vallette. It would be preferable, however, to give some weight to the element *com-* and to translate 'gnashing its teeth' (Valpy paraphrases 'terens inter se dentes').

quem primum insiliat: the narrator interprets the movement of the animal: for the narrative attitude of the present (sub-) narrator see the Introd. 4.2.1.2.

180, 3-4   Sed prior Tlepolemus iaculum, quod gerebat, insuper dorsum bestiae contorsit: "But Tlepolemus was first in throwing the missile he was carrying into the beast's back."

Similarly Adonis in Ov. *Met.* 10,710 f. wounds the boar before being attacked by it. Meleager ibid. 8,414 f. first wounds, then kills the Caledonian boar.

iaculum: the *uenabulum* of 179,24[1]. We hear of no other weapons: Tlepolemus is now unarmed, cf. below 1.9: *iacentem*.

insuper: used as a preposition (aptly chosen, since he is throwing from horseback); see *GCA* 1981, 200 on 7,17 (168,2), cf. KSt. 2,1,573. It is clear that the wound inflicted by Tlepolemus does not impair the beast's strength, at least for the time being: presently Thrasyllus will kill the boar *facili manu*, but see below on 180,17.

At Thrasyllus ferae quidem pepercit, set equi, quo uehebatur Tlepolemus, postremos poplites lancea feriens amputat: "Thrasyllus in turn however spared the animal but struck the hocks of the horse Tlepolemus was riding and cut them through with his lance." 180, 4-6

pepercit is an emendation by a clever second hand in φ. F has *pepercisset set*, an obvious instance of dittography.

lancea feriens: though, as noted above, the *lancea* was also used for throwing, it is obvious from the context that Thrasyllus cuts or thrusts, rather than throws, and that he retains his weapon. *Feriens* does not detail the number of thrusts needed to cut through two *poplites*; *amputat* gives the result. Bernhard 1927, 46 is mistaken in speaking of a redundancy in the expression *feriens amputat*.

Quadrupes reccidens, qua sanguis effluxerat, toto ⟨t⟩ergo supinatus inuitus dominum suum deuoluit ad terram: "The animal falling backwards where his blood had flowed came down on its back full length and involuntarily rolled its master down on the ground." 180, 6-8

Quadrupes: for the spelling see *GCA* 1981, 41, on 6,27 (149, 3-4).

reccidens: the spelling with *-cc-*, though more common in poetry for the form of the present stem, also occurs in prose e.g. Sen. *Ira* 3,39,3. *Met.* 1,11 (11,1) and 1,16 (15,8) show *recidens*. On our practice with regard to the adoption of spelling variants see Introd. 5.3. Since the result of the movement is that the horse lies on its back, Hildebrand imagined that it rears first and then falls backwards. It seems more likely though, that a horse *poplitibus amputatis* would sink down on its hindquarters, would try to raise itself and would then roll sideways, but the wording does not permit a really detailed picture. Andreae 1980 pl. 54,1 shows a sarcophagus with a lion hunt including a fallen horse, not however *supinatus*, but *praeceps*. Fallen horses in depictions of boarhunts proved hard to find.

toto tergo: F and φ have *ergo*; the correction occurs in ς.

supinatus: see below on 193,12.

---

[1] This is the only passage in the *Met.* in which the word is used for a weapon; cf. 10,32 (263,10), where it is used of flowers.

inuitus: projection of emotions or thoughts into the animal world is common enough in the *Met.*; also e.g. 3,26 (71,22, with *scilicet* in order to preserve the narrative perspective); 4,5 (77,24; for *scilicet* see *GCA* 1977,50 ad loc. and vdPaardt in *AAGA* 1978,79); 7,16 (166,13 see *GCA* 1981, 188 ad loc.). In the last instance *scilicet* is lacking, as it is here. Neither case necessarily presents an error of perspective: in 7,16 the subsequent action of the stallions enables us to assume a conclusion on the part of the narrator; in the present section the narrator assumes an attitude that closely resembles authorial omniscience.

The effect of the narrator's insight into the horse's emotional state is to invite pity for the plight of his *dominus*. At the same time *inuitus* marks the horse as faithful in contrast with the treacherous Thrasyllus.

180, 8-10 Nec diu, sed eum furens aper inuadit iacentem ac primo lacinias eius, mox ipsum resurgentem multo dente laniauit: "Nor did it take long before the raging boar attacked him as he was lying there, and first ripped his clothes, then with a lot of tusk work gored the man himself as he tried to get up."

Nec diu, sed: according to Helm it is not clear in F whether the *s* of *sed* was erased or has faded. However, since it was there originally, there is no reason to defend *et* with Oudendorp and Hildebrand. Helm compares 7,9 (160,16) *nec mora..., sed*; see also *GCA* 1981, 138 ad loc. The combination is less common than *nec diu, cum* or *nec diu, quod*.

furens aper: the process that had started above (line 1) in *incendio feritatis ardescens* is now complete.

primo lacinias eius: delaying tactics of the narrator in order to enhance the tension.

mox ipsum resurgentem: the participle is obviously used de conatu (LHSz 2, 316).

multo dente: the combination of *multus* and similar adjectives with a singular noun in plural or collective meaning belongs, according to LSHz 2,161, to popular language and is often used by poets; cf. *Met.* 7,15 (166,2) *multo...lapide*; see also Callebat 1968, 247.

laniauit: thus ς; *laniatum* F φ A. If *laniatum* is to be saved *ac* should be bracketed. The resulting syntax, though not impossible (cf. for supine with object LHSz 2,381 f.), is rather stilted, and there is no saving of surgery. The corruption could easily arise from the common compendium -*ū* for -*uit*. In view of the frequent confusion of *t,n,u* (cf. Helm Praef. *Fl.* xlii), one might also consider restoring *laniat*.

It should be noted that the picture presented in this sentence differs from that of Adonis' death in Ov. *Met.* 10,713-716: Adonis flees, is pursued by the boar, and killed subsequently.

180, 10-16 Nec coepti nefarii bonum piguit amicum uel suae saeuitiae litatum saltem tanto periculo cernens potuit expleri, sed percito atque plagosa crura [uulnera] contegenti suumque auxilium miseriter roganti per femus dexterum dimisit lanceam tanto ille fidentius, quanto crederet ferri uulnera similia futura prosectu dentium: "Nor did his good friend feel any horror at this unspeakable turn of events, nor could he be satisfied by seeing that his savagery had received at least due sacrifice by this great danger, but as Tlepolemus in a panic tried to protect his mauled legs and pitiably asked for his help, he threw his lance through the right thigh, all the more confidently since he believed that the wounds of the weapon would be similar to the cuts of the teeth."

The style of this period, which narrates the climax of the episode, is carefully ornamented, in particular by means of alliteration (*p, pl, s* and *f*). Unhappily the text is not entirely clear.

Nec...sed: note the contrastive character of the passage (179,24 *nec tantillum morati* – 26 *nec tamen illa* – 180,3 *sed prior* – 4 *at Thrasyllus* – 8 *nec diu sed* – 10 *nec coepti nefarii* – 16 *nec non tamen*.

coepti nefarii: Apul. uses *coeptum* only on four occasions, in the singular here only (*ThLL* enumerates about 50 instances of the singular as against about 130 of the plural).

bonum piguit amicum: a favourite Apuleian word-order cf. e.g. 7,16 (166,17-19), where the sequence adj. – verb – noun occurs twice. For the ironic use of *bonus* cf. 7,27 (174,23-25) and *GCA* 1981,260 ad loc.

suae saeuitiae litatum...cernens: a certain solemnity clings to the cultic metaphor, cf. 3,8 (57,28) and vdPaardt 1971,72 ad loc.

percito: 'participium *percitus* enixe adhibere amat Appulejus' (Oudendorp) and indeed there are thirteen instances in the *Met.* used of a variety of emotions ranging from joy (9,19: 217,18) to sexual desire (1,7: 7,14), violent grief (182,16) to panic (here). See also vdPaardt 1971,156; *GCA* 1977,203.

atque plagosa crura [uulnera] contegenti: F's reading cannot be construed; Armini 1928,309-310 tries to defend it by taking *plagosa crura* as an acc. resp., an exceedingly harsh construction; cf. LHSz 2,36 f.; asyndetic *plagosa crura, uulnera* is equally unlikely. It is not easy to decide whether the corruption consists of a copying error or rather in the insertion of a gloss. The former solution was tried by a series of scholars headed by Oudendorp's vir doctus who proposed *crurum uulnera*. *Plagosa* in that case should be taken with *crurum* through enallage – a bold instance indeed, but see below 199,6 *simulabat sauciam uecordiam*. Palaeographically almost as simple are Luetjohann's *plagosa et cruda uulnera* (a conjecture which might be improved upon by assuming asyndetic *plagosa, cruda*), Walter's *per plagosa crura uulnera contegenti* (see Walter 1916,126) and the solution proposed in *Mnem.* 1928,24 and 38 by Damsté and Kronenberg respectively and apparently independently. They propose *atque plagosa crura ulna contegenti*. However, *ulna* (especially in the singular) seems not to be used in defensive situations such as we have here, and the parallel of the wounded Spanish bull fighter adduced by Kronenberg does not really defend his choice. Somewhat less simple are the solutions proposed by Cornelissen (*percito atque plagoso, cruda uulnera contegenti*) and Robertson (*percito atque plagoso ac frustra uulnera contegenti*). Assumption of a gloss seems marginally preferable to the various conjectures listed above. It was made early: ς omit *uulnera* which was also deleted by Wower, whereas

Elmenhorst deleted *crura*. Since it seems more likely that *plagosa crura* would be glossed by *uulnera* than the other way round, deletion of *uulnera* is to be preferred.

plagosa crura: cf. 9,12 (212,3) *dorsum...plagosum*; the word *plagosus* is further attested in Horace only: *Ep.* 2,1,70 *plagosum.../ Orbilium*, where it is used in an active meaning. Ernout 1949, 25 does not discuss the remarkable difference in usage of this rare adjective.

contegenti: the participle is used de conatu, cf. *resurgentem* (l.10 above).

suumque auxilium miseriter roganti: in Charite's dream (4,27) Tlepolemus *conquerens populi testatur auxilium* (95,24 f.). *Miseriter* occurs here only in Apul., as against *misere* at 5,17 (116,14) and 183,8. Callebat 1968, 485 notes the use of an archaic form for stylistic ornamentation. It is obvious that Tlepolemus at this point still regards Thrasyllus as his good friend.

per femus dexterum: two problems arise: (a) why a thigh?, and (b) why the right thigh?; (a) It might be thought that a thigh wound would not be fatal. Bluemner 1905, 33 for that reason replaces *femus* by *pectus*. But even though a wound in the *pectus dexterum* would find a sympathetic echo at 187,21, where Charite commits suicide *ferro sub papillam dexteram transadacto* (see comm. ad loc.), the emendation removes much of the logic of Thrasyllus' subsequent consideration. In fact a deep thigh wound – in particular if an artery were severed – would prove fatal in a very short time. For the same reason it is unnecessary to take *femus* in the sense of 'groin' (cf. Anderson 1909, 545, who quotes a parallel in the Nibelungenlied and several passages in the Fathers, see *ThLL* s.v. *femur* 472,68).

The second question is harder: it may be that no more is involved than a slight element of ἐνάργεια But at 5,25 (121,19) Psyche desperately holds on to Amor's right leg as he flies away and one might argue that there as well as here and at 187,21 the right is selected for success. However, in other passages (e.g. 7,17 : 167,12; 9,37 : 231,23) such a notion makes no sense.

femus: cf. 201,28 with our comm. ad loc. See also Callebat in *AAGA* 1978, 169.

dimisit lanceam: *immisit* ς; *demisit* Colvius. Editors dismiss both conjectures, but they serve to point up the frequency of the confusion in the mss between *dimittere* and *demittere*. In fact there are very few if any certain instances of *dimittere* in the sense of e.g. Ov. *Met.* 4,119 *demisit in ilia ferrum* (*dimisit* in several mss.). Sen. *H.O.* 540 *deum...qui certa tenera tela dimittit manu* emphasizes the departure rather than the entry of the weapon, and that may well be the prevalent notion here.

tanto...dentium: for the narrator's insight into Thrasyllus' thoughts see below on 180,19 f. and Introd. 4.2.1.3.

tanto...fidentius, quanto...similia: see KSt. 2,2,484 for more instances of the positive after *quanto*; cf. Callebat 1968, 332.

prosectu: dative; cf. 4,17 (87,13) *lacu aliquo* with *GCA* 1977, 132 ad loc. The word is attested in Apuleius only, cf. below 199,18.

180, 16-17 Nec non tamen ipsam quoque bestiam facili manu transadigit:

"And furthermore he indeed transfixes also the beast itself with skilful hand."

Nec non together with *tamen* seems to have the effect of introducing an anticlimactic contrast: the killing of the boar is stated as an afterthought.

facili manu: the beast had been wounded by Tlepolemus (above line 3), but the text is not explicit on the question whether the easy kill is due to the wound or rather to Thrasyllus' skill. The implication that Thrasyllus could have saved Tlepolemus is obvious.

transadigit: see below on 187,22.

CHAPTER VI

Reactions.

180, 17-19 Ad hunc modum definito iuuene exciti latibulo suo quisque familia maesta concurrimus:
"When the young men had been finished off in this way, we, his sad family of slaves, came running together, each one of us aroused from his hiding place."

Ad hunc modum definito iuuene: the transition to the next scene is marked by a formal phrase with a striking use of *definito*.

Ad hunc modum: see our note on 187,3.

definito: here in the sense of 'finito', 'occiso'. No further instances of this usage have been found (cf. *ThLL* s.v. 344,27), but the verb is used for finishing a text etc. (e.g. Cic. *Orat.* 65; *Ver.* 4,115). The more normal *finire* (= *occidere*) is found at 7,26 (148,23), see *GCA* 1981, 39 ad loc. It should be noted that the English colloquialism 'finish off' does not reproduce the rarity-value of the word. Much the same type of etymologising change of meaning occurs below. (1. 21 *adseuerare*, an even more remarkable instance). For a list of words 'tirant leur sens de l'étymologie' see Médan 1927, 148 f. See also Loefstedt 1936, 100f. on Apuleius' pleasure in word-play ('er jongliert mit den Stilmitteln'). Obviously there is no need for the old conjecture *defuncto* (ς).

exciti latibulo suo quisque: the phrase refers back to 179, 16 f., where the hiding places were mentioned. For *latibulum* see *GCA* 1981, 249 on 7,25 (173,5).

Summers 1967, 267 notes a technical violation of the *Senatus consultum Silanianum* (*RE* Suppl. 6,812) whereby slaves are liable to render aid to their master if the latter is attacked violently. See however *GCA* 1981, 267 on *Met.* 7,27 (175,25); moreover it is highly questionable whether the reference to the *S. C. Sil.* is germane to the interpretation of the present passage: the slaves play no more than a subordinate part in the entire tale and the question of the culpability or otherwise of their behaviour is not raised or even hinted at.

familia maesta concurrimus: here the implication that the slaves could observe the events from their hiding-places seems obvious. However, see also on 179,17 above (*abscondimus*) and Introd. 4.2.1.3.

Familia refers to the group of hunting assistants only. They are to be distinguished from the present audience of *rustici*, who take flight in ch. 15 (188,9) *mutati dominii nouitatem metuentes*. For a discussion of the legal senses of the word *familia* see below on 194,1; Norden 1912, 140 and, more detailed, Summers 1967, 95. It should be noted that in the subject of *concurrimus* the narrator includes himself; cf. 179, 14 f. and 187,9 f.

At ille quanquam perfecto uoto, prostrato inimico laetus ageret, 180, 19-23
uultu tamen gaudium tegit et frontem adseuerat et dolorem
simulat et cadauer, quod ipse fecerat, auide circumplexus omnia
quidem lugentium officia sollerter adfinxit, sed solae lacrimae
procedere noluerunt: "But he, though he was glad his wish was fulfilled, his
enemy prostrated, nevertheless did not show his joy in his face, assumed a
sombre mien, feigned grief, and, closely embracing the corpse he had himself
produced, he slyly simulated all the other observances proper to mourners –
but the tears wouldn't flow."

At ille: Thrasyllus' feigned grief is placed in sharp contrast with that of the narrator and his colleagues.

quanquam...ageret: for the subjunctive see vdPaardt 1971, 31.

perfecto uoto, prostrato inimico: in addition to the contrastive phrasing (Bernhard 1927, 55 f.) alliteration and homoeoteleuton may be noted.

perfecto uoto: cf. 177,18 *cruento facinori quaerebat accessum*; ibid. 20 *sceleri, quod diu cogitarat, accingitur* and 178,1 *occultato consilio sceleris*. The combination *perficere uotum* also at Val. Fl. 4,538.

laetus: adjectives with *agere* = 'live', 'be' are fairly common, cf. 2,17 (39,11) *peruigiles egimus* and de Jonge 1941, 77 ad loc.; Sal. *Jug.* 55,2 and Koestermann ad loc.; Ov. *Met.* 13, 371, to mention but a few instances. See also below on 198,4 f. *partiarius agebat concubinus*.

et frontem adseuerat: *et* introduces the explanation of *uultu...tegit*. The verb *adseuerare* occurs in the same unusual sense at 3,13 (61,23), see vdPaardt 1971, 103 f. ad loc.[1], but is not attested anywhere else (cf. *ThLL* s.v. 876,47). Médan 1925, 169 notes a slight change of meaning, Bernhard 1927, 142 f. regards the present instance as one of Apuleius' most daring plays on etymology. E.g. Tac. *Ann.* 13,18,1 *uiros grauitatem adseuerantes*, Tert. *An.* 17,2 and 57,8 (cf. Waszink 1947, 241 and 583 ad loc.) use the word in a context of (implied) deceit; compare also Tert. *Or.* 22 (cf. Diercks 1947, 233 ad loc.). For the notion cf. Luc. 9, 1063 *adquiritque fidem simulati fronte doloris*.

et dolorem simulat: *et* places the phrase on the same level as *uultu...adseuerat*.

et cadauer...adfinxit: *et* introduces the details of Thrasyllus' simulated grief. It should be noted that we have no true polysyndetic series here in which all members have equal weight.

cadauer, quod ipse fecerat: the combination *cadauer facere* seems to occur here only (cf. *ThLL* s.v. *facere* 88,48 where it is listed under the not entirely appropriate heading *de vulneribus*). The harsh expression reflects the narrator's indignation which finds a climax in this chapter.

auide: in view of the narrator's attitude towards Thrasyllus no doubt he sees this as part of Thrasyllus' play-acting. However, he does not say so and therefore we possibly may glimpse an indication on the part of the (implied) author that the narrator's interpretation of Thrasyllus' actions is not to be trusted. See also Introd. 4.2.1.3.

---

[1] For 'Umdeutung', both as a phenomenon of the living language and as a creative attitude on the part of Apuleius, see Loefstedt 1936, 100. See also *GCA* 1981, 233 on 7,23 (171,18), where *detestatio* is used in the meaning 'castration'.

circumplexus: a number of younger mss. have *amplexatus*, possibly a gloss, possibly an attempt to make something of the almost vanished text (folio 159b, last three lines) of F. Applied to a *cadauer* the word occurs here only. Cf. Luc. 3,759 *amplexa cadauer* (sc. *coniunx*); Quint. *Decl*. 388 (434,6) *mulier, modo cadauer tamquam filium complexa, nunc filium tamquam cadauer fugit*. The deponent *circumplecti* occurs from Cic. *Phil*. 13,12 onwards, cf. Flobert 1975, 115 (for *circumplecto* ibid.287).

omnia...lugentium officia: in the immediate context one thinks of *plangere, lamentare*, throwing dust and ashes on hair and clothes, tearing one's hair, and similar shows of grief rather than of the more formal offices connected with burial (see Daremberg et Saglio s.v. *funus* 1387 f.: *oculos condere, conclamatio, unctura* etc.; also ibid. s.v. *luctus* 1347 f.; Kübler in *RE* s.v. *luctus* 1697 f.). The mourning scenes in the *Met*. (e.g. 4,34; 5,7; 9,30 cf. also 3,8) do not differ materially from the usual picture. The more formal rites are mentioned below at 181,25, Thrasyllus' *officia* (cf. 9,30:226,9 *peractisque feralibus officiis*) at 181,23.

sollerter adfinxit: the word *sollerter* has almost disappeared in F, but was restored by a second hand; in φ a second hand inserted it in a gap. The connotation here of slyness is due to the context. Elsewhere in the *Met*. (e.g. 4,14:85,22 and 4,15:86,7) *sollerter* and *sollers* simply denote expertise and cleverness. As to the narrator's interpretation see above on *auide*. For *adfinxit* see *GCA* 1977, 125 on 4,16 (86,21) *litteras adfingimus*, where we preferred the *ThLL* interpretation 'fictis nova addere falsa' also for the present passage.

sed solae lacrimae procedere noluerunt: cf. below c. 7 (181,15) *quas in primo maerore lacrimas non habebat, iam scilicet crescente gaudio reddere*. On the variation in the use of tenses (*tegit...adseuerat...simulat...adfinxit...noluerunt*) see Callebat 1968,427-429 after Bernhard 1927,152. Here it should be noted that the verbs describing Thrasyllus as he assumes his rôle are in the present, the performance itself (including its unsuccessful aspect) in the perfect tense.

180, 24-25 Sic ad nostri similitudinem, qui uere lamentabamur, conformatus manus suae culpam bestiae dabat: "Thus acting in conformity with the picture presented by us who were truly lamenting, he kept blaming the beast for the crime of his own hand."

ad nostri similitudinem: F has *ad nr̄i s...dinē*, but Robertson notes that the *s* is doubtful; φ left a gap which was filled by a second hand: *ad nr̄a amaritudine*. AU and other codd. have *ad nostri similitudinem* and there can be little doubt that this is the correct reading. For the gen. see vGeisau 1916,259.

qui uere lamentabamur: at 179,14 f. the contrast between the frightened slaves and the overbold Thrasyllus was underlined; here, at the end of the description of Tlepolemus' death, we find a similar contrast, now between feigned and true grief.

conformatus: cf. 2,21 (42,11) *ad instar oratorum conformat articulum*. The correction in ς for *confirmatus* F is certain; the mistake is very common. In addition to the contrast noted in the previous lemma, another one is implied here: at 179,20 Thrasyllus had scorned the *humilitas seruorum*, here he is reported to adjust his behaviour to that of those same slaves. Apparently it is expendiency rather than social status which dictates his behaviour.

manus suae culpam bestiae dabat: the imperfect may be taken 'de conatu' or in a durative sense. An interpretation of the tale which makes Thrasyllus the murderer (see Introd. 4.2.1.2) requires 'tried to blame the beast', one which makes Thrasyllus one of the victims of a tragic mistake (Introd. 4.2.1.3) requires 'kept blaming the beast'. *ThLL* 1307, 10f. s.v. *culpa* mentions one further instance of the combination *culpam dare*, but in an entirely different sense, at Paul. *Dig.* 9,2,45,4 *qui, cum aliter tueri se non possent, damni culpam dederint, innoxii sunt*.

manus suae culpam: the narrator uses a pointed phrase in order to neutralize Thrasyllus' attempt to exculpate himself. The combination seems to occur here only, but cf. Ov. *Am.* 1,14,43 *facta culpaque tua dispendia sentis*.

Necdum satis scelere transacto Fama dilabitur et cursus primos ad domum Tlepolemi detorquet et aures infelicis nuptae percutit: 181,1-3
"The crime hardly committed, Fame slips away and sets course first for Tlepolemus' house and strikes the ears of his unhappy bride."

Vergil was close to Apuleius' mind when he was writing this passage: when Dido has given herself to Aeneas *coniugium uocat, hoc praetexit nomine culpam./ Extemplo Libyae magnas it Fama per urbes* e.q.s. (*A.*4,172f.).

Necdum...transacto: cf. *extemplo* in the Vergil passage just quoted.

Fama: personified as in the Vergil passage though not all modern editors print a capital, cf. 11,18 (280,8) with Gwyn Griffiths and, in particular, Harrauer ad loc. for a short survey of *Fama* as *nuntia ueri* in ancient literature. For non-personified *fama*, which occurs 8 times in the *Met.*, see e.g. above 177,10; cf. 4,28 (97,4).

dilabitur: it is not easy to decide what picture is prevalent in *dilabitur*, that of diffusion as at 201,3 *infamia...per ora populi facile dilapsa* or that of escaping from the scene as at 5,5 (107,1) *eo* (sc.*Amore*) *simul cum nocte dilapso*. *ThLL* s.v. *dilabor* 1157,68 chooses the first possibility ('i.q. divulgatur') citing Cass. *Psal.* 88,1 *quod ex ore progreditur, cito dilabitur* as a further instance. However in that passage *dilabitur* must mean 'disappears', 'melts away', in itself a common enough meaning, but inapposite here. Against the meaning 'divulgatur' one may also point out that there is no strengthening of the notion as at 201,4 *per ora* as one would expect (cf. also 4,28:97,11 *prouincias...plurimas...peruagatur*; 5,4:106,9 *latiusque porrecta fama*; cf. also 10,19:251,15 *ibidem de me fama peruaserat*). The picture of departure is quite commonly associated with *dilabi* (*ThLL* s.v. 1159,5f. cites some 35 instances, some admittedly referring to groups of soldiers and the like departing in different directions). In our passage it produces a thoroughly acceptable sequence: the crime has just been committed, Fama departs from the scene and directs her course to the victim's house. Indeed the community reacts only when Charite starts loudly venting her grief (line 6f. below). On the other hand instances such as Verg. *A.* 4, 195f. *haec passim dea foeda uirum diffundit in ora./ Protinus ad regem cursus detorquet*

Iarban (a parallel quoted as early as Burmann and Oudendorp) and *A.* 9,473f. *per urbem/ nuntia Fama ruit matrisque adlabitur auris / Euryali* show that fame spreading and (yet) immediately reaching the ears of persons concerned cannot be regarded as impossible.

cursus primos: vGeisau 1912,24 notes a poetical plural. On this notion see LHSz 2,16f. Here the poetic quality is to be found in the Vergilian quotation.

infelicis nuptae: the comparison of Charite with Dido rests to some extent on the use of *infelix*, cf. *GCA* 1981,60 on 6,29 (151,18). Once the comparison has been suggested to the reader the fact that it is Dido's *culpa* which constitutes the message of Fama in *Aeneid* IV, whereas here Thrasyllus' *culpa* causes Fama to take a message to Charite, works like a neat inversion.

181, 3-7 Quae quidem simul percepit tale nuntium, quale non audiet aliud, amens et uecordia percita cursuque bacchata furibundo per plateas populosas et arua rurest⟨r⟩ia fertur insana uoce casum mariti quiritans: "As soon as she has heard the message – one such as she will not hear again – she is out of her mind, and stricken by madness she goes in a frenzied and furious rush through the populous streets and the fields of the countryside bewailing in an insane voice her husband's undoing."

For a comparison of the present scene with Charite's dream at 4,27 (95,20-21) see the Introd. 4.2.1.3.

quae quidem simul percepit: *quidem* marks the transition to the main actor of the remainder of the tale. *Simul* suggests little more than a rapid succession of events (Callebat 1968,432), see also *GCA* 1981,128 on 7,7 (159,11).

tale nuntium quale non audiet aliud: the narrator's comment on the terrible nature of the message. In fact Charite does receive another message of comparable impact, when Tlepolemus' ghost appears to her in ch. 8.

tale nuntium: for the gender cf. 7,1 (154,9) and *GCA* 1981,81 ad loc.

audiet: it is not easy to classify this future. Médan 1925,20 and Callebat 1968,103 regard it as a potential future comparing such instances as *Mun.* 27 (163,14) *multo magis deo inconueniens erit* (cf. Π. κοσμοῦ 398 b3 ἂν εἴη θεῷ) and *Met.* 2,4 (27,13) *sicunde de proximo latratus ingruerit, eum putabis de faucibus lapidis exire*. LHSz 2,310 however state that *audiet* is a historic future: the narrator puts himself in Charite's position in time and notes that she was not going to receive another such message. Cf. e.g. the narrator's intervention at Verg. *A.* 10,503 f. *Turno tempus erit magno cum optauerit emptum / intactum Pallanta, et cum spolia ista diemque / oderit*.

amens et uecordia percita: for pairs of synonyms in which the second expression elaborates on the first cf. Bernhard 1927,166. *Vecordia* also occurs below 199,7 (see comm. ad loc.), where it is used in a context of religious exaltation; cf. *Pl.* 2,24 (128,15) *uecordia* in association with tyranny. For the change in Charite's character from this point onwards see Heine 1962,239; Hijmans in *AAGA* 1978,116 and below on 187,26. Her reaction is described in terms first of madness (cf. below ch. 27 and comm. on 199,4-8), in chapters 7-8 of violent grief; cunning revenge follows in the remainder of the tale. For the combination cf. *Apol.* 84 *mulier obcantata, uecors, amens, amans.* See also Heine 1962,243.

cursuque bacchata furibundo: bacchari as a term for swift motion in a state of mental derangement also occurs 199,4 (see comm. ad loc.); the meaning at 3,20 (67,14) and 10,2 (237,17) is slightly different. Once Charite has completed her revenge she will once again run through the city *cursu furioso,* below 187,7. See comm. ad loc. also for Charite's epic predecessors.

per plateas populosas: according to Callebat 1968,65 'streets' rather than 'squares' are meant: *GCA* 1977,112 on 4,14 (85,13) is probably wrong in translating 'squares'.

et arua rurest⟨r⟩ia: the plural *arua* does not occur in prose before Apuleius (vGeisau 1912,23); it fits in very well in the poetic colour of the passage. For the correction in ς of *rurestia* F see *GCA* 1977,36.

fertur: the term may add to the epic flavour of the passage, cf. e.g. Verg. *A.* 2,725; 11,730 (*OLD* s.v. 4); *ThLL* s.v. 534,46 f.

quiritans: see also on 191,4. In the present passage there is no indication that Apuleius had the etymology cited there in mind. Callebat 1968, 78 lists the word under 'mots familiers de caractère expressif'. The *ThLL* material confirms the suggestion of *OLD* s.v. that there are no instances of the word in ancient poetry. It is possible then, that the sentence, full of poetic elements as it has been, ends on a remarkably prosaic note.

Confluunt ciuium maestae cateruae, secuntur obuii dolore socia- 181,7-8
to, ciuitas cuncta uacuatur studio uisionis: "Sad throngs of citizens come running together, passers-by follow with shared grief, the entire city empties itself eager for the spectacle."

Confluunt ciuium maestae cateruae: for a similar image cf. 4,20 (90,3) *populi circumfluentis turbelis. Confluere* of people also at 4,16 (87,3); 4,29 (97,14); 10,19 (251,12); 11,23 (285,3). Heine 1962,177 notes that the 'Anfangsstellung' of the verb directs the attention of the audience to a new aspect of the scene described.

secuntur obuii: sc. *Chariten.* The scene is carefully articulated: in the previous phrase crowds gather, in the present phrase people follow the young woman: the two phrases are connected by the elements of grief (*maestae...dolore sociato*). The third phrase collects the people, adding a new element: *ciuitas cuncta uacuatur studio uisionis*; the collected people follow Charite, thus emptying the city. Their grief obviously does not exclude curiosity *ut nouitas consueuit ad repentinas uisiones animos hominum pellere* (4,16: 87,1-2, see *GCA* 1977,127 ad loc.). Whether Heine 1962,286 f. is right in stating that *cuncta ciuitas* here, in contrast to 3,2 (a more elaborate description), is hyperbolic seems hard to determine. See also below 187,10 *omnis populus nudatis totis aedibus.* For the picture cf. Liv. 31,14,12; Vulg. *Matth.* 8,34.

studio uisionis: cf. 5,2 (104,14 f.) *prolectante studio pulcherrimae uisionis.* In the *Met. uisio* always refers to the thing seen (cf. also 2,13: 36,4; 4,27: 96,8), at *Pl.* 1,14 (98,1) the word refers to the sense or act of seeing (ὄψις cf. Pl. *Tim.* 45c). Nevertheless, for the picture Verg. *A.* 2,63 should be compared.

71

Apart from asyndeton and an obvious arrangement of sound effect (alliteration of *c*, preponderance of dark vowels) the sentence shows a slight increase in length in each of the cola (11,13,16 syllables) and is one of the instances of word-order showing at once parallelism and variation noted by Bernhard 1927,35.

181, 8-11 **Et ecce mariti cadauer accurrit labantique spiritu totam se super corpus effudit ac paenissime ibidem, quam deuouerat, ei red⟨d⟩idit animam**: "And, look, she ran up to her husband's lifeless remains and with failing spirit threw her entire body on the corpse and all but rendered up to him the life she had promised him."

Neither lapse of time nor geographical situation are indicated: the audience would have little difficulty in supplying both and the reader can do without. See Introd. 3.1 and 2.

Et ecce: marks the high point in this part of the chapter. Heine 1962, 174 n. 1 notes that the combination often occurs with verbs denoting (lively) action; Callebat 1968,424 collects instances of its usage; *GCA* 1977,157 discusses its function at 4,21 (90,8-12) using the phrase 'invites us to visualise'. The same is true here except that the narrator of the present tale invites his audience to visualise Charite's actual arrival.

mariti cadauer accurrit: the expression also at 2,26 (46,8) *nimio pauore perterritus cadauer accurro*. For the acc. with the verb see vdPaardt 1971,156; *GCA* 1977,113 on 4,14 (85,17) *passim iacentes epulas* (actually also *cadauera*) *accurrunt*. The word *cadauer* occurs some 22 times in Apuleius. Though he uses it on several occasions in contexts filled with horror (e.g. 2,20: 41,13 and 3,17: 65,7 in descriptions of magic) and as a term of invective (see 196,23 with comm.) he also uses the word in an emotionally neutral sense (e.g. 2,25: 45,13; 6,21:144,13). In the present chapter, too, the pathetic quality must be sought in the context (above 180,21 *quod ipse fecerat*; here *mariti*) rather than in the word itself. Nevertheless it is interesting to note that the word is avoided by several authors, whereas others use it with some gusto. For the distribution see *ThLL* s.v. 12,56 f.; Axelson 1945,49 f. and Bömer on Ov. *Met.* 7,602.

accurrit: F's *accursit* was corrected in φ. Leo proposed *occurrit*. His reasons remained unpublished. In view of 2,26 (46,8) quoted above the acc. cannot count as an objectoin to *accurrit*. It might be thought that Tlepolemus' body is being borne to the city and that Charite meets it on the way, in which case *occurrit* would be the appropriate term. However, the *pompa* is described below l. 12 f. and there is nothing in the text to indicate that it had started out before Charite's arrival. In view of *effudit* and *reddidit* the form is probably to be taken as a perfect.

labanti...spiritu: in connection with words denoting 'mind', 'spirit' the verb usually means 'waver', e.g. Verg. *A.* 4,22 *solus hic inflexit sensus animumque labantem/impulit* (said by Dido). *ThLL* s.v. *labo* 779,49 takes the present expression in the sense of *deficiente spiritu* but also compares Ov. *Ars* 3, 745 f. *exit et incauto paulatim pectore lapsus/excipitur miseri spiritus ore uiri* where *lapsus* refers to the escape of the last breath. It may well be that *spiritus* here refers at once to breath and spirit. In view of the many parallels between Charite and Dido, the Vergil passage cited may have played a part in Apuleius' choice of words.

paenissime: OLD regards the superlative as humorous; this is certainly true for Pl. *Aul.* 466; 668 and *Mos.* 656; the present passage, *Apol.* 99 (109, 15) and *Fl.* 16 (26,9) show no humorous intent. For the form see Neue-Wagener 2,759.

quam deuouerat ei reddidit animam: the expression is a strong one. For the combination *animam deuouere* cf. Stat. *Theb.* 3,232 f. *tibi* (sc. *Marti*) *praecipites animasque manusque/deuoueant*. Here the proper background is to be found in the motif, so common in the Greek romances, of the faithful lover or spouse dying or wishing to die when confronted with the death of his or her partner. See e.g. Charito 3,3,1;X.Eph. 3,10,2; Ach.Tat. 5,7,5; Hel.2,1,1. See also below comm. on 187, 19 f.; Petri 1963, 28. Merkelbach 1962, 77 notes that there are close parallels both with Aphrodite embracing the dead Adonis (cf. Bion 42-45) and with Isis embracing the dead Osiris (Plut. *Is.* 17). His suggestion that Isis brings Osiris back to life by means of this embrace is not borne out by Plutarch's text and such a suggestion is plainly impossible for our text.

reddidit ς; *redidit* F with a mark in the margin (·1·) which appears to indicate that the scribe suspected a mistake in the original, cf. Helm Praef. *Fl.* XXXIV.

Sed aegre manibus erepta suorum inuita remansit in uita, funus uero toto feralem pompam prosequente populo deducitur ad sepulturam: "But she was dragged away with difficulty by the hands of her people and – though against her will – remained alive. The deceased however was taken to his grave with all the people following the funeral procession." 181, 11-13

Sed aegre manibus erepta suorum: Damsté 1928,24 suggested *mānibus erepta manibus suorum*, a conjecture awarded a 'fortasse recte' by Robertson. Certainly its playfulness is entirely Apuleian, but there is no compelling reason for any conjecture here.

inuita remansit in uita thus ς: F has *inuita remansit inuita*. It is obvious that *in uita* should be written, but did ς separate the right *inuita*? Since the clausula hardly differs in the two cases it provides no argument; *in uita, funus uero*, however, provides a striking contrast; perhaps sufficiently so to approve the solution in ς. The striking paronomasia introduces one of the main themes of the remainder of the story, see above on 1. 10 *quam...animam*. Apuleius' use of paronomasia has been discussed often, see e.g. *GCA* 1977,52; 1981,184 and the literature mentioned there; add Tatum 1979,146.

funus uero...sepulturam: very similar phrasing occurs at 4,34 (101,18-20) where Psyche is led to her rock: *Perfectis igitur feralis thalami cum summo maerore sollemnibus toto prosequente populo uiuum producitur funus*. *Funus* meaning 'corpse' is largely confined to the poets. In Apuleius it occurs here and in the passage just quoted. See also below 201,9, where it means 'death'. Whether *sepultura* here is to be rendered 'burial' or 'grave' is hard to decide. See our discussion of 187,25 *inunita sepultura*. There we opted for 'grave' in view of the fact that in the present passage Tlepolemus is buried. In fact the text here provides no help to decide the question, but a pre-existent grave is certainly a possible implication, in particular since such a grave plays a role also in Greek novels, cf. e.g. Charito 1,6,5 and X. Eph. 3,7,4.

toto feralem pompam prosequente populo: see above on 1.8 *ciuitas cuncta*. Though the marked alliteration lends solemnity to the phrase, the reader realizes that nót much time can have been spent on arranging a formal *pompa* or on such *sollemnia* as are mentioned in the case of Psyche (4,35:102,15 f.).

deducitur: for the tenses *remansit/deducitur* see Callebat 1968,429 who notes narrative variation. A similar variation occurs above 180,4 f. *pepercit...amputat*, there, too, the result of an implied decision followed by a new moment of action.

The last two sentences pack a number of events into a few lines. Such quickening of pace[1] at the end of a chapter or episode may be observed several times in the *Met*. See for a discussion Introd. 5.2. The chapter shows various parallels with chapter 13 below, where again Charite is followed by throngs of people who wish to prevent her death.

---

[1] The category tempo as employed by vdPaardt in *AAGA* 1978,84-87 cannot be applied very well to these chapters in view of the absence of any detailed time stipulation. The impression of slower pace in chapters 4 and 5 is created by the detailed narration of a single event, in chapters 7 and 8 by the equally detailed narration of Charite's grief. In ch. 6 on the contrary several actions are narrated rather briefly.

CHAPTER VII

Thrasyllus woos his victim's widow.

Sed Thrasyllus nimium nimius clamare, plangere et, quas in primo maerore lacrimas non habebat, iam scilicet crescente gaudio reddere et multis caritatis nominibus Veritatem ipsam fallere: "But Thrasyllus went quite beyond the limit and cried out excessively, beat his breast and now – as his joy grew, of course – let flow the tears he did not have at the first lamentation and with his many expressions of devotion deceived Lady Truth herself." 181, 14-17

Thrasyllus nimium nimius clamare: note the careful interlocking wordorder, mitigated by the root of adverb and adjective. For the polyptoton cf. 3, 8 (73, 2) *opulentiae nimiae nimio* with vdPaardt 1971, 199 ad loc.

nimium nimius: we take *nimium* as a qualification of *clamare*. Translators are not always explicit in their rendering of the word group, cf. Vallette ('sans discrétion ni mesure'), Helm-Krenkel ('Aber Thrasyllus schrie überlaut'). There is no need for conjectures such as Colvius' *nimium nimiumque* or Bernhardy's *nimium naeniis*, even though the adj. *nimius* nowhere in the *Met.* qualifies (the name of) a person except here. See however *OLD* s.v. 3a for several instances. Usually in the *Met. nimius* qualifies an abstract noun, e.g. 4, 8 (81, 1) *nimia uirtus sua*, of Lamachus. In view of this penchant on the part of the author (there are some 30 instances) one may consider taking *nimius* here as alluding to the *temeritas* denoted by the name (see below on 182, 14 f.).

clamare, plangere et...reddere et...fallere: this series of historic infinitives is continued in the next period. Though hist. inf. occurs with some frequency in Apul. (vdPaardt 1971, 28 on 2, 1: 52, 20) the accumulation here is particularly striking and perhaps underlines Thrasyllus' highly active behaviour, cf. Marouzeau 1946, 212 f. See also Callebat 1968, 426. Note the asyndeton followed by *et* twice.

clamare, plangere...lacrimas...reddere: in the practice of ancient consolation it was customary to weep with the bereaved before starting on the actual task of consolation. Cf. e.g. Cic. *Fam.* 4, 5, 1 *coramque meum dolorem tibi declarassem*. For the *exordium* of an ancient consolation and its topoi see e.g. Kassel 1958, 51; von Moos 1971, 1, 48 f. See further below on *uerbis...nectere*.

quas...reddere: see above 180, 23 *sed solae lacrimae procedere noluerunt*. Two points arise. (1) In the narrator's interpretation the tears shed by Thrasyllus are tears of joy. The notion also occurs 1, 2 (11, 4 f.) *ut lacrimae saepicule de gaudio prodeunt*; 5, 7 (108, 23 f.); cf. Heine 1962, 249 n.3. In fact tears of joy well profusely throughout ancient literature from Homer onwards (e.g. *Od.* 19, 471 with Schol. ad loc. and Eustath. 1872, 64; Aesch.*Ag.* 270, with

Groeneboom ad loc. and 541; Soph. *El.* 1231; Plut. *Camill.* 30, 3; Longus 4, 22, 1; Pl. *Capt.* 419; Ter. *Ad.* 536; Liv. 5, 7, 11; 27, 19, 12; 34, 50, 1; Petr. 110, 3 and 89, 15 f. (poet.) etc. See the extensive listing in *ThLL* s.v. *lacrima* 837, 72 f.; see further von Moos 1971 index s.v. Freudenträpen. For the rhetorical theory of enacted emotions see e.g. Cic. *De orat.* 2, 189 (versus *Tusc.* 4, 55 and *Orat.* 130); Quint. *Inst.* 11, 3, 72 f. and, in particular, 75). A true parallel for the present situation as presented by the narrator is found in Luc. 9, 1035 f. : Caesar has been given the head of Pompey *Utque fidem uidit sceleris tutumque putauit/iam bonus esse socer, lacrimas non sponte cadentis/effudit gemitusque expressit pectore laeto/non aliter manifesta potens abscondere mentis/gaudia quam lacrimis.* Cf. also ibid. 1061 f. cited above on 180, 20. (2) The narrator marks his words as his own interpretation by *scilicet* (cf. *GCA* 1977, 50 on 4, 5: 77, 25 and vdPaardt in *AAGA* 1978, 79.) The narrator's point of view is marked as limited here, conforming with the strict adherence to the I-perspective. This means, however, that the author allows the reader some freedom to question all this narrator's statements that may be regarded as interpretations, e.g. 180, 10-16. For the entire problem see Introd. 4.2.1.3.

multis caritatis nominibus: the *nomina caritatis (amicum, coaetaneum* etc.) follow in the next sentence.

Veritatem ipsam fallere: at the level of communication between narrator and audience the expression denotes that Thrasyllus is lying so proficiently that Truth herself – let alone Charite – is deceived. At the level of communication between (implied) author and (implied) reader it is to be noted that apparently Thrasyllus' behaviour has aroused no suspicions in Charite and her circle. On the personification see *GCA* 1977, 110 f. Cf. 2, 22 (43, 16) *ut ipsos etiam oculos Solis et Iustitiae facile frustrentur*, a parallel noted by Pricaeus; see de Jonge ad loc. The frequency of deception in the *Met.* materially adds to its dismal atmosphere, cf. Heine 1962, 206 n. 4.

181, 17-24 Illum amicum, coaetaneum, contubernalem, fratrem denique addito nomine lugubri ciere, nec non interdum manus Charites a pulsandis uberibus amouere, luctum sedare, heiulatum cohercere, uerbis palpantibus stimulum doloris obtundere, uariis exemplis multiuagi casus solacia nectere, cunctis tamen mentitae pietatis officiis studium contrectandae mulieris adhibere odiosumque amorem suum perperam delectando nutrire: "He called upon him as his friend, his age-mate, his comrade and finally his brother, adding his mournful name. Also now and again he tried to keep Charite's hands from beating her breasts, to soften her mourning, to check her wailing, to dull the sting of her grief with soothing words, to knit a row of consolations from diverse instances of wide-ranging death – yet to all his offices of feigned piety he added his eagerness to touch the woman and nourished his hateful love by wrongly trying to attach her."

Illum amicum, coaetaneum, contubernalem: Schober 1904, 16 notes the string of cretics.

coaetaneum: the word occurs in Apul. here only; neither as a noun, nor as an adj. is it attested before Apuleius, though it appears several times in Tertullian (e.g. *An.* 31, 2, see Waszink 1947, 379 ad loc.) and later Christian authors. See Callebat 1968, 251.

contubernalem: Callebat 1968, 46 lists the word under the heading 'réalisme familier'; see also *GCA* 1977, 126 on 4, 16 (86, 26).

fratrem: for the affective use of this word cf. 1, 17 (15, 20) ; 2, 13 (36, 8); 9, 7 (207, 22). See also Callebat 1968, 74. Here it seems to function as the high point of a climactic list, and as such it is repeated by Charite in her speech, below 184, 14. According to Merkelbach's interpretation (1962, 77), Thrasyllus represents Seth, Osiris' brother, and he cites the present passage as evidence.

fratrem... addito nomine... ciere: a common solemn usage is *aliquem nomine ciere* e.g. Liv. 45, 38, 12; Suet. *Nero* 46, 2 or *nomen alicuius ciere* e.g. Tac. *An.* 1, 21. For the ritual call see also Verg. *A.* 3, 68; cf. below on 193, 7 (as against 191, 2).

addito nomine lugubri: F has *lugere*^{ubri}; the emendation is in the hand of the original scribe. The combination *nomen lugubre* is apparently unique, cf. *ThLL* s.v. *lugubris* 1804, 18 f. Pricaeus suggested *lugubriter*; Oudendorp *lugubri uoce* or *lugubri sono*, the first two of which Robertson praises with 'alteruter fort. recte'. Vallette's translation appears to adopt Oudendorp's emendation *lugubri uoce*: 'c'est ainsi qu'il appelait d'une voix lugubre celui dont en même temps il répétait le nom'. Oudendorp's reason ('tale enim non erat Tlepolemi nomen') is insufficient: though the expression is bold, *lugubris* may well be taken in the sense of 'that which induces mourning'. Prescott 1911, 350 defends the text of F noting that in the mouth of his murderer the significant name Tlepolemus ('Sturdy Fighter') truly becomes a *nomen lugubre*. This is not the sort of reasoning with which to defend a ms. reading, but it certainly marks an interesting implication once the text has been established. It is to be remembered that Charite does not yet know that Tlepolemus has been murdered by Thrasyllus. The implication, then, works at the level of the narrator and his audience.

addito nomine: the name Tlepolemus, present here by implication, is now used κατ' ἀντίφρασιν, just like the names Charite and Thrasyllus by the end of the story. For that reason we avoid the possibility of taking *lugubri* per hypallagen with the implied subject. (Should the reader also remember the name Haemus, now that Tlepolemus has been gored by animal and man? If the suggestion seems tasteless to a modern reader, this is not to say that it would seem so to an ancient one. Cf. 183, 9 *cruentam*).

amouere... nutrire: note that Thrasyllus' consolatory activities are strung together asyndetically, whereas the elements of the narrator's comment are linked by *-que*. The infinitives dealing with consolation have been translated 'de conatu'. See KSt. 2, 1, 121.

interdum: see vdPaardt 1971, 28, who points out that this is one of only three passages in the *Met.* in which the word has its usual meaning (= *nonnumquam*).

nec non... cohercere: unlike the soldier in Petronius, who presents the Ephesian widow with food (*Sat.* 111, 10), Thrasyllus touches Charite; see below on *studium contrectandae mulieris*.

a pulsandis uberibus: thus Ceres at the rape of Proserpine (Ov. *Met.* 5, 473) and Venus at the death of Adonis (Ov. *Met.* 10, 723) *percussit pectora palmis.* Further parallels in Bömer on Ov. *Met.* 3, 178 and 6, 248. See also e.g. 9, 31 (226, 13) *interdum pugnis obtundens ubera.* The grief of the *pistor's* daughter is markedly less intense than Charite's: here *interdum. . .amouere*, there *interdum. . .obtundens.*

uerbis. . .nectere: an abbreviated indication of *consolatio*. Walsh in *AAGA* 1978, 21 notes the inversion vis à vis Petronius' tale of the widow of Ephesus, in which the soldier similarly uses several elements of *consolatio*. In Petronius 111 the main topos is *omnium eundem exitum esse*; here the variety is stressed within the same topos (see below).

uerbis. . .obtundere: Weyman 1893, 355 notes the return of the phrase in Zeno of Verona 1, 5, 4 p. 48 (=2, 7, 4 Löfstedt 1971): *obtundam uerbis palpantibus aciem ueritatis.* For *palpare* see 5, 31 (128, 5), where Ceres and Juno try to soothe Venus' *ira* by means of a speech.

uariis exemplis multiuagi casus: one may think of lists of *exitus illustrium uirorum* as used in the *consolatio*; cf. e.g. Cic. *Div.* 2, 22 *clarissimorum hominum nostrae ciuitatis grauissimos exitus in Consolatione collegimus* (with Pease ad loc., who cites i.a. *Tusc.* 3, 70 and Hier. *Ep.* 60, 5, 3); see Ronconi in *RAC* 6, 1966, 1258-68 on the (sub)genre, also von Moos 1971/2 Testimonienband sub 552. *Multiuagus* should not be translated with 'similar' (e.g. Rode-Burck: 'ähnlich'), but rather in its basic meaning 'wide-ranging' (cf. e.g. Sen. *Her. F.* 533; Plin. *Nat.* 2, 48; Stat. *Theb.* 1, 499). The topos *de communi hominum condicione* is common enough, see e.g. Esteve-Forriol 1962, 150; Johann 1968, 65 f.

multiuagi casus solacia nectere, cunctis: Schober 1904, 10 and Médan 1925, 267 note the hexameter.

cunctis tamen mentitae pietatis officiis. . .adhibere: the phrase as a whole summarizes; *tamen* underlines the contrast between action and intention. It is not easy to decide whether *cunctis. . .officiis* should be taken as a dative with *adhibere* (thus e.g. Helm-Krenkel) or as an abl. of means (thus e.g. Vallette): 'by means of the offices of a feigned piety he put. . .into practice'. There is only a slight difference in meaning. Perhaps the first possibility is preferable in that it presents *studium* as a secondary aspect of the *officia*, just as the subsequent phrase denotes a side-effect.

contrectandae: specifically of sexual fondling, cf. *OLD* s.v. 2b, but in view of the fact that the word is also used for 'stealing' (cf. Summers 1967, 268; Gaius 3, 195), stealthy behaviour may well be implied. *ThLL* s.v. 774, 47 and 52 lists numerous parallels for both senses.

odiosumque amorem suum perperam delectando nutrire: several choices are open to the translator: (1) Oudendorp takes *delectando* in the sense of *ualde lactando* without specifying whether he means 'feeding' or 'deceiving', 'seducing'. *ThLL* s.v. *delectare* 422, 34-43 lists some instances of both meanings. If *delectando* is taken as *pascendo* the object is *amorem suum* (thus apparently Floridus). For this transferred sense of *delectare* cf. e.g. Cic. *Pis.* 45 *his ego rebus pascor, his delector, his perfruor.* The pleonastic phrasing need not surprise in Apuleius. If *delectando* is taken in the meaning 'seducing' (cf. e.g.

Enn. *scen.* 361 *set me Apollo ipse delectat, ductat Delphicus*), Charite is the implied object. In both cases *perperam* qualifies *delectando*. (2) Hildebrand follows Rode in taking *delectando* as referring to Thrasyllus himself 'qui eo, quod Chariten contrectat, perperam delectatur et paulatim maiore flamma incenditur'. Most translators take the phrase in this sense. (3) Helm-Krenkel ('und nährte so unsinnigerweise seine doch verhasste Liebe, indem er mit ihr spielte') take *perperam* with *nutrire* and *delectando* apparently as 'amusing himself by playing with her'.

A further complication lies in the fact that *perperam* may mean either 'by mistake' or, in a moral sense, 'wrongly', 'in an evil manner'. In the first case it is to be taken as a comment on Thrasyllus' procedure, in the second as a comment on his character. The second possibility is in keeping with the narrator's general attitude, the first may give a glimpse of the author behind the narrator (see Introd. 4.2.1.3).

On the whole it seems most natural to take *perperam* with *delectando* and to translate it at the level of the narrator. *Delectando* is best taken in the sense of *alliciendo* (the sense mentioned under (2) above occurs in the passive only).

odiosum. . .amorem: not to be taken as an oxymoron. Whereas at Pl. *Rud.* 1204 *nimis paene inepta atque odiosa eius amatiost* the happy father shows little more than a slight impatience, here the narrator shows considerable moral indignation: in his eyes Thrasyllus' love is just such a *calamitas animae* as described in Apul. *Pl.* 2, 13 (116, 22).

delectando nutrire: the section dealing with Thrasyllus ends with an impressive spondaic clausula (Médan 1925, 283).

Sed officiis inferialibus statim exactis puella protinus festinat ad maritum suum demeare cunctasque prorsus pertemptat uias, certe illam lenem otiosamque nec telis ullis indigentem, sed placidae quieti consimilem: inedia denique misera et incuria squalida, tenebris imis abscondita, iam cum luce transegerat: "But as soon as the rites of the dead had been completed the girl was immediately eager to go down to her husband, and she actually explored all methods, certainly that soft and leisurely one that is not in need of any weapons, but resembles peaceful rest: in short by a miserable fast and squalid neglect, hidden in deepest darkness, she had finally done with the light." 181, 25-182, 1

The narrator now turns his attention to Charite; her negative reaction to Thrasyllus' attempts at consolation is obvious; like many of her sisters in the Greek novel she wishes to die; see above on line 10.

officiis. . .exactis: at 9, 31 (226, 20 f.) the *pistor*'s daughter, too, waits until after the funeral rites have been completed (*iamque nono die rite completis apud tumulum sollemnibus*) before looking after her own business; cf. also 10, 27 (258, 10). The final rite of full mourning was the *cena nouendialis* at the grave-site. The vagueness of the present expression, however, makes it hazardous to use it for fixing a definite time element in the story. For a full discussion of funerary rites, see Toynbee 1971, 43-61. Funeral practices in the *Met.* are discussed below Appendix I.

The fact that Charite waits until after the rites have been performed fits in with her character: she is described below as being sensible of *religiosa necessitas* in other respects as well (182, 6). Toynbee 1971, 43 remarks that the two basic notions in Roman funerary practice were 'that death brought pollution and demanded from the survivors acts of purification and expiation; secondly that to leave a corpse unburied had unpleasant repercussions on the fate of the departed soul'.

inferialibus: ThLL s.v. gives only the present instance; the word is restored *per coniecturam* by Helm at 1, 6 (5, 21) and by Keller at Schol. Hor. *Epod.* 10, 17. Médan 1925, 116 lists it with other instances of the *-alis* group of adjectives, cf. LHSz 1, 350 f.

statim...protinus: the apparent redundancy is lessened by the fact that *statim* marks the end of one, *protinus* the beginning of the next activity.

exactis: F, after erasure and correction, now reads *factis* but may have had *eractis*. Robertson does not mention the reading in φ. Elmenhorst proposed *exactis*; Victorius' *peractis* is almost as good; Oudendorp proposed *stato more expletis* and notes, rightly, that the younger mss. have *expletis*, a reading that has disappeared from the more recent app. crit.

demeare: see Médan 1925, 128; Bernhard 1927, 121; Callebat 1968, 135; the last notes that the verb probably belonged to the contemporary sermo cotidianus. Comparison with 6, 7 (133, 5) and 1, 9 (17, 13) shows that Apuleius employs it both in highly stylized and in familiar narrative. Cf. also e.g. 11, 6 (271, 1f.) *cum spatium saeculi tui permensus ad inferos demearis*. See also Charite's own words at the end of the tale (187, 18 f.) *iam tempus est, ut isto gladio deorsus ad meum Tlepolemum uiam quaeram*.

cunctasque...uias: at 4, 25 (94, 7) Charite had mentioned three methods of suicide, see *GCA* 1977, 187 ad loc. For the topos see also Fraenkel 1932, 470 f. The ass is more restricted in his choices at 7, 24 (172, 5 f.) see *GCA* 1981, 239 ad loc.

pertemptat: *OLD* s.v. lists the present passage under 1 c ('try out a scheme'); we should prefer 1 b ('examine', 'explore'), since we do not think that several attempts at suicide are implied, rather that several modes were considered.

illam...consimilem, inedia: there are several passages in which this method of suicide is discussed, e.g. Cic. *Tusc.* 1, 84; Sen. *Ep.* 70, 9; Tac. *Ann.* 11, 3, 2 (Koestermann ad loc. gives background). Part and parcel of the irony of the relationships described in the present tale is the fact that in the end Charite chooses the 'hard' form of suicide, consonant with her *anima uirilis* (187, 24), Thrasyllus the 'easy' *inedia* (188, 6).

denique: the word indicates that *inedia* sums up *certe...consimilem*, cf. vdPaardt 1971, 43.

misera...squalida: the tone of these words differs markedly from the preceding *lenem otiosumque...placidae quieti consimilem*: the narrator's perspective replaces that of Charite. Merkelbach 1962, 77 compares the mourning goddesses Demeter (Hom. *Hymn. in Cer.* 49 f.) and Aphrodite (Bion 76 f.).

iam cum luce transegerat: a transferred business term; cf. 10, 8 (243, 5) *iam cum rei fortuna transacto*; Tac. *Agr.* 34, 3 *transigite cum expeditionibus* with

Ogilvie and Richmond ad loc.; Tac. *Ger.* 19, 2 with Anderson ad loc.; Calp. *Decl.* 46.

Sed Thrasyllus instantia peruicaci partim per semet ipsum, 182, 1-5
partim per ceteros familiares ac necessarios, ipsos denique
puellae parentes extorquet tandem, iam lurore et inluuie paene
conlapsa membra lauacro, cibo denique confoueret: "But with
stubborn importunity Thrasyllus, partly on his own, partly with the help of the
other members of the household and relatives, finally with that of the girl's
parents themselves, at last constrained her to sustain her limbs – almost
collapsed in pallor and dirt – with a bath and, finally, with food."

peruicaci: *pertinaci* A (and other younger mss.). *Peruicax* is always used *in malam partem* in Apuleius. See also 7, 25 (173, 4) and *GCA* 1981, 249 ad loc.

parentes: see 7, 13 (163, 22) and *GCA* 1981, 164 ad loc. Charite's parents play but a very slight role in this part of the story. See also below lines 5 f.

extorquet: for the construction with the subjunctive see Callebat 1968, 359; cf. 5, 6 (107, 18) *extorquet a marito, cupitis adnuat* with Fernhout 1949, 46 ad loc.

lurore: the word occurs in Lucr. 4, 333 (see Bailey ad loc.) and Apul. *Met.* 1, 6 (5, 14); 9, 12 (212, 7); 9, 30 (225, 19). Cf. also Claud. *Rapt. Pros.* 3, 238, where Parrhasius preferred *luror* to *liuor*.

lurore...inluuie...lauacro, cibo: an obvious a b b a arrangement: the *luror* is to be remedied *cibo*, the *inluuies* by a bath.

conlapsa membra: Médan 1925, 263 cites Verg. *A.* 4, 391. For several parallels see Pease ad loc. The word *conlapsam* is also used of the dying Dido at 664. The combination somewhat strengthens the comparison Charite / Dido; the latter first swoons, then dies by the sword; see below on 187, 18 *gladio*.

lauacro: see Callebat 1968, 132. The word occurs for the first time in the 2nd century A.D. :*CIL* XV 7247 *in*] lauacro Agrippinae is possibly datable to the period of Hadrian. See also Gel. 1, 2, 2. From this time onwards it is widely used. Apuleius uses it 19 times, usually in the sense of ablution; cf. *GCA* 1981, 52 on 6, 28 (150, 12); see also e.g. 11, 23 (284, 26), where the religious context allows a comparison with its frequent use for baptism in Christian authors. For the concrete meaning ('bathhouse') see e.g. 3, 12 (61, 9) and vdPaardt 1971, 97f. ad loc.

At illa, parentum suorum alioquin reuerens, inuita quidem, 182, 5-10
uerum religiosae necessitati subcumbens, uultu non quidem
hilaro, uerum ⌜pau⌝lo seneriore oboediens, ut iubebatur, uiuentium ⌜mu⌝nia pro[ru]rsus in[s] pectore, immo uero penitus i⌜n
medul⌝lis luctu ac maerore carpebat animum: "Being respectful of her
parents in other ways as well, she gave in, though unwilling, to the dictates of
duty and went about the tasks of the living as she was bidden, not actually with
a cheerful, but at least with a slightly more serene, face. But deep in her heart,

no, in the marrow of her bones, she utterly consumed her mind with grief and sorrow."

From this point onwards F's text has been damaged by a tear in fol. 160. The lost letters may be restored from later mss. The supplements have been marked by ⌐ ¬. This damage in F has been instrumental in establishing the relationship of the ca. 40 mss. of the *Met.* It was H.Keil who in 1849 announced that all other mss. depend on F, because the supplements added in φ in the fourteenth century (which he regarded as conjectures) are more or less faithfully repeated in all others. In essence Keil's opinion was accepted by subsequent editors including Helm (1907). However, in 1897 van der Vliet had suggested that the supplements were due, not to conjectures, but to F itself, through the intermediary of an early copy, now lost, but made before the damage to fol. 160 had occurred. Robertson's detailed examination of all the mss., published in 1924, confirmed the existence of a class of mss. deriving from F in its pristine state and more or less faithfully preserving not only the text elements lost through the mutilation of fol. 160 (roughly covering chapters 7, 8 and 9 of the present book) but also losses in many other passages caused by fading, correction and erasure. His description of the situation has now been generally accepted. See also Helm 1955 in app. crit. on 182, 7. For detailed information concerning the history of the stemma see Robertson's introduction to Robertson-Vallette (XXXVIII f.); for his classification of the mss. see Robertson 1924.

parentum...reuerens: the young widow returns to the *patria potestas*.

religiosae necessitati subcumbens: cf. 3, 9 (58, 26) *euictus tandem necessitate succumbo* with vdPaardt 1971, 80 ad loc. for the combination of *necessitas* and *succumbere* in one phrase. Below 185, 13 Thrasyllus in turn will yield to Charite's promise. The word *succumbere* underlines the element of inevitability almost as much as does *necessitas*. For the meaning of *religiosus* see below on 201, 19 f. Here the phrase further develops *parentum...reuerens*: *religiosa necessitas* for Charite, then, is tantamount to the inevitable familial circumstances in which she finds herself and in which she has her duties. For *religio* and *religiosus* in comparable contexts cf. 2, 6 (30, 3 *probi Milonis genialem torum religios⟨us⟩ suspice*); 5, 12 (113, 8 Amor demanding *religiosa continentia* on the part of Psyche); 10, 26 (257, 13 a murderess pretending to be a *religiosa uxor circa salutem mariti sollicita*). Compare, too, the robbers' military *religio* at 4, 11 (82, 22 with *GCA* 1977, 87 ad loc.) and the *religio* of the court room referred to at 10, 10 (244, 15); cf. 10, 8 (243, 14 f.).

hilaro: for the form see *GCA* 1977, 32 on 4, 2 (75, 15).

Oboediens: thus F, *obiens* ς and editors. At 4, 15 (86, 7) F reads *ad munus obediundum*. In *GCA* 1977, 119 ad loc. we thought that a defense of the ms. reading was not likely to succeed, but noted a number of passages in which *oboedire* is construed with a direct object. It should be noted that the two passages in which F construes *munus/munia oboedire* support one another. In addition to the passages collected in *GCA* 1977, cf. also 10, 17 (250, 6) *Atque haec omnia perfacile oboediebam*. Possibly however *haec omnia* should be regarded as an internal accus. (cf. Fron. 127, 10 vdH. *neque me puderet ea illum oboedire mihi, quae clientes...obsequuntur*) and, of course, that explanation is available for our passage. *Munus* is loosely associated with *oboedire* at *Pl.* 2, 7 (109, 15 f.) *ut unaquaeque portio ratione ac modo ad fungendum munus oboediat*. On the other hand Apuleius employs *munia...obibam* in the final sentence of the *Met*. Nevertheless, partly since *oboediens* is the lectio difficilior, partly because of the parallels noted above which indicate that *munus/munia oboedire* becomes a distinct possibility in later Latin, we prefer to retain the ms. reading.

pro[ru]rsus: the emendation occurs in ς. For similar duplications cf. 5, 15 (115, 1) *uaporo[ro]sis*; 5, 30 (127, 21) *lita[ta]tum*.

in pectore: F has *inspectore*; the emendation was made by one of φ's correctors.

⌜diesque to⌝tos totasque noctes insumebat l⌜uctuoso desi⌝derio et imagines defuncti, qu⌜as ad habitum dei⌝ Liberi for⟨m⟩auerat, adfixo s⌜eruitio diuinis percolens⌝ honoribus ipso se solac⌜io cruciabat⌝: "all her days and all her nights she spent in mournful longing. She worshipped the portraits of the deceased that she had ordered to be made in the appearance of the god Liber: she appointed servants to pay him divine honours; and so she tortured herself by her very consolation." 182, 10-14

diesque totos totasque noctes: note the a b b a arrangement. It is, of course, possible to translate 'whole days and entire nights', but in view of the frequency with which the word is used with the meaning 'all' (see e.g. *GCA* 1981, 72 on 6, 31: 153, 12 f.) that meaning seems preferable. The expression appears to indicate a fairly long period of time, see however Introd. 3.1 for the vagueness of the time element in this tale.

insumebat luctuoso desiderio: for the dative with *insumere* cf. e.g. Tac. *Ann.* 3, 1, 1 *illic paucos dies componendo animo insumit*; cf. 2, 53, 2. See further *ThLL* s.v. 2052, 63. *Luctuosus* is used here only in Apul.

imagines defuncti: the type of portrait is not specified. For the various possibilities see Hijmans, *Apuleiana Groningana VIII*, to be published in *Mnemosyne*.

ad habitum dei Liberi: the expression is as vague as the rest of this tantalising description. *Habitus* may refer to dress, but to attributes as well, cf. e.g. 10, 32 (263, 5 f.). It should be noted that Tlepolemus has undergone a number of metamorphoses of appearance (cf.7,5f. Haemus' (= the disguised Tlepolemus') tale, which includes a further disguise at 159, 26 f.; cf. 160, 8 *habitus alieni fallacia tectus*, which may refer to yet another disguise); the present phrase may well have to be placed in that list. For the question why Charite chooses Liber see Hijmans, *Apuleiana Groningana VIII*, to be published in *Mnemosyne*.

formauerat: *forauerat* F and φ; the ms. reading can hardly be retained: in two instances the word is used for drilling through stone in a context of sculpture (Hier. *in Is.* 54, 11 = 608, 22 Adriaen τρυπανισμοῦ ... *quod uerbum foratarum caelatarumque gemmarum sensum sonat*; Prud. *Psych.* 835 *caua per solidum multoque forata dolatu/gemma*) but neither context deals with portrait sculpture or even sculpture of human forms. The correction occurs in ς. Is the verb to be rendered 'shaped' as at 11, 17 (280, 4 f.) *argento formata* or rather

83

'adorned' as at 198, 12 *deformiter...formati*? If the suggestion made in the previous lemma, viz. that we have to do with Tlepolemus' final metamorphosis, is acceptable, the proper parallel is to be found at 7, 14 (164, 19) *quae me formauit non canem, sed asinum*.

adfixo seruitio: there are two main possibilities; either the expression is to be taken as an abl. abs. (*affigere* = 'attach': *seruitium* = 'a group of servants'), or as an abl. instr, (*affixo* = 'assiduous'; *seruitium* = 'service'). *OLD* s.v. *affigere* choose the first; for the concrete sense of *seruitium* cf. e.g. Cic. *Ver.* 2, 5, 9; *Har.* 25; Vell. 2, 82, 3. This possibility is preferred by Gwyn Griffiths in *AAGA* 1978, 151 and n. 72. See also vdPaardt 1971, 37 on 3, 2 (53, 21) *publica ministeria*. *ThLL* s.v. *affigere* 1216, 18 chooses the second, followed by e.g. Vallette, Brandt-Ehlers, Helm-Krenkel. For the abstract meaning of *seruitium* cf. e.g. 11, 15 (277, 14 f.). In view of the fact that for the adjectival usage of *affixus ThLL* s.v. *affigo* 1216, 17 produces but one parallel (*Decl. in Cat.* 105, at best a doubtful source), the first possibility seems preferable, but it should be admitted that the notion of a group of servants attached to this cult of Liber is not developed in the tale; certainly there is no reason to identify the *familiares* of 187, 24 with the (concrete) *seruitium* appointed here.

diuinis percolens honoribus: on the question of divine honours for departed loved ones see Hijmans, *Apuleiana Groningana VIII*, to be published in *Mnemosyne*.

Helm thinks *colens* may have to be read in view of the space available in F (cf. Praef. *Fl.* xxxii). Robertson's remeasurement (1924, 35) seems to have dealt with such doubts.

ipso se solacio cruciabat: note the oxymoron. Cicero, too, comforted himself by planning a shrine for Tullia, *Att.* 12, 18, 1 *ego, quantum his temporibus tam eruditis fieri potuerit, profecto illam consecrabo omni genere monimentorum ab omnium ingeniis sumptorum et Graecorum et Latinorum. Quae res forsitan sit refricatura uulnus*. See the detailed discussion concerning the origin of the notion and the planning of the details in Shackleton Bailey 5, 1966, 404 f. (Appendix III 'Tullia's Fane'). He notes that Roman parallels are lacking. For the instances of Harpalus and Hadrian see Hijmans, *Apuleiana Groningana VIII*, to be published in *Mnemosyne*.

CHAPTER VIII

An untimely proposal and a dream.

⌜Sed Th⌝rasyllus, praeceps alioq⌜uin et de ipso nomine⌝ temerarius, priusquam dolorem lacrimae satiarent et percitae mentis resideret furor et in sese nimietatis senio lassesceret luctus, adhuc flentem maritum, adhuc uestes lacerantem, adhuc capillos distrahentem non dubitauit de nuptiis conuenire et imprudentiae labe tacita pectoris sui secreta fraudesque ineffabiles detegere: "But Thrasyllus, overbold as he was and, because of his very name, headstrong, even before the tears could satisfy her grief and the fury of her shocked mind became quiet and mourning sank down in itself, fatigued through the duration of the excess, did not hesitate to approach her about marriage while she was still weeping over her husband, still tearing her clothes, still pulling out her hair, and to disclose – an imprudent slip – the silent secrets and unspeakable crimes of his heart."

Thrasyllus: on the name see Hijmans in *AAGA* 1978, 116; Tatum 1979, 72f. and vdPaardt in *SAG* 1981, 24 f.

praeceps...temerarius: Bernhard 1927, 167 notes that the second adjective develops the sense of the first adjective. Perhaps the period develops the untimely element of *praeceps* in *non dubitauit de nuptiis conuenire*; the more psychological characteristic of *temerarius* in *et (non dubitauit) imprudentiae...detegere*.

alioquin: for the position of *alioquin* following the adjective see Callebat 1968, 460: *GCA* 1977, 25 on 4, 1 (74, 8 f.) and 39 on 4, 3 (76, 5-11); *GCA* 1981, 188 on 7, 16 (166, 11-15).

de ipso nomine temerarius: *de* may mean 'because of' see Callebat 1968, 202; see also *ThLL* s.v. *de* 77, 75 f. and Scobie 1975, 105 on 1,12 (11,4) *de gaudio*, or 'as may be deduced from', cf. 192, 21.

The characterisation is seen here as the result of, or at least closely related to, the name: a neat narrative trick on the part of the author thus to have his narrator subscribe to the *nomen est omen* notion, after he had selected the name himself. It looks as if the author consciously underscores the exemplary function of the tale. For the effect of this trick, coupled with the fact that the narrator can hardly be aware of the *secreta pectoris* of his villain, see the Introd. 4.2.1.3 n.4. Heinsius' conjecture *et re et ipso nomine* shows that he neither appreciated the specific sense of *de* nor the author's playfulness here.

percitae mentis...furor: Heine 1962, 244 collects a large number of instances in which *furor* and the like are employed in a hyperbolic description of mourning etc. For Charite's *furor* see also above on 181, 5 *cursu...furibundo*; 187, 7 *cursu furioso*.

resideret: from *residēre*, see above on 176, 19 (*adsĭdens*).

in sese...lassesceret luctus: Hildebrand discusses at length the various conjectures occasioned by the fact that *in sese lassescere* is not attested elsewhere in Latin literature. Thus Heinsius proposed *et sensim nimietatis senio flaccesceret*; Stewech, Groslot and Oudendorp read *in sese...facesseret*. However *lassescere* (without *in sese*) does occur with reference to emotional states and the like, e.g. [Quint.] *Decl.* 17, 3 *ut lassesceret aliquando pro me iusta miseratio*; cf. Prud. *c. Symm.* 2, 101 *quis dubitet uicto fragilem* (sc. *aciem*) *lassescere uisu*. Doubtless Apuleius is attempting yet another variation on the proverbial theme 'time heals all' (see Otto n. 535, Nachträge 43, 155, 235). The addition *in sese* almost personifies *luctus*.

nimietatis senio: the correction (F has *ninietatis*) occurs in φ; *nimietas* is attested for the first time in Apuleius who has five instances. From Tert. onwards (*Herm.* 43: 172, 24) the word gains ground among the Fathers; cf. also Arn. 4, 10 *nimietatis...taedio*. The expression is somewhat bold in its combination of three abstract nouns.

adhuc flentem maritum(7), *adhuc uestes lacerantem*(8), *adhuc capillos distrahentem*(9): the anaphoric tricolon with 'wachsende Glieder', climactic in content, and chiastic placement of participle and object in the first two cola describes the object of *conuenire* in 24 syllables, almost perfectly balanced with its subject (*Sed Thrasyllus...temerarius*) which has 22 syllabes. Callebat 1968, 452 notes ellipsis of a pronoun in the accusative, Bernhard 1927, 69 the anaphora and 35 the chiasmus. The entire group serves to underscore Thrasyllus' haste, and at the same time gives carefully built expression to the narrator's indignation, cf. the stylistic features of Charite's speech in ch.12 below. For an emotional appeal in highly finished style see also our notes on ch. 20 below.

adhuc referring to past time underlines the contemporaneity of participle and main verb, see Bernhard 1927, 127.

de nuptiis conuenire: cf. 184, 10 *aures obseratas de nuptiis obtundens*.

In the narrator's presentation Thrasyllus had been one of Charite's suitors when she became nubile (177, 11 *inter praecipuos procos*), had subsequently discovered the impossibility of an illicit affair with Charite (178, 9 f.) and now, after murdering her husband approaches her once more *de nuptiis*. Notwithstanding the fact that *nuptiae* in the *Met.* does not always refer to a formal marriage (cf. 7, 22: 170, 24) it seems obvious that a formal marriage is what he proposes. Cf. also 183, 14 where the *umbra Tlepolemi* uses the expression *modo ne in...manum...conuenias*. Nevertheless Charite will presently set her trap substituting a secret rendezvous – later referred to as a *scaena feralium nuptiarum* (185, 23) – for *nuptiae* regarded as *immaturae* (185, 2).

imprudentiae labe: see 2, 14 (36, 23) *ac dehinc tunc demum Diofanes expergitus sensit imp⟨r⟩udentiae suae labem*, where there can be no doubt that *imprudentiae* is to be preferred to the transmitted *impudentiae*. The confusion is not uncommon, cf. *ThLL* s.v. *impudentia* 709, 24, but that is insufficient reason to assume, as most editors do, that here *impudentiae* is to be read with ς. Robertson prints *imprudentiae* but awards the ς reading a *fortasse recte*. But θρασύς, *praeceps* and *temerarius* are the very characteristics of *imprudentia*. For *imprudentia* as the result of all kinds of *uitia* cf. e.g. Sen. *Ira* 3, 26, 1. In this context the 'Umdeutung' of *labes* is particularly fitting: Löfstedt 1936, 101: 'Apul. dachte an *labi* im Sinne von 'dahingleiten', 'ausgleiten', (daher: 'zu weit gehen').

tacita...secreta...detegere: cf. e.g. 3, 15 (63, 5 f.) *domus huius operta detegere et arcana dominae meae reuelare secreta* with vdPaardt 1971, 114 ad loc. (cf. Schmidt 1982, 271) and 9, 26 (223, 4 f.) *detectis ac reuelatis fraudibus* for Apuleius' love of redundancy in this type of context.

fraudesque ineffabiles: explanatory *-que* identifies the *fraudes* with the *secreta*. It should be noted that these *fraudes* are not specified. Certainly the expression does not imply a confession of murder, since it is not until the dream that Charite is informed of the murder (see also Introd. 4.2.1.3). Once again the subnarrator is manipulating his audience. Note also the inner contrast between *ineffabiles* and *detegere*; cf. Verg. *A*. 2, 3 *infandum, regina, iubes renouare dolorem*.

Apart from the anaphoric tricolon noted above, the sentence shows a careful economy of sound in which alliteration (*praeceps...priusquam*; *lacrimae...lassesceret luctus...lacerantem...labe*; *distrahentem...dubitauit...de*), (near-)rhyme (*flentem...lacerantem...distrahentem*); assonance (*fraudes...ineffabiles*) and repetition (*adhuc*) vie for attention. The several (near-)synonyms (e.g. *praeceps...temerarius*, the tricolon, *tacita...secreta*) further enrich the texture of this instance of Apuleius' φιλολογία.

Sed Charite uocem nefanda⟨m⟩ et horruit et detestata est et uelut 183, 2-5 graui ton⟨i⟩tru procella[s]que sideris uel etiam ipso diali fulmine percussa corruit corpus et obnubilauit animam: "But Charite both abhorred and detested this sacrilegious speech and, as if struck down by heavy thunder and a star-sent storm or even by heaven's lightning itself, she collapsed bodily and a cloud covered her senses."

uocem nefandam: Thrasyllus' speech to Charite is reduced to the expression *de nuptiis conuenire*: the fact that the reader is left to guess at his actual words whets the reader's appetite. It is noteworthy that in the entire tale extraordinarily few utterances of Thrasyllus are directly quoted. See Introd. 4.2.1.3. Here the contrast with the ghost's speech below is obvious.

uelut...tonitru procellaque...uel etiam: for the interchange of disjunctive and copulative particles see Bernhard 1927, 83. See also 9, 2 (203, 22 f.) with our note ad loc. Thrasyllus' speech strikes Charite as (a) thunder; (b) the effusion of a baleful star or (c) lightning, but whereas (a) and (b) are linked together, (c) is separate. See below under *uel etiam ipso diali fulmine*.

uelut graui tonitru: though *grauis* is used several times of weather conditions, the present combination occurs only twice: here and in Lucr. 6, 121 f. (cf. *ThLL* s.v. *grauis* 2299, 8).

procellaque sideris: F and φ have *procellasque sideris*, the correction occurs in ς. The combination of the two words does not occur elsewhere in Latin literature according to the *ThLL* material. For the notion see Liv. 8, 9, 12 *haud secus quam pestifero sidere icti pauebant*; Mart. 7, 92, 9 *subito fias ut sidere*

87

mutus, cf. ibid. 11, 85, 1. The idea of wind associated with an unhealthy *sidus* is also found Petr. 2, 7: *Nuper uentosa. . .loquacitas. . .animos. . .iuuenum. . .ueluti pestilenti quodam sidere adflauit*; cf. [Quint.]*Decl.* 12, 22.

Such expressions may be seen against the background of the popular notion expressed in Plin. *Nat.* 18, 278, who notes two types of *caelestis iniuria* of which one is *tempestates. . ., in quibus grandines, procellae ceteraque similia intelleguntur, quae cum acciderint, uis maior appellatur. Haec ab horridis sideribus exeunt. . .ueluti Arcturo, Orione, Haedis.* Cf. also ibid. 223 *sidus uehemens Orionis. Procellosus* is an epithet of Orion at Rut. Nam. 1, 637; cf. Roscher 6, 989, 4 f. with Suppl. 2, 79 f. for comparable epithets of the same constellation. Hor. *C.* 3, 1, 27 has the expression *saeuus Arcturi cadentis impetus*, recalling Pl. *Rud.* 70, where Arcturus is made to cause the shipwreck of the *leno*, Cf.*AP* 7, 295, where Arcturus is referred to as causing storms (see also Gow and Page on 7, 273 (2345) on the notion καταιγίς; cf. Ps. Arist. Π. κοσμ. 395 a 5 = Apul. *Mun.* 12 : 147, 13). See further Gundel 1922 (^r1981), 173 and 230; Boll – Bezold – Gundel ⁵1966, 142 f.

uel etiam ipso diali fulmine: for *dialis* cf. 6, 15 (139, 16) *diales uias deserit* (*Iouis ales*). Apuleius appears to be the only one to use the word outside a context involving the *flamen dialis* cf. *ThLL Onom.* s.v. 126, 53. Not only *uel etiam*, then, but also the preciousness of the expression *diale fulmen* present the final notion as a climax.

corruit corpus et obnubilauit animam: is *corruit* to be taken transitively with *ThLL* s.v. 1061, 11 or intransitively with vGeisau 1916, 83 f. (*corpus* as a so – called acc. graecus)? We prefer transitive *corruere*, though it is not attested elsewhere in Apuleius, but see Lucr. 5, 368; (at Catul. 68, 52 Turnebus' *torruerit* is adopted by most editors); the phrase *obnubilauit animam*, though it hardly denotes a conscious activity, supports this possibility. vGeisau notes that Oudendorp and others take *corruit* in a transitive sense, Floridus *obnubilauit* in an intransitive sense, but he himself sees no reason to resort to either explanation and treats the contrast *corpus. . .animam* as a reason for the addition of *corpus* which in itself is superfluous. However *corruere* with internal acc. can not be supported by further instances in Apuleius (he uses the abl. at *Apol.* 52 (59, 2) *pede potius quam mente corruere*). For *obnubilare* see also 9, 24 (221, 15 f.) *odore sulpuris. . .obnubilatus*. Charite's collapse here works almost as a preview of her final collapse and death ([c̄]*corruit. . .efflauit animam uirilem*) at 187, 22 f., see comm ad loc.

183, 5-7 Sed interuallo reualescente paulatim spiritu, ferinos mugitus iterans et iam scaenam pessimi Thrasylli perspiciens, ad limam consilii desiderium petitoris distulit:"But after a while she gradually recovered the breath of life and again and again she lowed like an animal and, now seeing through the plot of despicable Thrasyllus, she deferred her wooer's desire in order to sharpen a plan."

At this point Charite is metamorphosed into an avenging fury of considerable cunning.

ferinos mugitus: when Apuleius wishes to describe grief, anger and the like in hyperbolic terms he often makes use of terms that are taken from animal life, see Heine 1962, 240, who compares Verg. *A.* 2, 222 f.

clamores simul horrendos ad sidera tollit:
qualis mugitus, fugit cum saucius aram
taurus et incertam excussit ceruice securim.

On the contrastive theme man/animal see Schlam, *SAG* 1981, 115 f. Here the discription clearly picks up *corpus...animam* of the previous period: *reualescente...iterans* corresponding with *corpus, et...perspiciens* with *animam*.

iam scaenam pessimi Thrasylli perspiciens: exactly what *scaena* does Charite see through? In our opinion the sub-narrator indicates that Charite now knows that Thrasyllus has arranged an accident for Tlepolemus. Her subsequent dream, then, simply provides further precision and does not have the function, so common in (ancient) literature, of a motivating link between sections of a narrative. See further Introd. 4.2.1.3 and below on 183, 20-21.

On Apuleius' metaphors from the theater see Heine 1962, 207. See also below 185, 23 *Placuit Thrasyllo scaena feralium nuptiarum*: Thrasyllus does not see through Charite's *scaena*.

ad limam consilii: for *ad* see vdPaardt 1971, 38 on 3, 3 (53, 23) *ad dicendi spatium*. The metaphor derives from the application of *lima* to literary work, cf. Bernhard 1927, 193 who cites Ov. *Tr.* 1, 7, 30 *defuit et scriptis ultima lima meis*; Hor. *Ars* 291 *poetarum limae labor et mora*. *ThLL* s.v. *lima* 1400, 55f. collects the passages in which *lima* is applied to literary work, most of them occurring in poets. In prose e.g. Plin. *Ep.* 5, 10, 3; Quint. *Inst.* 10, 4, 4 and Apul. *Fl.* 9 (11, 2). In the present context *consilii* should be taken as an obj. gen.; cf. Ennod. *Dict.* 9, 5 *magister...ingeniorum lima*.

desiderium petitoris distulit: thus Psyche asks 4, 34 (102, 12) *quid differo, quid detrecto uenientem* (sc. *maritum*). For *petitor* see below on 184, 10.

Tunc inter moras umbra illa misere trucidati Tlepolemi sane cruentam et pallore deformem attollens faciem quietem pudicam interpellat uxoris: "At that time, during the delay, the very shade of the miserably slaughtered Tlepolemus lifted up a face all bloody und ugly in its pallor and disturbed the chaste sleep of his wife." 183, 8-10

The narrator's knowledge of the dream is based on Charite's own information provided at 187, 19 f. See also Introd. 4.2.1.3.

Tunc inter moras: the operative word in the previous sentence was *distulit*.

umbra illa: there is no need for vdVliet's proposal to read *illas umbra*. Nevertheless the conjecture points up a slight difficulty in the interpretation of *illa* since the *umbra* has not been mentioned earlier. Callebat 1968, 278 notes a 'notion de notoriété' in *illa*, which does not explain our difficulty. The linear reader perhaps thinks of hypallage. (→ *illius Tlepolemi*). One may also think of the sub-narrator anticipating his audience's expectation, or the author playing with his readers' literary expectations ('of course at this point Tlepolemus' ghost must appear to Charite'): the situation almost demands the literary topos of the dream: cf. 185, 19 *nutricem istam meam*, the *nutrix* being equally topical, see our comm. ad loc.

89

sane: F. Meursius' *san⟨i⟩e* is seductive, but is it necessary? Though in the *Met. sane* usually has concessive force it also occurs in an affirmative sense e.g. 11, 12 (275, 26); 11, 27 (289, 3). *Sanie* was introduced per conjecturam by Lipsius at 2, 16 (38, 6), but not adopted there by modern editors; it is not attested elsewhere in Apul. Since *sanie*, however attractive the parallelism, does not materially add to the picture, we prefer to retain F's reading, though not without hesitation.

pallore deformem attollens faciem: one topical element in literary dreams is the description of the figure that appears to the dreamer. Tlepolemus' appearance has several parallels. In his list of Vergil's borrowings from earlier poets Macrobius (*Sat.* 6, 2, 18) notes that *A.* 2, 281 f. (*O lux Dardaniae* e.q.s.) had a model in Ennius' *Alexander*: *O lux Troiae, germane Hector/quid ita cum tuo lacerato corpore/miser ? aut qui te sic respectantibus tractauere nobis*? (*Sc.* 69-71 Jocelyn). Our description is to be compared with Verg. *A.* 2, 274-278 (Hector's appearance is described before the speeches start), and in particular with Sychaeus' appearance to Dido, *A.* 1, 353 f.: *ipsa sed in somnis inhumati uenit imago/coniugis ora modis attollens pallida miris;/crudelis aras traiectaque pectora ferro/ nudauit caecumque domus scelus omne retexit*; see also Austin's note ad loc. Not only does 183, 9 (*pallore deformen attollens faciem* – note the rhythmic quality) contain a verbal reminiscence of *A*.1,353 f., but Tlepolemus, like Sychaeus, reveals both the cause of his death and shows its visible marks. Cf. in epic poetry the dream of Alcyone in Ov. *Met.* 11, 686-692 (cf. 654-656: it is to be noted that there the dream-figure is Morpheus assuming the shape of Ceyx, marked by the signs of drowning); Luc. 3, 8 f. (Julia appears to Pompey *accenso furialis...sepulchro*); 7, 764 f.(various dreams of the survivors of Pharsalus); V.Fl. 1, 47-50 (a fictitious dream, but significantly containing the words *lacera...umbra*); Sil. 2, 561 f.; 8, 164 f.; Stat. *Theb.* 2, 89-127; in elegy Prop. 4, 7, 7 f. (Cynthia appears to Propertius as she was placed on the funeral pyre; she accuses Chloris of having brought about her death); Tib. 2, 6, 39 f.; in Statius' *epicedium* on Glaucias (*Silv.* 2, 1, 154 f.), where the link with the wish that one may die intact is obvious (see e.g. *GCA* 1981, 240); in prose Tac. *Ann.* 1, 65 (Caecina sees *Varum sanguine oblitum et paludibus emersum*); Apul. *Met.* 9, 31 (226, 15) *flebilis patris sui facies adhuc nodo reuincta ceruice*.

The notion that the dead continue marked by the causes of death is wide-spread in antiquity (see e.g. Norden on Verg. *A.* 6, 446; 450; 494 f.), but exists side by side with the notion that the dead appear as they were in life (at least in Homer, see Steiner 1952, 26 n.5).

deformem: Heine 1962, 150 f. discusses the repeated occurrence of *deformitas* in Apuleian description with many instances (e.g. 1, 6: 5, 14 (*Socrates*) *ad miseram maciem deformatus*; cf. Thelyphron in 2, 20). See also below 195, 16 with our note.

attollens faciem: together with *interpellat* the expression possibly represents the gesture of someone who is about to speak; cf. 9, 31 (226, 15) *ei per quietem obtulit sese*.

183, 11-16 'Mi coniux – quod tibi prorsus ab alio dici non licebit: etsi pectori tuo iam perman⟨e⟩at nostri memoria, uel acerbae mortis meae casus foedus caritatis intercidit. Quouis alio felicius maritare, modo ne in Thrasylli manum sacrilegam conuenias neue sermonem conferas ne ⟨c⟩ mensam accumbas nec toro adquiescas: " 'My wife – something no one else will be free to call jou: though you still continue to remember me in your heart, the event of my dire death has yet cut through the bond of love. Be married to anyone else in more auspicious circumstances, if only you do not confer yourself upon Thrasyllus' sacrilegious hands nor converse with him, nor lie down at his dinner-table, nor rest in his bed."

Apart from two minor blemishes [1], the text as presented by F faces the reader with some major uncertainties: (1) does the phrase *quod...licebit* qualify *mi coniux* on rather the advice Tlepolemus' ghost is about to give? (2) Do the words *etsi...memoria* convey the notion that Charite still remembers her husband, or rather that this memory is already starting to fade? In both cases *permanat* F presents difficulties. (3). Are the words *uel...intercidit* still dependent on *etsi*, or should they be taken as the apodosis of *etsi...memoria*, with a new sentence starting at *Quouis alio...maritare*?

The uncertainties are interconnected: if one decides that *quod...licebit* qualifies *mi coniux*, the phrase seems to be contradicted by the subsequent *quouis alio felicius maritare*. The measures that have been proposed to solve that contradiction have involved decisions concerning (2) and (3). [2]

(1) Scholars who decide that *quod...licebit* must refer to what follows, with reason attempt to insert a verbum declarandi (thus Helm III[2] and Helm-Krenkel: ⟨*quaeso audias*⟩ *quod* e.q.s.; *quod...non licebit ed*⟨*am*⟩*: si* Frassinetti).

Those who take it with *coniux* either try to give a deprecatory sense to *licebit*: (making the phrase roughly equivalent to *utinam ne liceat*; see Augello 1977, 179) or remove the negative (*dici iam licebit* Robertson), thus trying to remedy the apparent contradiction in *quouis alio...maritare*.

(2) The main problem with the phrase *etsi...memoria* is the fact that *permanare* is never construed with a dative. The history of corrections starts early: *permaneat* φ; *permanet* ς. Many scholars have sought to correct the relationship between the various thoughts by assuming a more serious corruption here, all of them assuming that Charite is here said to be on the way to forgetting her husband. Wiman 1927, 60 and Armini 1928, 310 f. take *permanat* in the sense of 'is ebbing away'; Frassinetti reads *promanat*; Helm III *permarcet*; Giarratano, Helm III[2], Helm-Krenkel and Terzaghi *tuo iam*⟨*non*⟩*permanet*; A.Y. Campbell, followed in part by Robertson *at si...tuo* ⟨*non*⟩ *permansit* (*etsi...permanet* Robertson). This approach is reasonable if *uel...intercidit* contains much the same thought, though presented from the other side. vThiel reads *etsi...nec*; *nec* for *uel* was first proposed by Colvius. This approach is equally reasonable. See further below.

The defence of the tradition undertaken by Wiman and Armini found no real

---

[1] *acerue* was corrected by a later hand; the correction *ne*⟨*c*⟩ occurs in ς
[2] Augello 1977, 178-180 separates his discussion of *mi coniux...licebit* from that of *etsi...memoria*. As a result he does not formulate the main problem.

response since it involves taking *permanare* in the sense of 'trickle away', which is not attested anywhere. On the other hand *perman⟨e⟩at* φ, which is hardly taken seriously in scholarly literature, may go well with *pectori tuo* if *uel* is taken in the sense of *saltem* (cf. Suet., *Nero* 47, 2 *ac, ni flexisset animos, uel Aegypti praefecturam concedi sibi oraret*).

(3) The possibility that *uel...intercidit* may be interpreted as the apodosis after the clause starting with *etsi* has not been considered. This would involve a semicolon or period after *intercidit* and a new sentence starting with *quouis alio*.

The phrase *quod...licebit* is most naturally taken with *Mi coniux*. It may be treated as a kind of parenthesis or even as an aside: the dead Tlepolemus knows what is in store for Charite: she is not going to be anyone else's wife. If he nevertheless says to her 'marry anyone else', this is not so much a suggestion that she should marry, as emphasizing the command not to marry Thrasyllus. The reason he presents sets in motion the series of deceit, vengeance and suicide which will make Charite his *perpetua coniunx* (187, 26).

V. Schmidt prefers Colvius' *nec* for *uel*; palaeographically it is a minor correction. If *nec* is read, the problem whether *quod...licebit* refers to *mi coniux* or rather to what follows is no longer of great importance. Tlepolemus knows that Charite embodies the ideal of the *uniuira* who abhors remarriage. Tlepolemus nevertheless advises her to do so; as her husband he may give this advice, since thus a worse evil, a sacrilegious marriage, is prevented. Schmidt objects to the solution presented above on the grounds that the omniscience of the ghost is not mentioned in the text and with *nec* a definite link is forged between the characterisation of Charite as *uniuira* and her burial at 187, 25 f.: *inunita sepultura...marito perpetuam coniugem reddidere*.

mi coniux: this form of the vocative of het possessive with a femine noun is not attested before Apuleius. See *GCA* 1977, 191; LHSz 1, 463. The nominative *coniu(n)x* is not attested in Apuleius, the vocative *coniux* here only, *coniuga* at 6, 4 (131, 6). See below on 186, 8-9 on the use of *coniux* and *maritus*.

uel acerbae mortis: for the notion *acerba mors* see Ter Vrugt-Lenz 1960.

casus foedus...intercīdit: Castiglioni 1938, 548 f., objecting to the clausula and the use of the verb *intercīdere* in this context, proposed *casu...intercĭdit* 'perished through the event of my death'. He was followed by Giarratano and Terzaghi. However, the spondaic clausula seems quite apt at this juncture and Sen. *Ben.* 7, 19, 8 uses the expression *intercisa iuris humani societas*; cf. also Aug. *Ciu.* 19, 8 *prohibeat...amica conloquia, interdicat amicalem uel intercidat affectum*.

foedus caritatis: cf. e.g. Catul. 64, 373 *accipiat coniunx felici foedere diuam* (in the context of the most famous wedding of ancient mythology).

Quouis alio felicius maritare: in view of the facts that *maritare* may be construed with either an abl. (see *ThLL* s.v. 402, 32) or a dative (*ThLL* ibidem), and that both *quouis* and *alio* may be either dative or ablative (see Neue-Wagener, 2, 487 and 536 and *Met.* 7, 3: 156, 3 with our comm. ad loc.), it is impossible to decide which case was intended by Apuleius. *Maritare* is pass. imperative; the verb occurs here only in the *Met. Felicius*: in contrast with the *casus mortis acerbae*.

modo ne...neue...nec...nec: Callebat 1968, 96 notes that *neue* occurs but rarely in the *Met*. Bernhard 1927, 183 lists several passages in which Apuleius employs a series of special expressions in preference to a single general one, a common type of rhetorical amplification. Here the notion of marriage is dissolved into the wedding and three of its results.

in...manum...conuenias: a common expression for marriage with the legal connotation of *in potestatem uiri uenire*. See *Met*. 6, 24 (146, 25); cf. above 177, 16.

sacrilegam adds a personal characteristic which rather strikingly modifies the legal aspect of the phrase. See Vallette *ad loc.* and *cruentam dexteram* below. The religious term is aptly used by the victim of betrayed friendship, as is *parricidio* (1.17 below).

sermonem conferas: also at 5, 11 (112, 10) where Amor is admonishing Psyche; the expression (first attested in Pl. *Curc.* 290) occurs in Latin of all periods; there appears to be no hint of formality.

mensam accumbas: for *accumbere* with simple acc. cf. Lucil. 452 K (= 443 Marx); Acc. *trag*. 217, then several instances in Apul.: *Met*. 2, 11 (34, 9); 4, 7 (80, 5: see *GCA* 1977, 68); 9, 22 (220, 9: *cenam...adcumbere*): 10, 17 (249, 29 f.).

toro adquiescas: for the dative cf. Catul. 31, 9-10 *labore fessi uenimus larem ad nostrum/desideratoque acquiescimus lecto*. Kirchhoff 1903, 24 proposed *torum*. There is no parallel for *acquiescere* + acc. and there is no reason to depart from a properly supported ms. reading, but the conjecture serves to underline the fact that the symmetry of expression is interrupted by the dative.

Fuge mei percussoris cruentam dexteram. Noli parricidio nuptias auspicari: "Shun the bloody right hand of my slayer. Do not start on a marriage under the auspices of parricide." 183, 16-18

percussoris cruentam dexteram: cf. 7, 11 (162, 28) *illi nescio cui recenti marito...hunc aduenam cruentumque percussorem praeponis?* The similarity of expression may be intentional: the slain Tlepolemus was once disguised as a bloodstained killer himself. It is noteworthy that the narrator of that passage soon proved to be mistaken. For possible doubts concerning Thrasyllus' guilt see Introd. 4.2.1.3.

parricidio: of course the narrator has Tlepolemus use a very strong word to refer to his own murder. At 4, 11 (83, 1 f.) the robbers refuse to kill their leader Lamachus, regarding the deed as an instance of *parricidium*. For the appropriate use of the word in that, and the present, context see *GCA* 1977, 90. See also 7, 3 (156, 6) for an instance of the use of *parricidium* as an exaggeration (*GCA* 1981, 96). It is used in a narrow technical sense of the murder of a close relative 5, 11 (111, 26); 10, 5 (240, 11 and 26; cf. *parricida* 10, 6: 241, 8); cf. the rather enjoyable use of *parricida* by Venus in her castigation of Amor 5, 30 (127, 5) and the comparison at *Apol*. 85 (94, 10 equally enjoyable though for a different reason) *uipera...exeso matris utero in lucem proserpit atque ita parricidio gignitur*.

nuptias auspicari: though *auspicari* is used quite often in the more general sense of 'start on', 'begin with', here the juxtaposition of the three terms (*parricidio, nuptias, auspicari*) guarantees a highly solemn, even awesome warning. *Nuptias auspicari* is not attested elsewhere, but cf. Hier. *Ep.* 22, 19, 2 *ficus folia* (of Adam and Eve) *auspicantia pruriginem nuptiarum*.

183, 18-20 Vulnera illa, quorum sanguinem ⌈tu⌉ae lacrimae proluerunt, non sunt tota dentium uul⌈nera⌉: lancea mali Thrasylli me tibi fecit alienum':"Those wounds whose blood your tears have washed away are not all wounds made by teeth: the spear of evil Thrasyllus has taken me away from you."

For the supplements see our note on 182, 5-10.

quorum...proluerunt: cf. 181, 9 *totam se super corpus effudit. Proluere* in the literal sense of 'wash away' is fairly rare. Cf. Caes. *Civ.* 1, 48, 2 *ex omnibus montibus niues proluit* (sc. *tempestas*); Apul. *Mun.* 23 (159, 17). The rhetorical technique (πάθος) is rather obvious.

tota: see vdPaardt 1971, 121 and e.g. above on 182, 10-14 for *tota = omnia* as commonly in Apuleius. The placement of the word gives it extra emphasis.

dentium uulnera: see 180, 10 *multo dente laniauit*. The similarity of the wounds made by the boar's teeth and Thrasyllus' spear was announced at 180, 16. For the rare subjective genitive with *uulnera* cf. e.g. Verg. *A.* 11, 40 *uolnus/cuspidis Ausoniae*: V.Fl. 6, 653 *Aesoniae uulnus fatale...hastae*.

mali Thrasylli: cf. above 183, 6 *pessimi Thrasylli*; 177, 16 *boni Tlepolemi*. The narrator is obviously concerned to underline the contrast as much as possible; it is hard to decide whether here the personal style of the narrator colours his rendering of Tlepolemus' speech or whether on the contrary the narrator's report, dependent as it is on information provided by Charite (187, 19 f.), takes its clue from Tlepolemus' very words.

me tibi fecit alienum: much the same expression is used when Psyche loses sight of Amor at 5, 25 (122, 17) - not the only link between the two ladies, see e.g. Schlam in *AAGA* 1978, 99. The expression occurs in a similar context in Ov. *Tr.* 4, 3, 67 *nec Semele Cadmo facta est aliena parenti/quod precibus periit ambitiosa suis*.

183, 20-21 ⌈Et addi⌉dit cetera omnemque scaenam sceleris inlumi⌈nat⌉:"And he added the rest and cleared up the entire plot of the crime."

Et addidit cetera: the story had already been told in chapters 4-5; together with the beginning of ch. 14 below this sentence indicates the source of the narrator's wealth of detailed information.

Compare Sychaeus' revelation and subsequent warning to Dido, Verg. *A.* 1, 353-359: see above comm. on 1.9.

omnemque scaenam sceleris: *-que* explicative. Note the alliteration.

scaenam: Callebat 1968, 66 translates 'mise en scène' and notes that Apuleius ordinarily employs *scaena* figuratively. See Heine 1962, 207 on 'Bühnenterminologie'. See also above 183, 6 and below 185, 23.

inluminat: It is by no means clear whether F had *inluminat* or rather *inluminauit*. The evidence of the later mss. points to *inluminat*, but φ, often a trustworthy guide as to readings now lost in F, shows *inluminat* written by a later hand in a lacuna. The evidence, therefore, is not strong. Robertson prints *inluminauit* and notes '*spatium uerbo* inluminauit *aptius*'; his comparative appears to indicate some hesitation. We share the hesitation. For more instances of change of tense see Callebat 1968, 427 f.

CHAPTER IX

Charite reacts to the vision.

184, 1-5 ⌐A⌐t illa, ut primum maesta quieuerat, toro ⌐faciem impressa, et⌐iamnunc dormiens lacrimis ema⌐nantibus genas cohu⌐midat et uelut quo[d]dam tormen⌐to inquieta quieti excussa⌐ luctu redintegrato prolixum he⟨i⟩ula⌐t discissaque interu⌐la decora b⟨ra⟩chia saeuientibus palmulis conuerberat: "But she, just as she had at first fallen asleep in her sadness, with her face pressed into the pillow, even now as she slept moistened her cheeks with welling tears. Then, restless as if through some torment, aroused from her rest, she started to mourn afresh, wailed profusely, tore her undergarment apart and beat her beautiful arms with savage little hands."

at illa: the text is as certain as that of any of the supplements filling the gaps caused by the tear in F's f. 160. The narrator turns his attention to the dreaming woman and her wakening.

ut primum: obviously the combination cannot have the usual meaning 'as soon as', not because of the less than usual pluperfect (e.g. 9,15:213,26 cf. vdPaardt 1971,83 on 3,10 (59,15) and LHSz 2, 626), but because of the subsequent phrase *etiamnunc dormiens*. Médan 1925,148 translates 'étant donné que d'abord' and indeed *primum* must refer back to the *quies pudica* of 183,10; however we prefer to render *ut* more simply with 'just as', cf. e.g. Vallette, Brandt-Ehlers. For a less problematical juxtaposition of *ut* and autonomous *primum* see 5,29 (126,15) *ut primum quidem tuae parentis...praecepta calcares...,uerum etiam* e.q.s.

maesta: Callebat 1968,411 f. notes that replacement of an expected adverb by an adjective contributes to narrative impact and vivacity. He distinguishes between adjectives expressing a modality of the action and those expressing 'une manière d'être du sujet pendant l'action'. In Apuleius the second type, of which we have an instance here, occurs rather more frequently than the first. See Callebat ibid.

quieuerat: Cod. Bertinianus (see Hildebrand LXXIV, the ms. so far has not been identified) had *coniuerat* or *conniuerat* (mistakenly reported by Helm as a conjecture by Bertin). Possibly the reading originated as a gloss on *quieuerat*; in any case there is no reason to adopt it as Pricaeus, Wower and Oudendorp do.

toro faciem impressa: the expression renders a topical situation, cf. Dido at Verg. *A.* 4,659 *dixit, et os impressa toro 'moriemur inultae/sed moriamur' ait* (see also Pease ad loc. on the question whether Dido kisses the couch or rather buries her face in it); Ov. *Met.* 10,410 f. *torumque/ore premens* (sc. Myrrha); Stat. *Theb.* 5,252; V. Fl. 8,9; Petr. 18,1 (*Quartilla*) *lacrimas rursus effudit gemitibusque largis concussa tota facie ac pectore torum meum pressit*. For similarities and contrast between Charite and Dido see Introduction 4.2.3.

etiamnunc dormiens: *etiam* is missing in φ; some of the later mss. read *non* for *nunc*, an emendation possibly occasioned by the belief that people do not shed tears while sleeping. However, Dr. Med. W.D.Müller-Wolf (Hamburg) kindly informs us that this is incorrect. (The references to weeping at 4,27:96,9 and e.g. Art. Dald. 2,60 do not apply here, since they deal with dreamt, not actual, tears.)

lacrimis emanantibus genas cohumidat: Keil and Cornelissen proposed *inundat*, but they were under the impression that F had ...*udat* or ...*ndat*; Robertson reports ...*midat* and thus *cohumidat*, the supplement of the a* group of mss., must stand. The fact that *cohumidare* is attested here only cannot count against it in view of the rather numerous hapax legomena in Apuleius (see Bernhard 1927, 120).

uelut quodam tormento inquieta quieti excussa: *quodam* is an emendation in ς for F's *quoddam*; *quieti* occurs in the best attested supplement. It was equally emended in ς to read *quiete*. Most editors follow ς, which reads more easily than *quieti*. The latter reading, which necessitates combining *quodam tormento inquieta*, a phrase which is then followed by the next stage in waking up, *quieti excussa*, is by no means impossible, and Giarratano-Frassinetti are right in keeping it. For *excutere* with a dative see e.g. Ov. *Met.* 1,155 (*pater omnipotens...*) *excussit subiectae Pelion Ossae*; see *ThLL* s.v. *excutere* 1309,56 and 1310,54. For the notion compare Numa's dream at Ov. *Fast.* 4,667 *excutitur terrore quies*. Juxtaposition of related words is a stylistic device Apuleius loves to use, cf. our note on 198,11 *deformiter...formati*.

luctu redintegrato: cf. 4,27 (95,17) *redintegratur...infortunium meum*; 5,11 (111,23) *simulatos redintegrant fletus*.

prolixum heiulat: F has *heula...la* (or *da*) *decora bc̄hia*, φ shows *heu heu eiulat*. *Discissaque interula decora brachia*, of which the first *heu* was written by the original scribe, the rest added later. The a* group has *(h)eiulat. Discissaque interula decora brachia*. Since the text in φ was added by a 14th cent. hand in an open space, the a* text is our best witness to the original reading in F. In F *interula* was added in the margin. For the rather imaginative addition of *heu* in φ² see Robertson 1924,36. On the adverbial neuter *prolixum* (cf. e.g. 6,2:129,20 *longum exclamat*) see Médan 1925,35; Callebat 1968, 185. The latter author discusses ibid. 408 the picturesque use of the word *prolixus* as well as the expressive verb *heiulare*. The derivation of *heiulare* (to cry '*heï*'; cf. *uapulare* 'to cry *uah*') is discussed in Hofmann, *LU*³1951,10 f.

interula: the subst. (cf. *Fl.* 9:12,9 *tunicam interulam* ex coni.) occurs here for the first time. The word remains rare; see e.g. Tert. *Pall.* 5,3. On the garment see Blümner 1911, 229 and Vallette ad loc.

decora brachia saeuientibus palmulis conuerberat: the spelling of *bracchium/ brachium* wavers both in general and in Apuleius. Here F's compendium *bc̄hia* and unanimous *brachia* in a* and φ² coincides with the most usual spelling in the Apuleian tradition, which shows *-cch-* only at 8,27 (198,17 f.). *ThLL* regards *bracchium* as both the older and more correct form, but there is no reason to assume severe spelling consistency on the part of ancient authors.

Cf.also Introd. 5.3. Cornelissen 1888,21 f. proposed *ubera* for *brachia*, arguing that women in mourning did not beat their lower arms. The expression as such, however, is supported by Sen. *H.O.* 1876 *centum populi bracchia pulsent*. The phrase carefully elaborates the contrast between beauty and savage treatment; the hypocoristic diminutive *palmulis*, placed between *saeuientibus* and *conuerberat* is clearly designed to arouse pity (cf. Abate 1978,58). *Conuerberare* is rare (*ThLL* lists in addition to our passage only *Met.* 9,40:233,30; Sen. *Ira* 3,19,5; *Ep.* 121,4; Curt. 7,2,5; Plin. *Nat.* 13,126; Suet. *Nero* 42; *Mul. Chir.* 766) and underscores the savagery.

184, 5-9 Nec tamen cum quoquam participatis nocturnis imaginibus, sed indicio facinoris prorsus dissimulato et nequissimum percussorem punire et aerumnabili uitae sese subtrahere tacita decernit: "Nevertheless she did not share her visions of the night with anyone, but kept the information concerning the deed wholly hidden and silently decided both to punish the wicked slayer and to depart from her mournful life."

Like Dido in Verg. *A.* 4, 456 (*hoc uisum nulli, non ipsi effata sorori* cf. ibid. 474 f.) Charite hides her vision and the decision resulting from it. See also below on *tacita decernit*.

cum quoquam participatis nocturnis imaginibus: this construction of *participare* in the sense of 'to share the knowledge of' is exceptional. Plautus usually has *participare aliquem* with gen., *de* or indir. quest. Cf. e.g. Pl. *St.* 33 with Petersmann ad loc. For the present construction, more common with tangible objects, see e.g. 9,24 (221,14) *mensam nobiscum secura participat*.

nocturnis imaginibus: at 11,27 (288,27) Lucius' *nocturna imago* is confirmed by an encounter the next morning. No such confirmation is forthcoming here. For *imagines*, common as a term for dream visions, see also 1,18 (16,16).

nequissimum percussorem: Apuleius has a rich vocabulary for pejorative characterisation with several intensive superlatives, of which *nequissimus* is the most frequent; see Callebat 1968, 399 f.; the present term depends on 183,16 *fuge mei percussoris cruentam dexteram*.

aerumnabili uitae: on Apuleius' penchant for *aerumna* and cognate words see 198,10 with our note and Tatum 1969, 45 n. 100.

sese subtrahere: the decision to commit suicide when the beloved husband or wife has died is a common motif in the ancient novel. See the forthcoming study by B. Wesseling.

decernit: in the narrator's presentation the *lima consilii* of 183,7 is discarded by Charite because of her dream vision. It is obvious that both Charite and the narrator unquestioningly accept the message of the dream. Nevertheless in interpreting the present section of the novel one may well wonder whether the author intends the reader to remember the doubts cast on the veracity of dreams by the *anus* at 4,27(96,5-14); see *GCA* 1977, 205 ad loc. For some of the problems involved see Introd. 4.2.1.3.

184, 9-11 Ecce rursus † imperor uide † uoluptatis detestabilis petitor aures obseratas de nuptiis obtundens aderat: "Lo and behold, again the detestable seeker ?of blind lust? was there to batter her locked ears about marriage."

Ecce: see Callebat 1968, 423, and in particular Heine 1962, 174 n. 1 who notes a theatrical element. See also *GCA* 1981,27 on 6,25 (147,6 f.) and ibid. 65, on 6,30(152,7 f.).

imperor uide: thus F; *impetor uide* φ; *improuidae* ς; *improuide* A. It is hard to choose between the many, sometimes very attractive, solutions proposed by generations of scholars. *Improuidae* is accepted by Robertson, Giarratano, Terzaghi, Frassinetti, Augello. Helm III[2] accepts *improuide* (cf. Helm-Krenkel). We cite a selection of conjectures: *Impetu turbidae* Luetjohann, *impetu toruidae* Koziol, *impetu auido* Bluemner, *impetu rabidae* Purser, all of them starting from the reading in φ (possibly influenced by *petitor*?). Cornelissen (*impiae et horridae*) and, more clearly, Helm (*nuper feruide*) take the reading in F as their base, as does Wiman who proposes *imperio orbidae* (taking *orbidae* in the sense of 'blind' with a reference to Cicero's *caeca cupiditas*: if the hapax legomenon *orbidus* is to be accepted, *uoluptatis* should be taken as a personification). This list might easily be increased (e.g. *imperio auidae*, *imperio rabidae* etc.). Though aware of the difficulty that if we read *improuide* or *improuidae* it is hard to account for the corruption, we prefer those to the other solutions. For *improuide* Helm (Addenda, 300) cites 3,6 (56,15) *improuide occurrentem* and 4,12 (84,4) *improuide conantem*: in both passages the adverb means 'heedlessly'. Whether it should be taken with *obtundens* or with *aderat* (or even *petitor*) may be no more than an academic question. Equally possible, and in view of the balance of the sentence perhaps slightly preferable, is *improuidae uoluptatis* (*detestabilis* to be taken with *petitor*). For *improuidus* = 'unheeding', 'blind' see 2,27 (47,5) *infausti ac improuidi sermonis*; cf. vdPaardt 1971,139 f. on 3,18 (65,20). This type of *uoluptas* in addition is in full accord with Thrasyllus' *imprudentia* of 182,19. The obeli indicate our desire to avoid a *labes imprudentiae*.

uoluptatis: in view of the uncertainty of the text it is not clear whether the word was qualified by a preceding adjective or by the subsequent *detestabilis*. Helm-Krenkel take *improuide* with *petitor* ('ohne jede Vorsicht seiner abscheulichen Lust nachjagend'). For *uoluptas* in the character of Thrasyllus as described see above 177,5 f., 178,5 f., in the *Met*. in general e.g. Tatum 1969, 167, Schlam in *AAGA* 1978, 95 f., 100.

detestabilis: if *improuidae* is read, the adjective must be taken with *petitor*. No etymological pun can be detected here as at 188,19 below (but see vdPaardt in *SAG* 1981,24); if we read *improuide*, the *uoluptas* is qualified as *detestabilis*.

petitor: cf. the expression *nuptiarum petitor* at 4,32 (100,6), without *nuptiarum* in the meaning 'suitor' above 183,7; *Apol*. 70 (78,21) and Sen. in Aug. *Ciu*. 6,10 (= frg. 39 Haase).

aures obseratas: the metaphor occurs also Hor. *Epod*. 17,53 (cf. Catul. 55,21 *obseres palatum*) V. Max. 6,5,5; 7,3 ext. 6, and in several Christian authors, see ThLL s.v. *obsero* 190,66 f.

de nuptiis: cf. 182,19 with comm. ad loc.

aures...aderat: Ruiz de Elvira 1954,116 notes a contamination between two phrases *obtundens uerbis de nuptiis* and *loquens de nuptiis obtundebat aures*. However *aures obtundere* occurs as early as Pl. *Cist.* 118, and in Cicero the verb, with or without *aures*, is used repeatedly of verbal violence. Cf. *Met.* 9,23 (220,27) *uxor...non cessat optundere, totam...fabulam promeret*. There is little sense, then, in using the term contamination to characterise the present phrase. *Obtundens*: possibly with final nuance, see LHSz 2,387 for final nuance with present participle.

184, 11-13 Sed illa clementer aspernata sermonem Thrasylli astuque miro personata instanter garrienti summisseque deprecanti: "But she mildly rejected Thrasyllus' words and playing her role with marvellous address (said) as he chattered pressingly and pleaded obsequiously:"

At this point the change in Charite's attitude expresses itself for the first time in her activity. Heine 1962, 207 notes the importance of the theatrical terms for the 'Maskendasein der Personen'. He also underscores the fact that the course taken by Charite almost mechanically leads to her own perdition (ibid. p. 240). See also Junghanns 1932,74 n. 111 concerning play-acting in the *Met.* (cf. *GCA* 1981,111 on Haemus' tale) and Schlam 1968,41 on the functioning of tales of trickery in the *Met.*

clementer aspernata: at 183,2 Charite *uocem nefandam et horruit et detestata est*; the fact that she rejects Thrasyllus' proposal in a mild manner here is due to her *astus*. *Aspernari* is not always used as a very strong word (at 1,17 : 15,23 it is qualified by *uehementer*; 1,23 : 21,16 f. *qui non est aspernatus...hospitium tenue* seems to imply no more than a simple rejection; cf. however 3,29 : 73,18) and it is unnecessary to assume a heavy oxymoron.

astuque miro: Heine 1962,240 notes the frequency of *mirus* in the *Met.* It may be regarded as a key-word, the world of the *Met.* being full of elements provoking astonishment. See also ibid. 180 concerning the rich vocabulary of amazed and stupefied reaction. Cf. also Scobie 1969, 46-54 on the thematic significance of 1,1 (1,6) *ut mireris*. Here the narrator's reaction is comparable to that at 10,4 (239,13 f.) *mulier ficta qualibet causa confestim marito miris persuadet artibus*. The term *astu* is emphatically repeated at the end of the story: *quoque astu Thrasyllum inductum petisset* (187,20).

personata: the same sense, but in malam partem, at 10,5 (240,15) *personata* (sc. dira femina) *nimia temeritate*. On *persona* see Fuhrmann 1979, 83-106.

instanter garrienti: the expression obviously picks up *aures obtundens* of the previous phrase. For *garrire* see 3,20 (67,12) and 9,22 (219,15), cf. *Fl.* 17 (33,8) where the word is used of *lusciniae*. Here it must denote rapid, continuous talk rather than inconsequential babbling.

summisse: the adverb occurs only here in Apuleius, cf. for *summissus* 9,40 (233,25) *simulansque sese ad commouendam miserationem genua...uelle contingere, summissus atque incuruatus*. The words *summisse deprecanti*, hardly in character for Thrasyllus as he is described by the narrator, indicate that he, too, is playing a role. There is some development of strategy after 182,18 f.

'Adhuc', inquit, 'tui fratris meique karissimi mariti facies pulch- 184, 14-17
ra illa in meis deuersatur oculis, adhuc odor cinnameus ambrosei
corporis per nares meas percurrit, adhuc formonsus Tlepolemus
in meo uiuit pectore: "'As yet that beautiful face of your brother and my
husband – most beloved as he was – still lingers in my eyes, as yet the cinnamon
fragrance of his ambrosial body wafts through my nostrils, as yet the comely
Tlepolemus is alive in my heart."

tui fratris: Callebat 1968,74 notes the expressiveness of this term of
friendship. In the present instance there is no doubt a reference to 181,18 where
Thrasyllus was reported to have used the term in his mourning. There the
narrator insisted on Thrasyllus' simulation, here the repetition of the term
enhances Charite's hidden purpose.

karissimi: F has kr̃mi, cf. 7,3 (156,5) *karissimū*. In our previous volume we
printed *carissimum*. However, *ThLL* s.v. *carus* 502,37 f. notes that there is
ample evidence for *karus*. In view of our rule of thumb (Introd. 5.3) we now
prefer to follow F. See also Sommer 1914,28 f.

facies pulchra illa: in marked contrast with Tlepolemus' *cruentam et pallore
deformen...faciem* (183,9). *Pulchra* here positive (cf. 3,23:69,14), usually
comparative or superlative in the *Met.*, and often ironic cf. Callebat 1968, 383.
Illa is emphatic and laudatory, see Callebat 1968, 275 f. See also below on
186,29 *uacuam faciem*.

in meis deuersatur oculis: for *deuersari* ('stay', 'dwell in') see e.g. *GCA* 1977,76
on 4,9 (81,8), *GCA* 1981, 93 on 7,2 (155,24).

odor cinnameus ambrosei corporis: note the chiastic word order. The phrase
may be read at two levels. At the level of the rôle Charite is now playing, she
refers to the living Tlepolemus and in this context it should be noted that
cinnameus (a rare adjective which apart from the *Met.* occurs in Aus.
Griph.Tern.Num. 17 (154 Prete) only) is used at 2,10 (33,15) in a sexual context.
Cf. 5,13 (113,21) where Psyche uses it of Amor's hair. At 10,29 (260,11) Lucius'
desired roses (curiously enough) spread *cinnameos odores*. The word *ambroseus*
(Apuleius is the first prose author to employ the adjective and, according to
ThLL s.v. 1867, 69, the only one to use forms with -*e*- rather than -*i*-) is also
used at least once in a sexual context (10,22: 253,16). Nevertheless the phrase as
a whole reminds the reader of the well-known fragrance of exalted persons and
divine beings. Among mortals Alexander was known for his fragrant body cf.
Plu. *Alex.* 4,4 (666 B-C), see Hamilton ad loc.; *Qu.Conv.* 1,6 (623 E); for
another mortal with a similar characteristic see *Def. or.* 421 B (cf. Nilsson *GGR*
2 (1961), 529). In the case of divine beings, in particular in a context of
epiphany, the topos is widespread. See e.g. Hom. *h.Cer.* 277 f. with Richardson
ad loc.; E. *Hipp.* 1392 with Barrett ad loc.; Verg. *G*.4,415; *A*.1,403; 12,419; Ov.
Fast. 5,376 with Bömer ad loc. and, of course, Isis at *Met.* 11,4 (269,10) *spirans
Arabiae felicia germina* with Harrauer ad loc. who refers to Lohmeyer 1919. Cf.
also Pfister in *RE* Suppl. 4,316; Kötting 1982. The reader is therefore justified
in suspecting a secondary level at which Charite chooses language which fits in
very well with her deification of Tlepolemus as described in the previous
chapter.

per nares meas percurrit: *percurrit* F; *re*- F in marg.; the marginal annotation is written by the same hand. Such marginal annotations deserve careful consideration, but it is not always clear whether they are to be seen as variants or as corrections. *Recurrit* was defended by Castiglioni 1938,550: Robertson's judgment is: 'fortasse recte'; it was adopted by Giarratano and Terzaghi and Augello 1977,181 who follows Paratore 1942,184 n. 50 in regarding *percurrit* as less in accordance with Apuleian grammar and usage. Indeed *percurro* is attested only here in Apuleius, whereas *recurro* occurs a number of times. On the other hand *OLD* cites no instances of *recurrere per*. Since moreover Apuleius' vocabulary includes many words, which, though common in Latin, he uses only once, there seems to be no compelling reason to adopt the marginal reading.

Charite's speech starts with a carefully phrased period showing cola of decreasing length (*Adhuc – oculis* 31, *adhuc – percurrit* 23, *adhuc – pectore* 17 syllables), varied clausulae, varied word order: each colon starts with a reference to Tlepolemus which is followed by a reference to Charite; the references to Tlepolemus show respectively genitive-nominative, nominative-genitive, nominative, those to Charite possessive-verb-noun, noun-possessive-verb, possessive-verb-noun. Anaphoric *adhuc* (cf. 182, 17 f.) introduces verbs of climactic force.

184, 17-185,4 Boni ergo et optimi consules, si luctui legitimo miserrimae feminae necessarium concesseris tempus, quoad residuis mensibus spatium reliquum compleatur anni, quae res cum meum pudorem, tum etiam tuum salutare commodum respicit, ne forte inmaturitate nuptiarum indignatione iusta manes acerbos mariti ad exitum salutis tuae suscitemus': "You will do well, therefore, very well indeed, if you allow a most unhappy woman the necessary time for her legitimate mourning, until the remaining part of the year is filled by the residual months: that matter regards not only my modesty, but also the preservation of your well-being, lest perchance through an untimely marriage we arouse the ghost of my husband – angered in just indignation – so as to put an end to your life'."

boni...et optimi consules: ThLL gives no further instances of the combination *boni et optimi*; the expression may be ascribed to a general penchant for abundance on the part of Apuleius, but here the abundance may also characterise the careful styling of Charite's simulated speech of encouragement (cf. her speech in ch. 12 below). The construction *boni consulere, si* occurs from Sen. *Ep.* 75,6 onwards. See also Sinko 1903,261 f., who relates the combination *bonum et optimum* to the well-known καλὸν κἀγαθόν. For the adverbial gen. see LHSz 2,71.

luctui legitimo miserrimae feminae: the chiastic word-order (also in the next colon *residuis mensibus spatium reliquum*), in combination with the assonance, further increases the impression of a carefully meditated speech. The word *legitimo* remains slightly ambivalent; its juxtaposition with *miserrimae* argues for 'legitimate', 'justifiable'; the subsequent colon, however, for 'fixed by law'.

tempus, quoad. . .compleatur: Callebat 1968,346 f. discusses the distribution of *quoad* followed by indicative and subjunctive (8 and 24 instances respectively). Most, but not all of the instances of the subjunctive construction show 'une nuance finale'.

spatium reliquum. . .anni: in referring to the customary period of mourning Charite mentions a year. Usually that period is fixed at 10 months (cf. *Dig.* 3,2,11,1, a passage which mentions the notion *legitimum tempus* and continues *uir. . .solet elugeri propter turbationem sanguinis* in connection with a possible pregnancy, and e.g. Sen. *Helv.* 16,1 *decem mensum spatium*, though Sen. applies the notion in a different sense), but *Cod.Iust.* 5,9,2 adds two months: *Si qua ex feminis perdito marito intra anni spatium alteri festinauit innubere (paruum enim temporis post decem menses seruandum adicimus, tametsi id ipsum exiguum putemus), probrosis inusta notis honestioris nobilisque personae et decore et iure priuetur.* See Norden 1912,121 f.; Vallette's note on the present passage; Summers 1967,269; Helm-Krenkel 413.

quae res. . .respicit: the phrasing seems rather heavy; in fact *res* summarizes the preceding description of the situation and thus is to be regarded as a repetition of the antecedent within the relative clause. The construction is relatively frequent in the archaising authors of the 2nd cent. and particularly frequent in juridical Latin, see LHSz 2,563.

meum pudorem: *pudor* in the sense of respect for public opinion fits the simulated encouragement.

salutare commodum: though *salus* and *commodum* occur in juxtaposition, the present combination is hard to parallel. Bernhard 1927, 175 is hardly right, however, in noting a redundancy: *salutare* adds to *commodum* the aspect which is elaborated in the final colon.

inmaturitate nuptiarum: the rarity of the word *inmaturitas* (in Apuleius it occurs here only, before him it is attested at Cic. *Quinct.* 82 and Suet. *Aug.* 34,2) further adds to the solemn style. We do not think there is a hidden reference to a possible pregnancy here since that notion is not hinted at anywhere in the text. The two causal ablatives are not placed in asyndetic juxtaposition as Médan 1925,338 suggests, but the present phrase gives the reason either for *indignatione*, which in turn gives the reason for *acerbos*, or for *suscitemus*.

manes acerbos: cf. 188,4 *infesti Manes*. It has proved impossible to turn up a parallel for the combination. The word *acerbus* rather often refers to a cruel or embittered person, even more often to a death experienced as bitter by the survivors. If the first sense is the most obvious one here, the second may well play a sub-surface role.

exitum: F. Helm, Robertson and others print *exit⟨i⟩um* with ς. Armini 1932,87 argues in favour of *exitum*. For the reverse situation at 188,2 see comm. ad loc. *ThLL* s.v. *exitus* 1532,7 f. notes confusion with *exitium* in the mss.; the present passage is listed under *exitium* 1531,32. There is no need for *exitium*. Cf. e.g. Sen. *Ira* 3,16,4 *Habuit. . .quem debuit exitum*; Val. Max. 5,1,3; Ulp. *Dig.* 3,2,11,3 *post huiusmodi exitum mariti*; Cypr. *Laps.* 30 *Si quem de tuis carum mortalitatis exitu perdidisses, ingemesceres dolenter et fleres.*

salutis: the choice of the word is doubtless influenced by *salutare commodum* above. Together the words acquire an ominous sound. The reader is aware of the fact that Charite intends to punish the murderer (184,8), but so far has no inkling of her method.

Chapter X

Charite seems to yield and allows herself to be persuaded into a rendez-vous.   185, 5-8

Nec isto sermone Thrasyllus sobriefactus uel saltem tempestiua pollicitatione recreatus identidem pergit linguae satia⟨n⟩ti⟨s⟩ susurros improbos inurguere, quoad simulanter reuicta Charite suscipit: "But Thrasyllus was not sobered by these words nor even comforted by the postponed promise. Again and again to satiety he kept urging Charite with shameless whispers of his tongue until, apparently giving in, she answered:"

isto: Callebat 1968, 273 points out the anaphoric use of *isto*; see also *GCA* 1977, 166.

sobriefactus: Médan 1925, 134 and Bernhard 1927, 139 speak of a neologism. The material of the *ThLL* offers no other occurrence of this word. We think that the metaphor should be brought out in the translation and therefore do not agree with Médan 1925, 134 'rendu sage' or Vallette 'sans vouloir entendre raison'. Our author seems to use the word with real point: Thrasyllus, who was already 177, 7 depicted as *diurnis potationibus exercitatus*, is drunk with love, and *nec...sobriefactus* points forward to the lethal drunkenness awaiting him 186, 2: the wine with the sleeping-draught which will mean his death. See also Heine 1962, 240 n. 2.

tempestiua: the translations vary: 'hope for the future' (Butler), 'hopeful promise' (Gaselee), 'quella promessa che rimandava la cosa a tempo debito' (Augello), 'de belofte van het ogenblik' (Schwartz), alii aliter. Apuleius uses the adjective a few times: 4, 17 (87, 22) *cibum* ('on schedule'); 177, 19 *occasionem* ('suitable occasion', see our comm. ad loc.); 193, 9 *uiae* ('at the right moment'); 9, 15 (214, 2) *prandio*; *Fl.* 15 (23, 16) *haud minus oportuni silentii laudem quam tempestiuae uocis testimonium consecutus* ('approbation pour l'à propos de mes discours', Vallette). Also *Apol.* 47 (54, 21) *conuiuium*; *Pl.* 2, 25 (130, 9) *ipsorum conubiorum quaeritur tempestiua coniunctio* ('le moment favorable', Beaujeu); *Mun.* 29, 24 (166, 4) *imbres*; See also *Apol.* 23(27, 18). With all its different gradations the fundamental meaning is 'what is in keeping with or appropriate to the circumstances (*tempora*)'. Charite requested 184, 18 *luctui legitimo...necessarium...tempus* in order that Tlepolemus' shade would not be incensed *inmaturitate nuptiarum* (185, 2). The *pollicitatio tempestiua* is the promise which takes this term, required by the circumstances, into consideration, hence our translation.

recreatus; its meaning must be weaker than that of *sobriefactus* in view of *uel saltem*, which contains a restriction. Thrasyllus is not refreshed or fortified by Charite's promise, given 184, 19-20, just as Psyche 5, 5 (107, 6) *nec cibo nec ulla denique refectione recreata*. More and more he becomes obsessed by his infatuation.

linguae satiantis: *linguę satiati* F (both words deleted by a different hand, at least according to Robertson and Frassinetti; according to Helm only *satiati* has been deleted). All editors consider this corrupt and numerous emendations have been proposed. Beroaldus: *linguae sauciantis* (followed by Gaselee); Colvius: *linguae satiantis* (followed by Giarratano; Frassinetti; Helm 1955, 300; Scazzoso); Hildebrand: *lacientis linguae*, Beyte: *linguae salacis*; vdVliet: *linguae lactantis*; Leo: *languidae satiati*; Blümner: *linguae astutia*; Brakman, Walter: *linguae fatuantis*; Kronenberg: *lingua satianti* (followed by Robertson, Terzaghi, Brandt-Ehlers, Helm-Krenkel, vThiel, Augello 1977, 181-182); Helm 1, 2, and 3: *lingua aestuanti*. The only one who attempts to defend the reading of F is Armini 1928, 311 f. Taking *satiati* as a dative of *satias* and *linguae* as a genitive, he paraphrases: 'linguae abundanti, linguae usque ad satietatem loquenti.' It is true that the noun *satias* occurs frequently, starting with Accius *ap.* Non. 172, 7 *satias sanguinis*; Lucr. 2, 1038 *fessus satiate uidendi* (5, 39 *ad satiatem terra ferarum/...scatit*); later e.g. Liv. 25, 23, 16 *uini satias* (30, 3, 4 *amoris*). However, no examples can be found for a combination like *satias linguae* in the meaning Armini wishes to attach to it; therefore we do not accept his proposal. Colvius' emendation is closest to F. Thus, *linguae satiantis* depends on *susurros*: whisperings of a tongue that never leaves off, that wears the other person out. That a tongue is able to whisper is elucidated by Ov. *Met.* 7, 824 *temerarius index/Procrin adit linguaque refert audita susurra*, where *susurrus* is used as an adjective; cf. the only other passage where this is the case: Ps. Hilar. *Hymn.* 2, 86 *adsensi numquam grunnienti Simoni/fauce susurra* (*aure* PJO). Kronenberg's proposal is more radical because in *lingua satianti* the first word is emended as well; also, 'whispering with the tongue' seems to us somewhat less expressive than 'whispering of the tongue'. For these reasons and in view of the Ovid passage we prefer Colvius' proposal.

satiantis: after *aures...obtundens* (184, 10), *identidem*, and *pergit* we have in *satiantis* another expression of Thrasyllus' persistent, irksome urging. *Satiare* occurs several times in the *Met.*, not only in an obvious combination like *cibo satio* (1, 7 : 6, 19) but also in a figurative sense like 5, 9 (110, 2) *haec autem nouissima* (viz. Psyche, the youngest) *quam fetu satiante postremus partus effudit*. This is the only occurrence in Apul. of the present participle; *satiatus* is found frequently.

susurros: here of the second declension, but *Fl.* 17 (32, 8) *susurru*. This variation is Apuleian; see Callebat 1968, 122.

improbos: often with an erotic connotation; cf. 7, 21 (170, 8) with our comm. ad loc.

inurguere: Apuleius shares the use of compounds instead of simple verbs 'mit den Altlateinern' (Bernhard 1927, 121). This verb – meaning '*sollicitando ingerere*'–occurs Lucr. 5, 1035 (*uitulus cornibus*) *iratus petit atque infestus inurget*; Zeno *Sermones* 2, 38 (*in conuiuio*) *obrutum pectus saepe crudis atque acidis uomitibus inurguetur*; the only other occurrence (except for our passage) may be *Met.* 5, 6 (108, 1) *imprimens oscula suasoria et inurguens* (conj. Traube, *ingerens* F) *uerba mulcentia*. (The mss. reading *ir*urgeri* at 9, 15:214, 2 is generally emended to *irrogari*.) For the form *inurguere* instead of *inurgēre* cf. Sommer 1914, 188, who mentions an inscription (to be dated around 148 *A.D.*) which reads *urguerer* instead of *urgerer* (see also LHSz 1, 152). Observe that a little later (185, 12) the simple verb *metiatur* is used rather than the expected compound; see or comm. ad loc.

simulanter: the material of the *ThLL* shows that this adverb is attested only here. *Simulate* is found before Apuleius, e.g. Cic. *N.D.* 2, 168; *simulans* from Cic. *Sest.* 118 onward, who mentions a *fabula togata* by L. Afranius titled *Simulans*. So one cannot call *simulanter* a neologism, as does Médan 1925, 124. Charite plays a part, pretends to be a different person from the one she really is, as Tlepolemus had done in his role of Haemus and Thrasyllus in his role of family friend. See our comm. on 178, 2 *mentiri* and on 185, 23 *scaena* and the theatrical metaphor, all of which fit into the play of masks, cf. Heine 1962, 197 f. After all, we are dealing with a story called *Metamorphoses*.

reuicta: the apparent result of Thrasyllus' *lingua satians*.

suscipit: cf. e.g. 2, 29 (49, 8) *suscipit ille de lectulo* with de Jonge ad loc.

'Istud equidem certe magnopere deprecanti concedas necesse est 185, 8-12 mihi, Thrasylle, ut interdum taciti clandestinos coitus obeamus nec quisquam persentiscat familiarium, quo ⟨a⟩d dies reliquos metiatur annus': " 'This at least you must grant me at my urgent request, Thrasyllus, that in the meantime we meet quietly and secretly and that no one in my house gets wind of it until the year brings the remaining days to a conclusion'."

equidem: in Apul. often used for *quidem*; cf. 7, 15 (165, 18) with *GCA* 1981, 180 ad loc.

interdum: synonymous with *interim* and *interea*, as in ten of the thirteen cases in the *Met.*; see Callebat 1968, 323 and e.g. 7, 11 (162, 21) with *GCA* 1981,154 ad loc., where further literature is mentioned.

(inter)dum taciti...obeamus makes a hexameter, as was pointed out by Schober 1904, 10 and Médan 1925, 268. At 178, 19-20 *oro...quorsum* the hexameter was in the middle of a sentence, here we must actually split a word *(interdum)* in order to obtain a 'verse'.

necesse est mihi is the obvious emendation by φ of *nec ecce ē m̃* in F (*mihi* depends on *concedas*). It does not seem necessary to read with Gruterus *mi* instead of *mihi* (Oudendorp follows this reading, too, in preference to his second suggestion *mihi, mi Thrasylle*; Helm's app. crit. is here imprecise), since *mi* as a dative occurs in Apuleius only once (202, 14) in the fixed phrase *mi ausculta* (attested from Pl. *Cas.* 204 onward).

clandestinos: see our comm. on 178, 10.

persentiscat: also found 194, 18 *dulcem ac mellitum corporis nidorem persentiscunt*, *Fl.* 12 (17, 7) and *P.* 1, 13 (97, 19). First attested Pl. *Am.* 527 *nunc ne legio persentiscat, clam illuc redeundum est mihi*, after Lucr. 3, 249 it is not found until Apul.

quoad: *qd̄* F, emend. ς, quite obviously. *Quoad*, which frequently occurs in Apul., has a final connotation when construed with a subjunctive (see Callebat

1968, 347): 'waiting until', 'in order that meanwhile'. Cf. also 184, 19 *quoad residuis mensibus spatium reliquum compleatur anni.*

metiatur: vdVliet 1887, 145 wanted to read *emetiatur* or *permetiatur* on account of 6, 1 (129, 9) *iamque nauiter emensis celsioribus iugis*; 9, 42 (235, 29) *emensis protinus scalis*; 188, 21 *siluosi montis asperum permensi iugum*; 11, 6 (271, 1) *spatium saeculi tui permensus.* But the simple verb *metiri* can be used in the required meaning, though *ThLL* s.v. 888, 3 mentions only two passages in addition to this one: Ov. *Met.* 8, 565 *iamque duas lucis partes Hyperione menso* and Cypr. Gall. *Heptateuchus Gen.* 1492 *(Joseph) postquam iam centum triuerat annos/atque decem, iuncti metitus tempora leti.*

185, 13-16 Promissioni fallaciosae mulieris oppressus subcubuit Thrasyllus et prolixe consentit de furtiuo concubitu noctemque et opertas exoptat ultro tenebras uno potiundi studio postponens omnia: "Overwhelmed, Thrasyllus gave in to the woman's deceitful promise. Eagerly he agrees on a covert union and longs himself, too, for the night and deep darkness. Everything had to give way to one thing: the desire of possessing her".

fallaciosae: in addition to this passage and 9, 6 (207, 4) *mulier fallaciosa* (the generally accepted conjecture of Pricaeus) this word is only found Gel. 6, 3, 34 *usum esse Catonem...argumentis...uafris ac fallaciosis* and 14, 1, 34 *ambages fallaciosae (Chaldaeorum).* Callebat 1968, 388 says therefore that Apul. seems to have borrowed the word directly from Gellius. Gargantini 1963, 38 classifies it among 'aggettivi di sua creazione'. Cf. also Ernout 1949, 83, who discusses the group of adjectives in *-osus*, which in their turn are derived from adjectives. The translators – among whom Callebat loc. cit. – connect *fallaciosae* with *promissioni* in spite of 207,4. In view of the position of the adjective between two nouns, taking it ἀπὸ κοινοῦ seems at least arguable, even if in our translation we take it with *promissioni*. If it is connected with *mulieris*, it contradicts the meaning of the name Charite (see Hijmans in *AAGA* 1978, 116). By the use of this adjective, incidentally, the narrating *iuuenis* entirely takes the point of view that Thrasyllus must have had afterwards, and betrays that he knows the outcome of the rendezvous. Elsewhere in his report the *iuuenis* gives evidence of a great sympathy for Charite and emphasizes her *masculi animi* (186, 6) and *anima uirilis* (187, 24). Cf. our comm. on 185, 26 *tandem*.

oppressus: we learn from the *OLD* that *oppressus* usually takes an instrumental ablative. But *oppressus* does occur by itself, e.g. Cic. *Mur.* 14, 31 *quam laudem ille Africa oppressa cognomine ipso prae se ferebat*; *Dom.* 10, 26 *oppressa captaque republica.* Thus there is no reason to read with Kronenberg *promissione*; *promissioni* depends on *subcubuit*.

prolixe: the adjective is mentioned by vdPaardt 1971, 179 and *GCA* 1977, 23. In the passages 3, 24 (70, 14) and 4, 2 (75, 24) it means 'wide' or 'lavishly' (cf. 4, 1:74, 12 *sermo prolixus*; 199, 15 and 10, 4 : 239, 4, where the adjective, too, has this meaning). Here the adverb means 'wholeheartedly, eagerly', as in Cic. *Att.* 7, 14, 2 *in quo (sc. dilectu) parum prolixe respondent Campani coloni*; 16, 6, 6 *ut...libenter, prolixe, celeriter facias.* This is the only occurrence of this meaning in the *Met.*

consentit: after the perfect *subcubuit* the story continues in the present tense. This is not uncommon for our author; cf. e.g. 177, 5 *erat* and 6 *fuit* with our comm. ad loc. and 179, 13 *interficit* and 14 *transabiit*. For the meaning 'to agree upon' cf. Cic. *Vat.* 23 *nos qui de communi salute consentimus*.

de furtiuo...opertas: these words, too, make a complete hexameter as in 185, 10 (Schober 1904, 10).

concubitus: 'sexual intercourse', as e.g. Pl. *Am.* 1136 *concubitu grauidam feci filio*; also *Met.* 5, 18 (117, 8); 10, 34 (265, 14) etc. Summers 1967, 271 remarks with reference to our passage that '*concubitus* is not well defined by the jurists, but it is cohabitation as in the case of concubinage as opposed to marriage'. We suspect that Thrasyllus was not very much concerned with exact juridical definitions but had a most concrete goal in mind.

noctemque et opertas...tenebras: again a case in which the second noun is a specification of the first; cf. Bernhard 1927, 166.

opertas: cf. Stat. *Theb.* 10, 18 *dux noctis opertae* (i.e. *obscurae*).

ultro: shows how much Thrasyllus is overcome by desire: Charite is not the only one to wish that night will come soon – but their motives are definitely not the same.

potiundi: here specialized to 'to win sexually', 'gain the submission of'; cf. Pl. *Cur.* 170 *ipsus se excruciat qui homo quod amat uidet nec potitur, dum licet*; Ov. *Met.* 10, 569 *nec sum potienda, nisi.../uicta prius cursu*. Apul. ex Menandro (*PLM* 4, 104, 1) *amare liceat, si potiri non licet*.

'sed heus tu', inquit Charite, 'quam probe ueste contectus omnique comite uiduatus prima uigilia tacitus fores meas accedas unoque sibilo contentus nutricem istam meam opperiare, quae claustris adhaerens excubabit aduentui tuo: "'But listen', Charite said, 'come, very well wrapped in your cloak and without any escort, quietly to my door in the first watch. One whistle will be enough; then wait for my nurse (remember?) who with her hand on the bolt will stand guard until your arrival.'" 185, 16-20

Charite: observe the reading of F *charitate*, a pretty example of miscopying by a scribe more familiar with Christian texts.

quam probe: *quam* is often used by Apul. to reinforce adverbs and adjectives; see *GCA* 1977, 44 (on 76, 25) with reference to vdPaardt 1971, 55, and the literature mentioned there. For *probe* = *bene* see vdPaardt 1971, 62.

uiduatus: this word is found in poetry and post-Augustan prose from Lucr. 5, 840 onward: (*portenta*) *orba pedum partim, manuum uiduata uicissim*; Verg. *G*.4, 517 *solus...aruaque Riphaeis numquam uiduata pruinis/lustrabat* (sc. *Orpheus*). In prose, cf. e.g. Suet. *Gal.* 5,1, where it has the special connotation of 'bereft of one's spouse'. It is not inconceivable that Vergil in the above-mentioned passage chose this verb deliberately in view of Orpheus' situation. In that case it is possible that Apuleius, too, has chosen this verb here because of its connotation, since Charite is *uiduata* as well. He uses it more often in its general meaning, e.g. 200, 24 with our comm.

accedas: a jussive subjunctive, frequent in early Latin and Cicero's letters and therefore regarded by Callebat 1968, 100 as 'langue de la conversation'; LHSz 2, 335 'in erster Linie umgangssprachlich'.

sibilo: whistling is an obvious means of attracting attention, as with the unsuspecting *maritus* returning home 9, 5 (206, 8) *sibilo...praesentiam suam denuntiante*. The purpose of the whistling in this passage – only once (*uno*) so as not to be too conspicuous – is to alert the *nutrix* to the lover's presence. Coughing can have this function, too, Tib. 1, 5, 74 *ante ipsas exscreat usque fores*. The lady-love in her turn may signal by snapping her fingers that her lover can come in, Tib. 1, 2, 31 *reseret modo Delia postes/et uocet ad digiti me taciturna sonum*. In Liv. 25, 8, 11 conspirators use a whistle-signal in capturing a town.

nutricem: the role of the nurse in love-affairs is known from epic (see Pease's extensive note on Verg. *A*. 4, 632) and drama (Phaedra). The *nutrix* also occurs – albeit not frequently – in elegy; Cynthia wants her nurse to be well provided for in her old age as a reward for her services, Prop. 4, 7, 73 *nutrix in tremulis ne quid desideret annis*.

istam: 'known to you'. It is also a hint to the reader: the context of the rendezvous practically requires a *nutrix*. For similar winks at the *lector doctus* cf. e.g. 190, 4 *tubam* with our comm. ad loc.

claustris: *claustrum* means anything by which one can lock or close something, but especially the bar by which the door is locked. For a technical discussion of *claustrum* see *GCA* 1977, 81 f.

adhaerens: for its meaning cf. Tac. *Ann*. 3, 21 *statiuis castris adhaerebat*.

excubabit: with a *datiuus commodi* (both of persons and of things) we find it also Luc. 9,910 *excubat hospitibus*; Plin. *Nat*. 6,66 *regi Ix peditum...excubant*; *Met*. 5, 4 (116, 14) *rebus tuis excubamus* (see *ThLL* s.v. 1289, 54). In elegiac poetry *excubare* has the specific meaning of the lover's watch-keeping at the *fores/ianua* of his lady in the hope of being let in (see Pichon ²1966, s.v. *excubiae*). The elegiac situation has shifted here: the nurse *excubat* – inside. She is doing what Delia's old mother does for Tibullus: 1, 6, 61 *haec foribus manet noctu me adfixa proculque/cognoscit strepitus me ueniente pedum*.

aduentui tuo: *aduenienti tibi*. Apuleius' penchant for abstract nouns has often been noted. See e.g. Médan 1925, 322; Bernhard 1927, 96 f.

185, 20-22 Nec setius patefactis aedibus acceptum te nullo lumine conscio ad meum perducet cubiculum: "She will also open the house for you, let you in, and bring you, without any witnessing light, to my bedroom'."

Nec setius: 'as well', as e.g. 5, 1 (104, 8) *sic cubicula, sic porticus, sic ipsae ualuae fulgurant, nec setius opes ceterae maiestati domus respondent*. *Setius* is regarded as a later comparative formation with *secus*; see Ernout-Meillet and Walde-Hofmann s.v. *secus*. For *secus* see *GCA* 1977, 147.

patefactis aedibus: we read the same expression 2, 32 (51, 24) *tumultu eo Fotide suscitata patefactis aedibus...inrepo*.

nullo lumine conscio: a case of personification; see Bernhard 1927, 190. Brakman 1917, 21 has no doubts that our passage was the example for Minuc. *Octavius* 9, 7 *euerso et extincto conscio lumine*; cf. also Sen. *Med*. 6 *conscium iubar* with Costa ad loc. The advice not to use any light in a situation like this is again found in elegiac poetry, Tib. 1, 2, 33 *parcite luminibus seu uir seu femina fiat/obuia: celari uult sua furta Venus.*

   ad meum perducet cubiculum: typically Apuleian word order; see Bernhard 1927, 18.

CHAPTER XI

Thrasyllus walks with open eyes into the snare laid for him by Charite.

185, 23 **Placuit Thrasyllo scaena feralium nuptiarum:** "The staging of this funereal wedding pleased Thrasyllus."

Placuit: the 'Anfangsstellung' of the verb achieves a close connection with the preceding sentence; cf. Bernhard 1927, 11.

scaena: 'mise en scène' (Callebat 1968, 65) seems to us the right meaning. The word is discussed *GCA* 1971, 151: in that passage (4, 20 : 89, 17) the correct rendition is 'role' whereas 'dramatic story' is the right translation 4, 25 (94, 20); see *GCA* ad loc. For Apuleius' use of theatrical imagery see Heine 1962, 207. Charite had seen through the *scaenam pessimi Thrasylli* mentioned 183, 6. Now the roles are reversed: Charite lays a snare for Thrasyllus but, unlike Charite a moment ago, he does not see through the plan.

feralium: although the reader may have understood from the preceding that Charite intends to punish Thrasyllus for his crime (184, 8), this is the first word indicating that Thrasyllus will die (the wider perspective of the narrator). *Feralis* is used a few times to give the reader a clue as to how events will develop, e.g. 10, 24 (255, 17) *sed haec bene atque optime plenaque cum sanctimonia disposita feralem Fortunae nutum latere non potuerunt*: by the *feralis Fortunae nutus* the *iuuenis* will presently, in spite of his pious intentions, become the sacrificial victim. Merkelbach 1962, 78 n. 4 also compares 4, 34 (101, 18) *perfectis...feralis thalami...sollemnibus...Psyche comitatur non nuptias, sed exequias suas*: according to the oracle Psyche will marry a *saeuum atque ferum uipereumque malum* (4, 33 : 100, 24). Cf. also e.g. Ov. *Met.* 9, 213 *feralia dona* (viz. the robe dipped in Nessus' blood).

nuptiarum: not in the meaning of a legal marriage but of *coitus*, as 7, 21 (170, 7) with our comm.

185, 23-24 **Nec sequius aliquid suspicatus, sed expectatione turbidus de diei tantum spatio et uesperae mora querebatur:** "Not suspecting any harm but bemused by anticipation, he only complained of the length of the day and the tardiness of the evening."

sequius aliquid: 'something bad'; cf. 9, 29 (225, 5) *quae res cum ei sequius ac rata fuerat proueniret* and e.g. Sen. *Ben.* 6. 42, 2 *uereor ne homines de me sequius loquantur*. The comparative has lost its meaning in our passage and in Seneca; see LHSz 2, 168 f. The form *sequius* with its variants *sectius* and *setius* is not found often after Plautus, and mainly in standard combinations with negations (LHSz 2, 248); it is regarded as a younger comparative formation with *secus* (Walde-Hofmann s.v.). Cf. also 185, 20 with our comm. At 7, 8 (160, 1) the expression *sequior sexus* is found; see *GCA* 1981, 134 ad loc.

aliquid: in post-classical times the use of *aliquis* is extended to sentences with a negative or with negative force; see LHSz 2, 195. That this hardly occurs anywhere in the *Met.*, as Callebat 1968, 284 maintains – he quotes only 10, 9 (243, 27) *ne forte aliquis...repperiatur* – does not seem to be entirely correct. We noticed this phenomenon already in our comm. on 7, 19 (169, 6).

expectatione turbidus: *turbidus* is the correct term to characterize the typical villain. Apuleius uses here the terminology of Cic. *Tusc.* 4,34 where the Stoic theory on *uirtus* and its opposite are discussed. We quote the passage extensively: *Virtus est adfectio animi constans conueniensque...ex ea proficiscuntur honestae uoluntates, sententiae, actiones omnisque recta ratio...huius igitur uirtutis contraria est uitiositas...ex qua concitantur perturbationes, quae sunt...turbidi animorum concitatique motus, auersi a ratione et inimicissimi mentis uitaeque tranquillae. Important enim aegritudines anxias atque acerbas animosque adfligunt et debilitant metu; iidem inflammant adpetitione nimia quam tum cupiditatem, tum libidinem dicimus, impotentiam quandam animi a temperantia et moderatione plurimum dissidentem.*The consequences of *turbidi animorum motus* are *auersio a ratione* (exemplified in our case in 185, 12 *promissioni fallaciosae mulieris oppressus subcubuit Thrasyllus* etc.), *cupiditas, libido*, and *impotentia animi* (cf. 185, 6 *nec...sobriefactus uel...recreatus*), all of which apply very well to Thrasyllus. Cf. also 178, 9-15 with our comm. and 178, 20 *furiosae libidinis...impetus* with our comm.

uespera: this is the form used by Apuleius, not *uesper*; see *GCA* 1977, 126.

querebatur: that the day seems long to the lover and the evening is slow in coming is a motif found in elegiac poetry, e.g. Prop. 3, 20, 11 *Tu quoque, qui aestiuos spatiosius exigis ignes, / Phoebe, moraturae contrahe lucis iter. / Nox mihi prima uenit* and Ov. *Met.* 4, 91 *lux tarde discedere uisa* (sc. *Pyramo et Thisbae*). Bömer 1976 observes that this is a motif from Hellenistic love poetry, which does not occur in Latin before Ovid. He quotes Longus 2, 8 θᾶττον εὐχόμεθα γενέσθαί τὴν ἡμέραν (but there the lovers wish for daybreak instead, so that they may meet again; this is also the case 2, 24, quoted by Bömer as well); Musaeus 231 πολλάκις ἠρήσαντο μολεῖν θαλαμηπόλον ὄρφνην (Kost 1971, 432 quotes many examples including the Longus passage just mentioned as well as passages from modern literature; Nonnus 7, 281 f. (Zeus) ἐθέλων Σεμέλης ἐπιβήμεναι εὐνῆς / δολιχὴν Φαέθοντος ἐμέμφετο δείελον ὥρην. From Latin literature Bömer quotes Sen. *Breu.* 10, 16, 3 *saepe illis longus uidetur dies, quod...tarde ire horas queruntur*, but fails to mention that this is said of people who can hardly wait for *condictum tempus cenae*.

Sed ubi sol tandem nocti decessit, ex imperio Charites ad-[h]ornatus et nutricis captiosa uigilia deceptus inrepit cubiculum pronus spei: "But when finally the sun had given way to the night, he stole, arrayed according to Charite's instructions and deceived by the nurse's ensnaring vigil, into the bedroom in an ecstasy of hope." 185, 25-28

sol...nocti decessit: a poetic turn of phrase; cf. Verg. *Ecl.* 8, 88 *nec serae meminit decedere nocti*, where again, because of the subject *bucula iuuencum quaerens*, we have an erotic connotation. Cf. also *Ecl.* 2, 67 *sol...decedens*.

tandem: again, as 185, 13 *fallaciosae* with our comm., the narrator, and hence the reader, takes Thrasyllus' point of view. Cf. Stanzel [8]1976, 42-43: 'die Fixierung des point of view der Darstellung im Bewusstsein einer Romangestalt'.

ad[h]ornatus: adhornatus (*n* changed into *t* by a different hand) F, *adornat* φ. The latter is the correct reading (cf. Augello 1977, 182). It does not seem necessary to read with Robertson and Scazzoso *adest ornatus*. *Adornatus* refers back, course, to 185, 17 *quam probe ueste contectus* etc.

captiosa: 9, 8 (209, 1) *diuinationis astu captioso* shows that *captiosa* need not be taken as a hypallage, even if it does apply to Charite. The word has clearly its etymological meaning here; (it is attested from Cicero onward; see Ernout 1949, 56;) the deceiver deceived by the *captiosa nutrix*.

inrepit cubiculum: 3, 24 (70, 4) has the same phrase; cf. vdPaardt 1971 ad loc.

pronus spei: the same expression is found 3, 27 (72, 6); see vdPaardt 1971 ad loc., who argues that it is hardly possible to decide whether *spei* is genitive or dative. But a passage like Suet. *Nero* 40, 2 *cui spei pronior* admits of no doubt. Von Albrecht 1971, 202 argues that it is a precious expression ('in seiner Hoffnung triebhaft') because *pronus* is used to depict both the animal's posture (bent formward) as contrasted to man's, and also its nature, ruled by instincts and passion.

185, 28-186,5 Tunc anus de iussu dominae blandiens ei furtim depromptis calicibus et oenoforo, quod inmixtum uino soporiferum gerebat uenenum, crebris potionibus auide ac secure haurientem mentita dominae tarditatem, quasi parentem adsideret aegrotum, facile sepeliuit ad somnum: "Then, according to her mistress's instructions, the old woman talked to him in friendly fashion and furtively brought out goblets and a wine jar which contained a sleeping-draught mixed into the wine. Several times he drained his cup eagerly and unsuspectingly, and while she falsely excused her mistress's tardiness with the story that she was sitting at her father's sickbed, she easily plunged him into a deep sleep."

de iussu: cf. 3, 2 (52, 24) *de iussu magistratuum*. Latin has a certain preference for the construction with *de* (rather than the ablative alone) to indicate that something happens in agreement with something else; see LHSz 2, 126.

furtim: the secrecy, which first purported to be to Thrasyllus' advantage (making the rendezvous possible), is now directed against him.

inmixtum: a rare word, also occuring 7, 12 (163, 12); see *GCA* 1981, 161 ad loc.

oenoforo: F, *oenophoro* ς, followed by Oudendorp, Hildebrand, vdVliet, Robertson, and Brandt-Ehlers. Our policy (see Introd. 5.3) in these matters is to follow the spelling of the principal manuscript. The word is attested from Lucil. 139 *uertitur oenofori fundus, sententia nobis* onward. In the *Met.* it is also found 2, 24 (45, 3), but written with *-ph-*.

soporiferum...uenenum: this combination occurs also 7, 12 (163, 15); see

GCA 1981, 162 ad loc. The addition *soporiferum* is not unnecessary, as is witnessed by *Dig.* 48, 8, 3 *adiectio... 'ueneni mali' ostendit esse quaedam et non mala uenena...nomen medium est et tam id, quod ad sanandum, quam id, quod ad occidendum paratum est, continet, sed et id quod amatorium appellatur*. The legal implications of the administration of a *uenenum soporiferum* are discussed by Rayment 1959, 50 f.

crebris potionibus auide ac secure haurientem: practically every word underlines the greed and carelessness with which Thrasyllus is drinking: another piece of evidence of the blindness with which he has been struck. That he drank too much on other occasions as well, the narrator had mentioned at 177,7.

mentita: 'give a false representation of the facts'; cf. 7, 21 (170, 7) and 7, 22 (171, 4) with our comm. ad loc. Cf. also 178, 2 *personam mentiebatur* and our comm. on lying and deception being one of the 'Leitmotive' in the *Met*. At this point Charite orders her *nutrix* to tell lies; this fact disrupts the reader's 'Erwartungshorizont' with regard to the (thus far) so sympathetic Charite. On the other hand, the reader has been prepared since 183, 6 (*ferinos mugitus iterans*) for the total change which takes place in her; cf. also 184,11 f. with our comm.

parentem: the narrator does not indicate where the father lives; apparently it is known to Thrasyllus and probably to the audience.

adsideret: the verb is here constructed with an accusative as 1, 22 (20, 18) *assidebat pedes uxor*; cf. e.g. Cic. *inc. fr.* 39 *neque adsidere Gabinium...quisquam audebat*. Cf. also 176, 19 *ignem propter adsidens* (with our comm.), where we prefer to regard *ignem* as an accusative dependent on the verb. It is constructed with a dative e.g. Liv. 21, 53, 6 *adsidens...aegro collegae*; Sen. *Con.* 9, 3, 7 *aegrotantibus adsedi*.

sepeliuit ad somnum: the turn of phrase is based on Verg. *A.* 2, 265 *inuadunt urbem somno uinoque sepultam* and 6, 424 *occupat Aeneas aditum custode sepulto* (see Austin ad loc. and cf. also *A.* 9, 189 [= 9, 236] *somno uinoque soluti*). Austin on *A.* 2, 265 mentions as Vergil's example Enn. *Ann.* 292 *nunc hostes uino domiti somnoque sepulti*. Before Vergil the expression had been used by Lucr. 1, 133 and 5, 974; after Vergil we find it in Ovid, Propertius (cf. Müller 1952, 10 f.), Petronius, Justinus – a good example of how the *sermo Ennianus* has become part of Latin literary traditon. Vergil, however, has changed the Ennian turn of phrase somewhat: Ennius speaks of *hostes* (*somno sepulti*), Lucretius of 'we' (the first human beings), but Vergil extends the usage to *urbem* (cf. Wigodsky 1972, 58). Norden remarks (comm. on *A.* 6, 424 f.) that the poets may have felt an – etymologically unjustified – connection between *sepelire* and *sopire*. It may also be pointed out that both in Ennius and Vergil, and now in Apuleius as well, the expression always refers to situations that lead to death; *sepelire* is therefore significant in this connection. This has probably contributed to the expression's popularity. Apuleius, on his part, gives a new shape to the Ennio-Vergillian phrase by replacing the ablative *somno* by *ad somnum*. Callebat 1968, 213 argues that these variants are not quite equivalent and that Apuleius, rather than implying an instrumental notion, wishes to suggest (by means of *ad*) the transition to a new condition, like e.g. Liv. 33, 29, 1 *efferauit ea caedes Thebanos...ad...odium.* For another Ennio-Vergilian phrase cf. 201, 4 *per ora populi* with our comm.

Charite shows herself here a wife worthy of her husband. As Tlepolemus had put the robbers into a lethal sleep with *soporiferum quoddam uenenum* (7, 12 ; 163, 15), so now Charite deals with Thrasyllus, with the help of her *nutrix*. Another verbal similarity can be found in *uino sepulti iacebant* (7, 12 : 163, 16); cf. Nethercut 1969, 112.

186, 5-8 Iamque eo ad omnes iniurias exposito ac supinato introuocata Charite masculis animis impetuque diro fremens inuadit ac supersistit sicarium: "And now that he was vulnerable to all kinds of violence and was lying on his back, Charite was called in. With masculine spirit and terrible speed she went at the assassin and stood over him, raving."

iniurias: 'physical injury', cf. Liv. 2, 29, 4 *rixa...in qua...sine lapide, sine telo plus clamoris atque irarum quam iniuriae fuerat*; Cels. 2, 10, 14 *opportuniores hic eae partes iniuriae sunt, quae iam male habent*. Summers 1967, 147 f. argues that at the time of the XII Tables the term *iniuria* was used for instances of physical violence only; later it was extended to anything done *non iure*. In view of what Charite is about to do to Thrasyllus, *iniuria* is the right word to anticipate the coming event (ibid. 272).

eo...supinato: a somewhat free use of the absolute ablative, not uncommon in Apuleius; see Bernhard 1927, 45 n.2; Callebat 1968, 321; and e.g. our comm. on 7, 21 (170, 10 f.).

exposito: cf. Liv. 9, 35, 6 *expositos ad ictus, cum iam satis nihil tegeret*; Sen. *Nat.* 1, 16, 4 *in perditis quoque et ad omne dedecus expositis*. See Callebat 1968, 212. For a figurative use cf. Liv. 42, 23, 9 *libertatem expositam ad iniurias Masinissae*.

supinato: post-Augustan, first attested Quint. *Inst.* 11, 3, 100 *manus modice supinata*; in poetry first found Stat. *Theb.* 6, 789 *aliquem in terga supinare*. Apul. uses this verb four times in book 8, once in book 9. One cannot help comparing *eo...supinato* with *pronus spei*, which typefied Thrasyllus only recently (185, 28).

introuocata: according to *ThLL* the word is used in a neutral, non-legal sense once in Cic. *Ver.* 2, 66 *cur ad nos filiam tuam non introuocari iubes*, four times in Apul., subsequently not before Amm. As a legal term (i.q. *in saepta uocare ad suffragium ferendum*) e.g. *Lex repetund.* (*CIL* I² 583, 72) *tribus intro uocabuntur*; Asc. Corn. 64 *intro uocare tribus Gabinius coepit, ut Trebellio magistratum abrogaret.*

introuocata...fremens: an ingeniously constructed chiasmus.

masculis animis: the ass said to himself 6, 26 (148, 19) *quin igitur masculum tandem sumis animum* (see *GCA* 1981, 38 ad loc.) and Plotina's *ingenium masculum* is mentioned 7, 6 (159, 4) (for Plotina foreshadowing Charite, see Introduction *GCA* 1981, 4). In either case the expression is used favourably, as Ov. *F.* 2, 847 describing Lucretia as *animi matrona uirilis*. In a derogatory sense Sen. *Ag.* 958 has Clytaemnestra tell Electra *animos uiriles corde tumefacto geris /, sed agere domita feminam disces malo* (see Tarrant ad loc.). Charite, in the episode of the robbers still a sweet, kind-hearted girl, has become a vindictive Kriemhild; earlier (184, 17) she had said about herself *Tlepolemus in meo uiuit pectore*); see Heine 1962, 238; Tatum 1969, 167; 1972, 309 n. 19; Scobie 1973, 66; 1975, 48; Schlam *AAGA* 1978, 100, 116; Tatum 1979, 32 n. 14. Psyche, at first a gentle girl, changes too (5, 22 : 120, 2 *sexum audacia mutatur*; see Hoevels 1979, 117 f.): she attacks Amor with a razor; in taking revenge on her sister she shows herself determined and cruel (5, 26 and 27); and when, at her wits' end, she has to call in Venus' aid, she uses the same words in her soliloquy as did the ass 6, 26 (148, 19).

fremens: a powerful word for a powerful emotion; cf. the *ferinos mugitos* (183, 6) uttered by Charite (*insana uoce* 181, 6) when she begins to see through Thrasyllus' sinister designs. In our passage the notion of fury prevails (cf. *ThLL* s.v. 1283, 4 f.) rather than that of indignation as in 4, 29 (98, 6) (*Venus*) *impatiens indignationis capite quassanti fremens altius sic secum disserit*.

supersistit: this verb also occurs 11, 24 (285, 25) *tribunal...superstiti*, again with an accusative. Its other occurrences are Amm. 29, 1, 31 *supersistit cortinulae sacerdos* (with a dative) and Iul. Val. 161, 21 *aquila aurea supersistebat* (absolutely). See Müller 1908, 142 and Bernhard 1927, 121.

sicarium: not just 'murderer' but 'assassin', 'professional bandit'; it is connected with *sica* 'considérée comme l'arme des brigands et des assassins' (Ernout-Meillet 1951 s.v. *sica*). Cf. Quint. *Inst*. 10, 1, 12 *per abusionem sicarios etiam omnes uocamus, qui caedem telo quocumque commiserint*. Cloud 1969, 269, who discusses the three passages in the *Met*. where this word occurs, argues that the notion *telo quocumque* is present 9, 37 (231, 22), since the *sicarius* had been called *ille cruentus et multis ante flagitiis similibus exercitatus percussor* (231, 15). The other occurrences are 10, 6 (241, 9), referring to the young man who had ostensibly threatened his stepmother with a sword (240, 23), and our passage, referring to Thrasyllus, who had been said to be *factionibus latronum male sociatus nec non etiam manus infectus humano cruore* (177, 8). Finally, observe the *s*-alliteration.

CHAPTER XII

Charite accuses the sleeping Thrasyllus in a flaming address showing great rhetorical skill.

186, 8-9 'En', inquit, 'fidus coniugis mei comes, en uenator egregius, en carus maritus: '"Here you are', she said, 'you faithful companion of my husband; you excellent hunter; you beloved spouse."

The rhetor Apuleius, who must have been familiar with ἠθοποιίαι like this, demonstrates his great technical skills in this monologue. Eicke 1956, 107-115 gives a detailed analysis of this speech. Eicke's analysis of the technical composition of the speech has been incorporated into this commentary without any explicit references.

En: in meaning close to *em*; see Callebat 1968, 90 and *GCA* 1977, 187 on 94, 5-7. In contrast to *em* it always occurs in Apul. in direct discourse, e.g. 7, 8 (160, 11). Cf. Heine 1962, 176 and 241 'wie eine leidenschaftliche Geste *ad spectatores*'.

fidus...maritus: the bitter irony is developed in a skilfully constructed anaphoric tricolon, in which the number of syllables decreases by equal amounts (10-8-6) and adjectives and nouns are placed chiastically in relation to one another. A similar triad, which also has a decreasing number of syllables and also contains an accusation, is found 3,3 (54, 25 f.); see vdPaardt 1971, 45 ad loc.

uenator: is significantly placed in the middle of the tricolon, linked to *coniugis*, whom he murdered at the hunt, and to *maritus*, in which quality he is about to be killed by Charite – the hunter hunted.

egregius: ironically, as so often in Apul., e.g. 2, 14 (36, 10) *Diophanes ille Chaldaeus egregius* (see de Jonge ad loc.); 2, 29 (49, 12) *uxor egregia*; 5, 9 (109, 19) *sorores egregiae*; perhaps 7, 18 (168, 5) *egregius agaso* (see *GCA* 1981, 201 ad loc.). Cf. also Bernhard 1927, 239.

maritus: Oudendorp remarks that Charite calls Thrasyllus *maritus* 'per amaram ironiam', as Ter. *An.* 792 uses *socer* of a future *socer* and Verg. uses *coniunx* for *sponsa* in *Ecl.* 8, 18 and in *A.* 9, 138, where Turnus refers to Lavinia, his future wife, as *coniuge praerepta*. But *maritus* can be used – especially in elegiac poetry – to mean 'lover', e.g. Ov. *Ars* 3, 611 (see Stroh 1979, 333 f. and *ThLL* s.v. 404, 70 '*de procis*'). If it means 'lover' here, *maritus* is not particularly ironical, but the context points firmly to the more ironical meaning. At 4, 26 (95, 2) Charite uses the term for Tlepolemus, naturally without irony.

186, 9-13 Haec est illa dextera, quae meum sanguinem fudit, hoc pectus, quod fraudulentas ambages in meum concinnauit exitium, oculi isti, quibus male placui, qui quodam modo tamen iam futuras tenebras auspicantes uenientes poenas antecedunt: "This is that right hand which shed my blood, this is the breast which hatched a treacherous plot for my perdition, those are the eyes which in an evil hour I pleased; yet somehow they already forebode the approaching darkness and anticipate the punishment that is coming to them."

Haec...placui: a most carefully constructed period. The anaphoric *haec, hoc* is alternated with (*oculi*) *isti*, which at the same time creates a chiasmus vs. *haec...dextera* and *hoc pectus: haec...dextera – hoc pectus – oculi isti*. The same anaphora and variatio is also observed in the relative clauses *quae meum sanguinem fudit* (8 syllables); *quod fraudulentas ambages in meum concinnauit exitium* (19); *quibus male placui* (17); *qui...antecedunt* (28). The first three clauses have either the first person singular of the possessive pronoun or the first person singular of the verb; in the fourth clause the first person singular does not occur at all. Cf. Bernhard 1927, 35.

meum sanguinem: Tlepolemus' blood is Charite's blood, just as the *ambages* devised against Tlepolemus bring about Charite's ruin.

fudit: the simple verb instead of the more usual *effundere, profundere* cf. *GCA* 1977, 127 on 87, 1-2 *pellere*, where we list discussions of the use of *simplex pro composito* in late Latin. Apul. does not use this figure of speech very often in the *Met.*, but it is not as rare as Eicke 1956, 109 suggests, who on p. 40 cites four examples from one chapter (10, 30). Furthermore it may be pointed out that *fudit* gives the most frequent clausula (cretic plus trochee; see Hijmans in *AAGA* 1978, 199), *profudit* an extremely rare one (*effudit* would give the same result as the simple verb because of elision).

ambages: for the meaning '(fraudulent) devices' cf. 9, 15 (214, 14) *scaenas fraudulentas in exitium miserrimi mariti subdolis ambagibus construebat*, where again we find also the words *fraudulentas* and *in exitium*.

concinnauit: 'devise', as e.g. 7, 20 (169, 24) with our comm.

male: cf. 177, 8 *factionibus latronum male sociatus* (*Thrasyllus*).

uenientes: Hildebrand observes that *uenire* is used more than once 'de re infausta atque improspera', e.g. Verg. *A*. 3, 137 *subito cum tabida membris / corrupto caeli tractu miserandaque uenit/...lues et letifer annus*; Hor. *S*. 1, 3, 87 *tristes misero uenere Kalendae*.

antecedunt: for the meaning 'anticipate an action or occurrence' cf. Sen. *Ben.* 1, 1, 13 *qui non dat, uitium ingrati antecedit*; *Ep.* 98, 7 *quae ista dementia est, malum suum antecedere?*

At 185, 23 the audience (and the reader) were prepared for the fatal ending of the *nuptiae* by the use of *feralis*; now they are prepared for the nature of Thrasyllus' punishment (*uenientes poenas*) by the words of Charite, who personifies Thrasyllus' sleeping eyes and thus foreshows the closed eyes of his blindness.

Quiesce securus, beate somniare: "Sleep sound, have happy dreams." 186, 13-14

Quiesce...somniare: a fine example of the *ars Apuleiana*. *Quiesce*, by its position at the beginning of the sentence, is closely linked with the previous sentence (see Bernhard 1927, 11 and 13) and once more underscores the connection between future blindness and present sleep. Observe the chiasmus of the imperatives, the variation of adjective and adverb, and the variation of the quality of the vowels: in the first member *u*'s (and *e*'s), in the second *a*'s (and *e*'s) and other clear vowels.

somniare: as a deponent this verb also occurs 3, 22 (68, 20); see vdPaardt 1971, 165 ad loc. Flobert 1975, 214 mentions, in addition to the two Apul. passages, Petr. 74, 14 *hic. . . aedes non somniatur* and three later passages from Christian Latin, e.g. *VL (e) Psalt. Cas.* 121, 5 *fuimus sicut somniati*. According to Flobert, the deponent is stronger than the active: 'se plonger dans des rêves'. *Somniari* can be regarded as vulgar since Caper *Gramm.* VII 95, 1 (Keil) emphatically rejects it (see Nelson 1947, 87). Wower's old conjecture *somnia. te non ego*, which removed the deponent, is unnecessary.

186, 14-16 Non ego gladio, non ferro petam; absit, ut simili mortis genere cum marito meo coaequeris: uiuo tibi morientur oculi nec quicquam uidebis nisi dormiens: "Not with a sword, not with iron will I assault you; I absolutely do not wish that by a similar kind of death you will be made my husband's equal. While you are alive, your eyes will die and you will see nothing except in sleep."

gladio: before this word Kronenberg 1892, 24 wants to read *te* (he gives no reasons, but he may have been influenced by Wower's conjecture mentioned above); this reading is adopted by Helm III (Robertson inaccurately says in his critical apparatus that Kronenberg wanted *te* before *petam*). There seems to be no cogent reason for this addition because the omission of pronouns, especially in the accusative, is characteristic of Apuleius' style (see Bernhard 1927, 160 n. 7; Augello 1977, 182).

non ego gladio, non ferro: Strilciw 1925, 116 regards this as a case of perissology. This term seems to be misleading: *gladio* and *ferro* are not necessarily identical.

ego...petam: although Callebat 1968, 94 gives many examples of the diminished strength of the pronoun when it is the subject, there still are examples of emphatic use; this seems to us to be the case here, too, because it marks the contrast with Thrasyllus, who had assaulted Tlepolemus with a weapon.

simili mortis genere: for a discussion of the manner in which Thrasyllus meets his death, see our comm. on 188, 6 *inedia*.

coaequeris: here constructed with *cum*; the ThLL gives as the only other example of this constuction Lact. *Inst.* 5, 14, 5 (*iustitiae*) *aequitatem dico non utique bene iudicandi..., sed se cum ceteris coaequandi*. More frequent is the construction with a dative, e.g. Gaius *Inst.* 3, 153 *ciuili ratione kapitis diminutio morti coaequatur*; Apul. *Soc.* 20 (31, 2) (*Socratem*) *cuiuis amplissimo numini sapientiae dignitas coaequarat*. The construction with a dative is used by Apul. at *Met.* 3, 19 (66, 8).

tibi...oculi: Callebat 1968, 261 f. discusses the substitution of a dative of the personal pronoun for a possessive; in addition to our passage he cites 9, 15 (214,

4) *mihi...genuinam curiositatem...ampliauerat*; 9, 38 (232, 14) *gulam sibi prorsus exsecuit*. This use, according to Callebat, is not an imitation from poetry; it rather has its origin in colloquial language because of its greater expressivity. We think that Callebat would have done better not to cite our passage; *tibi* must be taken with *uiuo* in the first place, so that there is no question of substitution; this is the dative of interest.

Sanders 1960, 114 f. maintains that for people in antiquity 'seeing' is the most comprehensive term which expresses the experience of 'living'. He demonstrates this on the basis of our passage: Charite will not kill Thrasyllus, but will put out his eyes instead. To this we wish to add that Charite herself regards the blindness as the appropriate punishment for Thrasyllus because the eyes, with which he had looked upon her with desire (186, 11), evoke this punishment.

Faxo, feliciorem necem inimici tui quam uitam tuam sentias: "I will see to it that you think your enemy's death more fortunate than your own life." 186, 17-18

Faxo: for *faxo* + subjunctive see *GCA* 1977, 190 on 4, 25 (94, 14). Callebat 1968, 504 remarks in connection with our passage that this *faxo* may, indeed, have been derived from comic language, but that in the monologue 'de style elaboré' spoken by the avenging Charite, the author is much less sensitive to the colloquial nature of the word than to its archaic colour.

For the notion that death is preferable to blindness, cf. Soph. *O.R.* 1368 where the chorus-leader says to Oedipus: κρείσσων γὰρ ἦσθα μηκέτ᾽ ὢν ἢ ζῶν τυφλός. Oudendorp on *errabis* etc. (1. 21 below) refers to Elmenhorst, who cites Chrysost. *in Ioh. hom.* 16 οὐ γὰρ οἱ τὸ φῶς τὸ ἡλιακὸν μὴ θεώμενοι παντὸς θανάτου πικροτέραν ὑπομένουσι ζωήν. In philosophical reflection on blindness, on the other hand, it is argued that blindness does not injure the wise: Cic. *Tusc.* 5, 112 *cuius* (sc. Antipater of Cyrene) *caecitatem cum mulierculae lamentarentur, 'quid agitis' inquit, 'an uobis nulla uidetur uoluptas esse nocturna'*; Sen. *Const.* 15, 1 *desinite itaque dicere: 'non accipiet ergo sapiens iniuriam, si caedetur, si oculus illi eruetur'* (with the comm. of Klei 1950 ad loc.). On a certain level Thrasyllus may be regarded as a spiritually blind man as well, who will not be granted the redeeming spiritual insight (see Appendix II 4.2.2); he will not suffer his blindness as a *sapiens*, either.

Lumen certe non uidebis, manu comitis indigebis, Chariten non tenebis, nuptias non frueris, nec mortis quiete recreaberis nec uitae uoluptate laetaberis, sed incertum simulacrum errabis inter Orcum et solem et diu quaeres dexteram, quae tuas expugnauit pupulas, quodque est in aerumna miserrimum, nescies de quo queraris: "This is certain: you will not see the light, you will need the hand of a companion, you will not possess Charite, you will not enjoy a marriage, you will neither be restored by the repose of death nor rejoice in the pleasure of being alive, but as a vague shade you will wander between underworld and 186, 18-23 sunlight. Long will you seek the hand that put your eyes out and – what is the worst fate in suffering – you will not know whom to blame."

Again a long period, as carefully constructed as 186, 8-13, but this time with different means. First, four cola (*lumen...frueris*) are joined asyndetically; they are followed by two clauses joined by *nec...nec*. This rigid division is softened because the rhyme obtained by repetition of the same verbal form (*uidebis, indigebis, tenebis, fruēris, recreaberis, laetaberis*) crosses the 4-2 partition (see Bernhard 1927, 86; 227 and Tatum 1979, 148 f. who maintains that the rhyme and rhythm of this passage accentuate 'Charite's vow to punish her husband's murderer'). Within these verbal forms a vowel harmony can be observed in the first three forms and again in the last two, while *frueris* clearly has a transitional function. Its rhyme, too, is less striking (*-ēris* vs *-bĕris*). From 186, 20 *sed incertum* the sentence continues with a variety of connectives: *sed...et* (plus a relative clause)*...-que*. There is a careful parallelism in the number of syllables:

lumen certe non uidebis (8)	*manu comitis indigebis* (9)
Chariten non tenebis (7)	*nuptias non frueris* (7)
nec mortis quiete recreaberis (11)	*nec uitae uoluptate laetaberis* (11)
sed...solem (18); *et...pupulas* (18);	*quodque...queraris* (19).

It is remarkable that, all careful construction notwithstanding, alliteration is practically absent here as well as in the entire chapter (only 12 *qui quodam*; 20 *uitae uoluptate*; 23 *quo queraris*).

lumen certe non uidebis: vdPaardt *SAG* 1981, 24 suggests the possibility that the implied author allows himself a pun in 182, 14 *Thrasyllus, praeceps alioquin et de ipso nomine temerarius*: the adjective *temerarius* may be connected with a noun **temus*, meaning 'darkness' (see Walde-Hofmann [3]1954 and Ernout-Meillet [4]1959 s.v. *temere*): 'Thrasyllus' fate is to see the light nevermore'.

manu comitis indigebis: cf. Cic. *Tusc.* 5, 113 *cum quidam quaereret* (sc. *Asclepiaden caecum*) *quid ei caecitas attulisset respondisse, puero ut uno esset comitatior*. The classical example is Soph. *O.R.* 444, where Teiresias says: ἄπειμι τοίνυν· καὶ σύ, παῖ, κόμιζέ με, and *O.C.* 181, where Antigone says to her father: ἕπεο μάν, ἐπε' ὧδ' ἀμαυρῷ κώλῳ, πάτερ, ᾇ σ'ἄγω.

tenebis: a word from the *sermo amatorius*; cf. Prop. 4, 7, 93, where Cynthia, appearing after her death in Propertius' dream, says: *nunc te possideant aliae; mox sola tenebo*. In the *Met.* it also occurs 3, 15 (63, 13) *amor is, quo tibi teneor*; see the comm. of vdPaardt 1971, 117 with more examples.

frueris: here constructed with an accusative as in e.g. Ter. *Haut.* 401 *me miserum non licere meo modo ingenium frui*; Cato *Agr.* 149, 1. See Callebat 1968, 487.

mortis quiete: the parallelism with the following colon is obvious: *mortis – uitae, quiete – uoluptate, recreaberis – laetaberis*. Thus *mortis quiete recreari* cannot mean anything else but 'be restored by the sleep of death' versus 'enjoy life'. For a further discussion of this expression we refer to Appendix II, 4.2.1.

incertum: according to *ThLL* s.v. 881, 43 the junction *incertum simulacrum* is found in our passage only. *Incertum* expresses the notion that Thrasyllus will not yet be a shade completely: he will not be entirely dead, but his blindness will give him a status close to death. The description of the *ThLL* 'caecus neque incolumis neque mortuus' seems correct to us. It is hard to describe the quality of Thrasyllus' existence in the shady realm between death and life; we attempt to render it here by 'vague'. Heine 1962, 241 points out how much this undefined state is dominated by the oxymoron, in which the mutually exclusive becomes real, e.g. *uiuo tibi morientur oculi nec quicquam uidebis nisi dormiens* (186, 15-16). Cf. also Amat 1972, 148. As an illustration of the notion that blindness is a twilight state between death and life Hildebrand cites Artem. 5,77 ἔδοξέ τις λέγειν αὐτῷ τινα 'ἀποθανεῖν μὲν μὴ φοβοῦ, ζῆν δὲ οὐ δύνασαι'. τυφλὸς ἐγένετο ὀρθῶς καὶ κατὰ λόγον ἀποβάντος αὐτῷ τοῦ τοιούτου· οὐκ ἐτεθνήκει μὲν γὰρ παρ' ὅσον ἔζη, οὐκ ἔζη δὲ παρ' ὅσον οὐκ ἔβλεπε τὸ φῶς. We refer for further discussion of this passage to Appendix II, 2.2 f.

incertum simulacrum: an implied simile which gives a poetic colour to the passage.

expugnauit: 'destroy an eye' is a meaning of *expugnare* not found elsewhere; cf. *ThLL* s.v. 1809, 62. It suggests that the eyes are Charite's adversaries and have to be fought, as Charite *conuulnerat tota lumina* a little later (187, 4). The choice of the verb may have been influenced by the assonances produced by *expugnauit pupulas*. About the feminine passion to pluck out someone's eyes, Don. *Eun.* 4, 6, 2 (with reference to Ter. *Eun.* 740 *atqui si illam digito attigerit uno, oculi ilico effodientur*) says: *femineae minae sunt et in libidinosos quam maxime...in oculos autem maxime saeuire feminas et tragoediae fere et comoediae protestantur*. Cf. Prop. 3, 8, 7 *tu* (Cynthia) *minitare oculos subiecta exurere flamma*, where Cynthia threatens Propertius whom she suspects of being unfaithful. In the Greek novel see e.g. Charito 6,5,8 Καλλιρόη...ὥρμησεν...τοὺς ὀφθαλμοὺς ἐξορύξαι. For further literature on putting eyes out, see *RAC* s.v. Blindheit 437 f.

quodque est in aerumna miserrimum etc.: cf. for the idea Sen. *Ag.* 491 *nec hoc leuamen denique aerumnis datur, / uidere saltem et nosse quo pereant malo*; see Tarrant ad loc., who also cites Luc. 3, 416 *tantum terroribus addit / quos timeant non nosse deos*.

queraris: Petschenig 1888, 765 proposes, without any further explanation, to read *quereris*.

At ego sepulchrum mei Tlepolemi tuo luminum cruore libabo et 186, 23-35
sanctis manibus eius istis oculis parentabo: "But I will pour out a libation on the tomb of my Tlepolemus with the blood of your eyes, and I will make a sacrifice to his sacred spirit with those eyes."

sepulchrum: F reads *sepulchrū* (but *ū* seems to have been written by another hand *in rasura*, which originally had *ŏ*); φα read -*um*. The accusative is here used to indicate the place where the libation is poured, not the direct object; a good parallel for this is Verg. *A.* 12, 173 *dant fruges manibus salsas et tempora ferro / summa notant pecudum, paterisque altaria libant*. Despite Hildebrand's earlier citation of this passage Helm and Brandt-Ehlers still change the text to *sepulchro*. Helm's reference to 4, 22 (91, 9 f.) does not make sense to us because *memoriae* in 91, 9 *memoriae defunctorum commilitonum uino mero libant* is a final dative. More worthy of consideration is the old conjecture of Colvius (adopted by Oudendorp) *ad ego sepulchrum*, but it is not compelling in view of the parallel from Vergil. Helm-Krenkel print *sepulchrum* again, with all modern editors. Augello 1977, 182 also defends this reading.

tuo luminum cruore: 'with your eye-blood', i.e. 'with the blood of your eyes'. *Tuo* is a hypallage in appearance only (differently Bernhard 1927, 215).

manibus: during the empire *manes* becomes the regular expression for the dead; cf. Latte 1960, 99. The combination *sanctis manibus* is found in grave inscriptions, e.g. *CIL* XIV 704 *dis manibus sanctis castis piis* and *CE* 1043, 3 *te, Tellus, sanctosque precor pro coniugis (!) Manes* (= *CIL* VI 14404). For the use of the plural see *GCA* 1981, 101 on 156, 20.

parentabo: during the Parentalia (February 13-21) sacrifices of bread, salt, wine and wreaths were made at graves (see Latte 1960, 98). Apuleius correctly distinguishes between *libare* (said of liquids, in this case *cruor*) and *parentare* (which has the general meaning 'perform the rites at the tombs of the dead'). This sharp distinction is not made elsewhere: cf. Liv. 24, 21, 2 *parentare sanguine*.

186, 25-27 Sed quid mora temporis dignum cruciatum lucraris et meos forsitan tibi pestiferos imaginaris amplexus? "But why grant you a respite from the torture you deserve and allow you to dream, perhaps, of my deadly embraces?"

mora temporis: *temporis* develops the notion of the word it complements (*mora*), so it is not 'sans utilité' (Médan 1925, 363).

lucraris: 'to be spared or relieved (from punishment or sim.)' (*OLD*); cf. Man. 5, 319 *non...poenam...lucretur noxius*; [Quint.] *Decl.* 4, 9 *ne supplicia properato...lucrarentur obitu*. For more examples see *ThLL* s.v. 1717, 23 f.

imaginaris: this word is attested from Sen. onward, e.g. *Const.* 6, 7 *tabellas, quibus auaritia...diuitias imaginatur*.

pestiferos: cf. Sil. 9, 37 *pestifero pugnae castra incendebat amore*. Of course Thrasyllus only dreams of *amplexus; pestiferos* is Charite's addition.

The hyperbaton *meos...pestiferos...amplexus* attracts the reader's attention. This figure of speech often occurs in ch. 12: lines 11, 22, 24, 26-27, 28, 31; 187, 1. The position of *forsitan* is remarkable, too.

186, 27-28 Relictis somnolentis tenebris ad aliam poenalem euigila caliginem: "Leave the darkness of your sleep and wake up to another gloom – your punishment."

In the ablative absolute the vowels *e, i, o* dominate, in the rest of the sentence *a* and *i*.

somnolentis: apart from this passage, this adjective occurs in the *Met.* 1, 26 (24, 10) and 10, 26 (258, 3). Gargantini 1963, 41 discusses adjectives in *-ulento-* (indicating an abundance of something), which are less frequent in the *Met.* than adjectives in *-oso-*. The adjective is not attested before Apul.; see Ernout

1949, 96. After Apul. it is found e.g. Solin. 20, 7 *somnolentam (bestiam) arbor sustinet*; Ambr. *Nab.* 15, 64 *somnolentae...mentis.*
   poenalem: this adjective occurs also 7, 21 (170, 18) *poenale...exitium.*
   euigila caliginem: the juxtaposition accentuates the paradox.

Attolle uacuam faciem, uindictam recognosce, infortunium intellege, aerumnas computa: "Raise your empty face, recognize vengeance, comprehend your misery, reckon up your adversities." 186, 28-30

The tetracolon consists of 9, 7, 8, 6 syllables respectively, if the elisions are counted as such. The last three cola are parallel, whereas the first and second colon are placed chiastically to one another; only the first noun has an attribute. For the 'Anfangsstellung des Verbums', see Möbitz 1924, 118. The sentence has many assonances: *attolle uacuam faciem*; many *c*'s in *uindictam recognosce; in* and *t* in *infortunium intellege.*
   atolle...faciem: cf. 183, 9 with our comm.
   uacuam faciem: 'an empty face', i.e. a face from which the eyes have gone; cf. Sen. *Oed.* 1011 *quo auertis caput / uacuosque uultus.* Of course it is used proleptically here.
   infortunium: 'misfortune', 'misery'. The word is discussed *GCA* 1977, 201 (4, 27 : 95, 18).

Sic pudicae mulieri tui placuerunt oculi, sic faces nuptiales tuos illuminarunt thalamos: "Thus have your eyes pleased a chaste woman, thus have the wedding torches illuminated your bridal chamber." 186, 30-31
   Sic: its consequence follows at 187, 3 f.
   tui placuerunt oculi: refers to 186, 11 *oculi isti, quibus male placui.* Thrasyllus' eyes, which Charite has pleased to her misfortune, have not only become her ruin, but also Thrasyllus'. *Male* (line 12) appears to refer to more than one person.
   illuminarunt: ironically, since he is about to lose his *lumina.*

Vltrices habebis pronubas et orbitatem comitem et perpetuae conscientiae stimulum': "Avenging matrons of honour you will have, blindness as a companion, and the prick of conscience for ever'." 187, 1-2
   pronubas: Sen. *Tro.* 1132 f. *thalami more praecedunt faces / et pronuba illi Tyndaris* shows the same combination of *thalamus, fax,* and *pronuba* as our sentence. The *pronubae*, whose part at the wedding is supportive (see the comm. of Pease on Verg. *A.* 4, 166), become *ultrices*, an adjective that is associated in the first place with *Dirae* (Verg. *A.* 4, 473 *ultricesque sedent in limine Dirae*), *Curae* (Verg. *A.* 6, 274 *ultrices posuere cubilia Curae*), or *Furiae* (Claud. *Carm. Min.* 22, 14 *ultrices Furias*). But it remains only an association, which should not be included explicitly in the translation as it is by Butler, Adlington-Gaselee, Carlesi, Brandt-Ehlers, Augello, Rode-Burck, Helm-Krenkel, and Schwartz. The oxymoron *ultrices pronubae* forms the climax of this perverted marriage.

orbitatem: the notion 'deprivation' normally becomes 'bereavement of parents or children'. For the meaning 'loss of one or two eyes > blindness' *OLD* can cite only our passage. Comparable is Apul. *Soc.* 7 (14, 15) *ut Hannibali somnia orbitatem oculi comminentur*. See Médan 1925, 159; Eicke 1956, 108; and Löfstedt 1933, 375, who speaks about *orbus* = *caecus* (cf. Italian *orbo* and Romanian *orb* in the same meaning). In that meaning we find *orbus* in *Met.* 5, 9 (109, 23) *orba et saeua et iniqua Fortuna*.

Purser 1906, 49 thinks that the reading used by us upsets the balance of this most rhetorical peroration. He supposes that something like *constantem famulum* should be read after *stimulum*. That would indeed give a balanced sentence : Furies as *pronubas*, *orbitatem* as *comitem*, and *stimulum* as *famulum*. But, as we have argued above, the Furies do not belong in the translation. The considerable effect of the final sentence is due not only to its content, but also – and especially – to the variatio. For *habebis* has three objects, which are all varied: 1. *habebis*, surrounded by the hyperbaton *ultrices...pronubas;* 2. *orbitatem* with *comitem* as a predicate accusative; 3. *stimulum*, with an explicative genitive; the objects, then, consist of a series of 'Wachsende Glieder' (respectively 6, 7 and 12 syllables). For the same reason we do not follow Robertson's suggestion to read ⟨*perpetuae noctis caliginem*⟩ *perpetuae conscientiae*. We agree, then, with Purser and Robertson in accepting three objects against e.g. Brandt-Ehlers who translate: 'Blindheit deine Begleiterin und der ewige Stachel deines Gewissens' and therefore treat *comitem* and *stimulum* as qualifiers of *orbitatem*. Though their translation makes good sense, we prefer ours, since thus a causal series is obtained in which *orbitas* is caused by the *ultrices pronubae* and the *stimulus* results from *orbitas*. In the other translation the causal link between *ultrices pronubas* and *orbitatem* with qualifiers seems a little less clear.

CHAPTER XIII

Only now does Charite carry out the punishment: she puts out Thrasyllus' eyes. After this deed she runs madly through the town.

Ad hunc modum uaticinata mulier acu crinali capite deprompta 187, 3-9
Thrasylli conuulnerat tota lumina eumque prorsus exoculatum relinquens, dum dolore[m] nescio crapulam cum somno discutit, arrepto nudo gladio, quo se Tlepolemus solebat incingere, per mediam ciuitatem cursu furioso proripit se procul dubi⟨o⟩ nescio quod scelus gestiens: "Having prophesied in this way, the woman took a hairpin from her head and pierced Thrasyllus' eyes completely, leaving him totally blind. While, under the influence of the unexplained pain, he was shaking off his intoxication with his sleep, she grasped the bare sword with which Tlepolemus used to gird himself and dashed right across town at a frenzied run, undoubtedly with every intention to do some dreadful thing."

Ad hunc modum: whereas we remarked in our comm. on 7, 22 (170, 19) that in book 7 Apul. often starts a new pericope with *talis*, we see in book 8 a distinct preference for expressions like *ad hunc modum* (180, 17 and our passage); *ad istum modum* (191, 28; 195, 20; 200, 10); *haec et huius modi* (197, 27). Cf. Callebat 1968, 214, who also points out the increased frequency of these expressions in the later books of the *Met*.

acu crinali: a preeminently feminine ornament, which excited the anger of Tert. *Virg.* 12, 2 *uertunt capillum et acu lasciuiore comam sibi inserunt, crinibus a fronte diuisis apertum professae mulieritatem*. As a weapon - albeit for a less cruel treatment - the *acus crinalis* is also used Petron. 21 *hinc Psyche acu comatoria cupienti mihi inuocare Quiritum fidem malas pungebat*. Also Hier. *Ruf.* 3, 11 *linguam ueridicam discriminali acu confodiebant*.

Masculis animis and fuming with anger Charite enters the room, holds forth to the sleeping Thrasyllus in a highly rhetorical fashion, and - presumably still *masculis animis* - stabs his eyes with... the feminine ornament par excellence. The irony is unmistakable. Eicke 1956, 115 may be right in his remark about this passage that 'alles ist nur burleskes Spiel'; yet its motif (piercing someone's eyes with pins) is not from burlesque, but from tragedy. Oedipus does it to himself with the brooches from Iocasta's dress (Soph. *O.R.* 1268 f.) and Polymestor is blinded by women in this way (Eur. *Hec.* 1170). Cf. also Erbse 1950, 111 'Ein Motiv...das ihm (Apuleius) aus hellenistischen Darstellungen wohlbekant war'.

crinalis: this adjective, originally used by poets only (Verg., Ov., Stat.), is found in prose from Apuleius onward; see *ThLL* s.v.

deprompta: α has the correct reading (adopted by Oudendorp, Hildebrand, vdVliet, Robertson, Brandt-Ehlers, Frassinetti, Helm-Krenkel, vThiel); F has *depta** in which *de* seems to have been added later *in rasura*; *depta* φ. Helm III (who uses the spelling *depromta* with Valpy, Giarratano, Terzaghi, and Scazzoso) adduces 4, 1 (74, 13) *rebus...depromptis* and 186, 1 *depromptis calicibus* as good parallels in which the mss. are not in doubt as to the spelling. Nor is there any question about the spelling in 6, 18 (142, 3), the remaining passage with *depromptus*.

conuulnerat: for the meaning 'to stab' cf. Fron. *Aq.* 27, 3 *quinariae impetratae, ne riuus saepius conuulneretur, una fistula excipiuntur*. The verb suggests that the eyes are regarded as enemies; cf. our comm. on 186, 22 *expugnauit pupulas*.

Heine 1962, 150 n. 1 offers several examples of detailed descriptions of cruelty, e.g. Venus' treatment of the pregnant Psyche (6, 9-10), the punishment which the robbers devise for Charite (6, 31-32), the *puer's* sadism (7, 17-19). Descriptions of this type fit into the picture of the 'deformierte Welt' (Heine) which the *Met.* presents.

exoculatum: in addition to our passage and 7, 2 (155, 21) *prorsus exoculatam...Fortunam* (likewise emphasized by *prorsus*) this verb is only found Plaut. *Rud.* 731 *ni ei caput exoculassitis...ego uos uirgis circumuinciam*.

dolore: F *dolorem*, emended by ς.

nescio: *nescius* in the passive meaning 'not known', 'unknown' is elsewhere found only in Plautus (e.g. *Rud.* 275 *in locis nesciis nescia spe sumus*, with a play upon the meaning 'unknown' and 'unknowing') and in Tac. *Ann.* 16, 14, 3 *neque nescium habebat Anteium caritate Agrippinae inuisum Neroni* (*Antistius Sosianus*). In the *Met.* compare 5, 12 (112, 20) *sarcinae nesciae rudimento miratur...incrementum...uteri* (said of Psyche, pregnant for the first time).

crapulam...discutit: this combination is found only a few times in Plin. *Nat.*, e.g. 20, 84 *sumpta (brassica) crapulam discuti*. See further *ThLL* s.v. 1097, 61.

per mediam ciuitatem etc.: cf. 181, 5 *cursuque bacchata furibundo per plateas populosas...fertur* when Charite learns about Tlepolemus' death. Charite's reaction has epic predecessors: Dido in Verg. *A.* 4, 300 *totam...incensa (regina) per urbem/bacchatur* (with the note by Pease, who compares *Ciris* 167 *infelix uirgo tota bacchatur in urbe*) and Amata in *A.* 7, 377 *immensam sine more furit lymphata per urbem*. We first noted the similarity between Charite and Dido in our comm. on 6, 29 (151, 18-20), where Charite calls herself *infelix*. See also Forbes 1943/4, 39, Walsh 1970, 54 and Introd. 4.2.3. Observe with regard to these parallel passages that, while the women's reaction is the same, its cause is not (although love usually plays a part).

For the meaning *ciuitas* = *urbs* see vdPaardt 1971, 41.

cursu furioso proripit se: Bernhard 1927, 178 treats *cursu* as a pleonastic substantive adverbial qualifier, a frequent Apuleian phenomenon. In his opinion the addition of a further pleonastic *furioso* is an even more remarkable Apuleianism. This conclusion has been endorsed by *GCA* 1977, 32 on 4, 2 (75, 16); our comm. on 7, 19 (168, 17) modifies it. Now we prefer to drop the qualification 'pleonastic' entirely: one can *se proripere fuga* and *se proripere cursu*; thus, *cursu* as a further qualification of *se proripere* is not redundant.

Heine 1962, 242 rightly remarks that *cursu furioso* is not a hyperbolical exaggeration: Charite really has gone mad, cf. *uaesanis manibus* 187, 11. Nor is there hyperbolical exaggeration in the passages quoted from Vergil. Cf. also 181, 5 *cursuque bacchata furibundo* (*Charite*). Charite's *furor* is a counterpart to Thrasyllus' *furiosae libidinis impetus* (178, 20).

procul dubio nescio quod scelus: apart from repeating a thought the present narrator may have had at the time the events took place, the phrase signals to the audience that the drama approaches its climax; at the same time it is a reminder of the fact that the audience already knows the outcome in general terms (176, 21 *fuit Charite*).

procul dubio: this expression, which has a solemn ring, is always used in passages in which an impending death is described: 4, 3 (76, 20) with our comm., 4, 25 (94, 8), and 7, 26 (174, 5).

Helm III and Brandt-Ehlers insert *et* before *procul*; vdVliet, Gaselee, and Robertson insert *et* before *recta* (below). The remaining editors follow the reading of the mss. and differ only on the manner of punctuation. Oudendorp and Valpy put a period after *se*. The objection against this is that a stop after *proripit se* is not in keeping with Apuleius' practice: nowhere, as far as we know, does he have a sentence ending in *se*. Hildebrand, Giarratano, Terzaghi, Frassinetti, and Scazzoso put a comma after *se*. In that case one has to assume an asyndeton; to avoid that, both Helm III and vdVliet with their respective followers propose additions. On the one hand we share the objection to the asyndeton; on the other hand, an addition seems too radical. Therefore we opt for a semicolon after *gestiens*: thus a new part of the sentence starts with *recta*, continuing through *manibus*; we do not make the new sentence start with *at nos*, as do Helm-Krenkel and vThiel. The clause *procul...gestiens* we take as an explanation of (*cursu*) *furioso*.

scelus: 'something terrible'; cf. Mart. 7, 14, 1 *accidit infandum nostrae scelus, Aule, puellae: / amisit lusus deliciasque suas* (viz. her pet bird).

gestiens: the construction of *gestire* with a direct object is not found until the *Met.*, e.g. 3, 18 (65, 19) *aditum gestientes*; see vdPaardt 1971,139 ad loc. and *ThLL* s.v. 1962, 23 f.

Recta monimentum mariti contendit, at nos et omnis populus 187, 9-12 nudatis totis aedibus studiose consequimur hortati mutuo ferrum uaesanis extorquere manibus: "She ran straight to her husband's tomb, but we and the whole population left our houses empty and followed her full of concern, urging each other to wrest the sword from her crazed hands."

recta: thus ς; F has *secta*, rewritten by a second hand. On the interchange of *r* and *s* see Helm, Praef. *Fl.* 45. *Recta* in this meaning is not uncommon in the *Met.*, e.g. 5, 14 (114, 8); see Callebat 1968, 250 n. 494.

totis = *omnibus*, e.g. 3, 16 (63, 22); see vdPaardt 1971, 121 ad loc.

nudatis: a military term (Médan 1925, 257), used elsewhere with the object *moenia* or *urbem*, e.g. Liv. 21, 11, 7 *cum...muros defensoribus nudassent*. Similarly, the houses are 'stripped' of their inhabitants now, because of the people's concern for Charite. For the meaning 'without inhabitants' with no further qualification, cf. Luc. 4, 148 *nudatos Caesar colles desertaque castra / conspiciens* and Amm. 24, 2, 17 *urbem nudatam irrupit*. Brantius' conjecture *uiduatis*, adopted by Hildebrand, is therefore unnecessary.

studiose: the translations vary considerably; e.g. Adlington 'incontinently', Vallette 'vivement', Brandt-Ehlers 'hastig', Helm-Krenkel 'eifrig', Schwartz 'in aller ijl', Scazzoso 'con ansia'. Our translation is based on the reflection that *studiose* pertains to the townspeople's anxiety about the prospective *scelus*, i.e. an attempt at suicide. Their *studium* is evident from the attempts to take Charite's sword away. They sympathize with her, are worried about her; cf. e.g. Cic. *Inv.* 2, 34, 104 *pro suo studio, quod in uos habuit semper*. The people's *studium* has already been evident at Tlepolemus' death 181, 7 *confluunt ciuium maestae cateruae, secuntur obuii dolore sociato, ciuitas cuncta uacuatur studio uisionis*, where there is the same combination of leaving the houses (*uacuatur*) and *studium*. Reactions on the part of the townspeople are similarly described more than once, e.g. 7, 13 (163, 21 f.) *tota ciuitas...effunditur*, where Charite, riding on the ass, is welcomed back; 3, 2 (53, 1) *ciuitas omnis in publicum effusa* and soon after (19) *studio uisendi*. vdPaardt 1971, 36 ad loc. suggests a reference to Verg. *A*. 2, 63 *undique uisendi studio Troiana inuentus / circumfusa ruit*. Compare also *A*. 12, 131 *tum studio effusae matres*.

hortati: here constructed with an infinitive. This usage is occasionally found as early as Cicero; it does not become frequent until the empire. See *ThLL* s.v. 3011, 43 f.

mutuo: this adverb is used frequently in the *Met.* to indicate a reciprocity; see *GCA* 1977, 194 on 94, 25.

187, 12-16 Sed Charite capulum Tlepolemi propter asssistens gladioque fulgenti singulos abigens, ubi fletus uberes et lamentationes uarias cunctorum intuetur, 'abicite', inquit, importunas lacrimas, abicite luctum meis uirtutibus alienum: "But Charite posted herself close to Tlepolemus' coffin, fending off everyone with the glittering sword, and said, when she saw the abundant tears and the varied laments of all: 'abandon your inappropriate tears, abandon your mourning which does not suit my valiant behaviour."

capulum: thus φ, generally accepted against F's *caput* (in margine add. *c̃apulũ*, paene erasum). The word means 'coffin' here as well as 4, 18 (87, 29) with our comm. The more usual sense of 'handle', 'hilt' occurs 1, 13 (12, 13) *capulo tenus*.

propter: should be taken as an adverb; see *GCA* 1977, 47 on 4, 4 (77, 13) and our comm. on 176, 19.

importunas...alienum: observe the chiastic position of the adjectives.

abicite...lacrimas, abicite luctum: a rhetorical anaphora in a pathetic context; see Médan 1925, 257; Strilciw 1925, 115; Bernard 1927, 235; Chodaczek 1932, 479. Repetition of a verb with different objects is also found e.g. 5, 1 (103, 10) *uidet lucum...uidet fontem*; 194, 9 *laqueum sibi nectit infantulumque...eodem funiculo nectit*. For *abicere* in the sense of 'give up', i.e. 'cease', cf. Cic. *Att*. 11, 21, 1 *dolorem...quem...iam abieceram*. Charite says *masculis animis* what Socrates said to his friends before his death: ἐγὼ μέντοι οὐχ ἥκιστα τούτου ἕνεκα τὰς γυναῖκας ἀπέπεμψα, ἵνα μὴ τοιαῦτα (i.e. weeping) πλημμελοῖεν (Pl. *Phd.* 117 D).

Vindicaui in mei mariti cruentum peremptorem, punita sum funestum mearum [mearum] nuptiarum praedonem: "I have taken revenge on the bloodstained killer of my husband, I have punished the death-dealing robber of my marriage." 187, 16-18

peremptorem: for Apuleius' preference for nouns in *-tor*, see Bernhard 1927, 104 f. *Peremptor* also occurs 7, 24 (172, 9); see our comm. ad loc.

punita sum: here used as a deponent, as Cic. *Tusc.* 1, 107; *Mil.* 13, 33. The active forms are found e.g. 5, 24 (122, 12); 8, 9 (184, 8). See Callebat 1968, 229; Flobert 1975, 203.

mariti cruentum: a striking juxtaposition when we consider that the *maritus* introduced himself as Haemus (αἷμα) at the time.

mearum: thus φ; F has *mearum mearum*. Chodaczek 1932, 479 seems to be the only one to take the double *mearum* as a *geminatio emphatica* to emphasize the πάθος. He refers to 3, 16 (64, 15) *iam de fuga consilium tenebam, sed istud quidem tui tui contemplatione abieci statim* where F has *tui tui*, φ deletes one *tui*, and the editors follow φ. So does vdPaardt 1971, 128 ad loc., who points out that '*geminatio* in genitive form of *tu* never occurs elsewhere'. This is an argument for us not to follow Chodaczek, even if (1) emphatic *geminatio* is generally quite frequent in Apul. (see LHSz 2, 809); (2) *geminatio* of pronouns occurs in the nominative (see Hofmann LU [3]1951, 59); (3) it remains curious that dittography of *complete* words seems to occur in F in these two passages only, both involving a pronoun in the genitive (Helm Praef. *Fl.* LIII does not mention any examples of this, either). A second argument for the deletion of the second *mearum* might be found in the fact that in case of deletion the number of syllables of *uindicaui...praedonem* would be 16 plus 17 (without deletion 16 plus 20), which makes for a more symmetrical structure; *abicite...alienum* has 16 syllables as well.

praedonem: for *praedo* followed by the genitive of what has been stolen, cf. Cic. *Ver.* 4, 95 *duo...sigilla...tollunt, ne...inanes ad istum praedonem religionum reuertantur.*

Iam tempus est, ut isto gladio deorsus ad meum Tlepolemum uiam quaeram', "Now is the time to seek with that sword a road down to my Tlepolemus'." 187, 18-19

tempus est ut: usually *tempus est* is followed by an infinitive; for the construction with *ut* cf. Cypr. *Ep.* 36, 3, 3 *tempus est..., ut agant delicti paenitentiam* (see Callebat 1968, 341). It is also followed by the genitive of the gerund, e.g. Cic. *Tusc.* 5, 10 *cuius de disciplina aliud tempus fuerit fortasse dicendi*; see LHSz 2, 349 and 375.

isto: one expects *hoc* but, as Callebat 1968, 271 rightly argues, *iste* can in this pathetic sentence very well suggest a gesture to the audience, as e.g. 5, 10 (110,

21) *fomentis olidis et pannis sordidis. . . manus tam delicatas istas adurens*, where *manus istas* refer to the speaker's hands. It may also be meant as a signal to the reader ('that well-known sword'), referring in this connection to Dido, Charite's illustrious epic predecessor; see the next lemma. Still another possibility is a reference to the sword of which Charite dreamt in the robbers' cave as one of the means to put an end to her life at the time; cf. vdPaardt *SAG* 1981, 22. For this use of *iste* see also our comm. on 4, 26 (94, 19).

gladio: when Charite, among the robbers, wanted to commit suicide in despair, she considered several ways: *laqueus aut gladius aut certe praecipitium procul dubio capessendum est* (4, 25 : 94, 7). Later (181, 28) she wanted to join Tlepolemus by means of *inedia*; see our comm. ad loc. Now it is the sword of her beloved husband that will kill her. In this, too, Charite follows her epic predecessor Dido, who committed suicide with Aeneas' sword: Verg. *A*. 4, 646 f.

A survey of the different ways in which women in classical literature committed suicide is given by Pease on *A*. 4, 475, from which appears that 'the favourite means employed were the dagger(. . .), the pyre (. . .), and hanging'.

deorsus: i.e. *ad inferos*. Neither *OLD* nor *ThLL* give another example of this use of *deorsus*. Comparable, however, is *VL Deut*. 32, 22 (*Lugd*.) *usque ad inferos deorsum* (LXX ἕως ᾅδου κάτω; Vulg. *usque ad inferni nouissima*) and the use of *demeare* 181, 26 with our comm. *ad loc*. Charite's last words are, of course, a paraphrase of her resolution to take her own life. As a model of the faithful wife who, separated from her husband and resisting the advances of others, commits suicide at the (false) news of her husband's death so as to prevent a second marriage Trenkner 1958, 61 offers Helen from the tragedy of the same name by Euripides. Another instance is found Ach. Tat. 3, 17, where the first person-narrator wants to die by his own hand because his beloved Leucippe has supposedly been murdered. We may also mention Pyramus, who commits suicide because he thinks that Thisbe has been devoured by a lion (Ov. *Met*. 4, 107 f.); Thisbe kills herself with Pyramus' sword shortly after (162 f.).

uiam: 181, 27 Charite was looking for several *uias*; now she has made up her mind (*uiam*).

CHAPTER XIV

The terrible deaths of Charite and Thrasyllus.

Et enarratis ordine singulis, quae sibi per somnium nuntiauerat maritus quoque astu Thrasyllum inductum petisset, ferro sub papillam dexteram transadacto [c̄] corruit et in suo sibi peruolutata sanguine postremo balbuttiens incerto sermone perflauit animam uirilem:"And after she had narrated in an orderly way everything her husband had told her in her dream and through what ruse she had enticed and attacked Thrasyllus, she thrust the sword under her right breast, right through, and collapsed. And writhing in her own blood, stammering some final, incomprehensible words, she breathed out her spirit, as courageous as a man's." 187, 19-24

enarratis ordine singulis: for the narrative problem involved, see Introduction 4.2.1.3.

ordine: the correct chronological order of the narrative is similarly stressed e.g. 7, 6 (158, 19) *rei noscendae carpo ordinem* and 9, 17 (215, 19) *ordine mihi singula retexe*: see also above on 177, 1 *referam uobis a capite*. Charite, then, heeds the advice of the rhetorical handbooks even in extremis: *Rhet. Her.* 1, 9, 15 *rem dilucide narrabimus si ut quidquid primum gestum erit, ita primum exponemus et rerum et temporum ordinem conseruabimus*. See further Lausberg 1960, 177 f.

somnium: for the dream motif see 183, 8-21 with our comm.

nuntiauerat...petisset: Callebat 1968, 343 notes that the shift from indicative to subjunctive sometimes is due to no more than an interest in variation. Here, however, the indicative clearly marks an objective fact, the subjunctive indicates that *quoque...petisset* is to be taken as an indirect question.

inductum: for the meaning 'lead on' with a connotation of deceit cf. 10, 21 (253, 4) *et cetera, quis mulieres et alios inducunt et suas testantur adfectationes* (where the aspect of deceit of course fits the narrator's point of view, not that of the active lady); the notion of deceit is explicit at 9, 21 (219, 10) *fallacia...iuuenis inductus*.

sub papillam dexteram: Otho proceeded more efficiently: *uno se traiecit ictu infra laeuam papillam* (Suet. *Otho* 11, 2); if Charite with her *anima uirilis* had acted as professionally, we would have missed the elements *peruolutare* and *incerto sermone balbuttire*. As a matter of fact Tlepolemus, too, receives his mortal wound on the right (*femus dexterum* 180, 14); see our note ad loc.

transaducto: *transadigere* is the accepted term in epic poetry since Verg. *A.* 12, 508 *transadigit costas et cratis pectoris ensem*, Stat. *Theb.* 5, 127. *aliquem ferro*, Sil. 10, 140 *aliquem iaculo*. Apul. is the first to use this poetic (Bernhard 1927, 122) word in prose (four times). After him it remains poetic: Prudentius,

133

Dracontius, Corippus; in prose the only other passage is Schol. on Stat. *Theb.* 10, 309. See above on 179, 14 (*transabiit*). Cf. also Löfstedt 1911, 92 on the tendency in late Latin to strengthen simple verbs by forming compounds and even to reinforce compounds by further compounding them, a procedure he calls 'Dekomposition'.

corruit: F and φ have *c̄ corruit*; the emendation occurs in ς. Oudendorp proposed to read *concorruit* but had to make up the verb for the purpose; Chodaczek 1930/31, 414 suggested *corpus corruit* as at 183, 2 f. *Charite...uelut...fulmine percussa corruit corpus*, but there is no proof that *c̄* can be used as a compendium for *corpus* and Chodaczek's reference to 1, 7 (7, 16) *[c̄]contraho* does not strengthen his case. *c̄ corruit* should rather be treated as a instance of dittography, *corruit* being the correct reading. Cf. e.g. 10, 28 (259, 17) *exanimis corruit* (also 9,38:232,22 and 2,17:39,9 *ambo corruimus inter mutuos amplexus*). A good parallel passage with an identical situation is Prop. 2, 8, 21 *Antigonae tumulo Boeotius Haemon / corruit ipse suo saucius ense latus.*

suo sibi: Callebat 1968, 258 f. discusses pleonastic reinforcement of the possessive by the dative of the reflexive pronoun, something which occurs quite regularly also in comedy. See *GCA* 1981, 269 on 7, 28 (176, 1), where further literature is mentioned.

peruolutata: a rare verb, which is attested only in Cic. *Att.* 12, 2 *meos...peruolutas libros* and *de Orat.* 1, 158 *scriptores eligendi et peruolutandi*, where it has a slightly more specialized sense.

balbuttiens: F has *balbultiens*, φ *balbutiens*. The verb *balbultire* is not attested elsewhere. Helm's spelling, adopted by all modern editors with the exception of Scazzoso, is based on 1, 26 (24, 11) and 10, 10 (244, 11), where F has *–tt–*. *ThLL* notes s.v. *balbutio* that *–tt–* is transmitted in many passages from Cic. *Ac.* 4, 137 (Non. 112 L) and Hor. *Sat.* 1, 3, 48 (cod. γ Porph.) onwards.

perflauit: this is the reading in F, but there is a dash or hyphen between *per* and *flauit* and a small erasure is to be noted above *fl.* φ has *perflauit* without dash or other markings; *perafflauit* α; *perefflauit* ς, the reading adopted by Hildebrand, Giarratano, Terzaghi, Frassinetti, Scazzoso; Pricaeus' conjecture *proflauit* was approved of by vdVliet, Gaselee and Robertson; Helm's *efflauit* was printed also by Brandt-Ehlers, Helm-Krenkel and vThiel. *Efflauit* is the verb to be expected in this situation but it has no support in the mss. *Perflauit*, the verb most strongly supported by the mss., is defended by Armini 1928, 312 who points out that *per –* is often used as a reinforcing prefix in popular language, cf. Löfstedt 1911, 92 and 124; see also e.g. our comm. on 188, 21 *permensi*, where we noted Apuleius' liking for compounds with *per-*. Hence we follow Armini, as does Augello 1977, 183. It is true of course that the argument based on the force of *per-* also goes for *perafflauit* (α) a reading which finds some support in the dash between *per* and *flauit* and possibly the erasure in F, but *perafflare* is not attested in Latin.

animam uirilem: Charite's manly courage is here mentioned for the second time. See our remarks on 186, 6 *masculis animis* and *GCA* 1981, 38 on 6, 26 (148, 19).

The tale, which up to this points has exhibited the characteristics of a Greek romance, changes into a tragedy (cf. Tatum 1979, 72 f.). Cf. also *GCA* 1981, 78 on 6, 32 (153, 27) where the robbers say Charite is to die of *inedia* without being able to commit suicide. The reverse is the case here, whereas Thrasyllus presently will in fact die of *inedia*.

Tunc propere familiares miserae Charites accuratissime corpus ablutum inunita sepultura ibidem marito perpetuam coniugem reddidere: "Then the friends washed poor Charite's corpse hastily but with great care and returned her right there to her husband in one and the same grave – to be his wife for ever." 187, 24-26

miserae: Hijmans *AAGA* 1978, 116 calls *miserae Charites* 'a very well developed oxymoron' and refers back to 176, 21 f. *fuit Charite nobisque misella*.

ablutum: the same rite at 9, 30 (226, 8) *summis plangoribus summisque lamentationibus atque ultimo lauacro procurant*. For washing as part of the funeral rites see *RAC* s.v. Bestattung 202.

accuratissime: notwithstanding the fact that everything is done *propere*, this aspect of the rite is carried out with every care.

inunita: Fφ read *munita*. Lipsius, unable to make anything of it, changed to *unita* since the mss. quite often duplicate the final *m* of a previous word at the beginning of the next (see Helm, *praef. Fl.* XLVII). Stewech proposes *unica*, an only slightly less simple suggestion. The modern editors adopt Lipsius' *unita*. *Munita sepultura* might be taken as 'a fortified grave', but there is nothing in the context that hints at fortification of the grave or its purpose and neither *ThLL* nor Toynbee 1971 have instances for imperial times. Combinations such as *munire uiam* do not provide proper parallels either. In the passages quoted in *OLD* s.v. 5 the building material is either specified in the ablative (e.g. Col. 8, 14, 1 *aditus...firmis ostiolis munitos*) or implied by the context (e.g. Verg. *G*. 4, 178 *grandaeuis (apibus) oppida curae / et munire fauos*; Gel. 20, 1, 29 '*arcera*' *autem uocabatur plaustrum tectum undique et munitum, quasi arca quaedam magna...qua...aegri portari cubantes solebant*). Therefore we prefer to adopt Brantius' *inunita*, palaeographically a minor change, approved also by Oudendorp, Rohde 1885, 104 and vdVliet.

At 11, 27 (288, 11) Fφ show the identical situation: *munita ratio* changed by most editors to read *unita ratio*. There, too, *inunita ratio* should be read with Hildebrand (who refers to our passage, where, however, he prints *unita*). He is followed by vdVliet and Fredouille. The two passages support one another. For *inunire* ThLL mentions Tert. *adv.Val*. 29 p. 204, 19 *triformem naturam (hominis) primordio professi (gnostici) et tamen inunitam* (PM, *unitatem* F) *in Adam*, and Ps. Vigil.Thaps. *Trin*. 5 p.275a *quemadmodum diuinitatem altitudinis dei poterat scrutans penetrare uel inuniri* (Chifflet; *unit(er)* ut uidetur O; *inire* Bulhart). The very rarity of the verb contributed to the corruption *munita*. Finally it may be pointed out that the present chapter contains other unusual compounds (*transaductu, peruolutata, perflauit*).

For the thought one may compare Ov. *Met*. 4, 154 f., where Thisbe says (*estote rogati...*) *ut quos certus amor, quos hora nouissima iunxit,/componi tumulo non inuideatis eodem*. Bömer on 4, 166 *una requiescit in urna* gives many instances of suicide on the grave of the loved one and burial in the same grave, including Shakespeare, *Antony and Cleopatra* (Act 5, scene 2): 'Take up her bed / and bear her, women, from the monument./ She shall be buried by her Antony./ No grave upon the earth shall clip in it/ a pair so famous.' The Greek romance, too, provides instances of the motif of lovers buried in one grave: Charito 3, 3, 6; X.Eph. 3, 10, 2. See also below on *perpetuam coniugem*.

sepultura: the present context demands the concrete meaning 'grave' rather than 'burial', 'funeral obsequies' since Tlepolemus' burial has taken place earlier (181,12f.). (Nevertheless Brandt-Ehlers translate 'in einem vereintem Begräbnis'.) For the meaning 'place of burial' *OLD* mentions *CIL* 5, 2090 only. In Christian Latin 'grave' is the prevalent meaning attested for the first time in Tert. *Res.* 48, 7 *ipsum enim quod cecidit in morte, quod iacuit in sepultura, hoc et resurrexit*. (We note on other occasions, too, that a specific meaning for which Tert. is the first author listed in the lexica occurs in Apul.; see our comm. on 199, 18 *praesumptione*.) Apul. uses the word also at 2, 20 (41, 16) and 10, 6 (241, 1), where 'burial' is meant, and 4, 12 (84, 11), 8, 6 (181, 13), 9, 30 (226, 10) and 10, 25 (256, 17), where there is room for doubt and where the translators disagree with one another. A possible case of similar concrete use of an abstract noun is noted ad 182, 13 *adfixo seruitio*.

Tlepolemus' grave should be imagined as a large monument such as described (e.g.) by Toynbee and Ward Perkins 1956, 64 (with plate 4). Since such a grave could comprise more than one chamber and even more than one story (see Toynbee 1971, 135) and therefore stairs, 'all the doorways (must) once have had doors or metal grilles, the slots and the holes by which they were secured can still be seen' (on the monument described by Toynbee on p. 65).

perpetuam coniugem: for the thought cf. Aesch. *Choeph.* 894 f. φιλεῖς τὸν ἄνδρα; τοιγὰρ ἐν ταὐτῷ τάφῳ / κείσει. θανόντα δ'οὔτι μὴ προδῷς ποτε. The thought is also found in funeral inscriptions, e.g. *CE* 1559, 3-5 *animus sanctus cum maritost, anima caelo reddita est./parato hospitium: cara iungant corpora / haec rursum nostrae sed perpetuae nuptiae* (see Lattimore 1962, 249). The expression *perpetuae nuptiae* is used by Apuleius, too, referring to the marriage of Psyche and Cupid (6, 23:146, 12).[1]

This, then, is the end of Charite, a character who shows a marked change of behaviour in the passages of the novel where she plays a role. There is quite a distance between the grief-stricken girl in the robbers' den (4, 24 f.) and the avenging fury of the present passage. But even in the robbers' den she showed determination when trying to escape (6, 27) and insistence in obtaining an honourable position for the ass after her marriage (*non destitit* 7, 14:164, 24). And she forbids her husband – himself no weakling seeing his way of dealing with a band of brigands – to hunt for big game (178, 23 f.), but all this is a far cry

---

[1] Those who (with Merkelbach 1962, 72) advocate an Isiac interpretation of the Charite episode will find it interesting that, in a grave monument dated to the 2nd century A.D. and found to the south of Rome, parents who were adherents of the Osiris cult caused an αἰώνιον νυμφῶνα to be built for their son, perhaps a mystic marriage with the god, as Toynbee 1971, 96 suggests. For the inscription see *Bollettino della Commissssione Archeologica Comunale di Roma* 41, 1933, 211-215.

from the *ferinos mugitus* (183, 6 with our comm.), when she sees through the scoundrel Thrasyllus (see Vallette 44 n.1; Heine 1962, 238 f. and our note with 186, 6 with more literature; for the possibility that she is mistaken see Introd. 4.2.1.3). This kind of metamorphosis is not unique in the *Metamorphoses*: the stepmother at 10, 4 (Heine 1962, 242) and in a sense, though in the other direction, Thrasyllus himself; cf. our note with 188, 6.

Thrasyllus uero cognitis omnibus, nequiens idoneum exitium praesenti clade reddere certusque tanto facinori nec gladium sufficere, sponte delatus ibidem ad sepulchrum...: "Thrasyllus had heard all, but since he was unable to pay a fitting penalty by dying instantly, and because he was convinced that for so great an offence not even death by the sword was enough, he was taken, at his own request, to the grave..." 188, 1-4

idoneum...reddere: the phrase is not without problems. F reads *exitium praesenti clade*, defended only by Hildebrand. Stewech proposes *exitum* and is followed by almost all editors. Helm, Gaselee and Augello 1977, 184 read *cladi* for *clade*. Robertson proposes *praesenti⟨cladi nisi noua⟩clade*. He is followed by Brandt-Ehlers. Stewech in addition replaces *reddere* by *reperire* and vdVliet *exitium* by *supplicium*.

Augello is right in rejecting Robertson's conjecture as too drastic. Since Apuleius always uses *idoneus ad* or *idoneus* with a dative, there are also objections to construing it with an ablative as proposed by Frassinetti, Terzaghi and Scazzoso: *ThLL* s.v. mentions only one passage: *Rhet.Her.* 3, 3, 5 *res humiles et indignas...uiros fortes...contemnere oportere nec idoneas dignitate sua iudicare*.

Helm reads *cladi* and translates 'sah er keine Möglichkeit, dem Unglück, das er jetzt angestiftet hatte, einen angemessenen Abschluss zu geben'. To this translation and to Frassinetti's proposal one must object with the question why Thrasyllus could not make his death fit the situation.

We retain *clade* as transmitted and take *praesens* in the meaning 'immediate', cf. e.g. Curt. 9, 1, 12 *quippe morsum praesens mors sequebatur*; Verg. *A.* 8, 495 *regem ad supplicium praesenti Marte reposcunt*; Tac. *Ger.* 19, 1 *adulteria, quorum poena praesens et maritis permissa*. The next part of the sentence indicates that a sword does not suffice for Thrasyllus' great offence: a sword would provide a quick end, but he understands that he deserves a heavier, i.e. slower, penalty. His *exitium* must not be effected by a quick execution – thus Hildebrand's correct reasoning. If this interpretation is correct, there is here, as at 187, 24, an inversion: in Charite's case, *inedia* was described as *lenis* and *otiosa*.

For *clades = caedes* see e.g. Var. *L.* 5, 116 *gladium...a clade, quod fit ad hostium cladem gladium*, a particularly apt parallel, since it, like the sequel of our passage, plays on *clades-gladius* (cf. *ThLL* s.v. *clades* 1243, 53 f. with many other instances).

For the meaning of *exitium* we start from Prud. *Perist.* 10, 91 *aequum est, ut...pro tantis caedibus primus exitium luas*, where *exitium = poena*, even *poena mortis*. This (rare) meaning is supported by 7, 21 (170, 18), where *poenale exitium* means 'death penalty' (see *GCA* 1981, 223 ad loc.). Hence *exitium reddere* may equal *poenas reddere* (cf. e.g. Sal. *Iug.* 14, 21 *ne ille...fratris mei necis...grauis poenas reddat*; Liv. 7, 19, 3 *id pro immolatis...Romanis poenae hostibus redditum.* In our text *idoneus* expresses the relation between offence and punishment as does *pro* in the Livy passage.

Once again the narrator shows himself aware of Thrasyllus' thoughts and motivations, though he does not mention how he has become aware of them. In the Introduction we have argued that the narrator's information about, and interpretation of, Thrasyllus' character and actions may be read as almost entirely dependent on Charite. This, of course, does not apply to Thrasyllus' end. In the words *nequiens...sufficere*, as interpreted above, the narrator continues Charite's interpretation. But these words can also be taken as indirectly rendering utterances by Thrasyllus himself. In that case *idoneum exitium praesenti clade reddere* requires the interpretation 'to bring about a fitting end in the present disaster'. *Tanto facinori* would then refer to the entire sequence of events unwittingly brought about by himself, for which he can think of only one expiatory sacrifice.

idoneum: for the meaning 'fitting' cf. *Rhet.Her.*4,8,12 *quis est uestrum,...qui satis idoneam possit in eum poenam ⟨ex⟩cogitare, qui prodere hostibus patriam cogitarit.* In the sequel of this passage the notion of punishment is also present: *quod maleficium cum hoc scelere comparari, quod huic maleficio dignum supplicium potest inueniri?* The thought is comparable to Thrasyllus': so horrible a crime has been committed that no fitting punishment exists for it. *Rhet.Her.* continues: *huic truculentissimo ac nefario facinori singularem poenam non reliquerunt (maiores)*. If a similar thought is present in our passage, F's reading, in the meaning offered, fits the sequel: Thrasyllus has become the repentant sinner (expressed by the narrator in the word *sponte*), who therefore offers himself as an *ultronea uictima*.

certusque...sufficere: *certus* followed by an infinitive occurs also e.g. at 11, 1 (266, 14) *certus...summatem deam praecipua maiestate pollere*. *-que* does not present a new possibility, but has explanatory force: a sword would cause a *praesens exitium* which in view of the gravity of Thrasyllus' *facinus* would not be an *idoneum exitium*.

nec = *ne...quidem*. Bernhard 1927, 123 and Callebat 1968, 334 list further instances in Apul.

ibidem ad sepulchrum: reinforcement of a preposition by an adverb also e.g. 7, 2 (155, 10) *ibidem in hospitio*. See Bernhard 1927, 181 and Callebat 1968, 523.

188, 4-6 'ultronea uobis, infesti Manes, en ades⟨t⟩ uictima' saepe clamitans, ualuis super sese diligenter obseratis inedia statuit elidere sua sententia damnatum spiritum: "... and crying repeatedly 'Here is your willing victim, hostile Shades', he carefully shut the leaves of the door upon himself and decided to expel the spirit he had condemned by his own sentence."

ultronea: a rare word, which, however, Apuleius uses five times; see *GCA* 1981, 212 on 7, 20 (169, 18). For the formation of the adjective cf. Gargantini 1963, 25. The word is given extra emphasis by the hyperbaton, cf. Bernhard 1927, 27.

infesti Manes: see above 185, 3 *manes acerbos*; it seems that the narrator has Thrasyllus refer back to Charite's words, which there fitted into her strategy. Here the *Manes Charites* must be remembered, too. Whether the editors, who by capitalizing *Manes* seem to indicate that the word refers to the underworld as a whole, are right is hard to decide.

en: not only in colloquial language, but also in fierce and pathetic passages, e.g. in Isis' epiphany 11, 5 (269, 12) *en adsum tuis commota, Luci, precibus*; cf. Callabat 1968, 90. The word is usually placed at the beginning of a sentence or colon. Its placement in the present sentence serves further to onderscore the emphatic position of *ultronea*. The only other passage in the *Met.* where *en* occurs in a similar position is 197, 16, where the stylistic effect is comparable.

saepe clamitans: in the *Met. clamitare* is always used for words uttered with considerable force, see Callebat 1968, 392; for the employment of an intensifying adverb here he uses ibid. 544 the term 'hypercaractérisation'.

ualuis: the difference between *ualuae* and *fores* is explained by Isid. *Orig.* 15, 7, 4 *fores et ualuae claustra sunt; sed fores dicuntur quae foras, ualuae quae intus reuoluuntur, et duplices conplicabilesque sunt*. (The etymology is not clear, see Walde-Hofmann 1954 s.v.) For *ualuae* in a grave monument see our note on 187, 25 *sepultura*.

super sese: many translators render 'behind', Butler and Gaselee 'upon'. One might defend 'above himself' if one imagines a large grave monument with a vault lying at a lower level and hence stairs (e.g. Toynbee 1971, 210). At 9, 2 (204, 10) *clausis obseratisque super me foribus* there is nothing in the context that argues for a lower level. Therefore we prefer to regard the phrase as an instance of Apuleian usage (Forcellini s.v. mentions only *Met.* 9, 2 for the meaning 'dopo', 'dietro').

inedia: Thrasyllus commits suicide using the method Charite had contemplated when she heard of Tlepolemus' death. The method is used by loving wives on other occasions, e.g. Petr. 111, 11 where the widow of Ephesus is addressed by her servant: *quid proderit...hoc tibi, si soluta inedia fueris? Si te uiuam sepelieris? Si, antequam fata poscant, indemnatum spiritum effuderis?* The final remark is interesting since the servant uses the fact that the woman's *spiritus* is *indemnatus* as an argument to make her end her hunger strike. In our passage the opposite argument (*sua sententia damnnatus spiritus*) is atributed to Thrasyllus. See also our note on 181, 25 f. and 187, 24 *animam uirilem*.

elidere...spiritum: the choice of verb underlines the violence of this manner of death: Sen. *Ep.* 70, 20 *lignum...in gulam farsit et interclusis faucibus spiritum elisit*. Cf. also 10, 26 (258, 6) *elisus uiolenter...medicus effundit spiritum*.

Thrasyllus, who commits suicide in the grave of the woman he desired, therefore in his choice of method is comparable to mourning wives. On the other hand the grave is also the resting place of the friend he had – in the narrator's view – so foully murdered. Thus Thrasyllus is comparable to

Adrastus in his choice of the place where he is going to die; see Hdt. 1, 34-45, where Adrastus, having accidentally killed Croesus' son Atys, kills himself on Atys' grave. The fact that Thrasyllus *infectus humano cruore* (177, 9) wishes to die of *inedia* is part of the irony (at the level of the narrator).

In the Greek novel suicide from feelings of remorse occurs only in Charito 1, 5, 2, where the hero wants to commit suicide because he discovers he has wrongly suspected his wife of being unfaithful.

The Charite story, then, ends as a double tragedy, Charite committing suicide because of Tlepolemus, Thrasyllus because of Charite.

Heine 1962, 245 notes that Charite's mental transformation (cf. our note with 187, 26) is more easily understood than Thrasyllus' transformation from scoundrel to remorseful sinner. Heine treats the change as one of the instances of surprising psychological transformations 'die wesentlich dazu beitragen, den Proteuscharakter einer unsicheren, unfesten, wandelbaren Welt aufzubauen'. This seems correct, at least at the level of the narrator. However, though surprising in itself, Thrasyllus' reaction rather strongly resembles that of Psyche's parents when she is led away to her death: *miseri quidem parentes eius tanta clade defessi, clausae domus abstrusi tenebris, perpetuae nocti sese dedidere* (4, 35: 102, 21 f.; Psyche's parents do not die however: 5, 4: 106, 8 f.).

For a discussion of the way Thrasyllus is characterised – in many respects he is Lucius' opposite – see vdPaardt in *SAG* 1981, 19 f.

CHAPTER XV

After the account of their master's and mistress' ruin the shepherds flee, taking all their worldly goods with them.

Haec ille longo⟨s⟩ trahens spiritus et nonnnunquam inlacrimans grauiter adfectis rusticis adnuntiabat: "This he reported, heaving deep sighs and sometimes weeping, to the deeply moved peasants." 188, 7-8

Here a new episode begins, see Introd. 1.

longo⟨s⟩: in F the *s* has been added by a different hand.

spiritus: this is the reading of F (*sps*). With some hesitation we accept this reading and not, as most modern editors do, Brantius' conjecture *suspiritus*. It appears from the context (the immediately following *inlacrimans* and the use of the verb *trahere*) that the meaning of *spiritus* must be 'sigh', not merely 'breath'. It must be conceded that, though Apul. often uses *spiritus*, he does not elsewhere use it in the meaning 'sigh', whereas he often uses *suspiritus* in this meaning. Cf. 1, 7 (6, 22) *cruciabilem suspiritum ducens*; 5, 25 (123, 3) *assiduo suspiritu*; Apol. 85 (94, 4) *suspiritus numeras*. We think, nevertheless, that the reading *spiritus* is correct here: the meaning 'sigh' is found e.g. Verg. *G*. 3, 505 (referring to a dying horse) *attractus ab alto / spiritus, interdum gemitu grauis* (inspired by Lucr. 6, 1186 *creber spiritus aut ingens raroque coortus*); Prop. 1, 16, 32 *surget et inuitis spiritus in lacrimis* where Enk paraphrases 'inuita suspirabit et flebit' and Camps notes 'it refers to sobbing'; in Prop. 2, 29, 37 *nullus...surgat / spiritus* the meaning is less clear ('heavy breathing' Camps); Hor. *Epod*. 11, 10 *latere petitus imo spiritus* probably suggests 'sigh'. See also e.g. Gel. 12, 5, 2 (referring to a sick person) *spiritusque et anhelitus e pectore eius euadere*. See also *GCA* 1981, 49 on 6, 28 (150, 1-3) *spirans altius*, where *spirare* has to mean 'sigh'.

trahens: a well-chosen verb, indicating how deeply moved the messenger is. In addition to the parallel passages quoted above, cf. Sil. 8, 79 *uerba trahens largis cum fletibus*; Ov. *Met*. 10, 402 *suspiria duxit ab imo / pectore*; 11, 709 *gemitus a corde trahuntur*.

inlacrimans: this compound is found in Apul. only here (the simple verb at 5, 6 : 107, 9 and 192, 11) but was used already in classical Latin, both in prose (e.g. Cic. *Cato* 27) and in poetry (e.g. Verg. *A*. 9, 303).

grauiter adfectis: the narrator in the novel suggests that not only the messenger but also his attentive audience is upset by the events; in fact, the author pays himself a compliment.

adnuntiabat: see 176, 20 *sic annuntiabat*; the messenger's story is now complete.

188, 9-10 Tunc illi mutati dominii nouitatem metuentes et infortunium domus erilis altius miserantes fugere conparant: "Then they prepared themselves for flight: they were afraid of the change – a new ownership – and commiserated deeply with the misfortune that had come upon their master's house."

dominii nouitatem: Médan 1925, 317 places this expression among the many instances of an abstract noun replacing an adjective; the phrase is equivalent to *dominum nouum*. This may go somewhat too far; the shepherds are afraid of the changes in their life (see our remark on 176, 16) which will accompany the transition to a new master. The motif 'fear of a new master' introduces another travel episode for Lucius.

domus erilis: see our comm. on 177, 16 *erilis puella*.

metuentes...miserantes: Strilciw 1925, 113 points out the homoioteleuton; The alliteration of *m*, too (in fact, the whole sentence is dominated by *m*'s, internal as well as initial) seems to illustrate the sadness of the group. One may compare the passage in Pl. *Cas.* 622 f., which seems a parody of a scene with a tragic female character, and which shows a variety of figures of speech, like repetition, alliteration, assonance, etc.: *cor metu mortuomst, membra miserae tremunt* (see MacCary-Willcock ad loc.). This phenomenon is also found in prose, e.g. Nep. *Them.* 10, 4 *illum ait Magnesiae morbo mortuum*. For further literature see Marouzeau 1946, 49 f. and Lausberg ²1973, 310 f.

altius: on similar comparatives with a weakened meaning see *GCA* 1977, 181 on 4, 24 (93, 10) *altius eiulans* and above on 185, 23 *nec sequius*; cf. also 4, 29 (98, 6) *fremens altius*.

miserantes: the elements of pathos, pointed out in the commentary on the *iuuenis*' story, appear not to have missed the mark.

fugere conparant: we do not understand why Robertson is so much in favour of Beroaldus' conjecture *fugae se. Comparare* with an infinitive is found, although rarely, in other authors: Ter. *Eu.* 47 *An potius ita me comparem / non perpeti meretricum contumelias*; Ov. *Tr.* 2, 267 *si quis tamen urere tecta / comparat*. See also Callebat 1968, 308 f.

188, 11-14 Sed quorum magister, qui me curandum magna ille quidem commendatione susceperat, quidquid in casula pretiosum conditumque seruabat, meo atque aliorum iumentorum dorso repositum a[d]sportans sedes pristinas deserit: "The head groom, the same who at such urgent recommendation had taken it upon himself to take care of me, loaded on my back and those of the other beasts of burden whatever he possessed of value and kept stored in his cottage; carrying it off he left his old home."

sed: indicating a transition, rather than an antithesis. See Callebat 1968, 326; LHSz 2, 487.

magna...commendatione: this refers to 7, 15 (165, 7-9) *Ergo igitur euocato statim armentario equisone magna cum praefatione deducendus adsignor*. On account of this passage Oudendorp even wants to read here *magna illa equidem commendatione*.

quidquid...seruabat: Ruiz de Elvira 1954, 128 collects the passages in which Apul. uses the indicative in iterative dependent clauses of this kind with a preterite verb. See e.g. 2, 14 (36, 16) *quodcumque...contraximus, id omne latrocinalis inuasit manus*; 194, 6 *quicquid horreo reconditum continebatur admoto combussit igne*; further 7, 17 (167, 17 f.); 10, 22 (254, 4 f.).

a[d]sportans: the verb is also used 4, 18 (88, 15), referring to the carrying off of gold and silver by a band of robbers; 9, 40 (234, 9) it is used of a sabre which is taken. The mss. agree in these passages; this is one of the reasons why ς's emendation of the word in our passage is most probably correct. The compound is found in Latin of all periods, used both of carrying off people and animals and of dragging away loot etc. See e.g. *B. Afr.* 91, 3 *ut secum coniuges liberosque asportaret*; Gel. 2, 29, 8 *pulli...circumstrepere orareque matrem, ut...in alium locum sese asportet.*

sedes pristinas: such a plural is a poeticism according to Médan 1925, 265. vGeisau 1912, 18 cites 6, 4 (131, 9) *beatas sedes*; 194, 28 *sedesque perpetuas*. The poeticism is emphasized by the prolepsis contained in the expression: the *sedes* become *sedes pristinas* only after he has left them. For the poetic quality of prolepsis see e.g. LHSz 2, 413 f.

deserit: the alternation in tense, which is found repeatedly in this chapter, gives an impression of liveliness and speed: *conparant...deserit...gerebamus...ambulabat...urguebat*. See also our comm. on 185, 13 f. *consentit*.

An attempt at flight is made by the group of slaves, who are apprehensive of passing into the hands of a new *dominus* after their good experience with Charite and Tlepolemus. Understandable as this is in every respect, they plunge into a generally desperate adventure (Apuleius does not say so explicitly but the reader will undoubtedly come to this conclusion). Norden 1912, 77 notes: 'Solches Entfliehen war...in den meisten Fällen recht aussichtslos'. On the cruelty of masters towards *fugitiui* see e.g. Hopkins 1978, 121.

Gerebamus infantulos et mulieres, gerebamus pullos, passares, aedos, catellos et quidquid infirmo gradu fugam morabatur, nostris quoque pedibus ambulabat: "We carried little babies and women, we carried pullets, pet birds, kids, and puppies, and whatever by feeble step slowed the flight, walked on our legs too." 188, 15-17

Gerebamus: the initial position and emphatic repetition of the verb suggest to the reader that the burden is enormous indeed. The entire sentence is constructed with great care, observing rhythm and parallelism (especially if one takes *infantulos et mulieres* as hendiadys 'women with children'), and at the same time variation: *pullos, passeres, aedos, catellos* with 2, 3, 2, 3 syllables respectively. The reader can easily visualize the whole scene, which might be met even today in any rural Mediterranean region.

infantulos: the word *infans*, strictly taken, already means 'baby', so the diminutive emphasizes the notion 'very small'. The *OLD* quotes only one additional passage, also from Apul. (194, 9); this noun is, indeed, found in Apul. for the first time but occurs regularly in later authors, especially the church fathers, e.g. Hier. *Tract. in Ps.* 1, 159; Aug. *Ep.* 149, 22 (p. 368, 9). See

143

ThLL s.v. 1352, 63 f.; the feminine form *infantula* is found 10, 28 (258, 24).

passares: thus the first hand in F, though the same hand possibly corrected to *passeres*, which was changed to *anseres* by a different hand. Two problems are involved here:

1. The first concerns the form *passares*. It is quite in keeping with linguistic developments to suppose that *passares* could be heard in Apuleius' time (see e.g. Väänänen ³1981, 35). The cautions in the App. Probi point in the same direction (see Keil 4, 198, 33). Cf. also Roensch ʳ1965, 21 for instances in the *V L*. In accordance with the policy announced in our Introd. 5. 3 we retain the spelling of the first hand in F (cf. 192, 18; 10, 22 : 254, 1 against 6, 6 : 132, 24).

2. Another question is whether the emendation *anseres* in F should be taken into consideration. Colvius denies this because *pulli*, *passeres*, and other birds were popular as children's pets; he quotes for this, among other sources, Pl. *Capt.* 1002, Arn. 7, 8, and Plin. *Ep.* 4, 2, 3. But *anseres*, too, are favourite children's toys. Oudendorp does not regard these animals as toys here but as a means of subsistence for the fugitives; therefore he opts for *anseres* and wants to read *capellas* rather than *catellos*, as had already been proposed by Piccartius. But psychologically it is quite acceptable that children take with them what they are very much attached to. Balsdon 1969, 91 gives under the heading 'children's pets' the following list: 'They kept pets, mice which pulled little carriages (Hor. *S.* 2, 3, 247), caged birds of all sorts, blackbirds, nightingales, parrots'; he cites the well-known passage in Petr. 46, 3 about Echion's son who *in aues morbosus est*; of course, children always played with dogs (Juv. 9, 61 *conlusore catello*) and there is a gruesome story in Pliny (*Ep.* 4, 2, 3) of how the abominable M. Regulus lost his son and then 'made a holocaust of the boy's pets around the funeral pyre: ponies, dogs, nightingales, parrots and blackbirds' (*ib.* 91). Whether this plays a part in Apuleius remains to be seen; but that it is a question here of domestic pets and not of animals necessary for subsistence is an opinion we share with Colvius, in view of the other animals listed by Apuleius. Accordingly, we opt for *passares* in the meaning of 'small song-bird'. See Fordyce 1961, 87 f. on Catul. 2, 1 on the possible meanings of *passer*.

et quidquid. . .ambulabat: the construction changes surprisingly into a new independent clause, ending in a truly Apuleian joke. One may compare e.g. 4, 27 (95, 23) *me pedibus fugientem alienis* and *GCA* 1977, 202 ad loc., where Plin. *Nat.* 29, 8, 19 is quoted on transportation in a sedan chair: *alienis pedibus ambulamus*. A similar playful thought is offered by 6, 29 (151, 19) *Quid meis pedibus facere contendis?* Mason, *AAGA* 1978, 5 rightly classes the phrase as one of Apuleius' 'characteristic additions' in respect to his Greek predecessor.

infirmo gradu: see also *Priap.* 12, 5 on an *anus* who *infirmo solet huc gradu uenire*. Often *gradus* is contrasted with *cursus*; it is usually a slow step.

188, 17-20 Nec me pondus sarcinae quanquam enormis urguebat, quippe gaudiali fuga detestabilem illum exectorem uirilitatis meae relinquentem: "But I was not troubled by the weight of the burden, enormous though it was, for by the joyful flight I left behind that detestable man who wanted to rob me of my virility."

Nec...relinquentem: we find the opposite situation at 6, 30 (152, 5 f.), where the ass reluctantly limps back to the robbers' cave: his gait is clearly related to his mood.

quanquam enormis: although the narrator of the novel maintains that as an ass he was not bothered by the weight at the time, still it is emphasized in strong terms to impress the reader.

quippe...relinquentem: Médan 1925, 80 quotes a few examples in Apul. of *forsitan, nescio an, quippe, utpote* with a participle and points out that *quippe* and *utpote* are often used in this way by Sall., Hor., and Liv. also. LHSz 2, 385 argue that the construction of *quippe* with a participle probably originated under influence of the Greek ἅτε; in poetry it is quite rare (oldest example Lucr. 3, 190) but in prose it is much more common.

gaudiali: Gargantini 1963, 37 lists the adjectives in *-lis* in Apul.; Médan 1925, 115 lists those in *-alis*, which actually occur quite frequently in later Latin. But *gaudialis* seems a typically Apuleian adjective: we find it also 2, 31 (50, 25) *gaudiali ritu*; 200, 12 *gaudiales instruunt dapes*; 11, 29 (290, 27) *animo gaudiali*. Observing the accompanying nouns one notices that the adjective has different connotations, like 'producing joy' and 'feeling joy'. As appears from the *ThLL* s.v. it is not found elsewhere in Latin literature.

detestabilem...uirilitatis: the reader may have almost forgotten him because of the lengthy intervening narrative, the ass has not – far from it; he is still panic-stricken at the thought of the threat of 7, 26 (174, 20) (see also our comm. on 7, 24 : 172, 5 and 20), fearing the actual intention to castrate him more than the threat to cut off his head. See also Junghanns 1932, 155. The use of *uirilitas* for animals is not uncommon, e.g. Col. 6, 26, 3; Plin. *Nat.* 23, 44. Cf. also 7, 25 (173, 1) *nec inuitus ego cursui me commodabam relinquens atrocissimum uirilitatis lanienam* with *GCA* 1981, 248 ad loc. The author permits himself a pun on *detestabilem*, see our comm. on 7, 23 (171, 18) *detestatione mansuetos*.

In *Onos* 34, 3 this flight with bag and baggage occurs too, but is dealt with quite briefly. The description of the laborious and perilous journey that follows is not found there at all; instead it is summarized in one short sentence καὶ τὴν νύκτα ὅλην ἐλθόντες ὁδὸν ἀργαλέαν.

Siluosi montis asperum permensi iugum rursusque repo[s]sita camporum spatia peruecti, iam uespera semitam tenebrante peruenimus ad quoddam castellum frequens et opulens, unde nos incolae nocturna, immo uero matutina etiam prohibebant egressione: "When we had crossed the rough ridge of a wooded mountain and had travelled over vast, remote fields again, we arrived, when evening already wrapped the path in darkness, at a populous, rich village; its inhabitants tried to keep us from leaving at night, or even in the early morning." 188, 21-25

siluosi: the equivalent of ὑλήεις. Ernout 1949, 28 says that it is attested during the Empire (Liv., Plin., Vitr.). See also *GCA* 1981, 254 on 7, 25 (174, 1) *montis illius siluosa nemora*; it may well be the same mountain.

permensi...peruecti...peruenimus: it would appear that Apul. has a preference for compounds with *per*, but it is more than that: the prefix emphasises the length of the journey.

reposita: F has *ss*, corrected by φ. There is some uncertainty as to the right translation: Helm-Krenkel have 'tiefliegend', Vallette 'qui s'étendait à ses pieds'. One may be reminded of 4, 6 (78, 25) *conualles...quaqua uersus repositae*, rendered in *GCA* 1977, 58 by 'stretching in all directions'; but when one recalls Verg. *A*. 3, 364 (see also 6, 59) *terras temptare repostas* and realizes that there are many Vergilian echoes in this passage of Apul., the translation 'remote' seems better. Thus also Médan 1925, 196 ('lointain' = *remotus*) and Castiglioni 1938, 551. In our opinion there is no reason at all for Leo's conjecture *supposita*: it is understood from the whole context (*camporum spatia*) that they are going now through a level valley.

tenebrante: in Apul. the word occurs only here. Before him it is not attested, after him it is not uncommon, as appears from the material of the *ThLL*; e.g. Amm. 19, 8, 5; Aug. *Eu.Io.* 13, 16.

castellum: 'village' as e.g. 200, 11 and 201, 6.

frequens et opulens: the passage recalls Xenophon, e.g. *Anab*. 1, 2, 7 εἰς Κελαινάς, τῆς Φρυγίας πολίν οἰκουμένην, μεγάλην καὶ εὐδαίμονα. *Onos* 34, 5 has ἐρχόμεθα ἐς πόλιν τῆς Μακεδονίας Βέροιαν μεγάλην καὶ πολυάνθρωπον. Other formulas used by Apul. to indicate the destination of a journey are e.g. 193, 20; 194, 27 *ciuitatem quandam populosam et nobilem...peruenimus* (see our comm.).

unde nos incolae: the inhabitants tell them that this region is in danger; nevertheless the shepherds continue their flight, but very cautiously. In ch. 19, too, after the first adventure, mention is made of a danger threatening the place where the shepherds are at that time. The threat of the present moment is about to be described in a long period with the key word coming emphatically first: *lupos...*

unde: it is difficult to determine whether one should take together *castellum, unde...prohibebant* or *unde...incolae*. LHSz 2, 208 f. discuss the latter usage, where the pronominal adverb takes the place of a pronoun; Callebat 1968, 293 cites 6, 9 (134, 21) *nobis turgidi uentris sui lenocinio commouet miserationem, unde me praeclara subole auiam beatam scilicet faciat* and 7, 11 (162, 13) *...pecua comminantes. Vnde praelectum grandem hircum...uictimant*. Taking *unde* with *prohibebant* forces one to take *egressione* as an abl. limitationis; however, if one takes *unde...incolae* together, *egressione* completes *prohibebant* in a more natural manner; hence our preference.

egressione: used literally, as here, this noun is not found before Apul. After him it occurs occasionally in Christian authors and in translations of the Bible, e.g. (in the sense of *egressus, exitus*) *VL Psalm*. 143, 13 *oues...abundantes in egressionibus suis*: Hil. *Trin*. 8, 19; Heges. 5, 6; Hier. *In soph*. 1, 13 p. 689 *uniuscuiusque mortis et egressionis a saeculo*.

In its other meaning 'digression' (παρέκβασις) in rhetoric the word is much more common, e.g. Quint. *Inst*. 3, 9, 4 *Egressio...uel...excessus...adiutorium uel ornamentum partium est earum, ex quibus egreditur*.

lupos enim numerosos, grandes et uastis corporibus sarcinosos, 188, 25-189, 4
ac nimia ferocitate saeuientes passim rapinis adsuetos infestare
cunctam illam regionem iamque ipsas uias obsidere et in modum
latronum praetereuntes adgredi, immo etiam uaesana fame rabidos finitimas expugnare uillas, exitiumque inertissimorum pecudum ipsis iam humanis capitibus imminere: "For wolves (they said), numerous, big, and powerfully built, savage and excessively fierce, accustomed to preying far and wide, were infesting that entire area. They were already taking over the very roads and attacking passers-by like brigands; worse still, furious with an insane hunger, they forced themselves into nearby country farms, and ruination threatened even human beings as if they were passive cattle."

lupos: Apul. clearly relishes the detailed description of these ferocious animals: their size, fierceness, and dangerousness are illustrated by no less than five attributes, all of them varied and sometimes arranged asyndetically. One may compare the description of the boar 179, 7 f. Heine 1962, 306 rightly remarks: 'Diese Flucht...geht in einer Atmosphäre vor sich, die durch die Drohung riesiger reissender Wölfe, am Wege liegende abgenagte Menschenleichen und den nächtlichen Angriff furchtbarer Hunde...einen etwas makabren, nicht ganz geheuren Gehalt erhält!'

This story belongs to a connected series of adventures: the following chapters of the shepherds' flight, too, are characterized by a macabre atmosphere in which gleaming bones and half-gnawed corpses play a part (ch. 21 and 22). The danger announced here does not become reality, but the future has increasingly bizarre adventures in store for the fugitives. Tension is mounting and uncertainty increasing.

numerosos...sarcinosos: Apuleius' preference for adjectives in *-osus* is evident: Gargantini 1963, 38 gives an impressive list, mostly 'derivati da nomi concreti'. *Numerosus* occurs quite frequently in the *Met.*, e.g. 4, 7 (79, 26) *panis numerosus*; 4, 9 (81, 8) *numerosa familia* cf. 4, 19: 89, 5); 11, 29 (290, 16) *numerosa serie*. Thus, there seems to be no reason to write with Castiglioni 1938, 546 *numero multos*.

According to Ernout 1949, 27 and the material of the *ThLL*, *sarcinosus* occurs only here and perhaps *Priap.* 79, 4; Plaut. *Poen.* 979 has *sarcinatus*. *Sarcinosos* is a descriptive attribute here: on account of their bulk, the wolves are a burden to themselves, as it were. We have placed commas after both *numerosos* and *sarcinosos* in order to mark off the cola more clearly and to accentuate the rhyme which seems, after all, to be intentional here. There is parallelism in content, too, between these cola: the first one concerns the quantity, the second the size of the monsters and the third their nature.

passim rapinis: our opinion (based, among other things, on the colometry) is that these words belong together; the author senses in *rapinis* the verbal function, which makes the addition of an adverb to the noun understandable. Blümner 1894, 309 disagrees: 'Da mit *passim* bereits der zum Subj. des Acc. c. Inf. gehörige Infinitiv beginnt, empfiehlt es sich wohl, *rapinis adsuetis* zu schreiben'.

infestare: the verb is also used 1, 15 (14, 1) *tu...ignoras latronibus infestari uias*?

iamque ipsas etc.: the descriptions become more and more vivid, and the wolves are compared finally to (human) highwaymen, to whom all kinds of military terms can be applied: *rapinis, infestare, obsidere, adgredi, expugnare.* See on the use of military terms in robber stories Appendix 1 in *GCA* 1977, 208.

immo etiam: the frightened villagers are using increasingly strong expressions.

inertissimorum pecudum: it is difficult to determine the correct reading: F has *inertissimorum pecodum* (the same hand wrote a *v* over the *o*). The neuter is defensible; see Médan 1925, 212 and Neue-Wagener 1³, 845. It is found e.g. Acc. *Medea* 409R³ *pecuda*; likewise Cic. *Rep.* 4, 1 and Sisenna *Hist.* 4, 76P. It is clearly an archaism, and the grammarians confirm this: Non. 234-5L *PECUA et PECUDA ita ut pecora ueteres dixerunt*; Prisc. *GLK* 6, 16, 86. Oros. *Hist.* 7, 37, 16 uses an expression similar to that of Apuleius, namely *uilissimorum pecudum*. We retain *inertissimorum,* with Giarratano-Frassinetti, Helm, and Augello 1977, 184-185. Pricaeus proposes *inertissimarum,* in which he is followed by Robertson. Blümner 1905, 34 prefers *insontissimorum,* for which we see no necessity.

humanis capitibus: this use of *caput* as a kind of *pars pro toto* is presumably the same as that of κάρη in Homer and the tragic poets. In the plural it often occurs in enumerations, especially in somewhat solemn and formulaic language, e.g. expressions relating to constitutional law: Liv. 42, 8, 6 *tot milia capitum innoxiorum*; Caes. *Ciu.* 3, 32, 2 *in capita singula...tributum imponebatur*; Gaius *Inst.* 3, 8 *non in capita, sed ⟨in⟩ stirpes hereditatem diuidi.* In such a context *caput* can be rendered by 'individual'.

189, 4-12 Denique ob iter illud, qua nobis erat commeandum, iacere semesa hominum corpora suisque uisceribus nudatis ossibus cuncta candere ac per hoc nos quoque summa cautione uiae reddi debere idque uel in primis obseruitare, ut luce clara et die iam prouecto et sole florido uitantes undique latentes insidias, cum et ipso lumine dirarum bestiarum repigratur impetus, non laciniatim disperso[s], sed cuneatim stipato commeatu difficultates illas transabiremus: "So, along the road we had to travel, half-eaten human bodies were lying about, and everything was glittering white because of the bones stripped of their flesh. Therefore we, too, ought to resume our journey with the utmost caution and pay attention in the first place to this: (to travel) in broad daylight, when the day was already well-advanced and the sun shining brightly, avoiding the ambushes hidden everywhere at the time of day when the fury of the dreadful animals is restrained by the light itself, not scattered in small groups but in a compact wedge-formation, to overcome those difficulties."

Denique: here clearly = *ergo*; see *GCA* 1977, 54 on 4, 5 (78, 13).

ob: this preposition is not found very often in the sense of 'in front of' or 'in the way of so as to block'; one may compare Pl. *Mil.* 1430 *qui ob oculum habebat lanam* and Gel. 5, 21, 4 *eas...quasi puluerem ob oculos...adspergebat.* In all probability, the meaning here is that the road is blocked by the half-gnawed corpses and carcasses.

erat: since the villagers' discourse continues, one would expect a subjunctive. LHSz 2, 548, however, discuss many cases in which this rule is not followed especially in later Latin. Another possibility is of course that the clause with *erat* is not part of the villagers' discourse, but a piece of factual information from Lucius.

Bernhard 1927, 52 f. maintains that Apul. generally prefers direct discourse because of its greater liveliness. On p. 53 he gives an enumeration of cases of indirect discourse in the *Met.*, from which it appears that those are more frequent in the second half of the novel than in the first; this stands in relation to the increasing tempo.

cuncta candere: observe the alliteration and assonance. The verb *candere* suggests 'glitter in the sunlight' and is more expressive than the usual *albere*, e.g. Ov. *F.* 1, 558 *squalidaque humanis ossibus albet humus*, the example for which may have been Verg. *A.* 12, 36 *campi...ossibus albent*. See on white-glittering bones also 194, 22.

per hoc: = *eam ob rem*.

uiae reddi: this is the reading in ς, accepted by Frassinetti and defended by Augello 1977, 185; F has *uia reddi*. Since there are no good parallels to be found for either reading, many emendations have been proposed: Walter 1916, 126 has *uia⟨m agg⟩redi*, accepted by Robertson; Helm has *ingredi*, which is paleographically quite radical and contextually rather dull (in the *Addenda* 300 he offers *uiare* without giving any explanation for *-ddi*). Terzaghi does take *-ddi* into account and proposes *uiare die*, following Beyte 1925, 749 *uiare de die*; a serious objection to this is that full attention is paid to this daylight in the very next line, which would cause a tautology. Armini 1928, 312 f. prefers *via⟨m⟩ reddi*, interpreting *uiam* as *in uiam* of *ad uiam* (sc. *nos reddere*), i.e. an accusative of direction. It is not quite clear why, in this context, he refers to 189, 16; 205, 19; 209, 3; 236, 16; all these passages have a preposition, namely *ad* (*uiam*).

If it is possible to translate *uiae reddi* as 'resume one's journey', then this meaning fits best into the context and keeps closest to the transmission. For the expression itself we could not find a good parallel, but normal is *thalamo, lecto, cubiculo se reddere*; Oudendorp, moreover, points out *poenae reddi* 7, 26 (174, 14) and *rursum se reddidit quieti* 9, 20 (218, 11).

obseruitare: 'watch or observe (regularly)'. cf. e.g. *Soc.* 19 (29, 8) *si omina obseruitaret*; Cic. *Diu.* 1, 2 *Assyrii...motus...stellarum obseruitauerunt* ('possibly a technical term', Pease); 1, 102 *deorum uoces Pythagorei obseruitauerunt*.

luce clara et die iam prouecto et sole florido: note the climactic tricolon.

florido: this adjective is used to describe the sun only here; accordingly, Médan calls it an 'expression nouvelle'. One could compare Lucr. 4, 450 *bina lucernarum florentia lumina flammis*. Apul. does use the adjective of bright colours e.g. 2, 8 (31, 19) *floridae uestis hilaris color*; 4, 13 (84, 25) *floridae picturae* (see *GCA* 1977, 107 ad loc.); 10, 34 (265, 12) *lectus...ueste serica floridus*. Neuenschwander 1912, 83 reminds us that in antiquity qualities of flowers often are transferred to fire (see e.g. Lucr. 1, 900 *flammai...flore*). In prose this is quite often the case with the verb *florere* 'sich hervortun', 'glänzen'; e.g. in the *Met.* 5, 12 (112, 17) referring to Psyche *laeta florebat* 'vor Freude strahlend'; 11, 16 (279, 3) *omnisque prorsus carina citro limpido perpolita florebat*; 3, 11 (60, 8) *lusus iste...florescit*; 5, 16 (115, 19) *adolescens modo florente lanugine barbam*. Metaphors of this kind pervade the modern languages as well.

cum...repigratur: here the indicative is less striking in view of temporal *cum*. Alternatively the subordinate clause can be taken as information offered by the narrator; see on *erat* (1.4).

repigratur: this rare verb (also occurring Mart. Cap. 1, 35 *uxoris Cyllenius fotibus repigratus*) is used by Apul. also 1, 9 (9, 7) *repigrato fetu*, but nowhere else. On Apuleius' preference for (unusual) compounds see Bernhard 1927, 121.

non laciniatim disperso[s], sed cuneatim stipato commeatu: the antithesis is marked both by the two rather unusual adverbs and by the well-differentiated verbal forms. The first adverb is hapax legomenon; it is derived from *lacinia* meaning 'the edge of a garment', 'fringe' (see 4, 23: 92, 15) and in an extended sense 'small group'. Both meanings fit well here: it is unwise to travel in small groups within a ribbon-like column. The second adverb is less rare: cf. Caes. *Gall.* 7, 28, 1; *ThLL* s.v. 1402, 74 f. quotes for *cuneatim* among others Serv. on *A.* 12, 457; Amm. 24, 2, 14; *Epit.Alex.* 9. *Commeatus* can be used as a military term, too, with the meaning 'convoy'; see e.g. *B.Afr.* 31, 30 *donec...legionum pars aliqua in secundo commeatu occurrisset*; 44, 1 *ex secundo commeatu...nauis una*.

transabiremus: this compound, formed with two prepositions, also occurs 7, 8 (160, 3) *per medias acies infesti militis transabiui* in a military context; see *GCA* 1981, 134. See also Bernhard 1927, 121.

CHAPTER XVI

On the run.

Sed nequissimi fugitiui ductores illi nostri caecae festinationis 189, 12-16
temeritate ac metu incertae insecutionis spreta salubri monitione
nec expectata luce proxuma circa tertiam ferme uigiliam noctis
onustos nos ad uiam propellunt: "But those good-for-nothing runaway
drivers of ours, in the rashness of blind haste and in fear of possible pursuit,
disregarded the sound advice. They did not wait for the next dawn but drove us,
heavily loaded, on to the road around the third vigil."

In this chapter for the first time pursuit by animals has an important function: an aspect of the inferno 'das auf das Purgatorio des 11. Buches vorbereitet' (Dornseiff 1938, 226 f.).

nequissimi...nostri: an abundance of attributes (adjective, adjective, pronoun, pronoun) with the central noun *ductores*; the combination *fugitiui ductores* results in an oxymoron (our passage is not mentioned by Bernhard 1927, 238 f. or Strilciw 1925, 118 in their discussions of this fugure of speech). For *illi nostri* see Bernhard 1927, 171 and Callebat 1968, 280.

caecae festinationis temeritate: the fugitives' blindness is reflected both by the adjective and by the noun *temeritas*, if we take the etymology (**temus* 'darkness') of the latter word into consideration; cf. Cic. *Inv.* 1, 2 *caeca et temeraria dominatrix animi cupiditas*. See vdPaardt in *SAG* 1981, 24 (with note 46) for the light-darkness symbolism, and our comm. on 186, 18 *lumen certe non uidebis*.

metu incertae insecutionis: placed chiastically vs. the previous combination, both as to part of speech and as to case. *Insecutio* is attested here for the first time; later e.g. Cassiod. *Var. Ep.* 10, 32. For Apuleius' preference for nouns in *-tio* see Gargantini 1963, 39. *Incerta* is an addition by the narrator: the *fugitiui* naturally do fear an *insecutio*. It is typical of the cruelty of the world (as depicted by Apuleius) that the fugitives are running towards danger and that they are taken for robbers because of their equipment, while real robbers can pass unhindered (3, 29; see vdPaardt 1971, 203 ad loc.)

spreta salubri monitione nec expectata luce proxuma: *salubri*, again, brings out the viewpoint of the narrator, who knows the outcome. This leads the reader to expect that the fugitives will be attacked by wolves, but (again!) *homines* will prove to be *hominibus lupi*.

circa tertiam ferme uigiliam noctis: the same indication of time in the same word order is found 1, 11 (10, 20), where Scobie 1975 ad loc. quotes from N. Remy, *Demonolatreia,* Lyons 1595, I, 14: 'They said that the two hours immediately preceding midnight were the most suitable and opportune, not only for these assemblies (sc. Sabbats) but for all other divilish terrors, illusive appearances and groanings...for experience teaches that these hours are chiefly notorious for spectres and terrible apparitions'. It cannot be denied that these indications of time suggest something sinister; this is also the case at 3, 3 (54, 13), the third passage in the *Met.* where *tertia uigilia* occurs, and where the prosecutor uses this point of time against him. For *circa* indicating time, which has completely superseded *circum* and *circiter* in Apuleius, see Callebat 1968, 217.

189, 16-20 Tunc ego metu praedicti periculi, quantum pote, turbae medius et inter conferta iumenta latenter absconditus clunibus meis ⟨ab⟩ adg⟨r⟩essionibus ferinis consulebam; iamque me cursu celeri ceteros equos antecellentem mirabantur omnes: "Then, for fear of the foretold danger, I sought as much as possible the middle of the crowd and, stealthily hidden among the huddling beasts of burden, I tried to save my rump from the attacks of the wild animals. And soon I surpassed in speed of running the horses in the group, to everybody's surprise."

metu praedicti periculi: accentuates the human aspect of the ass.

quantum pote: the reading of AE. F has *potui*, adopted by Hildebrand and Eyssenhardt; originally it probably also had *pote*. In φ *pote* has been completed to *poteram* by another hand (as in US), defended by Novák, who is of the opinion that the fixed combinations are *quam pote* and *quantum poteram*. However, Helm rightly refers in his app. crit. to Neue-Wagener 2, 174 f.; see also Callebat 1968, 116.

Robertson inserts *iam* between *pote* and *turbae* (referring for the combination *iam...iamque* to Verg. *Cat.* 9, 45), which he grounds palaeographically on the space in F ('e spatium non complet') and substantially on the logic of the narrative ('ne Lucius simul inter iumenta absconditus simul ceteros equos antecellere dicatur'). Neither argument is convincing: insignificant spaces occur more than once, and *antecellere equos* is a hyperbole with the function of Leitmotiv: 6, 30 (152, 9) *at paulo ante pim.* · *Pegasi uincebas celeritatem*; cf. 4, 2 (75, 17) *non asinum me, uerum etiam equum currulem nimio uelocitatis effectum*; 6, 27 (149, 4); 6, 28 (149, 24).

Callebat 1968, 116 disputes the theory that *pote* is an archaism (thus e.g. Tränkle 1960, 35 f.; Fordyce on Catul. 45, 5; vdPaardt 1971, 200) and opts for the possibility that it belongs to colloquial language. The reference material of Neue-Wagener 2, 174 f. and *OLD* s.v. *potis/pote* 2b supports his view; see also LHSz 2, 769 ('Konversationalismus').

turbae medius: for the extension of the use of *medius* with the genitive (possibly resulting form regular use of the adjective as a noun) see Callebat 1968, 188; KSt 2, 1, 445; LHSz 2, 78.

latenter absconditus: a pleonastic expression which occurs quite often in Apuleius; cf. 5, 20 (118, 14) *latenter absconde*; 6, 12 (137, 16); 179, 17; see Bernhard 1927, 177 f. for the different functions of pleonasm, cf. Callebat 1968, 541 f.

clunibus meis: Callebat 1968, 26 speaks of an 'expression ironiquement familière'. *Clunes* (in Apuleius only here) is used both of human beings and of animals, but most authors who use the word referring to people are comic authors and satirists. We may therefore assume that the somewhat 'low register' is intentional.

⟨*ab*⟩ *adg*⟨*r*⟩*essionibus ferinis consulebam*: F has *adgessionibus*; the addition of *ab* and the insertion of *r* are by ς. The addition of *ab*, which supposes haplography, seems entirely justified in view of 7, 18 (168, 1) *peronibus suis ab aquae madore consulens*; see *GCA* 1981, 199 ad loc.

cursu celeri ceteros: note the c-alliteration both here and in the whole sentence.

ceteros equos: vdVliet proposes ⟨*asinos et*⟩ *equos*, but one can explain these words as being said by Lucius who regards himself as 'one of the horses', but it is more probable that *ceterus* is used here in the sense of the Greek ἄλλος (and also *alius*), i.e. pleonastically; see vdPaardt 1971, 70 f. and 210. Cf. also 195, 5 *equi atque alii asini* with our comm. ad loc.

Sed illa pernicitas non erat alacritatis meae, sed formidinis indicium; denique mecum ipse reputabam Pegasum inclutum illum metu magis uolaticum fuisse ac per hoc merito pinnatum proditum, dum in altum et adusque caelum sussilit ac resultat, formidans scilicet igniferae morsum Chimaerae: "That fleetness, however, was not an indication of my enthusiasm but of my fear. And so I thought to myself that it was more through fear that the renowned Pegasus had been able to fly, and that he is therefore rightly represented as winged when he leaps up into the air and bounds sky-high, terrified of course of the bite of the fire-breathing Chimaera." 189, 20-26

Sed illa pernicitas: here we have a case of *occupatio*: a possible interpretation is contradicted. The noun *pernicitas* occurs in the *Met.* only here and at 4, 13 (84, 22) in a similarly sonorous passage (assonance of *a*, alliteration of *r*).

denique: here in the concluding sense, *ergo* or *igitur*; see Helbers-Molt 1943, 131. The reasoning is a typical example of projection.

Pegasum illum inclutum: for Pegasus (and Bellerophon) cf. 6, 30 (152, 10) and 7, 26 (174, 11) with *GCA* 1981, 65 and 257 ad loc.; also the *anteludia* passage at 11, 8 (272, 20) with Gwyn Griffiths ad loc. The interpreters of Apuleius' novel differ about the meaning of this and other mythological references. According to Helm-Krenkel (Einf. 24 and n. 413) these allusions are humorous; this view is shared by Rode-Rüdiger 1960, 336 n. 1; Vallette ad loc. ('parodie burlesque, semble-t-il, de certaines interprétations rationalistes des mythes'); Heine 1962, 192, n. 6; Tatum 1979, 82. At first sight this opinion seems to be supported by 11, 8 (272, 20 f.) *tamen rideres utrumque* but Gwyn Griffiths (*AAGA* 1978, 159) correctly writes: 'This last point, it may be conceded, does not decide the matter, for it is a part of the method often adopted by Apuleius to intertwine the comic and the serious. It is the tradition of the *spoudaiogeloion*.' We could also formulate it in this way: the fact that Lucius finds Pegasus etc. ridiculous does not imply that Apuleius attaches no deeper meaning to it; the opinions of narrator and (implicit) author need not necessarily coincide. Diametrically opposed to this humorous interpretation are those of Drake 1968 and

Nethercut 1968. The former identifies Pegasus with Candidus, 'the white horse of his immortal soul' (Drake 1968, 109), the latter sees in the allusions to Pegasus a reference to 'the ass's fear as a creature subject to the blind fortune of this world, his longing to go free' (Nethercut 1968, 118).

There is yet another allegorical approach to the Pegasus-figure. Apart from the connection of Pegasus (especially in Latin literature) with Apollo, the Muses, and Helicon (see Roscher 3, 1735 f. and Thibau 1965, 132 on the subject of *Met.* 11, 8 : 272, 20), there is the notion of Bellerophon 'als Tugendheld im Kampfe gegen Aphroditische Begierde' (Roscher 3, 1747). Thus, in the Pompeian wall-paintings of the first century, Bellerophon is the opponent of untrue love, embodied in the Chimaere (Hiller 1970). If we interpret the novel in its entirety as the account of someone who lays aside his *curiositas* and erotic *uoluptas* in favour of the spiritual *uoluptas* of the worship of Isis, then the allusions to Bellerophon and Pegasus can be taken as symbolical references to that struggle. The Chimaera symbolises the fiery powers of eroticism; she is called *ingnifera*, which calls to mind the well-known *ignes* of elegy (*morsus*, too, has erotic connotations).

uolaticum: this is the reading of φα*; F has *uolanticũ* in which, according to Robertson, the *n* may have been inserted by the same hand. The adjective rarely occurs in its literal sense, as appears from the *ThLL* material: Pl. *Poen.* 473 f.; *Paneg.* 12, 5, 3; *Epit. Alex.* (ed. Thomas) 18; *CGL* 5, 601, 29; in a figurative sense ('volatile', 'flighty', 'elusive') it is found e.g. Cic. *Har.* 46 and *Att.* 13, 25, 3; Tert. *Paen.* 11, 5; Apul. *Met.* 5, 31 (128, 2); see Fernhout ad loc. The passages suggest the 'langue familière' (Médan 1925, 177) rather than archaism (Gargantini 1963, 40).

pinnatum proditum: *prodere* primarily refers to written or oral transmission; cf. Cic. *Div.* 1, 7, 12 *nihil est autem quod non longinquitas temporum excipiente memoria prodendisque monumentis efficere atque adsequi possit*. It can also refer to depiction in the visual arts; cf. Apul. *Fl.* 7 (8, 16) *Alexandri illud praeclarum, quod imaginem suam, quo certior posteris proderetur, noluit a multis artificibus uulgo contaminari*. In this passage one can think both of literature and of the visual arts, especially the coins of Corinth.

sussilit ac resultat: the two verbs are synonymous; *resultare* means here 'jump up' as at 3, 21 (68, 14) *terra resultat (Pamphile)*; see Médan 1925, 364. Synonymy and sigmatism emphasize Pegasus' high and dangerous flight.

scilicet: more or less ironical, as so often; at the same time it accounts for the 'vision du dedans'.

igniferae morsum Chimaerae: a clearly poetic turn of phrase with clausula, hyperbaton, assonance of *i* and *ae*, and the poetic compound *ignifer* (*ThLL* s.v. describes it as 'vox poetica, raro in prosa' and cites as the only other example in prose Amm. 20, 11, 17). For the fire-breathing Chimaera cf. Lucr. 5, 906 *ore foras acrem flaret de corpore flammam*; Hor. *Carm.* 2, 17, 13 *Chimaerae spiritus igneae*. For references with illustrations see Austin on Verg. *A.* 6, 288; a well-known example is the Corinthian cup from Aegina (e.g. in De Bie 1979, 67).

Nam et illi pastores, qui nos agebant, in speciem proelii manus   189, 26-190, 4
obarmauerant; hic lanceam, ille uenabulum, alius gerebat spicula, fustem alius, sed et saxa, quae salebrosa semita largiter
subministrabat; erant qui sudes praeacutas attol⟨l⟩erent; plerique tamen ardentibus facibus proterrebant feras. Ne⟨c⟩ quicquam praeter unicam tubam deerat, quin acies esset proeliaris:
"Now those shepherds who drove us had armed themselves as if for battle: one carried a lance, another a hunting-spear, a third darts, a fourth a club; but they also carried stones, which the rugged road supplied in abundance. Some held up pointed stakes. Most of them, though, wanted to keep the wild animals at a distance with burning torches. The only thing lacking to make it a line of battle was a trumpet."

A somewhat ironical description of this disorderly band; Amat 1972, 141 notes: 'La scène est plaisante, sans être réellement burlesque, car le danger est réel.' Cf. the description of Catiline's army before the battle of Pistoria (Sall. *Cat.* 56, 3): *Sed ex omni copia circiter pars quarta erat militaribus armis instructa; ceteri, ut quemque casus armauerat, sparos aut lanceas, alii praeacutas sudis portabant*; also Verg. *A.* 7, 505 f. Undoubtedly we have here a standard scene; see Portalupi 1974, 63. The *faces ardentes*, however, are atypical.

Nam: vdVliet follows Colvius in reading *iam* here, probably reasoning as Blümner does (1894, 309): 'Von einer Begründung des Vorhergehenden ist hier nicht die Rede, daher besser *iam et*'. But Oudendorp had already pointed out that *nam* can be used as a transitional particle. See Callebat 1968, 329; in more detail Löfstedt 1911, 34 f.; commentators like Friedländer and Smith on Petr. 38, 4 *Nam mulam quidem nullam habet, quae non ex onagro nata sit*; LHSz 2, 505 f.

in speciem proelii: usually *in speciem* means 'in the manner of', 'like'; here it is used brachylogically for 'as if for', 'as if in'. See Callebat 1968, 232.

obarmauerant: this compound also occurs 2, 25 (45, 14) and 9, 1 (202, 22) *manus impias obarmabat*; besides Apuleius only Hor. *Carm.* 4, 4, 21 and Aus. *Epigr.* 25, 1 (44, 1 Prete). Médan 191 rightly calls it a poeticism.

hic...ille...alius...alius: variatio: see Bernhard 1927, 95. The 'close-up' is more effective than the 'total shot'; for this technique in Vergil see Heinze ³1915, 355 f.

salebrosa semita: cf. 7, 15 (166, 1) *furfures...multo...lapide...salebrosos*, where the adjective is again used literally; see *GCA* 1981, 182 ad loc. Note the sigmatism in this part of the sentence.

largiter: the 'classical' adverb *large* is not found in Apuleius; see Callebat 1968, 175.

nec quicquam...proeliaris: *nec* is φ's correction of *ne*. For the somewhat pleonastic combination *acies...proeliaris* (the hyperbaton with *esset* as the penultimate word is probably used for the sake of the clausula) cf. 3, 6 (65, 9) *dirigitur proeliaris acies*; see vdPaardt 1971, 59.

The irony of this sentence is twofold. Within the fiction the narrator ironises the actors; outside the fiction Apuleius ironises his own instrumentarium: the addition of one *tuba* would complete the topos of the *acies rustica*. Cf. Verg. *A.* 7, 513 f. *pastorale canit signum cornuque recuruo/Tartaream intendit uocem*; see

Fordyce ad loc.; Heinze³ 1915, 196. Similar winks at the *lector doctus* occur at 4, 6 (see *GCA* 1977, 62) and 185, 19 (the 'genre-bound' *nutrix*).

190, 4-10 Sed nequicquam frustra timorem illum satis inanem perfuncti longe peiores in⟨h⟩aesimus laqueos. Nam lupi, forsitan confertae iuuentutis strepitu uel certe nimia luce flammarum deterriti uel etiam aliorsum grassantes, nulli contra nos aditum tulerunt ac ne procul saltem ulli comparuerant: "But entirely in vain we suffered that utterly needless fear: we got entangled in much worse dangers. For the wolves, perhaps scared by the noise of the compact troop or at least by the bright light of the torches or even because they were prowling elsewhere, did not attack us at all and had not even been visible in the distance."

nequicquam frustra: Brandt deletes *frustra* (Helm: 'dubito an recte ut in loco singulari'); Robertson prefers to delete *nequicquam* as a marginal gloss. But Löfstedt 1911, 59 f. points out that pleonasm of particles is frequent in Latin of all periods, and especially in late Latin; cf. *ergo igitur, aliquando tandem*, (and cf. *propere celeriter* etc.). For Apuleius see Médan 1925, 364; Bernhard 1927, 172; Callebat 1968, 529; for the phenomenon in general KSt 2, 2, 573 f.; LHSz 2, 800.

timorem illum satis inanem perfuncti: Lipsius prefers *immanem* which is excellent paleographically and from the point of view of content, but unnecessary; *inanem* emphasizes the needlessness of the fear, and gives it an ironical accent. For *satis* (in the sense of *ualde*) as a favourite adverb in the *Met.* see Callebat 1968, 540 f.

perfuncti: the verb *perfungor* occurs in the *Met.* both with the accusative and the ablative; see vdPaardt 1971, 100. The construction with the accusative is not peculiar to Apuleius (despite Médan 1925, 33); KSt 2, 1, 383 mentions Lucr. 3, 956 (*perfunctus...praemia*) and Fronto 135, 10 (vdH 128, 6) *onera...perfunctus est*. Further Paul. Nol. *Carm.* 16, 229; *Cod. Theod.* 12, 6, 7; *CE* ed. Bücheler 744, 2 and 1203, 3 (according to the *ThLL*).

longe peiores in⟨h⟩aesimus laqueos: the correction is by φ. For *longe* with the comparative see *GCA* 1977, 47 on 4, 4 (77, 8). According to the *ThLL inhaeresco* with an accusative occurs only here. The metaphor of the snares is well-chosen in view of the situation which awaits Lucius the ass and the *fugitiui*: the expected danger is replaced by something worse. In this we disagree with vThiel 1971, 19 n. 55 who thinks that Apuleius apologizes for the fact that the wolves do not appear. There is no error of composition.

forsitan...uel certe...uel etiam: the variatio of words is the stylistic counterpart of the variatio of the three possible explanations; this seems to be typical of Apuleius.

grassantes: cf. *grassati* at 190, 19, where it refers to dogs. It seems to be a robbers' term; cf. Plin. *Nat.* 9, 145 *grassatur aries ut latro* and 188, 25 f. *lupos...in modum latronum praetereuntes adgredi*. It is questionable whether this metaphor should be regarded as ironical, as Callebat 1968, 393 maintains. It may have been the author's intention to bracket together the dangers of robbers and wild animals. For the relation of man and animal in the *Met.* see

Schlam in *SAG* 1981, 115 f., especially 125.

nulli: has the meaning of *non* here; see *GCA* 1981, 196 on 7, 17 (167, 12 f.).

aditum tulerunt: cf. 4, 9 (81, 22) *ferremus aditum* with *GCA* 1977, 79 ad loc.

ne...saltem: equivalent to *ne...quidem*; cf. 9, 32 (227, 14 f.) *ac ne suetis saltem cibariis uentrem meum replere poteram*. See Callebat 1968, 335; KSt 2, 2, 56.

comparuerant: the pluperfect is conspicuous; cf. 7, 2 (155, 5) *cum...idem profugisset nec exinde usquam compareret*. Callebat 1968, 104 thinks that in our passage we have a case of a plusquamperfectum pro perfecto and compares 201, 9 f. *accingunt se meo funeri ac...paene ad extremum confecerant mortem*. But that pluperfect has an entirely different explanation; see our comm. ad loc. It is true that variatio of tense occurs frequently in narrative texts (see Chausserie-Laprée 1969, 397-402) but, apart from a mechanistic explanation as clausulae causa, the simplest explanation of this pluperfect is that it indicates the pre-occurrence of *comparere* in relation to *aditum ferre*.

CHAPTER XVII

The fugitives are assaulted by dogs en stones.

190, 10-19 Villae uero, quam tunc forte praeteribamus, coloni multitudinem nostram latrones rati, satis agentes rerum suarum eximieque trepidi, canes rabidos et immanes et quibusuis lupis et ursis saeuiores, quos ad tutelae praesidia curiose fuerant alumnati, iubilationibus solitis et cuiusce modi uocibus nobis inhortantur, qui praeter genuinam ferocitatem tumultu suorum exasper[n]ati contra nos ruunt et undique laterum circumfusi passim insiliunt ac sine ullo dilectu iumenta simul et homines lacerant diuque grassati plerosque prosternunt: "But the farmers of the estate which we happened to be passing at the time, took our band for robbers. Most anxiously concerned about their property, with the usual cries and all kinds of shouting they set dogs on us, furious, huge, and more savage than any wolves and bears, which they had trained carefully for their protection. These dogs, who were (apart from their natural fierceness) maddened by the tumult of their masters, ran at us, surrounded our flanks on all sides, jumped up at us everywhere, and without any discrimination tore both pack animals and people to pieces. They raged on for a long time an threw most of us to the ground."

Between the subject *coloni* and the predicate is a great distance of five cola: *multitudinem...rati* (12 syllables), *satis...trepidi* (17), *canes...saeuiores* (22), *quos...alumnati* (20), *iubilationibus...nobis* (21). The relative clause which follows it also has extensive cola: *praeter...ruunt* (26), (*et*)*undique...insiliunt* (16), (*ac*)*sine...lacerant* (18), *diuque...prosternunt* (12).

uillae...coloni: the *uilla* must be a reasonably large agrarian settlement, in view of the number of *coloni* we may assume. Callebat 1968, 56 mentions the meaning 'village' only for 7, 8 (160, 9); id. *AAGA* 1978, 172.

latrones: the robber motif is present throughout the *Met.*; see e.g. Riefstahl 1938, 55; Heine 1962, 149 n.3; Scobie in *AAGA* 1978, 51 and n. 71.

In the Jungian approach of von Franz[2] 1980, 52 the robbers represent 'all the different aspects of a kind of crude primitive virility or masculinity, something which Lucius, the mother's boy, lacks to such an extent'. See also ibid. 199 f.

satis agentes rerum suarum: the meaning of *satis agere*, *sat agere* (or *sategere*), and *sat agitare* is 'have one's hands full', 'be in trouble'; cf. Cato *ap.* Charis. (*GLK* 218, 2) *iam apud uallum nostri satis agebant*: Gel. 3, 8, 1 *cum Pyrrhus rex in terra Italia esset...satisque agerent Romani*. For the combination with *rerum suarum* cf. Pl. *Bac.* 636 *agitas sat tute tuarum rerum*; Ter. *Hau.* 225 *is quoque suarum rerum sat agitat*. With all due respect to Gatscha 1898, 151, it is not necessary to see here a reminiscence of Plautus. See for the genitivus rei vGeisau 1916, 244; Callebat 1968, 513; LHSz 2, 74.

eximie: for the orthographical variant *exumie* cf. 201, 20 and our comm. ad loc. According to Callebat 1968, 535 Apuleius uses intensifying adverbs especially for the sake of expressivity, which is also characteristic of the language of the comic poets. The word *eximie*, however, is not found in comedy. It is quite rare in combination with adjectives (Colum. 8, 17, 1; Mela 1, 21; Plin. *Nat.* 22, 128); it is more common with verbs; see vdPaardt 1971, 58; Hofmann ³1951, 77 and 193; KSt 2, 1, 794; LHSz 2, 163.

canes rabidos et immanes: Elmenhorst compares Colum. 7, 12 *Villae custos eligendus est (canis) amplissimi corporis, uasti latratus canorique, ut prius auditu maleficum, dein etiam conspectu terreat*, on which Hildebrand remarks: 'Unde Pricaeus recte *immanes* ad mensuram corporis, non animi ferocitatem, id quod alii volebant, bene retulit'. For the descriptive adjectives see Portalupi 1974, 96. For the dogs 'hyperbolic savagery' see *GCA* 1977, 42 f. with a reference to Heine 1962, 149; see also Heitland 1921, 331; Schlam in *SAG* 1981, 125 f.

quos...fuerant alumnati: a 'verschobenes Plusquamperfekt'. According to Médan 1925, 121 its meaning is passive here: '*Quos* est une faute de copiste pour *qui*, causée par le voisinage de *os* dans *rabidos* une ligne plus haut'. It is indeed passive at 9, 36 (230, 19 f.) *canes pastoricios...transeuntium uiatorum passiuis morsibus alumnatos*, but in our passage it is active with *coloni* as the (not explicitly mentioned) subject; thus *ThLL*; Flobert 1975, 139. The verb is attested here for the first time; later it is found only Mart. Cap. 8, 813; 9, 892 (see Flobert ibid.)

ad tutelae praesidia: this seems to be a unique combination, in which *tutela* specifies the more general *praesidia*; for this genitivus identitatis see LHSz 2, 63.

iubilationibus: Heinsius wants to read *sibilationibus*, but Oudendorp points out Var. *L* 6, 68 *uicina horum* (sc. verbs like *fremere, clamare*) *quiritare, iubilare*; Fest. 104, 9 L *iubilare est rustica uoce inclamare*. The noun is attested in Apuleius for the first time; see *ThLL* s.v. 586, 56; after Apuleius *ThLL* lists only Christian authors.

Elsewhere it refers to shouting for joy (e.g. Aug. *Conf.* 4, 1, 1) and to lamenting (Sedul. *op.* 3, 11).

cuiusce modi = *cuiuscumque modi*. Cf. 9, 2 (204, 4) *arreptis cuiuscemodi telis*; 10, 13 (246, 18); 11, 7 (271, 18); 11, 22 (284, 17); *Apol.* 55 (62, 3); *Fl.* 15(20, 4). vdVliet 1896, 386 wants to read *cuiusce modi* also 9, 10 (210, 16), where F and φ have *huiusce modi* (Helm with Floridus *cuiusce modi*), and 11, 16 (279, 5), where the principal mss. have *huiusce modi* (adopted by Helm, but Brantius had already proposed *cuiusce modi*). The usual form *cuiusque modi* is found 2, 26 (46, 25). See Butler-Owen on *Apol.* 55; Gwyn Griffiths 1975, 169; also Sommer 1914, 450; Neue-Wagener 2, 453; LHSz 1, 126.

inhortantur: this verb is attested only in Apuleius; cf. 9, 36 (230, 23). See *ThLL* s.v.

exasper[n]ati: F originally had *exasp̄nati*, but a later hand corrected *p̄n* to *per*.

genuinam: see our comm. on 179, 26.

undique laterum: according to *ThLL* s.v. *latus* 1032, 21 this is a unique combination. Callebat 1968, 488 compares for the partitive genitive 2, 30 (50, 17) *hinc inde laterum* and *SHA* Fl.Vop. *Quadr. Tyr.* 5, 3 *undique gentium*.

grassati: see our comm. on 190, 8 above.

190, 19-24 Cerneres non tam hercules memorandum quam miserandum etiam spectaculum: canes copiosos ardentibus animis alios fugientes arripere, alios stantibus inhaerere, quosdam iacentes inscindere, et per omnem nostrum commeatum morsibus ambulare: "You could have seen a spectacle not so much, by heaven, noteworthy as tearworthy, too: a great many dogs in a fierce rage – some seized those who fled, others clung to those who stood their ground, some tore to pieces those who had fallen, and they went snapping all along our column."

According to Callebat 1968, 440 the asyndeton *prosternunt*. *Cerneres* has a consecutive value. This is not uncommon in a narrative which moves more or less logically.

Cerneres...spectaculum: cf. 7, 13 (163, 23) *pompam cerneres...nouumque et hercules memorandum spectamen* with *GCA* 1981, 164 f. ad loc. for the 'tableau' motif. The narrator summarizes the events (*memorandum*) and anticipates a few details (*miserandum*).

non tam...quam...etiam: vdVliet deletes *non*; Helm in his app. crit. compares 3, 4 (55, 3) *non tam hercules truculentam accusationem intuens quam meam miseram conscientiam*. Our passage, however, has in addition *etiam* (omitted in older editions); for that reason it is better to compare 3, 6 (56, 17) *non tam...uerum etiam*. It looks very much like a contamination, which we have retained in the translation.

hercules: Gaselee (with a few recentiores) *Hercule*. For the interjection see Heine 1962, 176; vdPaardt 1971, 48 f. Observe the full rhyme of *cerneres...hercules*; *memorandum...miserandum...spectaculum* (see Strilciw 1925, 113). The alliteration of *c* continues in *canes copiosos*, that of *m* in *nostrum commeatum morsibus*.

copiosos: with the same meaning as *multos*; cf. 4, 20 (89, 22) *canes...feri satisque copiosi*. See Ernout 1949, 15; Callebat 1968, 153.

ardentibus animis: for *animi* in the sense of *iracundia* cf. Acc. *trag.* 15 *iram infrenes, obstes animis*; Sal. *Hist.* 3, 48, 10 *quantis animis ierit in L. Quintium, uidistis*; Sen.*Med.* 174 *compesce uerba...animosque minue*.

iacentes inscindere: with some hesitation we retain the reading of F; most editors accept the obvious conjecture *inscendere* (the reading of φ). *Inscindere*, which is not attested elsewhere, is well defended by Hildebrand, who noted: 'Apuleium hoc compositum formasse, qui accuratius instantem canum rabiem hominumque lacerationem describeret, ad intima usque scissorum'. With Eyssenhardt we accept this reading. An argument for *inscindere* is that it takes up *lacerare* (1.18 above) and thus gives a climax. Besides, neologisms in Apuleius are often compounds; see the table in Bernhard 1927, 141. *Inscendere* is rather bland as is *insidere*, the reading of ς defended by Oudendorp.

commeatum: Brantius proposes *comitatum*, but cf. 189, 11 and our comm. ad loc. for the usual *concretum pro abstracto* meaning.

morsibus: for the ablative of manner see Médan 1925, 49.

ambulare: cf. 3, 5 (55, 26) *per totam domum caedes ambulet*. See also our comm. on 188, 17; for verbs indicating 'go' in Apuleius in general see Callebat 1968, 142 f.

Ecce tanto periculo malum maius insequitur. De summis enim tectis ac de proxumo colle rusticani illi saxa super nos raptim deuoluunt, ut discernere prorsus nequiremus, qua potissimum caueremus clade, comminus canum an eminus lapidum: "Lo and behold, this great danger was followed by a greater evil. For from the roofs and the nearest hill those farmers quickly rolled down rocks upon us so that we no longer could make out against which disaster we had best defend ourselves, the dogs close at hand or the stones at a distance." 190, 24-28

Ecce: calls the reader's attention to something unexpected or sudden, often something dangerous; see Heine 1962, 174; *GCA* 1977, 157 on 4, 21 (90, 11). *Ecce* takes up the visual element in *cerneres* (1.19 above).

malum maius: why is the attack by the villagers worse than that by the dogs? Helm points out 5, 4 (105, 19) *quouis malo plus timet quod ignorat* and refers in the app. crit. there to Publ. Syr. 596 R *semper plus metuit animus ignotum malum*. More important, however, seems the subjective point of view of Lucius the ass; the bites, however dangerous, have apparently not troubled him too much here; the rocks are much more dangerous to him. Observe the alliteration of *m* and *c*, and the sigmatism.

qua...caueremus clade: Callebat 1968, 491 says that *cauere* with an ablative is rare after the archaic period, so that there may be Plautine influence here. The only other certain occurrence of the ablative is Ambr. *Hex.* 5, 7, 17; ablative rather than dative, according to *ThLL*, at Pl. *Bac.* 147; 463; *Cas.* 411; 838; *Men.* 121; 249; *Persa* 369; 835; *Rud.* 945; 1089. Further Petr. 82; Lact. *Inst.* 3, 10, 3. See also KSt. 2, 1, 336; LHSz 2, 106.

Quorum quidem unus caput mulieris, quae meum dorsum residebat, repente percussit. Quo dolore commota statim fletu cum clamore sublato maritum suum pa⟨sto⟩rem illum suppetiatum ciet: "One of the stones suddenly struck the head of the woman who was sitting on my back. Immediately she started to weep and scream with pain and called for help to her husband, the shepherd mentioned earlier." 190, 28-191, 2

Quorum...unus: 'scene' replaces 'summary' here; cf. the remarks of Junghanns 1932, 98 and 166 n. 79 on 'Individualisierung'.

mulieris, quae residebat: Lucius has not explicitly mentioned this before; now it appears that the woman is part of *quidquid in casula pretiosum conditumque* (*pastor*) *seruabat* (188, 12 f.). The woman in question is the *auara equidem nequissimaque illa mulier* of 7, 15 (165, 18) who put Lucius to work at the mill and gave him a trashing, the wife of the *gregarius* (165, 16). We can compare the carrying of the sadistic *puer* (7, 18: 168, 2) and later the *dea Syria* (198, 16 below). In contrast to this is the joyous carrying of Charite; see Kerényi 1927,

187 and our comm. on 7, 13 (163, 25) *uirginem asino triumphantem* in *GCA* 1981, 165.

dorsum residebat: for the accusative cf. 10, 7 (241, 25) *consueta loca residentibus (patribus)*; 10, 18 (251, 5 f.) *me...exornatum ipse residens*. Médan 1925, 33 incorrectly calls it a 'construction nouvelle': the transitive use occurs already Cic. *Leg.* 2, 55 *dies denicales, quae a nece appellatae sunt, quia residentur mortuis*. The *ThLL* material shows that after Apuleius it occurs Drac. *Romul.* 10, 165 *impiger ales/nunc hanc nunc illam residet (columbam)*; id. 10, 273.

pastorem illum: Kronenberg wants to add⟨*meum*⟩ after *illum*, which is not necessary. The *pastor* is the *equorum magister*, as we mentioned above.

Sto in *pastorem* has been added later, according to Helm by a different hand, according to Robertson and Frassinetti by the same hand. In itself, the original *parem* would make sense; as a noun it can mean 'partner'. In that case we would have to assume an asyndeton bimembre with explanatory force, or regard *maritum suum* as a gloss. It seems better to follow the corrected version.

suppetiatum ciet: cf. 4, 10 (82, 15) *suppetiatum decurrunt anxii* with *GCA* 1977, 85 ad loc. The iteration of *c* suggests shock.

CHAPTER XVIII

The fugitives are allowed to move on; they seize the opportunity to nurse their wounds.

At ille deum fidem clamitans et cruorem uxoris ab⟨s⟩tergens altius quiritabat: 'Quid miseros homines et laboriosos uiatores tam crudelibus animis inuaditis atque obteritis? Quas praedas munitis? Quae damna uindicatis? At non speluncas ferarum uel cautes incolitis barbarorum, ut humano sanguine profuso gaudeatis': "And he, invoking the gods' help and wiping off his wife's blood, shouted and shouted even more loudly: 'Why do you so cruelly assault and destroy wretched, toiling travellers? What loot are you protecting? Against what damage are you defending yourselves? Surely you do not dwell in caves like animals or on crags like barbarians that you would take pleasure in shedding human blood?'" 191, 2-8

At ille: see Callebat 1968, 422: '*At* est dans bien des cas suivi de *ille, illa*, marquant un changement d'interlocuteur et introduisant un passage au style direct'. *At* followed by a pronoun generally has an enlivening effect and involves the reader directly in the events.

deum fidem clamitans: an intensification of the well-known *fidem clamare*; cf. Pl. *Men.* 1053 *clamabas deum fidem atque hominum; Aul.* 300; Caecil. *com.* 212. For similar intensives see Callebat 1968, 392.

ab⟨s⟩tergens: the correction is by φ.

altius: the man's shouting may be compared to his wife's, or to his own invocation of the gods. A third possibility, that the comparative should be translated 'rather loudly', is less likely here.

quiritabat: cf. 5, 29 (126, 11) *Haec quiritans properiter emergit e mari (Venus)*. Fernhout ad loc. and Callebat 1968, 78 cite Varro *L.* 6, 68 *Quiritare dicitur is qui Quiritum fidem clamans implorat.* If Apuleius knew this etymology – which seems quite probable in view of his etymological puns elsewhere – *deum fidem clamitans* is more pointed. For etymological puns in the *Met.* see *GCA* 1981, 184 on 7, 16 (166, 6) *pastor egregius*; 233 on 7, 23 (171, 18) *detestatione*; cf. also 180, 21 *adseuerat* above with our comm. Outside the *Met.* see e.g. Cairns 1979, 90 f.

miseros homines et laboriosos uiatores: the first member is explained by the second. For the miserable *uiator* see Schmidt 1979.

inuaditis atque obteritis: this is the reading of F; in the margin something has been added, probably by the same hand, that was deleted later. This addition, presumably *ac perteritis*, is regarded by Robertson as a varia lectio; being the lectio difficilior, it should certainly be taken into consideration. However, because neither the status of the varia lectio nor the reading is entirely clear, we

163

prefer to retain *obteritis*, parallels to which are found 1, 25 (23, 15); 9, 35 (229, 21). Some later mss. have a tricolon (AE *inuaditis ac prosternitis atque obruitis*; U *inuaditis ac perteritis atque obruitis*) but this seems somewhat too rhetorical in comparison with the following sentences; moreover, the second member of the tricolon may well have crept into the transmission by way of the marginal reading in F. For the putative relation between F and α* see Dowden 1980, 218.

Quas praedas munitis: F's reading *munitis* has often been assailed. Most editors (vdVliet, Gaselee, Robertson, Helm-Krenkel, vThiel, Scazzoso) adopt Eyssenhardt's conjecture *inhiatis*. Helm reads *uultis* in his three Teubner editions; Brandt-Ehlers have Novák's *cupitis*; Wiman 1927, 62 f. opts for *manetis* (= *cupitis*) after the analogy of *exspectare* which can have the same voluntary value. The reading *munitis* is defended by Kronenberg 1928, 39; Bernhard 1930, 310; Armini 1932, 88; Augello 1977, 39 (and obviously also Castiglioni 1943, unavailable to us); it appears in the texts of Giarratano-Frassinetti, Carlesi-Terzaghi, and Pagliano. The meaning of *munire* in our passage would have to be *defendere, custodire*, as at 5, 2 (104, 20 f.) *nullo custode totius orbis thensaurus ille muniebatur*. Bernhard defends *praedas munitis* against Wiman with the following paraphrase: 'Welche Beute habt ihr zu schützen, d.h. Seid ihr etwa Räuber und habt ihr die schon gemachten Beutestücke zu schützen'. The *uiatores*, however, take their attackers not for robbers but for *coloni*, who live in *uillae* (190, 10 above). Therefore one should take *praedas* proleptically, as do Kronenberg and Armini; in the paraphrase of the former: 'quas res, quasi nostram praedam futuram – nullas enim praedas agimus – defenditis (protegitis, tuemini)?'

cautes: Cornelissen 1888, 70 f. proposes *caulas* (= *cauernas*) because he thinks *cautes* meaningless. But *cautes* has the connotation of unfeelingness which is required here; cf. Verg. *A.* 4, 366 *duris gcnuit te cautibus horrens / Caucasus* with the extensive list of parallels of Pease ad loc.

191, 9-11 Vix haec dicta et statim lapidum congestus cessauit imber et infestorum canum reuocata conquieuit procella: "Scarcely had he said this when immediately the dense rain of rocks stopped, the aggressive dogs were called back, the storm subsided."

Observe the parallelism in this sentence: *lapidum...imber* vs. *canum...procella* with double enallage, double hyperbaton, assonance of *a*, alliteration of *c*.

uix...et: for the parataxis see Médan 1925, 86; Callebat 1968, 434.

imber...procella: for the synonymous expression see Bernhard 1927, 148; for the metaphor of *imber* cf. Enn. *Ann.* 284 *hastati spargunt hastas, fit ferreus imber* and (even more similar) Sil. 13, 181 *saxeus imber/ingruit*. According to the material of the *ThLL* no parallel exists for *procella canum* or for *procella* followed by the genitive plural of an animal. Liv. 30, 18, 4 *equestram procellam excitemus oportet si turbare...uolumus* and Tac. *Hist.* 3, 53 *dispersas...legiones equestri procella* are close. For *procella* in the sense of 'violent disturbance' (personified) many parallels exist: Cic. *Dom.* 137 *tu, procella patriae, turbo ac tempestas pacis*; Rufin. *hist.* 10, 29 (p. 991) *post haereticorum procellas et perfidiae turbines*; Petr. Chrys. *Serm.* 20 (p. 254 B) *Iudaeorum turbines, persecutorum procellae.* vThiel 1971, 1, 125 n. 154 remarks: 'Die Beendigung des Kampfes VIII 18, 3 ist ganz unwahrscheinlich: Die Bauern rufen ihre Hunde zurück, und diese folgen brav und unverzüglich. Wenn Apuleius glaubt, griechische Wachhunde liessen sich durch Rufen von ihrem Opfer abbringen, beweist er nur, dass er kaum einmal seinen Fuss vor die Stadt gesetzt hat'. Obviously vThiel is only aware of the realism in (the mimetic qualities of) the *Met.* Nevertheless, the (perhaps) unrealistic behaviour of the dogs clearly has a function here: it illustrates the sudden cessation of the emotional movement.

Vnus illinc denique de summo cupressus cacumine: 'At nos', inquit, 'non uestrorum spoliorum cupidine latrocinamur, sed hanc ipsam cladem de uestris protelamus manibus. Iam denique pace tranquilla securi potestis incedere': "One of them finally called from the highest top of a cypress: 'But we are no robbers and are not after your belongings – but we are warding off that very same disaster, which threatened us at your hands. Now you can safely go on in peace and quiet'." 191, 11-15

illinc: Médan 1925, 360 and Bernhard 1927, 181 take this pleonastically with *de... cacumine.* Callebat 1968, 293, on the other hand, rightly takes *illinc* in the sense of *illorum.* Thus also Hildebrand ad loc.: 'Interposita enim est *denique* particula, id quod aliis locis, ubi idem pleonasmus conspicitur, non reperi, unde *illinc* potius pro *ab illa parte* i.e. *illorum* dictum hic esse affirmo'. For the use of adverbs instead of pronouns see Callebat 1968, 293; LHSz 2, 208 f.

denique: the translation 'at last' seems the best; it achieves the effect of a 'lull after the storm', which fits well into this dramatic scene. It is also possible to consider *denique* in the sense of *ac* or *atque* (Becker 1879, 32).

de summo cupressus cacumine: remarkable iteration of *c* and *u*. Vallette ad loc. wonders why the man has chosen a cypress to climb into: 'Mais le croquant, que fait-il sur son cyprès? Mettons qu'il s'en serve comme d'un observatoire'. The funerary function of the cypress is well-known; according to Tatum 1979, 73 the tree is a symbol of death also in this passage: 'Every page of Book 8 reeks of death'. Cf. the old woman who hangs herself from a cypress; see *GCA* 1981, 67 on 6, 30 (152, 13). Fick presents a different view in her essay on vegetative symbolism in the *Met.*: 'Tandis que tous les habitants du village s'arment de pierre, cet homme, juché sur son cyprès où il n'a certainement pas fait monter de projectiles, n'a pas d'intentions belliqueuses; c'est lui, au contraire, qui prend l'initiative de déclarer la paix. Plus que d'observatoire, semble-t-il, le cyprès lui sert d'abri. En face de la menace des prétendus brigands, il ne choisit ni la violence, comme ses compatriotes ni le désespoir de la vieille femme, il s'arme de patience'. She refers to the interpretation of Artemidorus, who regards the cypress as 'le signe de la longanimité et de la temporisation, vertus féminines par excellence' (Fick 1971, 333). There seems to be no objection against combining the 'positive' and 'negative' aspects of the cypress (cf. 5, 24 : 121, 23 f. *inuolauit (Amor) proximam cupressum deque eius alto cacumine sic eam* (*Psychen*) *grauiter commotus adfatur*) and concluding that there is an ambivalence, as does De Gubernatis. He calls the cypress 'das ehrwürdigste und allgemeinste Symbol der weiblichen Gottheit in ihrer zweifachen Beziehung zu Zeugung und Tod' (*Kleine Pauly*, s.v. Cypresse, 1353, 19).

At nos: this is the emendation by ς of *ad nos*, the reading of F and φ which is adopted by Eyssenhardt and vdVliet; Müller proposes *ad nos ⟨'en'⟩, inquit*. Helm refers in his app. crit. to 196, 23 and 9, 21 (219, 3), where the transmission, obviously by mistake, has *ad* as well.

hanc ipsam cladem: sc. *latrocinium*.

de uestris protelamus manibus: Médan 1925, 65 remarks that *de* is used here to indicate the cause (so that *de...manibus* modifies *cladem*). In view of the word order one might wish to connect *de...manibus* with *protelamus* (so that *de* has a separative meaning), but according to the material of the *ThLL* there is no other occurrence of the combination *protelare de*. Apuleius has the verb also 9, 12 (204, 4 f.) *ut exitium commune protelarent*; earlier occurrences are rare (cf. Pl. *Merc. Arg.* 2, 12; Ter. *Ph.* 213; Sisenna *frg. hist.* Peter 27, 69). Callebat 1968, 478 notes a linguistic affinity between Sisenna and Apuleius.

denique: mildly concluding; see Molt 1943, 131.

pace tranquilla: cf. 10, 6 (241, 22) *in pace placida*. This 'pleonasm' has an expressive function: while sounding serious in the mouth of the speaker, the expression acquires an ironical connotation at the narrator's level in view of the following episode.

191, 16-18 Sic ille, sed nos plurifariam uulnerati reliquam uiam capessimus alius lapidis, alius morsus uulnera referentes, uniuersi tamen saucii: "Thus he spoke. We set out on the rest of our trip, wounded in many ways: one bearing wounds from a stone, another from a bite, but everyone with injuries."

Sic ille: ellipsis of the verbum dicendi. See Bernhard 1927, 157; Callebat 1968, 448; Hofmann ³1951, 169.

sed nos: since it does not appear anywhere that the ass is wounded, the word *nos* indicates his identification with the group; cf. *peruenimus* 1. 19 below, but from then on this solidarity is absent until 193, 18. Remarkably enough the ass refrains from bewailing the distressing situation, though he has many opportunities for doing so.

plurifariam uulnerati: cf. 6, 10 (135, 6) *uestem...plurifariam diloricat* and *Fl.* 17 (32, 4 f.) *ceterum ipsius uocis hominis exercendi cassus labor superuacaneo studio plurifariam superatur*, where the adverb means 'in many ways'. It is hard to determine whether it is used here locally or modally. For the modal meaning cf. Sol. 38, 12; Sid. *Ep.* 9, 3, 5; see Callebat 1968, 137.

uulnera referentes: an unusual combination, to which Tib. 1, 1, 66 *lumina...sicca referre domum* comes close.

tamen: not purely adversative; see LHSz 2, 495 f.

191, 18-22 Aliquanto denique uiae permenso spatio peruenimus ad nemus quoddam proceris arboribus consitum et pratentibus uirectis amoenum, ubi placuit illis ductoribus nostris refectui paululum conquiescere corporaque sua diuerse laniata sedulo recurare: "So, having covered a considerable distance, we arrived at a grove full of tall trees and pleasantly green meadows. There those drivers of ours decided to rest for a while in order to recuperate and to treat their various injuries carefully."

The *locus amoenus* is indicated explicitly by the use of the adjective in question.

permenso: in a passive sense also 10, 18 (250, 21); see our comm. on 188, 21. The first example of its use in an active sense is [Tib.] 3, 3, 9; see Flobert 1975, 366.

nemus...arboribus consitum: cf. 5, 1 (103, 10 f.) *lucum proceris et uastis arboribus consitum*; 10, 30 (261, 5) *mons...consitus uirectis et uiuis arboribus*; see further *GCA* 1977, 132 on 4, 17 (87, 14 f.).

pratentibus: this is a neologism according to Bernhard 1927, 139. The material of the *ThLL* has this passage as the only example of this word.

illis ductoribus nostris: cf. 189, 12 with our comm.

refectui: cf. 5, 3 (105, 7); 9, 22 (219, 28) with the same dative. The *ThLL* material does not give any examples before Apuleius. The only other occurrence is *Dig.* 36, 1, 80 (78), 12 (Scaevola) *ex refectu paupertatis* in the sense of 'proceeds'. See also Neue-Wagener 1, 760.

recurare: cf. 6, 25 (147, 8) *plagas recurantibus (latronibus)*. The verb is found first Catul. 44, 15 *et me recuraui otioque et urtica*, on which Kroll remarks: '*recurare* kennen Plin. Stat. Apul.: es mag ein vokstümliches Wort sein'. This assumption is more probable than the opinion of Médan 1925, 189 ('mot poétique rare') and 179 ('langue archaique'), in view of Plin. *Nat.* 12, 75; Stat. *Theb.* 3, 583; Tert. *ad Marc.* 1, 20, 1; id. *Nat.* 2, 14, 9; *Res.* 60, 7 (mentioned by the *ThLL* material); *CIL* 2, 5181; 9, 5804 (mentioned by *OLD*).

Ergo passim prostrati solo primum fatigatos animos recuperare ac dehinc uulneribus medelas uarias adhibere festinant, hic cruorem praeterfluentis aquae rore deluere, ille spongeis inacidatis tumores comprimere, alius fasciolos hiantes uincire plagas. Ad istum modum saluti suae quisque consulebat: "Consequently, sprawled everywhere on the ground, they tried as quickly as possible first to recover from their emotions and then to apply various remedies to their injuries. One washed off the blood with the water of a stream flowing by; another reduced his swellings with a sponge soaked in vinegar; a third bound up his gaping cuts with bandages. In this way each took care of his own well-being." 191, 22-27

fatigatos animos: they must recover emotionally before they can attend to their bodies (*primum...ac dehinc*).

festinant: for *festinare* with the infinitive see Médan 1925, 76; Callebat 1968, 311; KSt 2, 1, 667; LHSz 2, 346. This construction is less frequent in classical Latin.

hic...ille...alius: individualisation and variatio; cf. 189, 26 f. and see Bernhard 1927, 95.

praeterfluentis aquae rore: for *ros* = *aqua* cf. 1, 19 (18, 4) and 3, 18 (65, 11); see vdPaardt ad loc. with a list of references. The *praeterfluens aqua* is a fixed item in the *locus amoenus*. Here the water has no immediate association with death (as it often has in the *Met.*; see Nethercut 1968, 112), but with (renewing) life – an archetypal symbolism; cf. the water which saves the burning ass 7, 20 (169, 10 f.); for the cleansing power of water see Gwyn Griffiths 1975, 113. The chapters immediately following show, however, that this *locus 'amoenus'* does have associations with death.

inacidatis: a *hapax legomenon* meaning *aceto tinctis*. *Inacidatis* is the reading of F, φ, U, and E (in F *inaci* has been rewritten but it also was the original reading, says Helm; Robertson expresses himself more cautiously). A has *matidatis*. The reading of ς *madidatis* (followed by Hildebrand and Eyssenhardt) is a neologism, according to Médan 1925, 122; it occurs regularly in the church fathers. The objection of Pricaeus and others (as quoted by Hildebrand) against *inacidatis* is interesting: 'Aceto enim vulnera leniri ac dilui satis probavit Pric., qui hac de re conferatur et Intt. ad Petron. c. 136, licet ipse lectionem *madidatis* praeferat, quia non videantur illi, quorum fuga tam praeceps fuerit, acetum hic paratum habuisse, dum aquae ad quam prostrati iacuerint, copia abundarit' – a school example of an over-subtle reasoning.

CHAPTER XIX

Ominous words from a herdsman and the arrival of an old man.

Interea quidam senex de summo colle prospectat, quem circum capellae pascentes opilionem esse profecto clamabant. Eum rogauit unus e nostris, haberetne uenui lactem uel adhuc liquidum uel in caseum recentem inchoatum: "Meanwhile an old man stood looking out from the top of a hill. The goats grazing round about plainly announced that he was a herdsman. One of our people asked hem if he had milk for sale, either still liquid or curdled into new cheese." 191, 29-192, 2

Interea: the ability to describe simultaneous events (Quinn 1968, 84 f. speaks of 'parallel narrative', which is, strictly speaking, a *contradictio in terminis*) is naturally a consequence of the point of view taken by the narrator. In the *Aeneid interea* has almost become a transitional formula. Indeed, the perspectives in *Met.* and *A.* come close to each other; see vdPaardt in *AAGA* 1978, 76 f. and Stanzel 1979, 268 f. For *interea* in epic and historiography see Reinmuth 1933 and Chausserie-Laprée 1969, 29 f. respectively.

quidam senex: for *quidam* as an indefinite article see Graur 1969; *GCA* 1977, 38 on 4, 3 (76, 6).

prospectat: observe in this sentence the succession of tenses: *prospectat...clamabant...rogauit*: see Callebat 1968, 427 f.

quem circum...pascentes: Koziol 1872, 338 (followed by *ThLL* s.v. 1117, 59) regards *circum* as a preposition; Bernhard 1927, 28 demonstrates that anastrophe of a preposition does not occur elsewhere in Apuleius; he rightly sees the accusative *quem* as the subject of the infinitive *esse*, and *circum* as an adverb; thus also *Index Apul.* s.v. *circum* and Callebat 1968, 217; cf. our comm. on *propter* 187, 12. In *circum...pascentes* we therefore have 'abbildende Wortstellung' or iconicity.

opilionem: for the etymology of this noun see our comm. on 176, 21.

clamabant: the figurative meaning 'declare plainly' (cf. Catul. 6, 6 f. *te non uiduas iacere noctes...cubile clamat*) prevails, but the literal meaning (see *OLD* s.v. 1b) undoubtedly also plays a part here.

uenui: like UES, F has *uenui* (but the letters *ui* have been rewritten); φ has *uenu* (-*nu* is in an erasure and there are also traces of erasure over the word). The dative *uenui* is also found 195, 15 and 9, 10 (210, 12); Apuleius is the only author who uses this form of the dative instead of the usual *ueno*. See Neue-Wagener 1, 733 f.; LHSz 1, 450, whose findings are confirmed by the material of the *ThLL*.

lactem...inchoatum: this gives us an interesting view on the socio-economic aspects of the world described in the *Met.*; cf. Miller 1981, 73 'the world portrayed by Apuleius involves cash exchanges for produce right down to the lowest levels'. For cheese-making see Columella 12, 13; W. Richter in the Kleine Pauly s.v. Schaf und Ziege, with references.

lactem: this masculine accusative also occurs 199, 23 and 200, 4. In addition to *lac, lactis* there are also the forms *lacte, lactis* (neuter), as appears from Petr. 38, 1, and a masculine **lactis, -is*; see Stefenelli 1962, 51 f., who sees in the existence of *lactem* 'ein Zeugnis für das allmähliche Schwinden des lateinischen Neutrums.' See also vdPaardt 1971, 104 f. on 3, 13 (61, 26); Callebat 1968, 123.

in caseum recentem inchoatum: ς has *incoactum*; Heinsius proposes *recenter coagulatum*: Castiglioni hesitantly *recentem coactum*. There is, however, no reason to doubt the correctness of the reading of F (φ). This bucolic note is in keeping with the *locus amoenus* of the previous chapter and forms a strong contrast with the gruesome events which are to come.

192, 3-6 At ille diu capite quassanti: 'uos autem' inquit, 'de cibo uel poculo uel omnino ulla refectione nunc cogitatis? An nulli scitis, quo loco consederitis?', et cum dicto conductis ouiculis conuersus longe recessit: "But shaking his head for a long time, he said: 'How can you think of food or drink or any refreshment at all at a time like this? Don't you realise at all what kind of a place you have come to?' And with these words he gathered his sheep together, turned round, and went off into the distance."

quassanti: F has *quassante*, the correction by the same hand (thus also φ). vdVliet prefers *quassato*, but this seems unnecessary: cf. 2, 24 (45, 5) *capite quassanti* (correction in the margin); 3, 26 (71, 13) *quassanti capite*; 4, 29 (98, 6). Purser 1906, 49 compares also Pl. *Bac*. 305 *capitibus quassantibus* and *As*. 403 *quassanti capite*.

poculo: for this metonymy (*poculum* for *potio*) cf. 178, 4 *cena poculoque communi carior* with our comm. ad loc.; 1, 19 (18, 3) *auidus adfectans poculum*. For more examples of this figure of speech see Strilciw 1925, 109.

refectione: cf. 5, 7 (107, 6 f.) *nec lauacro nec cibo nec ulla denique refectione recreata flens ubertim decessit ad somnum*, where Fernhout 1949, 43 rightly notes for *refectio* 'omnia, quibuscumque homines recreari solent' (against Médan 1925, 159, who translates *refectio* as 'repas'). See also *GCA* 1977, 66 on 4, 7 (79, 20).

cogitatis: for the indicative cf. 9, 3 (204, 20 f.) '*Adhucine miserum istum asinum iugi furore iactari credimus?*'

nulli: has the meaning of an emphatic *non*; cf. 190, 6 f. *nam lupi... nulli contra nos aditum tulerunt*. See *GCA* 1981, 196 on 7, 17 (167, 14).

scitis, quo loco consederitis: since Elmenhorst's commentary it is traditional (cf. Gatscha 1898, 147) to refer for these lines to Verg. *A*. 4, 39 *nec uenit in mentem quorum consederis aruis*. On the verbal level the only parallel element is the verb, but the two situations are, indeed, identical: danger is imminent for 'fugitives'.

et cum dicto: this formula, indicating a transition, is frequently used in the *Met.*; see Bernhard 1927, 50; vdPaardt 1971, 104 on 3, 13 (61, 25 f.).

ouiculis: the noun *ouicula* is first attested here; later it is often found in Christian authors (because of the parable of the lost sheep) in prose only; see Callebat 1968, 49; *ThLL* s.v. It is remarkable that the *capellae* of 191, 30 have now become *ouiculae* – but this is not inappropriate in a novel about metamorphoses. It is possible that we have a 'mixed' flock here with the emphasis now on one kind of animal, now on the other; *ThLL* s.v. 1188, 48 probably means something similar by the comment 'variationis causa?'.

longe recessit: strictly speaking one can only observe the action of *recessit*. The additional *longe* and the explicative *fuga* in the following sentence are the result of the 'produktive Imagination' (Stanzel) of the narrating I; cf. 193, 19 f. *celerrime...longo itinere confecto*, which also is psychologically motivated.

Quae uox eius et fuga pastoribus nostris non mediocrem pauorem   192, 6-8
incussit: "These parting words of his struck our shepherds with considerable fear."

non mediocrem pauorem: cf. 6, 26 (148, 9) *nec me tamen mediocris carpebat scrupulus* and see *GCA* 1981, 35 ad loc. for the litotes.

incussit: the use of *incutere*, which not uncommonly governs words meaning emotions such as fear (for the combination with *pauor* cf. Liv. 25, 37, 12; Flor. *Epit*. 3, 10, 14; Amm. 25, 3, 11), and the dispondaic clausula underline the terror of the men. *Vox et fuga* are apparently regarded as a hendiadys, whence the singular form of the verb; see KSt 2, 1, 49 f.; LHSz 2, 433.

Ac dum perterriti de loci qualitate sciscitari gestiunt nec est qui   192, 8-14
doceat, senex alius, magnus ille quidem, grauatus annis, totus in baculum pronus et lassum trahens uestigium ubertim lacrimans per uiam proximat uisisque nobis cum fletu maximo singulorum iuuenum genua contingens sic adorabat: "And while they, terrified, were anxious to know what was the matter with the place and there was no one to tell them, another old man approached along the road. He was tall but burdened with years, leaning with his whole weight on a cane and dragging his weary steps along, weeping copiously. When he saw us, with many tears he touched the knees of the young men one by one, and imploringly spoke as follows:"

perterriti: this summarizes the substance of what precedes; cf. also *gestiunt*, which indicates the excitement. A fine touch of psychological insight is the detail that the people are looking for someone *qui doceat loci qualitatem*.

qualitate: this noun is first attested in Cic. *Ac*. 1, 25, where it is used to render the Greek ποιότης; in an agricultural context it occurs e.g. Col. 1, pr. 24 *quarum (terrarum) non nullae colore, non nullae qualitate fallunt*.

magnus ille quidem, grauatus annis: both Oudendorp and Hildebrand pay much attention to the adjective *magnus*, which looks innocent enough at first sight. Both reflect the opinion of Beroaldus, who proposed: 'vel pro *magno natu*, vel pro eo, *qui est longi corporis*, vel *qui primatum tenet inter pastores*'. Oudendorp rejects the third explanation arguing, 'Insigne aliquod tunc addere debuerat auctor; unde appareret, comites Lucii vel ipsum id scire potuisse'; and further 'ne pastor quidem ille senex erat, at viator, cui nepos itineris fuit comes'. The latter argument is decisive, the former based on narrow logic. Oudendorp, who finds the first two explanations as unsatisfactory as the third, mentions three possible emendations for the rejected *magnus*: 1) *ignarus*, in the sense of *ignotus*, with a reference to Verg. *A.* 3, 590 f. *cum subito e siluis macie confecta suprema/ignoti noua forma uiri miserandaque cultu/procedit supplexque manus ad litora tendit* (Pricaeus, too, assumes that Apuleius had this passage in mind); 2) *magnis*, in the sense of *multis*, to be connected with *annis*; 3) *magis*, a conjecture of Rover, 'sc. quam prior senex, de quo fuerat mentio'.

Magnus is, indeed, rather rarely used in the sense *procerus*, but we may compare e.g. Pl. *Am.* 1103 *puer ille...ut magnust et multum ualet!*; Ter. *Hec.* 440 *(homo) magnus*; Liv. 8, 6, 9 *uiri maioris quam pro humano habitu*. In view of later developments in the story it is probably not insignificant that *magnus* in this sense is used especially of animals (see *OLD* s.v. 1b): the *senex magnus* will become (193, 13) a *draco immanis* (Scobie 1977, 340: 'Apuleius does not explicitly say that the 'old man' and the dragon are one and the same person, but such a conclusion is supported by the emissary's remark that while the young man was being devoured by the dragon, 'the old man was nowhere to be seen'.').

The *ThLL* does not give a parallel for *grauatus annis* (again it just misses being a standard expression) but we may compare Verg. *A.* 2, 435 f. *Iphitus aeuo/iam grauior*; Hor. *S.* 1, 1, 4 *grauis annis/miles*; Apul. *Met.* 2, 2 (25, 16 f.) *senex iam grauis in annis*.

lassum trahens uestigium: *lassus*, which is avoided by e.g. Cicero and Caesar, is used by Apuleius more often for objects (parts of the body) than for persons; the distribution for *fessus* is just the opposite. See Axelson 1945, 29 f. and Callebat 1968, 165.

proximat: according to Callebat 1968, 140, this verb is first attested in Apuleius; *OLD* s.v. mentions that the codices at Plin. *Nat.* 15, 53 give the verb: *proximat is* (but *proxima iis* is usually read). The present tense in our passage increases the suspense and attention of the reader; we have also a change in tense (*gestiunt...proximat...adorabat*).

cum fletu maximo: the ablative indicating the concomitant circumstances is often constructed with *cum* in Apuleius; see Callebat 1968, 198 f.

iuuenum genua contingens: this is the classic gesture to invoke pity; cf. 9, 40 (233, 25) *simulans...sese ad commouendam miserationem genua eius uelle contingere*; 10, 6 (241, 5) *tum fletu, tum precibus genua etiam decurionum contingens*. For anthropological and literary details see *GCA* 1977, 95 f. on 4, 12 (83, 18). The *iuuenes* are approached because they are the only available source of help; cf. 192, 24 f.

adorabat: the meanings *adloqui* and προσκυνεῖν have merged here.

The sentence as a whole is a fine example of narrative art. The anxiety of the group gives way to curiosity and pity as the old man slowly approaches, almost like a snake (*lassum trahens uestigium*, an anticipation of his ability to change shape?). He evokes pity by his bent figure (*totus in baculum pronus*), his weary steps, and his sobbing, which is stressed by *ubertim* and *fletu maximo* and illustrated by the copious iteration of *m*. The old man is, however, completely master of the situation; this appears from his approach, which is psychologically powerful and geared to the individual, and from his effective speech; see the final remark on the next chapter.

CHAPTER XX

The old man addresses the fugitives with a supplication.

192, 14-17 'Per Fortunas uestrosque Genios, sic ad meae senectutis spatia ualidi laetique ueniatis, decepto seni subsistite meumque paruulum ab inferis ereptum canis meis reddite: "'By your Fortunes and Spirits, as you may reach my advanced age, happy and healthy – help a bereaved old man: rescue my little boy from the underworld and restore him to my grey hairs."

Per Fortunas uestrosque Genios: the beginning of the request belongs to the category of prayer formulas, but this particular example offers a unique combination. Adjurations of this kind, prayers in form, but addressed to human beings, are not uncommon in the *Met.*, e.g. 2, 28 (48, 11) *miserere per caelestia sidera*; 4, 31 (99,2) *'per ego te', inquit, 'materna caritatis foedera deprecor, per...'*; also 3, 23 (69, 9) and 6, 2 (130, 6).

Per Fortunas (printed with a capital in all editions) occurs 'in obsecratationibus et exclamationibus' (*ThLL* s.v. 1191, 74 f.) and is often used by Cicero, e.g. *Att.* 5, 11, 1 *ne nobis prouincia prorogetur, per fortunas, dum ades,...prouide*; see Shackleton-Bailey ad loc. In Cicero the plural relates to Fortune's double aspect (*uirilis* and *muliebris*); in our passage the plural refers to the *Fortuna* of each of the addressees individually, as *Genios* refers to each one's individual *Genius*. For the various aspects of Fortune, see *GCA* 1981, 50 on 6, 28 (150, 4); for the application to individuals and restricted groups, see *RE* 7, 32, 60 f. (Otto). The combination of *Fortuna* and *Genius* is found in inscriptions only, e.g. *CIL* 6, 216 *ginio et fortunae tutelaeque huius loci* and 13, 7610 *Ioui...caelesti fortun(ae) et genio loci*.

Fortuna with a possessive (indicating its attachments to a person or persons – see above) is found e.g. at Cic. *Fam.* 8, 16, 1 *Per fortunas tuas, Cicero, per liberos te oro* and in the *Met.* 195, 21; see our comm. ad loc. In the present passage, Rossbach conjectures *Fortunas ⟨uestras⟩*, which seems unnecessary; rather *uestrosque* is to be connected ἀπὸ κοινοῦ with *Fortunas*.

There is irony in the old man's invocation, since the event it provokes will have an *un*happy ending for the men, or at least one of them. Tatum 1969, 91 n. 175 finds a pun in *Per Fortunas*: the old man addresses the others 'by your fortunes' but the result is 'mala fortuna' for one of them.

sic...ueniatis,...subsistite...reddite: for *sic* with the subjunctive (= old optative, expressing a wish) followed by an imperative, see LHSz 2, 330 f. with bibliography, and Vallette on 5, 13, n. 1. In poetry this is found first in Catullus, e.g. 17, 5-7 *sic tibi bonus...fiat,...munus hoc mihi...da* with Fordyce ad loc. Cf. further Ov. *Ep.* 16, 281 *parce datum fatis, Helene, contemnere amorem/sic habeas faciles in tua uota deos* and Hor. *Carm.* 1, 3, 1 f. with Kiessling-Heinze and Nisbet-Hubbard ad loc. This idiom is also found in sepulchral inscriptions, e.g. *CE* 1181, 5 f. *te, pie possessor siue colone, precor,/ne partiare meis tumulis increscere siluas/sic tibi dona Ceres larga det et Bromius*. Similarly *ita* with the subjunctive (= optative), e.g. *CE* 196 *ita ualeas, scriptor, hoc monimentum praeteri*. For further examples, see Appel 1909 (repr. 1975), 152 and Lattimore 1962, 120.

ad meae senectutis spatia: cf. 11, 6 (271, 7) *ultra statuta fato tuo spatia uitam...prorogare*; Ov. *Met.* 15, 225 *spatiumque iuuentae transit*.

ualidi laetique: the old man wishes the young men the best for the future, at a moment when they are far from *ualidi* or *laeti*; they are recovering from the wounds inflicted upon them by dogs and stones, and so are not *ualidi*, and they are not *laeti*, either, on account of the recent threat about the place where they are (192, 5 f.). The contrast between this wish and the reality becomes even more marked when we learn the outcome of this adventure. The combination of *laetus* and *ualidus* does not occur elsewhere except Damig. *Lapid.* 34 (190, 11) *laetos et ualidos eos* (sc. *dentes*) *constituit* (sc. *lapis galactices*), in a totally different context.

decepto seni: F reads *decepti*; the conjecture *decrepito* in ς is adopted only by Helm III, who attributes it to Beroaldus. Of the other editors most retain *decepto*; Brant changes it into *defecto*. Wiman is right in opting for *decepto* but not in his argumentation that *deceptus* is equivalent to *interfectus, mortuus* in the sense of 'finished', 'wretched'. He adduces *Met*. 2, 27 (47, 15) *perempto ciui subsistite*, and is supported by *Armini*. But is is quite possible for *deceptus* to have the meaning of 'left behind', 'bereaved', referring to parents who have survived their children; see Vallette ad loc. Callebat 1968, 156 also takes *deceptus* in the sense of 'privé (de son enfant)'; literally 'trompé dans son espérance'; cf. Cic. *De Orat*. 2, 260 *decepti sumus expectatione*. Another example, mentioned by *ThLL*, is *CE* 1550 A1 *hunc titulum natae genetrix decepta paraui*. Finally, there is also an element of 'deception': the old man feels betrayed because his one and only grandchild and heir has fallen into a pit and is in danger of his life. Again, the irony is increased when we realize that the 'deceived' old man will turn out to be a cheat himself. The other occurrences of *deceptus* in the *Met*. are in the literal meaning only; 3, 18 (65, 20); 4, 12 (83, 21); 185, 27.

subsistite: cf. 2, 27 (47, 13) in a comparable context: *'per fidem uestram'*, *inquit, 'Quirites, per pietatem publicam perempto ciui subsistite'* and 6, 2 (130, 6) *per ego te...dexteram...deprecor...subsiste*. For the development in meaning of *subsistere* = 'help', see vdPaardt 1971, 175 on 3, 23 (69, 25).

ab inferis ereptum: two possibilities are to be considered here: 1. *ereptum* is used attributively, as e.g. Helm-Krenkel: 'meinen Jungen..., den mir die Unterirdischen entrissen'; 2. *ereptum* is used proleptically, as Vallette and Brandt-Ehlers: 'entreisst meinen Kleinen dem Totenreich und gibt ihn ... wieder'. This coheres with the question whether *ab inferis* (the ablative of *inferi*; the neuter plural *infera* is rare, according to *ThLL* s.v. 1390, 68 f.) is said 'de incolis Orci fere i.q. Manes' (*ThLL* s.v. 1390, 14 f.) or 'metonymice de ipso loco' (*ThLL* s.v. 1390, 27 f.). We prefer the second possibility, in view of expressions like 7, 24 (172, 3) *mediis Orci manibus extractus* (cf. *GCA* 1981, 238 ad loc.);

Ter. *Hec.* 852 *qui ab Orco mortuom me reducem... in lucem feceris*; Liv. 9, 6, 3 *uelut ab inferis extracti* (see Otto 1890, 258 s.v. Orcus).

canis meis: the noun *cani*, first attested in Cic. *Sen.* 62 and from then on occurring fairly often both in poetry and prose, is used by Apul. only here. This obvious metonymy for *senectus* is also found e.g. in Sen. *Const.* 12, 1 *post iuuentam canosque*. See also Tib. 1, 10, 43 with Kirby Flower Smith and Murgatroyd ad loc. The expression fits the elevated style employed by the old man.

192, 17-24 Nepos namque meus et itineris huius suauis comes, dum forte passarem incantantem sepiculae consectatur arripere, delapsus in proximam foueam, quae fructibus imis subpatet, in extremo iam uitae consistit periculo, quippe cum de fletu ac uoce ipsius auum sibi saepicule clamitantis uiuere illum quidem sentiam, sed per corporis, ut uidetis, mei defectam ualetudinem opitulari nequeam: "For while my grandson and sweet companion of this journey was trying by chance to catch a little bird singing charmingly on a hedge, he fell into a nearby pit below the brambles and is now in the utmost danger of his life, because I gather from his weeping and calling, as he cries again and again for his grandfather, that he certainly is still alive, but on account of my diminished strength, as you see, I am not able to help him."

This long and carefully built period (see our final remark on the present chapter) may serve to point up an important difference between the handling of style in Apuleius (and Latin literature in general) on the one hand and e.g. the modern novel on the other. In the latter the emotional state of the old man would probably have been expressed by phenomena such as near-speechlessness, broken sentences, and the like. Cf. Stankiewicz 1964, 239-26; Frier 1976, 287-292. Similar instances of highly emotional utterances in highly stylized form occur e.g. in Fotis' reaction to the result of her mistake at 3, 25 (70, 24-71, 5); in Charite's address (186, 8-187, 2 with our notes ad loc. passim); and perhaps in the *puer*'s speech at 7, 21 (170, 4 f.), although there the indignation is pretended (cf. *GCA* 1981, 219 ad loc.).

namque: in second place in the sentence; see *GCA* 1977, 142 on 88, 27-28.

passarem: the same hand in F has emended *passarem* to *passerem* by placing an *e* above the second *a*. See above on 188, 15. The meaning is 'small songbird', perhaps a thrush; see Fordyce's discussion on Catul. 1, 2 and Capponi 1979, 384 f.

incantantem: the actual meaning of *incantare* is 'enchant', 'formulas magicas cantare' (*ThLL*), but most translations give the meaning 'sing' for this passage, as does *ThLL*. But the meaning 'enchant', 'sing enchantingly' fits extremely well in this magical context: the boy is supposed to have been lured away by the charm of the bird's song. *Incantare* occurs only here in the *Met.*, and several times in the *Apol.* The dative with *incantare* is exceptional.

sepiculae: this diminutive of *saepes*(*sepes*) is hapax legomenon. Observe the paronomasia of *sepiculae... saepicule* (three lines below). Other examples in the *Met.* of a similar wordplay are 3, 18 (65, 10-12) *litat...libat*; 3, 23 (69, 8-10) *nidulum...nodulum*; 5, 15 (115, 7) *mellita...mollita*. See Bernhard 1927, 229 f.

consectatur: the construction of *consectari* with an infinitive seems to occur only here. Callebat 1968, 309 maintains that this construction is formed on the analogy of verbs like *consequi* with the infinitive; cf. Cic. *de Orat.* 1, 150 *uere...illud dicitur, peruerse dicere homines peruerse dicendo...consequi* with Sorof ad loc., explaining the 'gräzisierende' construction from the existence of a Greek parallel (S. *El.* 621 αἰσχροῖς γὰρ αἰσχρὰ πράγματ' ἐκδιδάσκεται). See further KSt. 2, 1, 674 and 683 for *consequi*. On the use of an infinitive after verbs meaning 'wish' or 'attempt', see Callebat 1968, 308 and cf. above 188, 10 *fugere conparant*.

subpatet: this verb, attested in Apuleius exclusively, also occurs 7, 24 (172, 19) *campis subpatentibus*; see *GCA* 1981, 244 ad loc.

in extremo...consistit periculo: of the expression *in periculo consistere* no other examples are given by the *ThLL*. Similar expressions are found *Met.* 4, 11 (82, 15 f.) *in ancipiti periculo constituti* (with *GCA* 1977, 86); PL. *Mer.* 122 *in periclo uortitur*; Cic. *Fam.* 4, 15, 2 *quo periculo...esse*. Cf. further Cic. *Fam.* 12, 10, 4 *in aliquo statu tolerabili consistet*.

sed: the contrast is expressed by *quidem...sed*: the *senex* does know that the boy is still alive, but – and now comes the more important statement – 'I cannot help him'.

de fletu ac uoce: for *de* with ablative indicating the cause, see our comm. on 182, 15 above.

ipsius...clamitantis: for *ipse* in the meaning of a demonstrative pronoun, see Callebat 1968, 283 f.; LHSz 2, 189 f.

auum sibi: sometimes Apuleius uses the dative (or the genitive *sui*) instead of the possessive pronoun; see Callebat 1968, 261 with other examples. The transmission of *auum* is not clear. In F a letter has been corrected; the original reading may have been *ouium*, later corrected to *auum*. In φ a later hand has written *auū* in rasura. Some of the later mss. have *auxilium*.

saepicule: the diminutive creates a pun with *sepiculae* (1.18). For diminutive adverbs see Callebat 1968, 520.

saepicule clamitantis: for the value of *clamitare*, see our comm. on 188, 5 above.

per corporis...mei defectam ualetudinem: the use of *per* + acc. instead of a causal ablative is found from Plautus onwards, but is more frequent in late Latin; see Callebat 1968, 220 and LHSz 2, 127. Cf. 2, 5 (29, 12) *per aetatem* and Ter. *Eun.* 113 *per aetatem etiam potis erat*. The participle *defectam* in the sense of 'weakened', 'worn out', 'tired' (*OLD*) is not found before the Augustan period; cf. e.g. Ov. *Met.* 13, 477 *defecto poplite labens*. After that it occurs quite frequently. In Apul. e.g. 4, 4 (77, 10) *uiae spatio defectus* and 5, 25 (122, 26) *sauciam Psychen atque defectam*; cf. also 198, 8 *defectis...lateribus*.

opitulari: in this chapter Apuleius uses three different words for 'help': *subsistite* (1.16), *opitulari* (1.23), and *suppetiari* (1.25). The meaning of these words does not differ very much; Apuleius probably uses them for the sake of variety.

192, 24-27 At uobis aetatis et roboris beneficio facile est suppetiari miserrimo seni puerumque illum nouissimum successionis meae atque unicam stirpem sospitem mihi facere': "But for you, thanks to your youth and vigour, it is easy to come to the aid of a most unhappy old man and save the life of that boy, the last of my line and my only descendant'."

The predominating *s*-sound of this sentence may reflect the ominousness of the old man's entreaty.

aetatis et roboris: this may be regarded as hendiadys: 'your vigorous age' or 'the vigour of your age'; at any rate they are interdependent notions. See LHSz 2, 782 f. and Bernhard 1927, 166: 'dat zweite Substantiv drückt die Folge des ersten aus'; cf. for the opposite notion *Met.* 7, 27 (175, 9) *senectam infirmitatemque*. *Aetas* stands for *adulescentia, iuuentus*; cf. *ThLL* 1127, 23 f. For the combination of *aetas* and *robur* cf. Cic. *S. Rosc.* 149 *si iam satis aetatis ac roboris haberet* and Tac. *Ann.* 13, 29 *deerat robur aetatis*.

beneficio + genitive: 'thanks to'. Here *beneficio* is preceded by the genitive, cf. 5, 25 (122, 29) *senectutis prolixae beneficio*. According to LHSz 2, 133 *beneficio* with a genitive instead of a causal ablative is 'spätlateinisch', but *OLD* and *ThLL* give examples of this construction in classical Latin, e.g. Cic. *Ver.* 2, 20 *beneficio Q. Metelli* and Sen. *Con.* 7, 6, 14 *aetatis beneficio*.

subpetiari: this verb probably does not occur before Apuleius; see *GCA* 1977, 85 on 4, 10 (82, 15).

nouissimum successionis: abstractum pro concreto = *progenies*. In this meaning it is found from Gellius onwards, e.g. 1, 9, 1 *ratio Pythagorae ac deinceps familiae ⟨et⟩ successionis eius*: Oros. *Apol.* 271 *peccante...homine, ex quo in uniuersam successionem dira contagia transierunt*. See Svennung 1922, 133.

sospitem...facere: this combination is found in this passage only. *Sospes* occurs in poetry and post-Augustan prose, e.g. Pl. *Capt.* 873 *saluum et sospitem/uidi*; Plin. *Pan.* 67, 5 *ut te sospitem incolumemque praestarent*. For descriptive *facere* (also with an adjective) see LHSz 2, 755.

Observe the rhetorical composition of the supplication: 1. the invocation, in a sentence of 23 words; 2. the reason for the supplication, in a long and carefully structured period with the main verb in the middle (54 words); 3. another appeal to the men, in a shorter sentence of 22 words. In each of these three sentences a variation of the notion 'help' occurs. There is further a remarkable succession of interrelated notions or complementary words, nouns and adjectives, always in sets of two: 1.14 *Fortunas...Genios*; 1.15 *ualidi laetique*; 1. 17-18 *nepos...et...comes*; 1.21 *fletu ac uoce*; 1.24 *aetatis et roboris*; 1. 25-26 *puerumque...atque stirpem*. See Bernhard 1927, 164 f. and *GCA* 1981, 234.

This chapter is characterized also by notions that indicate a contrast, e.g. the opposites young...old; happy and healthy...miserable. The examples are: *senectus...ualidi laetique*; *seni...paruulum...canis*; *nepos...auum*; *corporis defectam ualetudinem...aetatis et roboris beneficio*; *miserrimo seni...puerumque*; *in extremo...uitae consistit periculo...uiuere illum quidem*. By these contrasts the old man evokes a *miseratio*: an implicit reference is made to the former happy situation in which the old man was old, certainly, but also happy because he had a grandson. This is in accordance with the rhetorical rules of the *miseratio*. See Cic. *Inv.* 1, 107 and Lausberg 1960, 239 f., par. 439.

CHAPTER XXI

One of the young men sets out to help the old man but a horrifying thing happens.

Sic deprecantis suamque canitiem distrahentis totos quidem miseruit, sed unus prae ceteris et animo fortior et aetate iuuenior et corpore ualidior quique solus praeter alios incolumis proelium superius euaserat, exurgit alacer et percontatus, quonam loci puer ille decidisset, monstrantem digito non longe frutices horridos senem illum inpigre comitatur: "While he was pleading like this and tearing his grey hair, all indeed took pity on him, but one of them, who surpassed the others because he was more valiant in spirit, younger in age, and stronger in body, and who alone among the others had emerged from the previous fight unscathed, jumped up eagerly, asked exactly where the boy had fallen down and briskly accompanied the old man, who pointed with his finger to the dreadful thorny bushes not far away."

Against Helm III, Robertson, and Giarratano-Frassinetti, who punctuate with a period after *miseruit*, we punctuate with a comma, in order to accentuate the contrast in *totos quidem, sed unus*. The group is opposed to the individual, who will eventually take action, and who receives a detailed description.

deprecantis...distrahentis: ellipsis of a pronoun after a participle is frequent in the *Met.*, e.g. 184, 12 *garrienti...deprecanti*. See Callebat 1968, 451. For the alliteration, here of the two participles, see Bernhard 1927, 219 f.

distrahentis: cf. also 2, 26 (47, 1) *capillos distrahere* and 182, 18 *capillos distrahentem*.

canitiem: abstractum pro concreto. Cf. 7, 27 (175, 3) *trahens cinerosam canitiem* with *GCA* 1981, 261 ad loc. and 192, 16 *canis meis reddite*.

totos: in the sense of *omnes*; cf. 3, 16 (63, 22) with vdPaardt 1971, 121 ad loc.

miseruit: best taken here as an ingressive perfect; see LHSz 2, 318.

unus: in contrast to *totos*. Cf. Cic. *Att.* 6, 1, 3 *Pompeius...plus potest unus quam ceteri omnes* and Cic. *Q. Fr.* 1, 1, 16 *cui semper uni magis quam uniuersis placere uoluisti*. Similar descriptions of an individual who stands out in a group are found more than once in the *Met.*, e.g. 4, 8 (80, 16) *unus, qui robore ceteros antistabat* and 4, 14 (86, 1 f.) *ut unus e numero nostro, non qui corporis adeo, sed animi robore ceteris antistaret*.

prae ceteris: for the comparative use of *prae* see Callebat 1968, 209 and *GCA* 1977, 119 on 4, 15 (86,8).

et animo fortior et aetate iuuenior et corpore ualidior quique...euaserat: a polysyndetic construction, three short parallel phrases (ablative + comparative) connected by *et*, followed by a longer relative clause connected by *-que*.

One sentence contains all the young man's characteristics, the last of which, described in the greatest detail, will also turn out to be the most important. The three short cola are parallel in form and content and have approximately the same number of syllables. Variation is achieved by the fourth colon, which consists of 24 syllables and therefore receives most emphasis. For the parallelism in the first three cola see Bernhard 1927, 90.

iuuenior: ThLL s.v. *iunior* 737,58 cites of the form *iuuenior* one instance in each of the Elder and the Younger Seneca, the Elder and the Younger Pliny, Tacitus (but see also Sommer 1914, 461 and *OLD* s.v.; Sommer thinks the form was 'reconstructed' in the Imperial period). After Apul. the form remains rare and is confined to a few Christian authors.

solus praeter alios: variation on *unus prae ceteris*. Many examples of this idiom are to be found in Plautus, e.g. *Ps.* 801 *tu solus praeter alios*, but also at e.g. Hyg. *Fab.* 102, 1 *irata ei ob id quia solus praeter ceteros ausus fuit.*

solus...incolumis: this man will soon (193, 12) fall victim to a dragon. The fact that he is *incolumis* contradicts (perhaps ironically) 191, 18 *uniuersi tamen saucii*. On 'res neglegenter compositae' in the *Met.* see e.g. vdPaardt 1971, 74.

proelium superius: this refers to the attack in ch. 17 (191, 10 f).

The exuberant phrasing of the whole section *unus prae ceteris...proelium superius* is typically Apuleian. See Bernhard 1927, 177.

exurgit alacer: *alacer* is used predicatively as often in the *Met.*, e.g. 10, 31 (262, 21) *alacer demonstrabat Paridi* and 11, 6 (270, 14) *alacer continuare pompam*. See also Callebat 1968, 412. The young man's vitality is again emphasized, as it is by *inpigre* 1. 4.

monstrantem...senem illum: a hyperbaton. In the *Met.* Apuleius prefers *monstrare* to *ostendere*: 15 times vs. 3 times. In *Apol.* and *Fl. monstrare* is not used; *ostendere* occurs 12 times in *Apol.*, 2 times in *Fl.* Plautus and Ennius do not show a preference for either word; Terence and most prose authors before Apuleius prefer *ostendere*. Not until late Latin do some authors use *monstrare* more frequently. See *ThLL* s.v. *monstrare* 1440, 54 f. for a survey of *monstrare*, *ostendere*, and *demonstrare*.

frutices horridos: this combination is not found elsewhere in Latin literature. From the narrator's point of view *horridos* is used proleptically: the bushes are not only thorny, but also horrifying, as we will see later. Lämmert 1955, 185 speaks of 'zukunftsgewisse Voraussage'. *Frutices* is found in Apuleius only once elsewhere: 192, 19 *fruticibus imis*.

193, 5-10 Ac dum pabulo nostro suaque cura refecti sarcinulis quisque sumptis suis uiam capessunt, clamore primum nominatim cientes illum iuuenem frequenter inclamant, mox hora diutina commoti mittunt e suis arcessitorem unum, qui requisitum comitem tempestiuae uiae commonefactum reduceret: "And, having been restored, we by fodder and they by attention to their own needs, they took up each his own bundles and went on their way. In the meantime they first repeatedly cried out to the young man, loudly calling him by name; then, worried by the long time, they sent one of their number as a messenger to locate their companion, to urge him to a timely departure, and to bring him back."

pabulo nostro suaque cura: again Lucius makes a clear distinction between the animals to which he belonged and the people, thinking first of himself and the other animals. This distinction is in contrast to e.g. 191, 16 f., where Lucius the ass identifies with the whole group: we, animals and people. The separation of groups will be seen again shortly, at 193, 18 *se fuga proripiunt nosque pellunt*. Petschenig proposes to read *nostri* instead of *nostro* and to equate *pabulum* with *cibus*, so that the distinction between humans and animals is lost. But *pabulum* is the general term for the feed of many kinds of animal; see *ThLL* s.v. 5,37 f.; the few times it is used of food for humans, the humans in question are implicitly or explicitly compared to animals, ibidem 8,27. In Christian authors it becomes a common term also for human food. The contrast between *pabulum* and *cibus* is especially clear 11, 2 (267, 6). Petschenig offers no arguments for his conjecture; he probably takes exception to the incongruence of subject and verb, but such incongruencies often occur in the *Met.*, e.g. 198, 12 *quisque formati...prodeunt*. Observe the chiastic position of the possessive pronouns *nostro suaque*.

sarcinulis quisque sumptis suis uiam capessunt: observe the alliteration of *s*. *Quisque* is the subject of the sentence but is enclosed by the ablative absolute construction. For this see LHSz 2, 402. *Sarcinula* occurs a few more times in the *Met.*, notably in connection with *uiam capessere*; e.g. 1, 14 (13, 20) *et uiam...capessere. Sumo sarcinulam meam*; 1, 17 (16, 5) *Sumo sarcinulam et...capessimus uiam*.

clamore...nominatim cientes...frequenter inclamant: observe the 'Synonymenhäufung' (Bernhard 1927, 164 f.). By its context *nominatim ciere* evokes associations with the dead; cf. 2, 30 (49, 26) and Verg. *A.* 3, 68. For the solemn use of this expression see our comm. on 181, 18 above. It also occurs in the *Met.* without association with the dead, e.g. 4, 10 (82, 12); cf. also 5, 7 (108, 12).

inclamant: the compound intensifies the meaning, which is further strengthened by *frequenter*. Cf. Cic. *Inv.* 2, 14 *comitem illum suum inclamauit semel et saepius*.

nominatim: the only other occurrence of this adverb in the *Met.* is 7, 7 (159, 14) *miscuit milites suosque famulos nominatim*. See *GCA* 1981, 128 ad loc. and Callebat 1968, 477 for adverbs in *-tim*.

mox hora diutina: with Oudendorp, Hildebrand, and *ThLL* s.v. *diutina* 1643, 75 we retain the reading *hora* of F and φ. *Hora* in the sense of *spatium temporis* or *tempus* is quite possible; see *ThLL* s.v. *hora* 2961, 80 f. and 2962, 55 f. vdVliet retains *hora* but conjectures *diurna*; this is unnecessary and contrary to *ThLL* s.v. 1640, 19, which gives examples only of the plural.

arcessitorem: first attested in Pliny: *Ep.* 5, 6, 45 *altius ibi otium...nulla necessitas togae, nemo arcessitor* (var. lect. *accersitor*) *ex proximo*. In Apuleius the word occurs only here in the *Met.*; later it is found Amm. 29, 1, 44; Ambr. *Ep.* 6, 1; Heges. 1, 40, 12. For the suffix *-tor* in the *Met.* see Callebat 1968, 35 f., who, however, fails to mention *arcessitor*. Again we see here a 'Fülle des Ausdrucks' in the synonymous notions *arcessitor, requisitum, reducere*.

tempestiuae uiae: they must depart quickly because of the threat, expressed at

192, 3. Their companion's long delay makes their uneasiness about this place even greater. For *tempestiuae* cf. our comm. on 185, 6 above.

193, 10-12 At ille modicum commoratus refert sese buxanti pallore trepidus: mira super conseruo suo renuntiat: "But he returned after a short delay, trembling and pale as boxwood: he told an astonishing story about his fellow-slave."

At ille: in contrast to the lost companion. See Callebat 1968, 422 and our comm. on 197, 14 below.

modicum: Apul. is the first to use the word in the meaning *paulisper*, a meaning otherwise confined to Christian authors; see *ThLL* s.v. *modicus* 1235,40 f.

mira...renuntiat: the question is whether to take *buxanti pallore trepidus* with *refert sese* (thus e.g. Frassinetti and Helm-Krenkel) or with *renuntiat* (thus e.g. Robertson and Brandt-Ehlers). We prefer the former because we consider a stop after *sese* less probable (cf. 187, 8 *proripit se* with our comm. ad loc.); after *trepidus* we place a colon. The conjectures of Bluemner *renuntians* and Helm III ⟨*et*⟩ *mira* are not necessary. For the asyndeton (after *trepidus*) which enhances the drama of the sentence, see Bernhard 1927, 56 and Callebat in *AAGA* 1978, 176.

buxanti pallore: the adjective *buxans* is *hapax legomenon*, with the meaning 'of the colour of boxwood'. *Buxeus*, on the other hand, is used twice in the *Met.* each time in a lugubrious context and referring to someone's complexion: 1, 19 (17, 9) *pallore buxeo* and 9, 30 (225, 19) *lurore buxeo*. For *buxus*, proverbial for 'pallor', see Bömer on Ov. *Met.* 4, 134 *oraque buxo/pallidiora gerens*.

super: in the sense of *de*; see Callebat 1968, 237 f. and *GCA* 1977, 101 on 4, 13 (84, 15-16).

conseruo: for this noun see Callebat 1968, 46.

193, 12-15 conspicatum se quippe supinato illi et iam ex maxima parte consumpto immanem draconem mandentem insistere nec ullum usquam miserinum senem comparere illum: "For he had seen that on top of him, as he lay on his back and was already for the most part devoured, a frightful dragon was sitting, chewing; but the wretched old man was nowhere to be seen."

The dénouement of this event, which should be a dramatic climax since the narrative has been slowly leading up to it, via a long preamble in which the suspense grows (the locus amoenus in ch. 18; the shepherd's ominous words in ch. 19; the supplication of the other old man in ch. 20), is described in a single sentence. The words *arcessitor* and *renuntiat* indicate that we have here a 'messenger's account', told in oratio obliqua, as in historical writing. The historian's terse style is also suggested in the next sentence, starting with *qua re cognita*. We are strengthened in our opinion by the fact that indirect discourse is not often found in the *Met.*; see Bernhard 1927, 52 f. For a similar case see 9, 2 (203, 20 f.) with our comm.

conspicatum se...immanem draconem: the suspense is increased by the position of the object of *conspicatum*: *draconem* is not mentioned until ten words further on.

conspicari: the 'Anfangsstellung' of the verb, which often occurs in emotional passages, gives it emphasis. For the intensity of *conspicari* see vdPaardt 1971, 129.

supinato illi: the young man, only a short while ago *alacer* and *inpiger*, is now lying on his back. The situation is entirely reversed. In all five instances where Apuleius uses a form of *supinatus*, mention is made of the defencelessness of the 'victim': 180, 7; 186, 5; 200, 21 and especially 9, 40 (234, 1) *nec ille ut primum humi supinatus est, uel repugnare uel omnino munire se potuit*. See also our comm. on 186, 5.

consumpto: cf. 194, 22 *homine consumpto membra nudarunt*, in the same series of lugubrious stories in which people are eaten by animals.

immanem draconem...insistere: the verb *insistere* (hardly apt for a snake in spite of *ThLL* s.v. *draco* 2061, 54) makes 'dragon' a probable translation for *draco*. It is an indication of the world of fantasy in which this story takes place. Other passages in the *Met.* in which *dracones* occur are 6, 2 (130, 9) in the story of Psyche, where Ceres' chariot is drawn by *dracones*, and 6, 14 (139, 2) in the description of Psyche's journey to the Styx, where she is held back by *saeui dracones*. In the description of Lucius' cloak at 11, 24 (285, 29) Apuleius says of the dragons which are part of its decoration *quos...generat mundus alter*, thus characterising them as fabulous creatures. See Gwyn Griffith 1975, 313 and Scobie 1977, 342.[1]

immanis: 'fierce', 'brutal', 'huge', 'terrifying'. All these meanings apply to the dragon. Cf. Cic. *Diu.* 2, 63 (a quotation from Homer) *uidimus immani specie tortuque draconem/terribilem* and *Culex* 164 *immanis uario maculatus corpore serpens*. Cf. in the *Met.* 4, 18 (88, 23) *immani forma tantae bestiae* (referring to a bear); 5, 17 (116, 16 f.) *immanem colubrum multinodis uoluminibus serpentem* (Amor described by Psyche's sisters); 179, 7 *aper immanis*.

mandentem insistere: a sinister image; cf. our comm. on 194, 18-24 below. *Mandere = dilaniare, dilacerare*; cf. Lucr. 4, 639 (*serpens*) *receptaculum uentris ubi mansa et uorata decoquat uiscera*.

nec ullum usquam miserinum senem comparere illum: nec ullum...illum is a somewhat odd construction: for that reason vdVliet deletes *ullum*, Kirchoff and Oudendorp *illum*. Hildebrand, however, rightly defends this combination, arguing that *nec ullus* can be used for *nullus*, and *nullus* for *non*; cf. 190, 6-10 *lupi...nulli...ac ne procul saltem ulli comparuerant*. See Callebat 1968, 416. Mark the hyperbaton *nec ullum...senem comparere illum*. From the remarkable combination *nec ullum...illum* we can conclude that the supplicant *senex* of ch. 19 and 20 has changed into a dragon. For such an implicit

---

[1] Perhaps it is going a little too far to regard the dragon in this chapter as a symbol of evil, which represents a direct threat to Lucius (thus Scobie 1977, 242 following Merkelbach). For Lucius himself is not directly exposed to danger here – in fact, he has been in much more dangerous situations elsewhere. This dragon story reflects, in our opinion, the gruesome atmosphere of the world through which Lucius the ass must struggle. The next story (ch. 22) is characterized by the same macabre atmosphere.

metamorphosis cf. Ov. *Met.* 3, 508 f., where the metamorphosis of Narcissus is mentioned only implicitly: *iamque rogum quassasque faces feretrumque parabant;/nusquam corpus erat; croceumque pro corpore florem/inueniunt.* See also our comm. on 192, 9 above.

miserinum senem: *miserinum* is the reading of F and φ, which is defended by Leo and retained by Robertson, Terzaghi, and Helm III. The other editors read *miserrimum*. *Miserinus* is a rare word, often interchanged in the mss. with *miserrimus*; cf. Lucil. 733 M *ardum miserinum atque infelix lignum*; [Quint.] *Decl.* 1, 2 *miserini iuuenis*; 1, 5 *miserini adulescentis*. It is found also in inscriptions, e.g. *CE* 1826, 2 ⟨*fil*⟩*iu miserino* (see *ThLL* s.v.). For its formation see LHSz 1, 327. Apuleius' taste for variation and unusual words makes *miserinus* quite possible. A little earlier, at 192, 25, he writes *miserrimo seni*.

193, 15-19 Qua re cognita et cum pastoris sermone conlata, qui ⟨aequ-⟩ aeuum prorsus hunc illum nec alium tescorum inquilinum praeminabatur, pestilenti deserta regione uelociori se fuga proripiunt nosque pellunt crebris tundentes fustibus: "Learning this and comparing it with the words of the shepherd, who by his warning meant precisely that contemporary of his and no other inhabitant of this disastrous place, they left this baneful region, hurried on in even speedier flight and drove us on with continuous blows from their cudgels."

This sentence sums up what has happened and leads the reader towards what is going to happen, thus connecting the one scene with the other. Consequently we can speak of a 'summary'; see Genette 1972, 94 f.

Qua re cognita: a set formula, often used by historians to indicate a new turn in the narrative; cf. Caes. *Gal.* 7, 9, 6 and 7, 41, 5. See Chausserie-Laprée 1969, 61 f. and 71 f.

cum pastoris sermone conlata: the shepherd spoke his threatening words 192, 3-5.

qui. . .praeminabatur: the reading in F and φ is unintelligible: *q euū ƥɩſ* ; *hunc illū nec aliū cocorū Inqlinū p̄minebat*. Corrective measures start early: . . .*eū*. . .*locorum*. . .*praeminabatur* ς. *Eum* is barely supportable with *hunc illum* (however, see on gemination of pronouns below); the correction *locorum* for *cocorum* is the easiest way out but does not explain the corruption: possibly Oudendorp's *tesquorum* (better spelled *tescorum*) merits more attention than it has received; *praeminabatur* for *praeminebat* is acceptable. There remains F's *euū*. Eyssenhardt proposes ⟨*s*⟩*aeuum*, which makes good sense with *hunc illum nec alium*. . .*inquilinum*, though it was proposed in connection with his further conjecture *hunc [illum nec] anguem inquilinum*. Equally good sense (cf. 191, 29 *senex*) is produced by Kronenberg's *aequaeuum*. Palaeographically there is little to choose between the two and both are to be preferred to Leo's *dudum* as well as Helm's *eu*⟨*iden*⟩*ī*. For the sense of the passage Kronenberg's conjecture, which simply refers back, perhaps has a slight edge over Eyssenhardt's, which adds a judgement.

prorsus: the adjective is strengthened by an adverb; see Callebat 1968, 538.

hunc illum nec alium: strengthening of a pronoun by means of another pronoun is often found in the *Met.*, e.g. 2, 13 (35, 13) *hic iste*; 3, 1 (52, 16) *hanc illam*; 10, 24 (255, 20) *haec eadem*. See Callebat 1968, 267 f. This emphasizes the identification of the dragon with the *senex*.

tescorum: according to *OLD*, this is 'an augural term of uncertain sense, associated with *templum* and perhaps synonymous; by non-technical writers interpreted as a tract of wild or desolate land'. Cf. Apul. *Fl.* 17 (33, 7) *in remotis tesquis*.

uelociori: for the ablative in *-i* see LHSz 1, 435 f.

pestilenti...regione: the term *pestilens* is appropriate to a dragon-infested region. In Ovid five of the seven passages where *pestifer* occurs refer to a dragon; see Bömer on Ov. *Met.* 1, 459. The fact that these events take place in a locus amoenus (191, 18-22), usually a place of peace and security but now a *regio pestilens*, makes the story the more sinister.

praeminabatur: first attested in Apuleius, it also occurs *Met.* 5, 19 (117, 25) *malumque grande de uultus curiositate praeminatur* and 6, 15 (140, 6) *nolentes aquas et...praeminantes excipit*; it occurs only twice elsewhere: Tert. *Apol.* 21, 6 and *Marc.* 5, 19 (645, 23). See Flobert 1975, 141. The imperfect is perhaps 'de conatu'.

crebris tundentes fustibus: cf. 6, 25 (147, 12) *fustibus exinde tundentes producunt in uiam*, where Lucius the ass is hurried on by the robbers in the same way. Thus we return after this summary to the hard reality of the ass's life: he is beaten with sticks as he is driven on. One summarizing sentence creates the transition from the world of fantasy to the world of the ass and his fellow travellers.

CHAPTER XXII

A grisly tale.

193, 19-20 Cele⟨r⟩rime denique longo itinere confecto pagum quendam accedimus ibique totam perquiescimus noctem: "After we had gone a long way in great haste, we finally came to a village and there we had a good rest for the whole night."

In this chapter Lucius relates an event from hearsay. From chapter 15 onward (when Charite's slaves set out on their journey) his participation becomes progressively less active as the events become more gruesome: first he is threatened by dogs and stones, then he witnesses the death of one of the slaves, and finally he hears a story about a macabre event.

longo itinere confecto pagum...accedimus: a frequent syntactical pattern, which can be found with some variations e.g. 194, 25 *hac...deserta mansione,...rursum pergimus...ciuitatem quandam...peruenimus*; 9, 4 (205, 19 f.) *nec paucis casulis...oberratis deuertimus ad quempiam pagum*; 10, 1 (236, 21 f.) *confecta...uia ad quandam ciuitatulam peruenimus*. The ablative absolute is used to mark a transition to the next scene, as often in the historians. See Chausserie Laprée 1969, 65 f. Cf. also l. 15 above *qua re cognita* with our comm.

pagum quendam accedimus: for *pagum* without a preposition cf. 7, 13 (164, 12) *ciuitatem reuenimus* with *GCA* 1981, 168. The villages which Lucius the ass passes on his journey are nowhere mentioned by name, except at the end of the *Met.*, when Lucius escapes just before his metamorphosis back to human form, 10, 35 (266, 1) *Cenchreas peruado*.

perquiescimus: a rare word which, according to the material of the *ThLL*, occurs only here, at Ps. Ambr. *Serm.* 2, 5 *ibi perquiescat, ibi dormiat, ibi cum uoluerit, resurgat*, and Leo M. *Ep.* 167, 9 *si dolor parum perquieuerit*.

noctem: *nocte* has clearly been corrected to *noctē* in both F and φ (in F possibly, in φ certainly, by a different hand). See further on *ibi* below.

193, 21-22 Ibi coeptum facinus oppido memorabile narrare cupio: "A very noteworthy crime had been committed there which I wish to recount."

It will turn out that it is the punishment for the crime which is especially noteworthy.

Ibi: F has *ú* in quite a wide erasure, which Helm thinks originally contained *in*, or possibly *m*. Robertson thinks that *ḿ* (=*mihi*), the reading of φ, was the original reading in F (the implied chain of error is *noctemibi* to *nocte mihi* to *nocte ḿ*). Beroaldus' conjecture *noctem inibi* implies *noctem inibi* to *noctemmibi*

186

to *nocte mihi*, a more complicated solution. F's corrector's change of the unintelligible *m̀* to *ù*, though reasonable, is less probable on palaeographical grounds than either Beroaldus' or Robertson's conjecture.

coeptum: Castiglioni inserts *modo* before *coeptum*, but Apuleius does not specify when it took place. *Facinus incipere* is a familiar expression in Plautus and Terence (e.g. Pl. *Aul.* 460 *facinus audax incipit*); *conpertum* (Beroaldus) and *acceptum* (Brantius) are therefore unnecessary emendations.

facinus oppido memorabile narrare cupio: for similar metanarrative terms cf. e.g. 9, 4 (205, 23) *cognoscimus lepidam...fabulam, quam uos etiam cognoscatis uolo* and 9, 14 (213, 6) *fabulam...bonam...ad auris uestras adferre decreui, et en occipio*, with our comm. ad locos. For the manner of insertion see Heine in *AAGA* 1978, 29 ('clumsy') and Introd. 4.3. It is not quite clear, as a matter of fact, which is meant of the several *facinora* which make up the episode. Perhaps *facinus* refers to the whole story.

oppido memorabile: for *oppido* see vdPaardt 1971, 77 on 3, 9 (58, 12) and *GCA* 1981, 156 on 162, 24 f. Callebat 1968, 519 lists the passages in which it reinforces a qualifier.

Seruus quidam cui cuncta⟨m⟩ familiae tutelam dominus permi- 194, 1-5 serat suus quique possessionem maximam illam, in quam deuerteramus, uillicabat, habens ex eodem famulitio conseruam coniugam, liberae cuiusdam extrariaeque mulieris flag⟨r⟩abat cupidine: "A slave, to whom his master had committed the entire care of the house and who managed the enormous estate where we had put up, had as his wife a fellow slave from the same slave-family but was passionately in love with a free woman from elsewhere."

seruus quidam: like all the characters in this story, the slave is not mentioned by name. See Hijmans in *AAGA* 1978, 114 f.: when Lucius tells a story in the authorial mode, he does not name the characters.

cuncta⟨m⟩: F has *cuncta*. According to Helm III the ̄ was added by a second hand, according to Robertson probably by the first hand. Robertson reports *cunctam* for φ and ς.

familiae tutelam: *tutela* embraces the complete care, defense, and protection of the *familia* in the broadest sense of the word, i.e. family, servants, property, land, etc. *Tutela* should not be taken here in a strictly legal sense ('guardianship'), since this could not be entrusted to a slave. Cf. *Met.* 9, 18 (216, 9) *insignis tutelae nimietate instinctus atque inflammatus* and 9, 27 (223, 8) *senex claudus, cui nostra tutela permissa fuerat*. See Kaser [2]1975, 100 n. 5 and 222-234 on *tutela*.

permiserat: cf. *Met.* 9, 17 (215, 24) *suaeque dominae custodelam omnem permittit* and 9, 27 (223, 8) cited in the last note. The combination *tutelam permittere* is attested in Apuleius only.

dominus suus: for *suus* meaning *proprius* rather than as a substitute for a demonstrative, see *GCA* 1977, 74 on 81, 1-5.

deuerteramus: 'we had stopped at'. The verb is quite common in Plautus. In the *Met.* cf. 1, 7 (7, 9) *ad quandam cauponam...deuorto*; 3, 5 (55, 16) *ad bonum...Milonem...deuorto*; 4, 1 (74, 10) *in pago quodam apud...senes deuertimus.*

uillicabat: in the *Met.* the verb occurs only here. The transitive use is peculiar to this passage and *A.Epig.* 42-3,63,4. Apuleius does not use the noun *uillicus*, but *uilliconum* (from *uillico*) occurs once: *Apol.* 87 (96,23).

ex eodem famulitio: so φ; F has *familitio*. The correction of φ is right: *familitium* is found nowhere, but *famulitium* is first attested in Apul. himself (*Apol.* 17: 20, 18 and *Fl.* 22: 43, 7); after him e.g. in Macr. *Sat.* 1,7,1 (*unus e famulitio*) and Mart. Cap. A fem. noun *famulitio* is also known, though confined to Apul. (*Met.* 2,2 : 25,13 and 6,8:134,1). Both nouns mean 'crowd of servants', 'domestic staff'. The form *famuletium* occurs at Fest. 77 L. The suffix *-itium* is common in nouns indicating social position, cf. *seruitium*. See LHSz 1, 296. *Famulitium* is abstractum pro concreto, a common phenomenon in the *Met.*; see Bernhard 1927, 97 f.

conseruam coniugam: *coniugam* is used predicatively with *conseruam*; cf. e.g. 197, 20 *hominem seruulum*. In the *Met.* the word is found twice more, at 6, 4 (131, 6) and 9, 14 (213, 11); see also *CIL* 6, 13528 and 8, 5370. Apuleius uses the form *coniux* much more often. *Conseruam coniugam* forms a marked contrast with *liberae mulieris* in the next colon. *Conseruus* also occurs e.g. *Met.* 7, 3 (156, 17) *conseruum atque coniugem* (of an animal – literally a 'yoke-fellow'); 7, 27 (175, 21) *illo conseruo magistro*; in combination with *uxor* at Pl. *Cas. Arg.* 1 *conseruam uxorem duo conserui expetunt*. It is not unusual for slaves of the same house to be called *coniux, uxor* (1. 5), or *maritus* (1. 6), though a legal marriage between slaves was impossible. (On the advisability of not allowing one's slaves to marry slaves from another house, cf. Tert. *Ux.* 2, 8, 1 *nonne etiam...domini...seruis suis foras nubere interdicent, scilicet ne lasciuiam excedant, officia deserant, dominica extraneis promant*; see Norden 1912, 116.) Cato *Agr.* 143 and Paul. *Sent.* 3, 6, 38 also speak of a (slave) *uilicus* with his *uxor*. Here and in the next two sentences, the relationship between the two slaves is described in quite solemn terms; cf. 5,4 (105,20 f.) *ignobilis maritus et torum inscenderat et uxorem sibi Psychen fecerat; maritus, torus*, and *uxor* are used in both passages. Apuleius reverses the procedure, too: at *Met.* 6,10 (135,21) Psyche is called Amor's *contubernalis*: this term, when used in a marital context, generally refers to a slave.

extrariaeque: in the meaning 'strange', 'not belonging to the family' it is found in the *Met.* only here; elsewhere in Apuleius e.g. *Apol.* 68 (77,3). *si extrario nubsisset* and *Fl.* 18 (35, 7 and 24). The word is also found in this meaning in Ter. *Ph.* 579 and e.g. Quint. and Suet.

flag⟨r⟩abat cupidine: F and φ have *flagabat*, which was corrected by a different hand in F to *flagrabat*. For the variation of *flagrare* and *fraglare* see *GCA* 1977, 210. For the combination *flagrare cupidine* (usually not in an erotic sense) cf. e.g. Cic. *Ver.* 4, 75 *ita flagrare cupiditate atque amentia coepit*; Ov. *Met.* 2, 104 *flagratque cupidine currus*. In the *Met.* the only other occurrence (with erotic meaning) is 5, 23 (121, 6) *tunc magis magisque cupidine fraglans Cupidinis*.

This story again takes up the motif of adultery (cf. *Met.* 2,27 and Thrasyllus' attempts in ch. 3 above), and thus anticipates the series of adultery tales in book 9 (ch. 4-7 and 14-31) and 10 (ch. 23-29).

Quo dolore paelicatus uxor eius instricta cunctas mariti rationes et quicquid horreo reconditum continebatur admoto combussit igne: "His wife, moved with grief at this liaison, set fire to all her husband's accounts and whatever was kept stored in the granary, and burnt it." 194, 5-7

paelicatus: 'the fact or condition of being a *paelex*', (*OLD*). Cf. Cic. *Scaur.* 9 *Arinis uxorem paelicatus dolore concitatam*. In the *Met.* also 5, 30 (127, 8) *cui saepius in angorem mei paelicatus puellas propinare consuesti*; 10, 24 (256, 11) *Quodque frustra paelicatus indignatione bulliret*. The narrator does not say that the slave actually had an affair with the woman, as his wife suspects.

instricta: in the mss. often confused with *instinctus* or *distinctus*, e.g. Ov. *Met.* 11, 167 *instrictamque fidem* (variant readings: *instructam* and *distinctam*). In this meaning, 'rouse', 'incite', it also occurs Gel. 17, 20, 7 *sed instrinxit* (variant readings: *instinxit, instruxit*) *etiam nos*. Apuleius also uses *instinguere* with the same meaning, e.g. 9, 18 (216, 9) *et insignis tutelae nimietate instinctus atque inflammatus*. Given Apuleius' fondness for varying his vocabulary, we see no reason to change *instricta* into *instincta*, as does the editio Aldina. (*Instringere* in the sense of *ligare, amicire* also occurs in the *Met.*, e.g. 10, 12 : 245, 20).

mariti: for *maritus* of a slave, cf. e.g. 202, 9 and see our comm. on *coniugam* l. 4 above.

quicquid reconditum continebatur: as in the following *admoto combussit igne*, the narrator carefully indicates the order of events by the order of the verbs.

Nec tali damno tori sui contumeliam uindicasse contenta, iam contra sua saeuiens uiscera laqueum sibi nectit, infantulumque, quem de eo marito iam dudum susceperat, eodem funiculo nectit seque per altissimum puteum adpendicem paruulum trahens praecipitat: "Not content to have vindicated the insult to her marriage-bed by such damage, she now raged against her own flesh and blood, tied a noose around herself and with the same rope bound the little baby which she had had some time ago by that same husband. Then she threw herself down a very deep well, dragging down the little one attached to her." 194, 7-12

tori: cf. *Met.* 9, 14 (213, 11) *poenas extremas tori larisque sustinebat* and 9, 26 (222, 14) *pudore postposito torique genialis calcato foedere* (both stories about adultery); 10, 24 (255, 22) *uelut aemulam tori* (story about the *uilis aliqua* who suspects her husband of adultery). Cf. further Ov. *Met.* 1, 319 *Deucalion. . .cum consorte tori* and Bömer ad loc., who refers to this combination as 'hohe Sprache'.

contenta: with an infinitive; see *GCA* 1981, 181 on 7, 15 (165, 21).

contra sua saeuiens uiscera: for *uiscera* in the meaning of 'own flesh and blood', 'own child' see Bömer on Ov. *Met.* 6, 651; Costa on Sen. *Med.* 40; Tarrant on Sen. *Ag.* 27. Killing children to punish their father is a common motif in mythology (e.g. the myths of Medea, Procne and Philomela, Thyestes).

infantulum: first attested in Apuleius. See Callebat 1968, 32 and our comm. on 188, 15 above.

de eodem marito: for *de* with the ablative to indicate origin, see Callebat 1968, 200 f.

iam dudum: 'some time ago'. See *GCA* 1981, 106 on 7, 4 (157, 11).

eodem funiculo: *funiculus* has lost its diminutive value here as well as elsewhere in the *Met*. For the diminutives' development of meaning, see e.g. Hakamies 1951, 46-48 and LHSz 2, 772 f. Of the five passages in the *Met*. containing *funiculus*, four are scenes of suicide by hanging: 1, 16 (15, 2 f.) *obdita parte funiculi et altera firmiter in nodum coacta ascenso grabattulo ad exitium sublimatus et immisso capite laqueum induo*; 6, 30 (152, 13 f.); 202, 7 and this passage. The fifth passage (not a suicide) is 7, 19 (169, 1).

per...puteum adpendicem paruulum...praecipitat: observe the alliteration of *p*. Two methods of suicide are combined: the narrator does not specify whether the woman dies by hanging or from jumping into the well. The combination of jumping and hanging seems to be unique in classical literature. For the well as a means of suicide cf. Hld. 1, 17, 5 and Sen. *Ira* 3, 15, 4.

adpendicem paruulum: *appendix* as a noun, with the literal meaning 'appendage', is found in Apuleius only; cf. *Met*. 5, 24 (121, 18) *at Psyche...sublimis euectionis adpendix*. Elsewhere it is used figuratively meaning 'addition'; e.g *Apol*. 13 (15, 8) *has quoque appendices defensionis meae*; Liv. 9, 41, 16 *exiguam appendicem Etrusci belli conficere iubet*.

194, 12-18 Quam mortem dominus eorum aegerrime sustinens adreptum seruulum, qui causam tanti sceleris luxurie sua praestiterat, nudum ac totum melle perlitum firmiter alligauit arbori ficulneae, cuius in ipso carioso stipite in⟨h⟩abitantium formicarum †nidifici aburribant† et ultro citro commeabant multiiuga scaturrigine: "Their master took their death very hard: he seized the miserable slave who had been the cause of this great crime by his lust and firmly tied him, naked and smeared all over with honey, to a fig tree; right in its rotten trunk ?the nest-builders abounded? of the ants that lived there, who went to and fro in a continuous stream."

In this chapter, the story characterized as a *facinus memorabile* (193,21) consists of three *facinora*: the 'crime' of the slave, the revenge of his wife, and the punishment of the slave by his master; they take up $4\frac{1}{2}$, 7 and $11\frac{1}{2}$ (Teubner) lines respectively.

quam mortem...sustinens: the narrating I is interpreting here; see our comm. on 195, 11 *quae res*.

aegerrime sustinens: the only other examples of the combination *aegre sustinere* are found at *Met*. 1, 7 (6, 18) *aegerrime sustinens*; 10, 28 (258, 25) *sustinebat aegerrime*; Arn. 3, 11 *deos aegre et aegerrime sustinere dari...sibi...sexus*. Apuleius makes a variation on fixed expressions as *aegre ferre, aegre tolerare*, and *aegre pati*.

adreptum seruulum: the slave, who managed the estate and was responsible for the *familia*, is now scornfully called *seruulum* by the narrator. For the disparaging force of the diminutive see Callebat 1968, 508; Abate 50 f.

qui causam tanti sceleris...praestiterat; *causam praestare* is a legal term, found for the first time Quint. *Decl.* 270 (103, 14 f.) *Qui causa mortis fuerit, capite puniatur... Neque enim grauius quidquam aduersus eum, qui sua manu interfecerit, constituere potuit legum lator, quam aduersus eum qui causam praestitisset.* The expression is also found Ulp. *Dig.* 9, 2, 7, 6 *Celsus... multum interesse dicit, occiderit an mortis causam praestiterit* (a statement which contradicts that of Quintilian quoted above). Other expressions are *causam mortis praebere* (Ulp. *Dig.* 48, 8, 15) and *causa esse* (*Quint. Inst.* 7, 3, 32).

tanti sceleris: this refers not only to the burning of the *rationes* but also to the wife's suicide and the death of the child. The master takes the law into his own hands because the slave is entirely without rights; at 9, 21 (218, 17 f.), however, the master has his slave taken to the forum. Claudius and Hadrian both made attempts to deal with the arbitrary treatment of slaves; cf. Suet. *Cl.* 25, 2; *SHA*, Ael. Spart. *Hadr.* 18, 7 f. See also Vallette ad loc.

luxurie sua: F has *üxori sue* (·· is erased), but in the margin a variant reading has been erased; Robertson thinks that "l,,,/r.ẹs... can still be detected, which is consistent with *luxurie*, which was visible to Victorius. The fact that AUE have *luxurie sue* indicates that one of the earliest copies made of F adopted the marginal reading, which, indeed, makes good sense. It is, however, hard to choose between the two. Oudendorp, Hildebrand, Helm III, and Giarratano-Frassinetti prefer *uxori suae*, Robertson *luxurie sua*. We think that *luxurie sua* has a slight edge since it summarizes the reason for the punishment of the slave.

firmiter: for adverbs ending in *-iter* instead of *-e*, see *GCA* 1981, 33 f. on 148, 5-9 and 247 on 172, 22-24.

arbori ficulneae: the figtree probably has a sexual connotation. For the symbolism of figs and figtrees see e.g. Henderson 1975, 118 (including Greek comedy); Adams 1982, 113 f. In Latin literature cf. Hor. *S.* 1, 8, 1 (where the figtree is connected with Priapus); Mart. 1, 65, 3 f. *dicemus ficus, quas scimus in arbore nasci,/dicemus ficos, Caeciliane, tuos* and 7, 71. Trees mentioned by name in the *Met.* have a special meaning; cf. e.g. 6, 30 (152, 13), where the old woman has hanged herself from a cypress (death symbolism, see *GCA* 1981, 66 f.). *Ficulneus* is found in the *Met.* only here, and this is also the only passage in the *Met.* where a figtree is mentioned.

cuius in ipso cariosa stipite inabitantium formicarum nidifici aburrîbant: thus F[1]. Editors have followed φ in correcting *cariosa* to *carioso*, since no parallels can be found for feminine *stipes*. The obvious spelling correction *in⟨h⟩abitantium* φ may pass without comment. The difficulty of the passage lies in *nidifici aburrîbant*. In fact, what is now visible in F is *nidifici aborrîbant* and thus it was reported until Robertson noticed that the *o* was almost certainly written over an original *u*. Indeed φ, often witness to an earlier (and better) state of F, has *aburiebant*. It seems not impossible that F's corrector thought of *ab⟨h⟩orrebant* without paying attention to the context. Unable to make anything of the form *aburi(e)bant* or *aborri(e)bant* all editors have assumed a mistaken word-division, and most editors print *nidificia borriebant*. The verb *borrire* has thus reached the lexica, including Forcellini, Lewis and Short, Georges, *ThLL*, and *OLD*. Walde-Hofmann [3]1938 s.v. regard this verb as 'lautmalend', notwithstanding Hildebrand's scornful exclamation that he doubts that anyone has ever actually heard ants (this in reaction to a remark made by Beroaldus). Meyer-Lübke [5]1972, von Wartburg, Tobler-Lomatsch, Gamilscheg, Battisti-Alessio, and other etymological dictionaries of the Romance languages yield no support for the verb, nor do the dictionaries of Medieval Latin. However, *Gloss.* V, 563, 33 has an entry *borrit: uoce eleuat*.

Robertson understandably prints *bulliebant* with Beroaldus. Before this proposal can be accepted, however, we must decide whether *nidifici aburrĭbant* are incorrectly divided. If not, the nest-builders among the ants must be doing something, but it is quite clear that the verb needs considerable correction. One might think of *abhauriebant* (a hapax legomenon), to be taken in the sense of 'were carrying or digging away', which would entail the further correction *cuius cariosa in ipso stipite* in order to provide an object. Apart from the fact that the resulting Latin is rather less than satisfactory, the surgery required is prohibitive. Even less likely is *abhorrebant* (possibly suggested by F's corrector), explained by means of an Apuleian 'Umdeutung' with a reference to *horreus* (in itself a word often enough associated with ants). It is quite likely, then, that assuming a wrong word-division brings us closer to a solution.[1]

An attempt should be made, then, to explain *burrĭbant*. Apuleius indeed uses many hapax legomena; cf. e.g. Médan 1925, 107 f.; Bernhard 1927, 139. But it should be noted that his hapax legomena always have a clear link with well-known words; *burrire* (*borrire*) 'swarm' (*OLD*) would have no such link. To supply the link one might suggest *burrire* ⟨ *burrus* (= πυρρός; see André 1949, 121 and 299 f.) and suppose that Apuleius is speaking of nests covered with red ants. In that case Apuleius would have worked on the model *lippire*⟨*lippus*, *luscire*⟨*luscus*, *saeuire*⟨*saeuus*, etc. There are two objections: 1) the model is not used for colours. However, F's original scribe added an *e* over the *i* and may have intended a correction (cf. *Met.* 7, 14 : 165, 3 with *GCA* 1981, 174 on *utī*): if so, the model would be *albere*⟨*albus*. 2) There seems to be no mention of red ants in ancient literature.

Although the fact that a word is hapax legomenon constitutes no reason per se for rejecting it, and although it is not impossible that Apuleius has here created a word to render an optical impression (the teeming of an anthill or perhaps its colour), we print cruces since it is not clear what word it is that the author has coined.

ultro citro: without a conjunction; cf. e.g. 1, 5 (5, 5) *ultro citro discurrens*. For the combination with *commeare* cf. Cic. *N.D.* 2, 84 *sursus deorsus ultro citro commeantibus* with Pease ad loc.; see also KSt 2, 2, 151 for asyndetic combinations of antithetical adverbs.

multiiuga scaturrigine: a metaphor from water to indicate a swarm of ants. *Scaturrigo* combined with *multiiuga* provides a fine picture, since *iugis* ('everflowing', 'running', 'unbroken', from the root *iug*-) is often combined with words like *aqua, fons* etc. Cf. e.g. Cic. *N.D.* 2, 25 *uidemus. . . etiam ex puteis*

---

[1] If the words are wrongly divided, *nidificia* results, as read by most editors. *Nidificium* does not occur elsewhere, according to the *ThLL* material. The verb *nidificare*, however, occurs Col. 8, 8, 3 *loculamenta quibus nidificent aues* and Plin. *Nat.* e.g. 9, 81 *piscium sola (phycis) nidificat ex alga*; the adjective *nidificus* is found from Sen. *Med.* 714 *quodcumque tellus uere nidifico creat* onward.

iugibus aquam calidam trahi; Hor. *S.* 2, 6, 2 *iugis aquae fons, Multiiugis* is used elsewhere in the *Met.*: 4, 13 (84, 20); 6, 2 (130, 5); 199, 16; 11, 5 (269, 18). Its meaning varies, according to *OLD*: 1) of animals: 'yoked many together' and 2) transf.: 'having many parts or forms', 'performed by many together', 'many times as great'. See also *GCA* 1977, 104 f. on 4, 13 (84, 20). Here we have a combination of the aspect 'with many together' (referring to the ants) and that of 'in a continuous stream' (within the image of the *scaturrigo*).

Scaturrigo is also found 6, 13 (138, 11) *de summis fontis penita scaturrigine rorem...hauritum* (referring to the Styx); the verb *scaturrire* occurs 4, 6 (79, 1). *Scaturrigo* in a metaphorical sense occurs in Apuleius only, but *scaturrire* and *scatere* in that sense are also found elsewhere; see *OLD* s.v.

Quae simul dulcem ac mellitum corporis nidorem persentiscunt, paruis quidem, sed numerosis et continuis morsiunculis penitus inhaerentes, per longi temporis cruciatu⟨m⟩ ita, carnibus atque ipsis uisceribus adesis, homine consumpto membra nudarunt, ut ossa tantum uiduata pulpis nitore nimio candentia funestae cohaererent arbori: "As soon as they became aware of the honey-sweet smell of the body, they clung to him deeply with tiny but numerous and continuous nips; and in a long-lasting torment, in which the flesh and the very organs were eaten, the man was consumed and they laid bare the limbs in such a way that only his bones, stripped of flesh and shining with a bright glitter, were left bound to the fatal tree." 194, 18-24

A vivid and detailed description, in a long and carefully composed period. For Apuleius' liking for macabre scenes see *GCA* 1977, 136 on 87, 29-88, 3; cf. also our comm. on 193, 14 above. The cruelty is comparable to the treatment proposed by the robbers for Charite at 6, 31 (153, 12 f.); cf. also 153, 20 f. *cum uermes membra laniabunt...cum canes et uultures intima protrahent uiscera* with *GCA* 1981, 77. Cruel punishments for slaves were not unusual; Norden 1912, 75 with notes 1, 2, and 3 collects some examples. In view of this, the reaction of the cook, who for fear of punishment wants to commit suicide (202,3 f.) is perhaps not exaggerated. For the punishment described here cf. Plut. *Artox.* 16,2 f. and Ant. Lib. 11,7 with Papothomopoulos 1968, 95 n. 24 ad loc. for further references. See also Cazzaniga 1949, 1-5.

dulcem et mellitum...nidorem: the second adjective explains the first. For 'Synonymik koordinierter Begriffe' see Bernhard 1927, 166.

persentiscunt: an inchoative verb, reinforced by *per*: 'they became aware of the smell'. This verb is attested in comedy e.g. Pl. *Am.* 527; Ter. *Hau.* 916; and in Lucr. (3,249); later only in Apuleius: *Met.* 185, 11 *nec quisquam persentiscat familiarum*; *Fl.* 12 (17, 7); *Pl.* 1, 13 (97, 21).

morsiunculis: the ThLL mentions only this passage and Pl. *Pseud.* 65 *teneris labellis molles morsiunculae*, cf. *Gloss.* 2, 523, 19.

carnibus atque ipsis uisceribus adesis: when all the flesh has been eaten by the ants, the bones remain: *membra nudarunt*; the point is reinforced by *ossa tantum uiduata pulpis* – a horrifyingly detailed description.

homine consumpto: this happened also 193, 13 above.

uiduata: used in a figurative sense: 'bereft of', 'without'. See our comm. on 185, 17 *omnique comite uiduatus*.

pulpis: refers to human flesh, and also to meat as food; cf. 2, 7 (30, 15) *parabat...et pulpam frustatim consectam*.

ossa...nitore nimio candentia: we have already encountered the motif of glittering bones; they gleamed on the slaves' path in ch. 15 (189, 6): having learned of Charite's death the group fled and on the way was warned of prowling wolves by the inhabitants of a village: *iacere semesa hominum corpora suisque uisceribus nudatis ossibus cuncta candere*. Now the circle is closed: the image of glittering bones appears both at the beginning of the story of the slaves' wanderings and at the end of their journey. After hearing this story they set out once more; then the ass is sold and the fugitives disappear from the scene. For the image of 'glittering bones' cf. Verg. *A*. 12, 36 *campique ingentes ossibus albent*; Tac. *Ann*. 1, 61, 2 *medio campi albentia ossa*; Amm. 31, 7, 16 *albentes ossibus campi*.

funestae cohaererent arbori: the motif of death, which kept recurring in the previous chapters, is emphasized once more by *funestae*. The *arbor ficulnea* has now become an *arbor funesta*, an appellation more appropriate to the *cupressus*, e.g. 6, 30 (152, 13). Tac. *Ann*. 1,61,3 (mentioned in the last note) also contains a gruesome picture of corpses lying everywhere, with skulls hanging in trees: *truncis arborum antefixa ora*.

From the fact that Apuleius uses the imperfect subjunctive instead of the present, we may conclude that this is not the report of an eye-witness. Apuleius is not explicit here; he does not say whether the fugitive slaves actually saw the slave's skeleton hanging in the tree. But it appears from chapter 23 that the event took place only a short while ago: the fugitives leave the villagers in deep sorrow. This concludes the last of the three macabre events which Lucius experiences or hears about on his journey with the slaves. On the role of the number three in this narrative (three people die) and in the *Metamorphoses* in general, see Scobie in *AAGA* 1978, 53.

CHAPTER XXIII

An attempt is made to sell the ass.

Hac quoque detestabili deserta mansione, paganos in summo 194, 25-28
luctu relinquentes, rursum pergimus dieque tota campestres
emensi uias ciuitatem quandam populosam et nobilem iam fessi
peruenimus: "This detestable stopping-place we left too, leaving the villagers in deep sorrow. We set off again and, having travelled over country roads the whole day, at last arrived weary at a populous, well-known town."

The new chapter starts with a phrase which summarizes the preceding chapter and recalls its beginning; cf. vThiel 1971, 20 n.58.

mansione: the translations differ somewhat (e.g. Vallette: 'une ville'; Brandt-Ehlers: 'Herberg'). We prefer the meaning 'stopping-place', 'halt' as in 4, 5 (78, 12); see *GCA* 1977, 53 ad loc.

detestabili: the place is loathsome because of the gruesome event that happened there (ch.22).

in summo luctu: that event also causes the grief of the *pagani*.

dieque tota: for the ablative of the duration of time see Callebat 1968, 193 and e.g. 4, 7 (79, 21) *diebus ac noctibus* with *GCA* 1977, 66 ad loc.

ciuitatem: for the accusative without preposition after verbs of motion compare 7, 13 (164, 12) *ciuitatem reuenimus* with *GCA* 1981, 168 ad loc.

ciuitatem quandam: it is impossible to identify the *ciuitas*; see our comm. on 193, 20 *pagum quendam*.

populosam: this word is first attested in Apul. (also 5, 8 : 109, 4; 8, 6 : 181, 5; *Fl.* 6, 1 : 6, 3); but that is no reason to follow Gargantini 1963, 38 in classing it with 'aggettivi di sua creazione'. After Apul. it is found in Sid., Veg., Sol.; cf. Ernout 1949, 47.

Onos 34, 5 has μεγάλην καὶ πολυάνθρωπον; Apul. starts with *populosam*. In our comm. on 188, 23 *castellum frequens et opulens* we pointed out the formulaic nature of such expressions in accounts of travel; see also our comm. on 193, 19 f.

Inibi larem sedesque perpetuas pastores illi statuere decernunt, 194, 28-195, 2
quod et longe quaesituris firmae latebrae uiderentur et annonae
copiosae beata celebritas inuitabat: "The shepherds – you remember
them – decided to make their home and permanent abode there because they thought the hiding-place seemed a safe one, far from possible pursuers, and because a rich abundance of plentiful food attracted them."

sedes: on the poetic colouring of this noun see our comm. on 188, 14.

quaesituris: thus F, Hildebrand, Robertson, Terzaghi, Brandt-Ehlers,

Frassinetti, vThiel, Augello 1977, 189. ⟨a⟩ *quaesituris* Nolte, Helm, Giarratano, Scazzoso. *quaesituris* ⟨*nullae magis*⟩ *firmae latebrae* ⟨*fore*⟩ vdVliet, which seems to us much too drastic. If, as we think, (a) *quaesituris* means 'possible pursuers' (see LHSz 2, 157 for the nominalization of the masc. fut. part.) and (b) the reading of F is to be retained, we must explain the syntax of *quaesituris*. There are three possibilities:

1. It is a dative, to be connected with *uiderentur* (thus Hildebrand: quia pastores *putabant*, haec loca firmas latebras visum iri illis, qui se inquisituri essent). The difficulty with this suggestion is that the shepherds would found their decision on the views of their pursuers. We think that they should base themselves on firmer ground.

2. It is an ablative, to be connected with *firmae* (thus Kronenberg 1904, 444). The problem here is that *ThLL* s.v. gives no examples of *firmus* with a separative ablative (*firmus* with *contra* once: *ThLL* s.v. 816, 8 Plin. *Nat*. 14, 35 *mettica contra omne sidus firmissima*; with a somewhat different meaning Sal. *Iug*. 80, 1 *nihil satis firmum contra Metellum putat*, cf. *ThLL* 815, 77). Kronenberg himself mentions only passages like 190, 27 *qua...caueremus clade* and *Fl*. 14 (19, 9), where now *obtutu*⟨*m*⟩ is read. Kronenberg further proposes to link *longe* with *firmae* in the meaning of *firmissimae*, offering 1, 21 (19, 18) *longe opulentus* and 5, 11 (112, 4) *longe firmiter* as parallels. An argument against this is the hyperbaton in our passage which, consequently, elicits from *ThLL* s.v. *longus* 1649, 9 f. the comment 'vix recte'.

3. It is an ablative, to be connected with *longe*: 'far from'. In that case the only problem is whether we should follow Helm in inserting *a* before *quaesituris*. In classical Latin *a* or *e* is obligatory with *longe* (LHSz 2, 104), but there is one example of the ablative without a preposition: Enn. *Ann*. 481 *impetus* ⟨*h*⟩*aut longe mediis regionibus restat* (Festus explains that *restat* is used in the meaning *distat*; cf. *ThLL* s.v. *longus* 1646, 6). In view of Apuleius' preference for archaic forms and constructions we have decided – albeit with some hesitation – to retain *longe* without a preposition even in this locus vexatus. This also releases us from having to consider whether *quaesituris* is an incomplete ablative absolute.

firmae: here in the sense of *tutae, munitae*, as e.g. Liv. 28, 1, 8 *(castra) stationibus...tuta et firma*; Veg. 4, 1 *urbes atque castella aut natura muniuntur aut manu..., quod firmius ducitur*.

uiderentur...inuitabat: the alternation of the moods is not uncommon in our author; see our comm. on 187, 20-21. It is open to question, however, whether Bernhard 1927, 152 is right in including this passage: as our translation indicates, we think that the subjunctive *uiderentur* contains an element of subjectivity, whereas the indicative *inuitabat* expresses an undeniable and universally observable fact.

annonae copiosae beata celebritas: the chiastic word order brings the two adjectives together; thus the rich abundance is given additional stylistic emphasis.

beata: in the meaning *diues, locuples* it is used also 6, 20 (143, 19) *nec...sedile delicatum uel cibum beatum amplexa* (sc. Psyche). There is no need for Nolte's conjecture *lauta*.

celebritas: for the meaning *frequentia, copia* there are only four examples mentioned by *ThLL* s.v. 741, 78 f., e.g. Cic. *Fam.* 7, 2, 4 *in multitudine et celebritate iudiciorum*; Tac. *Ann.* 16, 29 *celebritate periculorum sueta iam senatus maestitia*.

The *pastores* were in fact *fugitiui*; all the officials of the empire were obliged to cooperate in tracking them down (see Summers 1967, 227 f.). But we may assume that their efforts did not amount to much; Millar 1981, 71 calls the world of the *Met.* 'one without policing by any Imperial forces...Justice is highly localized'. Cf. Aristomenes 1, 19, (18, 15), who flees to Aetolia in order not to be arrested, and remarries there without difficulty. The shepherds in our passage, too, are able to go as they please and settle elsewhere. The only instance in the *Met.* of immediate action by the imperial judiciary is found in Haemus' story, where the *nutus...magni principis* (7, 7 : 159, 22) eradicated the robbers' band *confestim*. But there the emperor was involved and, moreover, the whole story was made up by Heamus.

The *pastores* were mentioned in ch. 16 and 19; after the intervening episodes in ch. 20-22 they re-enter on the scene. After this they will disappear again from sight – this time for good: Apuleius keeps silent about their fate. One may compare 7, 26 (174, 10-14; see *GCA* 1981, 258 ad loc.) where the ass loses track of his *abactor*; as a consequence, the man disappears from our sight as well. See also Heine in *AAGA* 1978, 28.

Triduo denique iumentorum refectis corporibus, quo uendibiliores uideremur, ad mercatum producimur magnaque uoce praeconis pretia singulis nuntiantis equi atque alii asini opulentis emptoribus praestinantur; at me relictum solum ac subsiciuum cum fastidio plerique praeteribant: "After the pack animals' bodies had been fattened up for three days so that we would seem more salable, we were taken to a market; and to the accompaniment of the loud shouting of the auctioneer, who announced the price for each, one by one, the horses and other asses were purchased by wealthy buyers. But me, left over all by myself, most people kept passing by with disdain." 195, 2-7

triduo: vThiel 1, 161 calculates that in the *Onos* the journey to Beroë, which takes one night and three days, amounts to about 150 km. Such a distance can be covered in that time with pack animals, provided they are driven hard. According to vThiel, hard driving might explain Apuleius' insertion of a rest period of three days between arrival and sale. The question whether this three-day rest reflects a three-day journey in the Vorlage, we leave undecided; at any rate, Apuleius has established a connection between the three-day period (common to the *Onos* and the *Met.*) and the fattening of the animals to make them more marketable (a detail not found in the *Onos*).

denique: here merely transitional in function; see vdPaardt 1971, 43.

mercatum: a market held on a restricted and fixed number of days; see *GCA* 1981, 235 on 7, 23 (171, 21).

praeconis: 'auctioneer', as e.g. Cic. *N.D.* 3, 84 *eundem...haec...in forum protulisse et per praeconem uendidisse*.

equi atque alii asini: vGeisau 1912, 32, following Brakman 1906, 357 (cf. also Leky 1908, 13), puts this combination into the same category as 3, 10 (59, 16) *una de ceteris theatri statuis*. This is incorrect, for the *alii asini* are seen here as a separate group as opposed to the one ass Lucius. The clear contrast between him and the others is shown in the next line *at me*. That is, *alii* here means *ceteri*; see LHSz 2, 208.

opulentis emptoribus praestinantur: praestinare is a Plautine term, used some ten times in the *Met.*; e.g. 4, 15 (86, 17) with *GCA* 1977, 123 ad loc.; see also Callebat 1968, 484. The meaning 'buy', 'purchase' makes the translation of *emptoribus* 'by buyers' inevitable; consequently, we take *emptoribus* as a dative indicating the agent. vGeisau 1916, 63 demonstrates indeed that this dative is not often found in the *Met.* but nevertheless we have an example of it here. So we reject the translation 'werden an zahlungskräftigen Käufern verhandelt' (Brandt-Ehlers, and, following them, Schwartz 'aan rijke kopers verkocht').

at me: F reads *ac*, rightly corrected in ς. Heine 1962, 300 mentions the loneliness wich is so often experienced by Lucius the man and the ass. His horse and Milo's ass drive him out (*in solitudinem relegatus* 3, 27 : 71, 28; a case of professional jealousy); the stallions chase him out of the pasture because they see him as a rival (7, 16 : 166, 11 f.); and here, too, he is excluded from the *alii asini* – although for no apparent reason.

subsiciuum: derived from *subsecare*, this adjective means 'cut off and left remaining'; it is a technical term of the *agrimensores*. Apuleius uses it a few times, e.g. 3, 8 (58, 4; see vdPaardt 1971, 73 ad loc.) and *Apol.* 31 (36, 18) *quam (Italiam) subsiciuam Graeciam fecerat* (Pythagoras; Vallette: 'Italie, qu'il avait adoptée pour sienne'). The material of the *ThLL* shows that the adjective only occurs once to describe a living being: Lact. *Opif.* 12, 15 *duos sexus maris ac feminae machinatus est (Deus) quibus inter se per uoluptatis inlecebram copulatis subsiciua suboles pararetur, ne genus omne uiuentium condicio mortalitatis extingueret.* For the word-formation see LHSz 1, 304.

praeteribant: by using the imperfect the author emphasizes the ass's steadily deteriorating situation.

195, 7-11 Iamque taedio contrectationis eorum, qui de dentibus meis aetatem computabant, manum cuiusdam faetore sordentem, qui gingiuas identidem meas putidis scalpebat digitis, mordicus adreptam plenissime conterui: "And finally, fed up with being mauled by people who were trying to figure out my age by my teeth, I bit the dirty, stinking hand of a man who kept scratching my gums with his filthy fingers, and crushed it completely."

de dentibus: for this '*de* instrumental' see Callebat 1968, 202 f. and e.g. 202, 18 *salus de mea morte* with our comm.

aetatem computabant: cf. Hier. *Ephes.* 2, 8, 6 *aetatem (hinni) ex dentibus cognoscunt.* Col. 6, 29, 5 gives detailed information about the manner of computation. See also Plin. *Nat.* 11, 168 f. Presently (196, 8) a *mathematicus* will have a different method of calculating the ass's age.

scalpebat: Callebat 1968, 38 says that this verb frequently occurs in the comic poets. It occurs Calv. *poet.* 18 *digito caput uno scalpit* (cf. *Met.* 10, 10 : 244, 11 *capitis partem scalpere*) and e.g. Nov. *com.* 44 *scalpes dentes*; it does not occur in Plautus and Terence. In view of the 'caractère populaire' of this verb its occurrence in comic (and satiric) authors is hardly surprising. In addition the verb has the technical meaning (without 'caractère populaire', obviously) of 'carve' or 'engrave', attested from Cic. *N.D.* 2, 150 *ad pingendum fingendum, ad scalpendum...apta manus* and Plin. *Nat.* 36, 15 *ipsum Phidian tradunt scalpsisse marmora* onward.

gingiua: 'caro dentes in ore continens' (*ThLL*), attested from Catul. 39, 19. It is occasionally used of animals, e.g. Plin. *Nat.* 8, 107 (sc. *corocotta*) *nullis gingiuis dente continuo*.

mordicus: in the sense of 'mordendo dentibus', also used e.g. 3, 26 (71, 10) *mordicus adpetens*.

plenissime: this superlative also occurs 11, 26 (288, 5) *plenissime iam dudum uidebar initiatus*. Also Plin. *Ep.* 5, 8, 13 *quamuis illud plenissime, hoc restrictissime feceris*. It would be a mistake to weaken *plenissime* here to *paenissime*, as Lipsius does. Forceful language is a constant element in the descriptions of Lucius the ass, especially when he loses his temper: his first deliberation after he has been changed into an ass 3, 26 (71, 10) is *mordicus adpetens necare deberem* (sc. *Fotidem*); and 9, 27 (223, 15 (*digitos adulteri) ad summam minutiem contero*.

conterui: thus F;-*terui* has been written in an erasure by a different hand, possibly the original reading was *congerui* (a form not attested elsewhere) as found in φα. ς has *contriui*, undoubtedly the usual form for the perfect. *Conterui*, however, is not impossible: Char. *gramm.* 1, 248, 4 mentions as perfect forms of *terere: terui et triui iuxta Apuleium*. *ThLL* s.v. *conterere* 682, 44 f. mentions several passages in the *Vetus Latina*, Fulgentius, and Gregorius Turonensis. We find, moreover, *atteruisse* in Tib. 1, 4, 48, although this may be metri causa; see André ad loc. See also Callebat 1968, 127.

Quae res circumstantium ab emptione mea utpote ferocissimi deterruit animos: "This deterred the bystanders from buying me, obviously a very ferocious animal."

Quae res: No remarks of the bystanders are recorded: the narrator appears to supply his own interpretation for the fact that as an ass he remained unsold at this point. The *Onos* states merely that an auction takes place and the ass does not find a buyer; see Junghanns 1932, 88; Feldbrugge 1938, 68; vThiel 1, 14 n. 37.

circumstantium...animos: a notable hyperbaton.

ab emptione mea utpote ferocissimi: the apposition *utpote ferocissimi* (gen.) with *mea* (abl.) is by no means as curious as Médan 1925,26 and Callebat 1968, 337 suggest: see KSt 2,1,245; cf. also 7,12 (163,9) *contempta mea praesentia quasi ucrc mortui* see *GCA* 1981, 160 ad loc.

Tunc praeco dirruptis faucibus et rauca voce saucius in meas fortunas ridiculos construebat iocos: "Then the auctioneer, with a sore throat from opening his mouth so wide and shouting so raucously, started to arouse laughter by making jokes about my fate."

dirruptis faucibus: according to the *ThLL* 1266, 50 s.v. *dirumpere* this is a unique combination: Callebat 1968, 77 calls it a 'terme-image expressif'. Cf. e.g. 3, 2 (53, 6) *nemo... qui non risu dirumperetur*. The spelling *-rr-* occurs in F at 9, 28 (224, 19); 10, 22 (253, 20); 10, 29 (260, 10). More examples of this spelling are given *ThLL* s.v. 1264, 28 f.

faucibus et rauca uoce saucius: the use of *au* three times and of *au-i-u* twice is not accidental.

saucius: at 4, 22 (92, 2), also, throats are described as *sauciae*; on that occasion the cause is hunger: *fauces diutina fame saucias*. See *GCA* 1977, 169 ad loc.

in meas fortunas: 'sur ma personne' Vallette (also Callebat 1968, 86); Brandt-Ehlers 'auf meine Kosten'; Helm-Krenkel 'über mein Schicksal'. Though the distinction is slight, our preference is for the last translation: our author uses *fortuna* in the plural more than once in the sense of 'fate' and especially 'miserable fate', e.g. 3, 1 (52, 19) *fortunas meas heiulabam*; 3, 8 (57, 26) *paruuli huius... fortunis succurrite*. See vGeisau 1912, 21 for more examples.

ridiculos... iocos: up to now the ass may constantly have bemoaned his own bad fortune, that has caused him to fall into the clutches of cruel people, but this is the first time we hear him being ridiculed. As a man, Lucius had been the laughingstock at the Risus festival; now the same thing happens to him as an ass. In this respect, too, he has as an ass, retained a quality that characterized him as a human.

construebat iocos: the *ThLL* has no other example of this combination.

195, 14-17 'Quem ad finem cantherium istum uenui frustra subiciemus et uetulum ⟨et⟩ extritis ungulis debilem et dolore deformen et in hebeti pigritia ferocem nec quicquam amplius quam ruderarium crib⟨r⟩um?': "'How long will we unsuccessfully offer that nag for sale, old as he is, tottering on his worn-out hooves, unsightly through pain, and, for all his obtuse laziness, vicious? He's nothing more than a broken sieve."

Quem ad finem: cf. *quousque tandem... cantherium patiemur istum* 3, 27 (72, 12) with vdPaardt 1971, 194 ad loc. and Westerbrink, *AAGA* 1978, 66, who calls it a 'self-evident instance of parody'; the question whether the parodied passage is Cic. *Cat.* 1, 1 *quo usque tandem...* or Sal. *Cat.* 20, 9 *quae quo usque tandem*, is left unanswered. In our passage, however, the target is clearly Cicero, since his phrase *quem ad finem (sese effrenata iactabat audacia)* is repeated here. The other passages of parody that contain the phrases *quem ad finem* or *quo usque (tandem)* all refer to circumstances threatening to the ass: 3, 27 (72, 12) his mutilation; 6, 26 (147, 20) his death (cf. *GCA* 1981, 31 ad loc.); 7, 20 (169, 18) his torment. That is not the case here, where he is merely ridiculed.

cantherium: this word occurs twice elsewhere in Apul.: the passage quoted above 3, 27 (72, 12), and 9, 13 (212, 13). Generally it indicates a castrated horse, but in our passages it is used of the ass; see vdPaardt 1971, 194 on 3, 27 (72, 12) with additional literature.

et uetulum ⟨et⟩ extritis ungulis: F reads *et uetulum extritis ungulis* which is retained by Hildebrand; following a proposal of Oudendorp and Beyte, *et* is inserted before *extritis* by Giarratano, Helm, Robertson, Brandt-Ehlers, Frassinetti, Scazzoso, vThiel, Augello 1977, 189; Castiglioni 1938, 552 and Terzaghi delete *et* before *uetulum* (without inserting *et* before *extritis*). We agree with Oudendorp. With *et* before *extritis* we get a polysyndeton of four membra, of which Strilciw 1925, 119 gives more examples. The four membra (3, 9, 6, and 11 syllables respectively) are ingeniously varied: alle four adjectives consist of three syllables; the last three adjectives have homoeoteleuton; the first adjective has no additions, the second has an ablative (*ungulis*) with a qualification (*extritis*), the third has an ablative (*dolore*) without a qualification, and the fourth has an ablative (*pigritia*) with a qualification (*hebeti*) plus *in*. These four membra – all of them descriptions of the ass – are followed by another variant qualification *nec quicquam* etc.

extritis ungulis: the same combination is found 4, 4 (77, 11) where they are the consequence of a long journey; see *GCA* 1977, 47 ad loc. The material of the *ThLL* offers in addition only the combination *attritis...ungulis* in Curt. 8, 2, 34 and Plin. *Nat.* 11, 127. Palaeographically attractive, too, is Scriverius' suggestion *et uetulum et tritis ungulis*.

debilem: in 3,27 (72,15), already linked with the present passage by the parody of Cicero (see above) and by the word *cantherium*, the speaker threatens to make the ass *debilem claudumque*. That threat would be unnecessary now: after all his hardships the ass is already *debilis* and *deformis*.

dolore deformem: the older editors found this difficult; hence *colore* Beroaldus, *lurore* Oudendorp, *squalore* vdVliet. But the idea that one can become 'misshapen', 'unsightly' by pain does not seem astonishing; the ass is in a condition which Cic. *Att.* 2, 21, 3 in a different context would have called *deformatus corpore, fractus animo*. Moreover, comparable expressions are found in the *Met.* more than once: 1, 6 (5, 21) *luctu et maerore diuturno deformata* and 9, 30 (225, 18) *mulier reatu miraque tristitie deformis*. Cf. also e.g. Sal. *Iug.* 14, 7 *rex...deformatus aerumnis* and Prop. 1, 5, 16 *et timor informem ducet in ore notam* with Enk ad loc. Thus the ass's *deformitas* is comparable with that of human beings in comparable situations. Though not always, as here, caused by pain, *deformitas* plays an important part in the *Met.*; see Heine 1962, 150 f. Observe, finally, the alliteration in *debilem et dolore deformem*, which would be weakened by emendation.

in hebeti pigritia: our concessive translation 'for all...', 'in spite of...' is suggested by the context; Callebat 1968, 223 mentions our passage as the only example in the *Met.* of this construction. But cf. 202, 13 *si quid in ultimo fortunae turbine resipiscis* with our comm. ad loc.; see also *OLD* s.v. *in* 40 c.

ruderarium: evidently an Apuleian neologism (Bernhard 1927, 139) and, according to the material of the *ThLL*, attested here only. *Ruderarius* (LS 'of or belonging to rubbish', from *rudus, -eris*) is taken by some to describe a sieve that is fit for the rubbish-heap, i.e. already broken ('ein morsches Sandsieb' Helm-Krenkel; 'een kapotte zeef' Schwartz), by others a sieve for rubbish (thus Valpy; Butler; Vallette; Brandt-Ehlers and others). Certainty is impossible for lack of more passages; the obscurity may be conscious on the author's part if, as Vallette suggests, we have here a pun on the verb *rudere* 'to bray.' For the expression see vdPaardt 1971, 205 on 3, 29 (73, 20) *corium nec cribris iam idoneum relinquunt*, where this proverbial expression (see Otto² 1965, 98) means 'useless even as a sieve.'

cribrum: this the correct emendation of ς; F has *cribum*. Although in *Gloss.* 5, 495, 55; 639, 32 a form *cribus* is mentioned, this does not justify the form *cribum* in our passage. At 3, 29 (73, 20; see preceding lemma) F spells *cribris* correctly.

195, 18-19 **Atque adeo uel donemus eum cuipiam, si qui tamen faenum suum perdere non grauatur**': "Let us therefore give him to someone for a present instead, if that person at least does not object to wasting his hay'."

Atque adeo uel: F has *quare*, written in a larger erasure, according to Robertson (according to Helm's app. crit. it seems to have been originally *atque*); φ has *atque ideo uel*; ς has *atque adeo uel*; α has *atque adeoque uel*. F is followed by Hildebrand; α by vdVliet, Gaselee, Terzaghi, Brandt-Ehlers, Frassinetti, Scazzoso; φ by Helm; ς by Giarratano, Robertson, vThiel. We agree with this last group: *adeo* serves here as an introduction to a conclusion, and is so almost synonymous with *ideo* (see Waszink 1947, 90; for an example in the *Met.* see 3, 22: 68, 20 with vdPaardt 1971, 166 ad loc.) Therefore *ideo*, preferred by Helm (see his Praef. *Fl.* XXXII, where he says that this is one of the cases in which φ has retained the correct reading), is to be rejected as the *lectio facilior*. As an example of *adeo* = *ideo* Waszink quotes Tert. *An.* 1, 4 *adeo omnis illa tunc sapientia Socratis de industria uenerat consultae aequanimitatis, non de fiducia compertae ueritatis*.

uel: has here the function of a 'corrective without *potius*, implying an alternative the first member of which is omitted' (LS). The reasoning is: 'since selling the ass does not work, let's try the alternative of giving him away.' So it is not necessary to follow Stewech and delete *uel*.

si qui: *qui* instead of *quis* occurs a few times in classical authors, but it is used in particular in 'style familier' by later authors (see Callebat 1968, 290 with further literature); another example in the *Met.* is 2, 20 (41, 19) *nescio qui simile passus*; see de Jonge 1941 ad loc.

CHAPTER XXIV

A priest of the Dea Syria is interested in purchasing the ass.

Ad istum modum praeco ille cachinnos circumstantibus com- 195, 20-21
mouebat: "In this manner the auctioneer elicited roars of laughter from the bystanders."

Ad istum modum: for the frequency with which Apuleius in book 8 starts a new pericope with this or a similar phrase, see our comm. on 187, 3 *ad hunc modum*.

cachinnos: *cachinnus* is a much stronger word than *risus*, cf.*ThLL* s.v. 'risus nimius ac sonans'. See also Heine 1962, 290.

circumstantibus: cf. Cic. *Brut.* 216 *cachinnos alicuius commouere*, where the construction with the genitive is used. Callebat 1968, 490 f. discusses the phenomenon that Apuleius, as well as the comic poets, often has the dative where other authors have the genitive; cf. also 9, 12 (211, 23) *risum toto coetu* (dative) *commoueram*. Löfstedt 1928, 1, 167 and LHSz 2, 95 discuss this sympathetic dative, which is characteristic of the 'Volkssprache' but may rather be considered poetic in certain authors. In 7, 5 (158, 3) *Hauete...fortissimo deo Marti clientes* we pointed to something similar in our comm. ad loc. Note the *c* alliteration.

Sed illa Fortuna mea saeuissima, quam per tot regiones iam 195, 21-25
fug⟨i⟩ens effugere uel praecedentibus malis placare non potui, rursum in me caecos detorsit oculos et emptorem aptissimum duris meis casibus mire repertum obiecit: "But that utterly cruel Fortune of mine, whom I had not been able to escape on my flight through so many places now or to appease by my earlier adversities, turned blind eyes towards me again. Miraculously she found a buyer who exactly matched my harsh fate and threw him in my way."

Sed: at times *sed* underlines a turning point in the tides of fortune; see Tatum 1969, 95 n. 185 and our comm. on 4, 3 (76, 5) and 7, 20 (169, 8).

illa Fortuna mea saeuissima: for the combination of *ille* and *meus* see 7, 22 (171, 4) *accusator ille meus noxius* and Callebat 1968, 280. Wolterstorff 1917, 224 compares *Onos* 35, 4 ἡ δὲ πολλὰ πολλάκις δινουμένη καὶ μεταπίπτουσα Νέμεσις and concludes from this that *illa* has become an article. An objection against this is that Apuleius has mentioned *Fortuna* before, and repeatedly in book 7, where her latest appearance was 7, 25 (173, 4); now, at her re-appearance, we ought to be familiar with her (*illa*).

mea: a possessive pronoun with *Fortuna* is not often found in the *Met*.: apart from 192, 14 *per Fortunas uestrosque Genios* (see our comm. ad loc.) the only occurrences are this passage and 11, 15 (277, 25) where the possessive *sua* emphatically refers to what is here called *Fortuna mea:pristinis aerumnis absolutus Isidis magnae prouidentia gaudens Lucius de sua Fortuna triumphat: Fortuna uidens* triumphs over *Fortuna caeca*. See also Gwyn Griffiths ad loc.

saeuissima: Tatum 1969, 94 n. 184 gives a list of all epithets of Fortune in the *Met*. The epithet is often used to draw the reader's attention to Fortune's grimness and thus to prepare him for a deterioration in the ass's situation; cf. Heine 1962, 170.

fugiens effugere: Apuleius occasionally adds a participle of the same root to a finite verb; cf. 4, 11 (83, 2) *suadens persuadere* with our comm. and the literature listed there (add vGeisau 1912, 34).

uel: there are two ways in which one can try to escape *Fortuna saeuissima*: running away or appeasing her. The ass has not been able to do either.

caecos: for the blindness of Fortune, see *GCA* 1981, 91 on 7,2 (155, 21). The fact that the narrator attributes to this blind Fortune his association with the Dea Syria (next sentence: 196,4) suggests that his opinion of the Dea Syria is not high; see appendix IV 1. Observe the striking oxymoron. Cf. Valpy ad loc.: '(oculos) quibus aut nihil videt, aut tam perverse videt, ut bona malis, bonis mala decernat.'

detorsit: Becker 1879, 25 proposes *retorsit* because 'detorquere avertendi tantum vim habet, numquam advertendi'. This reasoning is too formal: *detorquere* here means 'turn towards' as at 2, 5 (29, 5) *simul quemque conspexerit speciosae formae iuuenem,...ilico in eum et oculum et animum detorquet* (Pamphile) and 181, 21 *fama...cursus primos ad domum Tlepolemi detorquet*. ThLL s.v. 819, 51 f. rightly defines the verb by 'convertere'.

emptorem: after Philebus, the ass will be sold to the baker (9, 10), the gardener (9, 31), and the brothers (10, 13); except in the last case, the sales are by public auction (cf. Heine *AAGA* 1978, 29, who points out that there is no connection at all between these episodes). The soldier (9, 39-42) will not buy the ass, but simply commandeer him.

aptissimum duris meis casibus: it will soon be revealed that the buyer is a *cinaedus*, who by definition indulges in sexual debaucheries. The narrator's words can therefore be interpreted as follows: 'unfortunate as I have been in the past, I am now, on top of it all, sold to a *cinaedus*!' But there is another way in which one can speak of a perfect match between the buyer and the misfortunes suffered by Lucius the ass: sexual debauchery is traditionally a characteristic of asses as well as *cinaedi* (see our comm. on 196, 19-21). This relationship would be broken by vdVliet's conjecture *durisque*, which we reject on that account.

mire: the translators – in so far as they commit themselves – connect *mire* either with *aptissimum* (e.g. Vallette 'merveilleusement adapté'; Schwartz 'wonderbaarlijk passend') or with *repertum* (e.g. Brandt-Ehlers 'wundervoll ausfindig gemacht'). Because of its position we prefer the latter view. The buyer is a *cinaedus* and – worse still – a priest of the Dea Syria, Isis' antithesis (see appendix IV); how miraculously blind, therefore, are the eyes of the false Fortune, who establishes contact between the ass (later to become a devotee of

Isis) and the Dea Syria. Cf. Heine 1962, 240 n. 1, who observes that *mirus, mirari* etc. occur 59 times in the Met.: 'vielleicht darf man dies als Indiz für die Unerklärbarkeit und Ungewöhnlichkeit der Welt der M. werten'.

Scitote qualem: cinaedum et senem cinaedum, caluum quidem, sed cincinnis semicanis et pendulis capillatum, unum de triuiali popularium faece, qui per plateas et oppida cymbalis et crotalis personantes deamque Syria⟨m⟩ circumferentes mendicare compellunt: "Let me tell you what he was like: a pervert, an old pervert, bald on top but with greying ringlets dangling, one of those utter dregs of society who go round the streets and the towns making a row with cymbals and castanets, carrying the Syrian goddess around and forcing her to beg." 195, 25-196,4

Scitote: Callebat 1968, 502 f. says that Apuleius' use of imperative forms in-*to*-shows that he is influenced by comic poetry. But LHSz 2, 340 f. point out that it is for formal reasons that, in certain verbs, only the imperatives in -*to*- are used; thus always *scito* and *memento*. By using the imperative the narrator makes contact with the reader (cf. e.g. 10, 2 : 237, 12 *scito te tragoediam...legere*) in the same way as by using the second person 7, 13 (163, 23) *pompam cerneres omnis sexus*; cf. Heine 1962, 220 n.3 and *GCA* 1981, 164 f. ad loc.

cinaedum...compellunt: a carefully constructed sentence, with alliteration of *c* all through the sentence and of *p* in the middle part. The position of the attributes deserves attention as well: first *senem* (used as an adjective, see below) with a noun; next *caluum* without any modifier; then *capillatum* preceded by a modifier consisting of four words (11 syllables); finally *unum...* followed by a modifier consisting of four words (12 syllables).

cinaedum: Callebat 1968, 62 describes this word as an expression of 'réalisme familier', borrowed from the Greek and accepted into colloquial language already in comedy. The rhetorical anaphora focuses the attention on the word (cf. Verg. *A.* 8, 71 *Nymphae, Laurentes Nymphae*); see vGeisau 1912, 32. The etymology of *cinaedus* (κίναιδος) is uncertain (see both Boisacq and Frisk s.v.); its original meaning is 'dancer', cf. Non. 5 (9L) *cinaedi dicti sunt apud ueteres saltatores uel pantomimi* ἀπὸ τοῦ κινεῖν σῶμα. (a folk-etymological explanation). Their dances were notorious for their lasciviousness; as a characteristic can be mentioned *clunem agitare* (Petr. 23,3 *spatalocinaedi...femore facili, clune agili et manu procaces, molles*). There are many indications of a connection with cults: *Galli* are often called *cinaedi* (Firm. *Math.* 7, 25, 4 *Gallos abscisos dicito et cinaedos*). From Plato *Gorg.* 494 E onward the word *cinaedus* is used to describe the *molles* and *pathici*, i.e. those who play the passive part in homosexual relationships (Firm. *Err.* 6, 7 *effeminatum cinaedum eum fuisse et amatorum seruisse libidinibus Graecorum gymnasiis decantatur*). Less often he plays an active part (Schol. Lukian. 211, 3 R κίναιδος ὅ τε ποιῶν ὅ τε πασχών παρὰ τὸ τὴν αἰδῶ κινεῖν; see also Petr. 23, 4 f.). These data are taken from *R.E.*11, 1, 459 f. s.v. *kinaidos* (Kroll). Because of the versatility of the *cinaedi*, as suggested above, we have a wide variety of translations to choose from: 'an old bawd' (sic! Butler), 'un bagascione' (Carlesi), 'an old naughty man' (Adlington-Gaselee), 'ein alter Päderast' (Rode), 'ein alter Kastrat' (Rode-Burck), 'einen Lüstling'

(Brandt-Ehlers), 'einen Buhlknaben' (Helm-Krenkel). 'un cinedo' (Scazzoso). Prof. Ph. Goold suggests that the rather un-specified 'pervert' will do nicely in English.

et: i.e. *et quidem*; cf. 7, 13 (156, 2) *in bestiam et extremae sortis quadripedem* with *GCA* 1981, 85 ad loc.

senem: must be used adjectivally, in view of the repeated *cinaedum*. Cf. 10, 4 (239, 9) *ad quendam compertae grauitatis educatorem senem...refert* where, in our opinion, *senem* is again used as an adjective.

caluum: baldness is considered ugly: Psyche's sister says contemptuously about her husband 5, 9 (110, 14) *ego misera primum patre meo seniorem maritum sortita sum, deinde cucurbita caluiorem et quouis puero pusilliorem*. In the *Apologia* baldness is a *deformitas* (74 : 83, 15) as it is in Petr. 108, 1 *turbatus...et deformis praeter spoliati capitis dedecus superciliorum etiam aequalis cum fronte caluities*. Worst of all are the baldheads who, as in this passage, accentuate their baldness by curls on the side of their heads; cf. Mart. 10, 83, 11 *caluo turpius est nihil comato*. See Heine 1962, 198, 1. Baldness is sometimes associated with debauchery; see Bramble 1974, 111 on Pers. 1, 56 *nugaris, cum tibi, calue, / pinguis aqualiculus propenso sesquipede exstet*. Bramble quotes in this connection Apul. *Apol.* 59 (67, 24) *caput iuuenis barba et capillo populatum...uocem absonam, manuum tremorem, ructus popinam*. For the religious significance of baldness (obtained by shaving, and not due to natural causes) see Appendix IV 2.2.

cincinnis: borrowed from the Greek (κίκιννος: etymology uncertain, according to Frisk), it is attested from Pl. *Truc.* 287 *istos fictos, compositos, crispos, cincinnos tuos,/unguentatos* onward, a passage which, like ours, suggests disapproval; cf. 610 (said of a priest of Cybele) *moechum, malacum, cincinnatum/...tympanotribam*; Ov. *Ars* 1, 505 *sed tibi nec ferro placeat torquere capillos* (Hollis remarks ad loc. 'Men did curl their hair in Rome, but this was considered foppish').

semicanis: according to the material of the *ThLL* this word is found only here and *Met.* 9, 30 (225, 20).

unum de: cf. 2, 26 (46, 21) *de famulis tuis unum* with de Jonge's comm. ad loc. *Unus* with the genitive is found already in early Latin but the construction with *de* occurs more frequently e.g. Cic. *Mil.* 65; see LHSz 2, 57. *Unus ex* is found 7, 22 (170, 22).

triuiali popularium faece: the adjective and the noun are juxtaposed somewhat pleonastically, which is not uncommon in our author; see Bernhard 1927, 175. The expression, like so many others, betrays the narrator's contempt (it is absent in the *Onos*; see Appendix IV note 44), but it is true that the followers of the Dea Syria belonged primarily to the lowest stratum of the population (see Appendix III). *Triuialis* is attested before Apuleius in Calp. *Ecl.* 1, 28; Quint., Iuv., Suet.

cymbalis: see our comm. on 201, 20. The *cymbala* were as a rule used in the cult of the *mater deum*, but also in that of the Dea Syria; see Wille 1967, 62.

crotalis: this word, which is used *Met.* 9, 4 (205, 18) as well, is found for the first time in Scip. *apud* Macr. *Sat.* 3, 14, 7 *eunt...in ludum saltatorium inter cinaedos uirgines puerique ingenui...uidi...puerum...cum crotalis saltare quam saltationem impudicus seruulus saltare non posset* (note that there, as in our passage, *crotala* are associated with *cinaedi*). The connotation of lasciviousness is also found in the combination of *crotalis* with *cymbalis*, as in *Priap.* 27, 3 *cymbala cum crotalis, pruriginis arma*. In *Copa* 1 f. *copa Syrisca, caput Graeca redimita mitella,/crispum sub crotalo docta mouere latus*, the provocative dance is performed by a Syrian *copa*.

personantes: compare as a contrast the sweet music at the Isis procession (11,9:273, 8) *Symphoniae dehinc suaues, fistulae tibiaeque modulis dulcissimis personabant* and Appendix IV 2.5.

deamque Syriam: see Appendix III.

mendicare compellunt: an exact rendering of *Onos* 35, 4 τούτων εἰς τῶν τὴν θεόν...ἐπαιτεῖν ἀναγκαζόντων. Morelli 1913, 174 compares Min. Fel. 22, 8 (= 24, 11) *mendicantes uicatim deos ducunt*. Cf. also Tert. *Ap.* 13, 6 *circuit cauponas religio mendicans* (concerning the cult of Isis and Cybele; see Waltzing ad loc.) and 42, 8 *hominibus et deis uestris mendicantibus* (referring to Roman gods, whose temples need the people's donations). Both the Christian apologists and the Isis-worshipping narrator in the *Met.* (for whom the author has borrowed the idea from the *Onos*) show a deep contempt by using this phrase.

compellunt: the priests exploit and misuse the goddess; cf. our comm. on 198, 2 *conlaticia stipe*.

Is nimio praestinandi studio praeconem rogat, cuiatis essem; at ille Cappadocum me et satis forticulum denuntiat: "In his great eagerness to buy me, this man asks the auctioneer where I come from. He states that I am Cappadocian and quite strong." 196, 5-7

praestinandi: see our comm. on 195, 6.

cuiatis: i.e. 'de qua patria, quibus parentibus natus' is occasionally found as a nominative in Plautus, Accius, and Cicero. Afterwards it appears in Gellius and Apuleius (Neue-Wagener 2, 27); the latter uses it also 1, 5 (5, 2; see Molt ad loc.) and 5, 9 (117, 21). In addition a form *cuias*, gen. *cuiatis* occurs Liv. 27, 19, 9 *cum percontaretur Scipio quis et...cuias* (sc. *esset*). In Cic. *Tusc.* 5,108 *Socrates...cum rogaretur cuiatem se esse diceret, 'mundanum' inquit* it is impossible to determine which nominative underlies the accusative.

Cappadocum: the plural *Cappadoces* is the most common form; *Cappadocius* is rare; *Cappadocus*, the form used here, is somewhat less rare (*ThLL* s.v.). Cappadocia was known as a source both of thoroughbred horses (Hildebrand quotes twelve passages to demonstrate this; according to *RE* s.v. Kappadokia 1911, 58 f., the name is derived from the Persian *Katpatuka* 'the land of the *tucha* or *ducha*', i.e. 'the land of beautiful horses') and also of good slaves (demonstrated by Valpy and more recently by Norden 1912, 82 n.7). For evidence of their strength see Mart. 6,77,1 f. *cum sis.../tam fortis quam nec cum uinceret Artemidorus,/ quid te Cappadocum sex onus esse iuuat?*, i.e. the corpse was carried on a bier borne by six Cappadocians (see Marquardt [2]1886,170: Cappadocians were in demand as pall-bearers because of their physical strength).

We agree with Helm-Krenkel 413 that the *praeco*'s reference to Cappadocia refers particularly to its reputation for good slaves, because

(1) the *praeco, lasciuiens* (8), will soon speak explicitly of the ass as a slave (12 *bonum et frugi mancipium*), as will the priest, more seriously, 197,16; cf. *Onos* 36,2, where the priest says: δοῦλον ἡμῖν ἐώνημαι καλὸν καὶ ἁδρὸν καὶ Καππαδόκην τὸ γένος. (Apuleius has moved the mention of Cappadocia to an earlier point in the narrative (see vThiel 1971,1,117 n.49), but the two passages convey the same idea, namely that Cappadocia is a country that supplies good slaves);

(2) the passage is much more comic if the *praeco* – with unconscious truth – presents the ass as a human being. Moreover, Lucius in his human shape was a distinguished young man; now, in the shape of an ass, he is presented as a slave, and, to top it all, a slave who is fit for hard labour. See Junghanns 1932,88 n. 134; 90 n.136. The *praeco* describes the ass in language appropriate to a human being also at 195,16 *dolore deformem* and 196,10 *professionibus*; see our comm. on *gladium* 7,22 (171,7).

satis forticulum: satis = ualde occurs frequently in our author (see Callebat 1968, 541); see e.g. 2, 21 (43, 6) *satis peregrinus* with the note of deJonge ad loc. The addition of *satis* may be an indication that both the notion of smallness and the affective value of the diminutive have disappeared; see Hofmann *LU*³1951, 140 f. Walsh *AAGA* 1978, 22 compares Petr. 63,5 *habebamus tunc hominem Cappadocem, longum, ualde audaculum et qui ualebat: poterat bouem iratum tollere*, an interesting passage in more than one respect: here we have a comparable combination of *ualde* with a diminutive, and a Cappadocian to boot. In Petronius, too, the Cappadocian (although not a slave) is praised because of his physical strength.

196, 7-10 Rursum requirit annos aetatis meae; sed praeco lasciuiens: 'mathematicus quidem, qui stellas eius disposuit, quintum ei numerauit annum, sed ipse scilicet melius istud de suis nouit professionibus: "He makes another enquiry – about my age. But the auctioneer says flippantly: 'An astrologer who drew his horoscope gave him four years, but he himself knows better, of course, from his own declarations to the registrar."

requirit annos aetatis meae; the *edictum aedilium curulium*, which regulated the sale of slaves, contained the clause that the slave's actual age had to be given at the sale: *Dig* 21, 1, 37 *praecipiunt aediles, ne ueterator pro nouicio ueneat* etc.; see Summers 1967, 279. We have no evidence that the age of animals had to be disclosed at the sale.

Dig. 21, 1, 38 says only *qui iumenta uendunt, palam recte dicunto quid in quoquo eorum morbi uitiique sit.* The farmers in 195, 8 had, in any case, their own method for determining an animal's age.

lasciuiens: for its meaning 'to joke' cf. Gel. 4, 20, 6 *censor eum quod intempestiue lasciuisset, in aerarios rettulit causamque hanc ioci scurrilis apud se dicti subscripsit.* The disrespect with which the *praeco* treats the priest is typical of the low esteem in which the worshippers of the Dea Syria were generally held; see Appendix IV note 44. The κῆρυξ ranked higher socially than his Latin counterpart *praeco*, who could be a *libertinus* (see von Albrecht 1977, 127); whether Apul. gives the *praeco* here the social status of the κῆρυξ in the *Onos*, or uses the Latin standard, does not make any difference to the jokes (which, incidentally, are absent in the *Onos*).

mathematicus: its general meaning is 'vir disciplinarum liberalium peritus' (*ThLL* s.v. 471, 41 f.) and may refer to arithmetic, geometry, and astronomy, cf. Var. *hist.* 6 (in Aug. *civ.* 21, 8) *Adrastos Cyzicenus et Dion Neapolites, mathematici nobiles* and Cic. *Luc.* 82 (*solem*) *mathematici amplius duodeuiginti partibus confirmant maiorem esse quam terram*. It acquired the further meaning 'astrologer': e.g. Sen. *Apoc.* 3, 2 *patere mathematicos aliquando uerum dicere*; Tac. *Hist.* 1, 22; and our passage.

stellas...disposuit: the *ThLL* 1423, 83 s.v. *disponere* has no other examples of this phrase, which must mean 'draw a horoscope'.

scilicet: as so often, *scilicet* gives an ironical colouring to the passage; see Callebat 1968, 461 and vdPaardt 1971, 194 on 3,27 (72,10) *pessima scilicet sorte*.

professionibus: a Roman citizen had to file his tax return himself at the census; see e.g. Quint. *Decl.* 341 *ea res...in professionem non uenit* ('was not filed in someone's tax return'); Hyg. Gr. *agrim.* p. 169 *nequa usurpatio* (of land) *per falsas professiones fiat*. Registration of the birth of a child was introduced by Marcus Aurelius (see Marquardt 1886 I 86 f.); in Apul. *Apol.* 89 (98, 9) Pudentilla's father registered his daughter thirty days after her birth. Consequently, the Roman citizen made *professiones* several times in his life, whence *suis* in our text.

The *praeco* continues to refer to the ass as a human being; here he does so by referring to the *professiones*, which are naturally made by people only. See our comm. on *Cappadocum* (196, 6) and on *modestum hominem* (196, 18 below). The *praeco* is really going to extremes when he has the ass make his own *professiones* at his birth; one should not attempt to explain this away as does Valpy on *professionibus*: 'i.e. tabulis quibus natum eum sibi professus est ejus pater apud acta'; cf. Rode's translation 'aus seinen Geburtsbriefen'.

Quanquam enim prudens crimen Corneliae legis incurram, si ciuem Romanum pro seruo tibi uendidero, quin emis bonum et frugi mancipium, quod te et foris et domi poterit iuuare?: "For altough I knowingly risk an indictment under the Cornelian law if I sell you a Roman citizen as a slave, why not buy this good and honest slave, who will be able to help you outdoors and in the house?" 196, 10-13

Corneliae legis: the adjectives derived from proper names, which come after the noun in classical authors, are often placed before the noun in Apuleius. Especially notable are *Cornelia lex* in this passage and *Romanus populus* 11, 17 (279, 22), because a fixed expression is changed, according to Bernhard 1927, 22.

Much has been said about this *Cornelia lex*. Legal sources mention laws *de falsis, de sicariis et ueneficiis* as *leges Corneliae*, but not a *lex Cornelia* dealing with the punishment of a person who sells a free Roman citizen as a slave – that

209

was done under the *lex Fabia de plagiariis*; see Ulp. *Dig.* 48, 15, 1 *uenditor quoque fit obnoxius, si sciens liberum esse uendiderit* (cf. Norden 1912, 82 f.). Is Apul. making a mistake here? This has been maintained by Elmenhorst; Mommsen 1899, 780 n. 2 cautiously adds 'perhaps'. We think, however, that an experienced lawyer like Apul. is unlikely to have made such a mistake; moreover, Mommsen did not make a distinction between *praeco*, narrator, and author. *Lasciuiens* in line 8 should not be forgotten: the joke is that the *praeco* is using quasi – legal terms 'pour épater le bourgeois', i.e. the *cinaedus*. Vallette says in his note that we may have 'un nom de fantaisie' here (thus Walsh 1970, 61 n. 4). Summers 1967, 282 does not wish, either, to exclude the possibility of a joke even though he finds the joke 'extremely flat'. The success of a joke is subjective; we see no reason to regard the reference to a *Cornelia lex* as a mistake. The unusual word order may be evidence that it is a 'nom de fantaisie'.

crimen...incurram: cf. *SHA* Capitol *Pert.* 7, 1 *si delationis crimen incurreret*; Arn. *Nat.* 4, 16 *ne...stultitiae crimen incurrat*.

ciuem Romanum: again the joke is that the *praeco* does not know that he is indeed selling a Roman citizen, or at least someone who used to be one in his pre-asinine period (cf. 196, 18 below). Although it is never said in so many words, we may safely assume that Lucius was a Roman citizen because of his famous ancestors (1, 2:2, 5 f.) and his activities as a lawyer in the Forum Romanum (11, 28:290, 4).

bonum et frugi: as is often the case in the *Met.*, it is difficult to determine what – if anything – is the difference between the two epithets; see Bernhard 1927, 167 and *GCA* 1981, 232 on 7, 23 (171, 14) *crassior atque opulentior*. *Frugi* is often used to characterize slaves, e.g. Hor. *S.* 2, 7, 2 *Dauus, amicum /mancipium domino et frugi quod sit satis*; see Kiessling-Heinze ad loc. and *ThLL* s.v. 1457, 7 f.

mancipium: for the implications which, in our opinion, the use of this word has in the case of the ass – a unique case, as it seems – see Appendix IV 2, 11.

foris et domi; later (198, 7-9) it will become clear that the services indoors are of a sexual nature; see our comm. ad loc.

196, 14-16 Sed exinde odiosus emptor aliud de alio non desinit quaerere, denique de mansuetudine etiam mea percontatur anxie: "But the detestable buyer does not stop asking continuously one question after another, and finally he even inquires anxiously whether I am gentle."

The ass is recommended as a *bonum et frugi mancipium*, but the *praeco*'s obligatory assurance is not sufficient for the buyer: his craving for information now focuses on the ass's *mansuetudo*. Norden 1912, 171 points out that before the second century AD Roman law did not recognize the seller's obligation to guarantee the quality of the object to be sold; this may explain why the buyer *non desinit quaerere*.

exinde: 'incessantly'. We assume the same typically Apuleian meaning at 7, 27 (175, 3) *heiulans et exinde proclamans*; see *GCA* 1981, 262 ad loc.

odiosus: sums up in one word the *emptor*'s many objectionable qualities already mentioned by the narrator.

aliud de alio: cf. Ter. *Hau.* 598 *dicam, uerum ut aliud ex alio incidit*; Cic. *Fam.* 9, 19, 2 *me cotidie aliud ex alio impedit*. Compare also e.g. Liv. 5, 48, 6 *diem de die prospectans*. See LHSz 2, 262; 267.

anxie: the use of the adverb here attracts attention because later Latin prefers the adjective; thus Bernhard 1927, 110. We have pointed out this phenomenon more than once, e.g. 7, 11 (162, 25) *adpetenter*.

CHAPTER XXV

The bargain is struck, to the ass's dismay.

196, 16-19 At praeco: 'ueruecem', inquit, 'non asinum uides, ad usus omnes quietum, non mordacem, nec calcitronem quidem, sed prorsus ut in asini corio modestum hominem inhabitare credas: "But the auctioneer said: 'What you are looking at is a wether, not an ass – he's quiet, whatever he's used for; he doesn't bite, he doesn't even kick – you'd be quite certain that a gentle human being was living in the ass's skin."

ueruecem: for the *ueruex* as an example of gentleness, see 7, 23 (171, 1): (*asinum amatorem*) *dissitis femoribus emasculare et quouis ueruece mitiorem efficere* with *GCA* 1981, 236 ad loc. The ass's situation in the present passage is different from the one just mentioned in that here he is not threatened with emasculation – quite the contrary, we shall soon see. If the ass really were a *ueruex* – i.e. castrated – the auctioneer's ambiguities would be even more comical. The manner in which *ueruecem* and *asinum* are contrasted is colloquial; cf. Ter. *Hec.* 214 *me omnino lapidem, non hominem putas*; Catul. 115, 8 *non homo, sed...mentula*. See LHSz 2, 728.

ad usus omnes quietus: on the modal use of *ad* see Callebat 1968, 212; *GCA* 1977, 198. Cf. 2, 16 (38, 4) *ad libidinem inquies* (see, however, app. crit.); as in line 13 above, the information is innocent in itself, but what follows gives it a double entendre.

non mordacem: the *praeco* knows his job: he ignores the fact that only a little while ago (195, 10) the ass completely shattered someone's hand.

calcitronem: this word, explained by Non. 64 L as *calcitrones qui infestent calcibus*, is found Pl. *As.* 391 (referring to a human being); Var. *Men.* 479 *equum mordacem, calcitronem, horridum*; Cael. Sab. (apud Gel. 4, 2, 5) *equus mordax aut calcitro*; and here. It is one of those words which are attested in early Latin and are found again in Apuleius; see Callebat 1968, 479, who speaks of authors 'archaïques et archaïsants' and rightly dismisses Bernhard 1927, 131, where these words are called vulgarisms. Observe the common combination with *mordax*.

prorsus: emphasizing *ut* it is also found 9, 34 (228, 27); cf. 199, 7 *prorsus quasi*. Callebat 1968, 538 traces this use from Pliny onward. See LHSz 2, 644 for *prorsus* with final and consecutive *ut*.

in asini corio modestum hominem inhabitare: as so often, the author makes the most of the irony of the situation, i.e. that the speaker unknowingly hits the nail on the head with *hominem*: 6, 29 (151, 9) with *GCA* 1981, 58 ad loc.; 7, 25 (173, 20) with *GCA* 1981, 253 ad loc. See Heine 1962, 302; Walsh 1970, 160 n. 3; vThiel 1, 119 n. 141. Cf. our note on line 11 *ciuem Romanum* above.

The double entendre of *modestum* may be compared with that of *foris et domi* (13). If the human aspect is emphasized, as the author seems to encourage, it means 'modest' or 'moderate'; in that case the irony consists in the inappropriateness of the adjective to Lucius with his *curiositas improspera* (11, 15: 277, 9). If one bears in mind the animal aspect, as the *praeco* undoubtedly does, the word means 'gentle', 'docile', 'tractable'. Cf. Sulp. Sev. *Dial.* 1, 13, 8 *fera* (= *leo*) *paululum...modesta secessit et constitit* (sporadically this meaning applies to human beings as well: Porph. ad Hor. *S.* 1, 3, 51 *simplices...pro mansuetis et modestis dicuntur*); Col. 6, 37, 1 *(admissarius) amoris saeuitiam labore temperat et sic ueneri modestior adhibetur*. The sexual connotation of this last passage plays a part in our passage too; 'gentle' seems to us the best translation.

Quae res cognitu non ardua. Nam si faciem tuam mediis eius feminibus i⟨m⟩miseris facile periclitaberis, quam grandem tibi demonstret patientiam': "And this is not hard to find out. For if you put your face right between his thighs, you can easily check what a huge...submissiveness he displays.'" 196, 19-21

res: the addition of *est*, inserted over *res* by a different hand in F, is unnecessary.

ardua: it is found followed by a supine from Liv. 8, 16, 8 *quia id arduum factu erat* onward.

si faciem...immiseris: a grotesque position but a necessary one if someone actually were to accept the invitation to observe the ass's *patientia*.

mediis...feminibus: *femina* are mentioned five times in the *Met*; three times they are the object of malicious or equivocal acts concerning the ass. In 7, 23 (172, 1) they are mentioned in connection with an attempt to castration; 202, 15 his *femus* in is danger of being cooked and served for supper; in our passage his *femina* are the target of cinaedic lechery, as we shall see. In the fourth case 10, 24 (256, 13) punishment is inflicted on the *femina* of an innocent girl who is falsely accused of adultery: *titione candenti inter media femina detruso crudelissime necauit (puellam insontem)*. In the fifth case 11, 14 (276, 26), when Lucius has been changed back into a man, his *femina* appear in a context of modesty: *compressis in artum feminibus et superstrictis accurate manibus...uelamento me naturali probe muniueram*.

immiseris: this is the correction made by ς; F has *emiseris*, which Hildebrand admits into the text although he rightly questions its correctness in the commentary. The interchange of *immittere* and *emittere* in the mss. is not unusual; see *ThLL* s.v. *emittere* 500, 40 and s.v. *immittere* 468, 41. *ThLL* mentions two passages where *immittere* is used in an erotic sense: Verg. *Cat.* 9, 34 *immitti expertae* (sc. *Semele et Danae*) *fulmine et imbre Iouem* (but see Westendorp Boerma ad loc.) and Petr. 131, 11 *toto...corpore in amplexus eius immissus*; the same connotation is found here.

periclitaberis: 'to put to the proof', 'try out' as 9, 3 (204, 25) *an iam sim mansuetus, periclitantur*; interestingly enough that passage, too, refers to the ass's gentleness. Cf. also Caes. *Gal.* 2, 8 *quid nostri auderent, periclitabatur* and

Solin. 19, 3 *periclitari fidem uoluit*. With this meaning for the verb, the addition *uidens* (written by a different hand over *quam*) is not necessary.

That *cinaedi* engage in sexual activities with asses may be illustrated from another source. Rostovtzeff 1939, 87 f. published a cup, which he dated to the first half of the third century B.C.; see now, however, *CVA* France 23, Louvre 15 (1968) 8 for description, recent bibliography, and discussion of origin (Thebes) and date (first half of the second century B.C.). The cup shows a scene at a mill, where μυλωθροί with an ass are busy grinding. Important for us is the fact that they appear to be attacked by five men who, according to the inscription, are κίναιδοι and are obviously sexually aroused. One of them is occupying himself with the ass's male organ, which appears to be in a state of sexual excitement as well; another *cinaedus* is standing behind the ass but it is not clear what exactly he is doing. Rostovtzeff (followed by Moritz 1958, 15) assumes that the presence of the *cinaedi* and the burlesque nature of the representation indicate the illustration of a mime. Mimes are known in which *cinaedi* play an important part; see *RE* s.v. *Mimos* 1735 about a mime (probably by Sophron, a contemporary of Euripides) in which a κίναιδος has to appear in court. It seems likely, therefore, that sexual relations between asses and *cinaedi* was a theme known from the mime, and that Apuleius in his portrayal of the Dea Syria priests could count on his readers' knowledge of this.

grandem: Callebat 1968, 406 rightly points out that *grandis* here retains its affective and expressive value in spite of the fact that in the 2nd century it is replacing *magnus*; cf. *GCA* 1977, 38. The hyperbaton of *grandem* provokes the reader's curiosity.

patientiam: the sexual connotation of the words used here and above (l. 13 and 20 f.) becomes increasingly clear; therefore we agree with Blümner 1905, 35, who regards the ending of the sentence in *patientiam* as an ἀπροσδόκητον. Although *patientiam* can be taken in the first place in a 'neutral' sense here, echoing *mansuetudine* of l. 15, one may compare for its sexual connotation Tac. *Ann.* 6, 1, 2 *tuncque primum ignota antea uocabula reperta sunt sellariorum et spintriarum ex foeditate loci ac multiplici patientia*; Petr. 9, 6 (said of Ascyltus) *muliebris patientiae scortum*; Sen. *Nat.* 1, 16, 2 *cum uirum ipse pateretur* (*pathicus*). It is not suggested here, however, that the ass is to play the female part: 197, 23 he is referred to as *maritum*.

196, 22-24 Sic praeco lurchonem tractabat dicacule, sed ille cognito cauillatu similis indignanti: 'at te', inquit, 'cadauer surdum et mutum delirumque praeconem . . . : "So the auctioneer dealt wittily with the glutton. But he, realizing that he was being mocked, said, the very image of indignation: 'You, you deaf and dumb cadaver, you raving auctioneer...''

lurchonem: Paul. Fest. 107 L derives this word as follows: *lura os cullei...unde lurchones*, which Walde-Hofmann 1938, 837 regard as 'blosse Volksetymologie' (*lura* is attested in this passage only). The correct explanation is that of Non. 16L *lurcones dicti sunt a lurchando; lurchare est cum auiditate cibum sumere* (the origin of *lurchare* is uncertain, according to the *ThLL*). *Lurcho*, which Bernhard 1927, 137 calls vulgar, is yet another example of a word that, after occurring in Plaut., Lucil. and Lenaeus (*libertus et comes Pompeii*; see Suet. *Gram.* 15, 2), is not found again before Apuleius, who uses it also *Apol.* 57, 7 (65, 5) *gumiae...et desperati lurconis*.

dicacule: 'wittily'; see 2, 7 (31, 6) *lepida...et dicacula puella*; 3, 13 (61, 22) *sermone dicaculo* with the note of vdPaardt. For the formation of the adverb of a diminutive cf. 4, 8 (81, 4) *timidule* and 4, 31 (99, 12) *pressule*; see LHSz 1, 308 f. See Bernhard 1927, 137 on diminutives in Apul. in general.

It is the narrator who uses the word *dicacule* with hindsight; Lucius the ass would hardly use this qualification, since the witticisms are mainly at his expense.

cauillatu: hapax legomenon. It belongs to the group of nouns in -*tu*- used by Apul. instead of nouns in -(*t*)*io*; see Gargantini 1963, 40.

similis indignanti: the same phrase as in 7, 1 (154, 15) *dolentique atque indignanti similis*. There the phrase is entirely natural, here it is conspicuous by its oddness: one would expect the priest to be genuinely indignant at the *praeco*'s mockery. We may suppose that after the unflattering depiction of the priest at his first appearance (195, 25 f.) the narrator now emphasizes the priest's artificiality and hypocrisy; on the other hand, his feigned indignation certainly plays a part in the negotiations about the price; cf. our comm. on 199, 6 *simulabat*; 199, 10 *conficto mendacio*; and appendix IV 2.9.1 and 2.9.2. Our translation agrees with most of the other translations, e.g. Butler 'made a great show of indignation' and Brandt-Ehlers 'wie in Entrüstung'; Vallette, Schwartz, Scazzoso omit the element 'quasi'. The author may have remembered a comparable expression at Verg. *A.* 8, 649 *illum indignanti similem similemque minanti/aspiceres*, referring to the picture of Porsenna, the cruel enemy of Rome, and borrowed it so as further to emphasize the unsympathetic aspect of the priest.

at te: the imprecation 9, 21 (219, 3) starts in the same way: *at te,...nequissimum et periurum caput...cuncta caeli numina...pessimum pessime perduint*; this is colloquial language; see Bernhard 1927, 126.

cadauer: ThLL s.v. 13, 57 mentions under the heading 'de homine improbissimo per convicium' only a few passages, starting with Cic. *Pis.* 9, 19 *ad hoc eiecto cadauere quicquam mihi...ornamenti expetebam* (for this and other words of abuse directed at Piso, see Opelt 1965, 143). Another instance in the *Met.* is 4, 7 (79, 17) *busti cadauer extremum*; see *GCA* 1977, 64 ad loc.

surdum et mutum: these qualifications seem rather curious after what has been said before; see 197, 1 *caecus* below.

delirum: this is the *cinaedus*' opinion of the *praeco*; the reader, however, realizes that the *praeco* has revealed the truth about the ass (above, lines 18-19) *ut in asini corio modestum hominem inhabitare credas*. It may be an example of Apuleian humor as in the case of the *anicula*, who, after having told the story of Amor and Psyche, is likewise described as *delira* 6, 25 (147, 3); see *GCA* 1981, 24 ad loc.

...omnipotens et omniparens dea[s] Syria et sanctus Sabadius et Bellona et mater ⟨I⟩daea ⟨et⟩ cum suo Adone Venus domina 196, 24-197, 2 caecum reddant, qui scurrilibus iam dudum contra me uelitaris iocis: "...may the all-powerful Dea Syria, mother of all, and the holy Sabadius and Bellona and the Idaean mother and lady Venus with her Adonis make you blind for harassing me all this time with your coarse jokes."

omnipotens: from Ennius onward used as an epithet of Jupiter, later also of Juno and other gods. Apul. uses it here as an epithet of the Dea Syria; he uses it once more 11, 16 (278, 8), this time referring to Isis; see Gwyn Griffiths ad loc. Soon (197, 5) we will see how all-powerful she actually is.

omniparens: the *r* has been corrected from *t* by a different hand in F. The word is found for the first time in Lucr. 2, 706 *per terras omniparentes* (borrowed by Verg. *A.* 6, 595). At *Met.* 6, 10 (135, 24) the word also occurs as an epitheton of *terra*; at 11, 11 (274, 23) it is used for Isis, the only other goddess so described in the *Met*. An adept of Isis would regard it as wrong for the priest to use the epithets *omnipotens* and *omniparens* to describe the Dea Syria; see Appendix IV 2.10.1. Observe the assonance and alliteration of *omnipotens* and *omniparens*.

dea Syria: F has *deásyria&*, with & (developed from an *s*) written by the first hand; the correction is by φ. For more information on the goddess see Appendix III.

Sabadius: for the spelling with *d* cf. Arn. 5, 21 *ipsa nouissime sacra et ritus initiationis ipsius, quibus Sebadiis nomen est* (viz. the followers of Sabadius); *CIL* III 12429 *Sabadio et Mercurio*; and *Gloss*. III 290, 16 Σάβαδιος. This evidence is enough to justify retaining the evidence of the mss. and rejecting the spelling *Sabazius*, although this form is found as well: Cic. *N.D.*3, 58 *Sabazia*; *Leg.* 2, 37; Tert. *Apol.* 22 *Sabazia mysteria*; (*CIL* XIV 4296 *ex imperio Iouis Sabazi uotum fecit*). *Sabazius* is actually the correct form, although the derivation of the Phrygian name is uncertain. *Sabadius* or *Sebadius* originated from an incorrect association with σέβομαι; see Fellmann 1981, 316.

Sabazius is originally a Phrygian-Thracian deity of vegetative fertility, essentially similar to Dionysus. He often fuses with Men, Attis, Helios, Mithras; but in Sabazius' case we never hear of castrated acolytes. In 139 B.C. he is known in Rome from the edict of Cn. Cornelius Hispalus (see Val. Max. 1, 3, 3) against Jewish adherents of Jupiter-Sabazius, who was identified by them with Sebaoth. We know of mysteries in his cult; see the passage from Arn. quoted above. See further Pease on Cic. *N.D.* 3, 58; Kl. Pauly s.v. Sabazios. Observe the angry sigmatism in *Syria et sanctus Sabadius*.

Bellona: the bloody war-goddess, who at the end of the republic was identified with Mâ of Kommana; the latter is a goddess from Asia Minor, who was worshipped with ecstatic rites (see Appendix IV 2.10. 1 and note 24). Bellona is one of the goddesses who are supposed to merge into Isis 11, 5 (269, 24).

mater Idaea: *maté idea* F, apparently corrected by a second hand from *materdea* (Helm and Frassinetti have a somewhat different notation). She, too, is mentioned 11, 5 (269, 20) as a goddess who merges into Isis; see Gwyn Griffiths ad loc. and Appendix IV 2. 10. 1 and note 21.

⟨*et*⟩ *cum suo Adone*: thus ς, adopted by almost all modern editors. Oudendorp, Valpy, and Hildebrand follow F, which does not have *et*.

Kronenberg 1928, 40 supplies *cum ⟨suo Attide et cum⟩ suo Adone*, adopted by Robertson; Petschenig 1881, 50 supplies *ac* which is paleographically attractive. We think, however, that the addition of *et* before *cum* is correct; without *et*, or with *ac*, the priest's otherwise repetitive enumeration *et...et...et* would end either in asyndeton or in variation - neither is very likely. This repetitiveness is used deliberately by the author – the catalogue is absent in the *Onos* – in order to emphasize the contrast with Isis, who, as she claims herself, absorbs all other deities, as we see in the Catalogue at 11, 5, where Isis is rightly called μυριώνυμος (269, 18) and *rerum naturae parens* (269, 12). In his prayer to the *regina caeli* (11, 2) Lucius uses for that reason the characteristic *siue...seu* (267, 4 f). The series of enumerating *et*'s in our passage emphasizes the fact that the deities in question exist *beside* the Dea Syria. See further Appendix IV 2.10.1 and note 27.

Adone: the genealogy and mythology of Adonis indicate an origin in Asia Minor, a characteristic shared by all the deities mentioned here. As a dying vegetation spirit Adonis is the parhedros of the great Syro-Phoenicean fertility goddess Astarte-Venus. Sometimes Astarte is interchanged with Atargatis (identical to the Dea Syria), e.g. Artem. 1, 8, 14; there are also references to her being interchanged with Isis (see *RAC* s.v. Astarte 809). As a deity of death and resurrection Adonis has much in common with Osiris; see *RAC* s.v. Adonis.

Venus: she, too, appears – although without her parhedros – in the catalogue of 11, 5 (269, 21). For the identification of Venus and Isis, see Gwyn Griffiths ad loc.

domina: *ThLL* s.v. 1940, 9 f. gives a list of the goddesses who are called *domina*: Cybele, Diana, Iuno, Proserpina, Isis. Apuleius calls the latter *domina* at 11, 5 (269, 13), 11, 7 (271, 24) and 11, 21 (283, 4). For Venus see e.g. Prop. 3, 3, 31 *Veneris dominae uolucres...columbae* (in an elegiac context). The *auis* calls Venus *domina* at *Met*. 5, 28 (126, 5 'my lady').

caecum: the worshipper of Isis believes that it is Isis who blinds those who anger her, e.g. Iuv. 13, 92 *decernat quodcumque uolet de corpore nostro/Isis et irato feriat mea lumina sistro* (cf. Courtney ad loc.); see Appendix IV 2.10.2. The priest had called the *praeco* deaf and dumb; now he wants him to be blind as well. The combination of *caecus* and *mutus* is also found in Pl. *Mer*. 630 *claudus, caecus, mutus, mancus, debilis*; cf. Opelt 1965, 231 n. 57.

reddant: F has *reddunt*; φ *reddant*. The latter reading appears already in F as a correction by a different hand. Oudendorp's conjecture *redduint* is palaeographically very attractive and is supported by 9, 21 (219, 6) in a comparable context. However, *u* for *a* is common enough (cf. e.g. Helm Praef. *Fl*. xliii) and hence φ's conjecture is acceptable.

qui...uelitaris: the relative clause has a causal connotation; for the use of the indicative in such circumstances, see LHSz 2, 559.

scurrilibus: 'characteristic of a *scurra*'. The etymology of the underlying noun is obscure; it may be Etruscan (Walde Hofmann[3] 1954 q.v.) For adjectives in *-ilis*, see LHSz 1, 350.

uelitaris: Apul. uses this word both literally, with a military meaning (e.g. 7, 16 : 166, 18 with the note of *GCA* 1981, 189 ad loc.), and metaphorically as in this passage and e.g. 5, 11 (112, 3).

197, 2-6 An me putas, inepte, iumento fero posse deam committere, ut turbatum repente diuinum deiciat simulacrum egoque misera cogar crinibus solutis discurrere et deae meae humi iacenti aliquem medicum quaerere?': "Or do you think, fool, that I can commit the goddess to a wild beast of burden, for him, in a sudden panic, to throw the divine image and poor me to have to run about with my hair in a mess and look for a doctor for my goddess as she lies on the ground?' "

iumento fero: the priest has not allowed himself yet to be convinced of the ass's *mansuetudo*; at least, that is the impression he gives. It may well be a trick to lower the price.

deam committere: what this means to the narrator (who is an initiate in the mysteries of Isis), viz. that the image of the goddess is being carried by an ass, the animal most hateful to Isis, is discussed in Appendix IV 2.11. For the motif ὄνος βαστάζων ἄγαλμα compare 198, 17, where the image is actually placed on the ass; see our comm. ad loc.

The priest's indirect accusation, that the ass might throw the image, may be set side by side with the accusation of Lucius' slave 3, 27 (72, 14), that the ass was *nunc etiam simulacris deorum infestus* when he tried to get hold of the wreath of roses worn by the image of the goddess Epona.

misera: thus φ; in F the *a* has been erased, according to Robertson; a* has *miser*, which is accepted in the older editions (Oudendorp, Valpy, Hildebrand, vdVliet, Helm II, Gaselee); the modern editors have *misera*. In view of the erasure in F, *misera* is the better-founded reading. Moreover, the feminine form is supported by 197, 16 *puellae* (the fellow-priests) and *seruum...mercata perduxi*; see our comm. ad loc. The classic example is Catul. 63, where feminine forms are used to describe the castrated Attis, e.g. 63, 8 *niueis citata cepit manibus leue tympanum*; cf. 12, where he addresses his fellow-castrates as *Gallae*. Kroll ad loc. compares Cic. *De Orat*. 2, 277 *quid tu, Egilia mea*, addressed to one Egilius *qui uideretur mollior*; and Verg. *Cat*. 13, 17 *quid palluisti femina*, addressed to an *impudicus*. Catullus does not, however, invariably use feminine forms in this poem; see Quinn on 63, 8. In this inconsistency he is also followed by Apul., who after *puellae* uses the form *rati* 197, 19. This may have contributed to the uncertainty in the tradition.

crinibus solutis: we observed earlier (on 196, 1 *caluum...sed cincinnis semicanis*) that the *cinaedus* tries to camouflage his baldness with long curls. The same motive now leads him to imagine himself with his hair flowing loose. *Crines soluti* are a sign of mourning (the priest will be mourning his fallen idol), e.g. Liv. 26, 9, 7, *matronae...crinibus passis aras uerrentes* and Ov. *Fast*. 6, 441 *flebant demisso crine ministrae*; but this sign of mourning is appropriate only to women (see *RE* s.v. Trauerkleidung 2231, 15 and s.v. Luctus 1699, 39); it certainly fits anyone describable as *misera*.

deae...aliquem medicum quaerere: the surprising suggestion – that the goddess will need a doctor – becomes intelligible when we recognize the constant attempt to point out the contrast between the Dea Syria and Isis: whereas Isis is famous for her powers of healing (see Appendix IV 2.10.2), a doctor will be needed to cure the fallen Dea Syria, apparently because she dwells in her image. Isis, too, dwells in her image (see Gwyn Griffiths on 11, 17:

279, 14 and 11, 24: 286, 10), but how different is the unspeakable joy inspired in the initiate by the contemplation of *her* image; see Appendix IV 2, 13.

These words of her own priest make the Dea Syria ridiculous in the eyes of a devotee of Isis. This is the goddess who was described as *omnipotens* 196, 24! Her priest is once more revealed as a charlaten.

Accepto tali sermone cogitabam subito uelut lymphaticus exilire, 197, 7-9 ut me ferocitate cernens exasperatum emptionem desineret: "Hearing these words, I intended to leap away suddenly like a madman so that, when he saw me wild with fierceness, he would give up the purchase."

cogitabam: the verb *cogitare* is used here in the meaning of *consilium inire* or *uelle* as in 4, 4 (77, 14) with *GCA* 1977, 48 ad loc.

lymphaticus: cf. 4, 25 (94, 1), where it refers to Charite's sudden awakening from her dream; see *GCA* 1977, 186 ad loc. Presently (198, 20) the word will be used of the priests' *tripudium*. Since the word *exsiliunt* (198, 19) is used there too, it seems that the narrator's formulation in this passage anticipates the activities of the ass's future owners; thus, by means of the same word, the ass is made equal to the priests. In his case the notion *lymphaticus* is somewhat weakened by *uelut*: like the priests' ecstatic behaviour later on (e.g. 199, 6 *simulabat*) the ass's is hardly genuine.

emptionem desineret: cf. e.g. 4, 3 (76, 24) *fugam desino* with *GCA* 1977, 43 ad loc. and 4, 24 (93, 18) *fletum desinere*. The construction belongs both to poetic and colloquial language.

Sed praeuenit cogitatum meum emptor anxius pretio depenso 197, 9-14 statim, quod quidem gaudens dominus scilicet taedio mei facile suscepit, septemdecim denarium, et ilico me stomida spartea deligatum tradidit Philebo; hoc enim nomine censebatur iam meus dominus: "But the buyer, in his anxiety, forestalled my plan; right away he paid the price, which my master happily accepted without hesitation because, obviously, he wanted to get rid of me; it was seventeen denarii. He tied a rope of flax around my mouth and immediately handed me over to Philebus; for that was the name of the man who was now to be my master."

Sed praeuenit: Bernhard 1927, 16 calls this 'gedeckte Anfangsstellung' of the verb. *Praeuenire* is found as a transitive verb from Liv. 8, 16, 13 *ut beneficio praeuenirent desiderium plebis* onward. See vGeisau 1916, 92: Waszink 1947, 226; Callebat 1968, 182. Another example in the *Met.* is e.g. 10, 5 (240, 18) *quod mortem praeuenisset puer*.

This passage may be compared to 4, 5 (77, 22) *sed tam bellum consilium meum praeuertit sors deterrima*. In both cases the ass's plan is thwarted: in the earlier passage by *sors deterrima*, in this one by the *emptor* whom *Fortuna saeuissima* had allotted him.

cogitatum: here used in the sense of *consilium* as at 4, 5 (77, 24) with *GCA* 1977, 50 ad loc. Apul. is the first to use it with this meaning; with the meaning 'deliberatio' it is found in Fr. *Str.*, *VL.* and Tert.

anxius: because the word lacks a modifier its meaning is not quite clear. We favour the view of the translators who add something to *anxius*: e.g. Butler ('he was anxious to get me'); Vallette ('soucieux de conclure'); Scazzoso ('ansioso di comperare'). These translations indicate that the priest, eager to own the ass for his own purposes, is worried that the purchase may not take place and therefore wants to complete the transaction quickly. This view is supported by 196, 5 *nimium praestinandi studium* and 196, 16 *anxie* (the priest is worried that the ass's wildness might prevent the purchase).

gaudens dominus: everyone in this pericope is pleased with the transaction: the ass's former owner (because he is rid of him), the new owner, and later the *puellae* (197, 17) and the *iuuenis corpulentus* (198, 1). These feelings of joy are in sharp contrast with the ass's emotions.

scilicet: for the justification of the 'vision du dedans' cf. 198, 25 with our comm.

facile: for the meaning 'without hesitation', 'readily' cf. Tac. *Ag.* 9,2 *facile iusteque agebat*; Fro. *Ar.* 2 p. 58 (238 N = 226, 3 vdH) *illi facile respondent.*

suscepit: for the meaning 'to accept (money)' cf. *Met.* 7, 5 (158, 4) *uirum...libentius uulnera corpore excipientem quam aurum manu suscipientem* and *Dig.* 22, 3, 25 *qui...negauit pecuniam suscepisse.*

septemdecim: in *Onos* 35, 5 the ass sells for thirty drachmae; later (46, 1) for twenty-five, which is not much of a difference. In the *Met.* the ass sells for twenty-four denarii 9, 10 (210, 13); for fifty 9, 31 (226, 25), paid by the *pauperculus hortulanus*, of all people; for only eleven 10, 13 (246, 6). Clearly the *Met.* shows quite a variation in the price (Nethercut 1969, 121, overlooking 10, 13, supposes that Lucius' price increases as he comes closer to the moment when he will change back into a human being). We make two observations in this context. First, Apuleius (as so often) exaggerates quantitatively in respect to the *Onos* (thus vThiel 1971, 12); the misery, too, that the ass has to go through in the *Met.* is much greater than in the *Onos*. Secondly, the price in the *Onos* is the regular price (thus Junghanns 1932, 89 n. 135, relying on Olck *RE* s.v. Esel 644; according to Olck, drachmae equal denarii in this case). The lower price in this passage can be explained by the ass's ferocity (195, 10 f.): his former owner wants to get rid of him at any price. In addition it marks the niggardliness of the *cinaedus*, who is only too happy to buy the ass cheaply. Duncan Jones 1974, 249 compares the price of the ass in the *Met.* with the price of asses in Egypt. His conclusion is that, even with the variations mentioned above, the price in the *Met.* is low; 'no doubt this was done deliberately, for comic or dramatic effect.'

denarium: GCA 1977, 143 gives a list of these genitive forms in the *Met.*

stomida spartea: F has *tumidas partea* (the first *t* written in an erasure which is sufficiently large for *st*); φ *stumidas partea*; *spartea* occurs in ς; Sittl *ALL* 1 (1884) 581 emended *stomida spartea*, accepted by all modern editors except vdVliet (who followed Scaliger's old conjecture *tumicla* ('little rope') *spartea*). Sittl bases himself on Non. 33 L *p⟨r⟩ostomis dicitur ferrum quod ad cohibendam equorum tenaciam naribus uel morsui imponitur, graece*, ἀπὸ τοῦ στομάτος.

Nonius quotes Lucilius (*Sat.* XV) *truleu' pro stomide huic ingens de naribu' pendet.* (511 M = 515 K). There are difficulties: the Nonius tradition has *postomis* in the heading and *postomide* in the quotation from Lucilius. Salmasius emended the heading to read *Stomis* and proposed *pro stomide* for the line from Lucilius. These conjectures are accepted by Marx and Krenkel, but Charpin prints *postomide* (apparently taking it as part of an abl. abs.: 'La muselière ⟨une fois enlevée⟩, un grand seau lui descend des narines'). There seems to be no evidence for στομίς (for the required sense of στομίς see Marx on Lucil. 511) in Latin texts apart from Salmasius' conjecture. Of course it is possible that a technical word is borrowed, but for the defence of Sittl's emendation we must assume in addition, that from the unattested loan word *stomis* the metaplasm *stomida* is formed (see Neue-Wagener 1, 492 f.). The basis of the conjecture, therefore is not very strong. We hesitantly accept it for want of a better proposal. Scaliger's above-mentioned conjecture *tumicla* (to be explained as a diminutive derived from *t(h)omix* ∾ θῶμιγξ), while resting on hardly firmer ground, suffers from the additional weakness that θῶμιγξ seems to refer to cord or string which is hardly appropriate for the present context, see Liddle-Scott s.v.

We have deliberately kept the translation vague because we do not have any further data; cf. Frei-Korsunsky 1969, 64 where *stomida* is translated with 'ein Teil des Zaumzeuges'.

tradidit: since the buyer has fulfilled his duty (*pretio depenso*), the seller now has the obligation to *rem tradere*; see Norden 1912, 169. Cf. 9, 6 (207, 2) *ut exobrutum* (sc. *dolium*) *protinus tradatur emptori*; 9, 32 (226, 30) *ibi uenditoribus tradita merce*.

Philebo: 'the Rev. Love-Boyes' (McLeod), an example of a significant name, which Apul. found in the 'Vorlage' (see *Onos* 36, 1) and without a doubt gladly adopted. *GCA* 1977, 102 gives a list of such names in the *Met*. The name Philebus is not very common: Hijmans *AAGA* 1978, 112 suggests that it may have been chosen to recall the beginning of Plato's dialogue of the same name. We observe that when the narrator – as in this case the narrator in the *Onos* – first introduces a name in the *Met*., he carefully explains how he came to know it; cf. 10, 18 (250, 18) *Thiasus – hoc enim nomine meus nuncupabatur dominus* (see Hijmans *AAGA* 1978, 114).

censebatur: in the meaning '*uocari*' found first in V. Max. 8, 7 ext. 2 *quo cognomine censeretur interrogatus*; frequent in late Latin (see Callebat 1968, 155). Cf. *Met*. 5, 26 (124, 7) *nomen quo tu censeris aiebat*.

iam meus dominus: many examples of *iam* connected with a noun are given by ThLL s.v. 89, 19. For adverbs connected with a noun, in general, see KSt. 1, 218 f.

The narrator has depicted the *praeco* to the life (for the characteristics of the *praeco* see Junghanns 1932, 38 f.). When all the other animals have been sold, he is faced with the problem of how to get rid of the unwanted (195, 6) ass – preferably at a profit. With his hoarse throat (*rauca uoce*) he goes at it professionally, presenting the ass as an old nag and a broken sieve. That does not raise the price, but with his coarse humor he does manage to draw an audience (195, 20). When the bald priest joins the bystanders, the *praeco* spots him immediately as a prospective buyer (196, 5); encouraged by his success with the bystanders, he is now getting under way in poking fun at the *cinaedus*. Asked for the animal's age, he gives a silly answer (196, 8 f.): the *cantherius* of a moment ago (195, 14) has now become a thoroughbred. He fully realizes that the *cinaedus* is intent on buying the ass for a low price, but that is exactly what he wanted in the first place: to get rid of the animal at any price. With great virtuosity he hints at his – and the bystanders' – knowledge of the end to which the *cinaedus* wishes to use the ass; his insinuations become more and more direct (196, 13 f.), culminating in the invitation to the *cinaedus* to put his face between the ass's thighs, with the brilliant ἀπροσδόχητον of *patientiam* (196, 21). With that he has reached his goal: the priest counts out the seventeen denarii at once (197, 11) – not much for an average ass but quite a lot for an unsalable one. The former owner pockets the money without hesitation; the *praeco*, his duty done, has played his part in the story and is heard of no more.

CHAPTER XXVI

Philebus shows his bargain at home.

At ille susceptum nouicium famulum trahebat ad domum statim- 197, 14-17
que illinc de primo limine proclamat: 'puellae, seruum uobis
pulchellum en ecce mercata perduxi': "Now he took his newly acquired
servant and dragged him home. Scarcely has he reached the threshold when he
calls loudly: 'Girls, look here what a darling slave I have brought you from the
market!' "

A sonorous sentence, beautifully constructed. Homoeoteleuton of the first
two verbs; six nouns ending in -*um*; *p*-alliteration; a b b a order of the first two
verbs and the prepositional phrases.

At ille: strongly marks the change of subject: a shift of focalisation.

nouicium famulum: the adjective is appropriate for the newly purchased ass.
Cf. 7, 10 (161, 23) *nouicii latronis* with *GCA* 1981, 146 and 9, 15 (213, 25)
nouicium...asinum.

famulum...seruum: the *praeco*'s joke, namely his ambiguous references to
the ass as if he were a human being (ch.24), is taken over by Philebus. For the
implications of the use of *famulus* and semantically related words in the episode
of the ass's stay with the priests, see our comm. on *mancipium* 196, 13 and
appendix IV 2. 11. In addition to the aspects mentioned there, a sexual
connotation is always present; this appears explicitly from the lines immediately following *mancipium* (196, 13-21) and from 197, 23-26 and 198, 7-10. Cf. in
this connection also 3, 22 (68, 26) *tuumque mancipium* and appendix IV n.
30.

trahebat: the imperfect is rather striking placed as it is between preceding
perfect tense forms (*suscepit* 1. 11, *tradidit* 1. 12) and subsequent present tense
forms (*proclamat* 1. 15, *intollunt* 1. 19, etc.): possibly the imperfect suggests
some passive resistance on the part of the ass. The transition to the present
tense is announced by *statim illinc* ('un "intermédiaire" temporel' in the
terminology of Callebat 1968, 428).

illinc de primo limine: Apuleius likes to use an adverb to reinforce a
prepositional phrase: see our comm. on 188, 3 *ibidem ad sepulchrum*.

puellae: cf. *egoque misera* 197, 4 with our comm. (Butler's translation 'My
children' is of some historic interest. Cf. *Onos* 36, 2: 'ὦ κοράσια, δοῦλον ὑμῖν
ἐώνημαι καλὸν καὶ ἁδρόν'.

pulchellum: a rare word, which occurs once elsewhere in the *Met.* 9, 27 (223,
26) *pulchellum puerum*. The material of the *ThLL* mentions in addition Cic. *de
Orat.* 2, 262; *Att.* 1, 16, 10; *Fam.* 7, 23, 2. The word is always used in an ironical
context; see Hofmann *LU*[3] 1951, 140 and Callebat 1968, 380. Characteristic of

the priests' mincing speech is their frequent use of diminutives: 197, 14-26 (in addition to *pulchellus*) *seruulus* 1. 20 (with 'vision du dedans'), *pullulus* 1. 25, and *palumbulus* 1. 26.

en ecce: this pleonastic combination of interjections is found four more times in the *Met.* (e.g. 1, 1: 1, 12; see Molt ad loc.) rarely elsewhere. Callebat 1968, 90 mentions, in addition to two passages in Seneca (*Oed.* 1004 and *Phoen.* 42, also mentioned by Molt), also [Quint.] *Decl.* 11, 9. It seems probable that this is a case of *sermo cotidianus*; cf. 188, 4 *en* with our comm. Observe its position in the sentence.

mercata: this undoubtedly correct reading of F and φ has been wrongly changed by a second hand in F to *mercat*; (=*mercatus*).

197, 17-20 Sed illae puellae chorus erat cinaedorum, quae statim exultantes in gaudium fracta e⟨t⟩ rauca et effeminata uoce clamores absonos intollunt, rati scilicet uere quempiam hominem seruulum ministerio suo paratum: "But those girls were a chorus of *cinaedi* who immediately shouted with joy and raised discordant cries in cracked, hoarse and effeminate voices, under the impression, of course, that indeed a little human slave had been procured to serve them."

illae; refers back; cf. 6, 27 (149, 16) *illa uirgo captiua*. See Callebat 1968, 279.

illae...chorus erat: the verb agrees with the predicate noun; for this common phenomenon see LHSz 2, 442.

chorus: their out-of-doors task consists of making music (196, 3 *cymbalis et crotalis personantes*) and dancing (198, 19 f. *exsiliunt...lymphaticum tripudium*).

cinaedorum: see our comm. on 195, 25 *cinaedum*.

quae: because of the preceding *puellae* the narrator, too, uses the feminine here for the priests; but from 197, 19 onwards he uses the masculine (see also our comm. on 197, 4 *egoque misera*).

exultantes in gaudium: for consecutive/final *in* (sometimes hard to distinguish) see Callebat 1968, 227 f. ThLL 1950, 17 f. s.v. *exsultare* does not give a parallel of this combination. Cf. 2, 26 (46, 19) *diffusus in gaudium*; 1, 8 (8, 4) *in stuporem attonitus*; 7, 23 (171, 13) *in uenerem...surgere*.

fracta...absonos: the many attributes emphasize how atrocious their voices sound to Lucius. This detail is absent in the *Onos*; the depiction of the priests in the *Met.* reveals a stronger aversion, see Apendix IV 1 f.

fracta e⟨t⟩ rauca: the text is not clear here. According to most editors F has *fractę* (*fracte* according to Robertson and Frassinetti, *fracta* according to Augello 1977, 190) **rauca*; all editors agree that the erasure probably had an *a* before *rauca*; a later hand wrote *rauca* again in the erasure (see Lütjohann 1873, 489). φ has *fractę ạrauca*; the *a* before *rauca* is by a second hand. ς has *fractae rauca* (*fracta et* according to Helm III²); A has *fracte et rauca*. The editors generally opt for *fractae rauca* (thus vdVliet, Giarratano, Terzaghi, Helm III) or for *fracta et rauca* (Helm I, II, and IV; Robertson, Frassinetti, vThiel, and Augello). An objection against the former reading is that it does not account for the *a* which was probably written in the erasure. (The same objection applies to Eyssenhardt's reading, after Cannegieter, *fracta [rauca]* and to Scazzoso's *fracta rauca*.) We prefer the latter reading on paleographical and stylistic grounds. A paleographical argument: according to Helm (Praef. *Fl.* XLI) there seems to have been confusion between *t* and *a* at 3, 4 (55, 9) as well: *persuaderes ea* instead of *persuadere. set*. If Helm's supposition is correct that the 'Vorlage' of F was written in Beneventan script, such confusion is very easy to understand. A stylistic argument is that *fracta et. . .uoce* makes a typically Apuleian syndetic tricolon.

fracta. . .uoce: this is a characteristic of the *effeminatus*; cf. Juv. 2, 11 f. *Hic turpis Cybeles et fracta uoce loquendi/libertas* with Courtney ad loc. It is not clear exactly how this kind of voice is supposed to sound. *RAC* 636 s.v. *effeminatus* gives the following possibilities: 'sie (i.e. the voice) ist hoch und zart oder schlaff und üppig, gebrochen und heiser, auch lispelnd oder zwitschernd'. See also *ThLL* 1252, 26 f. s.v. *frango*. It seems best to translate it literally 'broken', while bearing in mind the other implied connotations 'affected' (referring to the way of speaking) and 'debauched', 'vulgar' (referring to words' contents). The words *rauca* and *effeminata* complement aspects of *fractus*, viz. the sound and the manner of speaking. This phrase does not give a definite answer to the question whether the priests are castrated, but much – particularly their behaviour in ch. 29 – points in that direction.

rauca: used of the voice also 195, 13 *rauca voce* (of the *praeco*). Lütjohann 1873, 489 compares Juv. 6, 511 f. *Ecce furentis/Bellonae matrisque deum chorus intrat et ingens/semiuir. . ./cui rauca cohors, cui tympana cedunt*. The sound of the Phrygian flute, used by priests of the Dea Syria and other gods equated with her (see appendix IV 2. 5), is also described as *raucus*. Cf. 201, 21 *cantus. . .Frygii*; Lucr. 4, 544 *raucum. . .bombum*: Catul. 64, 263 *raucisonos efflabant cornua bombos*.

clamores absonos: cf. 198, 22 (where the priests are performing their ritual) *absonis ululatibus constrepentes*. Their present cries, as they hear the glad tidings, are almost ritualistic.

scilicet: account of the 'vision du dedans'; see our comm. on 189, 25.

hominem seruulum: it is hard to determine if *hominem* is used here adjectively or if this is an asyndeton bimembre. Cf. 3, 29 (73, 24) *rosae uirgines* with vdPaardt 1971, 205 f. ad loc. and 7, 11 (162, 27) *puella uirgo* with *GCA* 1981, 156 ad loc.

ministerio suo: the sexual connotation here remains implicit only.

paratum: a passive translation of this word fits better into the context (unlike Helm-Krenkel : 'ein Mensch, der als Sklave bereit stände') because the *puellae* are reacting to Philebus' words of 1. 16. Cf. 198, 2 *paratus*, where it is certainly passive (for its acceptability as a parallel, see our comm. on 198, 2).

Sed postquam non ceruam pro uirgine, sed asinum pro homine succidaneum uidere, nare detorta magistrum suum uarie cauillantur: non enim seruum, sed maritum illum scilicet perduxisse: "But when they saw not a hind instead of a maiden, but an ass instead of a man

197, 20-24

as a victim, they turned up their noses and mocked their master in various ways: that he had taken him along not as a slave but, of course, as a spouse for himself."

sed: introduces an anticlimax here; cf. 4, 3 (76, 5) with *GCA* 1977, 38.

ceruam pro uirgine: an allusion to the story of Iphigeneia, which is lacking in the *Onos*. In Greek this allusion was proverbial, according to Ach. Tat. 6, 2, 3 (cited by Heine 1962, 310 n. 2) θέαμα... τῆς κατὰ τὴν ἔλαφον ἀντὶ παρθένου παροιμίας and Lib. *Ep.* 1509, 3 (Foerster 534 = Strömberg 55) ἔλαφος ἀντὶ παρθένου (see vThiel 1971, 184 n. 54). This mythological allusion in a most 'realistic' context has a parodying effect; cf. 198, 7 *uenisti* etc. with our comm. ad loc. Heine 1962, 310 correctly speaks of an 'unpassende Überhöhung'. Observe the similarity between our passage and Mart. 3, 91, 11 f. *subpositam quondam fama est pro uirgine ceruam,/at nunc pro ceruo mentula subposita est.* That passage, too, refers to homosexual priests of the Dea Syria and the same allusion is combined with a similar 'realism'.

succidaneum: found in Apul. only here and once in Plautus (*Epid.* 140). From the second century A.D. onward it is more frequent; the material of the *ThLL* comprises (among others) Fest.393 L; Gel. 4, 6, 2-6; Cypr. *Ep.* 2, 2; Fronto 3, 19 vdH.; *Cod.Just.* 5, 34, 10 (written as *succed.*) Its original usage is *(hostia) succidanea*; see Ernout-Meillet and Walde-Hofmann s.v., who derive it from *sub-caedo* and refer to the expression *porca praecidanea* in Cato. Festus, too, knew this original usage: 393 L *succidanea hostia dicebatur, quae secundo loco caedebatur, scilicet sic appellata a succedendo*. Apparently he derives it from *cēdere*. Gellius, however, supports the view of Walde-Hofmann, cf. 4, 6, 6 (cited by Wissowa 1912, 415 n. 7) *aliae...hostiae caedebantur, quae, quia prioribus iam caesis luendi piaculi gratia subdebantur et succidebantur, succidaneae nominatae*. In late Latin the adjective is used exclusively as an equivalent of *succēdens* ('substituted', 'succeeding', e.g. Cypr. *Ep.* 2, 2 *qui uicarios substituit et qui pro se uno plures succidaneos suggerit*; see also Blaise s.v.) in accordance with the derivation from *succedere* mentioned by Festus. It seems quite probable that Apul. has the derivation from *caedo* in mind, both in view of the allusion to Iphigenia's sacrifice and because the ass is a *seruus* – slave and victim – of the perverted priests (see our comm. on *seruus* l. 16 above). But we do not exclude the possibility that the other meaning (= *uicarius* as in Cypr. *Ep.* 2, 2) should be assumed here. If so, we have another instance of Apuleius being the first to use a word in a meaning which becomes more frequent in later, in particular in Christian, authors; cf. e.g. *praesumptio* 199, 18 with our note.

nare detorta: Callebat 1968, 458 speaks of an 'image familiaire'; cf. 7, 9 (160, 24) *contorta et uituperanti nare* with *GCA* 1981, 140.

magistrum: this word can be understood here in two senses, first as the spiritual leader of the priests, and secondly as the 'old hand' who coaches his pupils in erotics. For a similar ambiguity cf. Juv. 2, 114 with Hottentot et al. 1982, 73.

uarie: this is followed by a selection of the priests' remarks; cf. 197, 27 *haec et huius modi mutuo blaterantes*. For a similar procedure cf. 6, 26 (147, 20 f.) with *GCA* 1981, 32.

cauillantur: although their master's joke was effective, the *puellae* show not so much disappointment (which the reader might have expected) as disdain and disapproval (*nare detorta*: 'ugh, an ass'). Nevertheless they pay him back in the same coin, indeed outdo him.

seruum...perduxisse: Bernhard 1927, 53 points out that indirect discourse is less frequent in the *Met.* than direct discourse, which, in fact, is used in the very next sentence. For the function of this variation, see our remarks at the end of this chapter.

seruum...maritum: *seruum* is a repetition of the term used by Philebus in 1. 16. *Maritum*: an unambiguous term instead of the ambiguous *seruus*: 'you said '*seruus*', but now that we see that ass we understand, knowing you, that you meant '*maritus*', of course.' The *puellae* pretend not to have had any ulterior thoughts; instead, they lay them jokingly at their master's door. It is not surprising that Apuleius makes the priests, whom he typifies as *cinaedi*, have sexual associations at the sight of an ass; see our comm. on 195, 24 *emptorem aptissimum duris meis casibus*.

maritus: cf. 7, 22 (170, 22 f.), where the ass is accused of perverted practices: *publicum istum maritum...immo communem omnium adulterum*. For *maritus* referring to animals cf. e.g. Verg. *G.* 3, 125 *quem* (sc. *equum*) *legere ducem et pecori dixere maritum*.

The combination *maritum...perduxisse*, too, may contribute to the ambiguity of the passage and evoke associations with an expression like *uxorem ducere* (*ThLL* 2143, 51 s.v. *ducere* mentions Hier. *Ep.* 49, 17, 5 *maritum ducere*); the verb *perducere* itself can mean 'seduce', as in Hor. *S.* 2, 5, 77 *perduci poterit tam frugi tamque pudica*?

scilicet: used ironically as in 1. 25; see Callebat 1968, 461 and our comm. on 196, 9.

Observe the *s*-alliteration and two tricola: the first tricolon consists of 1. 20-21 *sed...uirgine*, 1. 21-22 *sed...uidere*, 1. 22-23 *nare...cauillantur*; the second of 1. 23 *non...seruum*, *sed...illum*, 1. 24 *scilicet...perduxisse*.

Et 'heus', aiunt, 'caue ne solus exedas tam bellum scilicet pullulum, sed nobis quoque tuis palumbulis nonnunquam inpertias': "And they said: 'Hey, take care that you don't devour such an undoubtedly fine chick all by yourself, but share him sometimes with us, your little doves, too'."
197, 24-26

heus: this word, usually followed by *tu* (except here and e.g. 9, 33 : 228, 11), belongs to colloquial language; see *GCA* 1981, 225 on 7, 22 (170, 25).

exedas: used in the *Met.* only here. *ThLL* does not mention any other example of *exedo* in a comparable context.

bellum: correction of *uellum* by a second hand. The same confusion of *u* and *b* is found 4, 5 (77, 23) and 6, 25 (147, 5; see *GCA* 1981, 26 ad loc.). Although in most cases the diminutive value of *bellus* has weakened and is no longer felt as such, here it is functional, with an ironical connotation, as in 4, 5 (77, 23); 7, 23 (171, 10; see *GCA* 1981, 230 ad loc.) ; 9, 7 (207, 25). See also Callebat 1968, 379.

pullulum: 'young bird', 'chicken'; a rare diminutive. The only other examples mentioned in the *ThLL* material are Plin. *Nat.* 17, 65 (where it means 'young shoot'), *Fro.* 93, 28 vdH *pullulos tuos* (referring to Antoninus' sons), and a few glosses. *Pullus* is attested most often in the same meaning as *pullulus* (cf. Fro. 88, 23 vdH *Pullus noster Antoninus*), but also occurs with the meaning 'foal of a horse or ass' (cf. Var. *R.* 2, 8, 2 *pullum asininum*); finally it can mean 'beloved boy', 'catamite', cf. Fest. 285 L *puer, qui obscene ab aliquo amabatur, eius, a quo amatus esset, pullus dicebatur*. It is very probable that all these meanings of *pullus* are implied in *pullulus* in this passage, in view of the context and the use of πῶλος in *Onos* 36, 4 (cited at 197, 27 below). The meanings of πῶλος are comparable to those of *pullus* (see LS s.v.); for its erotical connotation cf. Eub. 84, 2 πώλους Κύπριδος (referring to prostitutes).

The question whether *pullulus* is a literary word (thus Callebat 1968, 373) or rather belongs to the sermo cotidianus (thus vWees 1972, 782) hardly adds to the understanding of the present passage.

palumbulis: cf. 10, 22 (254, 1), where again it is hypocoristic. According to the material of the *ThLL* the word is not attested before Apuleius. Gargantini 1963, 42 points out Apuleius' preference for words with the suffixes *-ulus* and *-culus* because of their musicality and expressiveness (cf. *pullulus* above). For a comparable combination of pet names cf. Pl. *Cas.* 138 *meus pullus passer, mea columba*.

Two cola with the same number of syllables: l. 24-25 *caue...pullulum* (17) and l. 25-26 *sed...inpertias* (17). Observe the frequent occurrence of the *u*-sound in l. 21-26.

The meaning of l. 24-25 (through *perduxisse*) is opposite to that of l. 22-26: 'we will have none of that ass, keep him for yourself' (l. 24-25) vs. 'please allow us to enjoy him, too' (l. 25-26).

197, 27-198, 1 **Haec et huius modi mutuo blaterantes praesepio me proximum deligant**: "While they were babbling back and forth in this way, they tied me nearby to a manger."

haec et huius modi: *Onos* 36, 4 exploits the association ass/sexuality even more: νυμφίον σαυτῇ (cf. *maritum...sibi*)...ὄναιο δὲ τούτων τῶν καλῶν γάμων καὶ τέκοις ταχέως ἡμῖν πώλους τοιούτους.

mutuo: see our comm. on 187, 11.

blaterantes: in addition to this passage the word occurs three more times in the *Met.*, e.g. 4, 24 (93, 4) *his et his similibus blateratis*; see *GCA* 1977, 179 for the other passages, etymology, and usage. It belongs to colloquial language; see Callebat 1968, 513. *Blaterantes* is here the comment of the experiencing I on the previous remarks of the priests, which Lucius/the ass evidently does not yet take seriously; only after the words of the *iuuenis* (198, 9) will he apply them to himself.

praesepio...deligant: it is impossible to determine whether *praesepium* means here 'stable' or 'manger'. If one chooses 'stable', then *praesepio* is an ablative and *proximum* does not govern any case (ς have *proximo*, probably because the enallage is not recognised); if one prefers 'manger', it is a dative depending either on *deligant* (cf. 7, 18: 168, 12-14 *spinas...caudae meae...de-*

ligauit) or on *proximum* (*OLD* prefers the latter, see s.v. *proximus* 3). For *praesepium* see *GCA* 1981, 170 on 7, 14 (164, 16) and 7, 27 (175, 6).

Erat quidam iuuenis satis corpulentus, choraula doctissimus, conlaticia stipe de mensa paratus, qui foris quidem circumgestantibus deam cornu canens adambulabat, domi uero promiscuis operis partiarius agebat concubinus: "There was a very stout young man, a most accomplished reed pipe player whom they had bought off the auction block with collected alms. Outside, when they carried the goddess around, he walked with them blowing his pipe. But inside he acted as the communal bedfellow, because everyone made use of his services." 198, 1-5

erat quidem iuuenis: the standard way to start a story, with 'Anfangsstellung' of the verb; see Möbitz 1924, 119. Cf. 7, 6 (158, 19) *fuit quidam* with *GCA* 1981, 119 and 177, 5 *erat...iuuenis* with our comm. For *quidam* with the approximate meaning of *aliquis* see *GCA* 1977, 38 on 4, 3 (76, 6) *iuuenis quidam*. Junghanns 1932, 92 observes that individualisation of a general situation is typical of Apuleius, in contrast to the *Onos* (198, 1-10 is not found in the *Onos*). Here the preceding description is concretised by the example of the man who plays the reed pipe. See also our comm. on 189, 26 f. and 190, 28 f.

satis: equal to *ualde*, as in 177, 6 and 196, 6; see Callebat 1968, 541.

corpulentus: often used by the comic poets; see *GCA* 1981, 232 on 7, 23 (171, 14).

choraula: thus F, which has in the margin a reading by the first hand *ceraula*. There is no reason to accept this form (as Robertson 1924, 26 considers – see also his app. crit.), because there are no certain examples of this form of the nominative (see *ThLL* 856, 39 s.v. *ceraules*). The nominative plural *ceraulae* does occur, e.g. *Fl.* 4 (5, 18) *quod monumentarii ceraulae tibicines dicerentur*. The form *choraula* (or *choraules*; see *ThLL* 1017, 10 f. s.v. *choraules*) is used by Apul. also *Soc.* 14 (22, 10 f.) *strepitu cymbalistarum et tympanistarum et choraularum*.[1] The *iuuenis* plays the Phrygian reed pipe (cf. 201, 21 *cantusque Frygii*) called *cornu* 198, 3, *tibia* 198, 19. This instrument which was regarded as typical of the Cybele-cult (but also used in the Bacchus-cult), consisted of two pipes, one straight and one, longer than the other, with a curved end; cf. e.g. Ov. *Met.* 11, 16 *infracto Berecyntia tibia cornu*. For additional passages and further details see Wille 1967, 55 f.

conlaticia stipe...paratus: this is the only occurrence of *conlaticius* ('collected') in Apuleius. *ThLL* s.v. 1557, 31 mentions Sen. *Marc.* 10, 1; *CIL* 10, 411; Tert. *Val.* 12 (191, 19) *ex aere collaticio*, and others. *Stips* means, in addition to

---

[1] The context of this passage, which deals with the mediating function of demons, is most interesting and demonstrates the necessity to keep the person Apuleius strictly separated from the author of the *Met.* There is no evidence in *Soc.* 14 of the distaste for savage, orgiastic rites shown by the narrating I in the *Met.* (see our comm. on ch. 27 and 28); all cult practices are valued equally. Cf. 22, 4 f. *unde etiam religionum diuersis obseruationibus et sacrorum uariis suppliciis fides inpertienda est*; 8 f. *uti Aegyptia numina ferme plangoribus, Graeca plerumque choreis, barbara autem strepitu cymbalistarum et tympanistarum et choraularum (gaudeant)*.

'coin' and 'wages', also 'alms', both a. requested by / given to beggars (cf. *Met.* 1, 6: 5, 15 and 7, 14: 157, 17; Amm. 14, 1, 4) and b. in connection with religion, especially the cult of the Magna Mater (see Bailey on Lucr. 2, 627): cf. Cic. *Leg.* 2, 9, 22 *praeter Idaeae matris famulos eosque iustis diebus ne quis stipem cogito* and Ov. *Pont.* 1, 1, 39 f. (cited by Helm) *ante deum Matrem cornu tibicen adunco / cum canit, exiguae quis stipis aera negat*? See also Bömer on Ov. *Fast.* 4, 350 f. At 2, 12 (35, 4) and 2, 13 (35, 17), *stips* is again used in a more or less religious context (it concerns the fee for the soothsayer Diophanes). The priests of the Dea Syria in the *Met.*, too, receive *stipes* after their 'performance' 200, 2. (For the numerous similarities between the priests of the Magna Mater Cybele and those of the Dea Syria, see Appendix IV 2. 10. 1.) It is typical of the priests' hypocrisy as pictured by the narrator, that the money they receive for their religious acts is used by them not only for their livelihood and for the preservation of the cult but also for their base lusts (see appendix IV 2. 9. 1).

de mensa: *mensa* is here the platform from which slaves are offered for sale – a rare meaning of the word; another example is *Apol.* 17 (21, 11) *duos pueros...de mensa emi*. According to Callebat 1968, 56 it is borrowed from the 'langue courante'. A more customary term for this platform is *catasta*; see *RE* 3, 1786.

foris quidem...domi uero: this antithesis points up the discrepancy in the priests' behaviour, alluded to above (see also Heine 1962, 307 n. 3) The same words were used by the *praeco* 196, 13 *quod te et foris et domi poterit iuuare*. Thus the ass and the *iuuenis* are comparable to each other in two respects: 1. like the *iuuenis*, the ass has been bought at the market (cf. 197, 16 *seruum...mercata perduxi* and 197, 20 where *paratum* corresponds with *de mensa paratus*) and 2. like the *iuuenis*, the ass is expected to be useful both indoors and outdoors. The passage 196, 13 can now be interpreted as an anticipation of the important part played by sexuality in ch. 26 (and in the entire episode of the ass among the priests).

All told, there are four passages in the *Met.* where mention is made of the ass's copulation with a human being: 7, 22 (170, 22 f.) he is falsely accused of it; in our chapter allusions are made to it – first covertly, later (from 198, 1 onward) more openly; 10, 19 f. it actually takes place with the *matrona* and 10, 34 it threatens to take place with the condemned woman. See also *GCA* 1981, 223 on 7, 21 (170, 18).

circumgestantibus deam: cf. 196, 4 *deamque Syriam circumferentes*. Apparently the priests themselves used to carry the image of the goddess before the task was given to the ass. Cybele's image was generally carried around on a cart; cf. Verg. *A.* 6, 784 f. and Ov. *Fast.* 4, 345.

adambulabat: this is a rather rare word, which also occurs 3, 12 (61, 11) and 11, 8 (272, 19), where, as here, it is constructed with the dative, see vdPaardt 1971, 98 ad loc. The only other occurrence is Pl. *Bac.* 768.

promiscuis operis: the final *s* of *promiscuis* has been deleted by a second hand in F; so too in φ and ς. With all modern editors we retain the *s* and take *promiscuis operis* as an ablative with the following *partiarius agebat concubinus*. Admittedly a genitive with *partiarius* is attested Tert. *Marc.* 1, 24, 2 and *Res.* 2,

2 (26, 12), but the word is used in an active sense there, as opposed to our passage. Moreover, there is more reason to link *partiarius* with the following words than with the preceding; see below.

operis: both the singular *opera* and the plural *operae* are customary terms for 'service' in re amatoria; see *ThLL* s.v. 662, 25 f.

partiarius agebat concubinus: this reading of F, altered by a second hand into *partiarios concubitus* (in φ only *concubinus* has been corrected, with *-us* written again over it), is rightly defended by Petschenig 1881, 143, who points out that the intransitive use of *agere* in the meaning 'act as' is not uncommon in the *Met.* (see Helm's app. crit.). An even more persuasive argument is advanced by Norden 1912, 89, who holds the view that *partiarius concubinus* is formed on the analogy of *partiarius colonus* (this opinion is adopted by Summers 1968, 282). In connection with the latter notion Norden cites *Dig.* 19, 2, 25 *partiarius colonus quasi societatis iure et damnum et lucrum cum domino partietur*. See also our comm. on 200, 13 and 201, 27. *Partiarius* is used actively (see quotation *Dig.*) and passively; the latter is the case here (cf. Robertson-Vallette 57 n. 2 and Helm-Krenkel 'in den sie sich teilten'). In the *Met.* it occurs twice more: 4, 30 (98, 9) *Venus...quae cum mortali puella partiario maiestatis honore tractor* and (as an adverb) 9, 27 (223, 27) *cum uxore mea partiario tractabo*. From the material of the *ThLL* it appears that the word is first attested in Cato (*Agr.* 16 and 137) and after that only from the second century onward (apart from Apul. also e.g. Gaius *Inst.* 2, 254 and 257; the Tert. passages mentioned above; *Cod. Iust.* 2, 3, 9 (8); see also Rönsch 136). Callebat 1968, 470 maintains that this is a case of unexpected irony resulting from the use of a legal formula in a non-legal context; this is questionable because *partiarius* is used elsewhere in non-legal connections.

Once again the period is built ingeniously. *Erat quidam iuuenis* (7 syllables) is followed by an anaphoric tricolon with 'wachsende Glieder', the third of which contains as many syllables as the first two together:

satis corpulentus (6).
choraula doctissimus (7)
conlaticia stipe de mensa paratus (13)

(observe the homoeoteleuton and *c*-alliteration). The tricolon is followed by contrasting relative clauses with isocoly. The first relative clause forms a unity with what precedes it by means of the *c*-alliteration; the second relative clause is linked to the first by the homoeoteleuton *promiscuis operis ∾ foris*; observe the *p*-alliteration. In the second relative clause verb and modifier are interchanged in respect to the first clause: *agebat concubinus ∾ canens adambulabat*; by means of the *c* and the ending *-us* a connection is made between the last word of the sentence and the beginning of the period (*satis...paratus*).

Hic me simul domi conspexit, libenter adpositis largiter cibariis gaudens adloquitur: 'uenisti tandem miserrimi laboris uicarius. Sed diu uiuas et dominis placeas et meis defectis iam lateribus consulas': "As soon as he had seen me at home, he eagerly supplied me with 198, 5-9 food in abundance and addressed me joyfully: 'Have you come at last to relieve me in my wretched work. May you live long, please your masters, and bring comfort to my already worn-out loins'."

domi: emphasizes the previous *domi* 1. 4. Blümner 1905, 35 regards it as an insertion, – paleographically defensible but not necessary.

libenter...largiter: Hildebrand and vdVliet take *libenter* with *conspexit*. This possibility should not be excluded, but the connection with *adpositis* is more plausible because 'Nachstellung' of the adverb is usually found with adverbs like *ualde* and *nimis* (see LHSz 2, 410). Médan 1925, 364 wrongly mentions our passage as an example of synonyms in juxtaposition: there is no question of synonyms, nor of juxtaposition (*largiter* also goes, almost adjectivally, with *cibariis*). For the form *largiter* see our comm. on 190, 1. The *l*-alliteration is noteworthy.

adpositis...cibariis: cf. 9, 11 (211, 3) *cibariis abundanter instruxit praesepium*. The *iuuenis* treats the ass well materially. The youth is *corpulentus* and the ass has now to be fattened, too, like the stallions in the rutting-season 7, 16 (166, 11 f.); see *GCA* 1981, 187.

gaudens: used here predicatively; cf. 7, 11 (162, 24) *offerebat hilaris* with *GCA* 1981, 155. The *iuuenis* is glad when he sees the ass (because he is being relieved), unlike the *puellae*, whose initial joy (197, 18) at Philebus' words turned to scorn (*nare detorta*) on seeing the ass; see also our remark on 197, 10 *gaudens*. Nothing more is said about the *iuuenis*; for a moment the spotlight is turned on him, then he disappears into the dark, a customary procedure in the *Met*.

uenisti tandem: these words are rightly compared with the initial words of Anchises at Verg. *A*. 6, 687 f. *uenisti tandem, tuaque exspectata parenti / uicit iter durum pietas*? (see Norden ad loc., Brakman 1906, 348, and Heine 1962, 326 n. 2). vdVliet's reading *uenistine* causes the allusion to Vergil to be lost; moreover, questions which are really exclamations or which express impatience (as here), surprise, or irritation, usually do not have an interrogative particle; see KSt 2, 2, 501 and LHSz 2, 460. The function of the 'quotation' in this passage is twofold: 1. Spoken by the *concubinus* to the ass, the epic words (observe the spondees) sound like a parody and again give expression to the antithesis between appearance and reality of the priests – an antithesis which Apul. uses continually (see below). 2. The context of the Vergil quotation (Anchises speaks to Aeneas in the underworld) seems significant too, if one attributes an important role to the theme of the underworld in the *Met*.[1]

miserrimi laboris: the implications of these words are not yet clear to the experiencing I at the moment they are spoken by the *iuuenis*; the reader, on the other hand, has been prepared by the previous passage 198, 1-5, narrated with 'vision par derrière'.

uicarius: means 1. 'substitute', 'deputy', e.g. Cic. *Ver*. 4, 81 *succedam ego uicarius tuo muneri*; and 2. 'under-slave', i.e. a slave kept by another slave (see *OLD* s.v. 2a), e.g. Pl. *As*. 432; Hor. *S*. 2, 7, 79; Mart. 2, 18, 7; *Dig*. 9, 4, 19. In the

---

[1] Examples of this theme are 1, 15(14, 12 f.); 2, 11 (34, 11 f.); 3, 9 (59, 3 f.); 3, 10 (59, 17 f.). These passages are connected with sinister Thessaly. Further e.g. 6, 15 f. (Psyche in the underworld) and 11, 21 and 23 (the symbolic journey of the underworld at the initiation into the mysteries). See Nethercut 1969 passim.

Met. it occurs once more, as an adjective with the first meaning, 2, 30 (50, 5 f.) *uicariam pro me lanienam sustinuit* (*sustinuit* is a conjecture of Helm). In our passage its meaning is primarily 1., but 2. plays a role as well.

Lucius has fallen low indeed, if the slave of the (in his eyes) repugnant *cinaedi* can address him as *uicarius*.

Sed: the opposition is: 'you have come late, but still you are most welcome.' The ass is addressed here as if he were a human being; cf. 7, 27 (175, 13 f.) with *GCA* 1981, 265.

sed diu...consulas: polysyndetic tricolon with 'Wachsende Glieder' and homoeoteleuton:

sed diu uiuas (5)
et dominis placeas (7)
et meis iam defectis lateribus consulas (14).

From the point of view of content, too, the tricola show a rising line or, if one prefers, a falling one. The solemn phrasing and lofty tone form a strong contrast with the *iuuenis*' intentions, which become apparent especially from his last words.

latera: *ThLL* s.v. 1027, 24 f.: 'h.l. respicitur genitalia uirorum'; cf. 200, 16 f. *rusticanum...industria laterum atque imis uentris bene praeparatum*; Catul. 6, 13 *non tam latera ecfututa pandas*. For *defectis lateribus* see Priap. 26, 11 (sc. *ecfututus*) *defecit latus*.

Haec audiens iam mea⟨s⟩ futuras nouas cogitabam aerumnas: 198, 9-10
"On hearing this, I already envisaged the new ordeals in store for me."

mea⟨s⟩: F reads *mea*; the *s* has been added by a second hand. It seems most plausible to opt for the reading *mea⟨s⟩* and reject the conjecture of Damsté 1928, 15 *mae⟨rens⟩* and that of Helm in his app. crit. ⟨*mente*⟩ *mea*. As Helm points out (Praef. *Fl*. XLVII), *s* before *s* or *f* is often omitted. Finally, the ending *-as* is conspicuous in this (once more carefully composed) passage (1. 8-10), so that *meas* fits in very well. For the plural cf. 195, 24 *duris meis casibus* and see LHSz 2, 178 f. for the preference for the possessive in colloquial language, a usage that increases after Augustus in literary language as well and is very frequent in late Latin.

cogitabam: ingressive imperfect with *iam*. The word underscores the ass's humanness. Observe that the ass does not qualify the *iuuenis*' words with a term like *blaterantes* (197, 27) or *cauillantur* (197, 23). He takes them dead seriously and is getting scared *now* (see above on *blaterantes*). However, what the ass/Lucius fears for himself (and the reader expects) will not happen (cf. the fear of the wolves 190, 8 and our comm. ad loc.). Lucius will, indeed, be a witness to homosexual acts (8, 29) abhorrent to him since they are committed by castrates, whom he detests because of his own fear of castration; for this last point see *GCA* 1981, 238 on 7, 24 (172, 3 f.) and appendix IV n. 4. Schlam 1978, 101, too, points out that the themes of deification of sexuality and fear of castration are developed in the passage concerning the priests. Furthermore, the description of the entire episode is an anticipation of the predominant role of sexuality and deceit in books 9 and 10. Junghanns 1932, 168 n. 83 draws attention to the fact that the first adultery story in book 9 is told even before the priests' ruin (9, 5-7); from this he rightly concludes the connection between the episode of the priests and the adultery stories.

aerumnas: Tatum 1969[a], 45 n. 100 remarks that this word is used more than once to describe Lucius' miseries; cf. 7, 16 (166, 3) *talibus aerumnis edomitum* with *GCA* 1981, 183.

Final remarks (partly applicable to 8, 27-30 and 9, 8-10 as well).

Apul. plays in this chapter a very subtle game with the antithesis of appearance and reality:

1. The *puellae* turn out to be no *puellae* but no true men either. In spite of the 'alteration' and their priesthood they are more than usually interested in sex, hypocritical, and sanctimonious. Their reactions are unpredictable; they go from one extreme to the other. Their bisexuality is expressed grammatically as well (1. 16 f. *puellae...quae*; 1. 19 *rati*).

2. The *seruus* proves to be not a human being but an ass. Nevertheless, people talk jokingly about him as if he were human (197, 23-26) ; seriously, too, he is addressed as a human being (198, 7-9); and after all the ass *is* a transformed human being.

3. It turns out that from now on the expectations that are raised will not be realized.

4. The antithesis is expressed also by means of style and use of words: rhetorical devices, mythological and literary allusions, rare and non-literary words, and legal terms are used in the context of banal and base matters.

CHAPTER XXVII

Gaudily bedizened, the priests set out and give a performance.

Die sequenti uariis coloribus indusiati et deformiter quisque 198,11-16
formati facie caenoso pigmento delita et oculis obunctis grafice
prodeunt, mitellis et cro [cro] cotis et carbasinis et bombycinis
iniecti, quidam tunicas albas, in modum lanciolarum quoquouersum fluente purpura depictas, cingulo subligati, pedes luteis
induti calceis: "The following day they deck themselves out in colourful clothes and they all make themselves hideously pretty: their face they smear with muddy make-up, their eyes they daub like a painter, and so they set out. They are dressed in caps and saffron-coloured, linen, and silk robes. Some are wearing white tunics striped with purple that runs, like lance-points, in all directions and tucked up high with a girdle. On their feet they have golden-yellow shoes."

The motley garb of the priests is described in one long, carefully built sentence (in the *Onos* not a word on the clothes). Observe the parallelism in the construction (five times participium coniunctum, twice ablative absolute), the approximately equal distribution of the syllables over the four cola from *uariis* onward, and the polysyndeton with homoeoteleuton *mitellis...bombycinis* (13 f.). Observe, too, 1. the strong hyperbaton *tunicas...depictas* and *quidam...subligati* and 2. the distribution of the syllables in e.g. the section *quidam...subligati*: *quidam tunicas albas*(7)
     in...depictas(21)
     cingulo subligati(7)

uariis coloribus: metonymic use of *color* is not uncommon; cf. Mart. 5, 23, 1 *Herbarum fueras indutus, Basse, colores* and *ThLL* s.v. 1714, 44 f.

indusiati: this is a rare word which, however, occurs twice more in the *Met.*: 2, 19 (40, 20 f.) *pueri calamistrati, pulchre indusiati* and 10, 30 (261, 9) *pulchre indusiatus adulescens* (in both cases, as here, referring to splendidly arrayed men). *ThLL* s.v. 1273, 25 f. gives as the only additional example Pl. *Epid.* 231 referring to a *tunica* of fashion-crazy women who keep creating new styles. The noun *indusium* is found only in Var. *L.* 5, 131 and Non. 870 L., which state that it is an overtunic, worn indoors by women. This garment early fell into disuse; see Blümner 1911, 231. The *ThLL* remarks on the three passages in the *Met.*: 'idem quod *vestitus*'. In our passage the word certainly has a more or less general meaning, because 1. 13-16 are best interpreted as a detailed description of the garments indicated in 1. 11. But in view of the original usage and the context here (the effeminate priests) it seems that *indusiatus* was chosen deliberately; it is not simply an arbitrary equivalent for *uestitus* or *indutus*. Another reason for choosing *indusiati* may well have been the assonance with *formati*.

deformiter quisque formati: oxymoron; *formare* means 'adorn', 'prettify'. Apul. likes to place two cognate words together; see vdPaardt 1971, 199 on 3, 28 (73, 2 f.) *opulentiae nimiae nimio* and our comm. on 184, 3 *inquieta quieti*.

deformiter: see our comm. on 201, 15. It is possible to regard *deformiter...formati* as an addition to what precedes it, or to connect it with what follows (viz. the make-up). For the meaning of the sentence as a whole it makes little difference; parallelism suggests the first possibility.

pigmento: this word is usually found in the plural; the singular (according to Callebat 1968, 246 probably 'vivant' in the 2nd century) is found e.g. *Apol.* 14 (17, 1) and Tert. *Cult. fem.* 2, 8, 2 *pigmento...muliebri*. White make-up (*creta*) and red make-up (*cerussa, fucus*) were used; see Blümner 1911, 437 and *RE* s.v. *pigmenta* 1232, 60 f. The use of make-up by (effeminate) men was not uncommon, although socially not accepted. See e.g. Petr. 23, 5 (referring to an old *cinaedus*) *profluebant* (var.: *perfluebant*) *per frontem sudantis acaciae riui, et inter rugas malarum tantum erat cretae, ut putares detectum parietem nimbo laborare*. For the use of make-up by the priests of the Dea Syria and Cybele, see *RAC* s.v. *Gallos* 1021. Our passage lacks details as to the colour of the paint (Aug. *Ciu.* 7, 26 says that in Carthage he has seen Galli with white make-up, *facie dealbata*).

oculis obunctis grafice: by this is meant the painting of eyebrows and lashes with a black powder, called *puluis niger* or *calliblepharum*, and made of soot (*fuligo*) or crushed antimony (*stibium*); see *ThLL* s.v. *calliblepharum* 167, 46 f. and Blümner 1911, 437. Cf. e.g. Plin. *Nat.* 33, 102 *plerique platyophthalmon id* (*stibium*) *appellauere, quoniam in calliblepharis mulierum dilatet oculos*; Juv. 6, 0, 20 f. (= Oxford fragment, see Courtney 304) *Haud tamen illi/semper habenda fides: oculos fuligine pascit/distinctus croceis et reticulatus adulter* (said of a *cinaedus*); Tert. *Cult. fem.* 1, 2, 1.

grafice: there is no reason to adopt the spelling *ph* found in ς, as Robertson does; see *GCA* 1981, 57 on 6, 29 (151, 7) *Frixum*. Apul. has this word also 10, 31 (262, 4). *ThLL* s.v. 2197, 1 f. mentions in addition a few Plautus passages (e.g. *Trin.* 767) and Gel. 10, 17 ,2; 14, 4; for this passage it gives the meaning: 'quasi in pictura', subest notio 'eleganter' (2197, 4 f.); cf. *OLD* s.v. 2 'in the manner of a painter'.

The *ThLL* places a comma after *obunctis*, but the colon *oculis obunctis* without a modifier would be out of keeping with this expressive passage.

mitellis: as in chapter 26, the diminutives in this chapter are quite numerous; see our remark on *lanciolarum* l. 15 below. A *mitella* is also worn by Haemus/Tlepolemus in his disguise as a woman; see *GCA* 1981, 133 on 7, 8 (159, 27). *Mitella* (= *mitra*) probably refers here to the Phrygian conical cap, also called *pilleus* (πῖλος). See Serv. on Verg. *A.* 4, 216 *utebantur et Phryges et Lydi mitra, hoc est incuruo pilleo* and *Met.* 11, 8 (272, 17), where at the *anteludia* of the Isis-procession Ganymedes is represented by a monkey: *simiam pilleo textili crocoti[i]sque Frygiis*. The *mitra* is often mentioned as being worn by the acolytes of orgiastic cults; cf. Prop. 4, 7, 62 *mitratisque sonant Lydia plectra choris* (see *RAC* s.v. *Gallos* 1020 f. and *effeminatus* 629 f. for more examples). Lucianus *Syr. D.* 42, too, says of the priests in Hierapolis πῖλον ἐπὶ τῇ κεφαλῇ ἔχουσιν. This remark is confirmed by the iconography of the local priestly garb; see Stucky 1976, 127-140. For the wearing of the *mitra* by priests of Cybele and the Dea Syria, see also Brandenburg 1966, 56 f.

cro[cro]cotis: the correction is by ς. F has *crocroco/tis*, where -*tis* probably is a correction of -*gis*, according to Helm; φ has *crocrocogis*.

A *crocota* is a saffron-coloured garment, worn by women and effeminate men; cf. Cic. *Har.* 44 *P. Clodius a crocota a mitra, a muliebribus soleis purpureisque fasceolis...est factus repente popularis* (Clodius disguised himself as a woman in order to be able to participate in the mysteries of the fertility goddess Bona Dea) and the passage from the *Met.* quoted under *mitella* above (11, 8 : 272, 16 f.) with Gwyn Griffiths 179 ad loc.

carbasinis: neuter plural of a rare adjective, which before *Apul.* is attested only at Caecil. *com.* 138 and Plin. *Nat.* 19, 23; after Apul. it is found at e.g. *Vulg. Esth.* 1, 6 (see *ThLL* s.v. 428, 57 f.).

bombycinis: cf. 10, 31 (261, 28) *tenui pallio bombycino*. The word does not occur very frequently (e.g. Plin. *Nat.* 11, 76; Mart. 14, 24, 1; Ulp. *Dig.* 34, 2, 23, 1). *Bombycina* are silk fabrics, named after the Assyrian purple-snail *bombyx*, and usually of a yellow colour; see Marquardt 1886, 491 f. and Kleine Pauly s.v. Schmetterling 19, 53 f. At first sight it seems attractive to take *carbasinis* and *bombycinis* as adjectives with *crocotis*: 'saffron-coloured robes of linen and silk' (thus Brandt-Ehlers and Helm-Krenkel), the more so as *bombyx* often is yellow; however, *et* before *carbasinis* presents a difficulty for this view. Our translation 'saffron-coloured, linen, and silk robes' is noncommittal as to the fabric of the former garments and the colour of the latter. In l. 11-16 an impressionistic, not a photographic, description is given (cf. also the lack of details about the make-up and the *tunicas albas* 1. 14 f.); by means of the polysyndeton in 13 f. extra emphasis is given to the motley dress of the priests; they are wearing garments of many different types.

in modum lanciolarum quoquouersum fluente purpura depictas: the noun *lanciola* (usualled spelled *lanceola*) is first found in Apuleius; see *ThLL* s.v. 918, 71 f. Remarkably frequent in this chapter are words formed with the suffix -*ulo* and -*culo*. In addition to the diminutives *lanciolarum* and 1. 20 *casulis* there are *cingulo* (1. 16), *amiculo* (1. 17), *pendulos* and *circulum* (199, 1) and *musculos* (199, 2), words which are not diminutives or are no longer regarded as such. It seems evident that the suffix has an expressive value here. For diminutives in general see Abate 1978, passim and *GCA* 1981, 102. The *ThLL* gives no comparable example for this metaphor with *lanciola*. It is clear that this passage refers to purple stripes, but it is hard to determine exactly what they look like.[1]

---

[1] The priests are wearing white tunics with purple stripes. With what technique these stripes have been applied, and what exactly they look like, does not become clear from this description, nor is there any adequate material for comparison available from other texts.

Depingere can mean 'paint', 'decorate', and 'embroider'. The translators do not agree. Krenkel opts for 'paint', Vallette for 'decorate', whereas *ThLL* s.v. 573, 50 f. explains our

Be this as it may, Apuleius describes in a most original and picturesque way red and white striped tunics (see also our comm. on *bombycinis* above). Colourful (yellow and red) robes as worn here by the priests of the Dea Syria are also typical of the priests of the Magna Mater (for the resemblances of the cults see *Met.* 9, 10 with our forthcoming comm.). The fact that striped robes are nowhere mentioned explicitly in connection with the above-mentioned cults does not seem important (see also our remark after 199, 4 *dissicant* below. At any rate, there is a great contrast between the multi-coloured garments here and the white linen tunics of the worshippers of Isis (see appendix IV 2, 6. and Gwyn Griffiths 192 on 11, 10: 273, 19 *lintea uestis*), a contrast which is possibly emphasised by the use of *albas* in this connection.

tunicas...cingulo subligati: compare this construction with the 'middle' participle (likewise 1. 16 *pedes...induti calceis*) with 9, 20 (218, 6) *tunicas...iniectus* and 6, 30 (152, 13) *induta laqueum* (with *GCA* 1981, 67 ad loc.). For the instrumental ablative cf. Verg. *A.* 1, 228 *lacrimis oculos suffusa*.

luteis calceis: the shoes, too, have the effeminate colour yellow (cf. *crocotis* above). Cf. 11, 8 (272, 7 f.) *soccis obauratis inductus...feminam mentiebatur* and Catul. 61, 9 f. *niueo gerens/luteum pede soccum* (sc. Hymenaeus, to whom a feminine appearance was ascribed). For women's shoes see *GCA* 1981, 133 on 7, 8 (159, 27 f.) *calceis femininis albis...indutus*.

induti: it is not necessary to adopt the reading of φ *inducti* (Robertson: 'fortasse recte', following Oudendorp). Both F and φ have *indutus* at 7, 8 (160, 1); see *GCA* 1981, 134 ad loc. *Inductus* occurs three times in the *Met.* (2, 28: 48, 9; 9, 21: 218, 14; 11, 8: 272, 8), which is too infrequent to draw a conclusion as to Apuleius' preference for either word. Asyndeton between participles (*subligati, induti*) is characteristic of Apul.; see vdPaardt 1971, 44. Though the make-up and women's clothes mentioned 1. 11-16 are in keeping with the effeminate

passage by 'acu pingere'. Assuming, for the present, that the description of the garments corresponds with reality, it is unlikely that the stripes were applied to the fabric with paint, because this technique was not much used in antiquity (see Bieber 1934, 13 and Forbes 1956, 137 and 207). Stripes and patterns were usually woven into the fabric by the Greeks, which accounts for the soft drape of the Greek garments. The patterns on Roman clothes, on the other hand, were usually embroidered or sewn on, which makes the Roman garments fall stiffly and heavily (see Bieber 1934, 40). The priests here are wearing softly draped garments, cf. *fluente purpura* (for *fluere* referring to clothes cf. Verg. *A.* 1, 320 (*uenatrix*) *nodoque sinus collecta fluentes*; see *ThLL* s.v. *fluere* 971, 4 f.); for that reason the stripes are probably woven in. Compare with our passage 10, 20 (252, 8 f.) *stragula ueste auro ac murice Tyrio depicta*, which is probably another case of a woven-in pattern (gold-thread was usually woven in; see Marquardt 1886, 536; but according to *ThLL* s.v. *depingere* 573, 50 f. the verb means 'embroider' there.

For striped garments Oudendorp compares X. *Cyr.* 8, 3, 16 ῥαβδωτοῖς ἱματίοις καταπεπταμένοι and Verg. *A.* 8, 660 *uirgatis...sagulis* (said of the Gauls). See also Ov. *Ars* 3, 269 *pallida* (sc. *femina*) *purpureis tangat sua corpora uirgis* and Sil. 4, 155 *auro uirgatae uestes*. Oudendorp maintains that these stripes were woven; see his comm. on *Fl.* 9 (12, 8 f.) *tunicam interulam tenuissimo textu, triplici licio, purpura duplici*. Servius' remark on Verg. *A.* 8, 660 points in the same direction: *quae habebant in uirgarum modum deductas uias*. According to Oudendorp and Hildebrand (who follow Beroaldus) *in modum lanciolarum* means here the same as *uirgatus*; see Oudendorp ad loc.: 'Cape χιτῶνας ῥαβδωτούς'.

Certainty about this question cannot be obtained, however. Therefore allowance must be made for the possibility that the garments do no exactly correspond with reality.

ways of the priests (see ch. 26), their main purpose is to exploit the public's craving for sensation and trick them out of their money (see 220, 2 f.).

Deamque serico contectam amiculo mihi gerendam imponunt bracchiisque suis umero tenus renudatis, adtollentes immanes gladios ac secures, euantes exsiliunt incitante tibiae cantu lymphaticum tripudium: "They put the goddess, wrapped in a silk cloak, on my back to carry. They leap up, their arms bare to the shoulder, lifting immense swords and axes, with the cry 'Euan', while the tones of the pipe incite a frenzied dance." 198, 16-20

serico...amiculo: the image is wrapped in a precious cloak; Chinese silk was regarded as a luxury item, more precious than *bombyx*. See Blümner 1911, 245 and *RE* 678, 19 f. s.v. *bombyx*; see also our comm. on 198, 14 *bombycinis* above.

mihi gerendam imponunt: whereas from 195, 6 onward much attention was paid to the narrator's experiences, in ch. 27-29 the 'I' appears mainly as witness. The role of the ass is most important, however: he is carrying the image of the goddess (that was the reason for his being bought). In Appendix IV, 2. 11 it is shown how unworthy the ass's *seruitium* is of an adept of Isis (see also our comm. on 197, 14). After his initiation Lucius will fulfill a worthier *seruitium* as a member of the college of *pastophori*, who have among their tasks the carrying of images and other sacred objects (cf. 11, 17: 279, 18 with Gwyn Griffiths ad loc.). The notion of an ass carrying the image of a god (and the baggage of the faithful) has a long tradition and is perhaps proverbial, according to the Scholiast on Ar. *Ra*. 159 ἐγὼ γοῦν ὄνος ἄγω μυστήρια; See also van Leeuwen and Radermacher ad loc. In the fable, too, it is a well-known theme; cf. Babrios 141 and 163, and Phaed. 4, 1 (= Aesop. 290 H.). The last fable reads, from vs. 4 onward: *Galli Cybebes circum in quaestus ducere/asinum solebant baiulantem sarcinas./Is cum labore et plagis esset mortuus,/detracta pelle sibi fecerunt tympana./Rogati mox a quodam, delicio suo/quidnam fecissent, hoc locuti sunt modo:/'putabat se post mortem securum fore;/ecce aliae plagae congeruntur mortuo'*. See further Weinreich 1931, 39 f. and Mason in *AAGA* 1978, 10.

renudatis: for *renudare* see our comm. on 201, 10.

adtollentes immanes gladios ac secures: for the function of the weapons see our comm. on 199, 3 f. Cf. Lucr. 2, 621 *telaque praeportant uiolenti signa furoris*. They are *immanes* in the eyes of the narrator: he is afraid; cf. 199, 20 f. (in other passages referring to self-mutilation by *Galli*, no mention is made of the size of the weapons; see e.g. V. Fl. 3, 231 f.; Mart. 11, 84, 3; Lucianus *Syr. D.* 51; Claud. *rapt. Pros.* 2, 270).

euantes: this is the reading of φ; F has **leuantes*, where **l* seems to be a correction of *h* by a second hand, according to Robertson; AU have *euhantes*. Therefore it is quite probably that *euantes* is the correct reading. The lectio facilior *leuantes* (adopted by Bernhard 1927, 148) can be explained by the preceding synonym *adtollentes*. *Euans* is found almost exclusively in poetry. Originally it is a term from the cult of Bacchus, but it is already used by Catul. 64, 391 and Verg. *A.* 6, 517 for worshippers of Cybele; see also our comm. on 199, 4 *bacchatur*.

tibiae cantu: see our comm. on 198, 2 *ceraula* (or *choraula*) and Kleine Pauly s.v. Tibia 818, 40 f. Cf. Catul. 64, 264 *barbaraque horribili stridebat tibia cantu*.

lymphaticum: cf. 197, 7 *uelut lymphaticus* with our comm. For the function of the motif of madness in the *Met.*, see Heine 1962, 243 f.

tripudium: 'dance'. From Catullus onward the word is found in a broader meaning than its original one ('three-step', referring in particular to the war-dance of the Salii); it can be used in connection with orgiastic dances, as it is here and e.g. Catul. 63, 26 *Quo nos decet citatis celerare tripudiis* and Ov. *Fast.* 6, 330 *et uiridem celeri ter pede pulsat humum*. See *RE* s.v. *tripudium* 233, 47 f.

198, 20-199, 4 Nec paucis pererratis casulis ad quandam uillam possessoris beati perueniunt et ab ingressu primo statim absonis ululatibus constrepentes fanatice prouolant diuque capite demisso ceruices lubricis intorquentibus motibus crinesque pendulos in circulum rotantes et nonnunquam morsibus suos incursantes musculos ad postremun ancipiti ferro, quod gerebant, sua quisque brachia dissicant: "After calling at several cottages in their wanderings, they arrive at the estate of a wealthy landowner. Scarcely have they set foot on it when they rush frantically forward, letting out discordant shrieks. For a long time, with heads bent, they turn their necks with smooth movements, they swing their hanging hair in circles, and from time to time they ram their teeth into their own flesh. Finally all of them slash at their own arms with the two-edged weapons they carried."

casulis: see *GCA* 1981, 214 on 7, 20 (169, 22); see also our comm. on *lanciolarum* 1. 15 above.

ad quandam uillam: *uilla* has here the broad meaning 'estate' (including the mansion), possibly 'village' as at 190, 10 (see our comm. ad loc.). At any rate we haven here a large, prosperous settlement with many inhabitants; cf. 200, 2 f.

ingressu: here is meant the entry into the settlement, not into the house in a narrower sense.

absonis: see our comm. on 197, 19.

ululatibus: cf. Catul. 63, 24 *ubi sacra sancta acutis ululatibus agitant* and Luc. 1, 567 *populis ululariunt tristia Galli*. In sharp contrast to this music stands the music at the Isis-procession 11, 9 (273, 8 f.) *fistulae tibiaeque modulis dulcissimis personabant...sequebatur chorus, carmen uenustum iterantes*; see also appendix IV 2. 5.

constrepentes: attested for the first time in Apul.; see *GCA* 1977, 196 on 4, 26 (95, 5).

fanatice: the adverb is found in this passage only. The adjective *fanaticus* is used especially in connection with followers of Oriental religions (see *ThLL* s.v. 270, 28 f.), e.g. Liv. 37, 9, 9 *fanatici Galli*; Quint. *Inst.* 11, 3, 71 *iactare id (caput) et comas excutientem rotare, fanaticum est*; Juv. 2, 112 and 4, 123 f.

prouolant: correction by Scriverius, adopted by vdVliet and most modern editors (e.g. Giarratano, Robertson, Helm-Krenkel, Frassinetti, vThiel). F. has *puolant (*p is the correction by a second hand of *po). Helm III, following Eyssenhardt, has *peruolant*; this reading is defended by Augello 1971, 191. φ has *pŭolant*; the correction is by the same hand. A has *perouolant*. We agree with Robertson 1924, 95, who thinks that the original reading of F supports Scriverius' proposal. *Prouolant* seems more appropriate to the context than *peruolant*: the priests are giving a performance; *peruolare* would be less effective in achieving their object, which is to be seen by everybody.

ceruices lubricis intorquentes motibus: *lubricus* has a sensuous connotation; cf. 2, 7 (30, 22) *membra sua leniter inlubricans* and 2, 17 (39, 6) *lubricis gestibus* (both times of Fotis). Limberness was an important characteristic of *cinaedi*; see our comm. on 195, 25 and e.g. Aug. *Ciu.* 7, 26 *qui* (sc. *molles*) *usque in hesternum diem madidis capillis facie dealbata, fluentibus membris incessu femineo per plateas uicosque Carthaginis etiam a propolis unde turpiter uiuerent exigebant* (compare 196, 2 f. *qui per plateas et oppida...personantes deamque Syriam circumferentes mendicare compellunt*).

crines pendulos: cf. 196, 1 f.

in circulum rotantes: cf. Var. *Men.* 132 *tibi nunc semiuiri/teretem comam uolantem iactant*; Luc. 1, 566 f. *crinemque rotantes/sanguineum...Galli;* Quint. *Inst.* 11, 3, 71 (cited above on *fanatice*). Observe in this sentence the *c*-alliteration, followed by *m*-alliteration.

morsibus suos incursantes musculos: for *incursare* cf. 7, 17 (167, 9) with *GCA* 1981, 194; also Pl. *Rud.* 722 (*te*) *pendentem incursabo pugnis*. Although there are frequent examples in Latin literature of self-mutilation by Galli, there does not seem to exist any parallel for the form of behaviour described here (*ThLL* s.v. *morsus* 1508, 77 f. mentions Calp. *Ecl.* 1, 48 (*Bellona*) *in sua uesanos torquebit uiscera morsus*). See further the remark after 199, 4 *dissicant*.

ad postremum: corresponds with 198, 21 *ab ingressu primo* and refers to the moment when, as a consequence of the rousing music and dance, the ecstasy has reached its climax.

sua quisque brachia dissicant: *dissicare* is a strong term; the narrator exaggerates, influenced by his low opinion of the priests. *Onos* 37, 2 has it slightly differently: τοῖς ξίφεσιν ἐτέμνοντο τοὺς πήχεις, καὶ τὴν γλῶτταν τῶν ὀδόντων ὑπερβάλλων ἕκαστος ἔτεμνεν καὶ ταύτην. So Apuleius adds some details to the story and omits others. Cf. also Lucianus *Syr. D.* 50 (referring to Galli in Hierapolis) Γάλλοι τέμνονταί τε τοὺς πήχεας; V. Fl. 3, 233 *tunc ensis placeatque furor, modo tela sacerdos/porrigat, et iussa sanguis exuberet ulna*; Sen. *Vit. B.* 26, 8 *cum aliquis secandi lacertos suos artifex brachia atque umeros suspensa manu cruentat*; Mart. 11, 84, 3; Tert. *Apol.* 25, 5. See further our comm. on 199, 14 f. and appendix V.

The numerous quotations and other references in the commentary on this chapter show that Apuleius' description of appearance and behaviour of the priests substantially agrees with the many other descriptions of *cinaedi* and Galli both in poetry (e.g. Lucr. 2, 614-628; Catul. 63; Phaed. 4, 1; Luc. 1, 565 f.; Juv. 2, 111 f.) and in prose (e.g. Lucianus *Syr. D.* 50 f.; Tert. *Apol.* 25,5; Aug. *Ciu.* 7, 26). This remark applies to ch. 28 as well.

In summary the points of agreement are these; the colourful, feminine dress and make-up; the ass with the image of the goddess; the weapons and the self-mutilation; the wild music, the screaming, and the frenzied dancing with specific movements of neck and hair. Some detail in Apuleius' description are not found elsewhere (the striped robes 198, 14 f. and the biting 199, 2), but these (as far as the colourful dress and the self-mutilation are concerned) are variations on, not deviations from, the general image. These descriptive and apparently original details together with such devices as rare words and forms (e.g. *indusiatus, carbasinus, lanciola, fanatice*) and sound-effects (e.g. expressive word-endings and rhyme), contribute to the poetic expressivity of the passage. Apuleius seizes the opportunity to give his own version of a favourite subject.

199, 4-8 Inter haec unus ex illis ba⟨c⟩chatur effusius ac de imis praecordiis anhelitus crebros referens uelut numini⟨s⟩ diuino spiritu repletus simulabat sauciam uecordiam, prorsus quasi deum praesentia soleant homines non sui f⟨i⟩eri meliores, sed debiles effici uel aegroti: "Meanwhile one of them is carrying on like a Bacchante even more excessively. Repeatedly heaving deep sighs from his chest as if he were filled with the heavenly inspiration of a deity, he pretended to be stricken with madness – as if the presence of the gods does not usually raise people above themselves, but makes them weak and ill".

unus ex illis: as at 198, 1 f., Apuleius specifies here. This *unus* is not mentioned in the *Onos*.

ba⟨c⟩chatur: the correction is by ς; a spelling with *-ch-* does not occur. Cf. Verg. *A*. 6, 78 *bacchatur uates* (sc. the Sibyl) and Sil. 17, 20 f. *semiuirique chori.../...qui Dictaeo bacchantur in antro*.

effusius: this word puts extra emphasis on the immoderation of the priests; the others exaggerate, but this person goes even beyond that. The narrator makes a critical comment (f. 198, 22 *absonis*).

de imis praecordiis: Médan 1925, 65 observes that *de* is used here instead of *ex*, as it is e.g. 5, 15 (115, 12) and 9, 7 (207, 19). *De* replaces *ex* in late Latin; see LHSz 2, 262 f. and *GCA* 1977, 201 on 4, 27 (95, 18).

anhelitus crebros referens: compare this description of 'prophetic' transports with that at 11, 16 (278, 4 f.) *sacerdos egregius fatigatos anhelitus trahens* (see Gwyn Griffiths ad loc.). The use of similar words in a totally different context supports our view (see appendix IV 2. 9. 1) that the cult of the Dea Syria and that of Isis are each others counterpart in the *Met*. The literary prototype of the raving priests in the eighth and eleventh books is Verg. *A*. 6, 48 f. *sed pectus anhelum/et rabie fera corda tument*; see also on *bacchatur* above. Other imitations of Vergil can be found in Luc. 5, 128 f. and Sen. *Ag*. 710 f.; see Norden on *A*. 6, 45 f.

uelut...repletus: for *uelut* with a participle, see KSt 2, 1, 790 f. and LHSz 2, 385.

numini⟨s⟩ diuino spiritu repletus: it is least drastic to accept *numini⟨s⟩*, a correction by ς of *numini* (F and φ). Oudendorp proposes *nimium*, about which Robertson in his app. crit. remarks 'fortasse recte'. It is no objection that *numinis*, in combination with *diuino spiritu* is pleonastic. For similar combinations cf. 9, 14 (213, 19 *diuinis numinibus* and 11, 1 (266, 17 f.) *diuino...numinisque nutu*. Moreover, by this terminology extra emphasis is given to the pretense of the priest that he is inspired by the 'true deity'. Cf. also Liv. 5, 15, 10 *diuino spiritu instinctus* and Verg. *A*. 6, 50 *adflata est numine*.

spiritu: for the different contexts in which this word occurs in the *Met.*, see *GCA* 1977, 158 on 4, 21 (90, 14). Compare with our passage 11, 28 (290, 3) *spiritu fauentis Euentus*. By *numinis diuino spiritu repletus* the narrator means 'the true inspiration, bestowed by the true deity'. The priest does not have this (*uelut*). See also the comment of another 'unbeliever'; Firm. *Err*. 4, 2 *deinde cum sic se alienos a uiris fecerint, adimpleti tibiarum cantu uocant deam suam, ut nefario repleti spiritu uanis hominibus quasi futura praedicant*.

simulabat: according to Heine 1962, 309 it is improbable that the priests would go so far as to mutilate themselves for the sole purpose of satisfying the mob's desire for sensation and their own greed. Thus, conscious play-acting cannot be an explanation for their ecstasy, and divine inspiration is explicitly dismissed by the narrator. Heine then draws the conclusion *ex silentio* that they are possessed by an evil power (cf. Firm. *nefario repleti spiritu* above); this madness is like a 'befremdlich sich verselbständigende Maske', which changes its wearer to such a degree that he is temporarily a different person, who can no longer distinguish between play-acting and reality. We think, however, that the narrator does interpret the behaviour of the priest(s) as conscious play-acting in view of formulations like *uelut, simulare, prorsus quasi*. Compare for this simulated, artificially evoked ecstasy Iamb. *Myst*. 3, 9, 118, where he says of the excitement, caused by music, of worshippers of Sabazios and Cybele φυσικά τε γάρ ἐστι καὶ ἀνθρώπινα καὶ τέχνης ἡμετέρας ἔργα · τὸ δὲ θεῖον ἐν αὐτοῖς οὐδ' ὁπωστιοῦν διαφαίνεται. Cf. also Flor. *Epit*. 2, 7, 4(3, 19) *Syrus quidam...fanatico furore simulato dum Syriae deae comas iactat*.

sauciam uecordiam: observe the attributive position of *saucius* with *uecordia*, for which the material of the *ThLL* offers no parallels. It seems to be some sort of enallage for *saucius uecordia*. *Saucius* in the sense of 'stricken with some deep emotion' (cf. *OLD* s.v. 5) is quite common; cf. 4, 32 (100, 12) (*Psyche*) *aegra corporis, animi saucia*; 5, 23 (121, 9) (*Psyche*) *saucia mente*; Enn. *scen*. 254 *Medea animo aegro amore saeuo saucia*; in these passages the emotion is always love. Compare with our passage Sen. *Her. O*. 701 *Baccho saucia Maenas* (var.: *Thyas*). Oudendorp remarks: '*sauciam* est a deo contacta' and translates (correctly, in our opinion): 'fingebat se correptum insania'. It appears, indeed from the narrator's presentation that the divine inspiration is regarded by the priest as something that taints and sickens the mind; cf. 199, 8 *debiles...uel aegroti*. Oudendorp cites for this (traditional) interpretation Luc. 5, 118 f. *stimulo fluctuque furoris/compages humana labat, pulsusque deorum/concutiunt fragiles animas*; cf. also 169 f. *Bacchatur* (sc. *uates*) *demens aliena per antrum/colla ferens*. Ch. 28 will elaborate on how this madness manifests itself.

prorsus quasi: cf. 196, 18 *prorsus ut* with our comm., and 9, 9(209, 18 f.) *prorsus quasi*. For *prorsus* see *GCA* 1981, 115 on 158, 9 f. *Quasi* with a subjunctive is ironical: the comparison is presented as a supposition; see KSt 2,

2, 453. The narrator gives his own interpretation of the event: the priests must have thought that carrying on like a Bacchante was proof of divine inspiration.

deum praesentia: means the same as *numinis diuino spiritu repletus*. Clearly Lucius the priest of Isis is speaking here (with 'vision par derrière'). Therefore we may interpret the words *prorsus quasi. . .aegroti* here as describing the true inspiration bestowed by Isis (for the plural *deum* in connection with Isis, see Appendix IV, 2, 10, 1). Vallette incorrectly identifies the narrator here with Apuleius himself (thus ignoring the distiction between author, implied author and narrator), see his remark p. 58 f. n. 1 'ce mot (*aegroti*), caractéristique d'une notion épurée de la religion, doit être d'Apulée lui-même'. See in this connection also our remark on *choraula* 198, 2.

sui f⟨i⟩eri meliores: *fieri* is a correction of *feri* by a second hand in F. For the genitive of comparison cf. 3, 11 (60, 20) *dignioribus meique maioribus* with vdPaardt 1971, 91 f. ad loc. and 9, 38 (232, 8) *sui molliorem*. Observe the repetition of the *s*-sound.

sed debiles effici uel aegroti: *aegrotus* originates from the 'langue familiaire'; see Callebat 1968, 170 for other examples. These words correspond with *sauciam uecordiam*; they indicate the result of a false religion, in contrast to the beneficial influence of the true religion. Cf. in this connection also the description of the facial expression of the prohesying priest of Isis 11, 14 (277, 2 f.) *sacerdos uultu geniali et hercules inhumano*. Penwill 1975, 64 f. points out 11, 15 (277, 5 f.) and 11, 25 (286, 20 f.), where the spiritual healing granted by Isis is symbolised by the image of the calming down of a storm: *tu. . .humani generis sospitatrix* and *depulsis uitae procellis salutarem porrigas dexteram*. For the power of physical healing ascribed to Isis see Appendix IV 2. 12. 1.

CHAPTER XXVIII

The self-mutilation, abhorrent to the ass, produces the effect desired by the priests.

Specta denique, quale caelesti prouidentia meritum reportauerit: 199, 9-10
"Now see what sort of reward he got through divine providence."

specta: the narrator makes direct contact with his audience; cf. 195, 25 *scitote* with our comm.; *tu...dixeris* 4, 6 (79, 8) with *GCA* 1977, 61; and 7, 13 (163, 24) with *GCA* 1981, 164 f.

denique: here transitional. vdPaardt 1971, 42 f. discusses the meanings of *denique* in the *Met*.

quale caelesti prouidentia meritum reportauerit: although there is a marked increase in the use of *de* in late Latin (see our comm. on 199, 5 *de imis praecordiis* and LHSz 2, 126 on *de* with the instrumental and causal ablative), yet the suggestion made by vdVliet (⟨*de*⟩ *caelesti*) has – rightly – not been followed.

caelesti prouidentia: *caelestis prouidentia*, also *diuina* or *deum prouidentia*, is in the eyes of the narrator identical with fickle Fortune. See e.g. 202, 12 with our comm. and 9, 1 (203, 14) with our comm.

meritum: 'gift of the gods' (see *ThLL* s.v. *mereo* 815, 12 f.), 'reward'. It appears from what follows that this refers to the self-mutilation, called *iustas poenas* by the priest l. 12 f. The linear reader will regard *quale...reportauerit* as the view of Lucius the ass, who has an intuitive aversion to the homosexual priests and their religious practises (see Appendix IV 3 and note 46). In that case *meritum* is used ironically: 'a fine reward', a punishment in the opinion of the narrator. The underlying thought is: 'if an artificially evoked ecstasy leads to bloodshed, and if that has to pass for the reward (*meritum*) for and the proof of being dedicated to the god, I must decline it with thanks'. With this interpretation it is incorrect to take *meritum* as the priest's 'deserts' for his behaviour, so repulsive to the narrator; from this point onward the narrator shows only revulsion and fear (l. 19 f.), not moral satisfaction. Moreover, the self-mutilation is willed by the priest himself (l. 13); he is immune to pain (l. 17 f.); in short, there is no evidence in the narrator's report that the priest experiences his penitence as something negative, even if the narrator himself refers to *iustas poenas noxii facinoris* (see also our comm. on l. 19 *spurcitia*). Sandy 1968, 90 ignores the narrator's point of view when he cites our passage as a typical example of Apuleius' notion that 'the universe is somehow watched over by a moral force and that wrongdoers receive their due'. The re-reader, on the other hand, paying attention to 199, 6 f. (see our comm. ad loc.) and the imperative *specta* l. 9, will interpret *meritum* in the first place from the perspective of the narrating I, the worshipper of Isis, who renounces bloody self-mutilation on religious grounds (see Appendix V). In this interpretation *meritum* means 'punishment' in a moral sense. Cf. 11, 15 (277, 9 f.) *curiositatis inprosperae sinistrum praemium reportasti*, where the *praemium* has turned out to be different from what Lucius had expected originally. These words are connected with *Fortunae caecitas* immediately afterwards; thus they correspond with *caelestis prouidentia* in our passage.

199, 10-13 Infit uaticinatione clamosa conf[l]icto mendacio semet ipsum incessere atque criminari, quasi contra fas sanctae religionis dissignasset aliquid, et insuper iustas poenas noxii facinoris ipse de se suis manibus exposcere: "Prophesying loudly, he starts to attack himself with trumped-up lies and to accuse himself as if he had trespassed against a commandment of his holy religion; moreover, he himself demands from himself and by his own hands an appropriate punishment for his sin."

infit: 'Anfangsstellung' of *infit*, which is followed by three infinitives. See for *infit* also *GCA* 1977, 186 on 4, 25 (94, 3-5) and *GCA* 1981, 251 on 7, 25 (173, 14-18).

uaticinatione clamosa conficto mendacio: observe the a b b a order and the *c*-alliteration.

uaticinatione clamosa: *uaticinatio* means here 'expression of ecstasy', 'inspiration', the psychological condition typical of a prophesying *uates*. The fact that the priests tell people's fortunes is not mentioned in detail until 9, 8.

clamosa: a person who is in a state of ecstasy will usually speak in a loud voice, so that *clamosa* accentuates here the noise made by the priest. Cf. *clamosis ululatibus* 6, 27 (149, 13) with *GCA* 1981, 44 and *clamoso strepitu* 9, 42 (235, 23).

conf[l]icto mendacio: the correction is by φ. Cf. for the same combination 5, 16 (115, 23 f.) *mendacia... confingere* and 200, 13 *fictae uaticinationis mendacio* with our comm.

incessere atque criminari: the second word explains the first; see Bernhard 1927, 168 and *ThLL* s.v. *incessere* 890, 6 f. 'fere idem quod *criminari*'. For *criminari* see *GCA* 1981, 231 on 7, 23 (171, 11), which states that *criminari* always has a connotation of 'accuse falsely'; see also *ThLL* s.v. Thus the priest's hypocrisy is strongly emphasized again by *conficto mendacio, criminari,* and *quasi* immediately below (cf. l. 6 *simulabat*). Gwyn Griffiths maintains (*AAGA* 1978, 153) that the portrait of this possessed priest forms a sympathetic element in the passage about the mendicant priests. If there is a sympathetic element, it must be discovered through discounting the narrator's scorn. On the level of the author it may well be implied. Cf. 199, 17 f. *contra plagarum dolores praesumptione munitus* with our comm.

quasi with subjunctive: here, differently from l. 7 above, 'under the pretext that', strongly subjective. This use often occurs after verbs meaning 'accuse', 'say'. See KSt 2, 2, 456; *GCA* 1981, 162 on 7, 12 (163, 15); and on *aliquid* below. LHSz 2, 596 says that in Fronto and Apul. *quasi* has superseded *tamquam*.

dissignasset aliquid: *ThLL* s.v. *designo* 714, 72 says about the spelling: 'in codicibus saepe confunduntur *des-* et *diss-*'; according to *OLD*, *diss-* may be the correct reading in some cases. The word is used here in malam partem, as is often the case in the meaning 'factum notabile edere'; see *ThLL* s.v. 719, 80 f. Cf. 10, 2 (237, 1 f.) *dissignatum scelestum ac nefarium facinus memini*. Leo compares Pl. *Mos.* 413 *quae dissignata sint et facta nequiter* and Ter. *Ad.* 87. Cf. further Hor. *Ep.* 1, 5, 16.

aliquid: the 'transgression' is not specified; see appendix V. The words *quasi...aliquid* indirectly reflect the substance of the self-accusation, which is attributed entirely to the priest; the narrator himself does not believe a word of it (see also on *conficto mendacio* above). Consequently, *fas sanctae religionis* refers to the cult of the Dea Syria from the priest's point of view.

iustas poenas noxii facinoris...exposcere: the quoted words should be closely linked with *conficto mendacio*. Again the priest's words are rendered indirectly. *Facinus* can have the connotation 'malicious intention' (see Wilhelm-Hooybergh 1954, 48), which is emphasized by *noxii*; cf. Butler's translation 'sin and wickedness' and Brandt-Ehlers' 'Verbrechensschuld'. Therefore the punishment is deserved (*iustus*).

Arrepto denique flagro, quod semiuiris illis proprium gestamen est, contortis taenis lanosi uelleris prolixe fimbriatum et multiiugis talis ouium tesseratum, indidem sese multinodis commulcat ictibus mire contra plagarum dolores praesumptione munitus: "Finally he seizes his whip, the attribute par excellence of those pansies, consisting of long tassels of ropes braided from woolly fleece, and equipped with numerous rectangular sheep's knuckle-bones; with that he flogs himself, hitting himself with the many knots, miraculously protected against the pain of the lashes by his stubbornness." 199, 14-18

denique: used here not transitionally as at 199, 9 above, but to indicate a climax.

semiuiris illis: said scornfully. *Semiuiri* is a customary designation of *Galli*; cf. Apul. *Mun.* 17 (153, 18) referring to priests in Hierapolis; Var. *Men.* 132; *Juv.* 6, 513.

contortis taenis: *taeniis* ς; the same difference between F and ς also 5, 26 (124, 9) *nuptis* and 10, 34 (265, 10) *bestis*. See also Verg. *A.* 5, 269 *taenis* and Neue-Wagener 1, 47. See further LHSz 1, 429. Cf. for the combination Tib. 1, 6, 46 *uerbera torta* in a comparable context.

lanosi uelleris: *lanosus* is a rare word, attested from Col. 7, 3, 7 onward (see *ThLL* s.v. and Gargantini 1963, 39) and occurring only twice elsewhere in the *Met.*, 5, 8 (109, 13) and 6, 12 (137, 18). Here it is used pleonastically with *uelleris*; see Bernhard 1927, 175 and cf. 191, 14 *pace tranquilla* with our comm.

fimbriatum: 'fringed'. According to *ThLL* s.v. 66 f. our passage is the only example of *fimbriatus* referring to a whip.

multiiugis: we prefer to translate 'numerous' rather than 'various'. For the several connotations and their frequency see our comm. on 194, 17 and *GCA* 1977, 105 on 4, 13 (84, 20).

talis: *talus* is 'a pastern or pastern-bone' (see *OLD* s.v. 1b), i.e. a small bone in the ankle joint of ungulates, strongly resembling a vertebra (see also Forcellini s.v. 2).

ouium: thus φ F has *ouiuā;* in the erasure was written ˆ; over the line was probably written *ouiû*. According to Helm in his app. crit. the *a* in *ouiua* may be explained from a reading *ŏuium*.

tesseratum: this adjective is found only here, according to the material of the *ThLL*. It is formed on an analogy with *tessellatum*, derived from *tessella*, the diminutive of *tessera*. *Tessellatum* is found Suet. *Jul.* 46 *tessellata... pauimenta* 'floors inlaid with mosaic tiles'. A *tessera* is a cube-shaped object, made of various materials, generally used as a die. *Tali*, too, served as dice; they differed from *tesserae* in being rectangular rather than square, and in being marked only on the four long sides instead of all six. For the difference between *tesserae* and *tali* in games see Mart. 14, 15 and Daremberg-Saglio s.v. *talus* 28 f. It is therefore possible to see a play on words in *talis... tesseratum*; the words *talus* and *tessera* are here synonyms meaning 'rectangular small knuckle-bone'.

The whip described here is referred to at 201, 11 f. as *flagro illo pecuinis ossibus catenato*; cf. *Onos* 38, 7 ἐκείνῃ, τῇ ἐκ τῶν ἀστραγάλων μάστιγι παίοντες. Apuleius' remark *quod semiuiris illis proprium gestamen est* is confirmed by Plu. 2, 1127 c (*adv. Colot.*) ἀλλ' οὐκ ἐλεύθερος οὗτος (γέλως), ὦ Μητρόδωρε, ἐστὶν ἀλλ' ἀνελεύθερος καὶ ἀνάγωγος καὶ οὐδὲ μάστιγος ἐλευθέρας δεόμενος, ἀλλὰ τῆς ἀστραγαλωτῆς ἐκείνης ᾗ τοὺς Γάλλους πλημμελοῦντας ἐν τοῖς Μητρῴοις κολάζουσιν and *AP* 6, 234, 1 f. Γάλλος ὁ χαιτάεις, ὁ νεήτομος, ὠπὸ Τυμώλου / Λύδιος ὀρχηστὰς μάκρ' ὀλολυζόμενος, / τᾷ παρὰ Σαγγαρίῳ τάδε Ματέρι τύμπαν' ἀγαυᾷ / θήκατο καὶ μάστιν τὰν πολυαστράγαλον. There is a well-known relief from Lavinium, originating from the time of Hadrian or the Antonines (see *RAC* s.v. *Gallus* 1013 and 1022), which represents a *Gallus* in full regalia. This *Gallus* is equipped with the kind of whip described here (see Daremberg-Saglio s.v. Gallus 1457, ill. 3482 and Cumont [4]1929, planche II, 1). The whip depicted there consists of three strands on which, at small intervals, small bones are strung which rather resemble cervical vertebrae.

indidem: here with an instrumental meaning, as at 7, 28 (176, 2); see *GCA* 1981, 270 ad loc.

multinodis ictibus: metonymic for 'with the lashes of the whip with its many knots'. *Multinodus* is first found in Apul.; in addition to this passage, 5, 17 (116, 17) *multinodis uoluminibus serpentem* and 10, 29 (260, 26) *multinodas ambages*. *ThLL* also mentions Prud. *Cath.* 7, 139 *flagellis multinodis* and Mart. Cap. 4, 423.

commulcat: the compound is hapax legomenon; see *ThLL* s.v. It seems to be a strong word, adding to the significance of *mire*.

mire: Colvius compares 10, 10 (244, 22) *offirmatus mira praesumptione* and wants therefore to read *mira* here as well, as do vdVLiet and Oudendorp. This is unnecessary, although all other passages in the *Met.* have *praesumptio* combined with an adjective. *Mire* is frequent in the *Met.* (e.g. 195, 25); see also the Quintilian passage in the next lemma.

contra plagarum dolores praesumptione munitus: as appears from the material of the *ThLL*, *praesumptio* is first found Sen. *Ep.* 117, 6 where it is used in approximately the same meaning as Quint. *Inst.* 9, 2, 16 *mire uero in causis ualet praesumptio, quae* πρόλημψις *dicitur, cum id, quod obici potest, occupamus.* In addition to this passage, Apul. uses it five more times: 9, 4 (205, 15), again referring to the priests, *contra uesanam eorum praesumptionem* 'in contrast to their mad assumption (that the ass was suffering of rabies); 9, 14 (213, 20) *mentita sacrilega praesumptione dei* 'the improper, blasphemous, unfounded belief in a god'; 10, 10 (244, 22) *offirmatus mira praesumptione nullis uerberibus ac ne ipso quidem succumbit igni* 'strengthened by his exceptionally unrepentant obstinacy he (the scoundrel) did not yield to the whip and not even to the fire.' Further *Apol.* 77 (86, 6) *praesumptione cassa* 'vain illusion', 'wrong notion'; and *Fl.* 9 (10, 19) *uestra de me benigna praesumptio* 'the favourable opinion you have formed of me in advance'. Apart from the last citation, *praesumptio* is always used in a pejorative sense: 'a (preconceived) incorrect opinion, to which one sticks stubbornly' (9, 4 and 9, 14) or 'obstinacy', 'wilfulness' (10, 10). The word occurs frequently in Tert. and later authors, usually in a religious context; e.g. Tert. *Cult. fem.* 2, 2, 2 *timor fundamentum salutis est, praesumptio impedimentum timoris*; Cypr. *Ep.* 34, 1 *in praesumptione et audacia sua pertinaciter perstiterunt*; Hilar. *Trin.* 6, 25 *tibi quaero, heretice, unde alia praesumptio sit*; Aug. *Ciu.* 18, 52. See also Blaise s.v. 5. A religious connotation, in malam partem, is apparent in our passage as well; cf. 9, 14 (213, 20). *Mire* expresses the astonishment of the unbeliever; the narrator finds the priest's behaviour curious and incomprehensible. *Praesumptio* can be paraphrased here as 'the (in the narrator's eyes) wilful and inappropriate assumption of the priest that he is possessed by the deity and that self-mutilation is part of that inspiration'. This (in the eyes of the narrator) stubbornly imagined, play-acted madness (cf. 1. 6) makes him insensitive to pain (*contra plagarum dolores munitus*). At 10, 10 (244, 22), too, the scoundrel is insensitive to (imminent) pain owing to his obstinately adhering to previous assertions. Cf. for this notion Tib. 1, 6, 45 f. *haec* (sc. *sacerdos*) *ubi Bellonae motu est agitata, nec acrem / flammam, non amens uerbera torta timet: / ipsa bipenne suos caedit uiolenta lacertos / sanguineque effuso spargit inulta deam, / statque latus praefixa ueru, stat saucia pectus.*

Cerneres prosectu gladiorum ictuque flagrorum solum spurcitia sanguinis effeminati madescere: "You could see, as a result of the cutting of the swords and the lashing of the whips, the ground getting soaked with the filth of effeminate blood." 199, 18-20

cerneres: cf. *specta* l. 9, but the imperfect subjunctive is more distant; cf. 7, 13 (163, 23 f.) *pompam cerneres* and 190, 19 *cerneres...spectaculum* with our comm.

prosectu: found in Apul. only according to the material of the *ThLL*; in addition to this passage also 180, 16.

prosectu gladiorum ictuque flagrorum: isocolon with homoeoteleuton; the pattern is a b a b.

solum spurcitia sanguinis effeminati madescere: cf. *Onos* 37, 2 ὥστε ἐν ἀκαρεῖ πάντα πεπλῆσθαι μαλακοῦ αἵματος, which also shows contempt. These words can be read at two levels: 1. from the point of view of the experiencing I, who has an aversion to the effeminate priests; 2. from the point of view of the narrating I, to whom self-mutilation and bloodshed have nothing to do with true religion. Such acts are labeled as dirty, unclean (*spurcitia*). See also our comm. on *meritum* (1. 9 above) and Appendix IV 2.12.2. To the priest however, the bloodshed is a rite of purification and demonstrates the ascetic desire to free the soul from matter (see Cumont [4]1929, 47).

spurcitia: this is the reading of ς; see the app. crit. of Robertson and Giarratano-Frassinetti. F has *spurcicie*, with *cie* written by a second hand in an erasure; in the margin the first hand has added *spurcitie* according to Robertson, *spurcitia* according to Helm III (see also Praef. *Fl.* XXXVI) and Giarratano-Frassinetti. φ has *spurcitie*; Robertson and Giarratano-Frassinetti note that this seems to be a correction of *spurcita* by a second hand. Thus it is difficult to recover the original reading of F. An argument for *spurcitie* could be that it is the lectio difficilior; see Neue-Wagener 1, 567 and Bailey on Lucr. 6, 977. The word is found once more in Apuleius, at *Fl.* 17 (31, 20) *aures spurcitie obseratae*, but there it is a conjecture for *spiritu*, adopted by both Helm and Vallette. Because of the uncertainty we follow the modern editors in printing *spurcitia* (Oudendorp, Hildebrand, Eyssenhardt, and vdVliet have *spurcitie*). *Spurcitia* (or *spurcities*) is found in a limited number of authors. *OLD* notes passages in Varro, Lucr., Col., Plin. *Nat.*; the *ThLL* material mentions in addition *SHA* Capitol. *Maximin.* 28, 4 and a few passages from *Mul. Chir.* (e.g. 162). For a comparable characterisation cf. 200, 19, where the priests are called *spurcissima illa propudia*. Observe the strong *s*-alliteration in 1. 19.

199, 20-200, 1 Quae res incutiebat mihi non paruam sollicitudinem uidenti tot uulneribus largiter profusum cruorem, ne quo casu deae peregrinae stomachus, ut quorundam hominum lactem, sic illa sanguinem concupi⟨s⟩ceret asininum: "This started to strike me with no small anxiety when I saw the blood flowing profusely from so many wounds: I feared that the stomach of the foreign goddess perhaps, as that of some people would crave the milk, so she would crave the blood of an ass."

incutiebat...non paruam sollicitudinem: cf. for this phrase 192, 7 f. *non mediocrem pauorem incussit. Incutiebat* contrasts with the predominant present tense in this passage: now the ass is in imminent danger of becoming involved himself.

largiter: cf. 190, 1 and 198, 6 with our comm.

deae peregrinae: one never knows what to expect of an unknown, foreign goddess whose priests behave so outlandishly. (But later Lucius will give himself up to Isis gladly, which shows again the strong contrast between the two goddesses; see Appendix IV passim).

quorundam hominum lactem: stomachus is linked ἀπὸ κοινοῦ with *hominum*; a typical Apuleian procedure, see vdPaardt 1971, 51.

lactem: masculine instead of neuter (also 200, 4); cf. 192, 1 with our comm. It is not certain, but quite probable, that *asininum* modifies *lactem* as well; at any rate, the translators so take it (see e.g. Butler, Vallette, Helm-Krenkel, Brandt-Ehlers, Rode). Ass's milk was extensively used as a medicine; see *RE* s.v. Milch 1575, 51 f. It was prescribed for many kinds of poisoning, for laryngitis, and fever. Plin. *Nat.* 28, 125 mentions in addition: *sunt inter exempla, qui asininum bibendo liberati sint podagra cheragraque.* The mocking remark about the milk is absent in the *Onos*.

sic illa sanguinem concupi⟨s⟩ceret asininum: it is not necessary to change *illa* to *illae* (Bursian) or something similar, because *illa* takes up the logical subject.

concupi⟨s⟩ceret: F and φ have *conspiceret*. Hildebrand retains the original reading; Beyte 1888, 60 f. defends it by interpreting the verb as *circumspiceret*. Beyte bases himself on 3, 17 (64, 19) *conspicio* (the reading of φ; Helm opts for *conspicor*, the reading of ς; see vdPaardt 1971, 129) *quendam...adtondentem*, where again, according to him, *conspicio* means 'look for'. But *conspicor* (or *conspicio*) means there 'catch sight of', 'see'; no passages are mentioned by *ThLL*, either, where *conspicio* has the connotation Beyte wants to give it. Oudendorp considers our passage corrupt and approves of Brant's conjecture *consitiret*; in his text, however, he prints *concupisceret*. This form he takes as a correction by Beroaldus, as do the other older editors and Helm (app. crit.); according to Robertson (app. crit.) and Giarratano-Frassinetti the correction is by ς. Eyssenhardt, vdVliet, and all modern editors adopt *concupisceret* and we follow them. *conspiceret* can be simply explained as a transposition of the consonants; Helm Praef. *Fl.* II gives as examples of similar transposition 3, 14 (62, 10) *suscipio* (F and φ *suspicio*) and 4, 2 (75, 16) *proripio* (F and φ *proprio*). The ass's fear becomes reality 201, 9 f., where he gets a lashing – although for a different, profane reason.

Sed ubi tandem fatigati uel certe suo laniatu satiati pausam 200, 1-9
carnificinae dedere, stipes aereas, immo uero et argenteas multis
certatim offerentibus sinu recepere patulo nec non et uini cadum
et lactem et caseos et farris et siliginis aliquid et nonnullis
hordeum deae gerulo donantibus, auidis animis conradentes
omnia et in sacculos huic quaestui de industria praeparatos
farcientes dorso meo congerunt, ut duplici scilicet sarcinae
pondere grauatus et horreum simul et templum incederem: "But when they were exhausted at last or at any rate had become bored with tearing their own flesh, they put an end to the torture. Many people vied with one another in offering copper and even silver coins as alms, which they received into the widely opened folds of their gowns, as well as a jar of wine, milk, cheeses, some spelt and fine wheat flour; some gave barley for the carrier of the goddess. All this they greedily scrape together, stuff it into bags specially made for this trade, and pile it on my back so that I, loaded as I was by the double weight of the burden, was simultaneously a walking storehouse and temple."

fatigati uel certe suo laniatu satiati: *fatigati* is corrected by the sceptical narrator to *uel certe...satiati*. *Vel certe* marks an emphatic correction of his first idea (cf. 5, 1: 103, 19 f. and Löfstedt 1936, 103 f.) and thus is entirely in keeping with his point of view as a narrator; apparently *fatigati* is not the right term for the raving, possessed priests. For the genuine inspiration cf. 11, 16 (278, 4 f.) *uaticinatus sacerdos...fatigatos anhelitus trahens conticuit*; see also our comm. on 199, 5 *anhelitus crebros referens*. Observe assonance and homoeoteleuton of *fatigati...suo laniatu satiati*.

carnificinae: literally 'torturing by the *carnifex*'; cf. 4, 24 (93, 16) with *GCA* 1977, 183 and 7, 27 (174, 25) with *GCA* 1981, 260. At 93, 16 *carnificina* is connected with *laniena*, here with *laniatus*: the pseudo-ritual is described in coarse terms, cf. *spurcitia* 199, 19.

stipes: see our comm. on 198, 2.

certatim: the narrator is full of scorn for the stupid audience, who will actually stand for this kind of thing.

nec non et: strengthened litotes; cf. *nec non etiam* 177, 9 with our comm. Callebat 1968, 417 f. says that this kind of combination always occurs in passages of high emotion. Here the narrator is surprised. The polysyndeton in l. 4-5 also emphasises the abundance of gifts.

uini cadum...hordeum: the priests receive everyday rations for themselves, and for the ass – the *deae gerulus* – barley, the regular feed for a beast of burden.

siliginis: (flour of) a fine type of wheat. According to the *ThLL* material the word is found from Cato *Agr.* 35, 1 onward; it occurs in professional literature; from Plin. *Ep.* 1, 20, 16 onward also in other contexts.

conradentes: cf. 7, 8 (160, 9 f.) *uiaticulum mihi conrasi* with *GCA* 1981, 136 and Bailey on Lucr. 1, 401, who regards it as a colloquialism.

sacculos: here *sacculus* = *saccus*, as at 9, 33 (227, 27); see Callebat 1968, 33.

huic quaestui...praeparatos: the priests are sly dogs and go about their work professionally. Their greediness is also expressed by numerous words: *auidis animis* (observe the assonance), *conradentes, farcientes, congerunt*.

et horreum simul et templum incederem: this ironic remark, which is absent in the *Onos*, seems to be an obvious allusion to the proverb ὄνος ἄγει μυστήρια; see our comm. on 198, 17.

Mendicant priests are not typical of the cult of the Dea Syria. Their origin is in the Greek world, where strolling soothsayers and beggars were a well-known sight (see Bömer 1961, 347 f.). They had a special name, ἀγύρτης which – significantly – also means 'charlatan' (see *RE* s.v. Agyrtes 915, 42 f., Cumont [4]1929, 42 f.). These beggar priests are mentioned as early as Plato (*Rep.* 2, 364B). They appear in various religions; most notorious were the Metragyrtes, in the service of Cybele (Antiphanes wrote a comedy with a title of that name, fr. 154 f. *CAF* 2, 74). Like them, our beggar priests misuse the name of the Dea Syria to make a profit. Cumont [4]1929, 97 remarks on *Met.* 8, 26 f.: 'Ce tableau pittoresque...est sans doute poussé très au noir. On a peine à croire que le sacerdoce de la déesse d'Hiérapolis n'ait été qu'un ramassis de charlatans et de maraudeurs.' Because the Dea Syria was relatively unknown in the Roman world, it was easy to bring her into disrepute (see Bömer 1961, 348); precisely because of her strong resemblance to Isis she invokes the anger of the worshipper of Isis. Although incidental examples are known of pursuit of gain by priests of Isis, there is not a trace of that to be found in the eleventh book; see

Appendix IV 2.7. The greed of the priests of the Dea Syria is thus diametrically opposed to the disinterestedness of the priests of Isis.

CHAPTER XXIX

The mendicant priests prepare a feast at which they indulge their passions with a country lad. The ass is shocked.

200, 10-12 Ad istum modum palantes omnem illam depraedabantur regionem. Sed in quodam castello copia laetati largioris quaesticuli gaudiales instruunt dapes: "Roving about in this fashion, they plundered that entire region. And in a village, where they rejoiced in a tidy little profit, larger than usual, they prepared a festive meal."

Ad istum modum: see our comm. on 187, 3 *Ad hunc modum*.

depraedabantur: this word emphasizes again that the priests are scoundrels and that their quasi-religious actions are nothing but a cover for their greed. The verb *depraedare* (*-i*) is not found before Apuleius; it occurs in the *Vetus Latina*, in Augustine and in other Christian authors, always with the meaning 'plunder', 'ravage'; it is also used by lawyers, e.g. Ulp. *Dig.* 3, 5, 5, 5 (3) and 47, 14, 1, 1 *qui pecora ex pascuis...subtrahunt et quodammodo depraedantur*. Médan 1925, 203 is therefore right to include it among the 'verbes de langue postérieure'; see also Bernhard 1927, 121; Flobert 1975, 142 and 371.

Sed: a transitional particle; cf. 188, 11 with our comm.

quodam: practically an indefinite article here; see e.g. *GCA* 1977, 38.

castello: see our remark on 188, 23.

largioris quaesticuli: the adjective shows that the diminutive has an affective connotation; see Callebat 1968, 378, who speaks of an 'emploi...surtout affectif correspondant aux expressions françaises du type: un bon petit gain, une belle petite somme'. Cf. Dutch 'een zoet winstje', English 'a tidy little sum'. Apul. uses the noun also 11, 28 (290, 3) and Brakman suggests it as a conjecture 9,32 (227,3).

gaudiales: see on this adjective our comm. on 188, 19 *gaudiali fuga* 'a flight which causes joy to the ass'. The position of the verb *instruunt* is typically Apuleian; see Bernhard 1927, 18.

200, 12-22 A quodam colono fictae uaticinationis mendacio pinguissimum deposcunt arietem, qui deam Syriam esurientem suo satiaret sacrificio, probeque disposita cenula balneas obeunt ac dehinc lauti quendam fortissimum rusticanum industria laterum atque imis uentris bene praeparatum comitem cenae secum adducunt paucisque admodum praegustatis olusculis ante ipsam mensam spurcissima illa propudia ad inlicitae libidinis extrema flagitia infandis uriginibus efferantur passimque circumfusi nudatum supinatumque iuuenem execrandis oribus flagitabant: "By means of a phoney story – a concocted prophecy – they demand from a farmer his fattest ram, which was to satisfy the hungry Syrian goddess by its sacrifice. When they had duly prepared the meal they went to take a bath. Then, after their bath, they brought a sturdy peasant along as a dinner guest, who was well equipped as to the power of his loins and the lower part of his belly. When they had only just tasted the vegetable hors d'oeuvre before the main course began, that filthy riff-raff got carried away in their abominable passion to commit the ultimate outrages of unnatural lust. From all sides they pressed round the young man, undressed him, laid him on his back, and kept falling upon him with their accursed mouths."

colono: Norden 1912, 88 f. discusses the social status of a *colonus* and remarks 89 n. 2 regarding our passage: 'Selbstverständlich handelt es sich hier lediglich um Klein-, bzw. Parzellenpächter'. Heitland 1921, 332 expresses himself more cautiously: 'And yet I cannot feel certain that Apuleius always means a tenant-farmer (see V 17, VII 15, VIII 17,29,31. Cf. Norden pp. 88-89) under a landlord whenever he uses the word *colonus*. Probably he does, as Norden seems to think' and 333 'The *coloni*, nominally free, were as yet only bound to the soil by the practical difficulty of clearing themselves from the obligations that encumbered them and checked freedom of movement. But they were now near to the time when they were made fixtures by law'.

fictae uaticinationis mendacio: from this entire chapter, as from the previous ones (cf. 199, 6 *simulabat sauciam uecordiam* with our comm. and 199, 10 *conficto mendacio*), it is obvious how much the narrator despises the priests of the Dea Syria and their – to him – objectionable cult; see Introduction 4.5. A comparison of this episode with its equivalent in the *Onos* shows that Apuleius must have borrowed the subject-matter and the name of the leading priest Philebus from the Vorlage; but he puts extra emphasis on everything, particularly on the perversion of the priests and the insincerity of their so-called religious activities. See Walsh 1970, 165; Gwyn Griffiths 1975, 29; Appendix IV 2.9.1 and 2.9.2. Their mendacity is even expressed pleonastically here: *fictae uaticinationis mendacio*.

arietem: the ram is of old one of the six customary sacrificial animals: cow, sheep, goat, pig, hen, and goose; see *RE* s.v. Opfer 590. The ram especially is commonly used in expiatory sacrifices (e.g. to Zeus Chthonios; see *RE* s.v. Schaf 395), also in later times, both in Greece and in Italy.

deam Syriam: see Appendix III. Observe the *s*-alliteration and the assonance in *Syriam esurientem suo satiaret sacrificio*.

esurientem: it is a common notion that the deity's appetite is satisfied by sacrifice; the god is present at the meal as a guest. Wilamowitz 1931/32, I 287 states that 'die Tischgemeinschaft des Gottes mit den opfernden Menschen die entscheidende Vorstellung war'. But from the preceding events in the story it becomes evident that the priests use the Dea Syria as a pretext (see our comm. on 196, 4 *deamque Syriam circumferentes mendicare compellunt* and the last note on chapter 28), so for *deam Syriam* in our passage one may understand 'the priests'.

In view of what happens l. 16 f. it is possible to read a double meaning into the words *pinguissimum arietem...sacrificio*: a) the ram was used, in Attic comedy at any rate, as a symbol of the male sexual organ; see Henderson 1975, 116 and 127 (the *ThLL* and *OLD* have no examples in Latin) ;b) for *deam Syriam* one may read 'the priests'; see above. c) Various words for 'eat', 'food', 'cook', 'heat', and 'sacrifice' are also used with a double meaning in Attic comedy (see Henderson 1975, 48, 60, 61, 177). There is a parallel at *Met.* 2, 7 (31, 1-10), where Lucius speaks to Fotis while she is preparing food in the kitchen, and 197, 21 f., where an allusion is made to the sacrifice of Iphigenia. The *ThLL* s.v. *esurire* gives, in addition to the literal meaning, the figurative meaning 'cupidum esse', 'vehementer appetere' without any specification; but cf. Pl. *Cas.* 801 and Catul. 21 for an ambiguous use of the verb. There are more examples of an erotic connotation of *satiare*: *Met.* 2, 17 (39, 7) *Veneris fructu me satiauit*; Prop. 2, 15, 23 *oculos satiemus amore* (one of the examples mentioned by *OLD* s.v. 3).

-que...ac...atque...-que: this variation in conjunctions is frequent in Apuleius. The same phenomenon is found in e.g. Valerius Maximus and Minucius Felix; see Bernhard 1927, 82 f.

disposita: the meaning of this verb is probably 'arrange in order or position', 'lay out' (*OLD*). In the same vein Sen. *Ep.* 84, 3 *apes...quidquid attulere, disponunt ac per fauos digerunt*; cf. 95, 28 *quae* (sc. *fercula*) *disponi solent, uno iure perfusa*; 110, 13 *disposita* (sc. *in cena*), *quae terra marique capiuntur*. Cf. also Apul. *Met.* 6, 10 (135, 14) *granis rite dispositis atque seiugatis*.

cenula: since they are about to eat a very fat ram as the pièce de résistance (cf. 200, 12 *gaudiales instruunt dapes*) preceded by – as we will hear presently – vegetables, it is likely that the diminutive has affective force here; presently (200, 18) the same dinner will be referred to as *cena*. The diminutive is quite common; it is attested from Varro *Men.* 103 onward. Apul. uses it also 2, 18 (39, 16) *apud eam (Byrrhenam) cenulae...interessem*; in that passage, too, the *cenula* is later called *cena* (39, 22 and 40, 11). Cf. also 3, 13 (61, 16); 9, 6 (206, 23); 9, 23 (220, 19).

balneas obeunt: 'ils vont se baigner' (Vallette). See *GCA* 1981, 235 on 7,23 (171,21) *mercatum proxumum obire statui*. Bathing took place before dinner, see Balsdon 1969,28 f. Even the robbers conform: 4,7 (80,3 f.). For the many public baths in towns and villages, both in Italy and in the provinces, see Mau in *RE* s.v. Bäder and, e.g., Plin. *Ep.* 2,17,26. In the Greek world bathing facilities were less elaborate than the Romans were used to, but it was perfectly normal in the second century A.D. to find them in a *castellum*, as in this passage.

quendam...bene praeparatum: it is interesting to compare this bold and expressive description with the sober version of the *Onos* (38,1): there the priests get hold of a young man and ἔπασχον ἐκ τοῦ κωμήτου ὅσα συνήθη καὶ φίλα τοιούτοις ἀνοσίοις κιναίδοις ἦν, which is followed by the information that the ass is so scandalised that he wants to bray ὦ Ζεῦ σχέτλιε.

industria: in combination with *laterum*: 'potency'; cf. *defectis...lateribus* 198, 8 with our comm.

imis uentris: a more detailed localization of the organ recently described by *laterum*. *Imis uentris* is the ablative of *ima uentris*, another example of the nominal use of a neuter adjective (singular or plural) connected with a partitive genitive; cf. e.g. 4,2 (75,18) *nimio uelocitatis* and 4,12 (83,13) *rerum singula* with *GCA* 1977, 32 and 94 respectively. See also Bernhard 1927, 106. Observe the juxtaposition of *industria*(abstract) and *imis* (concrete), both in the ablative.

bene praeparatum: slightly ironical, but used in an obscene sense, of course: '(flancs) comme bâtis sur mesure' (Vallette).

comitem cenae: again a striking alliteration. The young man has been lured with a dinner invitation. Does he know, one may wonder, what is in store for him?

olusculis: again a diminutive. *OLD* says the word usually has 'a depreciatory sense' and cites Cic. *Att.* 6, 1, 13 *in felicatis lancibus...holusculis nos soles pascere*; Hor. *Sat.* 2, 6, 64 *uncta satis pingui ponentur oluscula lardo*; Juv. 11, 79 *paruo quae legerat horto / ipse focis brevibus ponebat holuscula*; cf. also Gel. 19, 7, 1 *olusculis pomisque...* (*nos*) *inuitabat*. On the ground of these passages Callebat 1968, 35 concludes that it was a common word in the spoken language, scarcely different from (*h*)*olus*. It may be more correct to say that it generally connotes 'simple, plain food'. In our passage it seems to be used ironically: the simple hors d'oeuvre offers a contrast with what follows immediately afterwards.

spurcissima illa propudia: cf. 199, 19 *spurcitia sanguinis effeminati*, also referring to the priests. Heine 1962, 307 n. 2 observes that Apul. has an arsenal of vituperative adjectives to describe the moral indignation of Lucius the ass. Sandy 1969, 42 f. also discusses passages in which 'the ass is not content with simply passing judgment, but is driven by an affront to his moral sensibilities to intervene in the name of justice'. See also our comm. on 200,22 f. *nec...meis oculis tolerantibus*. From the other words in the phrase it is clear that *illa* is used here in a pejorative sense; see Callebat 1968, 277 who gives a series of examples, and *GCA* 1981, 180 on 7, 15 (165, 18) *nequissima...illa mulier*; cf. also 188, 19.

propudia: this word (*pro*+*pudet*+*ium*) can be used abstractly in the sense of 'shameful or immodest action', but it is often concrete: 'shameful creature', 'vile wretch', and in that sense is used as a term of abuse; e.g. Pl. *Bac.* 579 *ut pulsat propudium*; Cur. 190 *quid ais, propudium*?; Cic. *Phil.* 14, 8 *propudium illud et portentum L. Antonius*. Consequently, it is probably a borrowing from colloquial language; see Callebat 1968, 86. It is found in Apuleius only here: he has the adjective *propudiosus* at 9, 27 (223, 18) *propudiosae mulieris* and *Apol.* 75 (83, 22) *ipse propudiosus, uxor lupa, filii similes*.

ad inlicitae libidinis extrema flagitia infandis uriginibus efferantur: every word has been carefully chosen to contribute to the emphatic denunciation of the outrageous behaviour of priests who, doing only lip service to their cult, are out to indulge their lowest passions.

inlicitus: Callebat 1968, 164 maintains that this adjective had its origin in the sermo cotidianus and subsequently pervaded the literary language from the Empire onward. We dispute this on the ground of the absence of examples from comedy or Cicero's letters; the adjective is confined to literary Latin of the Empire, e.g. Sen. *Phaed.* 97 *stupra et illicitos toros...quaerit*; Stat. *Theb.* 8, 96 *Venerem illicitam*; Tac. *Ann.* 15, 37 *per licita atque illicita*. Apuleius uses it also 7, 21 (170, 5) *illicitas...libidines*, in an accusation addressed to the ass himself;

cf. also 4, 30 (98, 17) *inlicitae formonsitatis* and 6, 18 (142, 15) *inlicita...pietate*. All these cases contain a value judgment on the part of the narrator.

uriginibus: this post-classical noun, derived from *uro*, means 'lustful heat', 'desire', 'pruriency'. It occurs once more in Apuleius, 1, 7 (7, 14) (*Meroe*) *urigine percita (me) cubili suo adplicat*. Cf. also Arn. 5,44 *Semeleiae subolis urigo* (where *urigo* is Meursius' emendation for *origo* P). Bernhard 1927, 101 f. points out that Apuleius often uses the plural of abstract nouns, especially verbal nouns (as in this case). On the theme of *uoluptas* in the *Met*. see Scobie, *AAGA* 1978, 53; on 'Sex and Sanctity' see Schlam, *ibid*., 101.

efferantur: in the meaning of 'work up into a state of fury', 'madden' this verb is also found *Apol*. 28 (33, 21) (*puerum*) *in me ac matrem suam nefarie efferatum*. Variation in tense (*obeunt...adducunt...efferantur...flagitabant*) is quite frequent in Apuleius; see Bernhard 1927, 152. Callebat 1968, 427 observes a similar variation not only in the comic poets, but also in Livy, Petronius and Tacitus; he rightly considers it an enlivening element in the narrative style. Cf. also 188, 14 *deserit*.

supinatumque: see our comm. on 186, 5.

execrandis: this adjective, which will be used again l. 31 below, contains severe disapproval; cf. 9, 19 (217, 13) *execrando metallo (auro) pudicitiam suam...auctorata est*. It is often used in conjunction with *abominabilis* and *obscaenus*, e.g: Vulg. *Leu*. 11, 11 *abominabile uobis et execrandum erit*; Rufin. *Hist*. 1, 8, 7 *tentigo obscaena...et exsecranda*.

oribus: in F wrongly changed by a later hand to *uriginibus*; φ has retained the correct reading.

flagitabant: the verb is used on occasion in connection with *stuprum* (see ThLL s.v. 843, 67 f.), cf. the definition in Fest.110 L *inter cutem flagitatos dicebant antiqui mares qui stuprum passi essent*; see also Sulp. Sev. *Chron*. 1,6,4 *iuuentus...nouos hospites ad stuprum flagitabant*; Ulp. *Dig*. 47,1,2,5. Here the *stuprum* consists of *fellatio*, oral sex. Catul. uses it in connection with *irrumatio*: 21,8 *pedicare cupis meos amores...frustra: nam...tangam te prior irrumatione*; also *Priap*. 35,2; Mart. 2,47,4; 4,17,3.

Apuleius works up to the priests' debaucheries by means of a series of anticipations in ch. 24-26 (see e.g. our comm. on 195, 24 *emptorem aptissimum duris meis casibus*). However, what the ass feared for himself is now happening to someone else. Cf. Petr. *Sat*. 23 and 24, where another castrated *cinaedus* displays an equally great sexual activity.

200, 22-26 Nec diu tale facinus meis oculis tolerantibus 'porro Quirites' proclamare gestiui, sed uiduatum ceteris syllabis ac litteris processit 'O' tantum sane clarum ac ualidum et asino proprium, sed inoportuno plane tempore: "My eyes could not endure such misconduct and so I itched to call out 'Forward Romans', but 'O' came out alone, without the rest of the syllables and letters – clear and strong and appropriate to an ass, to be sure, but at an altogether untimely moment."

Nec...meis oculis tolerantibus: Lucius the ass several times shows his moral disapproval of certain forms of sexual behaviour; see *GCA* 1981, 223 on 7, 21

(170, 18). His attitude is ambivalent, however. a) In this passage his indignation seems to be caused by his aversion to the homosexual practices of priests (see our comm. on 198, 9-10 *cogitabam*). b) The ass resents the intimacies between Charite and Haemus 7, 11 (162, 26) *quae res oppido mihi displicebat*, because he thinks that Charite is being unfaithful to her fiancé. But there is every reason to suspect that his resentment is caused by jealousy, in view of his earlier words and actions 4, 23 (92, 19) and 6, 28 (150, 1). c) Lucius' disapproval of unfaithfulness and adultery seems also to be the reason for his abhorrence of the miller's wife 9, 26 (223, 1) *mihi penita carpebantur praecordia*. d) Lucius' own continuing preoccupation with *uoluptas* after his metamorphosis is clear not only from his attitude towards Charite (see above), but also from his regret at being no longer able to embrace Fotis (3, 24), from his fear of castration (e.g. 7, 24), and from the pleasure he derives from copulating with the *matrona pollens et opulens* (10, 21; 253, 8 f.). His later refusal to repeat the act (10,29) must therefore be attributed not to his ideas about sexuality, but to the facts that she is a criminal and that the event is to take place in public. See also *GCA* 1981, 156 on 7, 11 (162, 24-26).

porro Quirites: 'Forward Romans' (Heller 1941/42, 533). This fixed phrase – obviously somewhat elliptic – is found as early as Laberius (Ribbeck 361), *com. 125 Porro, Quirites, libertatem perdimus*; Priap. 26, 1 *Porro – nam quis erit modus? – Quirites*; Tert. *Adu. Valent.* 14, 3 *ut etiam inclamauerit in eam 'Iao'! quasi 'Porro Quirites' aut 'Fidem Caesaris'*. Apul. has found a truly Roman equivalent for ὦ Ζεῦ σχέτλιε (*Onos* 38,2).

Heller points out that the first *o* in *porro* is similar in sound with the Greek ω; see Sturtevant ²1940, 47 'In Attic of the fifth century B.C. ω was an open *o*, similar to Fr. *o* in *tort*'.

proclamare: F has *pclamare* (= *perclamare*), which has been corrected in ς; another mistake was made by the scribe of F in l. 24 *p̄cessit* (= *praecessit*), adopted by φ but corrected in ς. On the carelessness of the scribe of F regarding ligatures and compendia, see Helm, Praef. *Fl.* XLVI f.

gestiui: McKibben 1951, 170 n.8 says that in the *Met.* (where it occurs no fewer than 32 times) this verb always means 'intend', except at 2,6 (29,17) and 3,14 (62,10), where it means 'itch', 'burn', 'strongly desire'. In spite of this assertion, the word must have the latter meaning here, as also at 4,3 (76,5); see Dowden 1979, 69 against *GCA* 1977, 37.

uiduatum: used here in the sense of 'bereft of', 'without'. Apul. uses it also 4, 27 (95, 22); see our comm. on 185, 17.

'*O' tantum*: the motif of the wish to give expression to indignation in human words – doomed to failure in the ass's case – occurs two more times in the *Met.*: 3, 29 (see vdPaardt 1971,204 ad loc.) and 7, 3 (see *GCA* 1981,97 ad loc.). It obviously has its origin in the Vorlage: *Onos* 38, 2 has ἡ μὲν φωνὴ οὐκ ἀνέβη μοι ἡ ἐμή, ἀλλ' ἡ τοῦ ὄνου ἐκ τοῦ φάρυγγος, καὶ μέγα ὠγκησάμην. See Snell 1935, 355 f.; Heller 1941/42, 533 and 1942/43, 96 f.; Bianco 1956, 52 f.; Heine 1962, 302 n. 2.

sane clarum...proprium: Lucius the ass, who elsewhere complains that he can't get back his human shape, is now proud of the fact that he can bray so beautifully. See also our note with *ruditu* (1.29).

200, 26 - 201,1 Namque de pago proximo complures iuuenes abactum sibi noctu perquirentes asellum nimioque studio cuncta deuorsoria scrutantes intus aedium audito ruditu meo praedam absconditam latibulis aedium rati, coram rem inuasuri suam inprouisi conferto gradu se penetrant palamque illos execrandas foeditates obeuntes deprehendunt:"For several young men from the neighbouring village, who were looking everywhere for their ass, who had been driven off at night, were searching all possible lodgings with the greatest zeal. When they heard my braying inside the house they thought that the stolen goods had been hidden in a concealed spot in the house and, in order to take possession of their property in person, they unexpectedly and in close ranks burst in; and there they caught those creatures red-handed, engaging in their detestable foulnesses."

abactum: *abigere* in the meaning of 'drive off' of cattle, with the connotation 'steal'. Cf. Cic. *Ver.* 1, 28 *greges equorum eius istum abigendos curasse*; 3, 57 *familiam abduxit, pecus abegit*; Ovid. *Met.* 2, 686 *siluis occultat abactas* (sc. *boues*); also *Met.* 9,35 (229,20); many other examples in *ThLL* s.v. 96, 49 f.

perquirentes: 7,25 (173,6) mentions, with a slight variation in words, shepherds *perditam sibi requirentes uacculam*; they happen to find Lucius, who had been driven off by a passer-by. Here a stolen ass is sought, and Lucius who had not been stolen is found. Consequently, we may speak of a motif-reversal. See also our note on *praedam*.

asellum: the word, side by side with *asinus*, is used from the comic poets (e.g. Pl. *Aul.* 229) onward, by Varro, Cicero, Propertius, *Copa* 25, etc. Callebat 1968, 373 states that the diminutive is often used in a pejorative sense, and cites 6, 26 (147, 21); 9, 39 (233, 18); but this is not always the case: cf. 7, 8 (160, 2), *Apol.* 23 (27, 17), and our passage.

deuorsoria: presumably not so much 'inns' here as, more generally, 'possible lodgings'; after all, Apuleius does not localize this scene in an inn. Callebat 1968, 54 ('demeures') refers to Tert. *An.* 7, 4 and Hieron. *Ep.* 46, 10a. The verb *deuersari*, too, evolves in meaning from 'loger chez', 'descendre chez' to 'vivre à demeure', 'habiter'; see also 4, 9 (81, 8) with *GCA* 1977, 76 ad loc.

intus...aedium: this rare use of *intus* with a genitive is discussed by vGeisau 1916, 264; Löfstedt 1933, 2, 424; and LHSz 2, 278. It is explained as a Graecism on the analogy of ἐντός or εἴσω; this is presumably why Beyte inserts *intus* before *aedium* 10, 16 (248, 31). The construction also occurs both *Vetus Latina* and *Vulg. Matth.* 23, 26 *quod intus est calicis et parapsidis*; *Luc.* 11, 39 *quod autem intus est uestrum* (the translation of ἐντός and ἔσωθεν respectively). Sen. *Herc. Fur.* 679 may be another parallel passage: the *Etruscus* reads there *intus immensi sinus*, which is accepted as the correct reading in the editions of Leo ('*genitiuus ab* intus *pendet*'), Peiper-Richter, and Giardina. Löfstedt 1933, 424 n. 4 hesitatingly prefers the reading *immenso sinu* of the A-class, because he finds such a Graecism in Seneca 'höchst auffällig und kaum stilgerecht'. Be this as it may, it does not apply to the Bible translations or to Apuleius, of course. Both Helm 1904, 538 and Löfstedt *ibid.* point out *Apol.* 50 (57, 1) *foras corporis* (ἔξω τοῦ σώματος) and *Met.* 5, 9 (110, 2) *longe parentum* (ἀπάνευθε τοκήων). A similar genitive can be found *Met.* 3, 17 (65, 1) and 5, 2 (104, 16) *altrinsecus aedium*.

Our passage may also have been directly influenced by the Vorlage; cf. *Onos* 38, 3 παρέρχονται εἴσω.

ruditu: the *ThLL* material yields Serv. on *A.* 7,16 *ruditus... proprie est clamor asinorum* (also Schol. Persii, ed. Kurz, 3,9); Greg. M. *Dial.* 3,4 p. 225A *diabolus coepit imitari... roditus* (var.: *ruditus*) *asinorum*. For the word formation see Gargantini 1963, 40. The verb *rudere* is also used in the case of lions, deer and humans (see *OLD* s.v.). When Ovid uses it in the case of asses, it is qualified, e.g. *Ars* 3,289 *sonat raucum ut rudit... turpis asella*; *F.* 1,433 *ecce, rudens rauco Sileni... uector asellus/... edidit ore sonos*. Bömer ad loc. lists passages in which the 'heisere Geschrei' of asses frightens even the Giants. The fact that the narrator (above 1.25) qualified the braying of the ass with the word *clarum* is therefore rather striking.

praedam: the priests looted the entire region (1.10 *depraedabantur*). One item the priests were not guilty of stealing but which they had legitimately bought in the market was the very ass, whom the shepherds now mistakenly regard as stolen from them. After the shepherds have burst into the inn no further mention is made of stolen goods: this element was introduced by the narrator merely as a device to catch the priests at their erotic games.

latibulis aedium: Kaibel proposes to delete *aedium* as a dittography of *aedium* in the line above. However, Apuleius not infrequently repeats words (see Bernhard 1927, 232 f.) and, apart from that, *latibula* is qualified by a genitive noun in other passages as well, e.g. Amm. 24,4,12 *terrarum latibula concaua*.

latibulis: 'hiding place'. For the meaning of this word in the *Met.*, see *GCA* 1981,249 on 7,25 (173,5). For the abl. without a preposition (which may be taken as an instrumental abl.), see Médan 1925,57; cf. also Cic. *Rab.Post.* 42 *cum ferae latibulis se tegant*.

coram: 'ipse' (*ThLL* s.v. 943,22 f.); in the *Met.* e.g. 3,19 (66,14) *coram magicae cognoscendae ardentissimus cupitor*, with vdPaardt 1971, 146 ad loc. ('face to face').

inuasuri: 'in order to seize'; cf. *occupare* 7, 25 (173, 18) with *GCA* 1981, 252 ad loc. Perhaps comparable is Lucil. 260 ⟨*in*⟩ *suam enim* ⟨*hós*⟩ *inuádere* ⟨*rem*⟩ *átque innúbere cénsent*.

conferto gradu: a military term; cf. Tac. *Ann.* 12, 35 *hi conferto gradu, turbatis contra Brittanorum ordinibus* (sc. *inrupere*). Cf. also *Met.* 5, 14 (114, 13) *conferto uestigio domum penetrant*; see our comm. on 188, 28 *iamque ipsas* and *GCA* 1977, 208 f.

se penetrant: the transitive use of this verb with the reflexive, as in this passage, is not unusual; cf. e.g. Pl. *Trin.* 276 *quo... foras se penetrauit ex aedibus?*; *Amph.* 250; *Truc.* 44; Gel. 5, 14, 18. Elsewhere in the *Met.* the verb is transitive, e.g. 3, 23 (69, 16) *penetrauerint larem*; 5, 14 (114, 13) *domum penetrant*; 6, 20 (143, 19) *domum... penetrat*; 6, 22 (145, 3) *penetrato uertice*. Callebat 1968, 486 thinks that the reflexive use is typical of the language of the comic poets; in Plautus the verb is, indeed, always reflexive.

execrandas: cf. 1. 22 above. One may wonder whether the indignation is on the part of the *iuuenes* or of the ass. We presume the latter; cf. 201, 1 *turpissimam*. The *iuuenes* are inclined to ridicule the situation: 201, 2 *ridicule... laudantes*.

201, 1-3 iamiamque uicinos undique percientes turpissimam scaenam patefaciunt, insuper ridicule sacerdotum purissimam laudantes castimoniam: "at once they alerted the neighbours on all sides and exposed the utterly disgraceful scene; what's more, they jokingly praised the supremely pure chastity of the priests."

iamiamque: vdPaardt 1971, 110 on 3, 14 (62, 22) cites as parallels our passage and 202, 5 *iamiamque domino cenam flagitante*. The meaning here is a strengthened *iam*: 'at once'.

percientes: for the meaning 'rouse', 'stir', 'set in motion' cf. Lucr. 3, 184 *ocius ergo animus quam res se perciet ulla* and 4, 563 *uerbum saepe unum perciet auris/omnibus in populo*.

turpissimam: again intense disapproval.

scaenam: see our comm. on 185, 23.

ridicule...laudantes: the irony is carefully marked by the appropriate signal (see Büchner 1941, 339 f.), cf. Quint. *Inst.* 8,6,54 *aliquando cum inrisu quodam contraria dicuntur iis quae intellegi uolunt*. See also Lausberg 1960, 302.

purissimam laudantes castimoniam: many instances of irony in the *Met.* are to be found in Bernhard 1927, 239 f. See also vdPaardt 1971, 187 on 3, 26 (71, 15); *GCA* 1981, 32 on 6, 26 (148, 3) *mitissimi homines altercant de mea nece* and 63 on 6, 30 (151, 27) *probissima puella*.

Lucius' indignant braying which interrupts the priests' *extrema flagitia* toward the *rusticanus* has a precursor in the braying of Silenus' ass, which foiled Priapus' attempt to rape the sleeping nymph Lotis; cf. Ov. *F.* 1, 433 f. *ecce rudens rauco Sileni uector asellus/intempestiuos edidit ore sonos./territa consurgit nymphe manibusque Priapum/reicit*. But there is no question of moral indignation on the part of Silenus' ass.

CHAPTER XXX

The group makes off during the night and the ass is punished. They arrive in a large town, where they are hospitably received.

⟨H⟩ac infamia consternati, quae per ora populi facile dilapsa merito inuisos ac detestabiles eos cunctis effecera[n]t, noctem ferme circa mediam collectis omnibus furtim castello facessunt bonaque itineris parte ante iubaris exortum transacta[m] iam die claro solitudines auias nancti, multa secum prius conlocuti, accingunt se meo funeri deaque uehiculo meo sublata et humi reposita cunctis stramentis me renudatum ac de quadam quercu destinatum flagro illo pecuinis ossibus catenato uerberantes paene ad extremam confecerant mortem: "Disconcerted by this scandal, which had easily spread from mouth to mouth among the people and had made them deservedly hated and detestable to all, about the middle of the night they gathered everything together and furtively made off from the village; having covered a good part of the way before sunrise, they came – it was by now broad daylight – to a remote and desolate region. First they had a long conversation with each other and then they prepared to kill me. The goddess was lifted off me, her means of transportation, and put on the ground; I was stripped of all my coverings and tied to an oak; and then they flogged me with that whip, strung with sheep's knuckles – they all but killed me completely."

201, 3-13

⟨H⟩ac: F has ac; the emendation found already in the humanist mss., is adopted by all modern editors. The opinions in our group are divided: some think that the emendation is correct: ac (atque) as the initial word in a new sentence usually emphasizes what follows; cf. 1, 2 (2, 16); 1, 2 (3, 1); 1, 11 (10, 19); 1, 15 (14, 14); 2, 6 (29, 22); 2, 16 (37, 20); 2, 27 (47, 5); 9, 5 (206, 4); 9, 32 (227, 2); 10, 5 (239, 27). But our passage does not seem to call for an emphasis of this kind; moreover, the connection of these two sentences by ac does not seem stylistically pleasing. For these reasons hac is more attractive; cf. 9, 21 (219, 10) *Hac opportuna fallacia uigorati*; 9, 23 (220, 27) *His instincta uerbis mariti*; 2, 30 (50, 11) *his dictis perterritus*. The principal mss. make a similar mistake at the beginning of a sentence also 9, 22 (219, 15): instead of *Hactenus*, which is obviously the correct reading, they write *Acten;*.

Others in our group prefer Ac because it is the reading of the principal ms.; moreover, it is perfectly possible to argue that Ac infamia introduces a new element, to which Ac calls attention.

per ora populi: Ennius uses this expression; it occurs in an analogous form in the epitaph written by him and quoted by Cic. *Tusc.* 1, 15, 34 (= Enn. *Var.*

263

17-18) *Nemo me lacrimis decoret nec funera fletu / faxit. Cur? uolito uiuos per ora uirum.* Cf. Vergil's imitation in *G.* 3, 9 *uictorque uirum uolitare per ora* with Wigodzky 1972, 75. Another case is presumably *G.* 4, 561-562 *uictorque uolentis / per populos*; also *A.* 12, 235, where Juturna prophesies that Turnus *uiuusque per ora feretur.* Cf. also Macr. *Sat.* 5, 17, 5 (*fabula Didonis*) *pro uero per ora omnium uolitet.* We may assume that Apuleius knew this expression and that its use here is a conscious or unconscious echo. See also our comm. on 186, 4 *sepeliuit ad somnum.*

dilapsa: see our comm. on 181, 1 *fama dilabitur.*

merito: again a value-judgment by Lucius the ass on the sexual practices and (in his opinion) sinister procedures of the priests; see our comm. on 200, 19 *spurcissima illa propudia* and Appendix IV 2.3. One may compare the sober style of *Onos* 38, 3 f. καὶ γέλως ἐκ τῶν ἐπεισελθόντων πολὺς γίνεται. ἔξω ἐκδραμόντες ὅλῃ τῇ κώμῃ τῷ λόγῳ διέδωκαν τῶν ἱερέων τὴν ἀσέλγειαν, οἱ δὲ αἰδούμενοι δεινῶς ταῦτα ἐληλεγμένα τῆς ἐπιούσης νυκτὸς εὐθὺς ἔνθεν ἐξήλασαν. καὶ ἐπειδὴ ἐγένοντο ἐν τῇ ἐρήμῳ τῆς ὁδοῦ, ἐχαλέπαινον καὶ ὠργίζοντο ἐμοὶ τῷ μηνύσαντι τὰ ἐκείνων μυστήρια.

detestabiles: an interesting epithet for these castrated priests; see our comm. on 188, 19.

effecera[n]t: the emendation is already read in φ.

noctem ferme circa mediam: Apuleius is obviously fond of this turn of phrase; cf. 1, 11 (10, 20) *circa tertiam ferme uigiliam*; 3, 21 (68, 1) *circa primam noctis uigiliam*; 4, 1 (74, 9) *Diem ferme circa medium.* Of course it is a common expression; see *GCA* 1977, 22 on 4, 1 (74, 9). As at 189, 15 they depart by night; on both occasions this is sufficiently motivated. Travelling by night is in itself highly unusual in antiquity: consider how much emphasis Cic. *S. Rosc.* 97 lays on the fact that Glaucia pushes on through the night to report the death of Roscius Pater. The first books of the *Met.* never mention a night journey: when Aristomenes 1, 14 (13, 18) wants to depart with the injured Socrates at the crack of dawn, the doorman finds that a risky undertaking: 14, 1 *tu...ignoras latronibus infestari uias, qui hoc noctis iter incipis?*

castello facessunt: without a preposition; see *GCA* 1977, 149 on 4, 20 (89, 12) *domo facesso* and our comm. on 176, 15 *uenit...proxima ciuitate.*

bonaque...parte: for the use of *bonus* in the sense of *magnus*, see *GCA* 1977, 47 on 4, 4 (77, 9) *confecta bona parte itineris.*

ante iubaris exortum: cf. Verg. *A.* 4, 130 *iubare exorto* and Apul. 1, 18 (16, 7) *iubaris exortu*; 2, 1 (25, 6) *de...caelo et iubaris orbe*; 4, 4 (77, 7) *in meridiem prono iubare* with *GCA* 1977, 46 ad loc. See also Bernhard 1927, 212 (Poetismen).

transacta[m]: F has *transactā*, which has been emended in φ.

solitudines: the plural is quite common (as it is in classical prose, e.g. Caes. *Gal.* 6, 23 *solitudines renuntiauere missi milites ad explorandum*) but fits in well with Apuleius' preference for abstracts in the plural; see Bernhard 1927, 101 f. Cf. 3, 10 (59, 20) *obseruatis uiae solitudinibus.* Callebat *AAGA* 1978, 179 points out that Apuleius often places the attribute after the noun (as he places *auias* here) to give it greater emphasis; cf. in this chapter 1. 14 below *pudore illo candido*; 188, 25 *lupos enim numerosos, grandes*; etc.

nancti: in F a second hand has repaired the second *n*. There is no reason to read *nacti* with Helm: Frassinetti cites in his app. crit. 10 passages in which F has forms with a second *n*, against 3 without.

accingunt se meo funeri: again seen entirely from the ass's point of view, for it appears from 1. 15 below that, with one exception, the priests have not the slightest intention of killing him.

funeri: the meaning here, 'death', is found in Latin of all periods; e.g. Pl. *Am.* 190 *quod multa Thebano poplo acerba obiecit funera*: Prop. 2, 27, 1 *incertam...funeris horam / quaeritis*; Verg. *Ecl.* 5, 20 *Extinctum...crudeli funere Daphnin*. It occurs very often in the *carmina epigraphica*, e.g. in the expression *funere mersit acerbo* (= Verg. *A.* 6, 429 and 11, 28; see Hoogma 1959, 285 f. and 329).

deaque...mortem: this entire passage almost literally corresponds with that in *Onos* 38, 7 τὴν γὰρ θεὸν ἀφελόντες μου καὶ χαμαὶ καταθέμενοι καὶ τὰ στρώματά μου πάντα περισπάσαντες γυμνὸν ἤδη προσδέουσί με δένδρῳ μεγάλῳ, εἶτα ἐκείνῃ τῇ ἐκ τῶν ἀστραγάλων μάστιγι παίοντες ὀλίγον ἐδέησαν ἀποκτεῖναι. According to Perry 1923, 198, this confirms the remark by Photius *Bibl.* 129 that, apart from the omitted passages, the *Onos* resembled the Vorlage αὐταῖς τε λέξεσι καὶ συντάξεσι.

uehiculo meo: Vallette translates 'porteur', Helm-Krenkel 'von meiner Trage'; either translation rather deviates from the usual 'a means of transport' (*OLD*). If one were to opt for the meaning 'pack-saddle' (developed from the broader meaning 'a means of transporting something') it is hard to see what the distinction would be between this phrase and *stramentis* immediately following. Presumably we have a kind of word-play here 'me as a means of transportation', as at 7, 15 (165, 14) *honoribusque plurimis asino meo tributis* (see *GCA* 1981, 178 ad loc. with our motivation).

The element *uehiculo meo* is not present in the *Onos*. This addition by Apuleius may have its origin not only in the play on words, but also in the fact that Lucius wants to highlight his achievements as an ass; cf. 7, 9 (160, 21) *deque mea uectura*.

stramentis: this is a rather general notion 'anything covering the beast of burden'; the *Onos* has here στρώματα. It also occurs 7, 21 (170, 3) *ipsis stramentis abiectis*; see *GCA* 1981, 218 ad loc. Cf. Liv. 7, 14, 7 *mulis strata detrahi iubet*. Here, too, the word probably refers to a pack-saddle or a blanket with a pack-saddle on it.

renudatum: F had *renundatum* corrected by a later hand (thus Robertson; the same hand, according to Helm and Frassinetti). The compound is both first attested and quite common in Apuleius: 1, 6 (6, 9) *ut...cetera corporis renudaret*; 2, 17 (38, 16) *laciniis cunctis suis renudata* (where again F wrongly inserts a second *n*); 7, 16 (166, 20) *renudatis asceis*; 198, 18 *bracchiis...renudatis*. Bernhard 1927, 122 observes that Apuleius sometimes follows the usage of poetic language (which prefers the simple verb), sometimes that of colloquial language (which tends to use compounds), in order to express himself more precisely and graphically.

de quadam quercu: *quadam* has the force of an indefinite article; cf. e.g. 6, 30 (152,13) *de quodam ramo procerae cupressus* and 7, 24 (172,10) *de cuiusdam uastissimae ilicis ramo pendulo*.

Note that here, as in the two passages just cited (see our comm. ad locc.),

Apuleius is more specific than the *Onos*. Here he specifies the type of tree, whereas *Onos* 38,7 has merely γυμνὸν ἤδη προσδέουσί με δένδρῳ μεγάλῳ. See also Junghanns 1932, 16 n. 15.

flagro illo: the instrument was described at 199,14 f.; the pronoun has therefore its usual retrospective force. Curiously enough *Onos* 38,7 has ἐκείνῃ τῇ ἐκ τῶν ἀστραγάλων μάστιγι παίοντες although no mention has been made of a whip before, an omission presumably due to the epitomiser. For this problem see Mason, *AAGA* 1978, 3 f. with an extensive discussion and a list of references.

pecuinis ossibus: Apuleian style follows both colloquial and poetic usage in preferring the combination of a noun and an adjective to the combination of two nouns; see Bernhard 1927, 110 f. and *GCA* 1981,175 on 7,14 (165,6) *greges equinos*.

pecuinis: a rare word. It may occur in Cato *Agr.* 132,2 though the text is uncertain. Apuleius uses it also 11,1 (226,16) and *Apol.* 12 (14,4). The *ThLL* files in addition have four passages in Zeno (e.g. *Serm.* 1,12,15 (= 2,4,15 Löfstedt)). There is insufficient evidence to speak of an archaism. Apuleius' liking for adjectives with the suffix -*ino*- was noted by Gargantini 1963,36.

paene ad extremam mortem: again Lucius represents the situation in the worst possible light.

confecerant: the pluperfect indicative is used here instead of the customary perfect with *paene* (e.g. *paene dixi*). The first example is Petr. 88, 5 *paene...comprehenderat*. See LHSz 2, 327.

201, 13-17 fuit unus, qui poplites meos eneruare secure sua comminaretur, quod de pudore illo candido scilicet suo tam deformiter triumphassem: sed ceteri non meae salutis, sed simulacri iacentis contemplatione in uita me retinendum censuere: "There was one who threatened to cut my hamstrings with his hatchet because I had triumphed so infamously over that surely lily-white modesty of his, but the others were of the opinion that I ought to be kept alive, not out of consideration for my well-being, but in view of the image lying there."

fuit unus: again the verb comes first in the sentence; see Bernhard 1927, 11 f. on 'Anfangsstellung des Verbums'. Junghanns 1930, 93 points out that first all the priests beat the ass; then their rage is illustrated by the behaviour by one of them. This individualisation is absent in the *Onos*.

poplites: a real threat, in the *Met.* actually carried into execution a few times: 4, 5 (78, 6) it happens to an obstinate ass; 180, 5 Thrasyllus, in the execution of his malicious plan, inflicts it upon Tlepolemus' horse (*postremo poplites lancea feriens amputat*). The ass's fear of this cruel punishment is almost as strong as his constant fear of castration.

eneruare: here literally 'cut the sinews off'; cf. Sen. *Con.* 10, 4, 2 *alterius bracchia amputat, alterius eneruat*; Querol. 46, 18 *utinam (canis) tibi crura ipsa eneruasset, ne umquam inde mouisses pedem*.

secure: the ablative in -*e* is very rare but not unique; cf. Tert. *Pud.* 16. On the other hand the mss. read *securi* at *Met.* 7, 24 (172, 12); see our comm. in *GCA* 1981, 242 ad loc.

comminaretur: here combined with a present infinitive without an accusative of the subject, which is very unusual. Callebat 1968, 315 cites also Tert. *An.* 13, 3 *illam perdere in gehennam comminatur* and Hesych. *In Leu.* 20, 6, 8. See vGeisau 1916, 273, who lists it with the Graecisms. Elsewhere Apuleius has the usual construction of an accusative with a future infinitive; e.g. 9, 40 (234, 2) *comminabatur...sese concisurum eum...frustatim*; *Apol.* 99 (109, 21) *diuersurum me ab ea comminatus sum.* Apuleius uses the compound 17 times in the *Met.*, the simple verb 8 times.

de pudore illo candido; with biting irony, referring back to 201, 1 f. *OLD* translates *candido* here by 'morally pure', 'innocent'. Catullus, too, speaks of the *candida labella* of the *fellator* Gellius (80,2). The first connotation of *pudor* that comes to mind here is definitely 'chastity'; cf. *Lydia* 53 *castos uiolare pudores / sacratamque meae uittam temptare puellae.*

illo...suo: Callebat 1968, 279 f. regards the combination of *ille* with a possessive pronoun (see also our remark on 189, 13 *illi nostri* above) as a stylistic device of the author to express himself emphatically and graphically. We think this more plausible than the theory of Wolterstorff 1917, 197 f., who maintains that the meaning of *ille* in Apuleius is becoming weaker, approaching that of a definite article. Cf. also 1. 28 below *illi suo.*

scilicet: accentuates the ironical tone and retains the narrator's perspective. We may infer from its position that it should be connected closely with *candido.*

deformiter: 'in a disgraceful manner', 'shamefully', from the priest's point of view, of course. This adverb is found for the first time Quint. *Inst.* 8, 3, 45 *siue iunctura deformiter sonat.* The moral connotation present in this passage is also found Suet. *Nero* 49, 3 *uiuo deformiter, turpiter.* The only other occurrence in Apuleius is 198, 11; see our comm. ad loc. Although it remains a rare word in later Latin, Ammianus uses it occasionally, e.g. 22, 14, 4 *adulando deformiter.*

triumphassem: again a military metaphor, a common one. In Apuleius also 9, 38 (231, 31) *de prostratis tuis ciuibus...triumpha* and 11, 15 (277, 25) *Lucius de sua Fortuna trimphat.* Bernhard 1927, 196 points out that the Augustan poets, too, know this figure of speech, e.g. Prop. 2, 8, 40 *de me iure triumphat Amor*; Ov. *Am.* 2, 18, 18 *deque cothurnato uate triumphat amor.*

iacentis: all mss. have *tacentis*, but Beroaldus already proposed to read *iacentis*, which has been accepted into the text by all modern editors. An interchange of *i* and *t* occurs, indeed, rather often in the principal mss. of Apuleius as a consequence of the nature of the so-called Langobardic script; see Helm, Praef. *Fl.* XLV, who has more examples of this confusion, e.g. 3, 20 (67, 17) *alium* instead of *altum*. Observe that especially the verbs *tacere* and *iacere* are often confused by the scribes; cf. Luc. 10, 329 *tacens* (the correct reading of MU) vs. *iacens* (variant reading of Ω c); 5, 443 *stagna iacentis aquae* (ZGV) vs. *stagna tacentis aquae* (MPU, obviously wrong because of 440 *sonantem*); Pl. *Ps.* 1247 *iacentem* (Ital.) vs. *tacentem* (PA); Cic. *Att.* 12, 23, 2 *iaceam* (emendation by Victor.) vs. *taceam* (reading of the mss.).

It is plausible to read *iacentis* in our passage, too, in view of *dea...humi reposita* (1. 10 above) and 197, 5 *deae meae humi iacenti* (where all mss.

unanimously write *iacenti*). But to call *tacentis* an 'ineptissima lectio', as does Oudendorp, goes too far in our opinion. The image of the goddess is lying silent on the ground; it is not unthinkable that the priests expect some direction, a spoken word from their Dea Syria; when that is not forthcoming, it seems safer to let the ass live for the sake of transportation of their goddess. Cf. Lucian. *Syr. D*. 10 on the images of gods in Syria, which give signs and make prophesies in Hierapolis: ἱδρώει γάρ δὴ ὧν παρὰ σφίσι τὰ ξόανα καὶ κινέεται καὶ χρησμογορέει, καὶ βοὴ δὲ πολλάκις ἐγένετο ἐν τῷ νηῷ κλεισθέντος τοῦ ἱροῦ, καὶ πολλοὶ ἤκουσαν. A similar situation occurs in the Old Testament (1 Kings 18, 25 f.), where the priests of Baal invoke their god, expecting an answer. At Liv. 5, 22, 5 the image of Juno, when asked by someone '*uisne Romam ire, Iuno*', is said to have nodded and even spoken in answer (*uocem...dicentis auditam*). Elsewhere in our novel, too, the notion of 'active' images of gods is not unusual: 2, 1 (15, 4) Lucius expects to see in Thessaly, the centre of sorcery, *statuas et imagines incessuras, parietes locuturos*, etc.

contemplatione: this noun can be interpreted in two ways: 1) 'consideration', 'regard'. This meaning, developing from Apuleius onward, becomes quite common in late Latin (e.g. Tert. *Apol*. 39, 16 *penes deum maior contemplatio*), especially in the ablative, where it has the prepositional meaning 'in consideration of', 'for the sake of'. This construction is found in Apuleius, in addition to our passage, 3, 16 (64, 16) *istud...tui contemplatione abieci* 'for your sake'; see vdPaardt 1971, 78 and 128. The development of this noun is similar to that of *causa* and *gratia*; it is frequently found in legal texts; e.g. Ulp. *Dig*. 3, 5, 5, 5 *si quis negotia mea gessit non mei contemplatione, sed sui lucri causa*. See on this matter Callebat 1968, 150 who cites Ps. Hier. *Ep*. 7, 1 *contemplatione mediocritatis meae*; more examples are given by *ThLL* s.v. 648, 69 f.

2) Elsewhere in Apuleius, e.g. 3, 9 (58, 18) and 6, 26 (148, 10), the noun still has the original meaning 'an attentive viewing', 'observation'. This meaning would fit in well with the variant reading *tacentis* discussed above, but also with *iacentis*; see Appendix IV 2.13.

For the umpteenth time the ass has escaped death, once again thanks to utilitarian considerations on the part of his enemies.

201, 17-19 **Rursum itaque me refertum sarcinis planis gladiis minantes perueniunt ad quandam nobilem ciuitatem:** "So they loaded me with the baggage again and, treatening me with the flat of their swords, they arrived at a renowned town."

itaque: in Apuleius usually in second place; Bernhard 1927, 27 gives a long list of examples.

planis gladiis: this combination is found only here, according to *ThLL* s.v. *gladius* 2017, 77. Quite common is *plana manu* 'with the flat of the hand'; cf. Sen. *Ep*. 56, 1 *plana (manus)...aut concaua*; Juv. 13, 128 *plana...palma*.

minantes: Callebat 1968, 50 and *AAGA* 1978, 172 discuss the verb 'minare' in the sense of 'mener des animaux' with reference to this passage. One should be careful, however: although the meaning 'drive' seems, indeed, to be present 3,

28 (73, 3) *asinos et equum...minantes baculis exigunt*, so does the notion 'threaten' (*ThLL* s.v. 1031,47 hesitates). The notion 'lead', 'drive' of animals has undoubtedly developed in the agricultural sphere: it is obvious in Fest. 23 *agasones equos agentes i.e. minantes* and Vulg. *Reg.* 1, 30, 20 *minare boues*. Cf. 7, 11 (162, 13) *gregatim pecua comminantes* with *GCA* 1981, 151 ad loc. and 9, 27 (223, 8) *senex...nos iumenta...gregatim prominabat*; both compounds are found in Apuleius only. In our passage the author may well play with the double meaning: 'drive' from the point of view of the priests: they use the flat of their swords, 'threaten' from that of the ass: after all they use swords.

Inibi uir principalis, et alias religiosus et exumie deum reuerens, 201, 19-25
tinnitu cymbalorum et sonu tympanorum cantusque Frygii mulcentibus modulis excitus procurrit obuiam deamque uotiuo suscipiens hospitio nos omnis intra conseptum domus amplissimae constituit numenque summa ueneratione atque hostiis opimis placare contendit: "There a prominent man, in other respects, too, religious and outstandingly deferential to the gods, came running to meet us, attracted by the clashing of the cymbals, the sound of the tambourines, and the stirring melodies of the Phrygian song; he welcomed the goddess hospitably: his prayers were answered. He installed us within the precincts of his very spacious house and hastened to propitiate the deity with the highest worship and fat victims."

uir principalis: vThiel 1971, 13 n. 36 remarks that, as so often in the *Met.*, this character remains without a name. We note that this is desirable from the narrator's point of view: how is Lucius to know the man's name?

et alias: cf. 9, 39 (233, 3) *et alias Latini sermonis ignarus*. One can conclude from this that *religiosus* has a broader meaning here than 'pious'; this is not brought out by the translations of Vallette ('dévot') and Helm-Krenkel ('fromm'). The connotation is rather 'dutiful', 'scrupulous', 'conscientious' (cf. 10, 3 : 238 , 24 *religio patris*); this gives a certain climax in the characterization.

exumie: this is the spelling of F, changed to *eximie* by φ. Our policy is to adhere to F and we do so here. The spelling is unusual but not unique: F has *exumie* 9, 12 (211, 27), too (but the same hand has written an *i* over it); at 10, 16 (248, 24) F has *exumie*, φ *eximie*. Cf. Pl. *Mer.* 210 and Pl. *St.* 381, where some mss. have the spelling -*u*- ('vix antiqua forma' Lindsay). On the use of this adverb see our comm. on 190, 12.

deum reuerens: F and φ write d̄m, the most probable interpretation of which is *deum*, adopted by most editors. The phrase describes the all-embracing enthusiasm of this *uir principalis* who welcomes each deity with rapture. Therefore we reject specifying conjectures as Beroaldus' *dominae*, de Rooy's *deam*, and Helm's (hesitant) *deum ⟨matris⟩*.[1]) For *deum = deorum* see 199, 7

---

[1] Robertson remarks regarding Helm's conjecture that Apuleius makes a distinction between the mother of the gods and the Dea Syria. This is in itself correct, but an uncritical *uir principalis* certainly could confuse them. For the many points of

deum praesentia and Armini 1928, 314, who for the genitive cites 182, 5 *parentum... reuerens.*

cymbalorum: metal plates which are clashed together; they are often used also by the priests of Cybele.

sonu: this ablative is quite rare; it is cited by Non. 789L in a fragment from Sisenna, *Hist.* 3 (frgm. 26 Peter) *Postquam sonu signorum proelium magno cum clamore uirorum commissum est.* After Apuleius the form is found a few times in Ammianus, e.g. 14, 6, 18 and 18, 8, 5; see Neue-Wagener 1³, 786. Apuleius may have chosen the form for the sake of assonance.

tympanorum: tambourines covered with leather, often used by Bacchants and followers of Cybele. Both these instruments and the cymbals are often mentioned side by side in descriptions of the Cybele-cult, which are often modelled on Lucr. 2, 618 *tympana tenta tonant palmis et cymbala circum / concaua, raucisonoque minantur cornua cantu, / et Phrygio stimulat numero caua tibia mentis.* Clearly influenced by these lines is Ov. *Fast.* 4, 183 and *Met.* 4, 29; similar passages are found Catul. 63, 9 f. and 64, 261; Verg. *A.* 9, 617 f. mentions the same attributes.

cantusque Frygii: F has *frygij*, the last letter in the erasure; φ and α have *frygii*; ς, on the other hand, reads *Phrygii*, which is adopted by Robertson. The *modi* (or *moduli*) *Phrygii* are a violent, wild kind of music, particularly in vogue at the ecstatic Cybele festivals; cf. Apul. *Fl.* 4 (5, 16). Cf. Ov. *Ib.* 456; Tib. 1, 4, 70; Ov. *Fast.* 4, 214. As to the arrangement of the three elements *tinnitu cymbalorum*, *sonu tympanorum*, and *cantusque Frygii mulcentibus modulis*, one might speak, as Bernhard 1927, 71 does, of a 'crescendo'. The assonance and alliteration accentuate the colourful entry of the motley crowd. One can see the entire scene in one's mind and hear the accompanying sounds.

excitus procurrit: this describes the haste and excitement with which the man comes running to offer his hospitality.

uotiuo: 'quod erat in uotis'; cf. 5,20 (119,2) *uotiuis nuptiis*; 7,13 (163,21) *uotiuum conspectum* with *GCA* 1981, 164 ad loc. Cf. Callebat 1968, 154 f. The visit of this (or any) deity is exactly what this *uir principalis* is always praying for. This meaning becomes much more frequent after Apuleius; e.g. *SHA* Treb. Poll. *Gall.* 3, 9 *uotiuum illi fuisse quod... non haberet*; Prud. *Peri.* 2, 330 *uotiua mors est martyri.* It is dubious whether it is right to cite 11,8 (272,5) *uotiuis cuiusque studiis* (as Callebat does), firstly because the text is uncertain, and secondly because the religious context makes the interpretation 'durch fromme Gelübde der Gottheit geweiht' (see Harrauer ad loc.) attractive. See also Gwyn Griffiths ad loc.

suscipiens: 'support', 'receive', e.g. Cic. *Leg.* 2, 2, 5 *in ciuitatem populi Romani susceptus est.*

conseptum: 'enclosure', 'precincts'. The expression suggests a complex of buildings enclosed by a wall. Cf. 11, 91 (281, 1) *intra conseptum templi* with the extensive comm. of Gwyn Griffiths ad loc.

hostiis opimis: in this combination the adjective means 'choice', 'in prime

---

resemblance between the two goddesses see Appendix IV 2. 10. 1. We reject Helm's conjecture on an entirely different ground.

condition'; cf. Fest. 202L referring to *spolia opima*: *hostiae opimae praecipue pingues*. Apuleius uses it quite often in the *Met*.; cf. 2, 11 (33, 25) *porcum opimum* (an emendation, though); 2, 13 (35, 17) *mercedes opimas* (here, too, the mss. read *optimas*); 5, 3 (105, 12) *opimas dapes*; 8, 5 (179, 22) *opimam praedam*; 10, 7 (250, 10) *opimum pabulum*. Cf. also 200, 13 *pinguissimum*.

placare: the use of this verb implies that an angry deity has to be propitiated; cf. 195, 21 *illa Fortuna mea saeuissima, quam. . .placare non potui*. Might the priests have suggested to the *uir principalis* that the Dea Syria is displeased? If so, that could be a reason for using the word *numen* here rather than *deam*. Cf. the priests' tactics 200,13 *uaticinationis mendacio pinguissimum deposcunt arietem*.

CHAPTER XXXI

Once again the ass's life is in danger.

201, 26-202, 3 Hic ego me potissimum capitis periclitatum memini. Nam quidam colonus partem uenationis inmanis cerui pinguissimum femus domino illi suo muneri miserat, quod incuriose pone culinae fores non altiuscule suspensum canis adaeque uenaticus latenter inuaserat, laetusque praeda propere custodientes oculos euaserat: "Here I ran into the most imminent danger, as I recall. For a farmer had sent as part of the hunting bag the haunch of an enormous stag for a gift to that gentleman, his landlord. They had carelessly hung it behind the kitchen door, not very high up, and a dog – equally a hunter – had slyly got hold of it and, pleased with his catch, had hurriedly got away from the watching eyes."

Hic: in the house of the *uir principalis* (cf. above 1. 19).

capitis periclitatum: the verb *periclitari* is construed here with a genitive like the verba iudicialia, instead of the usual ablative. The *ThLL* material comprises only one other instance: Mamert. *St.an. praef.* 20, 16 *ego conscriptionis periclitabor, sed tu editionis*, where the genitive seems to be causal, and therefore is not an exact parallel. For *Met.* 3, 21 (68, 13) *sui periclitabunda* ('testing out her new shape') see vdPaardt 1971, 162 ad loc.

memini: one of many passages in which the reader is reminded of the distinction between narrating and experiencing I. Cf. e.g. Encolpius in Petr. 30, 3 *si bene memini*; 65, 1. See Stöcker 1969, 136.

colonus: see above on 200, 13. As so often, Apuleius is more specific than *Onos* 39, 3 τῶν φίλων τις.

cerui: another difference from the account in the *Onos*, where an ὄνου ἀγρίου μηρόν is mentioned. The single dog who goes out 'hunting' below (202, 2) is another innovation (cf. *Onos* κυνῶν πολλῶν λαθραίως εἴσω παρελθόντων. On the one hand Apuleius obviously attempts to render the tale more realistic, on the other he enhances the colours (*inmanis, pinguissimum*) and the dramatic effects, see 202, 5-7 and Junghanns 1932, 94 n.144. Perry 1923, 199 collects a list of similar differences between the *Met.* and the Vorlage; see also Walsh 1970, 166.

femus: for this rare form (the usual nominatives are *femur* and *femen*) see Prob. *Inst. Gramm. GLK.* 4, 130, 16. It occurs in some late treatises, e.g. *Epit. Alex.* 75, *Mul. Chir.* 875, *Tab. devot. Audollent* 135 A 3, and in some glosses; see *ThLL* s.v. *femur* 470, 39 f.; Callebat in *AAGA* 1978, 169. Apuleius has forms of *femur* (-s) some ten times against *coxa* once (7, 17:167, 12 with *GCA* 1981, 195 ad loc.).

illi suo: see above on 201, 14.

muneri miserat: note the prevalence of *m* in *Hic...miserat* as against the subsequent lines. Bernhard 1927, 220 speaks of 'echt apuleianischen Künsteleien' – we do not share his disdain. See also above on 189, 9 f.

altiuscule: this adverb occurs only in Apuleius; cf. 2, 7 (30, 19) with de Jonge ad loc. on Apuleius' use of diminutives and 11, 11 (275, 10) with Gwyn Griffiths ad loc. See also Abate 1978 passim. The adjective *altiusculus* occurs in Suet. *Aug.* 73 and Aug. *Psal.* 38, 2.

canis adaeque uenaticus: like the *colonus* the dog is a hunter.

adaeque: 'equally', 'likewise', cf. 4, 8 (80, 8) with *GCA* 1977, 69 ad loc. and 10, 2 (237, 8). For the latter passage as well as the present one Kronenberg 1892, 26 tries the meaning 'eo ipso tempore', but he has no parallels. The adverb occurs several times in Plautus; subsequently in Fro. 199, 20 vdH. See Bernhard 1927, 134.

uenaticus: see *GCA* 1977, 147 on 4, 19 (89, 10).

inuaserat: 'to seize possession of'; see above on 200, 30. Note the homoioteleuton *miserat...inuaserat...euaserat*.

praeda propere: the sound effect seems to illustrate the speed of this hunter.

custodientes oculos: Robertson's proposal *custodientis* eliminates the neat personification of the eyes. Presently the reader will note that it is the responsible cook's eyes that have been outwatched.

Quo damno cognito suaque reprehensa neglegentia cocus diu lamentatus lacrimis inefficacibus iamiamque domino cenam flagitante maerens et utcumque metuens altius filio suo paruulo consalutato adreptoque funiculo mortem sibi nexu laquei comparabat: "When the cook had noticed the loss, he cursed his own negligence and lamented for a long time with unavailing tears; and as the master demanded his dinner at once, he said goodbye to his little son, sadly and above all in great fear, grabbed a rope and made ready to end his life by tying a noose." 202, 3-8

inefficacibus: the adj. does not occur before Seneca, but is quite common from that author onward. Apuleius uses it in combination with *lacrimis* also 4, 34 (102, 1); see also e.g. 1, 5 (5, 11); 7, 22 (171, 7).

iamiamque: see vdPaardt 1971, 110 and above on 201, 1; the master's impatience is also underscored by *flagitante*; no such impatience is mentioned in the *Onos*.

utcumque: Callebat 1968, 322 notes that this indefinite adverb (=*utique*) occurs rather often in the *Met*. He cites i.a. 4, 8 (81, 1) *illum...utcumque nimia uirtus sua peremit*, but there the word probably is a conjunction, as at 1, 20 (18, 23), see *GCA* 1977, 74; for the indefinite adverb cf. 4, 19 (89, 3) *et utcumque cunctis in domo uisa pronuntiat* ('somehow or other'); 6, 31 (153, 1). The usage occurs from Livy onward and is particularly common in late Latin; see Fernhout 1949, 149 and LHSz 2, 635.

altius: a weakened comparative, see *GCA* 1977, 181 on 4, 24 (93, 10) *altius eiulans*. For *altus* in a context of fear cf. e.g. Petr. 128, 6, 5 *mentem timor altus habet.* (See also Verg. *A.* 1, 208 f.). Cornelissen 1888, 24 argues that *alte metuere* is impossible Latin and proposes *metuens acrius* referring to Lact. *De mort. pers.* 9, 4 *metuebat acerrime*, Apul. *Met.* 3, 16 (64, 14) *acriter commoueri* and *Apol.* 1 (1, 19) *acrius motum*. The conjecture is as unnecessary as Colvius' *artius*.

filio suo...consalutato: the cook, then, says goodbye to his son, but not to his wife (who will presently keep him from committing suicide, 1.8 *fidam uxorem*; as in the account of the *Onos*). vThiel 1971, 1, 12 n. 30 lists a number of situations in which Apuleius employs dramatic effects without paying much attention to verisimilitude, including the introduction of 'handlungsunwichtige Nebenrollen' (as the *filius paruulus* here) which fortwith disappear again without leaving a trace.

consalutato: the context demands the translation 'say (or kiss) goodbye'. It is curious however that the *ThLL* lemma discusses the verb in the following contexts only: 1) the greeting of friends on arrival; 2) the *consalutatio* of the emperor; and 3) with *res* as an object; for the nuance required here no instances are given.

adreptoque funiculo: chiastically placed vis à vis *filio...consalutato*.

mortem sibi...comparabat: on the motif of failed or prevented suicide see vdPaardt in *AAGA* 1978, 92 n. 73; for the real danger presented by an irate master see Sen. *Ira* 3, 5, 4 *Iracundus dominus quot in fugam seruos egit, quot in mortem*.

202, 8-10 Nec tamen latuit fidam uxorem eius casus extremus mariti, sed funestum nodum uiolenter inuadens manibus ambabus....: "However, the fatal situation of her husband did not escape his faithful wife: firmly seizing the deadly noose with both hands..."

fidam uxorem: the motif of wives who assist their husbands occurs e.g. 4, 3 (76, 14 f.: the anonymous wife of the gardener) and 7, 6 (158, 23: Plotina); Apuleius' own experiences also come to mind (*Apol.* 68 f.).

casus extremus: *casus* is frequently used for '(danger of) death', e.g. Verg. *A.* 10, 350 f. *tris quoque Threicios.../per uarios sternit casus (Clausus)*; see also *Met.* 7, 4 (157, 3) *fortissimum quemque (commilitonum) uariis quidem, sed inpigris casibus oppetisse*.

uiolenter...ambabus: note the assonance.

inuadens: see above on 202, 2.

202, 10-12 'adeone', inquit, 'praesenti malo perterritus mente excidisti tua nec fortuitum istud remedium, quod deum prouidentia subministrat, intueris?': "...she said 'Are you so terrified by the present misfortune, that you've lost your reason, and don't you see there that fortuitous remedy, which the gods' providence provides?'"

mente excidisti tua: ThLL s.v. *excido* 1239, 2 gives for the combination *mente excidere* (='animo linqui') also Rufin. *Hist. Mon.* 8 p. 421 c *(puer) uisu draconis exterritus mente exciderat*; cf. Dict. 1, 4 *regem ira atque indignatione stupefactum consilio excidisse.*

istud: explained by *istum asinum* in the next sentence.

deum prouidentia: Heine 1962, 138 (also quoted in *GCA* 1981, 55 on 6, 29: 151, 1-4) notes that the expression has no religious depth (e.g. 2, 28:48, 3; 3, 3:54, 21; 3, 7:57, 8) and sometimes is to be taken ironically (e.g. 9, 27:223, 8). We disagree: in the first three passages mentioned the phrase has a clear function in characterising the speaker. For the passage mentioned last see our forthcoming comm. ad loc. In book 11 *prouidentia* refers to the power of Isis (and Osiris 11, 27: 289, 10); see Heine ibid. n. 6.

For *deum* see above on 201, 20 *deum reuerens*.

Nam si quid in ultimo fortunae turbine resipiscis, expergite mi ausculta et aduenam istum asinum remoto quodam loco deductum iugula femusque eius ad similitudinem perditi detractum et accuratius in protrimentis sapidissime percoctum adpone domino ceruini uicem': "For if you recover your wits a little in this extreme blast of fortune, you'll wake up and listen to me: take that stranger, that ass, to a remote spot, cut his throat and tear off a haunch that looks like the one that was lost; then cook it in a savoury stew until it is tender, and serve it to the master instead of the stag's'." 202, 13-17

in ultimo fortunae turbine: the combination occurs here only (*ThLL* s.v. *fortuna* 1190, 52), but cf. 11, 15 (277, 5) *magnis...Fortunae tempestatibus et maximis actus procellis* and *Paneg.* 6(7), 3, 4 *fortunae uertex*. At first sight it is a bold image, but wind metaphors are common in all languages (cf. e.g. vNes 1963, 7 f.); e.g. Cic. *Dom.* 53, 137 *tu, procella patriae, turbo ac tempestas pacis atque oti*; Catul. 64, 149 *ego te in medio uersantem turbine leti/eripui*; Ov. *Am.* 2, 9, 28 *nescio quo miserae turbine mentis agor*; Ov. *Met.* 7, 614 *attonitus tanto miserarum turbine rerum*.

For concessive *in* see *ThLL* s.v. 782, 2 f. (see also above on 195, 16). The concessive nuance is sometimes marked by *tamen* (e.g. Pl. *Capt.* 404 *ero gessisse morem in tantis aerumnis tamen*; Ter. *An.* 94; Cic. *Clu.* 3 (to mention but a few passages), sometimes to be culled from the context (e.g. Cic. *Tusc.* 1, 39 *in molestia gaudeo*; *Ver.* 4, 74; Stat. *Th.* 2, 640 with Mulder ad loc.).

resipiscis: the opposite of *mente excidisti* above 1.11. The verb is commonly used from Plautus (e.g. *Mil.* 1332) onward.

expergite: the adverb ('uigilanter, attente' *ThLL*) occurs only in Apuleius: also at 2, 23 (44, 12) *uide...quam expergite munus obeas*. The participle *expergitus* is found at 2, 14 (36, 23) and 2, 26 (46, 8).

ausculta mi: the dative of the person is not often found with this verb, but see e.g. Pl. *Cas.* 204 and Ter. *Ad.* 906. Prisc. *GLK* 3, 281, 7 teaches *ausculta tibi et te. Attici* ἀκροῶμαι σοῦ καὶ σέ, but Diom. *GLK* 1, 313, 4 and several other grammarians allow only the dative.

aduenam istum asinum: Médan 1925, 26 gives a list of nouns used in the *Met.* to qualify another noun. Cf. e.g. 3, 29 (73, 24) *rosae uirgines* with vdPaardt 1971, 205 f. ad loc.; see also LHSz 2, 157.

In several situations the 'accidental' presence of the ass creates direly needed opportunities (e.g. 3, 28, where the robbers use him to carry their booty; 7, 12 (163, 19), where Charite rides him home; 7, 28, where the *uiator* usurps him as a useful means of transport).

remoto quodam loco: *quodam* has the force of an indefinite article, see Graur 1969, 379; *loco* must be dative, though usually *deducere* takes *in* or *ad* or the accusative of motion towards, as (e.g.) at 9, 23 (226, 29). Consequently *quodam* is dative as well, cf. 3, 3 (53, 24) *uasculo quodam...infusa* with vdPaardt 1971, 38 ad loc; cf. also *GCA* 1981, 95 on 7, 3 (156, 3) *quouis*.

detractum: a strong term which makes the prospects for the listening[1] ass all the more frightening. The woman, of course, does not know the ass is listening: the choice of term must be ascribed to the narrator's strategies: the author causes him to express the danger he encounters in the shrillest possible colours. There is no need for *detruncatum* proposed by Rohde 1885, 104; *Onos* 39, 7 has τὸν μηρὸν ἀποτεμών. Rohde uses that phrase to defend his conjecture, but it is a typically Apuleian procedure to enliven flat terminology; see above on 201, 26 *cerui*. For a similar strong term see Verg. *A.* 1, 211 *tergora diripiunt costis* with Austin ad loc.

accuratius: another comparative with weakened meaning (cf. *altiuscule* 1.1 above). Such comparatives are common in popular language and frequent in Apuleius. See LHSz 2, 168 f.

in protrimentis: the expression is not entirely clear. The word *protrimenta* is not attested anywhere else. *OLD* s.v. suggests 'herbs', Vallette translates 'ragoût', Helm-Krenkel 'Brühe'. André 1961 does not mention it. The more important question is, whether *in protrimentis* equals a kind of modal ablative (thus Ruiz de Elvira 1954, 105) and signifies that the haunch is to be cut into very small pieces to make a hash, or whether it refers to the type of sauce or trimmings in which the haunch is first cooked and then served. In view of the wife's insistence that the piece must resemble the original *cerui femus*, the latter possibility is to be preferred. This detail is lacking in the *Onos*.

See Gargantini 1963, 37 for a list of nouns in *-mentum*, usually built on verbal stems (as here *proterere*) and often rare.

sapidisssime: 'savourily', the adverb is hapax legomenon; curiously enough the adj. *sapidus* is also first attested in Apuleius (2, 7:30, 17 *tuccetum...sapidissimum*; 10, 13:246, 9 *sapidissimis intrimentis*); after him it occurs a few times in Aug. and later authors. There is no need for vdVliet's proposal *sapidissimis*, a conjecture based on the passage in 10, 13 just quoted.

percoctum: Apuleius' liking for compounds with *per-* was noted on 200, 27. The verb also occurs at 4, 7 (79, 25). Its force (cooked until tender) is underlined by *sapidissime*.

uicem: φ has *uice*, but the acc. is correct Latin (LHSz 2, 47 cites Pl. *Capt.* 397 *ut eum...remittat nostrum huc amborum uicem*) and is unanimously read at 9, 14 (213, 12) *eius uicem*; 11, 3 (268, 20); *Fl.* 2 (3,2).

The programme proposed by the cook's wife might seem to require rather a lot of time in view of the master's impatience (above 1. 5 f.). Possibly *iamiamque*

---

[1] The ass's situation is not dissimilar to *Met.* 6, 31-32, where he hears the robbers discuss appropriate punishments for himself and Charite.

domino cenam flagitante should be interpreted as representing the cook's panicky thoughts rather than as an indication of 'objective' time.

Apuleius omits *Onos* 39, 8 ὁρᾷς δὲ ὡς ἔστιν ἔνσαρκος καὶ τοῦ ἀγρίου ἐκείνου πάντα ἀμείνων; Indeed the episode has been considerably rewritten in its details. See Mason in *AAGA* 1978, 5 for the procedure in general.

Nequissimo uerberoni sua placuit salus de mea morte et multum conseruae laudata sagacitate destinatae[t] iam lanienae cultros acuebat: "The utterly depraved scoundrel was delighted to save his own life by means of my death. He showered praise on his fellow-slave for her acute wits and started sharpening the knives for the slaughter now destined for me." 202, 18-20

Nequissimo: another instance of Lucius' selective indignation. The narrator uses the adjective rather frequently; he repeats it with reference to the cook at 9, 1 (202, 21).

uerberoni: Callebat 1968, 75 speaks of a 'mot expressif fréquent dans la langue des comiques mais appartenant d'abord au parler familier'; cf. e.g. Pl. *Am.* 284 *Aïn uero, uerbero? Capt.* 551. It occurs several times in the later books of the *Met.*, cf. 10, 7 (242, 23); 10, 9 (243, 23); 10, 10 (244, 7). The combination *nequissimus uerbero* is almost tautological; see Bernhard 1927, 175.

de mea morte: Callebat 1968, 202 f. notes an instance of instrumental *de*, which is used increasingly often in the popular language of Apuleius' times. Compare 7, 22 (171, 3) *mortem de lupo* with *GCA* 1981, 227 ad loc. Médan 1925, 66 regards the use of *de* in these two passages as 'extrêmement hardi'. See also Ruiz de Elvira 1954, 117 and LHSz 2, 264.

Onos 39, 9 has ὁ δὲ μάγειρος τῆς γυναικὸς ἐπαινέσας τὸ βούλευμα, "'Άριστα', ἔφη, 'σοι, ὦ γύναι, ταῦτα, καὶ τούτῳ μόνῳ τῷ ἔργῳ τὰς μάστιγας φυγεῖν ἔχω, καὶ τουτό μοι ἤδη πεπράξεται.' The element *salus de mea morte* represents τούτῳ μόνῳ τῷ ἔργῳ: once again Apuleius enhances the threat to the ass; on the other hand the punishment which threatens the cook is left out.

conseruae: the fact that the cook and his wife are slaves had been suggested by *domino* (1.5 and 17).

destinatae: F has *destinata* (the second *a* changed to *e* by a second hand) *etiã*; the correction was made by Lipsius.

lanienae: see vdPaardt 1971, 42 on 3, 3 (54, 7); *GCA* 1977, 183 on 4, 24 (93, 17) and *GCA* 1981, 248 on 7, 25 (173, 2).

cultros acuebat: cf. 7, 22 (171, 7) *protinus gladium cotis adtritu parabat*. The sharpening of the knives is lacking in the *Onos*: Apuleius leaves nothing undone to enhance the threat to the ass. The tale continues in the next book with the ass's escape.

APPENDIX I

Funeral practices in the *Met.*

The picture of funeral practices in the *Met.* is reasonably homogeneous if allowance is made for the requirements of the particular stories in which they occur. The treatment is usually allusive: one or two elements of the various ceremonies are allowed to stand for a totality. Of the three possibilities mentioned by Lucr. (3, 890–893):

*ignibus impositum calidis torrescere flammis
aut in melle situm suffocari atque rigere
frigore, cum summo gelidi cubat aequore saxi,
urgeriue superne obtritum pondere terrae*

only the last one occurs: there is no mention of embalment, whereas in the *Met.* both the words *bustum* and *rogus* must refer to graves rather than funeral pyres. When the bereft father at 10,6 (241, 1) has attended the funeral of his youngest son, he hurries to the forum *statim ab ipso eius rogo*; at the end of the story this son is revived: a sleeping draft had been administered to him rather than the intended poison. Comparison with 2, 20 (41, 12 f.) shows that *rogus* is in fact used for 'grave': *Nam ne mortuorum quidem sepulchra tuta dicuntur, sed ex bustis et rogis reliquiae quaedam et cadauerum praesegmina ad exitiabiles uiuentium fortunas petuntur*. This in a description of Thessaly's magic practices. For *rogus* in the sense of 'grave' compare Prop. 3, 7, 10 and 4, 11, 8, where Richardson 1977, 341 and 483 ad loc. notes that we have to do with the tombs of cremated remains. See also 4, 18 (88, 1) where the word *iam* in the expression *puluerei et iam cinerosi mortui* seems to indicate that *cinerosus* describes the result of decay rather than cremation.[1] In fact the situation within the *Met.* accords with the general shift towards inhumation in the 2nd and 3rd centuries A.D., cf. Toynbee 1971, 40.

The death-rites mentioned vary, of course, with the circumstances dictated by the particular story; Aristomenes buries Socrates hastily and furtively: *defletum pro tempore comitem misellum arenosa humo in amnis uicinia sempiterna contexi* (1, 18 : 18, 10). This hurried burial stands in shrill contrast to the elaborate wake and burial described in the tale of Thelyphron (2, 21–27). The robbers, too, dispose of their dead with some expedition (4, 11 Lamachus, 4, 12 Alcimus). They discard the body of their old housekeeper, who has committed suicide after the flight of Charite, with remarkable crudity: 6, 30 (152, 15) *cum suo sibi funiculo deuinctam dedere praecipitem* – a crudity which is not without a touch of (religious) superstition, see *GCA* 1981, 67 ad loc.[2] On the other hand the *anus* herself had described the funeral rites for Psyche in rather

---

[1] Certainly the expression cannot be adduced as an indication for the practice of cremation.

[2] They are themselves dealt with (7, 13 : 164, 9 f.) entirely without ceremony, as are all criminals in the *Met.*

more detail, with an appropriate admixture of wedding-elements.

The allusive character of the treatment of death-rites in the *Met.* is illustrated clearly by a comparison of the sequence of activities after the deaths of Tlepolemus, Charite and the *Pistor* in book 9:

Tlepolemus		Charite		Pistor	
180, 22	1. *omnia...lugentium officia* (Thras.)	187, 25	1. *corpus ablutum*	226, 8	1. *summis plangoribus*
	2. *lamentatio seruorum.*		2. *inunita sepultura*[4]		2. *ultimo lauacro*
181, 12	3. *feralis pompa*[3]		3. *perpetuum coniugem*		3. *peractis feralibus officiis*
	4. *toto...prosequente populo.*				4. *frequenti prosequente comitatu*[3]
	5. *sepultura*				5. *tradunt sepulturae*
181, 19	6. *planctus Charites.*			226, 18	6. *diutinus plangor filiae*
181, 25	7. *officiis inferialibus...exactis*				7. *nono die rite completis apud tumulum sollemnibus.*
182, 12	(8. *imagines defuncti*)				

Obviously Tlepolemus (7) corresponds with Pistor (7) rather than (3). The washing of the body is lacking in the case of Tlepolemus, whereas in the case of Charite it is the only truly ritual element mentioned.

---

[3] For the *pompa funebris* see also 10, 6 (241, 1).
[4] See also comm. ad loc. on the concrete meaning of *sepultura*.

APPENDIX II

Apuleius *Met.* 8, 12 (186, 19–21).

1. Before blinding the sleeping Thrasyllus, Charite delivers a fiery speech in which she describes his fate to him: *lumen certe non uidebis, manu comitis indigebis, Chariten non tenebis, nuptias non frueris,* followed by the words which concern us here: *nec mortis quiete recreaberis nec uitae uoluptate laetaberis, sed incertum simulacrum errabis inter Orcum et solem.*

It is remarkable that, as far as we know, these words are not discussed in the literature on Apuleius and have apparently escaped the attention of scholars, although in our opinion they are worthy of attention for several reasons.

2.1. The narrator of this passage, the *iuuenis* of 176, 15, tells his audience that Charite says these words just before she puts out Thrasyllus' eyes *without killing him*. The notion that being blind is a twilight condition between death and life was formulated in antiquity: cf. Sen. *Oed.* 949 f.,[1] where Oedipus says just before he blinds himself *mors eligatur longa, quaeratur uia / qua nec sepultis mixtis et uiuis tamen / exemptus erres...sedibus pulsi suis (oculis) / lacrimas sequantur...fodiantur oculi*. Both the Seneca passage and 186, 21 contain the verb *errare*; the idea that a swift death is too light a punishment is stated explicitly in Seneca, and may be presumed to underlie Charite's words *absit, ut simili mortis genere cum marito meo coaequeris* (186, 14 f.). To the linear reader Charite's words may seem to describe the situation of a blind person; especially the words *nec mortis quiete recreaberis nec uitae uoluptate laetaberis* (being no longer truly alive, but not yet dead) reasonably describe the blind man's life which Charite plans for Thrasyllus.

2.2. But to wander around as a *simulacrum incertum*, and on earth too – for that must be the meaning of *inter Orcum et solem*, a phrase not found elsewhere in the Latin language[2] – is a singular combination; moreover, the expression *simulacrum incertum* is not attested elsewhere.[3] Since (a) from Lucretius onward *simulacrum* is the technical term for εἴδωλον[4], and (b) the expression *incertum simulacrum errare* is reminiscent of the situation in Verg. *G.* 4, 472 *umbrae ibant tenues simulacraque luce carentum* and *A.* 6, 292 f. *tenuis sine corpore uitas...uolitare, caua sub imagine formae* (describing the shades in the

---

[1] Our comm. on 186, 21 *incertum* also cites Artem. 5, 77.
[2] The material of the *ThLL* offers no further instances.
[3] See *ThLL* s.v. *incertus* 881, 43. Nor does *ThLL* mention another example of *errare* referring to *simulacra*, though *errare* is the technical term with respect to shades; see *ThLL* s.v. 807, 19 f. 'de animis mortuorum'.
[4] Cf. Lucr. 1, 120 f. *Acherusia templa / ...quo neque permaneant animae neque corpora nostra, / sed quaedam simulacra modis pallentia miris*; see Bailey ad loc.

underworld), it seems not impossible that the author has chosen these expressions in order to put the reader on a different track.[5]

2.3. If this is correct, though Charite does not know when she utters these words that Thrasyllus' blindness will result in suicide, the sub-narrator does know it and puts words into Charite's mouth which can only be understood with his knowledge of Thrasyllus' end. The sub-narrator knows that Thrasyllus will end as a *biothanatus*.[6] The most famous description of *biothanati* is found at Verg. *A.* 6, 426 f. To this category belong those *qui sibi letum / insontes peperere manu lucemque perosi / proiecere animas* (434 f.), i.e. suicides like Thrasyllus (though the sub-narrator would not describe him as *insons*). Thrasyllus is also one of those *quos durus amor crudeli tabe peredit* (442): he, too, perishes *crudeliter* (by *inedia*) in consequence of a *durus amor*. Another person who belongs to this category in *Aeneid* 6 is Dido, who – as a *simulacrum*, although that word is not used here by Vergil – *errabat silua in magna* (451). The verb *errare* is curious here, although it is possible that other connotations play a part.[7] At any rate it should be stated that suicides and victims of *durus amor* in Vergil are found in the same place – and that Thrasyllus belongs to both categories.

2.4. Tert. *An.* 56, 4 tells us that *biothanati* are forced to wander on earth (!) until they have completed the number of years which they would otherwise have lived: *aiunt et immatura morte praeuentas eo usque uagari istic* (i.e. *in terra*), *donec reliquatio compleatur aetatum, quacum peruixissent, si non intempestiue obissent*;[8] only then are they allowed to enter the underworld.

Servius (*in Aen.* 4, 386) makes a similar statement about *animae biothanatorum: dicunt physici biothanatorum animas non recipi in originem suam, nisi uagantes legitimum tempus fati compleuerint*. Observe again *uagantes* (= *errantes*). The expression *incertum simulacrum errare inter Orcum et solem* accurately describes the twilight condition in which the soul wanders on earth before being admitted to the underworld.

3. *Incertum simulacrum errare inter Orcum et solem* is, then, a reformulation in positive terms of what Charite has earlier visualised in negative terms: *nec mortis quiete recreaberis nec uitae uoluptate laetaberis. Quiete recreare*,

---

[5] Cf. *Met.* 1, 6 (6, 3) *at tu hic laruale simulacrum* ('like a ghost'), said to Socrates, a victim of *uoluptas Veneria* and *scortum scorteum* (1, 8 : 8, 1). *Perlucidum simulacrum* 11, 3 (268, 2), on the other hand, refers to Isis' luminous image in the shape of the rising moon.

[6] Βιαιοθάνατος, Lat. *biaeothanatus* (Tert.) or with contraction *biothanatus*. See Cumont 1949, 306 f.; Norden 1957, 11 f.; *RAC* s.v. (Waszink).

[7] See Norden 1957, 251 'typisch ist...*errare*', who compares e.g. Prop. 1, 1, 11 *Partheniis amens errabat in antris*, referring to the exemplary *seruus amoris* Milanion. This verb describes Dido as someone still tormented by a *durus amor* (cf. Verg. *A.* 4, 444 *curae non ipsa in morte relinquont*), but its 'technical' connotation with reference to shades certainly plays a part here, too (cf. note 3 above).

[8] See Waszink ad loc., 565 f., who says that Tert. and Servius are the only ones who inform us of this doctrine. See also Cumont 1949, 397.

referring to natural sleep, is a regular combination; e.g. Plin. *Pan.* 79, 5 *labores...otio...et quiete recreasset*; Amm. 24, 3, 9 *uictu se recreauit et quiete nocturna* (variant reading *uictui...quieti*). But neither the lexica nor the material from the *ThLL* offer a passage which has *recreari quiete mortis* or anything comparable; again we have a unique expression.

No parallels are given, either, in the detailed and well-documented article by M.B. Ogle, *The Sleep of Death* (*MAAR* 11, 1933, 81 f.) or by Lattimore 1962. The metaphorical identification of sleep with death is already found in Homer (e.g. *Il.* 14, 482–483) but is not very frequent afterwards until in the Hellenistic period; cf. Cumont 1942, 361 '(cette idée) est une figure littéraire de la poésie, non pas un emprunt au language où à la mentalité populaires'. In Greek poetry we can refer to Ἐπιτάφιος Βίωνος 102 f. ἄμμες δ'οἱ μεγάλοι καὶ καρτεροί, οἱ σοφοὶ ἄνδρες, / ὁππότε πρᾶτα θάνωμες, ἀνάκοοι ἐν χθονὶ κοίλαι / εὕδομες εὖ μάλα μακρὸν ἀτέρμονα νήγρετον ὕπνον and in Latin poetry to Catul. 5, 5–6 *nobis cum semel occidit breuis lux, / nox est perpetua una dormienda*; Verg. *A.* 6, 522 *dulcis et alta quies placidaeque simillima morte* (where Homer's identification has become *simillima*); Hor. *C.* 3, 11, 38–39 *surge, ne longus tibi somnus, unde / non times, detur*. In Christian texts death and sleep continue to be compared, but death is no longer an eternal sleep, which would be a negation of immortality, but a temporary sleep, which will end on the Day of Judgment, in the resurrection of the dead; cf. Paul. Nol. *Ep.* 13, 9 *in Christo mortuos dormire Apostolus dicit, ut de somno intelligas temporalem esse mortem. Dormienti enim consequens est excitari et surgere. Recreare* is found in the context of this idea in Christian inscriptions, e.g. Diehl, *Inscr. lat. Christ.* 1, 2425 (in which a *pontifex* prays to God) *efflue astrigeros de caeli conclaue nimbos / et recrea cineres protinus inde meos*; Le Blant, *Inscr. chrét. de la Gaule* 42^c *ut ⟨r⟩e⟨cr⟩e⟨en⟩tur sede perenni* (i.e. *ut fruantur quiete aeterna in caelo*). The notion of being refreshed refers here to what, according to Christian belief, will follow death.

Logically, the notion of 'being refreshed by the sleep of death' can only mean that the sleep of death is followed by something, for a refreshment which presupposes an eternal sleep cancels itself out. This is a remarkable thought for pagan antiquity (except in the mysteries and in gnosticism), the uniqueness of which is underlined by the unusual combination of words. At any rate, these words *may* suggest more than a mere description of the situation of a blind person. It is possible that the narrator of this passage expresses with these words his own judgement on the fate of the *biothanatos* Thrasyllus, cf. 2.3 above.[9]

4. It is possible to take another course and suppose that there is a relation between the implicit author, who is concealed behind the *iuuenis*, and the concrete author, Apuleius himself, who can be characterized in two ways.

---

[9] The narrator's words *nec mortis quiete recreaberis* may also allude to something else. Referring to Nisus, Verg. says *A.* 9, 44 f. *tum super exanimum sese proiecit amicum / confossus placidaque ibi demum morte quieuit*. Nisus, the exemplary friend, who tried to protect Euryalus, obtains the rest of a *placida mors*; Thrasyllus, who did not protect his friend, is not granted *mortis quies*.

4.1. First he can be described as *philosophus Platonicus*; in that case it should be possible to find some statements in Apuleius' philosophical writings to clarify our text. In *De deo Socratis* he mentions a kind of demon which is the *animus humanus emeritis stipendiis uitae corpore suo abiurans* (15 : 23, 20 f.) Such spirits are the *Lemures*; one of them is the *Lar familiaris*, whose influence is beneficial but, says Apuleius (24, 5 f.), *qui uero ob aduersa uitae merita nullis sedibus incerta uagatione ceu quodam exilio punitur, inane terriculamentum bonis hominibus, ceterum malis noxium, id genus plerique Laruas perhibent.* At *Soc.* 8 (15, 13) where he discusses the four elements, he says that they all possess their *propria animalia.*[10] The element *aer* (9 : 17, 4 f. *quod si manifestum flagitat ratio debere propria animalia in aere intellegi*) is the abode of the demons: *habeant igitur haec daemonum corpora et modicum ponderis, ne ad superna inscendant, ⟨et⟩ aliquid leuitatis, ne ad inferna praecipitentur* (9 : 17, 16 f.). Thus the *daemonum corpora* belong to the *propria animalia* of the *aer*; among them the *Laruae* (see 15 : 24, 5 quoted above) can be included, whose *incerta uagatio* has its counterpart in *incertum* and *errare* in our text. It is the fate of people with *aduersa uitae merita* to wander as *Laruae* after their death, and their residence is between heaven and earth; they have little weight *ne ad superna inscendant* (i.e. *ad solem*)[11] and *ne ad inferna praecipitentur* (i.e. *ad Orcum*). We think that it is possible, but not certain, that *inter Orcum et solem* can simply be equated with *aer*, the element mentioned at *Soc.* 9 (17, 4 f.).

Still the remarkable fact remains that both in the case of *biothanati* and of the *Laruae* as harmful shades of criminals – and in the view of the sub-narrator Thrasyllus can be counted among both groups – the shade (*simulacrum*) remains wandering about, in the first case on earth but not (yet) in the underworld, in the second case in the *aer*. But be this as it may, the notion *inter Orcum et solem* remains vague and therefore we want to consider another possibility.

4.2. The author may also be characterised as an initiate of many mystery cults. Apuleius *Apol.* 55 says about himself: *sacrorum pleraque initia in Graecia participaui;...ego...multiiuga sacra et plurimos ritus et uarias cerimonias studio ueri et officio erga deos didici*; the mysteries of Isis will certainly have been among these. Cf. what Lucius says about himself *Met.* 3, 15 (63, 8): *sacris pluribus initiatus.*[12] Since we believe that the whole novel leads up to the

---

[10] *Soc.* 8, 137 *cum quattuor sint elementa notissima...sintque propria animalia terrarum, ⟨aquarum⟩, flammarum...cur hoc solum quartum elementum aëris...desertum a cultoribus suis natura pateretur, quin in eo quoque aëria animalia gignerentur?*

[11] This fits in with the opinion, more and more prevalent from the first century A.D. onward, that the abode of deceased evildoers is in the sphere above the earth rather than under the earth; see Cumont 1949, 189 f. ('Transformations des Enfers') and e.g. I.P. Culianu, *Démonisation du cosmos et dualisme gnostique* (*Revue de l'histoire des religions* 3, 1979), 3 f.

[12] Cf. F. Rohde, *Kleine Schriften* (Leipzig 1901, repr. Hildesheim 1969), 2, 54: 'es ist nicht zu verkennen, wie hier Apuleius an einen flüchtigen Durcheinanderschillern des Lucius und seines lateinisch redenden Doppelgängers sich ergötzen wollte', cited by vdPaardt on *Met.* 3, 15. See also vdPaardt 1981, 96 f. on *Madaurensem, sed admodum pauperem* (*Met.* 11, 27 : 289, 7) which is said of Lucius, 'but through these words can also be heard the extra-diegetical I, Apuleius' (106).

eleventh book, where Lucius, thanks to Isis, regains his human shape and is initiated into her mysteries, we think it likely that our passage, too, should be connected with the mysteries of Isis.

4.2.1. First we may point out that *mortis quiete recreari* is a unique phrase, but the notion is far from unique in a religious context. Cumont[13] discusses Lucius' initiation in Rome into the mysteries of Osiris (*Met.* 11, 27), which includes a ritual meal and the presence of thyrsus and ivy (288, 16), characteristics of Dionysus 'à qui Osiris et Sérapis sont constamment assimilés...ce banquet devait se reproduire dans l'autre monde et se transformer en une frairie éternelle'. The refreshment (*refrigerium*) which the god gives to his faithful servants 'se transformera en un festin céleste auquel participeront les âmes pieuses, et il finira par désigner la béatitude et le réconfort spirituels qui sont réservés aux Élus'.[14]

It is therefore possible that the words *nec mortis quiete recreari* indicate the contrast between Thrasyllus' fate and that of the person initiated into the cult of Isis: initiation in this cult has no other purpose than to give the initiate certainty about a happy life after death.[15] The *uoluntaria mors* is a necessary condition for the acquisition of that certainty and precedes the contemplation of the light. By the symbolical death the initiate becomes a new person. *Recreari* has in this context the same meaning as *renasci*.[16] Thus the words *nec mortis quiete recreari* have a very special meaning for the adept of Isis.

Thrasyllus comes indeed to his end by a *uoluntaria mors* (188, 6 *inedia*), but it is a perversion of the *uoluntaria mors* of the adept of Isis. Hence Thrasyllus is told: *lumen certe non uidebis* (186, 18). The *uoluntaria mors* is also a necessary condition for the *uoluptas* which is accorded to the initiate after his journey *per omnia elementa* and after his 'resurrection'. This *uoluptas* is acquired by the contemplation of the divine image, which is so characteristic of the cult of Isis, and which is experienced by Lucius after his initiation: *inexplicabili uoluptate simulacri diuini perfruebar* 11, 24 (286, 12).[17] It is conceivable that the complementary negative description of Thrasyllus' situation, *nec uitae uoluptate laetaberis*, should also be seen against the background of the *inexplicabilis uoluptas* of the adept of Isis; or, to put it positively, it is precisely the follower of Isis who will be allowed *mortis quiete recreari* and to enjoy the subsequent *uitae uoluptas*.

4.2.2. In that case, the words *simulacrum incertum errare inter Orcum et solem* say the same thing as *nec mortis quiete recreaberis nec uitae uoluptate laetaberis* but use a different image. For the combination *Orcus* and *sol*, and the space bounded by them, also play a part elsewhere, namely 11, 23, at Lucius' first initiation. Under the protection of the *domina elementorum* (Isis) the initiate

---

[13] 1949, 267 f.
[14] Ibid. 268. Cf. Cumont 1942, 387 f.
[15] See Witt 1971, 85; Gwyn Griffiths 1975, 296 f.
[16] See Gwyn Griffiths 1975, 51 f.; 258 f.
[17] Cf. Appendix IV 2.13. Cf. 186, 19 *non frueris*, addressed to Thrasyllus, although in a different context.

makes a journey through all the elements (*per omnia uectus elementa* 285, 15). *Orcus* is referred to in this journey (*accessi confinium mortis et calcato Proserpinae limine* 285, 14). Part of this is the contemplation of a marvellous light (φῶς τι θαυμάσιον)[18] and of the sun, as Lucius himself says: *nocte media uidi solem candido coruscantem lumine*. The same combination of *Orcus* and *sol* underlies the immediately following *deos inferos et deos superos accessi coram*. In the theology of Isis, Osiris is king and leader of the *dei inferi*; the *superi* are ruled by Re who, although lord of the *superi*, is assumed to be present in the underworld.[19] As *domina elementorum* Isis rules the cosmos and also maintains special relations with the underworld. Her rule over both domains appears also from 11, 25 (286, 28) *te superi colunt, obseruant inferi*. The visit to and contemplation of *Orcus* and *sol* mark the spiritual journey undertaken by the initiate *ad instar uoluntariae mortis* (11, 21 : 283, 7). He undergoes the fate of Osiris,[20] after his symbolical death he is reborn,[21] which implies an awakening. For the Isis adept it is especially true that by undergoing a *uoluntaria mors* he *mortis quiete recreabitur*.

Thrasyllus, however, perverts the *uoluntaria mors*, as pointed out 4.2.1. For him, therefore, no spiritual journey *inter Orcum et solem* but *simulacrum incertum errare*. He will become literally blind. At the superficial level his blindness is the result of Charite's revenge; at a higher level it is Isis' punishment for *seruiles uoluptates*.[22] But Thrasyllus is also blind spiritually; he is the uninitiated and will not be granted redeeming spiritual insight as the Isis adept will.[23] It will be his fate to wander about between heaven and earth, as the *philosophus Platonicus* has explained in other works. The same fate is invoked on him by the narrator at a different level, in formulas which are appropriate to situations occurring during the initiation into the mysteries of Isis.

Apuleius manages to condense the three levels at which our text can be approached into one sentence by means of peculiar phrasing, making use of the narrator of this passage as the reporter of Charite's words, who is at the same time familiar with Thrasyllus' suicide, and with his own (i.e. Apuleius') interest in philosophical and religious ideas.[24]

---

[18] Thus Plut. *Fr.de an.* 178; see Gwyn Griffiths 1975, 305. Cf. also *Met.* 11, 6 (271, 1) *cum... ad inferos demearis,... in ipso subterraneo semirutundo me... Acherontis tenebris interlucentem Stygiisque penetralibus regnantem, campos Elysios incolens ipse,... frequens adorabis.*
[19] Ibid. 306.
[20] Ibid. 298 (on 285, 11-12).
[21] Ibid. 305. Cf. our remarks on 4.2.1 *renasci*, and note 16 above.
[22] In the cult of Isis blindness is the typical punishment of him who angers the goddess; cf. Appendix IV 2.10.2.
[23] See Reitzenstein 1920, 118 and Gwyn Griffiths 1975, 330 on 11, 27 (288, 10) *inlustratum*.
[24] Merkelbach 1962, 75 f. sees in Charite 'eine Doppelgängerin der Isis' and assigns to Thrasyllus the part of Seth. Although we do not follow Merkelbach in detail, we share his opinion that certain ideas from the theology of Isis are present here, so that Thrasyllus' fate may be compared in certain respects to that of a person not initiated into the mysteries of Isis.

* We wish to thank Dr. I. P. Culianu (University of Groningen) for his suggestions, which have been most useful to us in writing this appendix.

APPENDIX III

The Dea Syria

Dea Syria (Συρία θεός) is in the Graeco-Roman world the title of Atargatis-Derketo, who was worshipped in Northern Syria and had her main temple in Hierapolis-Bambyce. This temple and the cult connected with it are described in great detail by Lucian in his treatise περὶ τῆς Συρίης θεοῦ. The Dea Syria resembles other mother goddesses and fertility goddesses of Asia Minor, such as Aphrodite-Astarte (Phoenicia) and Rhea-Cybele; with the cult of both of these she has much in common: procession to the sea, hydrophory, lavatio, ecstatic dancing, castration, phallolatry (see Fauth 1402).

From the third century B.C. onward her cult spread through merchants over the Greek world; inscriptions relating to her have been found in Beroea (the very town in Macedonia where Lucius arrives in the *Onos*), Phistyon (in Aetolia), Thuria (in Messenia), and on the island Astyphale. In the second century B.C. temples were dedicated to her on Delos and in Piraeus (Lambrechts 264 f.). No traces of her cult have been found in Africa.

Especially the inscriptions from Beroea and Phistyon show that Atargatis is associated with the liberation of slaves: she buys the slave in order to give him freedom; she becomes his patron. This type of manumission in the temple is found in the second century only. The close connection with the liberation of slaves is in itself an indication that the followers of the Dea Syria should be looked for especially in that social group.

The cult of the Dea Syria arrived in Rome in Nero's time; according to Suetonius (*Nero* 56) the emperor was himself a follower of her cult for a short time. The fact that she was worshipped by such a highly-placed person may be attributed to a whim on Nero's part. Only under Severus was a temple dedicated to her in Rome.

The observation that her adherents should be looked for primarily in the lowest social groups is confirmed by the fact that in Latin inscriptions her name is often spelled incorrectly or even completely mutilated: Diasura (e.g. *CIL* 6, 115), Diasuria (e.g. *CIL* 3, 10393), Dasyr(ia) (*CIL* 10, 1554); see Latte 1960, 346 note 2.

Unlike Isis, the Dea Syria is not mentioned in the Greek novel – with the exception, of course, of the *Onos*.

Literature: W. Fauth in Kleine Pauly 1964 s.v., whose bibliography includes Lambrechts (mentioned above). Add M. Hörig, *Dea Syria: Studien zur religiösen Tradition der Fruchtbarkeitsgöttin in Vorderasien* (Kevelaer 1979; Alter Orient und Altes Testament Bd. 208); H. J. W. Drijvers, *Cults and Beliefs at Edessa* (*EPRO* 82, Leiden 1980) and *Die Orientalischen Religionen im Römerreich* (*EPRO* 84, Leiden 1981) 241 f.

APPENDIX IV

Lucius' representation of the Dea Syria and her priests as the antitheses of Isis and her worshippers.

1. In his commentary on book 11 of Apuleius' *Metamorphoses* Gwyn Griffiths points out that Apuleius' account of the priests of the Dea Syria betrays contempt – natural in an author who is a devotee of a superior religion, that of Isis. Gwyn Griffiths later elaborated this point: in the cult of Isis the emphasis is on moderation, abstinence, and chastity, in sharp contrast to the homosexual practices of the Dea Syria's priests, their obtrusive begging, kleptomania, and unscrupulous use of oracles. Contempt for the Dea Syria's priests is also manifest in the *Onos:* 35, 4 τὸν δεσπότην, οἷον οὐκ ἂν εὐξάμην. Κίναιδος γὰρ καὶ γέρων ἦν, τούτων εἷς τῶν τὴν θεὸν τὴν Συρίαν εἰς τὰς κώμας καὶ τοὺς ἀγροὺς περιφερόντων καὶ τὴν θεὸν ἐπαιτεῖν ἀναγκαζόντων; also 38, 1 ἀνοσίοις κιναίδοις.

The contempt expressed here is on a par with that expressed in the *Met.*, but in the *Onos* Lucius is not converted to Isis-worship. If, as we think, Apuleius' description of the Dea Syria implies comparison with Isis, it is reasonable to conclude that Apuleius intends the comparison.[1]

We will try here to elaborate on Gwyn Griffiths' observations on the basis of the description of the Dea Syria's priests, i.e. from *Met.* 8, 24 onward; it may then be possible to answer the question why and at which narrative level Apuleius intended this comparison to be made.

2.1. The first striking fact is that Lucius' contact with these priests (and consequently with the cult of the Dea Syria) is emphatically attributed to *Fortuna mea saeuissima* (195, 21), who again turned her blind eyes (*caecos...oculos* 195, 23–24) towards him. This immediately puts Lucius' contact with this goddess in a special, unfavourable light.

A reference to Fortuna's fickleness is standard in the *Met.* whenever a new, disastrous event in the ass's life occurs.[2] But because the reference to Fortuna at 195, 21 has been preceded by a long period of silence from the point of view of narrated time,[3] special emphasis is given to the reference to Fortuna and her blind eyes that introduces the Dea Syria. This becomes even more significant when we realise that the fickle and blind Fortuna is also mentioned in connection with the redemptive power of Isis 11, 10 (277, 10) *sed utcumque Fortunae caecitas, dum te pessimis periculis discruciat, ad religiosam istam beatitudinem inprouida produxit malitia;* but now Fortuna has changed in one

---

[1] *AAGA* 1978, 152 f.
[2] Cf. *GCA* 1981, 91 f. on 7, 2 (155, 21). This is also the case in the picaresque novel; see van Gorp 1978, index s.v. Fortuin.
[3] See our comm. ad loc.

aspect: *in tutelam iam receptus es Fortunae, sed uidentis.*[4] When Fortuna's *caeci oculi*, in the context of the Dea Syria, are contrasted thus with *Fortuna uidens*, in the context of Isis, the cult of the Dea Syria is at once characterised as contrasted with that of Isis, at least at the level of the narrator.

2.2. When, after this introduction, the priest of the Dea Syria appears, the narrator at once describes him in unflattering terms: he is a *cinaedus* (195, 25), and an old one to boot, *unum de triuiali popularium faece* (196, 2), who immediately falls a prey to the *praeco's* mockery (196, 7 f.). Moreover, he is bald. Religious baldness was mandatory for the disciples of the Dea Syria on certain occasions. Lucian reports that pilgrims to Hierapolis, her holy city, shave off their hair and eyebrows.[5] Although no explicit allusion is made in our passage to a religious meaning, it is not inconceivable that it is assumed implicitly; another possibility is that the narrator's limited perspective makes it impossible for him to know the religious meaning. At any rate, the baldness of our priests is contrasted with that of the priests and acolytes of Isis. Plutarch maintains that the priestly habit of shaving in the cult of Isis has a religious origin: the desire for cleanness and purity (κάθαρσις).[6] This baldness is for outsiders a standard element in the description of worshippers of Isis, e.g. Mart. 12, 28, 19 *linigeri fugiunt calui sistrataque turba* and Iuv. 6, 533 (a priest who represents Anubis) *grege linigero circumdatus et grege caluo*. For the acolyte of Isis (11, 28: 289, 26 (*Lucius*) *deras⟨o⟩ capi⟨te⟩*) it is a reason for pride and joy: *qua⟨m⟩ raso capillo collegii uetustissimi...munia, non obumbrato uel obtecto caluitio, sed quoquouersus obuio, gaudens obibam*, as Lucius says about himself (11, 30: 291, 17 f., which deals with his third initiation).[7] It seems reasonable to infer that this is a statement of the narrating I; Apuleius himself wore his hair long, at least during the time of his Apology: *Apol.* 4 (6, 8) *capillus ipse, quem isti aperto mendacio ad lenocinium decoris promissum dixere, uides quam sit amoenus...et congestus.*

In religious baldness a *shaved* head is at issue, its most important element being the connection between a shaved head and celibacy.[8] But celibacy – and chastity in general – is completely alien to the Dea Syria's priests in the *Met.* (see 2.3 below). Moreover, so far we have disregarded the fact that the Dea Syria's priest does not have a *shaven* head; he is bald, but *cincinnis semicanis et pendulis capillatus* (196, 1).[9] An adept of Isis expects a priest to have a

---

[4] Cf. also 11, 12 (275, 19: now thanks to Isis) *quod...deae maximae prouidentia adluctantem mihi saeuissime Fortunam superarem.* See also the extensive comm. of Gwyn Griffiths on 277, 5 *Fortunae*.

[5] Luc. *Syr. D.* 55. Cf. *RAC* s.v. Atargatis p. 855 on the baldness of the priests.

[6] Plut. *De Isid. et Os.* 4. See Gwyn Griffiths on 273, 17 (= 273, 21 H) *capillum derasi funditus.*

[7] Except at *Met.* 5, 9 (110, 15) and 2, 8 (32, 6: a hypothetical reference to a woman) the words *caluus* and *caluitium* occur in the *Met.* only with reference to the priests of the Dea Syria and Isis.

[8] See Rudy Kousbroek, *Het avondrood der magiërs* (Amsterdam 1970), who bases himself on E. R. Leach, *Magical Hair* (*Journal of the Royal Anthropological Institute* 88, 1958).

[9] Mockingly the narrator has the priest speak of his loose-hanging hair (197, 4).

clean-shaven head; our priest however, who is naturally bald, tries to compensate for his baldness. This makes him not only reprehensible but also ridiculous; Mart. 6, 57, 1-2 says of a certain Phoebus: *mentiris fictos unguento, Phoebe, capillos / et tegitur pictis sordida calua comis.*

It is possible that the very outward resemblance between the priests of the Dea Syria and Isis is one of the reasons why the narrator describes the cult of the Dea Syria so disparagingly: the cults of the Dea Syria and Isis are, at least to the outsider, similar in many respects,[10] which increases the need of the adept of Isis to underline the dissimilarities. That the ideas of this adept play a part here may be deduced from the fact that the priest's baldness (and the *praeco's* mockery) are mentioned in the *Met.* but are absent in the *Onos,* even though the *Onos* refers to the priests contemptuously (see 1 above). The qualification *unum de triuiali popularium faece* is also absent in the *Onos.*

2.3. It appears that the notion of purity (κάθαρσις), mentioned at 2.2 above, generally plays an important part in the description of Isis and her cult, as does impurity in that of the worshippers of the Dea Syria. We sum up: 200, 19 *spurcissima illa propudia;* 201, 2 (the neighbours) *ridicule sacerdotum purissimam laudantes castimoniam;* 208, 6 *purissimi illi sacerdotes;* 9, 9 (209, 12) *sacrilegos* (the priests of the Dea Syria) *impurosque compellantes;* 9, 10 (210, 1) *impuratissima illa capita.* On the other hand the priest of Isis: 11, 16 (278, 19) *sacerdos...de casto praefatus ore;* 11, 21 (282, 17) another of Isis' priests is *grauis et sobriae religionis obseruatione famosus.* Cf. also 11, 21 (283, 18) *arcana purissimae religionis;* 11, 10 (273, 19) *candore puro luminosi,* referring to acolytes of Isis. Thus it appears that, with one exception, *purus* is always used in the *Met.* in connection with the cult of Isis, or antithetically with that of the Dea Syria.[11]

2.4. After the notion of purity in general, we come to some of its particular manifestations. The religious bath (*purissime circumrorans*) in the *balneae* (11, 23: 284, 25) as a preparation for fasting[12] can be contrasted with *balneas obeunt* (200, 15), where the Dea Syria's priests prepare for a meal accompanied by

---

[10] See M. Malaise, *Les conditions de pénétration et de diffusion des cultes égyptiennes en Italie* (*EPRO* 22), Leiden 1972, 171-172. Schlam *AAGA* 1978, 101 says that the Dea Syria's cult is comparable to that of Isis, at least in its devotion to a Great Goddess. The cults of the two goddesses were interchangeable in the view of some devotees: Witt 1971, 294 n. 11 mentions a certain L. Pacilius Taurus, who was a priest of the Magna Mater, the Dea Syria, and Isis simultaneously; see also *ibid.* 72 and 294 n. 13. Simultaneous priesthoods of Isis and of the Mater Deum are also found; see *Sylloge Inscriptionum Religionis Isiacae et Sarapiacae,* ed. S. Vidman (Berlin 1969), nr. 543 and 579.

[11] The exception is 10, 21 (253, 2) *pura atque sincera* (*basiola*). Cf. also 11, 16 (278, 20) *quam purissime purificatam nauem Isidis*) and 11, 23 (284, 27) *purissime circumrorans.* The adjective *purus* already plays a part in Cicero's discussion of the cult: *N.D.* 2, 71 *cultus...deorum est optumus idemque castissimus..., ut eos semper pura, integra, incorrupta et mente et uoce ueneremur* (see further Pease ad loc.). An adept of Isis would agree with every word of Cicero's remark.

[12] See the extensive comm. of Gwyn Griffiths ad loc. When the ass, awakened on the beach of Cenchreae, sees the goddess rising from the sea, he immerses his head seven times in the water, *purificandi studio* (11, 1: 266, 24).

sexual dissipation. The meal taken by Lucius after his initiation (*suaues epulae* 11, 24: 268, 8) forms a sharp contrast to the above-mentioned meal of the Dea Syria's priests.

2.5. The same adjective *suauis* also qualifies the music which is heard at the procession of Isis: 11, 9 (273, 8) *symphoniae dehinc suaues, fistulae tibiaeque modulis dulcissimis personabant*. This presents a striking contrast to the Dea Syria's priests: 196, 3 *per plateas et oppida cymbalis et crotalis personantes*. In our comm. ad loc. we have argued that *crotalum* in particular is often associated with immoral behaviour; here we cite only Priap. 27, 3 *cymbala cum crotalis, pruriginis arma*. Thus here, too, *prurigo* and *impudicitia* vs. modesty and purity.

The musical instrument par excellence in the cult of Isis is the *sistrum*, a dominant feature of which is the cathartic effect of the music.[13] Here we have the same contrast: immoral vs. purifying and beneficial.[14]

2.6. We also note the disapproving terms which describe the motley garb of the priests on their begging tour: 198, 11 *uariis coloribus indusiati et deformiter quisque formati facie caenoso pigmento delita et oculis obunctis graphice prodeunt*.[15] Admittedly some are described wearing *tunicas albas* (198, 14), but that is still far from the luminous beauty (*candidus, luminosus*) of the garments of the priests of Isis 11, 10 (273, 24) *antistites sacrorum...candido linteamine* and of her worshippers 11, 9 (272, 24) *mulieres candido splendentes amicimine;* 11, 10 (273, 18) describing the *pompa* of the worshippers of Isis, which is thus contrasted with the begging of the priests of the Dea Syria: *uiri feminaeque...linteae uestis candore puro luminosi* (observe the adjective *purus*). Cf. also the *Olympiaca stola* 11, 24 (286, 2) which Lucius is allowed to wear after his initiation.[16]

2.7. The itinerant priests of the Dea Syria force her to beg, as is stated 196, 4; ch. 27 contains a colourful description of how this is put into practice. Influenced by their wild dervish-dances, self-mutilation, and self-accusations, the spectators open their purses (200, 3), trying to surpass one another is generosity (*certatim*). These activities are summed up by the narrator with *omnem illam depraedabantur regionem* (200, 10), after making the biting remark earlier *quasi deum praesentia soleant homines non sui fieri meliores, sed debiles effici uel aegroti* (199, 7 f. in reference to their self-mutilation). Isis' priests also

---

[13] See Wille 1967, 63 with many examples of the benevolent and healing activity of Isis, accompanied by the rattling of the *sistrum*.

[14] At 201, 21 *tympana* are also mentioned as musical instruments of the Dea Syria's priests. Apuleius mentions *cymbala* and *tympana* scornfully as belonging to *numina barbara*, as contrasted to the *Aegyptia numina*: *Soc*. 14 (22, 8) *Aegyptia numina ferme plangoribus, Graeca plerumque choreis, barbara autem strepitu cymbalistarum et tympanistarum et choraularum* (*gaudent*). See J. Beaujeu, *La religion romaine à l'apogée de l'empire* (Paris 1955), 230.

[15] See our comm. ad loc., which shows that the description of the garments of the priests of the Magna Mater is a stereotype.

[16] See the comm. of Gwyn Griffiths ad loc.

live by their cult[17] and although it is of course possible to find examples of pursuit of gain even among them (see Nock 153 for the bribery of a priest who was to be a go-between at a rendezvous, as related by Josephus *Ant. Iud.* 18, 65 f.), we cannot detect any regret or complaint in Lucius' words as to the extent of his financial contribution to the cult of Isis or Osiris.[18] This applies both to his first initiation (11, 21: 282, 23; 11, 22: 283, 26; 11, 23: 284, 23) and the second and third initiations in Rome into the cult of Osiris (ch. 28 and ch. 36). He himself says 11, 25 (287, 5) *at ego referendis laudibus tuis exilis ingenio et adhibendis sacrificiis tenuis patrimonio:* rich as he is, he would never be rich enough to be able to make sufficient sacrifices. The absence of an undertone of regret or complaint is the more striking in view of his complaint in ch. 28 about the high cost of living in Rome; to pay for his initiation he has to sell his clothes: *ueste ipsa mea quamuis paruula distracta, sufficientem conrasi summulam* (11, 28: 289, 19 f.) But *do ut des* has seldom been fulfilled more rapidly: *quae res* (the inititation) *summum peregrinationi meae tribuebat solacium nec minus etiam uictum uberiorem subministrabat, quidni, spiritu fauentis Euentus quaesticulo forensi nutrito per patrocinia sermonis Romani* 11, 28 (290, 1 f.). Neither do we read a word of disapproval or regret on the occasion of his third initiation, when he says 11, 20 (291, 2) *instructum teletae comparo largitus.* In fact, he says explicitly *nec hercules laborum me sumptuumque quidnam... paenituit* because *do ut des* also functions here: *liberali deum prouidentia iam stipendiis forensibus bellule fotum* (11, 30: 291, 5 f.). Thus the purity of Isis' cult (and in its wake that of Osiris), which turns out to be profitable for its followers, is clearly contrasted to the rapacity of the Dea Syria's priests, who force their goddess to beg (a description full of contempt, taken over from *Onos* 35, 4 (τῶν... τὴν θεὸν ἐπαιτεῖν ἀναγκαζόντων) and who are found even to steal (9, 9: 209, 17 f.). Their greed (cf. 200, 6 *auidis animis*) pays off handsomely, but what do they use the profit for? For the acquisition of a *iuuenis satis corpulentus* to satisfy their sexual lusts (see our comm. on 198, 4–9).

2.8. At 199, 9 f. the narrator described how the priests make a public confession, which he characterizes at once with *conficto mendacio.* The cult of Isis also includes confession but characteristically it is unattended by self-mutilation with knives and scourge, in contrast to the cult of the Dea Syria from 199, 14 onward. The cult of Isis puts far more emphasis on purity of heart than of body; cf. 2.3 f. above. For further details of the confession, see Appendix V.

2.9.1. The contrast between greed on one side and purity on the other is also found elsewhere. The priests of both goddesses prophesy. In the case of the Dea Syria priests, this is at once qualified as a swindle: 199, 10 *infit uaticinatione clamosa conficto mendacio;* 200, 12 f. *fictae uaticinationis mendacio.* In addition to the fact that the priests are frauds, they prophesy for the sake of filthy lucre: at 200, 13 they use their prophetic skills to trick a farmer out of a

---

[17] See A. D. Nock, *Conversion* (Oxford 1933, ʳ1961), 150.
[18] Gwyn Griffiths, *AAGA* 1978, 152 comes to a different conclusion.

pinguissimum. . .arietem and at 9, 8 (208, 5) we read *uaticinationis. . .crebris mercedibus suffarcinati purissimi* (sic!) *illi sacerdotes nouum quaestus genus sibi comminiscuntur* (i.e. by giving oracles). The chapter ends with *ad istum modum diuinationis astu captioso conraserant non paruas pecunias* (209, 1–2).

Isis' priest also prophesies, or rather speaks with divine *inspiration* (*uaticinatus* 11, 16: 278, 4) when he admonishes Lucius, now changed back into human shape, to devote himself to the service of Isis: *tunc magis senties* (the prophetic future) *fructum tuae libertatis* (11, 15: 278, 3). This priest is called *egregius* (vs. the sarcastic *purissimi illi sacerdotes*) and he *fatigatos anhelitus trahens conticuit*. This is a poetic turn of phrase, inspired by Vergil's description of the Sibyl.[19] A similar turn is used 199, 5 *anhelitus crebros referens*, referring to the Dea Syria's priest, who *uelut numinis diuino spiritu repletus simulabat sauciam uecordiam*. *Velut* underlines the insincerity of the Dea Syria's priest; the contrast between the two priests is strikingly emphasised by the use of *uelut, simulare*, and similar phraseology.

2.9.2. The mendacity mentioned above is indicated by the narrator in many ways. It starts with the characterization of the Dea Syria's priest as *similis indignanti* (196, 23) at the beginning of his curse (cf. 2.10.1 below); 199, 6 *simulabat. . .uecordiam* and 199, 10 *conficto mendacio* (see our comm. ad locos) are meant to accentuate the contrast with Isis' priest (*uultu geniali et hercules inhumano in aspectum meum attonitus*).[20]

2.10.1. This brings us to the difference between the two cults from a 'theological' point of view. From 196, 23 onward the Dea Syria's priest, who wants to buy the ass, utters a malediction, which we need not take completely seriously: the priest is *similis indignanti*, which at once demonstrates his insincerity at this moment (cf. his insincerity in connection with his fortune-telling, 2.9.1 and 2.9.2). In this malediction he starts with his own goddess, *omnipotens et omniparens* (l. 24), followed by a series of other gods: *sanctus Sabadius et Bellona et mater Idaea et cum suo Adone Venus domina*. All the gods mentioned here *beside* the Dea Syria show, with the exception perhaps of Sabadius, many points of similarity with the Dea Syria, but identification has seldom taken place. The points of similarity apply especially to the *mater Idaea*,[21] whom the priests themselves call a sister of the Dea Syria (9, 10: 210, 5),

---

[19] Cf. Verg. *A.* 6, 48 f. *sed pectus anhelum / et rabie fera corda tument;* see Gwyn Griffiths ad loc. Fredouille 15 compares also *A.* 6, 79 *ille* (sc. *Phoebus*) *fatigat / os rabidum* (sc. *uatis*).
[20] See also our comm. on 198, 7 *uenisti tandem*: the use of epic language indicates that the sincerity of the Dea Syria's priest is more apparent than real.
[21] See *RE* s.v. Dea Syria 2240 (Cumont). Lambrechts and Noyen, 1954 268: the cults of the two goddesses have many traits in common; page 276 deals with the close relation of the Dea Syria with the *mater deum* and Aphrodite. M. Hörig, *Dea Syria: Studien zur religiösen Tradition der Früchtbarkeitsgöttin in Vorderasien*, Kevelaer 1979, 237–239. We note *I.G.* IX^2, no. 100 of the 3rd century B.C., from Phistyon in Aetolia, an important center of the cult of Atargatis = Dea Syria (Lambrechts and Noyen 266), where the Dea Syria is called Ἀφροδίται Συρίαι (dative); and *ibid.* no. 105, where she is called μάτερι θεῶν. The scholars mentioned above point out that 'equal to' is not the same as 'identical with'; but this distinction may not always have been clear to 'the man in the street'.

a relationship which also appears 210, 10 when, after the arrest of the stealing priests, the image of the Dea Syria is donated and dedicated to the temple of Cybele; another example is 201, 20 f., where the Dea Syria's priests wander along, accompanied by the sound of *cymbala, tympana* and the *cantus Frygius* – terms ordinarily used in the context of the cult of the *mater deum*.[22] Venus[23] and Bellona, who was identified with the Near Eastern goddess Ma after Sulla had become acquainted with this goddess in 92 during his campaigns in the East, and whose cult was quite similar to that of the Magna Mater,[24] belong to the same sphere as the Dea Syria.

Another passage in the *Met.* containing a long series of gods' names is 269, 12 f., where Isis reveals herself to Lucius: *en adsum tibi.* She is there μυριώνυμος (Plut. *De Isid. et Os.* 53, 372 E), or, as Apuleius puts it: *deorum dearumque facies uniformis* (15) and *cuius numen unicum multiformi specie, ritu uario, nomine multiiugo totus ueneratur orbis* (17; cf. also 284, 10 *dea multinominis*). These formulations 'reveal the monotheistic trend in the concept, but with it goes a recognition of other gods subsumed in the godhead'.[25] The following lines contain an enumeration of Isis' names: the Phrygians call her *Pessinuntiam deum matrem,* the Cyprians *Paphiam Venerem,* etc. This catalogue of Isis' names is preceded by a prayer of Lucius the ass to the rising moon on the beach of Cenchreae: *regina caeli, – siue tu Ceres alma. . .seu tu caelestis Venus. . .seu Phoebe soror. . .seu. . .horrenda Proserpina.* Admittedly Lucius is represented as not yet aware of the fact that it is actually Isis that he is addressing, but that does not alter the fact that to the devotee of Isis it is beyond all doubt that the *regina caeli* is Isis.[26] An interesting point is that the formula *siue. . .seu* corresponds to εἴτε. . .εἴτε as e.g. in an epigram from the time of Antoninus Pius, where it is used to introduce five appellations of the *same* goddess.[27] This is diametrically opposed to the copulative *et. . .et. . .et* in the curse of the priest of the Dea Syria.

The formulations at *Met.* 267, 4 f. and 269, 12 f. are for the adept of Isis the correct ones for his goddess: *te tibi una quae es omnia* (*CIL* X, 3800 = Dessau, *Inscr. Sel.* 4362). All other gods merge into her, so that the phrase *rerum naturae parens* may justifiably be applied to her. This is not true of the Dea Syria: her priest calls her *omniparens* (196, 25) and includes in his catalogue the names of several goddesses mentioned in the Isis-catalogues cited above (Mater Idaea (= *deum mater*), Bellona, Venus), but these goddesses, though in some respects similar to the Dea Syria, are not fully identified with her and certainly do not merge into her. Similarly, Isis is called *omnipotens* at 278, 8 and the Dea Syria's priest calls his goddess *omnipotens* at 196, 24 (and these are the only two

---

[22] See our comm. on 210, 5, which mentions the possibility that Apuleius thought here of Catul. 63, 9 and 64, 261, and of Verg. *A.* 9, 617 f. See also note 15 above for the equation of the Dea Syria with the Magna Mater.
[23] See note 21 above.
[24] See *RAC* s.v. Bellona 127 and s.v. Gallos 992. See also Gwyn Griffiths on 269, 18 (= 269, 24 H).
[25] Gwyn Griffiths on 269, 11–12 (= 269, 15 H).
[26] See Gwyn Griffiths ad loc. Cf. also Harrauer 1973, 11.
[27] See Y. Grandjean, *Une nouvelle arétalogie d'Isis à Maronée* (*EPRO* 49) Leiden 1975, 68 n. 153.

occurrences of the word in the *Met.*), but the priest's claim is given the lie in the course of ch. 25, when it emerges that he believes that the Dea Syria needs a *medicus* (see 2.12.1 below). In the eyes of the narrating I, Isis is the universal goddess,[28] while the Dea Syria is a private deity, whose cult is objectionable and who is wrongly described in terms which belong to Isis. Consequently she is not mentioned in the catalogue of Isis.

2.10.2. The substance of the priest's curse is to invoke the set of above-mentioned gods to blind the *praeco* for ridiculing the priest (197, 1). Again, the priest does this *similis indignanti*; this does not increase the strength of the malediction, which, moreover, is to be fulfilled by more than one deity. For the follower of Isis, on the other hand, it is Isis who blinds those who anger her (cf. e.g. Iuv. 13, 92 *decernat quodcumque uolet de corpore nostro / Isis et irato feriat mea lumina sistro* with the comm. of Friedlaender ad loc. with further references). She can restore the eyesight of those who ask her forgiveness; cf. Ov. *Pont.* 1, 1, 51 *uidi ego linigerae numen uiolasse fatentem / Isidis Isiacos ante sedere focos;* 55 *talia caelestes fieri praeconia gaudent;* 57 *saepe leuant poenas ereptaque lumina reddunt / cum bene peccati paenituisse uident.* This passage from Ovid shows that in addition to her blinding power Isis also has a healing power, which is especially concerned with the eyes. The recently discovered Isis-aretalogy from Maronea (late second or early first century B.C.) was drawn up after the miraculous cure of an eye-disease; cf. line 6 ὥσπερ οὖν ἐπὶ τῶν ὀμμάτων, Ἴσι, ταῖς εὐχαῖς [ἐπήκ]ουσας.[29]

The malediction of the priest of the Dea Syria, however, does not suggest any benevolent power similar to that suggested by the passage cited from Ov. *Pont.* 1, 1, 57. In the maledictions of the two goddesses we can see the contrast between a healing, benevolent power and a negative, malevolent one.

2.11. In his attempts to sell the ass to the Dea Syria's priest, the *praeco* recommends the ass as *bonum et frugi mancipium* (196, 12). At first sight this does not seem peculiar: the *praeco* is playing his own ironical game with the ass, which may account for the fact that *mancipium* is not used with reference to the ass in any other passage.[30] But when the bargain is struck and the priest shows his bargain to the *'puellae'*, he uses a similar term: 197, 14 *susceptum nouicium famulum, ...seruum...pulchellum;* cf. *Onos* 36, 2 δοῦλον ὑμῖν ἐώνημαι καλόν. The words used by the priests, *famulus* and *seruus*, also occur only here with

---

[28] This narrating I is not identical with the author; Apuleius does not mention Isis in the *Apology* and at 55 (62, 25) says only *multiiuga sacra et plurimos ritus et uarias cerimonias studio ueri et officio erga deos didici.* Cf. also what has been said at 2.2 about Apuleius' long hair.

[29] See Grandjean 25 f. on the role of Isis in the cure of eye diseases, with references. Witt 1971, 258 and *RAC* s.v. Blindheit, 438 f. Merkelbach 1962, 68 n. 1 and 7 also points out magical texts describing Isis as a healing goddess. See further 2.12.1 below.

[30] The other two passages in the *Met.* in which *mancipium* occurs are 3, 22 (68, 26), where Lucius says to Photis *tuum...mancipium*, and 4, 24 (93, 14) *praeda et mancipium*, referring to Charite. The *ThLL* gives no specific examples of *mancipium = seruus* referring to an animal. Isid. *Orig.* 9, 4, 45 says *mancipium est quidquid manu capi subdique potest ut homo, equus, ouis*, but this refers to the possibility of selling.

reference to the ass.³¹ It seems that there is a connection between *mancipium, famulus,* and *seruus,* used here in such a conspicuous way. The nature of the servile work which the ass is to perform, is clearly stated; he will transport the image of the goddess, without exposing it to danger: 197, 2 *me putas. . .iumento fero posse deam committere, ut turbatum repente diuinum deiciat simulacrum.*³²

It would be unthinkable for the image of Isis to be transported by an ass, for the ass is hateful to Isis: at 270, 16 she says to Lucius, when appearing to him right before his metamorphosis back into a human being: *pessimae mihique detestabilis iam dudum beluae istius corio te protinus exue.* This is in keeping with the theology of Isis, in which the ass is associated with Seth-Typhon, the incarnation of evil, who kills Osiris.³³ It is interesting that the word *famulus,* which occurs 18 times in the *Met.,* is used only twice of Lucius: in addition to the above-mentioned passage, which refers to Lucius the ass, it is used once more, this time referring to Lucius changed back into a man, at 288, 13 *me quoque peti magno etiam deo famulum sentire deberem.* Isis has delivered him from his ass's shape, in which he was the *famulus* of the Dea Syria through her priest; thanks to Isis he can now, at his second initiation as a human being, be a *famulus* of Osiris – the only true and pure service.³⁴

Therefore, when at 277, 16 the priest of Isis says to Lucius, who has regained his human shape, *quid latrones, quid ferae, quid seruitium. . .nefariae Fortunae profuit,* we think that *seruitium* refers not only to the heavy burdens he had to carry at the robbers' den or to the heavy work in the grain mill,³⁵ but certainly also to his unworthy *seruitium* to the Dea Syria (in which *Fortuna saeuissima* had a hand, cf. 2.1). This is the more probable because line 14 refers to those *quorum sibi uitas ⟨in⟩ seruitium deae nostrae maiestas uindicauit;* they can be contrasted to those who render *seruitium* to another, unworthy goddess, in this case the Dea Syria.³⁶

It is remarkable that in inscriptions of the 3rd century B.C. from Beroea (Macedonia) and Phistyon (Aetolia), Atargatis (= Dea Syria) is connected with the liberation of slaves;³⁷ as the inscriptions show, the goddess buys the

---

³¹ *ThLL* s.v. 267, 73 mentions four examples of *famulus* referring to animals, beginning with Verg. *A.* 5, 95 *incertus geniumne loci famulumne parentis / esse putet (anguem).* The other passages, in Ov., Val. Fl., and Sil., which also refer to snakes, are inspired by the Vergil passage. Apuleius himself uses the word once of his horse, directly after Lucius' metamorphosis: 3, 26 (71, 27) *illi gratissimo famulo,* in an ironical sense (see vdPaardt ad loc.).
³² The transportation of the goddess by the ass is described 198, 16 f.; 200, 8 f.; 201, 17 f.; 9, 4 (205, 18 f.); 9, 10 (209, 22 f.).
³³ See Gwyn Griffiths 25 and his comm. on 270, 13–14; also *RE* s.v. Seth 1899. For the Typhonian nature of the ass cf. Plut. *De Isid. et Os.* 30–31. See also Wlosok 1969, 80 n. 1 with references.
³⁴ 'Being a slave' is used here as a term to express religious service; cf. 278, 2 *nam cum coeperis deae seruire* with the comm. of Gwyn Griffiths ad loc. See also Harrauer 1973, 98.
³⁵ Thus Fredouille ad loc.
³⁶ *Seruitium* 277, 15 can also refer to being a captive of *uoluptas,* for Lucius calls himself at 3, 22 (68, 26) *tuum* (i.e. Photis') *mancipium;* cf. n. 30. For this passage see Schmidt 1982.
³⁷ See Appendix III.

295

slaves to give them their freedom: she becomes their patron. We have seen that in the *Onos* the priest of the Dea Syria uses the word δοῦλος. Could the author of the *Onos* (or of the Vorlage) have known about this function of the goddess so that he now, ironically, has the ass sold as a slave to the priest of a goddess whose activity had so often been connected in those regions with the liberation of slaves? If this is the case, the narrating I has the priest of Isis react to this in his address to Lucius (277, 5 f.) mentioned above, for it ends with *nam cum coeperis deae seruire, tunc magis senties fructum tuae libertatis* (278, 2). *Seruitium* to Isis brings *libertas* (this word is to be understood on several levels); *seruitium* to the Dea Syria, who redeems slaves, did not bring *libertas* to the ass.

2.12.1. At a certain moment the priest of the Dea Syria entertains the idea, repulsive to him, that the recalcitrant ass may shake off the image of the goddess which he is carrying. In that case the only solution for the priest would be to *deae meae humi iacenti aliquem medicum quaerere* (197, 5). This is a somewhat surprising utterance, which can be fully understood only in contrast with the cult of Isis. In Egyptian tradition Isis' miraculous deeds are often associated with healing;[38] cf. 2.10.2 above. This ability of the goddess is also known in Latin literature, e.g. Tib. 1, 3, 27 *nam posse mederi / picta docet templis multa tabella tuis*. Lucius' return to human form at 11, 13 is therefore described in detail, as is customary in tales of miraculous cures, though in this case there is no explicit mention of Isis' healing power. Examples of descriptions of miracle-cures (e.g. the Sarapis-aretalogy from Delos) are cited by Gwyn Griffiths in his comm. on 276, 4 *protinus mihi dilabitur* etc.

In the *Onos* the change back into human form is merely adumbrated (54, 2 ἀφανὴς ἐκεῖνος ὁ πάλαι ὄνος, ὁ δὲ Λούκιος αὐτὸς ἔνδον μοι γυμνὸς εἰστήκει) and the priest's remark about possible medical help for the Dea Syria is absent. We may conclude that the additions in the *Met.* emphasize the contrast between the worthlessness of the Dea Syria who cannot heal but needs a doctor, and the healing power of Isis. We have already pointed out that the proof of this worthlessness is found in the very chapter in which the Dea Syria was called *omnipotens* and *omniparens*.

2.12.2. Isis the healer is further contrasted with the Dea Syria the non-healer when the latter's acolytes wound themselves in a hideous manner, as described 199, 2. It does not seem accidental that the expression *spurcitia sanguinis* is used here; underlying the literal meaning lies the notion of impurity (see 2.3 above, where we quote 200, 29 *spurcissima illa propudia,* referring to the priests of the Dea Syria).[39]

2.13. Finally, book 11 mentions more than once that the contemplation of

---

[38] See Gwyn Griffiths on 276, 12 (= 276, 14 H.). Cf. D.S. 1, 25 (= *FRA* 104) φασὶ δ' Αἰγύπτιοι τὴν Ἶσιν φαρμάκων τε πολλῶν πρὸς ὑγίειαν εὑρέτιν γενομέναι καὶ τῆς ἰατρικῆς ἐπιστήμης μεγάλην ἔχειν ἐμπειρίαν. See also Wittmann 1938, 74 f.

[39] *Spurcus* and *spurcitia* are also found 7, 10 (161, 29), referring to a *lupanar;* 1, 13 (13, 2) and 1, 17 (15, 22), referring to the urine of the witches Meroe and Panthia.

the image of the goddess gives unspeakable joy to the believer, who is entirely absorbed in this contemplation. The most striking description is found at 11, 24 (286, 11 f.) *paucis dehinc ibidem commoratus diebus inexplicabili uoluptate simulacri diuini perfruebar;* the *uoluptas* consists in the adoration of the goddess, who is completely present within the image.[40] This contemplative adoration is one of the most striking features of the religious experience in book 11 (cf. also 280, 6 *intentus in deae specimen pristinos casus meos recordabar;* 280, 22 *me rursum ad deae gratissimum mihi refero conspectum;* 281, 3 *numinis magni cultor inseparabilis;* 281, 26 *deae uenerabilem conspectum adprecamur.*[41]

It almost goes without saying that in Lucius' view such an experience is unthinkable in the case of the Dea Syria. Her image is mentioned once in book 8: at 201, 16 the image, which used to be carried by the ass, is lying on the ground. Reflecting that the ass must carry it, the priests decide to keep him alive: *simulacri iacentis contemplatione in uita me retinendum censuere.* The contemplation of the image (by the priests) has, indeed, a directly beneficial effect on the ass as far as his physical well-being is concerned, but can hardly be compared to the religious experience brought about by the contemplation of the image of Isis. In book 9 the image of the goddess is mentioned 209, 21 *in ipso deae, quam gerebam, gremio,* where it is used as a depository for a cantharus stolen from the *mater deum* – not exactly an elevated picture. Finally, at 9, 10 (210, 10 f.) the image with the returned cantharus is placed *apud fani donarium* of the *mater deum*. This proves that, in spite of the narrator's aversion, there is a close relation between the two goddesses in the eyes of the uncomplicated believers, which is what we may assume the *pagani* are (cf. above note 10).

3. We conclude that the author causes the narrating I of the story to cast on the priests and cult of the Dea Syria as unfavourable a light as possible, and to represent the servants and cult of Isis as pure and true. This is not surprising in view of the initiation of Lucius into the cult of Isis, which will be treated in the eleventh book.[42] There is no question of an initial sympathy for the Dea Syria which later turns to antipathy: the narrating I[43] reports an aversion on the part of the experiencing I from the very first appearance of the Dea Syria's priest: his first reaction (as reported) is to flee: 197, 7 *accepto tali sermone cogitabam subito uelut lymphaticus exilire, ut...emptionem desineret (cinaedus).*[44]

---

[40] See Gwyn Griffiths on 286, 10 (= 286, 12 H) and 279, 14 (= 279, 16 H) *simulacra spirantia*. A. J. Festugière, *Personal Religion among the Greeks* (University of California Press 1960), 80 f. also points out that Lucius' happiness consists in the contemplation of the goddess's image. No parallels are known in the Greek mysteries such as those of Eleusis.

[41] 275, 3 *summi numinis uenerandam effigiem* refers to the image of Osiris; see Gwyn Griffiths ad loc.

[42] P. Thomas, *Revue de l'instruction publique en Belgique,* N.S. 14, 1871), 135 maintains that the Platonic philosopher is indignant about the disciples of the goddess; this is incorrect: Apuleius and Lucius need not coincide in their views.

[43] Bohm 1972/3, 231 again argues that the pious attitude with which Apuleius treats the religious aspect in book 11 is the result of his own experiences. This is possible, but not necessary; and since the narrating I and the author need not be identical, even putting the question is inappropriate.

[44] The presence of castrates in the cults of the Dea Syria and the Magna Mater is one of

It is true that at first the ass is treated well at the priests' house by the *iuuenis* (198, 5 f.). But it is going too far to say, as Thibau 1965, 127 does, that 'avec sa lucidité accrue Lucius a tôt compris qu'il s'est trompé sur la valeur de cette religion'.

If we are right in recognizing a conscious confrontation from the first moment onward between the cult of the Dea Syria and that of Isis, we must agree that those interpreters are on strong ground who regard book 11 not as an appendix, but as an integrated part – even the climax – of the *Met*.

the obvious ways in which those cults differ from that of Isis (see Witt 1971, 131). In view of his fear of castration (see e.g. *GCA* 1981, 238 on 7, 24: 172, 3-4), Lucius the ass is naturally antipathetic to those cults. It is possible, too, that some of the scorn he expresses for the cult of the Dea Syria has a snobbish origin. This is suggested by the description of the priest of the Dea Syria as *unum de triuiali popularium faece* (see 2.2 above). It is a fact that the worshippers of the Dea Syria were for the most part Syrian slaves (see Cumont [4]1929, 95 f.), whereas the cult of Isis was protected by emperors like Caligula and Domitian, which gave it greater social prestige.

APPENDIX V

Public Confession

Public confession, attended or not by public penance, was a familiar phenomenon in oriental religions, especially in the cult of the Dea Syria (see the *RE* article by Schwenn s.v. Kybele 2281, 21 f.; Kittel s.v. ὁμολογέω; Pettazoni 1954, 55 f.; Wilhelm-Hooybergh 1954, 84 f.). Many second and third century A.D. inscriptions from Phrygia and Lydia bear witness to this. These confessional stones deal with the failure to observe ritual cleanliness and, most frequently, with sexual offenses. Apart from Apuleius, penitence for guilt is mentioned by other literary sources, e.g.Plu. *de Superst.* 7,168 D (sc.δεισιδαίμων) ἐξαγορεύει τινὰς ἁμαρτίας αὐτοῦ καὶ πλημμελείας, ὡς τόδε φαγόντος ἢ πιόντος ἢ βαδίσαντος ὁδὸν ἣν οὐκ εἴα τὸ δαιμόνιον. For example, the acolytes of the Dea Syria were forbidden to eat fish. It was said that as a punishment their feet and stomach would swell up; cf. Menander in Porph. *Abst.* 4, 15 (fr. 544 *CAF* 3, 164); Plu. *de Superst.* 10, 170 D; Pers. 5, 186 f.; Mart. 4, 43, 7 *iuro per Syrios tibi tumores*. It is clear that 199, 11 f. *quasi contra fas sanctae religionis dissignasset aliquid* can refer to sexual offenses.

Confession was part of the Isis cult in very early times, as is proved by inscriptions dated as early as the 19th dynasty (Wittmann 1938, 218 n. 556 mentions catalogues of sins from early Egyptian to late Roman times; see also Pettazoni 1954, 55). Cf. for the later period Ov. *Pont.* 1, 1, 51 f. *uidi ego lanigerae numen uiolasse fatentem / Isidis Isiacos ante sedere focos. / alter, ob huic similem priuatus lumine culpam, / clamabat media se meruisse uia*. Observe that, as in our passage (*aliquid*), the offense is not mentioned by name. Juv. 6, 522 f. describes the penance of a worshipper of Isis: *Hibernum fracta glacie descendet in amnem, / ter matutino Tiberi mergetur et ipsis / uerticibus timidum caput abluet, inde superbi / totum regis agrum nuda ac tremibunda cruentis / erepet genibus; si candida iusserit Io, / ibit ad Aegypti finem calidaque petitas / a Meroe portabit aquas ut spargat in aede / Isidis, antiquo quae proxima surgit ouili*. According to the Scholiast this is punishment for a sexual sin, which is true of the sequel 535–541 at any rate. Finally cf. Sen. *Vit. B.* 26, 8.

In Rome, orgiastic rites like those described in our chapter were subject to severe restrictions until the time of Claudius. Before that time Roman citizens were not allowed to participate in the cult of Cybele. Afterwards measures were taken to regulate the cult; the rules applied to the eunuchs in particular. Self-castration was officially allowed to Phrygian Galli only (see *RAC* s.v. Gallos 1002 f.). Lucianus *Syr. D.* 50 mentions that in Hierapolis, too, rites were celebrated at which people mutilated themselves (Γάλλοι...τάμνονταί τε τοὺς πήχεας). In ch. 51 he describes how a young believer emasculates himself.

Self-mutilation with knives and lashes by way of penance is nowhere mentioned in connection with Isis. The absence of these practices is one of the

299

reasons why in the second century the Isis cult became such an important religion in the Roman world. Wittmann 1938, 163 says: 'Der Mensch, der erst duch Selbstvernichtung, durch Sünde und Busse gehen musste, besass für einen Römer keine Menschenwürde'. In the second century one can observe in religion a strong tendency toward spirituality and an emphasis on ethical values; see Wittmann 1938, 160 f. According to Cumont [4]1929, 86, in the second century a change takes place in the Isis cult as well, in the sense that it requires of the believer purity of the spirit, rather than of the body.

The attitude of Lucius the ass is in keeping with the above. He mentions explicitly that the priest accuses *himself* (199, 11 *semet ipsum*) and mutilates *himself* (199, 13 *ipse de se suis manibus*). We may deduce from this that the narrator disapproves of such behaviour (see our comm. on 199, 5–9). The 11th book does not speak anywhere of confession and penitence, but it does mention rites of purification. It is curious, however, that the priest prays for forgiveness before purifying Lucius: 11, 23 (284, 26) *praefatus deum ueniam*. Gwyn Griffiths 287 remarks on this: 'The prayer is a prelude to the main baptism of initiation, and its stress on forgiveness is in accord with the central spiritual experience of the work: Lucius is saved through the grace and mercy of Isis'. So the cults of the Dea Syria and Isis are described in the *Met.* as direct opposites also on the point of confession and penitence.

GENERAL INDEX

abigere   200, 26-201, 1
ablativus absolutus   178, 24-179, 5   182, 10-14   186, 5-8   186, 27-28
   193, 19-20   198, 11-16
   ambiguous   intr. 4.2.1.3
   incomplete   194, 28-195, 2
   causal   184, 17-185, 4
   concomitant circumstances   192, 8-14
   duration of time   194, 25-28
   instr.   179, 5-11   182, 10-14   198, 11-16
   manner   190, 19-24
   modal (with *in*)   202, 13-17
   respect   179, 5-11
abstract noun   176, 18-20   185, 16-20
   concrete use of   187, 24-26
   plural   178, 24-179, 5   200, 12-22   201, 3-13
   replacing an adjective   188, 9-10
abstractum pro concreto   179, 20-24   192, 24-27   192, 28-193, 5   194, 1-5
abundance ('Fülle des Ausdr.')   193, 5-10
abuse   196, 22-24   200, 12-22
ac (first word of sentence)   201, 3-13
accessus   177, 15-19
accingi (+ final dative)   177, 19-20
Accius *trag.*   15   190, 19-24;   217   183, 11-16;   443   179, 5-11
   Medea   409   R³   188, 25-189, 4
   ap. Non.   172, 7   185, 5-8
accumbere + acc.   183, 11-16
accurrere + acc.   181, 8-11
accusative adverbial   177, 10-15
   direction   189, 4-12   194, 25-28
   graecus   177, 5-10
   internal   182, 5-10
   predicate   187, 1-2
acerba mors   183, 11-16
acerbus   184, 17-185, 4
Achilles Tatius   2, 34   intr. 4.2.2;   3, 16, 2   intr. n. 7;   3, 17   187, 18-19;   5, 7, 5   intr. n. 7   181, 8-11;   6, 2, 3   197, 20-24;   7, 6, 1   intr. n. 7
acus crinalis   187, 3-9
ad (modal use of)   196, 16-19
adaeque   201, 26-202, 3
adambulare   198, 1-5
adeo   195, 18-19
adfingere   180, 19-23
adhuc (anaphora of)   182, 14-183, 1   184, 14-17
ad hunc modum   180, 17-19   187, 3-9
ad istum modum   195, 20-21   200, 10-12
adj. in -alis   188, 17-20
   in -eus   179, 5-11
   in -ilis   196, 24-197, 2
   in -inus   178, 9-15   201, 3-13
   in -osus   185, 13-16   186, 27-28   188, 25-189, 4
   in -ulentus   186, 27-28
   instead of adverb   184, 1-5
   neuter used as noun   200, 12-22
   repeated comparative   178, 2-6

Adonis   intr. 4.2.2   179, 20-24   180, 3-4   180, 8-10   181, 8-11   181,
    17-21   196, 24-197, 2
    genealogy and myth   196, 24-197, 2
adquiescere + dative   183, 11-16
Adrastus   188, 4-6
adseuerare   180, 17-19   180, 19-23
adsidere   185, 28-186, 5
adulterer   see motifs
adulterinus   178, 9-15
adultery   intr. 4.3   178, 9-15   194, 1-5
    story   198, 9-10
adverb in -iter   194, 12-18
    instead of adj.   196, 14-16
    instead of pronoun   188, 21-25   191, 11-15
    intensifying   188, 4-6
    in -ter   177, 15-19
    in -tim   193, 5-10
    'Nachstellung'   198, 5-9
    reinforcing prepositional phrase   197, 14-17
aegre sustinere   194, 12-18
aerumna   176, 15-18
aerumnabilis   184, 5-9
Aesch. *Ag.*   270   181, 14-17;   541   181, 14-17
    Choeph. 894 f.   187, 24-26
agere + adjective   180, 19-23
agreement   193, 5-10   197, 17-20
ἀγύρτης   200, 1-9
alacer (predicative)   192, 28-193, 5
Alcimus   app. I
Alexander the Great   184, 14-17
alii   195, 2-7
alio (abl. or dat.)   183, 11-16
alioquin   182, 14-183, 1
aliquis   185, 23-24
aliud de alio   196, 14-16
alliteration   intr. 5. 1   177, 20-178, 2   178, 9-15 bis   179, 5-11   179,
    11-14   179, 14-19   180, 10-16   180, 19-23   181, 7-8   181, 11-13   182,
    14-183, 1   183, 20-21   186, 5-8   186, 18-23   189, 16-20   189, 26-190,
    4   190, 19-24   190, 24-28   190, 28-191, 2   191, 11-15   192, 8-14   193,
    5-10   194, 7-12   195, 20-21   195, 25-196, 4   196, 24-197, 2   197,
    14-17   197, 20-24   198, 1-5   198, 5-9   198, 20-199, 4   199, 4-8   199,
    10-13   200, 12-22 bis   201, 19-25
    and assonance   177, 15-19   178, 24-179, 5   179, 5-11 bis   188, 9-10
    189, 4-12   189, 20-26   191, 9-11
allusion (mythological)   197, 20-24
altiusculus/-e   201, 26-202, 3 bis
altus (in context of fear)   202, 3-8
Amata   187, 3-9
ambages   186, 9-13
ambroseus   184, 14-17
Ambrosius *Ep.*   6, 1   193, 5-10
    Hex.   5, 7, 17   190, 24-28
    Nab.   15, 64   186, 25-27
    Psalm.   118, 12, 31   178, 9-15
Ps. Ambr. *Serm.*   2, 5   193, 19-20
amburere   178, 6-8
Ammianus   14, 1, 4   198, 1-5;   14, 6, 18   201, 19-25;   14, 11, 1   178,

    9-15;   18, 8, 5   201, 19-25;   19, 8, 5   188, 21-25;   20, 7, 9   178,
    9-15;   20, 11, 17   189, 20-26;   22, 14, 4   176, 15-18   201, 13-17;   22,
    15, 19   179, 11-14;   24, 2, 14   189, 4-12;   24, 2, 17   187, 9-12;   24, 3,
    9   app. II   3;   24, 4, 12   200, 26-201, 1;   24, 5, 2   179, 20-24;   25,
    3, 11   192, 6-8;   29, 1, 31   186, 5-8;   29, 1, 44   193, 5-10;   29, 5, 52
    178, 9-15;   31, 7, 16   194, 18-24
amor   intr.   4.2.1.1
Amor and Psyche   intr.   4.2.1.1   177, 5-10 bis
amplification   see rhetoric
anaphora   179, 20-24   182, 14-183, 1   184, 14-17   185, 5-8   187, 12-16
    195, 25-196, 4
anastrophe   191, 29-192, 2
anastrophe of preposition   176, 15-18   176, 18-20
'Anfangsstellung' of verb   181, 7-8   185, 23   186, 28-30   193, 12-15
    197, 9-14   198, 1-5   199, 10-13   201, 13-17
animal world   180, 6-8
animals   193, 5-10
    devouring humans   193, 12-15
    relation with man   183, 5-7   190, 4-10
    sacrificial   200, 12-22
animam deuouere   181, 8-11
anima uirilis   179, 20-24   181, 25-182, 1
animi = iracundia   190, 19-24
Année Épigraphique   42/43   194, 1-5
annuntiare   176, 18-20
antecellere equos   189, 16-20
anticlimax   197, 20-24
Antigone   186, 18-23
Antiphanes   fr. 154 f. (= *CAF* 2, 74)   200, 1-9
antistare   177, 10-15
antithesis   189, 4-12   198, 1-5   198, 5-9
    see also contrast
Antoninus Liberalis   11, 7   194, 18-24
ants   194, 12-18
anxie   196, 14-16
anxius   197, 9-14
Anthologia Palatina   7, 273   183, 2-5;   7, 295   183, 2-5
anus (body discarded)   app. I
Aphrodite   181, 8-11   181, 25-182, 1
    Astarte   app. III
    Syria   app. IV n. 21
Apollo, the Muses and Helicon   189, 20-26
appearance vs reality   198, 9-10
appendix   194, 7-12
appetite (of deity)   200, 12-22
apposition (in gen. with possessive)   195, 11-12
ἀπροσδόκητον   196, 19-21   197, 9-14
apud   178, 24-179, 5
Apuleius   intr. 4. 2. 4   intr. n. 12
    initiated in mysteries of Isis   app. II 4.2
    humor   196, 22-24
    irony   189, 26-190, 4
    long hair   app. IV 2. 2   app IV n. 28
    philosophus Platonicus   app. II 4. 1   app. II 4. 2. 2   app IV n. 42
    sources   intr. 4. 2. 3   intr. 4. 2. 4   176, 15-18
Apul. *ex* Menandro (*PLM* 4, 104, 1)   185, 13-16
Apul. *Apol.*   1 (1, 19)   202, 3-8;   4 (6, 8)   app. IV 2. 2;   10 (12, 8)   176,

21-177, 1 176, 21-177, 1; 12 (14, 4) 201, 3-13; 13 (15, 8) 194, 7-12; 14 (17, 1) 198, 11-16; 17 (20, 18) 194, 1-5; 17 (21, 11) 198, 1-5; 23 (27, 17) 200, 26-201, 1; 23 (27, 18) 185, 5-8; 28 (33, 21) 200, 12-22; 31 (36, 18) 195, 2-7; 35 (41, 8) 179, 20-24; 47 (54, 21) 185, 5-8; 50 (57, 1) 200, 26-201, 1; 52 (59, 2) 183, 2-5; 55 app. II 4, 2; 55 (62, 3) 190, 10-19; 55 (62, 25) app. IV n. 28; 57 (65, 5) 196, 22-24; 59 (67, 24) 195, 25-196, 4; 68 f. 202, 8-10; 68 (77, 3) 194, 1-5; 70 (78, 21) 184, 9-11; 71 (80, 6) 178, 24-179, 5; 74 (83, 15) 195, 25-196, 4; 75 (83, 20) 179, 20-24; 75 (83, 22) 200, 12-22; 77 (86, 6) 199, 14-18; 83 (92, 16) 178, 2-6; 84 (92, 19 f.) 181, 3-7; 85 (94, 4) 188, 7-8; 85 (94, 10) 183, 16-18; 87 (96, 23) 194, 1-5; 87 (96, 24) 176, 21-177, 1; 89 (98, 9) 196, 7-10; 92 (102, 11 f.) 178, 9-15; 98 (108, 23) 177, 5-10; 99 (109, 15) 181, 8-11; 99 (109, 21) 201, 13-17

Apul. *Fl.* 2 (3, 1) 178, 19-20; 2 (3, 2) 202, 13-17; 3 (3, 16) 176, 21-177, 1; 4 (5, 16) 201, 19-25; 4 (5, 18) 198, 1-5; 6, 1 (6, 3) 194, 25-28; 7 (8, 16) 189, 20-26; 9 (10, 19) 199, 14-18; 9 (11, 2) 183, 5-7; 9 (12, 8 f.) 198, 11-16; 9 (12, 9) 184, 1-5; 12 (17, 7) 185, 8-12; 12 (17, 7) 194, 18-24; 14 (19, 9) 194, 28-195, 2; 15 (20, 4) 190, 10-19; 15 (23, 16) 185, 5-8; 16 (26, 9) 181, 8-11; 16 (27, 20) 177, 5-10; 17 (31, 20) 199, 18-20; 17 (32, 4 f.) 191, 16-18; 17 (32, 8) 185, 5-8; 17 (33, 7) 193, 15-19; 17 (33, 8) 184, 11-13; 18 (35, 7) 194, 1-5 (bis); 18 (36, 10) 179, 14-19; 22 (43, 7) 194, 1-5

Apul. *Met.* compared with Vorlage 188, 15-17 201, 26-202, 3
compared with *Onos* 197, 9-14 201, 26-202, 3 201, 3-13

Apul. *Met.* 1, 1 intr. 4. 2. 4 177, 5-10 184, 11-13 197, 14-17; 1, 2 179, 5-11 181, 14-17 196, 10-13 201, 3-13 bis; 1, 4 179, 20-24; 1, 5 intr. n. 4 178, 24-179, 5 194, 12-18 196, 5-7 202, 3-8; 1, 6 181, 25-182, 1 182, 1-5 183, 8-10 195, 14-17 198, 1-5 201, 3-13 app. II n. 5; 1, 7 180, 10-16 185, 5-8 188, 7-8 194, 1-5 194, 12-18 200, 12-22; 1, 8 177, 5-10 197, 17-20 app. II n. 5; 1, 9 181, 25-182, 1 189, 4-12; 1, 11 176, 18-20 180, 6-8 201, 3-13 bis; 1, 12 182, 14-183, 1 197, 14-17; 1, 13 176, 21-177, 1 187, 12-16 app. IV n. 39; 1, 14 193, 5-10 201, 3-13; 1, 15 188, 25-189, 4 198, 5-9 201, 3-13; 1, 16 176, 15-18 177, 5-10 177, 10-15 180, 6-8 194, 7-12; 1, 17 179, 20-24 181, 17-24 184, 11-13 193, 5-10 app. IV n. 39; 1, 18 184, 5-9 201, 3-13 app. I; 1, 19 176, 21-177, 1 177, 15-19 178, 2-6; 1, 19 179, 20-24 191, 22-27 192, 3-6 193, 10-12 194, 28-195, 2; 1, 20 202, 3-8; 1, 22 176, 18-20; 1, 23 176, 18-20 179, 20-24 184, 11-13; 1, 24 177, 19-20; 1, 25 191, 2-8; 1, 26 186, 27-28 187, 19-24

Met. 2, 1 177, 10-15 181, 14-17 201, 3-13 201, 13-17; 2, 2 192, 8-14 194, 1-5; 2, 4 181, 3-7; 2, 5 177, 10-15 178, 19-20 192, 17-24 195, 21-25; 2, 6 178, 2-6 182, 5-10 200, 22-26 201, 3-13; 2, 7 179, 11-14 194, 18-24 196, 22-24 198, 20-199, 4 200, 12-22 201, 26-202, 3 202, 13-17; 2, 8 189, 4-12 app. IV n. 7; 2, 10 184, 14-17; 2, 11 183, 11-16 198, 5-9 201, 19-25; 2, 12 intr. n. 3 177, 1-4 198, 1-5; 2, 13 176, 18-20 176, 21-177, 1 179, 20-24 181, 7-8 181, 17-24 193, 15-19 198, 1-5 201, 19-25; 2, 14 182, 14-183, 1 186, 8-9 188, 11-14 202, 13-17; 2, 15 177, 10-15; 2, 16 178, 19-20 183, 8-10 196, 16-19 201, 3-13; 2, 17 180, 19-23 198, 20-199, 4 200, 12-22 201, 3-13; 2, 18 176, 21-177, 1 200, 12-22; 2, 19 198, 11-16; 2, 20 181, 8-11 183, 8-10 187, 24-26 195, 18-19 app. I; 2, 21-27 app. I; 2, 21 180, 24-25 196, 5-7; 2, 22 181, 14-17; 2, 23 176, 18-20 202, 13-17; 2, 24 185, 28-186, 5 192, 3-6; 2, 25 177, 19-20 178, 2-6 181, 8-11 189, 26-190, 4; 2, 26 181, 8-11 bis 190, 10-19 192, 28-193, 5 197,

17-20	202, 13-17;	2, 27	184, 9-11	192, 14-17 bis	194, 1-5	201, 3-13;
2, 28	192, 14-17	198, 11-16	202, 10-12;	2, 29	185, 5-8	186, 8-9;
2, 30	193, 5-10	198, 5-9	201, 3-13;	2, 31	188, 17-20;	2, 32
185, 20-22						

Met. 3, 1 193, 15-19 195, 12-14; 3, 2 177, 5-10 179, 5-11 181, 7-8 182, 10-14 185, 28-186, 5 187, 9-12 195, 12-14; 3, 3 176, 15-18 183, 5-7 189, 12-16 202, 10-12 202, 13-17 202, 18-20; 3, 4 197, 17-20 190, 19-24; 3, 5 190, 19-24 194, 1-5; 3, 6 177, 10-15 184, 9-11 189, 26-190, 4 190, 19-24; 3, 7 202, 10-12; 3, 8 180, 10-16 180, 19-23 195, 2-7 195, 12-14; 3, 9 178, 2-6 182, 5-10 193, 21-22 198, 5-9 201, 13-17; 3, 10 176, 15-18 184, 1-5 195, 2-7 198, 5-9 201, 3-13; 3, 11 189, 4-12 199, 4-8; 3, 12 182, 1-5 198, 1-5; 3, 13 180, 19-23 191, 29-192, 2 192, 3-6 196, 22-24 200, 12-22; 3, 14 177, 19-20 199, 20-200, 1 200, 22-26 201, 1-3; 3, 15 182, 14-183, 1 186, 18-23 app. II 4. 2 app. II n. 12; 3, 16 178, 24-179, 5 179, 5-11 187, 9-12 192, 28-193, 5 201, 13-17 202, 3-8; 3, 17 181, 8-11 199, 20-200, 1 200, 26-201, 1; 3, 18 184, 9-11 187, 3-9 191, 22-27 192, 14-17 192, 17-24; 3, 19 186, 14-16 200, 26-201, 1; 3, 20 181, 3-7 184, 11-13 201, 13-17; 3, 21 189, 20-26 201, 3-13 201, 26-202, 3; 3, 22 179, 20-24 186, 13-14 app. IV n. 30 app. IV n. 36; 3, 23 184, 14-17 192, 14-17 192, 17-24 200, 26-201, 1; 3, 24 185, 13-16 185, 25-28 200, 22-26; 3, 25-28 intr. 2; 3, 25 192, 17-24; 3, 26 178, 9-15 180, 6-8 192, 3-6 195, 7-11 bis 201, 1-3 app. IV n. 31; 3, 27 178, 24-179, 5 179, 5-11 bis 179, 14-19 185, 25-28 195, 2-7 195, 14-17 ter 196, 7-10 197, 2-6; 3, 28 181, 14-17 198, 11-16 201, 17-19 202, 13-17; 3, 29 184, 11-13 195, 14-17 197, 17-20 200, 22-26 202, 13-17

Met. 4, 1 178, 21-24 182, 14-183, 1 185, 13-16 187, 3-9 194, 1-5 201, 3-13; 4, 2 182, 5-10 185, 13-16 187, 3-9 189, 16-20 199, 20-200, 1 200, 12-22; 4, 3 176, 15-18 178, 24-179, 5 182, 14-183, 1 185, 16-20 187, 3-9 195, 21-25 197, 7-9 197, 20-24 198, 1-5 191, 29-192, 2 200, 22-26 202, 8-10; 4, 4 176, 18-20 bis 187, 12-16 190, 4-10 192, 17-24 195, 14-17 197, 7-9 201, 3-13 bis; 4, 5 177, 10-15 180, 6-8 189, 4-12 194, 25-28 197, 9-14 bis 197, 24-26 bis 201, 13-17; 4, 6 188, 21-25 189, 26-190, 4 194, 12-18 199, 9-10; 4, 7 183, 11-16 188, 25-189, 4 192, 3-6 194, 25-28 196, 22-24 200, 12-22 202, 13-17; 4, 8 177, 10-15 181, 14-17 192, 28-193, 5 196, 22-24 201, 26-202, 3 202, 3-8; 4, 9 184, 14-17 188, 25-189, 4 190, 4-10 200, 26-201, 1; 4, 10 179, 20-24 190, 28-191, 2 192, 24-27 193, 5-10; 4, 11 177, 10-15 182, 5-10 183, 16-18 192, 17-24 195, 21-25 app. I; 4, 12 184, 9-11 187, 24-26 192, 8-14 192, 14-17 200, 12-22 app. I; 4, 13 189, 4-12 189, 20-26 193, 10-12 194, 12-18 199, 14-18; 4, 14 179, 5-11 180, 19-23; 181, 3-7 181, 8-11 192, 28-193, 5; 4, 15 180, 19-23 182, 5-10 192, 28-193, 5; 4, 16 178, 9-15 bis 180, 19-23 181, 7-8 bis 181, 17-24; 4, 17 177, 5-10 180, 10-16 185, 5-8 191, 18-22; 4, 18 187, 12-16 188, 11-14 193, 12-15 194, 18-24 app. I; 4, 19 178, 24-179, 5 188, 25-189, 4 202, 3-8; 4, 20 181, 7-8 185, 23 190, 19-24 201, 3-13; 4, 21 176, 21-177, 1 bis 181, 8-11 190, 24-28 199, 4-8; 4, 22 177, 5-10 186, 23-25 195, 12-14; 4, 23 intr. 2 189, 4-12 200, 22-26; 4, 24 178, 6-8 188, 9-10 197, 7-9 197, 27-198, 1 200, 1-9 202, 3-8 202, 18-20 app. IV n. 30; 4, 25 181, 25-182, 1 185, 23 186, 8-9 186, 17-18 187, 3-9 187, 18-19 197, 7-9 199, 10-13; 4, 26 intr. 4.2.1.1 intr. n. 6 177, 10-15 177, 20-178, 2 178, 9-15 179, 24-26 186, 8-9 187, 18-19 198, 20-199, 4; 4, 27 176, 18-20 176, 21-177, 1 180, 10-16 181,

305

3-7   181, 7-8   184, 1-5 bis   184, 5-9   186, 28-30   188, 15-17   199,
4-8   200, 22-26;   4, 28   intr. 4.2.1.1   177, 5-10 bis   181, 1-3 bis;   4,
29   181, 7-8   186, 5-8 bis   188, 9-10   192, 3-6;   4, 30   198, 1-5;
200, 12-22;   4, 31   179, 5-11   192, 14-17   196, 22-24;   4, 32   184,
9-11   199, 4-8;   4, 33   185, 23;   4, 34   180, 19-23   181, 11-13   183,
5-7   185, 23   202, 3-8;   4, 35   181, 11-13   188, 4-6

Met.   5, 1   177, 10-15   185, 20-22   187, 12-16   191, 18-22;   5, 2   181,
7-8   191, 2-8   200, 26-201, 1;   5, 3   201, 19-25;   5, 4   177, 10-15
181, 1-3   185, 16-20   188, 4-6   190, 24-28   194, 1-5;   5, 5   181,
1-3   185, 5-8;   5, 6   178, 9-15   182, 1-5   185, 5-8   188, 7-8;   5,
7   180, 19-23   181, 14-17   192, 3-6   193, 5-10;   5, 8   178, 9-15
194, 25-28   199, 14-18;   5, 9   185, 5-8   186, 8-9   187, 1-2   195,
25-196, 4   196, 5-7   200, 26-201, 1   app. IV n. 7;   5, 10   187, 18-19;
5, 11   183, 11-16   183, 16-18   184, 1-5   194, 28-195, 2   196, 24-197,
2;   5, 12   176, 18-20   177, 20-178, 2   178, 9-15   182, 5-10   187,
3-9   189, 4-12;   5, 13   184, 14-17;   5, 14   187, 9-12   200, 26-201,
1;   5, 15   177, 5-10   182, 5-10   192, 17-24   198, 1-5   199, 4-8;   5,
16   189, 4-12;   5, 17   180, 10-16   193, 12-15   199, 14-18;   5, 18
178, 9-15   185, 13-16;   5, 19   193, 15-19;   5, 20   189, 16-20   201,
19-25 bis;   5, 21   177, 5-10;   5, 22   186, 5-8;   5, 23   194, 1-5   199,
4-8;   5, 24   187, 16-18   191, 11-15   194, 7-12;   5, 25   176, 21-177,
1   179, 14-19   180, 10-16   183, 18-20   188, 7-8   192, 17-24   192,
24-27; · 5, 26-27   186, 5-8;   5, 26   197, 9-14   199, 14-18;   5, 28
176, 18-20   178, 9-15   196, 24-197, 2;   5, 29   184, 1-5   191, 2-8;   5,
30   182, 5-10   183, 16-18   194, 5-7;   5, 31   181, 17-24   189,
20-26

Met.   6, 1   185, 8-12;   6, 2   184, 1-5   192, 14-17 bis   193, 12-15   194,
12-18;   6, 4   176, 15-18   183, 11-16   188, 11-14   194, 1-5;   6, 5
178, 19-20   179, 20-24;   6, 6   188, 15-17;   6, 7   178, 24-179, 5   181,
25-182, 1;   6, 8   194, 1-5;   6, 9   188, 21-25;   6, 10   191, 16-18   194,
1-5   196, 24-197, 2   200, 12-22;   6, 11   176, 15-18;   6, 12   179,
14-19   189, 16-20   199, 14-18;   6, 13   178, 9-15 bis   194, 12-18;   6,
14   193, 12-15;   6, 15   179, 11-14   183, 2-5   198, 5-9;   6, 18   187,
3-9   200, 12-22;   6, 20   194, 28-195, 2   200, 26-201, 1;   6, 21   181,
8-11;   6, 22   200, 26-201, 1;   6, 23   178, 19-20   187, 24-26;   6, 24
177, 15-19   183, 11-16;   6, 25   177, 1-4   184, 9-11   191, 18-22   193,
15-19   196, 22-24   197, 24-26;   6, 26   186, 5-8 bis   192, 6-8   195,
14-17   197, 20-24   200, 26-201, 1   201, 1-3   201, 13-17;   6, 27   177,
19-20   180, 6-8   187, 24-26   189, 16-20   197, 17-20   199, 10-13;   6,
28   182, 1-5   188, 7-8   189, 16-20   192, 14-17   200, 22-26;   6, 29
intr. n. 3   177, 1-4   181, 1-3   187, 3-9   188, 15-17   196, 16-19   198,
11-16   202, 10-12;   6, 30   176, 21-177, 1   178, 19-20   184, 9-11   188,
17-20   189, 16-20   189, 20-26   191, 11-15   194, 7-12   194, 12-18
194, 18-24   198, 11-16   201, 1-3   201, 3-13   app. I;   6, 31 f.   202,
13-17;   6, 31   182, 10-14   194, 18-24   202, 3-8

Met.   7, 1   181, 3-7   196, 22-24;   7, 2   184, 14-17   187, 3-9   188, 1-4
190, 4-10   195, 21-25   app. IV n. 2;   7, 3-14   intr. 2;   7, 3   183,
11-16   183, 16-18   194, 1-5   200, 22-26   202, 13-17;   7, 4-12   intr.
2;   7, 4   178, 24-179, 5   194, 7-12   202, 8-10;   7, 5 f.   182, 10-14;
7, 5   195, 20-21   197, 9-14   199, 4-8;   7, 6   176, 15-18   177, 5-10
187, 19-24   198, 1-5   202, 8-10;   7, 7   intr. 5.3   177, 10-15   178,
24-179, 5   181, 3-7   194, 28-195, 2;   7, 8   179, 11-14   185, 23-24
186, 8-9   189, 4-12   190, 10-19   198, 11-16   200, 1-9   200, 26-201, 1;
7, 9   177, 5-10   177, 19-20   178, 24-179, 5   180, 8-10   197, 20-24
201, 3-13;   7, 10   intr. 4.2.4   178, 21-24   197, 14-17   app. IV n. 39;
7, 11   177, 5-10   179, 5-11   183, 16-18   185, 8-12   188, 21-25   196,
14-16   197, 17-20   198, 5-9   200, 22-26 bis   201, 17-19;   7, 12   intr.

4.2.1.1   178, 19-20   185, 28-186, 5 bis   195, 11-12   199, 10-13   202, 13-17;   7, 13   intr. n. 6   176, 15-18   177, 19-20   177, 20-178, 2   182, 1-5   187, 9-12   190, 19-24   190, 28-191, 2   193, 19-20   194, 25-28   195, 25-196, 4 bis   199, 9-10   199, 18-20   201, 19-25   app. I n. 2;   7, 14-27   intr. 3.1;   7, 14-28   intr. 3.1;   7, 14   177, 15-19   178, 9-15   179, 20-24   182, 10-14   187, 24-26   197, 27-198, 1   198, 1-5   201, 3-13;   7, 15   intr. 3.2   176, 21-177, 1   185, 8-12   188, 11-14   189, 26-190, 4   190, 28-191, 2 bis   194, 7-12   200, 12-22   201, 3-13;   7, 16   177, 1-4   178, 24-179, 5   179, 5-11   180, 6-8   180, 10-16   182, 14-183, 1   191, 2-8   195, 2-7   196, 24-197, 2   198, 5-9   198, 9-10   201, 3-13;   7, 17-19   187, 3-9;   7, 17   180, 3-4   180, 10-16 bis   188, 11-14   190, 4-10   192, 3-6   198, 20-199, 4   201, 26-202, 3;   7, 18   intr. 4.4   179, 24-26   186, 8-9   190, 28-191, 2   197, 27-198, 1;   7, 19   178, 6-8   185, 23-24   187, 3-9   194, 7-12;   7, 20   186, 9-13   195, 14-17   195, 21-25   198, 20-199, 4;   7, 21   177, 20-178, 2   178, 19-20   185, 5-8   185, 23   185, 28-186, 5   186, 5-8   186, 25-27   188, 1-4   192, 17-24   198, 1-5   200, 12-22   200, 22-26   201, 3-13;   7, 22   177, 20-178, 2   182, 14-183, 1   185, 28-186, 5   187, 3-9   195, 21-25   195, 25-196, 4   196, 5-7   197, 20-24   197, 24-26   198, 1-5   202, 3-8   202, 18-20 bis;   7, 23   180, 19-23   188, 17-20   191, 2-8   195, 2-7   196, 10-13   196, 16-19   196, 19-21   197, 17-20   197, 24-26   198, 1-5   199, 10-13;   7, 24   179, 5-11   181, 25-182, 1   187, 16-18   188, 17-20   192, 14-17   192, 17-24   198, 9-10   200, 22-26   201, 3-13   201, 13-17   app. IV n. 44;   7, 25   intr. 4. 4   180, 17-19   182, 1-5   188, 17-20   188, 21-25   195, 21-25   196, 16-19   199, 10-13   200, 26-201, 1 bis   202, 18-20;   7, 26   intr. 4. 1   180, 17-19   187, 3-9   188, 17-20   189, 4-12   189, 20-26   194, 28-195, 2;   7, 27   176, 21-177, 1 bis   180, 10-16   180, 17-19   192, 24-27   192, 28-193, 5   194, 1-5   196, 14-16   200, 1-9;   7, 28   intr. 4. 4   176, 18-20   187, 19-24   199, 14-18   202, 13-17

Met.   8 cc. *1-14*   intr. 3.2   intr. n. 11;   *6*   187, 24-26   194, 25-28;   *15-16*   intr. 4.3;   *15*   179, 5-11;   *19-21*   intr. 4.1;   *21*   179, 5-11;   *22*   intr. 4.1;   *23-25*   intr. 4.1;   *27-30*   198, 9-10;   *27*   181, 3-7;   *31*   178, 24-179, 5

(Helm)   *176, 15-20*   intr. 1;   *176, 15*   intr. 3.1   intr. 3.2   201, 3-13;   *176, 16*   188, 9-10   app. II 2. 1;   *176, 19*   intr. 4.2.4   intr. n. 11   *179, 20-24*   182, 14-183, 1   179, 26-180, 2   185, 28-186, 5;   *176, 20*   188, 7-8;   *176, 21*   187, 3-9   191, 29-192, 2;   *176, 21 f.*   187, 24-26;   *177, 1*   187, 19-24;   *177, 3 f.*   intr. 4.2.4   intr. n. 3;   *177, 3*   intr. 5.1;   *177, 5 f.*   intr. 4.2.1.1   184, 9-11;   *177, 5*   185, 13-16;   *177, 6*   198, 1-5;   *177, 7*   185, 5-8;   *177, 8*   177, 15-19   186, 5-8   186, 9-13;   *177, 9*   188, 4-6   200, 1-9;   *177, 10*   intr. 4.2.1.1   181, 1-3;   *177, 11*   intr. 4.2.1.1   178, 9-15   182, 14-183, 1;   *177, 16*   183, 18-20   188, 9-10;   *177, 17*   178, 2-6;   *177, 18-20*   179, 14-19;   *177, 18*   180, 19-23;   *177, 19*   178, 9-15   178, 19-20   185, 5-8;   *177, 20 f.*   intr. 3.1;   *177, 20*   180, 19-23;   *178, 1*   180, 19-23;   *178, 2*   185, 5-8   185, 28-186, 5;   *178, 4*   192, 3-6;   *178, 5 f.*   184, 9-11;   *178, 6-8*   intr. 4.2.4;   *178, 9 f.*   intr. 4.2.2   182, 14-183, 1;   *178, 10*   185, 8-12;   *178, 19 f.*   intr. 4.2.4   185, 8-12;   *178, 20*   185, 23-24   187, 3-9;   *178, 23 f.*   187, 24-26;   *178, 23*   179, 14-19   179, 20-24;   *178, 24-179, 5*   179, 11-14;   *178, 25*   179, 14-19;   *178, 26*   179, 14-19;   *179, 1*   179, 5-11;   *179, 7*   193, 12-15;   *179, 9*   179, 26-180, 2;   *179, 13*   185, 13-16;   *179, 14 f.*   180, 17-19   180, 24-25;   *179, 14*   intr. 4.2.1.3   178, 19-20   179, 20-24   179, 24-26   179, 26-180, 2   187, 19-24;   *179, 16 f.*   intr. 4.2.1.3   180, 17-19;   *179, 16*   178, 24-179, 5;   *179, 17*   180, 17-19;   *179, 20*   180, 24-25;   *179, 21*   176, 18-20   179, 14-19;   *179, 22*   201, 19-25;   *179, 24*   180, 3-4;   *180, 1*   176, 18-20;   *180, 3*

307

179, 20-24; *180, 4 f.* 181, 11-13; *180, 5* 201, 13-17; *180, 7* 193, 12-15; *180, 10-16* 179, 20-24 181, 14-17; *180, 10* 183, 18-20; *180, 14* 187, 19-24; *180, 16* 179, 11-14 183, 18-20 199, 18-20; *180, 17* 180, 3-4 187, 3-9; *180, 17-19* 179, 14-19; *180, 19* 180, 10-16; *180, 20* 181, 14-17; *180, 21* 181, 8-11 191, 2-8; *180, 23* intr. 4.2.3 181, 14-17; *180, 25* intr. 4.2.1.3; *181, 1 f.* intr. 4.2.3 intr. 5.2; *181, 1* 201, 3-13; *181, 5* 182, 14-183, 1 187, 3-9 bis; *181, 6* 186, 5-8; *181, 7* 187, 9-12; *181, 9* 183, 18-20; *181, 11-13* intr. 5.2; *181, 15* intr. 4.2.3 177, 20-178, 2 180, 19-23; *181, 18* 184, 14-17 193, 5-10; *181, 19 f.* intr. n. 9; *181, 21* 195, 21-25; *181, 23* 180, 19-23; *181, 25 f.* 188, 4-6; *181, 25* 180, 19-23; *181, 27* 187, 18-19; *182, 5* 201, 19-25; *182, 10-14* 183, 18-20; *182, 12* intr. 4.2.2; *182, 13* 187, 24-26; *182, 14 f.* intr. n. 4 181, 14-17; *182, 15* 177, 5-10; *182, 16* 180, 10-16; *182, 17 f.* 184, 14-17; *182, 18 f.* 184, 11-13; *182, 18* 192, 28-193, 5; *182, 19* 184, 9-11 bis; *183, 2* 184, 11-13; *183, 6* 183, 18-20 183, 20-21 185, 5-8 185, 23 185, 28-186, 5 187, 24-26; *183, 7* 184, 5-9 184, 9-11; *183, 8-21* 187, 19-24; *183, 9* 181, 17-24 184, 14-17; *183, 14* 177, 15-19 182, 14-183, 1; *183, 16* 184, 5-9; *183, 20-21* intr. 4.2.1.3 183, 5-7; *184, 1 f.* intr. 4.2.3; *184, 3* 198, 11-16; *184, 8* 184, 17-185, 4 185, 23 187, 16-18; *184, 10* 182, 14-183, 1 183, 5-7; *184, 11 f.* intr. 4.2.2 185, 28-186, 5; *184, 12* 192, 28-193, 5; *184, 14* intr. 5.3 181, 17-24; *184, 18* 185, 5-8; *184, 19 f.* intr. 3.1; *184, 19* 185, 8-12; *185, 2* 176, 18-20 182, 14-183, 1 185, 5-8; *185, 6* 185, 23-24 193, 5-10; *185, 10* 178, 9-15; *185, 11* 194, 18-24; *185, 13 f.* 188, 11-14; *185, 13* 182, 5-10; *185, 17* 194, 18-24 200, 22-26; *185, 19* 183, 8-10 189, 26-190, 4; *185, 20* 185, 23-24; *185, 23* 177, 20-178, 2 182, 14-183, 1 183, 20-21 185, 5-8 186, 9-13 201, 1-3; *185, 26* 185, 13-16; *185, 27* 179, 14-19 192, 14-17; *185, 28* 186, 5-8; *186, 1 f.* intr. 4.2.2; *186, 1* 187 3-9; *186, 2* 185, 5-8; *186, 4* 176, 18-20 201, 3-13; *186, 5* 193, 12-15 bis; *186, 6* 179, 20-24 185, 13-16 187, 19-24; *186, 8-187, 2* intr. 5.1 192, 17-24; *186, 8-9* 183, 11-16; *186, 11* 177, 5-10 186, 30-31; *186, 14 f.* app. II 2.1; *186, 15 f.* 186, 18-23; *186, 18* 189, 12-16 app. II 4.2.1; *186, 19* app. II n. 17; *186, 21* app. II n. 1; *186, 22* 187, 3-9; *186, 25* 176, 21-177, 1; *186, 29* 184, 14-17; *187, 3 f.* intr. 4.2.3 186, 30-31; *187, 3* 180, 17-19 195, 20-21 200, 10-12; *187, 4* 186, 18-23; *187, 7 f.* intr. 4.2.3; *187, 7* 181, 3-7 182, 14-183, 1; *187, 8* 193, 10-12; *187, 9 f.* 180, 17-19; *187, 9* intr. 4.2.1.3; *187, 10* 181, 7-8; *187, 11* 187, 3-9 197, 27-198, 1; *187, 12* 176, 18-20 191, 29-192, 2; *187, 18 f.* 181, 25-182, 1; *187, 18* 182, 1-5; *187, 19 f.* intr. 4.2.1.3 181, 8-11 183, 8-10 183, 18-20; *187, 20 f.* 194, 28-195, 2; *187, 20* 184, 11-13; *187, 21 f.* intr. 5.2; *187, 21* 180, 10-16 bis; *187, 22 f.* 183, 2-5; *187, 22* 180, 16-17; *187, 24* 182, 10-14 185, 13-16 188, 4-6; *187, 25* 181, 11-13 188, 4-6; *187, 26* 181, 3-7 183, 11-16; *188, 1 f.* intr. 4.2.2; *188, 1* intr. 4.2.1.3; *188, 2* 184, 17-185, 4; *188, 3* 197, 14-17; *188, 4* 176, 21-177, 1 184, 17-185, 4 197, 14-17; *188, 6* 177, 5-10 179, 20-24 181, 25-182, 1 187, 24-26 app. II 4.2.1; *188, 7-14* intr. 1; *188, 8* 176, 18-20; *188, 9 f.* 179, 20-24 201, 26-202, 3; *188, 9* 176, 18-20 179, 14-19 180, 17-19; *188, 10* 192, 17-24; *188, 12 f.* 190, 28-191, 2; *188, 14* 194, 28-195, 2 200, 12-22 bis; *188, 15* 194, 7-12; *188, 17 f.* intr. 4.1; *188, 17* 190, 19-24; *188, 19* 184, 9-11 200, 10-12 200, 12-22 201, 3-13; *188, 21* 185, 8-12 187, 19-24; *188, 22* intr. 3.1; *188, 23* 194, 25-28; *188, 25 f.* 190, 4-10; *188, 25* 201, 3-13; *188, 28* 200, 26-201, 1; *189, 6* 194, 18-24; *189, 11* 190, 19-24; *189, 12* 179,

11-14; *189, 13* 201, 13-17; *189, 15* intr. 3.1 201, 3-13; *189, 16 f.* intr. 4.1; *189, 18* 179, 14-19; *189, 20 f.* intr. 4.3; *189, 25* 197, 9-14 197, 17-20; *189, 26 f.* intr. 4.3 198, 1-5; *190, 1* 198, 5-9 199, 20-200, 1; *190, 4* 185, 16-20; *190, 6 f.* 192, 3-6 193, 12-15; *190, 12* 201, 19-25; *190, 19* 190, 4-10 199, 18-20; *190, 27* 194, 28-195, 2; *190, 28 f.* 198, 1-5; *191, 2* 181, 17-24; *191, 4* 181, 3-7; *191, 10 f.* 192, 28-193, 5; *191, 16 f.* intr. 4.1; *191, 16* 193, 5-10; *191, 18* 192, 28-193, 5; *191, 28* 187, 3-9; *191, 29* 193, 15-19; *191, 30* 176, 21-177, 1 192, 3-6; *192, 1* 199, 20-200, 1; *192, 3-5* 193, 15-19; *192, 3* 193, 5-10; *192, 7* 199, 20-200, 1; *192, 9* 193, 12-15; *192, 14* 195, 21-25; *192, 16* 192, 28-193, 5; *192, 18* 188, 15-17; *192, 19* 192, 28-193, 5; *192, 21* 182, 14-183, 1; *192, 24 f.* 192, 8-14; *192, 25* 193, 12-15; *192, 29* 179, 5-11; *193, 7* 181, 17-24; *193, 9* 185, 5-8; *193, 11* intr. 4.3; *193, 12* 180, 6-8; *193, 13* 194, 18-24; *193, 19 f.* 194, 25-28; *193, 19* 192, 3-6; *193, 20* intr. 3.1 188, 21-25 194, 25-28; *193, 21 f.* intr. 1; *193, 21* 194, 12-18; *194, 1* 180, 17-19; *194, 6* 188, 11-14; *194, 9* 187, 12-16 188, 15-17; *194, 17* 199, 14-18; *194, 18 f.* 193, 12-15; *194, 18* 185, 8-12; *194, 22* 193, 12-15; *194, 25* 193, 19-20; *194, 27* 188, 21-25; *194, 28* 188, 11-14; *195, 1* 176, 18-20; *195, 2* intr. 3.1; *195, 5* 189, 16-20; *195, 6* 196, 5-7 197, 9-14 198, 16-20; *195, 8* 196, 7-10; *195, 10 f.* 197, 9-14; *195, 10* 196, 16-19; *195, 11* 194, 12-18; *195, 13* 197, 17-20; *195, 14* 197, 9-14; *195, 16* 183, 8-10 196, 5-7 202, 13-17; *195, 20* 187, 3-9 197, 9-14; *195, 21* 192, 14-17 201, 19-25; *195, 24* 197, 20-24 200, 12-22; *195, 25* intr. n. 11 196, 22-24 197, 17-20 198, 20-199, 4 199, 9-10 199, 14-18; *196, 1 f.* 198, 20-199, 4; *196, 1* 197, 2-6; *196, 2 f.* 198, 20-199, 4; *196, 3* 197, 17-20; *196, 4* 195, 21-25 198, 1-5 200, 12-22; *196, 5* 197, 9-14 bis; *196, 6* 198, 1-5; *196, 8* 195, 7-11 197, 9-14; *196, 10* 196, 5-7; *196, 13 f.* 197, 9-14; *196, 13* 198, 1-5 bis; *196, 16* 197, 9-14; *196, 18* 199, 4-8; *196, 21* 197, 9-14; *196, 23* 181, 8-11; *196, 24* 197, 2-6; *197, 1* 196, 22-24; *197, 4* 197, 17-20 app. IV n. 9; *197, 10* 198, 5-9; *197, 11* 197, 9-14; *197, 14* 193, 10-12; *197, 16* 196, 5-7 197, 2-6 198, 1-5; *197, 17* 197, 9-14; *197, 18* 198, 5-9; *197, 19* 197, 2-6 197, 17-20 198, 20-199, 4; *197, 20* 194, 1-5 198, 1-5; *197, 21 f.* 200, 12-22; *197, 23* 196, 19-21 198, 9-10; *197, 27* 187, 3-9 197, 20-24 198, 9-10; *198, 1 f.* 198, 5-9 199, 4-8; *198, 1* 177, 5-10 197, 9-14; *198, 2* 195, 25-196, 4 197, 17-20 198, 16-20 199, 4-8; *198, 3* 198, 1-5; *198, 4 f.* 180, 19-23; *198, 6* intr. 4.4 199, 20-200, 1; *198, 7 f.* 196, 10-13; *198, 7* 197, 20-24 app. IV n. 20; *198, 8* 197, 17-24 200, 12-22; *198, 9 f.* 200, 22-26; *198, 9* 197, 27-198, 1; *198, 10* 184, 5-9; *198, 11* intr. 3.1 184, 1-5 201, 13-17; *198, 12* 182, 10-14 193, 5-10; *198, 14 f.* 198, 20-199, 4; *198, 16* 190, 28-191, 2; *198, 17 f.* 184, 1-5; *198, 17* 197, 2-6; *198, 18* 201, 3-13; *198, 19 f.* 197, 17-20; *198, 19* 197, 7-9 198, 1-5; *198, 20* 197, 7-9; *198, 21* 198, 20-199, 4; *198, 22* 199, 4-8 197, 17-20; *199, 2* 198, 20-199, 4; *199, 3 f.* 198, 16-20; *199, 3* app. V; *199, 4-8* 181, 3-7; *199, 4* 181, 3-7 198, 11-16 198, 16-20 198, 20-199, 4; *199, 5 f.* app. V; *199, 5* 199, 9-10 200, 1-9; *199, 6 f.* 199, 9-10; *199, 6* 196, 22-24 197, 7-9 200, 12-22; *199, 7* 181, 3-7 196, 16-19 201, 19-25; *199, 10* 196, 22-24 200, 12-22; *199, 11 f.* app. V; *199, 14 f.* 198, 20-199, 4; *199, 14* 201, 3-13; *199, 15* 105, 13-16; *199, 16* 194, 12-18; *199, 18* 180, 10-16 197, 20-24; *199, 19* 200, 12-22; *199, 20* intr. 4.4 198, 20-199, 4; *199, 23* 191, 29-192, 2; *200, 2 f.* 198, 11-16 198, 20-199, 4; *200, 2* 198, 1-5; *200, 4* 191, 29-192, 2 199,

309

20-200, 1; 200, 10 f. intr. 3.1; 200, 10 187, 3-9; 200, 12 188,
17-20; 200, 13 198, 1-5 201, 19-25 201, 26-202, 3; 200, 16 f. 198,
5-9; 200, 19 199, 18-20 201, 3-13; 200, 21 193, 12-15; 200, 22
f. intr. 4.4; 200, 24 185, 16-20; 200, 27 202, 13-17; 200, 30
201, 26-202, 3; 201, 1 f. 201, 13-17; 201, 1 intr. 4.4 202, 3-8;
201, 3 181, 1-3; 201, 4 181, 1-3 185, 28-186, 5; 201, 9 f. 199,
20-200, 1; 201, 9 177, 19-20 181, 11-13 190, 4-10; 201, 10 198,
16-20; 201, 11 199, 14-18; 201, 14 201, 26-202, 3; 201, 15 198,
11-16; 201, 19 f. 182, 5-10; 201, 20 190, 10-19 195, 25-196, 4;
201, 21 197, 17-20 198, 1-5 app. IV n. 14; 201, 26 202, 13-17;
201, 27 198, 1-5; 202, 2 202, 8-10; 202, 3 f. 194, 18-24; 202, 5
201, 1-3; 202, 7 194, 7-12; 202, 9 194, 5-7; 202, 12 199, 9-10;
202, 13 195, 14-17; 202, 15 196, 19-21; 202, 18 f. intr. 4.4; 202,
18 195, 7-11
Met. 9, 1 189, 26-190, 4 199, 9-10; 9, 2 178, 16-17 178, 24-179, 5
183, 2-5 188, 4-6 190, 10-19 193, 12-15; 9, 3 192, 3-6 196,
19-21; 9, 4 193, 19-20 193, 21-22 195, 25-196, 4 199, 14-18; 9,
5 176, 21-177, 1 177, 19-20 185, 16-20 201, 3-13; 9, 6 178,
24-179, 5 197, 9-14 200, 12-22; 9, 7 181, 17-24 197, 24-26 199,
4-8; 9, 8 f. 198, 9-10; 9, 8 179, 14-19 185, 25-28 199, 10-13
app. IV 2.9.1; 9, 9 177, 5-10 199, 4-8 app. IV 2.3 app. IV 2.7; 9,
10 intr. 1 intr. 4.3 176, 15-18 190, 10-19 195, 21-25 197,
9-14 198, 11-16 app. IV 2.3 bis app. IV 2.10.1; 9, 11 198, 5-9; 9,
12 180, 10-16 182, 1-5 191, 11-15 195, 20-21 201, 19-25; 9,
14 193, 21-22 194, 1-5 194, 7-12 199, 4-8 199, 14-18 bis 202,
13-17; 9, 15 184, 1-5 185, 5-8 bis 186, 9-13 186, 14-16 197,
14-17; 9, 17 f. intr. n. 8; 9, 17 176, 18-20 187, 19-24 194, 1-5;
9, 18 177, 19-20 194, 1-5 194, 5-7; 9, 19 180, 10-16 200,
12-22; 9, 20 176, 15-18 189, 4-12 198, 11-16; 9, 21 187,
19-24 194, 12-18 196, 22-24 196, 24-197, 2 198, 11-16 201,
3-13; 9, 22 183, 11-16 184, 11-13 201, 3-13; 9, 23 178, 24-179,
5 184, 9-11 200, 12-22 201, 3-13 202, 13-17; 9, 24 183, 2-5
184, 5-9; 9, 26 177, 5-10 182, 14-183, 1 194, 7-12 200, 22-26; 9,
27 194, 1-5 bis 195, 7-11 197, 14-17 198, 1-5 200, 12-22 201,
17-19 202, 10-12; 9, 28 195, 12-14; 9, 29 185, 23-24; 9, 30
176, 18-20 180, 19-23 bis 182, 1-5 187, 24-26 bis 193, 10-12 195,
14-17 195, 25-196, 4; 9, 31 intr. 4.3 181, 17-24 181, 25-182, 1
183, 8-10 bis 195, 21-25 197, 9-14; 9, 32 190, 4-10 197, 9-14
201, 3-13; 9, 33 176, 15-18 179, 5-11 197, 24-26 200, 1-9; 9,
34 196, 16-19; 9, 35 191, 2-8 200, 26-201, 1; 9, 36 178, 24-179,
5; 190, 10-19 bis 9, 37 179, 14-19 180, 10-16 186, 5-8; 9, 38
186, 14-16 199, 4-8 201, 13-17; 9, 39 f. 195, 21-25; 9, 39 176,
15-18 178, 19-20 200, 26-201, 1 201, 19-25; 9, 40 177, 15-19
184, 1-5 184, 11-13 188, 11-14 192, 8-14 193, 12-15 201, 13-17;
9, 41 178, 24-179, 5; 9, 42 intr. 4.3 185, 8-12 199, 10-13
Met. 10, 1 193, 19-20; 10, 2 178, 6-8 179, 5-11 181, 3-7 195,
25-196, 4 199, 10-13 201, 26-202, 3; 10, 3 179, 5-11 201, 19-25;
10, 4 184, 11-13 185, 13-16 187, 24-26 195, 25-196, 4; 10, 5 179,
20-24 183, 16-18 197, 9-14 201, 3-13; 10, 6 183, 16-18 186,
5-8 187, 24-26 191, 11-15 192, 8-14 app. I app. I n. 3; 10, 7
190, 28-191, 2 201, 19-25 202, 18-20; 10, 8 181, 25-182, 1 182,
5-10; 10, 9 176, 15-18 177, 5-10 185, 23-24 202, 18-20; 10,
10 182, 5-10 187, 19-24 195, 7-11 199, 14-18 bis 202, 18-20; 10,
12 194, 5-7; 10, 13 intr. 4.3 190, 10-19 195, 21-25 197, 9-14
202, 13-17; 10, 14 178, 9-15; 10, 15 179, 5-11; 10, 16 178,
24-179, 5 200, 26-201, 1 201, 19-25; 10, 17 intr. 4.3 182, 5-10
183, 11-16; 10, 18 178, 24-179, 5 190, 28-191, 2 191, 18-22 197,

9-14;   10, 19   181, 1-3   181, 7-8   198, 1-5;   10, 20   198, 11-16;   10, 21   187, 19-24   200, 22-26   app. IV n. 11;   10, 22   184, 14-17   188, 11-14   188, 15-17   195, 12-14;   10, 24   178, 9-15   178, 24-179, 5   179, 14-19   185, 23   193, 15-19   194, 5-7   194, 7-12   196, 19-21;   10, 25   187, 24-26;   10, 26   178, 24-179, 5 bis   182, 5-10   186, 27-28   188, 4-6;   10, 27   181, 25-182, 1;   10, 28   194, 12-18;   10, 29   184, 14-17   195, 12-14   199, 14-18   200, 22-26;   10, 30   191, 18-22   198, 11-16;   10, 31   192, 28-193, 5   198, 11-16 bis;   10, 32   180, 3-4   182, 10-14;   10, 33   176, 21-177, 1;   10, 34   185, 13-16   189, 4-12   198, 1-5   199, 14-18;   10, 35   intr. 4.3   193, 19-20;
Met.   11, 1   188, 1-4   199, 4-8   201, 3-13   app. IV n. 12;   11, 2   176, 15-18   177, 20-178, 2   178, 19-20   193, 5-10   196, 24-197, 2   app. IV 2.10.1;   11, 3   178, 21-24   202, 13-17   app. II n. 5;   11, 4   184, 14-17;   11, 5   188, 4-6   194, 12-18   196, 24-197, 2 quater   app. IV 2.10.1 bis   app. IV n. 25 bis;   11, 6   179, 5-11   181, 25-182, 1   185, 8-12   192, 14-17   app. II n. 18   192, 28-193, 5   app. IV 2.11   app. IV n. 33;   11, 7   190, 10-19   196, 24-197, 2;   11, 8   189, 20-26 bis   198, 1-5   198, 11-16 ter   201, 19-25;   11, 9   195, 25-196, 4   app. IV 2.5   app. IV 2.6;   11, 10   177, 5-10   198, 11-16   app. IV 2.1   app. IV 2.3   app. IV 2.6 bis   app. IV n. 6;   11, 11   178, 24-179, 5   196, 24-197, 2   201, 26-202, 3;   11, 12   176, 15-18   183, 8-10   app. IV n. 4;   11, 13   179, 5-11 bis   app. IV 2.12.1 bis;   11, 14   196, 19-21   199, 4-8;   11, 15   176, 15-18   182, 10-14   195, 21-25   196, 16-19   199, 4-8   199, 9-10   201, 13-17   202, 13-17   app. IV 2.9.1   app. IV 2.11 ter   app. IV n. 34;   11, 16   189, 4-12   190, 10-19   196, 24-197, 2   199, 4-8   200, 1-9   app. IV 2.3   app. IV 2.9.1   app. IV 2.10.1   app. IV n. 11;   11, 17   182, 10-14   197, 2-6   198, 16-20   app. IV 2.13   app. IV n. 40;   11, 18   181, 1-3;   11, 19   app. IV 2.13 bis;   11, 20   app. IV 2.3   app. IV 2.7;   11, 21   196, 24-197, 2   198, 5-9   app. II 4.2.2   app. IV 2.3   app. IV n. 40;   11, 22   190, 10-19   app. IV 2.10.1;   11, 23   181, 7-8   182, 1-5   198, 5-9   app. II 4.2.2   app. II n. 20   app. IV 2.4   app. IV n. 11   app. V;   11, 24   186, 5-8   193, 12-15   197, 2-6   app. II 4.2.1   app. IV 2.4   app. IV 2.6   app. IV 2.13;   11, 25   177, 5-10   app. II 4.2.2   app. IV 2.7;   11, 26   195, 7-11;   11, 27   intr. n. 12   183, 8-10   184, 5-9   187, 24-26   202, 10-12   app. II 4.2.1   app. II n. 12   app. II n. 23   app. IV 2.11;   11, 28   192, 10-19   199, 4-8   app. IV 2.2   app. IV 2.7 bis;   11, 29   178, 19-20   188, 17-20   188, 25-189, 4;   11, 30   app. IV 2.2   app. IV 2.7
Mun.   12 (147, 13)   183, 2-5;   17 (153, 18)   199, 14-18;   23 (159, 17)   183, 18-20;   27 (163, 14)   181, 3-7;   29, 24 (166, 4)   185, 5-8
Pl.   1, 13 (97, 19)   185, 8-12;   1, 13 (97, 21)   194, 18-24;   1, 14 (98, 1)   181, 7-8;   2, 4 (107, 14 f.)   178, 19-20;   2, 7 (109, 15 f.)   182, 5-10;   2, 11 (114, 4)   179, 20-24;   2, 13 (116, 22)   181, 17-24;   2, 14 (117, 3)   178, 6-8;   2, 24 (128, 15)   181, 3-7;   2, 25 (130, 9)   185, 5-8
Soc.   5 (12, 10)   176, 21-177, 1;   7 (14, 15)   187, 1-2;   8 (15, 13)   app. II 4.1;   8 (15, 14)   app. II n. 10;   9 (17, 4 f.)   app. II 4.1;   9 (17, 16 f.)   app. II 4.1;   12 (20, 16)   179, 20-24;   14   198, 1-5;   14 (22, 4-22)   intr. 4.5;   14 (22, 8)   app. IV n. 14;   14 (22, 10 f.)   198, 1-5;   15 (23, 20 f.)   app. II 4.1;   15 (24, 5 f.)   app. II 4.1;   19 (29, 8)   189, 4-12;   20 (31, 2)   186, 14-16;   22, 4 f.   198, 1-5
arcessitor   193, 5-10
archaism   180, 10-16   189, 16-20   189, 20-26   194, 28-195, 2   196, 16-19
aries   200, 12-22
Aristomenes   intr. n. 4   194, 28-195, 2   app. I
Aristophanes *Ra.* 159   198, 16-20
Ps. Aristoteles Π.κοσμοῦ   398 b 3   181, 3-7;   395 a 5   183, 2-5

311

armare   178, 21-24
Arnobius   3, 11   194, 12-18;   4, 10   182, 14-183, 1;   4, 16   196, 10-13;   5, 21   196, 24-197, 2;   5, 44   200, 12-22;   7, 8   188, 15-17
Arnobius *ad Greg.* 13   179, 11-14
Artemidorus Daldianus   191, 11-15;   1, 8, 14   196, 24-197, 2;   2, 60   184, 1-5;   5, 77   186, 18-23   app. II n. 1
arts (visual)   189, 20-26
arua   181, 3-7
Asconius *Corn.* 64   186, 5-8
asellus   200, 26-201, 1
ass   intr. 4.2.1.3   195, 7-11
 age   195, 7-11
 beaten   193, 15-19
 carrying image of the goddess   198, 16-20   198, 20-199, 4   app. IV n. 31
 disapproval (moral)   200, 22-26
 ecstasy of - not genuine   197, 7-9
 fears   intr. 4.3
 hateful to Isis   197, 2-6   app. IV 2.11
 human aspect   189, 16-20   196, 5-7   196, 7-10   198, 5-9   198, 9-10
 identifies with animals   193, 5-10
 's milk   199, 20-200, 1
 point of view   201, 3-13
 presence creates opportunities   202, 13-17
 prices paid for the -   197, 9-14
 proud of braying   200, 22-26
 sale   intr. 1   intr. 3.1   intr. 4.1   intr. 4.3   intr. 4.4   195, 21-25
 of Silenus   201, 1-3
 slave   196, 5-7
 threatened   202, 18-20
 Typhon   app. IV n. 33
 value-judgement of   201, 3-13
asses   195, 21-25
 sexual activities with   196, 19-21
assidere/assīdere   176, 18-20
assonance   intr. 5.1   182, 14-183, 1   184, 17-185, 4   186, 18-23   186, 28-30   189, 20-26   196, 24-197, 2   198, 11-16   200, 1-9   200, 12-22   201, 19-25   202, 8-10
Astarte-Aphrodite   app. III
Astarte = Isis   196, 24-197, 2
Astarte - Venus   196, 24-197, 2
astu miro   184, 11-13
asyndeton   178, 17-19   181, 7-8   181, 14-17   181, 17-24   186, 18-23   187, 3-9   198, 11-16   190, 19-24   194, 12-18
 bimembre   190, 28-191, 2   197, 17-20
at   191, 2-8
 at te   196, 22-24
Atargatis   app. IV n. 5   app. IV n. 21
Atargatis = Astarte   196, 24-197, 2
Atargatis = Derketo   app. III
Attis   intr. 4.2.4   196, 24-197, 2
Atys   intr. 4.2.2   178, 21-24   179, 20-24   188, 4-6
auctioneer see praeco
auscultare + dative   202, 13-17
audience   intr. 4.2.1.1   intr. 4.2.4   intr. n. 5   177, 5-10 bis   178, 19-20   180, 17-19   181, 14-17   181, 17-24   182, 14-183, 1   186, 9-13   188, 7-8

Augustinus *Ciu.* 7, 26   198, 11-16   198, 20-199, 4 bis;   18, 52   199, 14-18; 19, 8   183, 11-16
   Conf.   4, 1, 1   190, 10-19
   Ep.   149, 22   188, 15-17;   211, 10   179, 11-14
   Eu. Io.   13, 16   188, 21-25
   C. Jul. op. imp.   5, 24   178, 9-15
   Psal.   38, 2   201, 26-202, 3
Ausonius *Epigr.*   25, 1 (44, 1 Prete)   189, 26-190, 4
   Griph. Tern. Num.   17 (154 Prete)   184, 14-17
auspicari nuptias   183, 16-18
author   intr. 4.2.1.3   intr. 4.5   intr. 5.2   181, 14-17   182, 14-183, 1   196, 16-19   199, 4-8   app. IV 3   app. IV n. 28   app. IV n. 43
   see also irony
   behind narrator   181, 17-24
   concrete   app. II 4
   implied   intr. 4.2.1.3   intr. 4.2.4   intr. n. 12   180, 19-23   181, 14-17   186, 18-23   189, 20-26   199, 4-8   app. II 4
   initiate in mysteries   app. II 4.2
   intention of   190, 4-10
   omniscience of   see omniscience
authorial mode   194, 1-5

Babrios   141   198, 16-20;   163   198, 16-20
bacchari   181, 3-7
Bacchus cult of   198, 1-5   198, 16-20
   see also Liber
balbuttire   187, 19-24
baldness   195, 25-196, 4   app. IV n.5
   religious   195, 25-196, 4   app. IV 2.2
baptism see initiation
barathrum   178, 2-6
bath(ing)   see also lauatio
bath (religious)   app. IV 2.4
bathing   200, 12-22
baths public   200, 12-22
beatus   194, 28-195, 2
begging priests   app. IV 1   app. IV 2.7
Bellerophon   189, 20-26
Bellona   196, 24-197, 2   app. IV 2.10.1
B. Afr.   31, 30   189, 4-12;   44, 1   189, 4-12;   91, 3   188, 11-14
bellus   197, 24-26
beneficio + gen.   192, 24-27
Beroea   app. III
βιαιοθάνατος   app. II n. 6
Bible, O.T.   1 Kings 18, 25 f.   201, 13-17
Bible,   see also Vetus Latina
   see also Vulgata
Bion   42-45   181, 8-11;   76 f.   181, 25-182, 1
biothanatus   app. II 2.3
   wanders on earth   app. II 2.4
   Thrasyllus   app. II 3
birth (registration of)   196, 7-10
bisexuality   198, 9-10
bitch   178, 24-179, 5
blinding   see also motifs
blinding   186, 18-23

blindness   185, 28-186, 5   186, 9-13   186, 13-14   186, 14-16   186, 17-18
    186, 18-23   189, 12-16   app. IV n. 29
    of Fortuna   195, 21-25   app. IV 2.1
    Isis' punishment   app. II 4.2.2   app. II n. 22
    result of Charite's revenge   app. II 4.2.2
    twilight condition   app. II 2.1
boar   179, 20-24   188, 25-189, 4
boarhunting   179, 20-24
bombycinus   198, 11-16
Bona Dea   198, 11-16
boni et optimi   see consulere
bonum et frugi   196, 10-13
bonus = magnus   201, 3-13
book-endings intr. 2
*borrire   194, 12-18
bracchium (spelling)   184, 1-5
burial (in the same grave)   187, 24-26
    see also Charite
    see also Tlepolemus
busequa   176, 21-177, 1
bustum = grave   app. I
buxans   193, 10-12
buxeus   193, 10-12

cachinnus   195, 20-21
cachinnum commouere + gen. or dat.   195, 20-21
cadauer   181, 8-11   196, 22-24
    facere   180, 19-23
Caecilius *Com.*   138   198, 11-16;   212   191, 2-8
Caelius Sabinus *apud* Gel.   4, 2, 5   196, 16-19
Caesar   intr. 4.2.3   181, 14-17
    Civ.   1, 48, 2   183, 18-20;   3, 32, 2   188, 25-189, 4
    Gal.   2, 8   196, 19-21;   6, 23   201, 3-13;   7, 9, 6   193, 15-19;
    7, 28, 1   189, 4-12;   7, 41, 5   193, 15-19
calamitas animae   181, 17-24
calcitro   196, 16-19
Caledonian hunt   179, 20-24   180, 3-4
Caligula   app. IV n. 44
Calpurnius *Ecl.*   1, 28   195, 25-196, 4;   1, 48   198, 20-199, 4
Calpurnius Flaccus *Decl.*   26   177, 15-19;   46   181, 25-182, 1
Calvus *poet.*   18   195, 7-11
Camma   intr. 4.2.2
candere   189, 4-12
Candidus   189, 20-26
cani   192, 14-17
cantherius   195, 14-17   197, 9-14
cantus Frygius   app. IV 2.10.1
Caper *Gramm.*   VII 95, 1 (Keil)   186, 13-14
Cappadoces   196, 5-7
Cappadocius   196, 5-7
Cappadocus   196, 5-7
caprea   179, 5-11
captiosus   179, 14-19   185, 25-28
capulus   187, 12-16
carbasinus   198, 11-16
carnificina   200, 1-9

Cassianus *Coen.* 9, 6   178, 2-6
Cassiodorus *Psal.*   88, 1   181, 1-3
    Var. Ep.   10, 32   189, 12-16
castellum   188, 21-25   200, 10-12
castrates   app. IV n. 44   app. V
castrate (feminine used for)   197, 2-6
castration   intr. 4.1   188, 17-20   197, 17-20   198, 9-10   app. III
    self-   app. V
casus   202, 8-10
Cato   *Agr.*   16   198, 1-5;   35, 1   200, 1-9;   132, 2   201, 3-13;   137   198, 1-5;   143   194, 1-5;   149, 1   186, 18-23
    ap. Charis.   (*GLK* 218, 2)   190, 10-19
Catullus   1, 2   192, 17-24;   2, 1   188, 15-17;   3, 6   176, 21-177, 1;   5, 5 f.   app. II 3;   6, 6 f.   191, 29-192, 2;   6, 13   198, 5-9;   17, 5-7   192, 14-17;   21   200, 12-22;   21, 8   200, 12-22;   31, 9 f.   183, 11-16;   36, 12   197, 2-6;   39, 11   179, 5-11;   44, 15   191, 18-22;   55, 21   184, 9-11;   61, 9 f.   98, 11-16;   61, 204   177, 20-178, 2;   63   198, 20-199, 4;   63, 8   197, 2-6;   63, 9 f.   201, 19-25;   63, 9   app. IV n. 22;   63, 24   198, 20-199, 4;   63, 26   198, 16-20;   64, 149   202, 13-17;   64, 261   201, 19-25   app. IV n. 22;   64, 263   197, 17-20;   64, 264   198, 16-20;   64, 341   179, 5-11;   64, 373   183, 11-16;   64, 391   198, 16-20;   68, 52   183, 2-5;   80, 2   201, 13-17;   115, 8   196, 16-19
cauere + abl.   190, 24-28
cauillatus   196, 22-24
cautes   191, 2-8
CE (*Carmina Epigraphica*)   196   192, 14-17;   744, 2   190, 4-10;   1043, 3   186, 23-25;   1181, 5 f.   192, 14-17;   1203, 3   190, 4-10;   1550 A 1   192, 14-17;   1559, 3-5   187, 24-26;   1826, 2   193, 12-15
celebritas   194, 28-195, 2
celibacy   app. IV 2.2
Celsus   2; 10, 14   186, 5-8
cena nouendialis   181, 25-182, 1
cenula   200, 12-22
ceraula   198, 1-5   198, 16-20
Ceres   181, 17-24
cerneres   199, 18-20
certus + inf.   188, 1-4
ceterus   189, 16-20
characterisation   177, 5-10   182, 14-183, 1
    pejorative   184, 5-9
characters (disappearance of)   intr. 5.2   194, 28-195, 2   197, 9-14
Charisius *gramm.*   1, 248, 4   195, 7-11
Charite   intr. passim   ch. 1-14 passim   app. II passim
    blinding Thrasyllus   app. II 1
    burial of   intr. 5.2
    characterisation of   intr. 4.2.3
    's death   194, 18-24
    death-rites   app. I
    mental transformation   181, 3-7   188, 4-6
    parents of   187, 1-5
Chariton   1, 5, 2   intr. n. 7   188, 4-6;   1, 6, 5   181, 11-13;   3, 3, 1   intr. n. 7   181, 8-11;   3, 3, 6   187, 24-26;   3, 10, 4   intr n. 7;   6, 5, 8   186, 18-23
chastity   app. IV 1   app. IV 2.2
cheese-making   191, 29-192, 2

315

chiasmus   177, 20-178, 2   182, 1-5   182, 10-14   184, 14-17   184, 17-185, 4
    186, 5-8   186, 8-9   186, 9-13   186, 13-14   186, 28-30   187, 12-16
    189, 12-16   197, 14-17   193, 5-10   194, 28-195, 2   199, 10-13   202, 3-8
Chimaera   189, 20-26 bis
choraula   198, 1-5
Chrysostomus *in Joh. hom.*   16   186, 17-18
cibus   193, 5-10
Cicero *Ac.*   1, 25   192, 8-14;   2, 108   176, 15-18;   4, 137   187, 19-24
    Agr.   1, 15   177, 5-10
    Arch.   5   177, 20-178, 2
    Att.   1, 16, 10   197, 14-17;   2, 21, 3   195, 14-17;   5, 11, 1   192, 14-17;   5, 12, 2   187, 19-24;   6, 1, 3   192, 28-193, 5;   6, 1, 13   200, 12-22;   7, 14, 2   185, 13-16;   11, 21, 1   187, 12-16;   12, 18, 1   182, 10-14:   12, 23, 2   201, 13-17;   13, 25   189, 20-26;   16, 6, 6   185, 13-16
    Brut.   216   195, 20-21
    Cael.   23   177, 10-15
    Cat.   1, 1   195, 14-17
    Cato   27   188, 7-8
    Clu.   3   202, 13-17
    de Orat.   1, 150   192, 17-24;   1, 158   187, 19-24;   2, 189   181, 14-17;   2, 260   192, 14-17;   2, 262   197, 14-17;   2, 277   179, 2-6
    Diu.   1, 2   189, 4-12;   1, 12   189, 20-26;   1, 102   189, 4-12;   2, 22   181, 17-24
    Dom.   26   185, 13-16;   137   191, 9-11   202, 13-17
    Fam.   4, 5, 1   181, 14-17;   4, 15, 2   192, 17-24;   7, 2, 4   194, 28-195, 2;   7, 23, 2   197, 14-17;   8, 16, 1   192, 14-17;   9, 19, 2   196, 14-16;   12, 10, 4   192, 17-24
    Har.   25   182, 10-14;   44   198, 11-16;   46   189, 20-26
    inc. fr.   39   185, 28-186, 5
    Inv.   1, 2   189, 12-16   1, 107   192, 24-27;   2, 14   193, 5-10;   2, 104   187, 9-12
    Leg.   2, 2, 5   201, 19-25;   2, 9, 22   198, 1-5;   2, 37   196, 24-197, 2;   2, 55   190, 28-191, 2
    Luc.   82   196, 7-10
    Mil.   13, 33   187, 16-18;   65   195, 2596, 4
    Mur.   14, 31   185, 13-16
    N.D.   2, 25   194, 12-18;   2, 71   app. IV n. 1!;   2, 84   194, 12-18;   2, 121   178, 21-24;   2, 150   195, 7-11;   2, 168   185, 5-8;   3, 58   196, 24-197, 2 bis;   3, 84   195, 2-7
    Orat.   65   180, 17-19;   130   181, 14-17
    Part.   80   177, 20-178, 2
    Pis.   9, 19   196, 22-24;   45   181, 17-24
    Phil.   13, 12   180, 19-23;   14, 8   200, 12-22
    Quinct.   82   184, 17-185, 4
    Q. Fr.   1, 1, 16   192, 28-193, 5
    Rab. Post.   42   200, 26-201, 1
    Rep.   4, 1   188, 25-189, 4
    Scaur.   9   194, 5-7
    Sen.   62   192, 14-17
    Sest.   93   178, 2-6;   118   185, 5-8
    S. Rosc.   97   201, 3-13;   149   192, 24-27
    Top.   3   177, 15-19
    Tusc.   1, 34   201, 3-13;   1, 39   202, 13-17;   1, 84   181, 25-182, 1;   1, 107   187, 16-18;   3, 70   181, 17-24;   4, 34   185, 23-24;   4, 55   181, 14-17;   5, 10   187, 18-19;   5, 90   178, 24-179, 5;

```
   5, 108       196, 5-7;       5, 112       186, 17-18;       5, 113       186, 18-23
   Vat.      23       185, 13-16
   Ver.      1, 28       200, 26-201, 1;       2, 9       182, 10-14;       2, 20       192, 24-27;
   2, 66       186, 5-8;       3, 57       200, 26-201, 1;       4, 74       202, 13-17;       4, 75
   194, 1-5;       4, 81       198, 5-9;       4, 95       187, 16-18;       4, 115       180, 17-19;
   6, 92       178, 6-8
   ap. Quint. Inst.      8, 3, 66       177, 5-10
CIL (Corpus Inscriptionum Latinarum)       I       583, 72       186, 5-8;       1, 2525
   176, 21-177, 1;       2, 5181       191, 18-22;       3, 12429       196, 24-197, 2;
   6, 216       192, 14-17;       6, 13528       194, 1-5;       8, 5370       194, 1-5;
   9, 5804       191, 18-22;       10, 411       198, 1-5;       10, 3800       app. IV 2.10.1;
   13, 7610       192, 14-17;       14, 704       186, 23-25;       14, 4296       196, 24-
   197, 2;       15, 7247       182, 1-5
ciere aliquem nomine       181, 17-24
cinaedi       196, 19-21       197, 20-24       198, 5-9       198, 20-199, 4 bis
cinaedus       195, 21-25       195, 25-196, 4       198, 11-16       app. IV 2.2
cincinnus       195, 25-196, 4
cinnameus       184, 14-17
circa      189, 12-16
circum       191, 29-192, 2
circumplecti       180, 19-23
Ciris       167       187, 3-9
ciuis Romanus       196, 10-13
ciuitas       176, 15-18       187, 3-9
clades = caedes       188, 1-4
clamare       191, 29-192, 2
clamitare       188, 4-6       192, 17-24
clamosus       199, 10-13
clandestinus       178, 9-15
Claudianus carm. min.       2, 5       178, 24-179, 5;       22, 14       187, 1-2
   rapt. Pros.       2, 270       198, 16-20;       3, 238       182, 1-5
Claudius (emperor)       194, 12-18       app. V
clausula       see rhythm
cleanliness (ritual)       app. V
climax       176, 18-20       177, 5-10       178, 19-20       178, 24-179, 5       179, 5-11
   181, 17-24       182, 14-183, 1       183, 2-5       190, 19-24       199, 14-18
   of the Met.       app. IV 3
close-up       189, 26-190, 4
clunes       189, 16-20
coaequare cum       186, 14-16
coaetaneus       181, 27-29
Cod. Just.       2, 3, 9(8)       198, 1-5;       5, 9, 2       184, 17-185, 4;       5, 34, 10
   197, 20-24;       5, 60, 3       177, 10-15
Cod. Theod.       12, 6, 7       190, 4-10
coeptum       180, 10-16
cogitare       197, 7-9
cogitatum       197, 9-14
cohumidare       184, 1-5
colometry       179, 5-11       181, 7-8       182, 14-183, 1 bis       184, 14-17       188, 25-
   189, 4       192, 28-193, 5       195, 14-17       197, 24-26       198, 11-16
   isocoly       198, 1-5       199, 18-20
   tetracolon       186, 28-30
   tricolon       179, 5-11       191, 2-8       197, 20-24
      anaphoric       186, 8-9       198, 1-5
      climactic       189, 4-12
      polysyndetic       197, 17-20       198, 5-9
coloni       intr. 4.4       190, 10-19       191, 2-8       200, 12-22       201, 26-202, 3
```

317

Columella   1, pr. 24   192, 8-14;   6, 26, 3   188, 17-20;   6, 29, 5   195, 7-11;   6, 37, 1   196, 16-19;   7, 3, 7   199, 14-18;   7, 12   190, 10-19;   8, 8, 3   194, 12-18;   8, 14, 1   187, 24-26;   8, 17, 1   190, 10-19;   9, 8, 10   178, 24-179, 5;   12, 13   191, 29-192, 2
comedy (language)   186, 17-18
comminus conferre   179, 11-14
commodum salutare   184, 17-185, 4
commulcare   199, 14-18
comparare + inf.   188, 9-10
comparative   185, 23-24
    weakened   188, 9-10   202, 3-8   202, 13-17
compound (intensifying)   193, 5-10
compounds instead of simple verbs   185, 5-8
    unusual   187, 24-26   189, 4-12
concinnare   186, 9-13
concretum pro abstracto   190, 19-24
concubitus   185, 13-16
conferto gradu 200, 26-201, 1
confession (public)   app. IV 2.8   app. V
    confessional stones   app. V
confluere   181, 7-8
coniuga   183, 11-16   194, 1-5
coniugalis   178, 9-15
coniu(n)x (nom.)   183, 11-16
conjunctions (varied)   200, 12-22
conlaticius   198, 1-5
connectives (variety of)   see variation
conradere   200, 1-9
consalutare   202, 3-8
consecare   179, 11-14
consectari + inf.   192, 17-24
conseptum   201, 19-25
conseruus   193, 10-12   194, 1-5
consolation   181, 14-17   181, 17-24   181, 25-182, 1
conspicere/conspicari   199, 20-200, 1
constrepere   198, 20-199, 4
consulere boni et optimi   184, 17-185, 4
contemplatio   201, 13-17
contentiosus   178, 16-17
contentus + inf.   194, 7-12
conterui   195, 7-11
contrast   180, 10-16   180, 19-23 bis   180, 24-25   183, 5-7   183, 18-20   192, 24-27
    anticlimactic   180, 16-17
contrectare   181, 17-24
contubernalis   181, 17-24
conuenire in manum   183, 11-16
conuerberare   184, 1-5
conuulnerare   187, 3-9
Copa   1 f.   195, 25-196, 4;   25   200, 26-201, 1
copiosi = multi   190, 19-24
coram   200, 26-201, 1
corium   179, 5-11
Cn. Cornelius Hispalus (edict of)   196, 24-197, 2
correction (uel certe)   200, 1-9
corruere with obj.   183, 2-5
cost of living in Rome   app. IV 2.7

coxa   201, 26-202, 3
crapula   187, 3-9
cremation   app. I
cribrum   195, 14-17
criminari   199, 10-13
criminals deceased   app. II n. 10
    harmful shades of   app. II 4.1
crinalis   187, 3-9
crines soluti   197, 2-6
crocota   198, 11-16
Croesus   178, 21-24
crotalum   195, 25-196, 4   app. IV 2.5
cruelty   187, 3-9   194, 18-24
    of masters   188, 11-14
    of the world   189, 12-16
cuias   196, 5-7
cuiusce modi   190, 10-19
Culex   164   193, 12-15
culpa   see also manus
culpam dare   180, 24-25
cum primum + subj.   177, 10-15
cuneatim   189, 4-12
curiositas   intr. 4.2.1.1   189, 20-26
    improspera   196, 16-19
curiosity   181, 7-8
cursus   187, 3-9
Curtius   6, 8, 10   178, 24-179, 5;   7, 2, 5   184, 1-5;   8, 2, 34   195, 14-17; 9, 1, 12   188, 1-4
cutis   179, 5-11
Cybele   195, 25-196, 4   198, 16-20   200, 1-9   app. IV 2.10.1
    cult   198, 1-5 bis   app. V
    priests   198, 11-16
    see also Rhea
cymbala   195, 25-196, 4   201, 19-25
cypress   194, 12-18   194, 18-24
    funerary function   191, 11-15
Cyprianus *Ep.*   2, 2   197, 20-24 bis;   34, 1   199, 14-18;   36, 3, 3   187, 18-19;   76, 4   177, 20-178, 2
    Laps.   30   184, 17-185, 4
Cyprianus Gall. *Heptateuchus Gen.*   1492   185, 8-12

daemonum corpora (belong to the air)   app. II 4.1
Damigeranus *Lapid.* 34 (190, 11)   192, 14-17
dammula   179, 5-11
dances (ecstatic)   198, 16-20   app. III   app. IV 2.7
danger   intr. 4.4
Dasyr(ia)   app. III
dative agent   195, 2-7
    ethic   176, 21-177, 1
    of interest   186, 14-16
    instead of possessive   186, 14-16   192, 17-24
    purpose   178, 24-179, 5
    sympathetic   195, 20-21
    in -*u*   180, 10-16
de   176, 15-18   185, 28-186, 5   191, 11-15   192, 17-24   199, 4-8   199, 9-10
    causal   182, 14-183, 1

instrumental 195, 7-11 202, 18-20
 to indicate origin 194, 7-12
Dea Syria intr. 4.4 190, 28-191, 2 195, 25-196, 4 196, 24-197, 2 app. III app.IV passim
 antithesis of Isis 195, 21-25 197, 2-6
 ass's association with 195, 21-25
 =Atargatis 196, 24-197, 2
 confused with Mater Deum 201, 19-25
 cult 199, 4-8 199, 10-13 200, 1-9 app. IV n. 44 app. V bis
 cult, interchangeable with Magna Mater app. IV n. 10
 distinguished from Mater Deum 201, 19-25
 doctor needed for 197, 2-6
 followers of 195, 25-196, 4
 dwells in her image 197, 2-6
 omniparens 196, 24-197, 2
 omnipotens 196, 24-197, 2 197, 2-6
 disrespect for priests 196, 7-10
 priest intr. 2 intr. 4.1 intr. 4.4 intr. 4.5 196, 19-21 197, 14-17 197, 17-20 passim 197, 20-24 passim 197, 27-198, 1 198, 1-5 198, 5-9 198, 9-10 198, 11-16 bis 198, 20-199, 4 199, 4-8 passim app. IV passim
 priests characterised intr. 4.2.4. 196, 22-24
 priests debauched 195, 21-25
 priests, ecstacy not genuine 197, 7-9
 priests, greed 200, 1-9
 priests, hypocrisy 199, 10-13
 priests, insincere 200, 12-22 see also insincerity
 priests, perversion 200, 12-22
 priests, possessed 199, 10-13
 =priest of the Dea Syria 200, 12-22
 sexual practices of priests 201, 3-13
 priests, sly 200, 1-9
death light punishment app. II 2.1
 threatening intr. 4.4
 -rites app. I
 =sleep app. II 3
 symbolical - of initiate app. II 4.2.1 app. II 4.2.2
deception 181, 14-17
deceptus 192, 14-17
decipula/um 179, 14-19
Decl. in Cat. 105 182, 10-14
declamations intr. 4.2.3
defectus 192, 17-24
definire 180, 17-19
deformis 195, 14-17
deformitas 183, 8-10 187, 3-9 195, 14-17 195, 25-196, 4
deformiter 201, 13-17
'Dekomposition' 187, 19-24
delabi 177, 15-19
delectare 181, 17-24
delirus 196, 22-24
Demeter 181, 25-182, 1
demon app. II 4.1
demonstrare 192, 28-193, 5
denarium (gen.) 197, 9-14
denique 177, 19-20 178, 19-20 189, 4-12 189, 20-26 191, 11-15 bis 195, 2-7 199, 9-10 199, 14-18

deorsus   187, 18-19
depingere   198, 11-16
depraedare (-i)   200, 10-12
desinere +obj.   197, 7-9
detestabilis   184, 9-11   188, 17-20   201, 3-13
detestatio   180, 19-23
detorquere   195, 21-25
deuersari   184, 14-17   200, 26-201, 1
deum prouidentia   202, 10-12
    reuerens   201, 19-25
deuorsorium   200, 26-201, 1
dialis   183, 2-5
Diasura/ia   app. III
dicacule   196, 22-24
Dictys Cretensis 1, 4   202, 10-12
Dido intr. 4.2.3   181, 1-3 bis   181, 8-11   182, 1-5   183, 8-10   183, 20-21
    184, 1-5   184, 5-9   187, 3-9   187, 18-19   app. II 2.3   app. II n. 7
dies   178, 21-24
Dig. 3, 2, 11, 1   184, 17-185, 4;   9, 2, 45, 4   180, 24-25;   9, 4, 19   198, 5-9;
    19, 2, 25   198, 1-5;   21, 1, 37 f.   196, 7-10;   22, 3, 25   197, 9-14;   36,
    1, 80 (78), 12   191, 18-22;   48, 8, 3   185, 28-186, 5 see also Ulpianus
dilabi   181, 1-3   201, 3-13
diminutive   179, 11-14   192, 17-24 bis   194, 7-12   196, 22-24   197, 14-17
    197, 24-26   198, 11-16
    adjective   177, 19-20
    adverb   196, 22-24
    affective   196, 5-7   200, 10-12   200, 12-22
    hypocoristic   176, 21-177, 1   184, 1-5   197, 24-26
    pejorative   194, 12-18   200, 12-22   200, 26-201, 1
    suffix -ulus and -culus   197, 24-26   198, 11-16
Diomedes *GLK*   1, 313, 4   202, 13-17
Dionysus   196, 24-197, 2
Diophanes   intr. n. 3
Dioskouroi   179, 20-24
dirruptus   195, 12-14
discourse direct   189, 4-12   197, 20-24
    indirect   193, 12-15   197, 20-24
disponere stellas   196, 7-10
distrahere   192, 28-193, 5
dittography   180, 4-6   182, 5-10   187, 19-24   200, 26-201, 1
diu   177, 19-20
diu denique   178, 9-15
divine honours for the dead   182, 10-14
divine image (contemplation of)   app. II 4.2.1
doctiores   177, 1-4 bis
dogs   intr. 4.1   intr. 4.4   178, 24-179, 5   190, 4-10   190, 10-19   191,
    9-11   192, 14-17   193, 19-20
domina (epithet of goddesses)   196, 24-197, 2
Domitian   app. IV n. 44
domum (without *in*)   177, 20-178, 2
Donatus Ter. *Eun.*   4, 6, 2   186, 18-23
double entendre   196, 16-19 bis
draco   192, 8-14   193, 12-15
Dracontius *Romul.*   10, 165   190, 28-191, 2;   10, 273   190, 28-191, 2
dragon tale   intr. 4.1   intr. 4.3
dramatic effects   202, 3-8
dream intr. 4.2.1.3   179, 14-19   183, 5-7   183, 8-10   184, 5-9   187,

321

19-24
   Charite's -   180, 10-16   181, 3-7
   literary topos   183, 8-10
drinking   177, 5-10   178, 2-6
dum + pluperf.   177, 15-19
durus amor   app. II 2.3   app. II n. 7

eating (words for - with double meaning)   200, 12-22
ecce   184, 9-4   190, 24-28
edict concerning sale of slaves   196, 7-10
effeminacy   198, 11-16
efferari   200, 12-22
egregius (ironically)   186, 8-9
egressio   188, 21-25
elegy   185, 16-20 passim   185, 20-22   185, 23-24   186, 8-9
elements   app. II 4.1
Eleusis   app. IV n. 40
elidere spiritum   188, 4-6
elision   186, 9-13   186, 28-30
ellipsis   179, 20-24
   of pronoun   192, 28-193, 5
   of verbum dicendi   191, 16-18
emittere (confused with immittere)   196, 19-21
emotion(s)   see pathos
   enacted -   181, 14-17
   projection of -   see also animal world
en   186, 8-9   188, 4-6
   + imperative   179, 20-24
      en ecce   197, 14-17
enallage   178, 16-17   185, 25-28   186, 23-25   191, 9-11   197, 27-198, 1
   199, 4-8
ἐνάργεια   180, 10-16
eneruare   201, 13-17
Ennius *Ann.* 190   178, 24-179, 5;   284   191, 9-11;   292   185, 28-186, 5;
   481   194, 28-195, 2
   Sat. 7   179, 5-11
   scen. 69-71 Jocelyn   183, 8-10;   102   176, 15-18;   254   199, 4-8;
   361   181, 17-24
   Var. 17-18   201, 3-13
Ennodius *Dict.* 9, 5   183, 5-7
epic flavour   181, 3-7
   language   app. II n. 20
epiphany   184, 14-17
Ἐπιτάφιος Βίωνος   102 f.   app. II 3
Epit. Alex. 9   189, 4-12;   18   189, 20-26;   75   201, 26-202, 3
Epona   197, 2-6
equidem = quidem   185, 8-12
equiso   176, 21-177, 1
erilis   177, 15-19
errare   app. II 2.1   app. II 2.3
'Erwartungshorizont'   185, 28-186, 5
Et ecce   181, 8-11
et = et quidem   195, 25-196, 4
et explicative   180, 19-23
   repetitive   196, 24-197, 2
ἠθοποιίαι   186, 8-9
etiam   177, 5-10

etymology   176, 15-18   180, 17-19   180, 19-23
euare   198, 16-20
Eubulus 84, 2   197, 24-26
eunuchs   see castrates
Euripides   187, 18-19
   Hec.   1170   187, 3-9
   Hipp.   1392   184, 14-17
Eustathius 1872, 64   181, 14-17
ex (instrumental)   179, 24-26
exaestuare   178, 6-8
exaggeration   187, 3-9   see also hyperbole
exanclare   176, 15-18
excutere + dat.   184, 1-5
execrandus   200, 26-201, 1
exedere   197, 24-26
exercitatus   177, 5-10
eximie (exumie)   190, 10-19   201, 19-25
exinde   196, 14-16
exitium   188, 1-4
exoculare   187, 3-9
'Exordialtopik'   177, 1-4
expergite = uigilanter   202, 13-17
explicit (in ms.)   intr. n. 1
expugnare   186, 18-23
extrarius   194, 1-5
eye-witness   intr. 4.2.1.3   179, 14-19

fabella/fabula   177, 1-4
facessere (without preposition)   201, 3-13
facies   184, 14-17
facile   197, 9-14
facinus   199, 10-13
fairy-tale   177, 5-10
fallaciosus   185, 13-16
fama   intr. 4.2.1.1   181, 1-3
Fama   intr. 5.2   181, 1-3
familia   180, 17-19
   rustica   intr. 2   intr. 3.2   intr. 4.1   intr. 4.2.1.1
famulitio/ium   194, 1-5
famulus   197, 14-17   app. IV 2.11   app. IV n. 31
fanaticus   198, 20-199, 4
fantasy (world of)   193, 12-15
faxo +subj.   186, 17-18
fellatio   200, 12-22
femus   180, 10-16   196, 19-21   201, 26-202, 3
feralis   185, 23
fertur   181, 3-7
feruidus   178, 24-179, 5
Fest. 23 L   201, 17-19;   77 L   194, 1-5;   104, 9 L   190, 10-19;   105, 17 L   179, 20-24;   107 L   196, 22-24;   110 L   200, 12-22;   202 L   201, 19-25;   285 L   197, 24-26;   393 L   197, 20-24 bis
festinare + inf.   191, 22-27
ficulneus   194, 12-18
fig (symbolism of)   194, 12-18
fig-tree   194, 18-24
fimbriatus   199, 14-18
finire   180, 17-19

323

Firmicus Maternus *Err.* 4, 2   199, 4-8;   6, 7   195, 25-196, 4
   Math.   7, 25, 4   195, 25-196, 4;   8, 21, 3   178, 6-8
fish (forbidden)   app. V
flagitare   200, 12-22
flamma amoris   178, 6-8
flammeus   179, 5-11
floridus   189, 4-12
Florus *Epit.*   2, 7, 4   199, 4-8;   3, 10, 14   192, 6-8
flute (Phrygian)   197, 17-20
focalisation (shift of)   197, 14-17
fomentum   178, 6-8
forare   182, 10-14
formulaic expressions   194, 25-28
fortuna   195, 12-14
Fortuna   195, 21-25   199, 9-10   app. IV 2.1
   caeca   195, 21-25   199, 9-10   app. IV 2.1
   epithets   195, 21-25
   false   195, 21-25
   mea   195, 21-25
   saeuissima   197, 9-14
   uidens   195, 21-25   app. IV 2.1
Fortunae (per -as)   192, 14-17
fractus   197, 17-20
fragrance   184, 14-17   see also topos
frater (affective use of -)   181, 17-24   184, 14-17
frondosus   178, 24-179, 5
Frontinus *Aq.*   27, 3   187, 3-9
   Str. 4, 1, 8   179, 26-180, 2;   4, 1, 19   179, 14-19
Fronto   3, 19 vdH   197, 20-24;   88, 23 vdH   197, 24-26;   93, 28 vdH
   197, 24-26;   127, 10 vdH   182, 5-10;   128, 6 vdH   190, 4-10;   199, 20
   vdH   201, 26-202, 3;   226, 3 vdH   197, 9-14
frugi   see bonum
frui + acc.   186, 18-23
fugitiui   194, 28-195, 2
fulmineus   179, 5-11
funeral practices   app. I
funeral rites   181, 25-182, 1
funiculus   194, 7-12
funus   181, 11-13   201, 3-13
furatrina   178, 9-15
furor   182, 14-183, 1
future historic   181, 3-7
   potential   181, 3-7

Gaius *Inst.*   2, 254   198, 1-5;   2, 257   198, 1-5;   3, 8   188, 25-189, 4;
   3, 153   186, 14-16;   3, 195   181, 17-24
Gallae   197, 2-6
Galli   195, 25-196, 4   199, 14-18   app. V
gallicinium   176, 15-18
Ganymedes   198, 11-16
gaps (in the tale)   177, 5-10
garments of priests   app. IV 2.6   app. IV n. 15
garrire   184, 11-13
gaudialis   188, 17-20   200, 10-12
gaudibundus   177, 20-178, 2
Gellius   1, 2, 2   182, 1-5;   1, 8, 1   177, 1-4;   1, 9, 1   192, 24-27;
   1, 11, 8   179, 20-24;   2, 29, 8   188, 11-14;   3, 8, 1   190, 10-19;

4, 6, 2-6	197, 20-24;	4, 6, 6	197, 20-24;	4, 20 6	196, 7-10;
5, 11,10	178, 24-179, 5;	5, 14, 7	179, 5-11;	5, 14, 18	200, 26-
201, 1;	5, 18, 6	177, 1-4;	5, 21, 4	189, 4-12;	6, 3, 34	185, 13-
16;	7, 3, 1	179, 5-11 bis;	10, 17, 2	198, 11-16;	2	188, 7-8;
14, 1, 34	185, 13-16;	14, 4	198, 11-16;	17, 20, 7	194, 5-7;
19, 7, 1	200, 12-22;	19, 7, 3	179, 5-11;	20, 1, 29	187, 24-26

geminatio emphatica   187, 16-18
gena   179, 11-14
generosus   178, 24-179, 5
genitive adverbial   184, 17-185, 4
    causal   177, 10-15
    charge   177, 10-15
    comparison   199, 4-8
    explicative   178, 2-6   187, 1-2
    identity   190, 10-19
    partitive   176, 15-18   190, 10-19
    partitive with neuter adj.   200, 12-22
    rei   190, 10-19
    relation   177, 5-10   178, 24-179, 5
    subjective   183, 18-20
Genius   192, 14-17
geography   intr. 3   intr. 3.1
gestire   187, 3-9   200, 22-26
gingiua   195, 7-11
Gloss.   2, 234, 14   178, 9-15;   2, 523, 19   194, 18-24;   3, 290, 16   196, 24-197, 2;   4, 50, 13   179, 14-19;   4, 522, 21   179, 11-14;   5, 76, 23   179, 20-24;   5, 416, 37   179, 14-19;   5, 495, 55   195, 14-17;   5, 601, 29   189, 20-26;   5, 639, 32   195, 14-17;   5, 657, 10   176, 21-177, 1
graecism   192, 17-24   200, 26-201, 1   201, 13-17
grafice   198, 11-16
grandis   196, 19-21
grassari   190, 4-10
Grattius *Cyneg.*   185   178, 24-179, 5
grave   see tomb
grauis   183, 2-5
Gregorius Magnus *Dial.*   3, 4 p. 225A   200, 26-201, 1

habitus   182, 10-14
Hadrian   194, 12-18
Haemus   181, 17-24   194, 28-195, 2
hapax legomenon   184, 1-5   189, 4-12   191, 22-27   192, 17-24   194, 12-18 bis   196, 22-24   199, 14-18   202, 13-17
haplography   189, 16-20
Hegesippus   1, 40, 12   193, 5-10;   5, 6   188, 21-25
heiulare   184, 1-5
Helen   187, 18-19
Heliodorus   1, 17, 5   194, 7-12;   1, 31, 6   intr. n. 7;   2, 1, 1   intr. n. 7   181, 8-11;   2, 4, 4   intr. n. 7;   5, 24, 3   intr. n. 7;   10, 20, 2   intr. n. 7
Helios   196, 24-197, 2
hendiadys   188, 15-17   192, 6-8   192, 24-27
hercules   190, 19-24
Herodotus   1, 34 f.   intr. 4.2.2   178, 21-24   179, 20-24   188, 4-6
Hesychius In *Leu.*   20, 6, 8   201, 13-17
heus   197, 24-26
hexameter   see rhythm

hic ille 193, 15-19
Hierapolis 198, 11-16 198, 20-199, 4 app. III app. IV 2.2 app. V
Hieronymus *Ephes.* 2, 8, 6 195, 7-11
  Ep. 22, 19, 2 183, 16-18; 46, 10a 200, 26-201, 1; 49, 17, 5 197, 20-24; 60, 5, 3 181, 17-24; 98, 5 179, 14-19; 100, 16 178, 2-6
  Ruf. 3, 11 187, 3-9
  in *Soph.* 1, 13 p. 689 188, 21-25
  Tract. in Ps. 1, 159 188, 15-17
Ps. Hier. *Ep.* 7, 1 201, 13-17
Hilarius *Trin.* 6, 25 199, 14-18; 8, 19 188, 21-25
Ps. Hilarius *Hymn.* 2, 86 185, 5-8
hilarus 182, 5-10
Hirtius *Gal.* 8, 25, 2 177, 5-10
historia 177, 1-4 bis
historiae specimen intr. 4.2.1.1 intr. 4.2.4
historians 193, 19-20
  see also style
hoc (anaphoric) 186, 9-13
Homerus *h. Cer.* 49 f. 181, 25-182, 1; 277 f. 184, 14-17
  Il. 3, 8 f. 179, 20-24; 9, 529 f. 179, 20-24
  Od. 19, 471 181, 14-17
homoeoteleuton 179, 5-11 179, 14-19 180, 19-23 188, 9-10 195, 14-17 197, 14-17 198, 1-5 198, 11-16 198, 5-9 199, 18-20 200, 1-9 201, 26-202, 3
homosexuality 195, 25-196, 4 198, 9-10 app. IV 1
honey punishment intr. 4.1 intr. 4.2.1.1 intr. 4.3
hora = tempus 193, 5-10
Horatius *Ars* 291 183, 5-7
  C. 1, 1, 28 179, 11-14; 1, 3, 1 f. 192, 14-17; 2, 17, 13 189, 20-26; 3, 1, 27 183, 2-5; 3, 11, 38 f. app. II 3; 4, 4, 21 189, 26-190, 4
  Ep. 1, 5, 16 199, 10-13; 2, 1, 70 180, 10-16
  Epod. 11, 10 188, 7-8; 17, 53 184, 9-11
  S. 1, 1, 4 192, 8-14; 1, 3, 48 187, 19-24; 1, 3, 87 186, 9-13; 1, 8, 1 194, 12-18; 2, 3, 247 188, 15-17; 2, 5, 77 197, 20-24; 2, 6, 2 194, 12-18; 2, 6, 64 200, 12-22; 2, 7, 2 196, 10-13; 2, 7, 79 198, 5-9
hordeum 200, 1-9
horoscope 196, 7-10
horror 181, 8-11
hortari + inf. 187, 9-12
humiliation intr. 4.3 intr. 4.4
hydrophory app. III
Hyginus *Fab.* 102, 1 192, 28-193, 5
Hyginus Gromaticus *agrim.* p. 169 196, 7-10
hypallage see enallage
hyperbaton 177, 20-178, 2 186, 25-27 187, 1-2 188, 4-6 189, 20-26 189, 26-190, 4 191, 9-11 192, 28-193, 5 194, 28-195, 2 195, 11-12 196, 19-21 198, 11-16
hyperbole 182, 14-183, 1
'hypercaractérisation' 188, 4-6

I distinction between narrating and experiencing I 201, 26-202, 3
  experiencing intr. 3.1 197, 27-198, 1 198, 5-9 app. IV 3
    point of view of 199, 18-20
  extra-diegetical app. II n. 12

    narrating   192, 3-6   194, 12-18   198, 1-5   app. IV 2.2   app. IV 2.10.1   app. IV 2.11   app. IV 3   app. IV n. 28   app. IV n. 43
        perspective of   181, 14-17   199, 9-10
        point of view of   199, 18-20
iaculum   180, 3-4
iam dudum   194, 7-12
iamiamque   201, 1-3   202, 3-8
iam + noun   197, 9-14
iconicity   191, 29-192, 2
id genus   177, 10-15
idoneus + *ad* or + dative   188, 1-4
Inscriptiones Graecae IX^2 100   app. IV n. 21
ignifer   189, 20-26
ille   184, 14-17   191, 2-8   195, 21-25
    approaching definite article   201, 13-17
    pejorative   200, 12-22
    referring back   197, 17-20
ille suus   201, 13-17   201, 26-202, 3
illinc = illorum   191, 11-15
ima uentris   200, 12-22
image contemplation of the goddess'   app. IV 2.13   app. IV n. 40
    of the goddess   app. IV 2.12.1   see also ass
    transport of the goddess'   app. IV 2.11   app. IV 2.13
imaginari   186, 25-27
imagines defuncti   182, 10-14
imagines (dream visions)   184, 5-9
imitation of character   179, 20-24
immanis   193, 12-15
immittere   178, 24-179, 5   196, 19-21
imperative in -to-   195, 25-196, 4
imperfect de conatu   180, 24-25
    duration   195, 2-7
    ingressive   198, 9-10
    between other tenses   197, 14-17
impetus   179, 26-180, 2
    plur.   178, 19-20
improbare   177, 10-15
improuide   184, 9-11
imprudentia   182, 14-183, 1   184, 9-11
impurity   app. IV 2.3
in concessive   195, 14-17   202, 13-17
    consecutive/final   197, 17-20
in speciem   189, 26-190, 4
in ultimo fortunae turbine   202, 13-17
inacidatus   191, 22-27
incantare   192, 17-24
inclamare   193, 5-10
indicative instead of subj.   189, 4-12   192, 3-6
    in iterative dependent clauses   188, 11-14
indidem   199, 14-18
indignation (moral)   181, 17-24
    sub narrator's - 182, 14-183, 1
indipisci   179, 20-24
individual vs group   192, 28-193, 5
individualisation   191, 22-27   198, 1-5   201, 13-17
inducere   187, 19-24
indusiatus   198, 11-16

industria   200, 12-22
inedia   181, 25-182, 1   187, 19-24   188, 1-4   188, 4-6 bis   app. II 4.2.1
inefficax   202, 3-8
infantulus (-a)   188, 15-17   194, 7-12
inferi   192, 14-17
inferialis   181, 25-182, 1
infestare   188, 25-189, 4
infinitive de conatu   181, 17-24
    historic   181, 14-17
infit   199, 10-13
information (chain of)   intr. 4.2.1.3   179, 14-19
infortunium   176, 18-20   186, 28-30
inhaerescere + acc.   190, 4-10
inhortari   190, 10-19
inhumation   app. I
initiate of Isis   intr. n. 10
    journey through elements   app. II 4.2.2
    rebirth   app. II 4.2.2
initiation   198, 5-9   app. IV 2.7   passim
    baptism of   app. V
    of Lucius   198, 16-20
iniuria   186, 5-8
inlacrimare   188, 7-8
inlicitus   200, 12-22
inmaturitas   184, 17-185, 4
inmixtus   185, 28-186, 5
inmunitus   179, 14-19
innoxius   179, 14-19
inscendere   190, 19-24
Inscr. chrét. de la Gaule 42c (Le Blant)   app. II 3
Inscr. lat. Christ. 1,2425 (Diehl)   app. II 3
insecutio   189, 12-16
insertion of tale   see tale
insigniter   177, 20-178, 2
insilire + acc.   179, 24-26
insincerity of the priests of the Dea Syria   app. IV 2.9.1   app. IV 2.9.2   app. IV
    2.10.1   see also Dea Syria
instinguere   194, 5-7
instringere   194, 5-7
insumere + dative   182, 10-14
insuper   180, 3-4
insurgere   179, 5-11
intercīdere   183, 11-16
interdum   181, 17-24   185, 8-12
interea   191, 29-192, 2
interula   184, 1-5
introuocare   186, 5-8
intus + genit.   200, 26-201, 1
inunire   187, 24-26
inurguere   185, 5-8
inuadere   201, 26-202, 3   202, 8-10
invective   181, 8-11
inversion literary   intr. 4.2.3   181, 1-3   181, 17-24   188, 1-4
inuisitatus   179, 5-11
inuoluere   177, 1-4
Iphigeneia   197, 20-24 bis
ipse (demonstrative)   192, 17-24

irate masters   202, 3-8
irony   180, 10-16   181, 25-182, 1   186, 8-9   186, 30-31   187, 3-9   190, 4-10   192, 14-17 bis   196, 7-10   196, 16-19   197, 20-24   198, 1-5   199, 4-8   199, 9-10   200, 1-9   201, 1-3   201, 13-17   202, 10-12   app. IV 2.11   app. IV n. 31
   at the level of the author   177, 1-4
   ironical connotation   191, 11-15   197, 24-26
   ironical context   197, 14-17
   ironical description   189, 26-190, 4
   of the metaphor   190, 4-10
   narrator's -   188, 4-6   189, 26-190, 4
irrumatio   200, 12-22
Isidorus *Orig.*   1, 41   177, 1-4;   9, 4, 45   app. IV n. 30;   15, 7, 4   188, 4-6;   19, 31, 7   179, 11-14
Isis   intr. 4.2.4   intr. n. 10   181, 8-11   184, 14-17   189, 20-26   195, 25-196, 4   196, 24-197, 2   198, 11-16   198, 16-20   199, 4-8 passim   app. III   app. IV passim
  adept of   app. IV n. 11
  aretalogy   app. IV 2.10.2
  blinding power   app. 2.10.2
  = Bellona   196, 24-197, 2
  catalogue of names   app. IV 2.10.1
  cult of   199, 4-8   app. II 4.2.1   app. II n. 22   app. V bis
  domina elementorum   app. II 4.2.2
  healing power   197, 2-6   app. IV 2.10.2   app. IV 2.12.1 bis   app. IV 2.12.2   app. IV n. 13   app. IV n. 29
  image   197, 2-6   app. II n. 5
  Isiac interpretation of the novel   187, 24-26
  μυριώνυμος   196, 24-197, 2   app. IV 2.10.1
  omniparens   196, 24-197, 2
  omnipotens   196, 24-197, 2
  power   202, 10-12
  priest(s) of   199, 4-8   app. IV passim
  procession   see procession
  pursuit of gain by priests of   200, 1-9
  theology   app. II n. 24
  = universal goddess   app. 2.10.1
  = Venus   196, 24-197, 2
isocoly   see colometry
iste (anaphoric)   185, 5-8
ita + subj.   192, 14-17
itaque   201, 17-19
iubilatio   190, 10-19
Iulius Valerius   2, 26   178, 9-15;   30, 39   179, 5-11;   161, 21   186, 5-8
ivy   app. II 4.2.1

Jamb. *Myst.* 3, 9, 118   199, 4-8
joke (Apuleian)   188, 15-17
Josephus *Ant. Jud.*   18, 65 f.   app. IV 2.7
joy (of Isis' initiate)   197, 2-6
Jung   intr. 4.2.4   190, 10-19
Iuno   196, 24-197, 2
Jupiter   196, 24-197, 2
  -Sabazius (identified with Sebaoth)   196, 24-197, 2
Juv.   2, 11 f.   197, 17-20;   2, 112   198, 20-199, 4 bis;   2, 114   197, 20-24;   4, 123 f.   198, 20-199, 4;   6, 0, 20 f.   198, 11-16;   6, 424 f.   177, 5-10;   6, 511 f.   197, 17-20;   6, 513   199, 14-18;   6, 522 f.

app. V;   6, 533   app. IV 2.2;   9, 61   188, 15-17;   11, 79   200, 12-22;   13, 92   196, 24-197, 2   app. IV 2.10.2;   13, 128   201, 17-19
juxtaposition   186, 25-27   187, 16-18
   of related words   184, 1-5

κάθαρσις   app. IV 2.2   app. IV 2.3
καλὸν κἀγαθόν   184, 17-185, 4
karissimum   intr. 5.3
karissimus   194, 14-17
Katpatuka   196, 5-7
κῆρυξ   196, 7-10
kleptomania   app. IV 1

labare   181, 8-11
Laberius *com.*   125   200, 22-26
labes   182, 14-183, 1
laciniatim   189, 4-12
Lactantius *De mort. pers.*   9, 4   202, 3-8
   Inst. 3, 10, 3   190, 24-28;   5, 14, 5   186, 14-16
   Opif.   12, 15   195, 2-7
lactem accus.   191, 29-192, 2   199, 20-200, 1
Lamachus   183, 16-18   app. I
lancea   179, 20-24   180, 4-6
lanciola   198, 11-16
landscape   intr. 3.2   179, 14-19
language (colloquial)   see sermo cotidianus
laniena   202, 18-20
lanosus   199, 14-18
largiter   189, 26-190, 4   199, 20-200, 1
Laruae   app. II 4.1
lasciuire   196, 7-10
lassescere   182, 14-183, 1
lassus   192, 8-14
latera   198, 5-9
latibulum   180, 17-19
   + genit.   200, 26-201, 1
lauacrum   182, 1-5
lauatio   app. III
   as part of funeral rites   187, 24-26
lector doctus   177, 5-10   185, 16-20
   winks at the -   189, 26-190, 4
lector, intende: laetaberis   intr. 4.2.4
legal terms (quasi -)   196, 10-13
Lemures   app. II 4.1
Leo Magnus *Ep.* 167, 9   193, 19-20
Leucippe   187, 18-19
Lex Cornelia   196, 10-13
Lex Fabia de plagiariis   196, 10-13
Lex repetund. CIL I² 583, 72   186, 5-8
Libanius *Ep.*   1509, 3   197, 20-24
Liber   182, 10-14
liberation of slaves   app. III   app. IV 2.11
libertas   app. IV 2.11
libido   intr. 4.2.1.1   intr. 4.2.4   178, 9-15
   furiosa   178, 19-20
life after death   app. II 4.2.1
lima consilii   183, 5-7   184, 5-9

litotes   177, 5-10   192, 6-8   200, 1-9
Livius   1, 57, 7   179, 20-24;   2, 29, 4   186, 5-8;   4, 58, 7   176, 15-18;   5, 7, 11   181, 14-17;   5, 15, 10   199, 4-8;   5, 22, 5   201, 13-17;   5, 48, 6   196, 14-16;   7, 14, 7   201, 3-13;   7, 19, 3   188, 1-4;   8, 6, 9   192, 8-14;   8, 8, 10   179, 5-11;   8, 9, 12   183, 2-5;   8, 16, 8   196, 19-21;   8, 16, 13   197, 9-14;   9, 6, 3   192, 14-17;   9, 35, 6   186, 5-8;   9, 41, 16   194, 7-12;   21, 11, 7   187, 9-12;   21, 53, 6   185, 28-186, 5;   24, 21, 2   186, 23-25;   25, 23, 16   185, 5-8;   25, 8, 11   185, 16-20;   25, 37, 12   192, 6-8;   26, 9, 7   197, 2-6;   27, 19, 9   196, 5-7;   27, 19, 12   181, 14-17;   28, 1, 8   194, 28-195, 2;   30, 3, 4   185, 5-8;   30, 18, 4   191, 9-11;   31, 14, 12   181, 7-8;   33, 4, 2   178, 24-179, 5;   33, 29, 1   185, 28-186, 5;   34, 9, 6   178, 24-179, 5;   34, 50, 1   181, 14-17;   37, 9, 9   198, 20-199, 4;   42, 8, 6   188, 25-189, 4;   42, 23, 9   186, 5-8;   45, 38, 12   181, 17-24
locality   see geography
locuples   177, 5-10
locus amoenus   intr. 4.3   191, 18-22   191, 22-27   191, 29-192, 2   193, 12-15   193, 15-19
   association with death   191, 22-27
loneliness of Lucius   195, 2-7
longe + abl.   194, 28-195, 2
   + *ab* or *ex*   194, 28-195, 2
   + comparative   190, 4-10
Longus   2, 8   185, 23-24;   2, 22   intr. n. 7;   2, 24   185, 23-24;   4, 22, 1   181, 14-17
λόγχη   179, 20-24
love poetry (Hellenistic)   185, 23-24
lubricus   198, 20-199,4
Lucanus   1, 566 f.   198, 20-199, 4 bis;   3,8 f.   183, 8-10;   3, 416   186, 18-23;   3, 759   180, 19-23;   4, 148   187, 9-12;   5, 104   178, 24-179, 5;   5, 118 f.   199, 4-8;   5, 128 f.   199, 4-8;   5, 443   201, 13-17;   7, 764 f.   183, 8-10;   9, 910   185, 16-20;   9, 1035 f.   intr. 4.2.3   181, 14-17;   9, 1061 f.   intr.   4.2.3   181, 14-17;   9, 1063   180, 19-23;   10, 329   201, 13-17
Lucianus *Jup. Conf.*   12   intr. 4.2.2
   Syr. D.   1, 25   app. IV n. 38;   10   201, 13-17;   42   198, 11-16;   50   198, 20-199, 4 bis   app. V;   51   198, 16-20;   55   app. IV n. 5
Lucilius   139 M   185, 28-186, 5;   260 M   200, 26-201, 1;   443 M   183, 11-16;   511 M   197, 9-14;   733 M   193, 12-15;   1083 M   176, 15-18
Lucius   intr. 1   intr. n. 10   177, 5-10   179, 14-19   193, 5-10   195, 2-7
   ass   intr. 3.1   intr. 4.3   201, 3-13
   subjective point of view   190, 24-28
   aversion to homosexuals   199, 9-10
   cloack of -   193, 12-15
   in human shape   196, 5-7
   initiation   197, 2-6   app. II 4.2.1   app. IV 3
      in various mysteries   app. II 4, 2
   initiation (after)   app. IV 2.4   app. IV 2.6
   initiation (before)   app. IV 1
   lawyer   196, 10-13
   loneliness of -   195, 2-7
   man and ass   195, 12-14
   metamorphosis   intr. 2
   misfortunes   195, 21-25
   returns to human form   193, 19-20   app. IV 2.11   app. IV 2.12.1 bis
   Roman citizen   196, 10-13

331

selective indignation   202, 18-20
uoluptas   200, 22-26
lucrari   186, 25-27
Lucretia   186, 5-8
Lucretius   1, 120 f.   app. II n. 4;   1, 133   185, 28-186, 5;   1, 401   200, 1-9;   1, 900   189, 4-12;   2, 618   201, 19-25;   2, 627   198, 1-5;   2, 614 f.   198, 20-199, 4;   2, 621   198, 16-20;   2, 706   196, 24-197, 2;   2, 1038   185, 5-8;   3, 184   201, 1-3;   3, 190   188, 17-20;   3, 249   185, 8-12;   3, 249   194, 18-24;   3, 890 f.   app. I;   3, 956   190, 4-10;   4, 333   182, 1-5;   4, 450   189, 4-12;   4, 544   197, 17-20;   4, 563   201, 1-3;   4, 639   193, 12-15;   5, 39   185, 5-8;   5, 368   183, 2-5;   5, 840   185, 16-20;   5, 906   189, 20-26;   5, 974   185, 28-186, 5;   5, 1035   185, 5-8;   6, 121 f.   183, 2-5;   6, 977   199, 18-20;   6, 1186   188, 7-8
luctuosus   182, 10-14
lugubris   181, 17-24
lurchare   196, 22-24
lurcho   196, 22-24
luror   182, 1-5
luxuria/ies   177, 5-10   194, 12-18
Lydia   53   201, 13-17
lying and deceit   177, 20-178, 2   185, 28-186, 5   187, 19-24
lymphaticus   197, 7-9   198, 16-20

Mâ of Kommana   196, 24-197, 2   app. IV 2.10.1
macabre atmosphere   188, 25-189, 4   193, 12-15
    events   194, 18-24
    scenes   194, 18-24
Macrobius *Sat.*   1, 3, 12   176, 15-18;   1, 7, 1   194, 1-5;   5, 17, 5   201, 3-13;   6, 2, 18   183, 8-10
Madaurensis   intr. n. 12   app. II n. 12
magic   181, 8-11
magis magisque   178, 9-15
Magna Mater cult of   198, 1-5   app. IV n. 44
    priests of   198, 1-5   198, 11-16
magnus   196, 19-21
    = procerus   192, 8-14
make-up (effeminate men)   198, 11-16
malediction   app. IV 2.10.1
Mamertus *St.an.praef.*   20, 16   201, 26-202, 3
Manilius   5, 319   186, 25-27
mancipium   196, 10-13   197, 14-17   app. IV 2.11   app. IV n. 30   app. IV n. 36
mandato   178, 24-179, 5
mandere = dilaniare   193, 12-15
manes acerbos   184, 17-185, 4
Manes (plural)   186, 23-25
Manis   176, 21-177, 1
mansio   194, 25-28
manus suae culpam   180, 24-25
manuscripts Beneventan script   197, 17-20
    F: marginal annotations   184, 14-17
    F: tear in f. 160   182, 5-10
    F: confusion in compendia   200, 22-26
        of *t* and *a*   197, 17-20
        of *u* and *b*   197, 24-26
    mistaken word-division   194, 12-18

332

transposition of consonants   199, 20-200, 1
maritare + abl. or dat.   183, 11-16
mariti   177, 20-178, 2
maritus   186, 8-9   194, 5-7   197, 20-24
Martialis   1, 65, 3 f.   194, 12-18;   2, 18, 7   198, 5-9;   2, 47, 4   200, 12-22;   3, 91, 11 f.   197, 20-24;   4, 17, 3   200, 12-22;   4, 43, 7   app. V;   5, 23, 1   198, 11-16;   6, 57, 1 f.   app. IV 2.2;   6, 77, 1 f.   196, 5-7;   7, 14, 1   187, 3-9;   7, 71   194, 12-18;   7, 92, 9   183, 2-5;   10, 83, 11   195, 25-196, 4;   11, 58, 1   183, 2-5;   11, 84, 3   198, 16-20   198, 20-199, 4;   12, 28, 19   app. IV 2.2;   14, 15   199, 14-18;   14, 24, 1   198, 11-16;   14, 221, 2   179, 5-11
Martianus Capella   1, 35   189, 4-12;   4, 423   199, 14-18;   8, 813   190, 10-19;   9, 892   190, 10-19
Mater deum   195, 25-196, 4   201, 19-25   app. IV n. 21
    Pessinuntia   app. IV 2.10.1
Mater Idaea   196, 24-197, 2   app. IV 2.10.1
mathematicus   196, 7-10
maturescere   177, 10-15
maturus   177, 10-15
medius + gen.   189, 16-20
Mela (Pomponius) 1, 21   190, 10-19
Meleager   179, 5-11   179, 20-24   180, 3-4
memento   195, 25-196, 4
Men   196, 24-197, 2   (see also Mâ)
Menander *in* Porph. *Abst.*   4, 15   app. V
mendicant priests   200, 1-9
mensa   198, 1-5
mente excidere   202, 10-12
mentiri   177, 20-178, 2
mercatus   195, 2-7
meretrix   177, 5-10
meritum   199, 9-10
Meroe   app. IV n. 39
messenger in tragedy   176, 21-177, 1
metamorphosis   187, 24-26   192, 3-6
    of Charite   183, 5-7
    of Tlepolemus   182, 10-14
metanarrative terms   193, 21-22
metaphor   178, 9-15   179, 14-19   180, 10-16   185, 5-8   190, 4-10   194, 12-18   196, 24-197, 2   app. II 3
    see also irony
    abyss   178, 6-8
    agricultural   177, 10-15
    imber   191, 9-11
    military   177, 5-10   201, 13-17
    mixed   177, 15-19
    nautical   176, 15-18
    snares   190, 4-10
    sprinkling   177, 10-15
    theatrical   177, 20-178, 2   183, 5-7   185, 5-8   see also theatre
    wind   202, 13-17
metaplasm   197, 9-14
metiri   185, 8-12
metonymy   192, 3-6   192, 14-17   198, 11-16   199, 14-18
Metragyrtes   200, 1-9
mi coniux   183, 11-16
military term   187, 9-12   188, 25-189, 4   189, 4-12 bis

333

Milo 179, 14-19
mime (illustrated) 196, 19-21
minare 201, 17-19
Minucius Felix *Octavius* 9, 7 185, 20-22; 22, 8 (= 24, 11) 195, 25-196, 4
mirabilia intr. 4.2.4 intr. 4.3 intr. n. 11
mirari 195, 21-25
mire 199, 14-18
mirus 184, 11-13 193, 10-12 195, 21-25
miscere 178, 24-179, 5
misellus 176, 21-177, 1
miseratio (rhetorical) 192, 24-27
misere 180, 10-16
miserinus 193, 12-15
miseriter 180, 10-16
mitella 198, 11-16
Mithras 196, 24-197, 2
mitra 198, 11-16
modestus 196, 16-19
modicum = paulisper 193, 10-12
modi Phrygii 201, 19-25
molles 195, 25-196, 4
monstrare 192, 28-193, 5
moods (alternation) 194, 28-195, 2
moralism intr. 4.2.4
    moral indignation intr. 4.4 180, 19-23 200, 26-201, 1
    selective indignation 202, 18-20
mordicus 195, 7-11
morsiuncula 194, 18-24
mors placida app. II n. 9
    uoluntaria app. II 4.2.1
      perverted app. II 4.2.2
mortis quies app. II n. 9
mortis quiete recreari (applies to Isis' initiates) app. II 4.2.1
motif-reversal 200, 26-201, 1
motifs intr. 4.2.3
    blinding intr. 4.2.2
      of adulterer intr. 4.2.3
    custodia pudicitiae uxoris intr. 4.2.2 intr. n. 8
    death 194, 18-24
    faithful husband intr. n. 7
    faithful lover dying 181, 8-11
    faithful wife intr. 4.2.2 intr. 4.2.3 intr. n. 7 187, 18-19
      assisting husband 202, 8-10
    glittering bones 194, 18-24 bis
    imagines defuncti intr. 4.2.2
    killing children to punish their father 194, 7-12
    madness 198, 16-20
    ὄνος βαστάζων ἄγαλμα 197, 2-6
    ruse intr. 4.2.2
    suicide intr. 4.2.2 intr. n. 7
      failed 202, 3-8
      in/on the grave of the beloved 187, 24-26 188, 4-6
    treacherous friend intr. 4.2.2
    see also adultery, robbers
mourning 180, 19-23 197, 2-6
    see also officia
    period of 184, 17-185, 4

rites   180, 19-23
scenes   180, 19-23
Mul. Chir.   162   199, 18-20;   766   184, 1-5;   875   201, 26-202, 3
multiiugus   199, 14-18
multinodus   199, 14-18
multus + collective singular   180, 8-10
munire   191, 2-8
μυριώνυμος   see Isis
Musaeus   231   185, 23-24
music   app. IV 2.5
  at Cybele festival   201, 19-25
musitatio   178, 24-179, 5
mutuo   187, 9-12
mythological references   189, 20-26

nam   189, 26-190, 4
nameless characters   201, 19-25
names (Isis)   app. IV 2.10.1
  significant   intr. n. 5   182, 14-183, 1   197, 9-14
  κατ' ἀντίφρασιν   181, 17-24
namque   192, 17-24
nanctus   201, 3-13
nanque   intr. 5.3
narrative   see also pace
  attitude   179, 26-180, 2
  chronological order   187, 19-24
  economy   intr. 5.2
  elliptical   178, 24-179, 5
  familiar   181, 25-182, 1
  levels (ignored)   196, 10-13
  parallel   191, 29-192, 2
  perspective   see perspective
  strategy   intr. 4.2.1.3
  style   see style
  stylized   181, 25-182, 1
  technique   176, 21-177, 1   177, 5-10
  trick   182, 14-183, 1
narrator   intr. n. 4   178, 6-8   178, 9-15   178, 19-20 bis   179, 5-11
  185, 13-16   185, 25-28   185, 28-186, 5   187, 3-9   188, 1-4 passim
  188, 4-6   188, 7-8   188, 17-20   189, 4-12   189, 12-16   194, 5-7 bis
  194, 7-12   194, 12-18   195, 21-25 bis   195, 25-196, 4   196, 14-16
  196, 22-24   197, 17-20   198, 1-5   198, 16-20   198, 20-199, 4   199, 4-8 passim   app. IV 2.1   app. IV 2.7   app. IV 2.8   app. IV 2.9.2   app. IV n. 9
  see also irony
  author behind the -   177, 1-4   178, 19-20
  aversion   app. IV 2.3
  characterisation of chief -   intr. 4.5
  chief   intr. 4.2.1.1   intr. 4.2.1.3   intr. 4.2.4   intr. n. 10   183, 16-18
  197, 2-6   197, 9-14
  conclusion of   180, 6-8
  critical   199, 4-8
  despises priests of the Dea Syria   200, 12-22
  direct contact with audience   199, 9-10
  disapproval of   177, 5-10   app. V
  experiences   198, 16-20
  first person   intr. 5.2

335

    hindsight   196, 22-24
    interpretation of   188, 4-6   195, 11-12
    level   191, 11-15
    limited perspective   app. IV 2.2
    opinions   189, 20-26
    point of view   187, 19-24   189, 12-16   191, 29-192, 2   200, 1-9
    presentation of facts   177, 1-4
    revulsion and fear   199, 9-10
    sceptical   200, 1-9
    strategy   202, 13-17
    sub -   intr. 1   intr. 2   intr. 4.2.1.1   intr. 4.2.1.2   intr. 4.2.1.3   intr. 4.2.4   intr. 5.1   intr. n. 5   intr. n. 10   177, 5-10 bis   177, 10-15   177, 20-178, 2   179, 14-19   179, 26-180, 2   180, 17-19   180, 19-23 bis   181, 14-17   181, 17-24   181, 25-182, 1   182, 14-183, 1 bis   184, 1-5   184, 5-9   app. II 2.1   app. II 2.3   app. II 3   app. II 4.1
    sub- characterised   179, 20-24
    delaying tactics of sub-   180, 8-10
    information of sub-   183, 8-10   183, 18-20   183, 20-21
    insight of sub-   180, 6-8   180, 10-16
    interpretation of sub-   180, 19-23 bis   181, 14-17 bis   182, 14-183, 1
    personal style of sub-   183, 18-20
    point of view of sub-   181, 14-17
    reaction of sub-   184, 11-13
    summarizes the events   190, 19-24
    unreliability of   intr. 4.5
natales   177, 5-10
ne...saltem   190, 4-10
nec = ne...quidem   188, 1-4
nec non et   177, 5-10
nec non etiam   177, 5-10
nec ullum...illum   193, 12-15
nec ullus = nullus   193, 12-15
necessitati succumbere   182, 5-10
neologism   185, 5-8 bis   190, 19-24   191, 18-22   191, 22-27
Nepos *Alc.*   3, 6   177, 10-15
    Them.   10, 4   188, 9-10
nequissimus   184, 5-9   202, 18-20
Nero   app. III
nescius   187, 3-9
Nestor   179, 14-19
Nibelungen   178, 21-24
nidificare   194, 12-18
nidificus   194, 12-18
nimietas   182, 14-183, 1
nimium/nimius   181, 14-17
nomen est omen   182, 14-183, 1
    lugubre   181, 17-24
nominatim ciere   193, 5-10
Nonius   5 (9 L)   195, 25-196, 4;   16 L   196, 22-24;   33 L   197, 9-14;   64 L   196, 16-19;   234-5 L   188, 25-189, 4;   789 L   201, 19-25;   848 L   178, 9-15;   870 L   198, 11-16
Nonnus   7, 282   185, 23-24
nos (identification with group)   191, 16-18
noun qualifying noun   202, 13-17
nouns in -ius   178, 9-15
    -itio   189, 12-16   194, 1-5
    -mentum   202, 13-17

-(t)io   177, 5-10   196, 22-24
-tor   187, 16-18
-tu-   196, 22-24
novel   see also Isis
novel greek   188, 4-6   app. III   see also romance
  picaresque   app. IV n. 2
Novius *com.*   44   195, 7-11
nudare   187, 9-12
nulli = non   190, 4-10   192, 3-6   193, 12-15
numerosus   188, 25-189, 4
nuntium (neuter)   181, 3-7
nuptiae   182, 14-183, 1   185, 23
nutrix   185, 16-20   185, 28-186, 5 bis   189, 26-190, 4

ob   189, 4-12
obarmare   189, 26-190, 4
obesus   179, 5-11
obnubilare   183, 2-5
oboedire + object   182, 5-10
obseruitare   189, 4-12
obtundere aures   184, 9-11
ociter   179, 20-24
ocius   179, 20-24
occupatio   189, 20-26
Oedipus   187, 3-9
oenoforum   185, 28-186, 5
officia lugentium   180, 19-23
olusculus   200, 12-22
Olympiaca stola   app. IV 2.6 bis
omniparens   196, 24-197, 2
omnipotens   196, 24-197, 2
omnipotens et omniparens   app. IV 2.10.1
omniscience (authorial)   180, 6-8
ὄνος ἄγει μυστήρια   200, 1-9
Onos   179, 5-11   197, 17-20   197, 20-24   198, 1-5   198, 11-16   199, 4-8   app. III bis   app. IV 1   app. IV 2.2   app. IV 2.11   resembling Vorlage   201, 3-13
  34, 1   intr. 4.2.3.;   34, 3   188, 17-20;   34, 5   194, 25-28;   35, 4   195, 21-25   195, 25-196, 4   app. IV 1   app. IV 2.7;   35, 5   197, 9-14;   36, 1   197, 9-14;   36, 2   196, 5-7   197, 14-17   app. IV 2.11;   36, 4   197, 24-26   197, 27-198, 1;   37, 2   198, 20-199, 4   199, 18-20;   38, 1   200, 12-22;   38, 2   200, 22-26 bis;   38, 3 f.   201, 3-13;   38, 3   200, 26-201, 1;   38, 7   199, 14-18   201, 3-13 bis;   39, 3   201, 26-202, 3;   39, 7   202, 13-17;   39, 8   202, 13-17;   39, 9   202, 18-20;   54, 2   app. IV 2.12.1
opilio   176, 21-177, 1
opimus   201, 19-25
oppido   193, 21-22
oppressus   185, 13-16
ὄψις   181, 7-8
oracles (unscrupulous use)   app. IV 1
orbidus   184, 9-11
orbitas   187, 1-2
orgiastic rites   198, 11-16   app. V
oro   178, 19-20
Orosius *Apol.*   271   192, 24-27
  Hist.   7, 37, 16   188, 25-189, 4

337

Osiris   intr. 4.2.4   181, 8-11   181, 17-24   196, 24-197, 2   202, 10-12
    app. IV 2.7 bis   app. IV 2.11   app. IV n. 41
    cult   187, 24-26
    initiate undergoes fate of   app. II 4.2.2
    king of inferi   app. II 4.2.2
    ritual meal   app. II 4.2.1
ostendere   192, 28-193, 5
ouicula   192, 3-6
Ovidius *Am.*   1, 14, 43   180, 24-25;   2, 9, 28   202, 13-17;   2, 18, 18
    201, 13-17
    Ars   1, 505   195, 25-196, 4;   2, 373   179, 5-11;   3, 269   198, 11-16;   3, 289   200, 26-201, 1;   3, 611   186, 8-9;   3, 745 f.   181, 8-11
    Ep.   4, 83   179, 20-24;   12, 107   179, 5-11;   16, 281   192, 14-17;   17, 143   178, 9-15;   20, 183   177, 20-178, 2
    Fast.   1, 433 f.   201, 1-3;   1, 433   200, 26-201, 1;   1, 558   189, 4-12;   2, 847   186, 5-8;   4, 183   201, 19-25;   4, 214   201, 19-25;   4, 345   198, 1-5;   4, 350 f.   198, 1-5;   4, 667   184, 1-5;   5, 376   184, 14-17;   6, 330   198, 16-20;   6, 441   197, 2-6
    Ib.   456   201, 19-25
    Met.   1, 155   184, 1-5;   1, 319   194, 7-12;   1, 459   193, 15-19;   1, 496   177, 15-19;   2, 104   194, 1-5;   2, 686   200, 26-201, 1;   3, 140   178, 24-179, 5;   3, 178   181, 17-24;   3, 508 f.   193, 12-15;   4, 29   201, 19-25;   4, 91   185, 23-24;   4, 107 f.   187, 18-19;   4, 119   180, 10-16;   4, 134   193, 10-12;   4, 154 f.   187, 24-26;   4, 166   187, 24-26;   5, 473   181, 17-24;   6, 107   179, 11-14;   6, 248   181, 17-24;   6, 651   194, 7-12;   7, 602   181, 8-11;   7, 614   202, 13-17;   7, 824   185, 5-8;   8, 142   179, 24-26;   8, 338 f.   179, 5-11;   8, 366 f.   179, 14-19;   8, 372 f.   179, 20-24;   8, 414 f.   180, 3-4;   8, 419   179, 20-24;   8, 565   185, 8-12;   9, 213   185, 23;   10, 402   188, 7-8;   10, 410 f.   184, 1-5;   10, 545   178, 21-24;   10, 569   185, 13-16;   10, 710 f.   179, 20-24   180, 3-4;   10, 713 f.   180, 8-10;   10, 713   197, 20-24;   10, 723   181, 17-24;   11, 16   198, 1-5;   11, 167   194, 5-7;   11, 654 f.   183, 8-10;   11, 686 f.   183, 8-10;   11, 709   188, 7-8;   13, 371   180, 19-23;   13, 477   192, 17-24;   14, 335   177, 10-15;   14, 617   177, 10-15;   15, 225   192, 14-17
    Pont.   1, 1, 39 f.   198, 1-5;   1, 1, 51 f.   app. IV 2.10.2   app. V;
    Tr.   1, 7, 30   183, 5-7;   2, 267   188, 9-10;   4, 3, 67   183, 18-20;   5, 1, 63   178, 6-8
oxymoron   184, 11-13   186, 18-23   187, 1-2   187, 24-26   189, 12-16
    195, 21-25   198, 11-16
ὦ Ζεῦ σχέτλιε   200, 22-26

pabulum   193, 5-10
pace   change of narrative -   intr. 5.2
    narrative   181, 11-13
paelicatus   194, 5-7
paene + pluperf.   201, 3-13
paenissime   181, 8-11
pagum (without preposition)   193, 19-20
Paneg.   2, 25, 2   177, 20-178, 2;   6 (7), 3, 4   202, 13-17;   8, 1, 1   178, 9-15;   12, 5, 3   189, 20-26
Panthia   app. IV n. 39
Papinianus   24, 1, 52   177, 20-178, 2
paradox   186, 25-27
parallelism   181, 7-8   186, 18-23   188, 15-17   188, 25-189, 4   191, 9-11
parataxis   178, 24-179, 5   191, 9-11

παρέκβασις 188, 21-25
Parentalia 186, 23-25
parentare 186, 23-25
parenthesis 178, 21-24
parody intr. 4.2.3 178, 21-24 195, 14-17 198, 5-9 197, 20-24
paronomasia 181, 11-13 192, 17-24
parricidium 183, 16-18
pars pro toto 188, 25-189, 4
partiarius 198, 1-5
participare (constructions of) 184, 5-9
participle future 178, 21-24
    fut. -masc. nominalized 194, 28-195, 2
    middle 198, 11-16
    present - de conatu 180, 8-10 180, 10-16
       final 184, 9-11
particles (disjunctive - interchanged with copulative -) 183, 2-5
pastophori 198, 16-20
pathici 195, 25-196, 4
pathos see also rhetoric 177, 1-4 187, 16-18 187, 18-19 188, 9-10
patientia (sexual connotation of -) 196, 19-21
Paulus *Sent.* 3, 6, 38 194, 1-5
Paulinus Nolensis *Carm.* 16, 229 190, 4-10
   Ep. 13, 9 app. II 3
pecuinus 201, 3-13
Pegasus intr. 4.3 189, 20-26
penetrare (se) 200, 26-201, 1
penitence app. V
per (instead of causal abl.) 192, 17-24
per- 187, 19-24 188, 21-25 202, 13-17
perciere 201, 1-3
percitus 180, 10-16
peremptor 187, 16-18
perficere uotum 180, 19-23
perflare 187, 19-24
perfungi + acc. 190, 4-10
periclitari 196, 19-21
   + genit. 201, 26-202, 3
perissology 186, 14-16
permanare 183, 11-16
permetiri 191, 18-22
peroration 187, 1-2
perperam 181, 17-24
perquiescere 193, 19-20
persentiscere 185, 8-12 194, 18-24
Persius 1, 56 195, 25-196, 4; 5, 186 f. app. V
persona 177, 20-178, 2 184, 11-13
personata 184, 11-13
personification 182, 14-183, 1 201, 26-202, 3
perspective (narrative) 180, 6-8
pertemptare 181, 25-182, 1
peruicax 182, 1-5
peruolutare 187, 19-24
pestilens regio 193, 15-19
petitor 183, 5-7 184, 9-11
Petronius 2, 7 183, 2-5; 9, 6 196, 19-21, 18, 1 184, 1-5;
   21 187, 3-9 23 f. 200, 12-22; 23, 3 195, 25-196, 4; 23, 4 f.
   195, 25-196, 4; 23, 5 198, 11-16; 30, 3 201, 26-202, 3; 31

339

177, 5-10;   38, 1   191, 29-192, 2;   38, 4   189, 26-190, 4;   46, 3
188, 15-17;   62, 3   176, 15-18;   63, 5   196, 5-7;   65, 1   201, 26-
202, 3;   65, 10   176, 21-177, 1;   74, 14   186, 13-14;   82   190, 24-
28;   88, 5   201, 3-13;   89, 15 f.   181, 14-17;   96, 6   179, 20-24;
108, 1   195, 25-196, 4;   110, 3   181, 14-17;   111   intr. n. 7   intr. n.
9;   111, 10   181, 17-24;   111, 11   188, 4-6;   128, 6, 5   202, 3-8;
131, 11   196, 19-21
Petrus Chrysostomus *Serm.*   20 (p. 254 B)   191, 9-11
Phaedra   185, 16-20
Phaedrus   4, 1 (= Aesop. 290 H)   198, 16-20
phallolatry   app. III
Philebus   195, 21-25   197, 9-14   197, 14-17   197, 17-20   197, 20-24
198, 5-9   200, 12-22
Philesitherus   intr. n. 8
Photius *Bibl.*   129   201, 3-13
pigmentum   198, 11-16
pistor (death-rites)   app. I
plagosus   180, 10-16
plana manu   201, 13-17
planis gladiis   201, 13-17
platea   181, 3-7
Plato   178, 6-8
   Gorg.   494 E   195, 25-196, 4
   Phd.   117 D   187, 12-16
   Tim.   45 C   181, 7-8
Plautus *Am.*   190   201, 3-13;   284   202, 18-20;   527   185, 8-12
194, 18-24;   1103   192, 8-14;   1136   185, 13-16
   As.   391   196, 16-19;   403   192, 3-6;   432   198, 5-9;   540
176, 21-177, 1
   Aul.   148   177, 20-178, 2;   229   200, 26-201, 1;   300   191, 2-8
460   193, 21-22;   466   181, 8-11;   668   181, 8-11
   Bac.   79   177, 5-10;   147   190, 24-28;   305   192, 3-6;   463
190, 24-28;   579   200, 12-22;   636   190, 10-19;   768   198, 1-5
   Capt.   397   202, 13-17;   404   202, 13-17;   419   181, 14-17;
551   202, 18-20;   873   192, 24-27;   1002   188, 15-17
   Cas. arg. 1   194, 1-5;   138   197, 24-26;   204   202, 13-17;   411
190, 24-28;   491   178, 19-20;   622 f.   188, 9-10;   801   200, 12-
22;   838   190, 24-28
   Cist.   118   184, 9-11
   Cur.   170   185, 13-16;   190   200, 12-22;   290   183, 11-16;
312   179, 20-24
   Epid.   96   179, 20-24;   140   197, 20-24;   231   198, 11-16
   Men.   121   190, 24-28;   249   190, 24-28;   1053   191, 2-8
   Mer. arg. 2, 12   191, 11-15;   122   192, 17-24;   210   201, 19-25;
630   196, 24-197, 2
   Mil.   235   179, 5-11;   1332   202, 13-17;   1430   189, 4-12
   Mos.   413   199, 10-13;   656   181, 8-11
   Persa   369   190, 24-28;   835   190, 24-28
   Poen.   473 f.   189, 20-26;   979   188, 25-189, 4
   Ps.   65   194, 18-24;   801   192, 28-193, 5;   1247   201, 13-17
   Rud.   70   183, 2-5;   275   187, 3-9;   722   198, 20-199, 4;   731
187, 3-9;   945   190, 24-28;   1089   190, 24-28;   1204   181, 17-24
   St.   33   184, 5-9;   139   178, 24-179, 5;   211   177, 5-10;   381
201, 19-25
   Trin.   276   200, 26-201, 1;   767   198, 11-16
   Truc.   44   200, 26-201, 1;   287   195, 25-196, 4;   610   195, 25-
196, 4

play-acting   184, 11-13
plenissime   195, 7-11
pleonasm   see redundancy
Plinius *Nat.*   2, 48   181, 17-24;   2, 139   179, 20-24;   6, 66   185, 16-20;   8, 107   195, 7-11;   9, 81   194, 12-18;   9, 145   190, 4-10;   10, 132   179, 5-11;   11, 76   198, 11-16;   11, 127   195, 14-17;   11, 168   195, 7-11;   11, 227   179, 5-11;   12, 75   191, 18-22;   13, 126   184, 1-5;   14, 35   194, 28-195, 2;   14, 143   177, 5-10;   15, 13   192, 8-14;   17, 65   197, 24-26;   18, 223   183, 2-5;   18, 278   183, 2-5;   19, 23   198, 11-16;   20, 84   187, 3-9;   22, 128   190, 10-19;   23, 44   188, 17-20;   28, 125   199, 20-200, 1;   29, 8, 19   188, 15-17;   32, 102   198, 11-16;   36, 15   195, 7-11
Plinius *Ep.*   1, 20, 16   200, 1-9;   2, 19, 5   178, 16-17;   4, 2, 3   188, 15-17 bis;   5, 6, 45   193, 5-10;   5, 8, 13   195, 7-11;   5, 10, 3   183, 5-7;   10, 18, 2   178, 24-179, 5
Pan.   67, 5   192, 24-27;   79, 5   app. II 3
Plotina   186, 5-8
pluperfect (conspicuous)   190, 4-10
    'Verschobenes'   190, 10-19
plural poetic   181, 1-3   188, 11-14
plurifariam   191, 16-18
Plutarchus *Alex.*   4, 4   184, 14-17
    Amat.   22   intr. 4.2.2
    Artox.   16, 2 f.   194, 18-24
    Camill.   30, 3   181, 14-17
    Def. or.   421 B   184, 14-17
    Is.   4   app. IV n. 6;   17   181, 8-11;   30 f.   app. IV n. 33;   53   app. IV 2.10.1
    Fr. de an.   178   app. II n. 18
    Mul. virt.   20   intr. 4.2.2
    Qu. Conv.   1, 6   184, 14-17
    de Superst.   7   app. V;   10   app. V
poculum   178, 2-6
    = potio   192, 3-6
poenalis   186, 25-27
poetic colour   179, 5-11   181, 3-7
    language   197, 7-9
    sound   177, 20-178, 2
    use of singular   178, 21-24
poeticism   177, 15-19   189, 26-190, 4
poetic usage   201, 3-13
point of view   181, 14-17   185, 25-28
    see also ass, I, Lucius, narrator
Polyaenus   8, 39   intr. 4.2.2
Polymestor   187, 3-9
polyptoton   181, 14-17
polysyndeton   192, 28-193, 5   195, 14-17   196, 24-197, 2   198, 11-16 bis   200, 1-9
Pompey   intr. 4.2.3   181   14-17
populosus   194, 25-28
Porphyrio *ad* Hor. *S.*   1, 3, 51   196, 16-19
Porro Quirites   200, 22-26
possessive in colloquial language   198, 9-10
postomis/prostomis   197, 9-14
potatio   177, 5-10
pote   189, 16-20
potiri   185, 13-16

prae   192, 28-193, 5
praeco   195, 2-7   196, 16-19   196, 22-24   196, 24-197, 2   197, 14-17
    198, 1-5   app. IV 2.2   app. IV 2.10.2   app. IV 2.11
    characterised   197, 9-14
    disappears without a trace   197, 9-14
    social status of -   196, 7-10
praedo + genet.   187, 16-18
praenobilis   177, 5-10
praesens   188, 1-4
praesepium   197, 27-198, 1
praestinare   195, 2-7   196, 5-7
praesumptio   187, 24-26   199, 14-18
praeuenire (trans.)   197, 9-14
pratens   191, 18-22
prayer formulas   192, 14-17
prefixes (reinforcing)   177, 5-10
preposition reinforced by adv.   188, 1-4
Priapus   194, 12-18   201, 1-3
Priapea   12, 5   188, 15-17;   26, 1   200, 22-26;   26, 11   198, 5-9;
    27, 3   195, 25-196, 4   app. IV 2.5;   35, 2   200, 12-22;   79, 4
    188, 25-189, 4
price(s) of the ass   see ass
priesthood (simultaneous)   app. IV n. 10
priests of the Dea Syria   see Dea Syria
Priscianus *GLK*   3, 281, 7   202, 13-17;   6, 16, 86   188, 25-189, 4
probe = bene   185, 16-20
Probus *Inst. Gramm. GLK*   4, 130, 16   201, 26-202, 3
procella canum   191, 9-11
    sideris   183, 2-5
procession of Isis   198, 11-16   198, 20-199, 4   app. IV 2.6
    to the sea   app. III
proci   177, 10-15
professiones   196, 7-10
projection of emotions   180, 6-8
prolepsis   191, 2-8   192, 14-17
    poetic quality of   188, 11-14
prolixe   185, 13-16
prolixity   177, 10-15
prolixum (adv. neuter)   184, 1-5
pronoun (omission of)   186, 14-16
    strengthened by pronoun   193, 15-19
    (weakened force)   186, 14-16
pronuba   187, 1-2
pronus   185, 25-28
Propertius   1, 1, 11   app. II n. 7;   1, 5, 16   195, 14-17;   1, 12, 5
    177, 15-19;   1, 16, 32   188, 7-8;   2, 8, 21   187, 19-24;   2, 8, 40
    201, 13-17;   2, 15, 23   200, 12-22;   2, 27, 1   201, 3-13;   2, 29, 37
    188, 7-8;   3, 3, 31   196, 24-197, 2;   3, 7, 10   app. I;   3, 8, 7   186, 18-
    23;   3, 20, 11   185, 23-24;   4, 7, 7 f.   183, 8-10;   4, 7, 62   198, 11-
    16;   4, 7, 73   185, 16-20;   4, 7, 93   186, 18-23;   4, 11, 8   app. I
prophesy   app. IV 2.9.1
propter   176, 18-20
propudiosus   200, 12-22
propudium   200, 12-22
prorsus   193, 15-19
    quasi   196, 16-19   199, 4-8
    ut   196, 16-19

prosapia   177, 20-178, 2
prosectu   180, 10-16   199, 18-20
Proserpina   181, 17-24
prospectus   178, 24-179, 5
prospicere   178, 24-179, 5
prostituta   177, 5-10
prostitute   197, 24-26
protelare de 191, 11-15
protrimentum 202, 13-17
proverbial phrase 178, 17-19
prouidentia   199, 9-10   202, 10-12
   caelestis 199, 9-10
prouolare   198, 20-199, 4
proximare   192, 8-14
Prudentius *Cath.*   7, 139   199, 14-18
   Perist. 2, 330   201, 19-25   10, 91   188, 1-4
   Psych.   835   182, 10-14
   c. Symm.   2, 101   182, 14-183, 1
Psyche   181, 11-13   185, 5-8   185, 23   186, 5-8   194, 1-5
Publilius Syrus   596 R   190, 24-28
pudor   184, 17-185, 4
puella = filia   177, 15-19
pulchellus   197, 14-17
pullulus   197, 24-26
pun   177, 1-4   188, 17-20   192, 14-17   192, 17-24   195, 14-17
   etymological   191, 2-8
   see also word-play
puniri (depon.)   187, 16-18
purification (blood in rite of -)   199, 18-20
purity   app. IV 2.3   app. IV 2.5   app. IV 2.7   app. IV 2.8   app. IV 2.9.1
   of the spirit   app. V
Pyramus and Thisbe   187, 18-19
purus   app. IV n. 11

qua   179, 11-14
qua re cognita   193, 15-19
qualitas   192, 8-14
quam   185, 16-20
quanquam + subj.   177, 10-15   178, 9-15   180, 19-23
quanto + positive   180, 10-16
quantum pote   189, 16-20
quasi + subj.   199, 4-8   199, 10-13
-que explicative   182, 14-183, 1   183, 20-21
quem ad finem   195, 14-17
Querol.   46, 18   201, 13-17
qui (interrogative)   179, 20-24
qui = quis   195, 18-19
quidam   191, 29-192, 2   198, 1-5   200, 10-12   202, 13-17
quidem   181, 3-7
quidni   178, 6-8
Quintilianus *Decl.*   270 (103, 14 f.)   194, 12-18;   341   196, 7-10;   357 intr. 4.2.3;   363   intr. 4.2.3;   388 (434, 6)   180, 19-23
   Inst.   1, 6, 40   176, 15 18;   3, 9, 4   188, 21-25;   7, 3, 32   194, 12-18;   8, 3, 45   201, 13-17;   8, 6, 54   201, 1-3;   9, 2, 16   199, 14-18;   10, 1, 12   186, 5-8;   10, 4, 4   183, 5-7;   11, 3, 71   198, 20-199, 4 bis;   11, 3, 72 f.   181, 14-17;   11, 3, 75   181, 14-17;

343

11, 3, 100   186, 5-8
[Quintilianus] *Decl.*   1, 2   193, 12-15;   1, 5   193, 12-15;   4, 9   186, 25-27;   11, 9   197, 14-17;   12, 22   183, 2-5;   17, 3   182, 14-183, 1
  Decl. exc. Monac.   12, p. 376, 25   179, 5-11
quiritare   181, 3-7   191, 2-8
quippe + partic.   188, 17-20
quoad + indicative or subjunctive   184, 17-185, 4
  + subj.   185, 8-12
quod + subj.   178, 9-15
quod = quoad   178, 21-24
quodam (dative)   202, 13-17
quoque   177, 5-10
quorsum   178, 19-20
quouis (abl. or dative)   183, 11-16
quo usque (tandem)   195, 14-17

raucus   197, 17-20
Re (king of superi)   app. II 4.2.2
reader(s)   intr. 4.2.1.1   intr. 4.2.1.2   intr. 4.2.1.3   intr. n. 4   177, 1-4   177, 5-10   177, 10-15   181, 14-17   185, 25-28   186, 9-13   186, 25-27   188, 17-20   189, 12-16   190, 24-28   191, 2-8   192, 8-14   198, 5-9   198, 9-10
  expectations   183, 8-10
  hint to   185, 16-20   187, 18-19
  implied   181, 14-17
  linear   183, 8-10   199, 9-10   app. II 2.1
  re-   199, 9-10
realism   195, 25-196, 4   201, 26-202, 3
recreare quiete   app. II 3
recreari quiete mortis   app. II 3
recreari = renasci   app. II 4.2.1
recta   187, 9-12
recurare   191, 18-22
redundancy   177, 15-19   179, 14-19   180, 4-6   181, 17-24   181, 25-182, 1   182, 14-183, 1   187, 19-24   189, 3-9   189, 16-20 bis   189, 26-190, 4   191, 11-15   195, 25-196, 4   199, 14-18   200, 12-22
  of particles   190, 4-10
reedpipe Phrygian   198, 1-5
refectus (-us)   191, 18-22
regina caeli   196, 24-197, 2
relative clause (causal connotation)   196, 24-197, 2
religio   182, 5-10
religiosa necessitas   181, 25-182, 1   182, 5-10
religiosus   182, 5-10
reminiscences literary   intr. 4.2.3
  verbal   intr. 4.2.3
renudare   201, 3-13
repentance   188, 1-4
repetition   178, 9-15   182, 14-183, 1
  emphatic   188, 15-17
  of the same verbal form   186, 18-23
  see also anaphora
repigrare   189, 4-12
repulsa   177, 10-15
'res neglegenter compositae'   192, 28-193, 5
residēre   182, 14-183, 1
residēre + acc.   190, 28-191, 2

revenge   181, 3-7
Rhea-Cybele   app. III
Rhet. Her.   1, 9, 15   187, 19-24;   3, 3, 5   188, 1-4;   4, 8, 12 f.   188, 1-4
rhetoric   intr. 4.2.1.2   intr. 4.2.3   intr. 4.2.4   intr. 5.1   179, 20-24
    181, 14-17   187, 19-24
    amplification   183, 11-16
    composition   192, 24-27
    devices   198, 9-10
    effect   179, 5-11
    miseratio   192, 24-27
    pathos   176, 15-18   177, 1-4   183, 18-20
rhyme   intr. 5.1   176, 18-20   178, 24-179, 5   179, 5-11 ter   182, 14-183, 1   186, 18-23   188, 25-189, 4   190, 19-24   198, 20-199, 4
rhythm   183, 8-10   184, 14-17   188, 15-17
    clausula   189, 20-26   189, 26-190, 4;   190, 4-10
       cretic plus trochee   186, 9-13
       dispondaic   192, 6-8
       heroica   176, 21-177, 1   178, 24-179, 5
       spondaic   181, 17-24   183, 11-16
    cretics   178, 9-15   178, 19-20   181, 17-24
    dactylic   178, 21-24   178, 24-179, 5
    hexameter   178, 19-20   181, 17-24   185, 8-12   185, 13-16
ridicule   intr. 4.3   intr. 4.4   195, 12-14
risus   195, 20-21
Risus festival   195, 12-14
robbers   194, 18-24   app. IV 2.11
    motif   190, 10-19
    term   190, 4-10
rogus = grave   app. I
romance (greek)   187, 19-24   187, 24-26   see also novel
ros = aqua   191, 22-27
roses   197, 2-6
ruderarius   195, 14-17
rudimentum   178, 9-15
ruditus   200, 22-26   200, 26-201, 1
Rufinus *Hist.*   1, 8, 7   200, 12-22;   10, 29   191, 9-11
    Hist. Mon.   8 p. 421c   202, 10-12
    Orig. in Num.   1, 3   178, 9-15
    Orig. in Rom.   7, 6   178, 9-15
ruina   178, 2-6
rupina   178, 9-15
Rutilius Namatianus   1, 637   183, 2-5

Sabadius / Sabazius / Sebadius   196, 24-197, 2   app. IV 2.10.1
sacculus   200, 1-9
sacrilegus   183, 11-16
sale (quality of goods not guaranteed)   196, 14-16
    see also ass
salebrosus   189, 26-190, 4
Salii   198, 16-20
Sallustius   intr. n. 1
    Cat.   20, 9   195, 14-17;   56, 3   189, 26-190, 4
    Hist.   3, 48, 10   190, 19-24
    Iug.   11, 7   195, 14-17;   14, 21   188, 1-4;   55, 2   180, 19-23;   80, 1   194, 28-195, 2
sane   183, 8-10
sapidissime   202, 13-17

sarcinosus   188, 25-189, 4
sarcinula   193, 5-10
satiare   185, 5-8
satias   185, 5-8
satis = ualde   190, 4-10   196, 5-7   198, 1-5
    agere   190, 10-19
saucius   195, 12-14   199, 4-8
scaena   183, 20-21   201, 1-3
scalpere   195, 7-11
scaturrigo   194, 12-18
scelus   187, 3-9
scene   190, 28-191, 2
    articulated   181, 7-8
    standard   189, 26-190, 4
Schol. Hom. *Od.*   19, 471   181, 14-17
    Hor. *Epod.*   10, 17   181, 25-182, 1
    Lucian.   211, 3 R   195, 25-196, 4
    Stat. *Theb.*   10, 309   187, 19-24
scilicet   180, 6-8   181, 14-17   189, 20-26   196, 7-10   197, 9-14   197, 20-24   201, 13-17
Scip. *ap.* Macr. *Sat.*   3, 14, 7   195, 25-196, 4
scito   195, 25-196, 4
scortum   177, 5-10
scurrilis   196, 24-197, 2
secure (abl.)   201, 13-17
sed   178, 19-20   188, 11-14   197, 20-24   200, 10-12
sedes   194, 28-195, 2
Sedulius *op.* 3, 11   190, 10-19
self-accusation   app. IV 2.7
    -mutilation   198, 16-20 bis   198, 20-199, 4 bis   199, 4-8   199, 9-10
    app. IV 2.7   app. IV 2.8
seller (obligation of)   197, 9-14
semicanus   195, 25-196, 4
semiuir   199, 14-18
Senatus consultum Silianum   180, 17-19
Seneca *Con.*   2, 2, 1   intr. 4.2.3;   7, 6, 14   192, 24-27;   9, 3, 7   185, 28-186, 5;   10, 4, 2   201, 13-17
Seneca *Ag.*   27   194, 7-12;   491   186, 18-23;   710 f.   199, 4-8;   958   186, 5-8
    Apoc.   3, 2   196, 7-10
    Ben.   1, 1, 13   186, 9-13;   1, 14, 2   179, 11-14;   6, 42, 2   185, 23-24;   7, 19, 8   183, 11-16
    Breu.   10, 16, 3   185, 23-24;   14, 4   178, 24-179, 5
    Cons. H.   16, 1   184, 17-185, 4
    Cons. M.   10, 1   198, 1-5
    Cons. P.   8, 1   177, 15-19
    Const.   6, 7   186, 25-27;   12, 1   192, 14-17;   15, 1   186, 17-18
    Ep.   16, 6   177, 15-19;   25, 4   177, 1-4;   56, 1   201, 17-19;   70, 9   181, 25-182, 1;   70, 20   188, 4-6;   75, 6   184, 17-185, 4;   84, 3   200, 12-22;   95, 28   200, 12-22;   98, 7   186, 9-13;   102, 23   177, 10-15;   110, 13   200, 12-22;   117, 6   199, 14-18;   121, 4   184, 1-5;   122, 6   177, 5-10
    Her. F.   533   181, 17-24;   679   200, 26-201, 1
    Her. O.   540   180, 10-16;   701   199, 4-8;   1876   184, 1-5
    Ira   2, 35, 2   179, 11-14;   3, 4, 2   179, 5-11;   3, 5, 4   202, 3-8;   3, 15, 4   194, 7-12;   3, 16, 4   184, 17-185, 4;   3, 19, 5   184, 1-5;   3, 26, 1   182, 14-183, 1;   3, 39, 3   180, 6-8

Med. 6   185, 20-22;   40   194, 7-12;   174   190, 19-24;   714 194, 12-18
Nat.   1, 16, 2   196, 19-21;   1, 16, 4   186, 5-8
Oed.   949 f.   app. II 2.1;   1004   197, 14-17;   1011   186, 28-30
Phaed.   97   200, 12-22
Phoen.   42   197, 14-17
Tro.   1132 f.   187, 1-2
Vit. B.   26, 8   198, 20-199, 4   app. V
  ap. Aug. *Civ.*   6, 10   184, 9-11
senex (adj.)   195, 25-196, 4 bis
sentences (short)   177, 5-10
sepelire ad somnum   185, 28-186, 5
sepicula   192, 17-24
sepultura   181, 11-13   187, 24-26
sequius   185, 23-24
sermo amatorius   186, 18-23
  cotidianus   177, 5-10   179, 5-11   181, 25-182, 1   185, 16-20   186, 14-16   186, 17-18   189, 16-20   189, 20-26   195, 18-19   195, 20-21   196, 22-24   197, 7-9   197, 14-17   197, 24-26   197, 27-198, 1   198, 1-5   199, 4-8   200, 12-22 ter   201, 3-13
sermonem conferre   183, 11-16
seruare   178, 24-179, 5
seruitium   182, 10-14   app. IV n. 36
  to the Dea Syria   app. IV 2.11
Servius on Verg. *A.*   3, 587   176, 15-18;   4, 138   179, 11-14;   4, 216 198, 11-16;   4, 386   app. II 2.4;   7, 16   200, 26-201, 1;   8, 660 198, 11-16;   12, 457   189, 4-12
seruus   app. IV 2.11
Seth   intr. 4.2.4   177, 5-10   181, 17-24   app. IV n. 33
  -Typhon   app. IV 2.11
setius   185, 20-22
Severus (emperor)   app. III
sex   198, 9-10
  depraved   intr. 4.4
  dissipation   195, 21-25   app. IV 2.4   app. IV 2.7
  offenses   app. V
  sin   app. V
  see also ass
sexuality   198, 1-5
SHA, Ael. Spart. *Hadr.*   18, 7 f.   194, 12-18
  Capitol. *Maximin.*   28, 4   199, 18-20
  Pert.   7, 1   196, 10-13
  Treb. Poll. *Gall.*   3, 9   201, 19-25
  Fl. Vop. *Quadr. Tyr.*   5, 3   190, 10-19
Shakespeare *Antony and Cleopatra* Act 5, scene 2   187, 24-26
shape-shifting   intr. 4.3
shaving   app. IV 2.2
Sibyl   app. IV 2.9.1
sic + subj.   192, 14-17
sicarius   186, 5-8
Sidonius Apollinaris *Carm.* 23, 293   179, 5-11
  Epist.   1, 6, 3   176, 21-177, 1;   9, 3, 5   191, 16-18
sigmatism   192, 24-27   196, 24-197, 2
  see also alliteration
silence of divinity   201, 13-17
siligo   200, 1-9
Silius Italicus 2, 561 f.   183, 8-10;   4, 155   198, 11-16;   8, 79   188, 7-8;

347

8, 164 f.   183, 8-10;   9, 37   186, 25-27;   10, 140   187, 19-24;
13, 181   191, 9-11;   17, 20 f.   199, 4-8
silk   198, 16-20
siluosus   188, 21-25
simile (implied)   186, 18-23
similis indignanti   196, 22-24
simplex pro composito   186, 9-13
simul   181, 3-7
simulacrum = εἴδωλον   app. II 2.2
    (wandering)   app. II 2.2   app. II 4.1
simulanter   185, 5-8
Sinatus   intr. 4.2.2
Sinorix   intr. 4.2.2
si qui   195, 18-19
Sisenna *Hist.*   4, 76 Peter   188, 25-189, 4;   26 Peter   201, 19-25
    frg. hist.   27, 69 Peter   191, 11-15
sistrum   app. IV 2.5   app. IV n. 13
siue...seu   app. IV 2.10.1
slave(s)   179, 14-19   179, 20-24   180, 17-19   180, 24-25
    arbitrary treatment   194, 12-18
    death   193, 19-20
    flight   194, 18-24
    legal marriage   194, 1-5
    Lucius'   197, 2-6
    punishment   194, 12-18   194, 18-24
    sale   196, 7-10
    Syrian   app. IV n. 44
    see also Cappadoces
sleep of death followed by something   app. II 3
sobriefactus   185, 5-8
society (lower strata)   179, 14-19   195, 25-196, 4
Socrates   187, 12-16   app. I
Solinus   19, 3   196, 19-21;   20, 7   186, 25-27;   38, 12   191, 16-18
solitudines   201, 3-13
sollers   180, 19-23
sollerter   180, 19-23
somniari   186, 13-14
somnolentus   186, 27-28
somnus   see sepelire
sonax   179, 5-11
sonu (abl.)   201, 19-25
Sophocles *El.*   621   192, 17-24;   1231   181, 14-17
    O.C.   181   186, 18-23
    O.R.   444   186, 18-23;   1268 f.   187, 3-9;   1368   186, 17-18
sospitem facere   192, 24-27
soul wandering in twilight   app. II 2.4
sound(s)   201, 26-202, 3
    effect   181, 7-8   201, 26-202, 3
    expressive   179, 20-24
speaker   196, 16-19
    characterisation   intr. 5.1
specimen historiae   177, 1-4
spelling   intr. 5.3   180, 6-8   184, 1-5   184, 14-17   185, 28-186, 5
    188, 15-17   190, 10-19 bis   195, 12-14   195, 14-17   198, 11-16   199, 4-8   201, 19-25 bis
spiritus   181, 8-11   188, 7-8
spoudaiogeloion   189, 20-26

spumare   179, 5-11
spurcitia   app. IV n. 39
   /spurcities   199, 18-20
Statius *Silv.*   2, 1, 154 f.   183, 8-10
   Theb.   1, 499   181, 17-24;   2, 89 f.   183, 8-10;   2, 130   179, 11-14;   2, 640   202, 13-17;   3, 232 f.   181, 8-11;   3, 583   191, 18-22;   5, 127   187, 19-24;   5, 252   184, 1-5;   6, 789   186, 5-8;   8, 96   200, 12-22;   10, 18   185, 13-16;   10, 290   179, 11-14
stipes   200, 1-9
Stoa   185, 23-24
stomida/stomis   197, 9-14
stramentum   201, 3-13
studiose   187, 9-12
stuprum   200, 12-22
style   intr. 5   184, 1-5   184, 17-185, 4   186, 14-16   192, 17-24   198, 9-10
   abundance of attributes   189, 12-16
   emotional   182, 14-183, 1
   emphatic   194, 28-195, 2
   historian's   193, 12-15
   narrative   intr. 5.2   200, 12-22
   ornamentation   180, 10-16
   ornate   177, 10-15
   see also compounds
suauis   app. IV 2.5
subjunctive   178, 24-179, 5
   imperfect for present   194, 18-24
   jussive   185, 16-20
   shift to   187, 19-24
   without conjunction   182, 1-5
suboles   177, 20-178, 2
subpatere   192, 17-24
subpetiari   192, 24-27
subsiciuus   195, 2-7
subsistere   192, 14-17
succidaneus   197, 20-24
Suetonius *Aug.*   34, 2   184, 17-185, 4;   73   201, 26-202, 3
   Cl.   25, 2   194, 12-18
   Gal.   5, 1   185, 16-20
   Iul.   46   199, 14-18
   Nero   3, 2   177, 10-15;   22, 2   178, 9-15;   40, 2   185, 25-28;   42   184, 1-5;   46, 2   181, 17-24;   49, 3   201, 13-17;   56   app. III
   Otho   11, 2   187, 19-24
   Tib.   42, 2   177, 5-10
   Gram.   15, 2   196, 22-24
suicide   187, 18-19   187, 19-24   188, 4-6 bis   194, 12-18   194, 18-24   app. II 2.3
   methods   181, 25-182, 1   194, 7-12 bis
   see also motifs
Sulpicius Severus *Chron.*   1, 6, 4   200, 12-22
   Dial.   1, 13, 8   196, 16-19
summary   181, 17-24   190, 28-191, 2   192, 8-14   193, 15-19 bis   194, 25-20
summissus/-e   184, 11-13
super   188, 4-6
   = de   193, 10-12

349

superlative (humorous)   181, 8-11
supersistere   186, 5-8
superstition   app. I
supinare   186, 5-8
supine + obj.   180, 8-10
suscipere   197, 9-14   201, 19-25
suspense   intr. 2
susurrus, -i   185, 5-8
suus   194, 1-5
Sychaeus   183, 8-10   183, 20-21
synonyms   181, 3-7   182, 14-183, 1   193, 5-10   194, 18-24

tableau   190, 19-24
Tab. devot. Audollent.   135 A 3   201, 26-202, 3
Tacitus *Agr.*   9, 2   197, 9-14;   34, 3   181, 25-182, 1
   Ann.   1, 21   181, 17-24;   1, 61, 2   194, 18-24;   1, 61, 3   194, 18-24;   1, 65   183, 8-10;   2, 53, 2   182, 10-14;   3, 1, 1   182, 10-14;   3, 21   185, 16-20;   6, 1, 2   196, 19-21;   11, 3, 2   181, 25-182, 1;   11, 27   178, 9-15;   12, 35   200, 26-201, 1;   13, 18, 1   180, 19-23;   13, 29   192, 24-27;   15, 37   200, 12-22;   15, 54   176, 15-18;   16, 14, 3   187, 3-9;   16, 29   194, 28-195, 2
   Ger.   19, 1   188, 1-4;   19, 2   181, 25-182, 1
   Hist.   1, 22   196, 7-10;   3, 53   191, 9-11;   4, 20, 1   179, 14-19
tale exemplary function   182, 14-183, 1
   framing   intr. 4.2.1.1
   function   intr. 4.2.4
   insertion   intr. 4.2.1.1   intr. 4.3   193, 21-22
   patterns   intr. 4.2.3
   significance   intr. 4.2.4
tales of trickery   184, 11-13
talis   187, 3-9
talus   199, 14-18
tamen   191, 16-18
tautology   202, 18-20
tax return   196, 7-10
tears of joy   181, 14-17
tegmen   178, 24-179, 5
tempestiuus   185, 5-8   193, 5-10
tempo   181, 11-13
   increasing   189, 4-12
*tempestillus   177, 19-20
tenebrare   188, 21-25
tense(s)   180, 19-23
   variation   177, 5-10   179, 20-24   181, 11-13   188, 11-14   190, 4-10   191, 29-192, 2   192, 8-14   200, 12-22
tension   180, 8-10
Terentius *Ad.*   87   199, 10-13;   536   181, 14-17;   906   202, 13-17
   An.   94   202, 13-17;   792   186, 8-9
   Eu.   47   188, 9-10;   113   192, 17-24;   740   186, 18-23
   Hau.   225   190, 10-19;   401   186, 18-23;   598   196, 14-16;   916   194, 18-24
   Hec.   214   196, 16-19;   440   192, 8-14;   852   192, 14-17
   Ph.   213   191, 11-15;   579   194, 1-5
Tertullianus *An.*   1, 4   195, 18-19;   7, 4   200, 26-201, 1;   13, 3   201, 13-17;   17, 2   180, 19-23;   31, 2   181, 17-24;   38, 1   178, 9-15;   56, 4   app. II 2.4;   57, 8   180, 19-23
   Apol.   13, 6   195, 25-196, 4;   22   196, 24-197, 2;   25, 5   198, 20-

199, 4 bis;   39, 16   201, 13-17;   42, 8   195, 25-196, 4
Cult. fem.   1, 2, 1   198, 11-16;   2, 2, 2   199, 14-18;   2, 8, 2   198, 11-16
Exh. Cast.   9   177, 20-178, 2
Herm.   43 (172, 24)   182, 14-183, 1
Marc.   1, 20, 1   191, 18-22;   1, 24, 2   198, 1-5
Nat.   2, 14, 9   191, 18-22
Or.   22   180, 19-23
Poen.   11, 5   189, 20-26
Pall.   5, 3   184, 1-5
Pud.   7   178, 24-179, 5;   16   201, 13-17
Res.   2, 2 (26, 12)   198, 1-5;   48, 7   187, 24-26;   60, 7   191, 18-22
Spect.   1, 5   178, 24-179, 5
Test. An.   4   176, 21-177, 1
Ux.   2, 8, 1   194, 1-5
Val.   12 (191, 19)   198, 1-5;   14, 3   200, 22-26;   29   187, 24-26
tescum/tesquum   193, 15-19
tessellatus   199, 14-18
tessera   199, 14-18
tesseratus   199, 14-18
text constitution   intr. 5.3
theatre (imagery)   184, 11-13   185, 23   see also metaphor
Thelyphron   app. I
Thessaly   198, 5-9
t(h)omix   197, 9-14
Thrasyllus   intr. 1   intr. 4 passim;   intr. 5.1   intr. 5.2   ch. 1-14 passim   app. II passim
   blinded   app. II 1
   characterisation   intr. 4.2.4   intr. n. 5   178, 19-20
   contrasted with initiate of Isis   app. II 4.2.1
   perverts mors uoluntaria   app. II 4.2.2
three (role of the number)   194, 18-24
thyrsus   app. II 4.2.1
Tibullus   1, 1, 66   191, 16-18;   1, 2, 31   185, 16-20;   1, 2, 33   185, 20-22;   1, 3, 27   app. IV 2.12.1;   1, 4, 70   201, 19-25;   1, 5, 74   185, 16-20;   1, 6, 45 f.   199, 14-18;   1, 6, 61   185, 16-20;   1, 10, 43   192, 14-17;   2, 6, 39 f.   183, 8-10
[Tib.]   3, 3, 9   191, 18-22;   3, 7, 179   177, 19-20;   3, 18, 1   178, 24-179, 5
time   intr. 3   195, 2-7
   experienced   intr. 3.1
   objective   intr. 3.1
   indication   189, 12-16
   narrated   app. IV 2.1
   subjective   202, 13-17
   unspecified   177, 20-178, 2
Titinius *Com.*   53   176, 15-18
Tlepolemus   intr. 1   intr. 2   intr. 4 passim;   intr. n. 6   ch. 1-14 passim   176, 15-18   198, 11-16
   burial   intr. 5.2
   death-rites   app. I
   degeneration   178, 21-24
tomb   intr. 4.2.2   181, 11-13   187, 24-26   188, 4-6
topos   intr. 4.2.3
   acies rustica   189, 26-190, 4
   literary   184, 1-5
   divine fragrance   184, 14-17

totus = omnis   178, 24-179, 5   182, 10-14   183, 18-20   187, 9-12   192, 28-193, 5
tragedy   187, 3-9   187, 19-24
transabire   179, 11-14   189, 4-12
transadigere   187, 19-24
transigere cum   181, 25-182, 1
transition-formula   192, 3-6
travel episode   188, 9-10
   by night   201, 3-13
trickery   see tales
tripudium   197, 7-9
triuialis   195, 25-196, 4
triumphare   201, 13-17
Tullia's shrine   182, 10-14
tumicla   197, 9-14
tutela   194, 1-5
tympanum   201, 19-25
Typhon   see ass, Seth

Ulpianus *Dig.*   3, 2, 11, 3   184, 17-185, 4;   3, 5, 5, 5 (3)   200, 10-12;   3, 5, 5, 5   201, 13-17;   9, 2, 7, 6   194, 12-18;   33, 7, 12, 12   178, 24-179, 5;   34, 2, 23, 1   198, 11-16;   47, 1, 2, 5   200, 12-22;   47, 14, 1, 1   200, 10-12;   48, 8, 15   194, 12-18;   48, 15, 1   196, 10-13   see also *Dig.*
   Reg.   5, 2   177, 10-15
ultro citro   194, 12-18
ultroneus   188, 4-6
'Umdeutung'   180, 19-23   182, 14-183, 1   194, 12-18
uncinus   178, 9-15
unde   188, 21-25
underworld   198, 5-9
undique gentium   190, 10-19
uniuira   183, 11-16
unus de/ex/ + gen.   195, 25-196, 4
upilio   176, 21-177, 1
urigo   200, 12-22
ut + pluperf.   184, 1-5
utcumque = utique   202, 3-8
ut mireris   184, 11-13
   primum   184, 1-5
uxor pudica   intr. 4.2.3
   uniuira   intr. 4.2.3
ualde + diminutive   196, 5-7
Valerius Flaccus   1, 47 f.   183, 8-10;   3, 231 f.   198, 16-20;   3, 233   198, 20-199, 4;   4, 538   180, 19-23;   6, 653   183, 18-20;   8, 9   184, 1-5
Valerius Maximus   1, 3, 3   196, 24-197, 2;   5, 1, 3   184, 17-185, 4;   6, 5, 5   184, 9-11;   7, 3 ext. 6   184, 9-11;   8, 7 ext. 2   197, 9-14;   9, 10 ext. 1   intr. 4.2.3;   9, 14, 3   177, 10-15
ualuae   188, 4-6
variation   177, 15-19   178, 17-19   179, 5-11   180, 19-23   181, 7-8   186, 9-13   186, 13-14   187, 1-2   187, 19-24   188, 15-17   189, 26-190, 4   190, 4-10   191, 22-27   192, 17-24   192, 18-193, 5   194, 5-7   194, 12-18   197, 20-24
   of connectives   186, 18-23
   of fixed expression   196, 10-13
   of proverbial theme   182, 14-183, 1

stylistic   179, 20-24
Varro *hist.*   6 *ap.* Aug. *civ.* 21, 8   196, 7-10
  L.   5, 94   178, 24-179, 5;   5, 116   188, 1-4;   5, 131   198, 11-16; 6, 68   190, 10-19   191, 2-8
  Men.   103   200, 12-22;   132   198, 20-199, 4   199, 14-18;   479   196, 16-19
  R.   2, 8, 2   197, 24-26
  fr.   108 Ag.   179, 20-24
uaticinatio   199, 10-13
uecordia   181, 3-7
Vegetius *Mul.*   2, 42, 2   178, 24-179, 5;   4, 1   194, 28-195, 2
uehiculo meo   201, 3-13
uel   195, 18-19
  certe   200, 1-9
uelitari   196, 24-197, 2
Velleius Paterculus   2, 82, 3   182, 10-14
uelut   app. IV 2.9.1
uelut + part.   199, 4-8
uenabulum   179, 20-24
uenaticus   201, 26-202, 3
uenatio   178, 24-179, 5
uenatus   178, 21-24
uenire   186, 9-13
uenui (dat.)   191, 29-192, 2
Venus   181, 17-24   196, 24-197, 2   app. IV 2.10.1
  Paphia   app. IV 2.10.1
  and Adonis   178, 21-24
verba intensiva   191, 2-8
uerbero   202, 18-20
Vergilius *A.*   1, 208 f.   202, 3-8;   1, 210   177, 19-20;   1, 211   202, 13-17;   1, 228   198, 11-16;   1, 320   198, 11-16;   1, 324   179, 5-11; 1, 353 f.   183, 8-10   183, 20-21;   1, 403   184, 14-17;   2, 3   182, 14-183, 1;   2, 63   187, 9-12;   2, 222 f.   183, 5-7;   2, 265   185, 28-186, 5;   2, 274 f.   183, 8-10;   2, 281 f.   183, 8-10;   2, 298   178, 24-179, 5;   2, 325   176, 21-177, 1;   2, 435 f.   192, 8-14;   2, 511   178, 21-24;   2, 725   181, 3-7;   3, 68   181, 17-24   193, 5-10;   3, 137   186, 9-13;   3, 207   179, 5-11;   3, 364   188, 21-25;   3, 590 f.   192, 8-14;   4, 22   181, 8-11;   4, 39   192, 3-6;   4, 130   201, 3-13; 4, 131   179, 20-24;   4, 158   179, 5-11;   4, 160   178, 24-179, 5; 4, 166   187, 1-2;   4, 172 f.   181, 1-3;   4, 195 f.   181, 1-3;   4, 300   187, 3-9;   4, 366   191, 2-8;   4, 391   182, 1-5;   4, 444   app. II n. 7; 4, 456   184, 5-9;   4, 473   187, 1-2;   4, 474 f.   184, 5-9;   4, 475   187, 18-19;   4, 579   179, 5-11;   4, 632   185, 16-20;   4, 646 f.   187, 18-19;   4, 659   184, 1-5;   4, 664   182, 1-5;   5, 73   177, 10-15;   5, 95   app. IV n. 31;   5, 269   199, 14-18;   6, 48 f.   199, 4-8 app. IV n. 19;   6, 50   199, 4-8;   6, 78   199, 4-8;   6, 79   app. IV n. 19;   6, 191   176, 15-18;   6, 274   187, 1-2;   6, 288   189, 20-26; 6, 292 f.   app. II 2.2;   6, 424   185, 28-186, 5;   6, 426 f.   app. II 2.3; 6, 429   201, 3-13;   6, 434 f. app. II 2.3;   6, 442   app. II 2.3;   6, 446   183, 8-10;   6, 450   183, 8-10;   6, 494 f.   183, 8-10;   6, 517   198, 16-20;   6, 522   app. II 3;   6, 595   177, 5-10   196, 24-197, 2;   6, 612   178, 9-15;   6, 687 f.   198, 5-9;   6, 784 f.   198, 1-5;   7, 377   187, 3-9;   7, 488   179, 5-11;   7, 505 f.   189, 26-190, 4;   7, 513 f.   189, 26-190, 4;   8, 71   195, 25-196, 4;   8, 351   178, 24-179, 5;   8, 495   188, 1-4;   8, 649   196, 22-24;   8, 660   198, 11-16;   9, 44 f.   app. II n. 9;   9, 138   186, 8-9;   9, 189   185, 28-186, 5;   9, 303   188, 7-8; 9, 442   179, 5-11;   9, 473 f.   181, 1-3;   9, 617 f.   201, 19-25   app. IV

353

n. 22;   9, 798   178, 6-8;   10, 350 f.   202, 8-10;   10, 503 f.   181, 3-7;   10, 724   179, 5-11;   11, 28   201, 3-13;   11, 40   183, 18-20; 11, 730   181, 3-7;   12, 36   189, 4-12   194, 18-24;   12, 131   187, 9-12;   12, 173   186, 23-25;   12, 235   201, 3-13;   12, 419   184, 14-17;   12, 508   187, 19-24;   12, 894   178, 24-179, 5
Cat.   9, 34   196, 19-21;   13, 17   197, 2-6
Ecl.   1, 1   178, 24-179, 5;   2, 67   185, 25-28;   5, 20   201, 3-13; 8, 18   186, 8-9;   8, 88   185, 25-28
G.   3, 9   201, 3-13;   3, 125   197, 20-24;   3, 505   188, 7-8;   4, 80   176, 15-18;   4, 178   187, 24-26;   4, 415   184, 14-17;   4, 472   app. II 2.2;   4, 517   185, 16-20;   4, 561 f.   201, 3-13
Vergil allusion to   198, 5-9
   imitations of   199, 4-8
Vergilian echoes   188, 21-25
Veritas   181, 14-17
ueruex   196, 16-19
uespera   185, 23-24
uestigator   178, 24-179, 5
uicarius   198, 5-9
uiduatus   200, 22-26
Ps. Vigilius Thaps. *Trin.*   5 p. 275a   187, 24-26
uilla   190, 10-19   191, 2-8
uillicare   194, 1-5
violence   intr. 4.4
Virgilius *Gramm. Ep.*   5 p. 166, 19   177, 20-178, 2
uirilitas   188, 17-20
uirtus   185, 23-24
uiscera   194, 7-12
uisio   181, 7-8
'vision du dedans'   189, 20-26   197, 9-14   197, 14-17   197, 17-20
   'par derrière'   199, 4-8
VL Deut.   12, 22   179, 5-11;   32, 22 (Lugd)   187, 18-19
   Matth.   23, 26   200, 26-201, 1
   (e) Psalt. Cas.   121, 5   186, 13-14
   Psalm.   143, 13   188, 21-25
uolaticus   189, 20-26
uoluptas   intr. 4.2.1.1   intr. 4.2.4   178, 9-15   184, 9-11   189, 20-26   200, 12-22   app. IV 2.13   app. IV n. 36
   of initiate   app. II 4.2.1
'Vorlage'   intr. 4.2.3   197, 17-20   200, 12-22   200, 26-201, 1   app. IV 2.11
   differences from *Met.*   201, 26-202, 3
uotiuus   201, 19-25
vowel harmony   186, 18-23
   sounds   intr. 5.1
Vulg. Esth.   1, 6   198, 11-16
   Leu.   11, 11   200, 12-22
   Luc.   11, 39   200, 26-201, 1
   Matth.   8, 34   181, 7-8;   23, 26   200, 26-201, 1
   Reg.   1, 30, 20   201, 17-19

'wachsende Glieder'   178, 9-15   179, 5-11   182, 14-183, 1   187, 1-2   198, 1-5   198, 5-9
wake   app. I
washing   see lauatio
water   191, 22-27
whip in cult of Dea Syria   199, 14-18

widow of Ephesus   intr. n. 9   181, 17-24   188, 4-6
wolves   intr. 4.3   179, 5-11   188, 21-25   188, 25-189, 4 bis   189, 12-16   190, 4-10   194, 18-24   198, 9-10
women   179, 20-24
word-order   180, 10-16   181, 7-8   185, 20-22   196, 10-13 bis
   interlocking   181, 14-17   199, 18-20
   position of attributes   195, 25-196, 4
      verb   200, 10-12
   -play   180, 17-19   180, 19-23   188, 1-4   192, 17-24   201, 3-13
   see also pun
world of *Met.* (socio-economic aspects)   191, 29-192, 2

Xenophon *Anab.*   1, 2, 7   188, 21-25
   Cyn.   3, 1   178, 24-179, 5
   Cyr.   8, 3, 16   198, 11-16
Xenophon Ephesius   3, 6, 3   intr. n. 7;   3, 7, 4   181, 11-13;   3, 10, 2   intr. n. 7   181, 8-11   187, 24-26;   5, 4, 11   intr. n. 7

yellow (effeminate colour)   198, 11-16

Zeno of Verona *Sermones*   1, 5, 4   181, 17-24;   1, 12, 15   201, 3-13;   2, 38, 1   185, 5-8

355

Printed in the United States
By Bookmasters